EASTERN INFLUENCI
WESTERN PHILOSOPHY

A READER

Edited by
Alexander Lyon Macfie

EDINBURGH UNIVERSITY PRESS

The author would like to thank the editorial staff of Edinburgh University Press for their help in preparing the manuscript for publication; also Helen Johnston for her help in editing the text, and the library staff of the University of London and School of Oriental and African Studies libraries for their help in assembling the various articles and extracts.

Edinburgh University Press Ltd
22 George Square, Edinburgh

Typeset in Sabon and Gill Sans
by Bibliocraft Ltd, Dundee, and
printed and bound in Great Britain by
Antony Rowe Ltd, Chippenham

A CIP record for this book is available from
the British Library

ISBN 0 7486 1740 X (hardback)
ISBN 0 7486 1741 8 (paperback)

CONTENTS

INTRODUCTION

In the last fifty years or so academic opinion, mainly in the West, has tended to divide between those who take it for granted that, in the modern period, Oriental ideas have had a significant effect on European (Western) thought, and those who for a variety of reasons either doubt the possibility of Oriental influence or, whilst admitting the possibility, find the concept of influence in one way or another problematic.

The former group might include Raymond Schwab, *La Renaissance orientale* (1950); Dale Riepe, 'The Indian Influence in American Philosophy: Emerson to Moore' (1967); P. J. Marshall (ed.) *The British Discovery of Hinduism in the Eighteenth Century* (1970) (Introduction, pp. 26–44); and Heinrich Dumoulin, 'Buddhism and Nineteenth-Century German Philosophy' (1981). The latter group might include Raghavan Iyer (ed.), *The Glass Curtain Between Asia and Europe* (1965); Edward Said, *Orientalism: Western Conceptions of the Orient* (1978); Samuel P. Huntington, 'The Clash of Civilisations' (1993); J. J. Clarke, *Oriental Enlightenment: The Encounter Between Asian and Western Thought* (1997); Richard King, *Orientalism and Religion* (1999); and presumably also the editors of many of the histories of, and guides to, modern philosophy, such as *The Oxford History of Western Philosophy* (1994) and *The Blackwell Guide to the Modern Philosophers* (2001) published in recent years, which contain little or no material concerning the possibility of Oriental influence. Not that it is possible to be precise about the nature and extent of Oriental influence on Western thought in the modern period, as is shown by a number of the articles contained in this collection, including in particular that concerning Hume.

European (Western) thought is defined here as the thought of a series of leading European thinkers and philosophers – starting with Malebranche, one of the earliest leading European thinkers to take an interest in Oriental (Chinese) philosophy, and ending with Heideggar, whose considerable interest in Oriental (again Chinese) philosophy is not usually appreciated – whose works are generally included in the standard canon of significant philosophical works.

Of the two principal accounts of the engagement of European thinkers with the Orient – Raymond Schwab's *La Renaissance orientale* (English translation, *The Oriental Renaissance*,1984) and J. J. Clarke, *Oriental Enlightenment* – Schwab's *The Oriental Renaissance* must be considered the most influential. For Schwab, the Orient was not so much a geographical area – more or less synonymous in the classical period with Persia and the Near East – as an idea, supposedly separating 'some vague Asia' from 'our [European] world' (Schwab 1984: p. 1). According to Schwab, this idea of the Orient remained fixed, rooted in the European imagination, for almost eighteen centuries, until in the modern period, as a result of the age of discoveries, the imaginary wall, dividing Europe from Asia, was penetrated, broken down, giving rise in the process not only to a new view of Asia – which might now be seen as including China, India and the East Indies – but also to substantial changes in the literary and philosophical culture of Europe, changes identified by many contemporaries at the time, including Edgar Quinet, Arthur Schopenhauer, Pierre Leroux and Eugène Burnouf, as an 'Oriental Renaissance' – an event as significant, in Schwab's opinion, as the first Renaissance. As for the starting points of this great 'event' in the history of European thought, designated by the title 'Oriental Renaissance', these could, according to Schwab, be identified with precision: in 1771, when Abraham-Hyancinthe Anquetil-Duperron, the effective founder of Indic studies in France, published a translation, from the Persian, of the *Zend Avesta*, a collection of Zoroastrian ritual hymns; and in the 1780s, when Charles Wilkins and an élite group of scholars, employed for the most part by the British East India Company, published translations, from the Sanskrit, of a series of classical Hindu texts, including, in particular, the *Bhagavad Gita*, a work described by Schwab as the 'summit of metaphysical poetry'. According to Schwab, Anquetil-Duperron's translation of the *Zend Avesta* embodies the 'first approach to an Asian text totally independent of the biblical and classical traditions', and represents the 'first time anyone had succeeded in breaking into one of the walled languages of Asia' (Schwab 1984: 7 and 17). The end of the 'event' could, in Schwab's view, be discovered in 1869, when Theodor Benfy published *Geschichte der Sprachwissenschaften Orientallischen Philogie in Deutschland* (History of the Study of Oriental Philology in Germany); in 1870, when a 'Bibliothèque orientale' was added to a series entitled 'Chefs-d'œuvre de l'esprit humain', published in Paris; and in 1875, when Max Müller published in London a series entitled 'Sacred Books of the East' – all works which, in Schwab's opinion, indicated that knowledge of Oriental learning and religion was now fully available in the West. Between these dates, according to Schwab, there occurred in Europe an 'oriental eruption of the intellect', which entailed a widening of the historical vision, a reminting of the 'current coin of ideas', a reshaping of the (Christian) images of space and time, a breaking out of Europe's 'hermetic little Mediterranean room', a discovery (in Sanskrit and the Aryans) of common origins, a counter to Cartesian absolutism, the appearance of 'the masses', the dislocation of the rational, a mania for excavation, the discovery of the unconscious, an end to limitation, a discovery of negation, and, surprisingly perhaps, the origins of radicalism and the rise of the Franco-German antagonism.

If Schwab's *The Oriental Renaissance* may be considered the most influential of the numerous books and articles published on the subject of the impact of Oriental ideas on European thought, Clarke's *Oriental Enlightenment* may be considered the most wide-ranging. In *Oriental Enlightenment*, Clarke, like Schwab, concludes that, for the Europeans, the Orient was not so much a geographical term, identifying a particular area or continent, as an idea signifying cultural difference. Europeans, concerned with the Orient, that is to say, generally tended to view Asia not only as a source of inspiration, a fount of ancient wisdom and the location of a culturally rich civilisation, far superior to that of Europe, but also as an alien region of 'looming threat and impenetrable mystery', from which little or nothing was to be learned (Clarke, 1997: 1). Only in the modern period, Clarke concludes, was the deep chasm that divided East from West finally bridged – an event which, in Clarke's opinion, not only opened the West to the influence of Oriental (mainly Chinese, Indian and Japanese) ideas, but also gave rise to an 'Oriental Enlightenment', comparable in the range and profundity of its effects to the Oriental Renaissance, earlier identified by Schwab.

In Clarke's opinion, the Oriental Enlightenment began in the period of the Renaissance, expanded in the period of the Enlightenment, flourished in the age of (European) imperialism, and survived well into the periods of post-colonialism and post-modernism that followed the collapse of the Great European empires. Evidence of a significant engagement with Oriental ideas, of one kind or another, can in Clarke's opinion be found in the works of numerous European writers, including Montaigne, Bayle, Montesquieu, Malebranche, Leibniz, Voltaire, Diderot, Adam Smith, Herder, Goethe, Schelling, Hegel, Schlegel, Schopenhauer, Gobineau, Wagner, Nietzsche, Emerson, Jung, Pound, Eliot, and Santayana, not to speak of the Theosophists, the 'beat' movement and the hippies. Like Schwab, therefore, Clarke believes that the Western discovery of Oriental culture and civilisation had a significant effect on European culture, in particular European (Western) thought. But unlike Schwab, Clarke concludes that the new light, coming from the East, was welcomed in Europe and the West, not so much because it contributed to the rise of the new humanism, the Romantic movement and the new comparatism (secularism, agnosticism, pluralism) – though he recognises that it did all of these things – as because it assisted Europe in answering the numerous questions, regarding the nature of the world, the self, truth, civilisation, culture, progress, reason, and faith, raised by the Renaissance, the Reformation, the scientific revolution and the rise of capitalism – all developments which, by dissolving the Christian theological, philosophical and political synthesis, created in Europe in the early Middle Ages, gave rise in the West to an acute sense of uncertainty, insecurity and anxiety.

In *Oriental Enlightenment*, Clarke, sceptical regarding the concept of influence, as employed in the context of the intercultural relations of Europe and Asia, seeks merely to 'recover and re-examine the serious intellectual involvement – with all its incongruities and contrarieties – of the West with Eastern ideas', and to show that 'throughout the modern period from the time of the Renaissance onward, the East has exercised a strong fascination over Western minds, and has entered into Western cultural and intellectual life in ways which are of considerably more than passing significance within the history of Western ideas' (Clarke 1997: 5 and 7). This approach he adopts because, following Hans-Georg Gadamer, whose hermeneutical philosophy he finds useful, he believes that all human understanding has to be construed as a kind of dialogue, an encounter in which a text or tradition is addressed and which answers questions, or itself questions the interpreter. Such a dialogue would involve 'the interplay of the movement of tradition and the movement of the interpreter' (Gadamer 1975: 261), a continuing exchange in which the sense of a text is sought by reiterative interplay of meaning between interpreter and interpreted. One consequence of this approach (according to Gadamer) is that we must avoid any supposition that we can enter into and fully recover the meanings and mentalities of past ages and their symbolic products (see Clarke 1997: 12–13).

Other authors proved even more sceptical regarding the possibility of Oriental influence on European (Western) thought. In *The Glass Curtain* (1965), Raghavan Iyer, the noted Indian historian, argued that Oriental influence on European thought in the modern period remained limited, as for the most part Europeans persisted in viewing the Asian peoples and their cultures 'through a glass darkly', thereby sustaining the 'obstinate schism', 'irresoluable dichotomy' and 'meridian of cleavage', previously created by prejudice and ignorance. In Iyer's view the 'glass curtain' thus created (or, better still perhaps, reinforced), though merely a psychological barrier, supported by a tissue of lies, half truths and delusions, might well prove – as, indeed, according to some accounts it eventually did – more intransigent than the Iron Curtain. Nor would it be possible to remove the glass curtain even if one wanted to, for if a few thinking men were to shatter the curtain with their analytical tools, it would be rapidly replaced, as words like 'Oriental' and 'Westerner' are periodically redefined to suit changing prejudices:

> We are faced not merely with meagre knowledge or a mild suspicion of
> strangers but, what is worse, a seemingly invincible ignorance and a

self-perpetuating sense of superiority reinforced by a basic failure in communication. Travel too often only confirms instead of removing the preconceptions with which Asians come to Europe or Europeans to Asia. Alternatively, there are brown or yellow 'Europeans' and white 'Asians', as it were, who have lost their own roots in their effort to respond to those beyond the curtain.

In general, the inability to explain the unfamiliar in terms of the familiar results in attempts to explain away even the familiar (in thought and in conduct, art or music, politics and society) by reference to the mystique already imposed upon the 'inscrutable Orient' or the 'decadent West'. Propagandists and even scholars – whether 'Orientalists' or nationalists – give a new lease of life to stale clichés and pernicious myths such as 'Oriental despotism' or 'Western materialism', 'Oriental cunning' and 'European hypocrisy', 'Asiatic fatalism' and 'Western aggression', the meretricious 'glamour' of Asia and the 'vulgar' fascination of Europe. The supposed 'thought-barrier' between the East and the West may be the result of divergent conceptions of God, man, and nature as well as of the state, the individual, and society. It is certainly heightened by the rival claims and mutual misrepresentations of the dominant religions, although they all arose in Asia, and of competing political ideologies which originated in Europe. Furthermore, even universal values, beliefs, and tendencies are often made the basis of exclusive claims to uniqueness on both sides of the Glass Curtain, which in this is essentially different from the Iron Curtain. Altogether, the less people are rooted in their cultures and creeds, the more they need to make far-fetched claims and to denigrate the cultures and creeds of those they cannot intimidate. (Iyer 1965: 6)

In *Orientalism: Western Conceptions of the Orient* (1978), Edward Said, an American (Palestinian, Arab Christian) student of English and comparative literature, similarly argued that Europeans (Westerners) in general and orientalists, in particular, heirs to a 'narcissistic' tradition of European writing, founded by among others Homer and Aeschylus, are as a result of their conditioning largely incapable of viewing the Orient objectively. Rather, driven by racist, imperialist and ethnocentric attitudes, they collectively create a series of self-sustaining myths, according to which Europe (the West, the 'self') is seen as being essentially rational, humane, advanced, masculine and superior, while the Orient (the East, the 'other', a sort of surrogate, underground version of the West or 'self') is seen as being irrational, aberrant, backward, feminine and inferior. The outcome, in Said's opinion, is the creation of a European 'style of thought', based on an ontological and epistemological distinction between Orient and Occident, which not only assists in the creation of a 'saturating hegemonic system', designed consciously or unconsciously to dominate the Orient, but also makes any worthwhile intellectual contact between Orient and Occident unlikely, if not impossible. The relationship of Europe to Asia, in other words, remains throughout the modern period one of power, domination and exploitation – a relationship that makes the possibility of Oriental influence on European thought remote.

Finally, in 'The Clash of Civilisations', in *Foreign Affairs* (1993), an article concerned not so much with the past as with the future, Samuel P. Huntington, an American student of international politics, concluded, from an analysis of recent events, that the interaction of peoples of different civilisations – defined here as cultural entities, based on ethnicity, nationality and religion – far from promoting mutual understanding, usually produces merely awareness of difference, hostility and animosity – a conclusion which would appear to rule out the possibility that in the period of the Oriental Renaissance/Enlightenment, Oriental religion and philosophy could have influenced significantly European thought.

The thesis advanced by Said, in *Orientalism*, has, it may be noted, been widely challenged. David Kopf, in 'Hermeneutics versus History' (1980), for instance, citing the work of the British orientalists (Jones, Colebrooke, Wilkins, Wilson and Prinsep), employed mainly by the East India Company, in the period of the Orientalist–Anglicist controversy, challenges Said's conclusion that Europeans were incapable of observing the Orient objectively. On the contrary, by the time of the founding of the Asiatic society of Bengal, the British in south Asia had acquired a curiosity about the 'whole range and substance' of what has subsequently been called Indian civilisation. Orientalism as history, that is to say, exists and has existed outside Said's personal conception of it. Historical orientalism has a concrete reality, was complex, internally diverse, changed over time, and was never monolithic. It was quite independent of Said's 'discourse'. Bernard Lewis, in 'The Question of Orientalism' in *New York Review of Books* (1982, revised version in *Islam and the West*, 1993), accuses Said of misunderstanding the history of orientalism; of misunderstanding the relations between Europe, the Islamic world and India; of promoting anti-Westernism; and of ignoring the work of many leading orientalists, who made important contributions to the understanding of the Orient, or at least those parts of it with which they were concerned. Orientalists were, for the most part, more than capable of contributing to the understanding of the Orient, parti-cularly the Arab countries, as many Arab scholars would themselves admit. Of course, some orientalists might be guilty of bias, but they were in a minority. The significant difference lies between those who recognise their bias and try to correct it and those who give it free reign. Beyond the question of bias there lies the larger epistemological problem of how far it is possible for scholars of one society to study and interpret the creations of another.

> The accusers complain of stereotypes and facile generalisations. Stereo-typed prejudices certainly exist – not only of other cultures, in the Orient or elsewhere, but of other nations, races, churches, classes, professions, generations and almost any other group one cares to mention within our

own society. The Orientalists are not immune to these dangers, nor are their accusers. The former at least have the advantage of some concern for intellectual precision and discipline.

Dennis Porter, 'Orientalism and its Problems', in P. Hulme, M. Iverson and D. Loxley (eds), *The Politics of Theory* (1983), finds Said's thesis to be both ahistorical and inconsistent. On the one hand Said appears to argue that all knowledge is tainted because the Orient is a construction, and on the other he appears to suggest that there might well be a real Orient, capable of being both known and understood. Said's thesis, based as it is on the conflicting theoretical positions of Gramsci (hegemony) and Foucault (discourse), excludes the possibility that a counter discourse, operating within the given hegemonic discourse, may emerge. The Orientalist discourse is in fact far more heterogeneous than Said supposes. Aijaz Ahmad, the noted Indian student of comparative literature, in 'Between Orientalism and Historicism', *Studies in History* (1991), finds Said's analysis of orientalism incoherent, as it attempts to uphold simultaneously the 'absolutely contrary traditions of Auerbachian High Humanism and Nietzschean anti-Humanism'; it defines orientalism – as an interdisciplinary area of academic knowledge, a style of thought, originating in the days of Homer and Aeschylus, and a corporate institution, designed for dealing with the Orient, established in the late eighteenth century – in ways which are both illogical and contradictory; it assumes that orientalism necessarily inferiorises the 'other'; and it essentialises the West in the same way that Said accuses the West of essentialising the East. In rejecting the possibility that European representation of the Orient might actually correspond to the non-European facts, Said effectively makes it impossible for the Oriental to examine the relevance of that representation to his own historical and political condition. Finally, John MacKenzie, a student of imperial history and culture, in *Orientalism: History, Theory and the Arts* (1995) – a work concerned not so much with the history of ideas as with the arts, in particular, art, architecture, design, music and the stage – finds that Said's thesis (that the West inhabits a hermetic and stereotypical world, closed to the influence of the Oriental 'other') cannot be sustained. Far from inhabiting a closed world, impervious to Oriental influence, Western culture, in the modern period at least, has been one of 'constant change, instability, heterogeneity and sheer porousness'. That is to say, in the world of the arts, at least, the European 'self' and the Oriental 'other', as defined by Said, have throughout been locked in a process of mutual modification, sometimes 'slow but inexorable', sometimes running as fast as a 'recently unfrozen river'.

Wilhelm Halbfass, 'Research and Reflection: Beyond Orientalism', in E. Franco and K. Preisendanz (eds), *Beyond Orientalism: The Work of Wilhelm Halbfass* (1997), repeats many of the criticisms of Said's *Orientalism* made in the preceding paragraph and draws attention to a number of others, one or two of which might be considered very damaging to Said's case. Said, according to

Halbfass, in *Orientalism*, never proposes any non-Western alternatives to Western Orientalist ways of dealing with 'self' and 'other', 'Orient' and Occident'. He speaks within the Western world, as a Palestinian Arab (*not* a Muslim), living and educated in the West. The causal and conceptual relationship between textual and academic Orientalism and actual political and economic subjugation of the Orient, which Said assumes to exist, remains in his account of the subject unclear and ambiguous. Barthélemy d'Herbelot's *Bibliothèque Orientale* (1697), which Said views as a major step in the 'Orientalizing of the Orient', was inspired, and to a certain extent guided, by a bibliographical dictionary – found by Galland, the French orientalist and editor of d'Herbelot's work, in Istanbul in 1682 – written by the great Ottoman scholar and compiler of encyclopaedias Hājjī Khalīfa (or Kātib Celebi, 1609– 1657). It was Hājjī Khalīfā who first established the systematic and alphabetic principle, later adopted by d'Herbelot in his work, which Said assumes to be characteristic of the Orientalist attitude. Goethe, whose work Said sees as just another instance of common Orientalist discourse, had in fact tried to engage, in a 'literal' sense, in a dialogue with Hafiz, the fourteenth-century Persian poet, whom he treated as his poetic and spiritual twin brother. Missing from Said's account of orientalism is any mention of the Muslim scholar of India, al-Burani (973–c.1050), whose work, according to Halbfass, exhibits many of the characteristic features of the subject, as described by Said: his 'essentialisation' of Indian society in terms of caste; his ideas concerning Indian irrationalism and traditionalism; his appeals to rationality and disinterested theory; and his notion of a fundamental and pervasive Indian otherness.

Certainly we have to accept the historical actuality and legitimacy of the 'Orientalism debate', but we should not overestimate its significance. Of course we want to go 'beyond orientalism', to go 'beyond' European and Eurocentric claims to a higher or absolute authority, the epistemic subjugation of non-Western traditions, and indulgence in false essentialisations and reifications. But do we want to go 'beyond' the quiet and patient pursuit of understanding, which has also been part of the history of Indian and 'Oriental' studies? And do we want to go 'beyond' legitimate generalisations, which are inherent in the process of understanding itself? Once we commit ourselves to the pursuit of understanding, we have to live with the constant presence of misunderstanding and the inevitability of prejudice. But we also have to be aware of the positive potential, the seeds inherent within prejudice, which call for its transcendence and make understanding possible. For the time being, the pursuit of understanding has not become obsolete. For those who work in the field of Indian studies, this means listening to the ancient documents as well as the modern representatives of the tradition; it means meeting them, conversing with them, in a realm of shared or shareable meanings and questions.

The arguments put forward by the critics of *Orientalism* in the 1980s and 1990s made little impression on Said. In 'Orientalism Reconsidered', *Race and Class* (1995), for instance, he continued to identify the Orient, not as Europe's interlocutor, but as its 'silent Other', a product of imaginative geography; and orientalism as a 'scientific movement whose analogue in the world of empirical politics was the Orient's colonial accumulation and acquisition by Europe'. And in the Afterword of the 1995 edition of *Orientalism*, he made it clear that his critique of orientalism was not an attack on the West, a defence of Islam and the Arabs, or a defence of the downtrodden and the abused. It was simply an attempt to show that concepts such as 'Orient' and 'Occident' correspond to no stable reality. Far from being natural facts, such concepts are constructs, designed to create a sense of identity – a sense of identity that might be further strengthened by the construction of an 'other', against which the self can be contrasted. Yet in 'Orientalism and After', an interview published in *Radical Philosophy* (1993), Said admitted that, in *Orientalism*, his use of the Foucauldian perspective, combined with a Gramscian theory of hegemony, had created tensions, and that in later years, whilst not abandoning Foucault, he had tended to lose interest in his work, particularly when he had begun to view him not as a theorist of power but as a *scribe* of power. Gramsci's concept of hegemony he still made use of, but it was not an easy concept to employ in practice. Increasingly distrustful of theory, he now preferred to concentrate on the historical study of texts; and as regards the opposition of Orient and Occident, to talk about overlapping areas of experience. The whole point is that imperialism was not of one side only, but of two sides, and the two are always involved with one another. In order to understand the relationship between them you have to have a concept of overlapping territories – what he called 'interdependent histories'. Only in this way would it be possible to talk about liberation, decolonisation and integration.

THE EUROPEAN DISCOVERY OF ASIA

Europe's discovery of the Orient, mainly China, India and Japan, in the modern period, might reasonably be divided into four parts: the discovery of Confucianism (China), the discovery of Hinduism (India), the discovery of Buddhism (India, Tibet, China and Japan) and the discovery of Taoism (China). The European discovery of Islam (the Near East and North Africa), an important development in the inter-cultural relations of Asia and Europe, is not here considered, as it was already well advanced in the Middles Ages. Indeed, as Norman Daniel, *Islam and the West* (1960) and Richard Southern, *Western Views of Islam* (1962), have shown, by the end of the twelfth century many European scholars had acquired an adequate knowledge of Islam, sufficient for them to understand its principal features. But unfortunately their understanding was in many cases vitiated by a polemical desire to distort the religion, denigrate its followers, and where possible secure their conversion to Christianity. The result was that, until the end of the sixteenth century, at least, understanding of Islam and Islamic society in Europe remained confused, distorted by an unwillingness or inability to appreciate the significance of a number of central Muslim conceptions, regarding the unity of God, the nature of creation, the role of Muhammad and the nature of the Koran. Nor, according to Daniel, was any correction of this misunderstanding likely, for in time the prejudice and distortion displayed by Christian scholars and polemicists created an accepted canon, a constituted body of belief about Islam – that it was inherently irrational, mysterious, idolatrous, violent and licentious – substantially different from what Muslims themselves believed. Needless to say, it was the powerful polemic against Islam, forged by Christian scholars and polemicists in the Middle Ages, that gave the type of orientalism analysed by Said its peculiar force and resonance; and it was the accepted canon, the constituted body of belief about Islam, that prevented European thinkers in the modern period, increasingly confident in their supposed intellectual superiority, from looking to Islam for new insights and enlightenment.

Early European knowledge of Confucianism was – as Knut Lundbaeck makes clear in his article 'The Image of Neo-Confucianism in *Confucius Sinarum Philosophus*', in Julia Ching and Willard G. Oxtoby (ed.), *Discovering China* (1992) – derived mainly from accounts of the subject written by Jesuit and other Christian missionaries, dispatched to China in the sixteenth and seventeenth centuries. These included Matteo Ricci (1552–1610), who in 1582 established the first Catholic mission in China, and Niccollo Longobardi (1565–1655), who succeeded Ricci as Superior of the Chinese Mission in 1610. Where Ricci, with a view to making the conversion of the Chinese easier, generally sought to accommodate Christianity to Confucianism, Longobardi rejected the so-called accommodation policy, which in his opinion tended merely to promote superstition. As a result there broke out in missionary circles a dispute that was eventually to lead to the notorious Terms and Rights controversy, divide Christian opinion in Europe for more than a century and incidentally provoke in Europe an immense interest in Chinese culture and civilisation. Works written in this period include Niccollo Longobardi, *De Confucio ejusque doctrina tractatus* (A treatise on Confucius and his Doctrine) (c.1623), a work later translated into Spanish (Madrid, 1676) and French (Paris, 1701); Martin Martini, *De bello Tartarico in Sinis historia* (1654); Athanasius Kircher, *China monumentis qua sacris qua profanis* (Amsterdam, 1667); Domingo Fernandez Navarette, *Tratados históricos, políticos, éticos y religiosos de la Monarchia de China* (Rome, 1674); Philip Couplet, *Confucius Sinarum philosophus* (Paris, 1687); and Father Jean Baptiste Du Halde, *Description de l'Empire de la Chine* (1735). Among these works, Philip Couplet's *Confucius Sinarum philosophus* – a work which contains translations, by a number of Jesuit scholars, of parts of the Chinese Four Books (Analects, Great Learning, Doctrine of the Mean, Book of Mencius) – was from a philosophical point of view probably the most significant; and du Halde's *Description de l'Empire de la Chine* – a work which influenced writers as diverse as Voltaire, Montesquieu, Rousseau, Hume and Goldsmith – the most popular. Such works as these, which frequently emphasised the exccllence of the Chinese system of government and administration – the education system, the examination system, the tax system and the grain storage system – and the quality of the Confucian–Taoist ethical system on which it was supposedly based, were often cited by the so-called *physiocrats* and *philosophes*, as evidence in support of their case against the rottenness of government at home.

While the European discovery of Confucianism took place mainly in the seventeenth and early eighteenth centuries, the discovery of Hinduism – as Peter Marshall (ed.), *The British Discovery of Hinduism* (1970), makes clear – took place mainly in the second half of the eighteenth century, and the first quarter of the nineteenth, when in order to facilitate the good government of their newly acquired empire in the East, a number of senior British East India Company officials, later known as orientalists, led initially by Warren Hastings, the governor, decided to undertake the study of Hindu law and culture, and the translation of a number of classical Hindu texts. Not that information regarding the nature of Hinduism was then entirely lacking. On the contrary, in the first quarter of the eighteenth century Danish Lutheran missionaries, who had established a mission on the Coromandel Coast, published a series of letters, containing much information about Hinduism, many of which were later translated into English; and in the same period Jesuit missionaries published a similar collection. In 1767 John Zephaniah Holwell published *Interesting Historical Events relative to the provinces of Bengal and the Empire of Industan*, and in 1768 Alexander Dow published a *History of Hindostan*. Meanwhile, Etienne Mignot and Joseph de Guignes published a series of articles, concerning Hinduism, in *Mémoires de l' Académie royale des Inscriptions et Belles Lettres* (1761–3,1770–2, 1773–6 and 1780–4); and in 1782 Pierre Sonnerat published a comprehensive survey of the religion in *Voyages aux Indes Orientales*. But such works, the product of limited knowledge, remained generally unreliable. Only in the last quarter of the eighteenth century, when the so-called British East India Company orientalists got to work, was substantial progress made. There then followed the publication of a number of significant translations and other works. These include Nathaniel Brassey Halhed, *Code of Gentoo Laws* (1776); Charles Wilkins, the *Bhagavad Gita* (1785) and the *Hitopadesha* (1801) (a collection of Hindu fables); William Jones – probably the most influential of the British orientalists – *Sakuntala* (1789) (a classical Hindu drama by Kalidasa), *Ritusamhara* (1792) (by the same author), *Gita Govinda* (1792) (a Hindu love poem) and the *Institutes of Hindu Law, or the Ordinances of Menu (Manu)*; Henry Thomas Colebrooke, *Essays on the Religion and Philosophy of the Hindus* (1837); and H. H. Wilson, *A Sketch of the Religious Sects of the Hindus* (1846). Meanwhile numerous articles and dissertations, concerning various aspects of Hindu culture and civilisation, were published in *Asiatic Researches*, the journal of the Asiatic Society of Bengal, a society founded by Jones and others in Calcutta in 1784. These include three articles by Jones, 'On the Hindus', 'On the Gods of Greece, Italy, and India', and 'On the Chronology of the Hindus', all of which were published in the first two issues of the journal. Most of these books, articles, dissertations and translations, in particular, Jones's translation of *Sakuntala*, which made an immense impression on writers as diverse as Goethe, Herder, Friedrich Schlegel, Chateaubriand, Michelet, Hugo, Lamartine and de Maistre, were later translated, or retranslated, into French, German and many of the other European languages.

Not that the contribution made by the British to the discovery of Hinduism in the modern period was in any sense unique. About the same time in France, Anquetil-Duperron, who might with some justification be described as the 'angry young man' of French orientalism, following a visit to India, undertaken in 1754–61, and a series of extraordinary adventures – these involved trips to Benares, Surat, Chandernagore (then a French settlement), Cossimbazar, Pondicherry, Goa and Mahé (also a French settlement), experience of war, a duel (resulting in the death of an adversary) and a series of extraordinary attempts to acquire possession of a Sanskrit alphabet –published his translation of the *Zend Avesta* (1771), and a retranslation, from the Persian, of fifty-two Upanishads (1801–2) – both immensely influential works.

Significant progress in the European discovery of Buddhism, on the other hand, occurred only in the middle years of the nineteenth century, when Eugène Burnouf, the French orientalist, published his *Introduction à l'histoire du Buddhisme indien* (1844), a work which included translations of numerous Buddhist texts, taken from a collection of eighty-eight manuscripts, given by Brian Houghton Hodgson, an Englishman living in Nepal, to the Société Asiatique in 1837. As J. W. de Jong makes clear, in 'A Brief History of Buddhist Studies in Europe and America' (1987), already in the Middle Ages, the period of the Renaissance and the period of the Enlightenment, Europeans had acquired some knowledge of Buddhism from the reports and letters of Franciscan and Dominican friars, dispatched by the Pope to visit the Mongol Khans in Karakorum (Mongolia), Marco Polo's *Description of the World*, travellers' tales, such as John Mandeville's *Voyages* (1365), and the reports and letters of Jesuit missionaries, such as Franciscus Xaverius and Antonio d'Andrade, despatched by the Pope to China, Japan, Ceylon, Siam and Indochina in the sixteenth and seventeenth centuries. But it was only with the publication of Burnouf's work that a real breakthrough was made. There followed the publication of a series of significant works. These include R. Spence Hardy, *Eastern Monachism* (1850); *Manual of Buddhism in its Modern Development* (1853), and *The Legends and Theories of the Buddhists* (1866); P. Bigander, *The Life of the Gaudama* (1858); and Siam Henry Alabaster, *The Wheel of Law: Buddhism Illustrated from Siamese Sources* (1871). Not that Burnouf's contribution to the discovery of Buddhism was entirely unprecedented. In 1836 Abel-Rémusat, first professor of Chinese at the Collège de France, published *Foe Koue Ki ou Relations des royaumes bouddhiques de Fa hian* (1836); and in 1832–7 Isaac Jacob Schmidt, a Russian orientalist, published a number of important articles on the Tibetan sources of Buddhism in *Mémoires de l'Academie*.

Knowledge of Taoism, like Confucianism, was, according to J. J. Clarke, *The Tao of the West* (2000), first brought to the West by Jesuit missionaries in the late seventeenth and eighteenth centuries. But the concentration of the Jesuits on Confucianism meant that little or no attention was paid to its more spiritual competitor, seen at the time as degenerate and idolatrous. In 1667, for instance, Athanasius Kircher, *China Illustrata*, characterised Taoism as a religion of the common people, full of 'abominable falsehoods', and in 1669, Johann Hoornbeck, *De Conversione Indorum & Gentilium*, condemned it for promoting superstition. Nor, when interest in Confucianism declined in the late eighteenth century, did interest in Taoism greatly increase, though Hegel did find a place for it in his historical dialectic. Only in the second half of the nineteenth century, following the foundation of chairs of Chinese studies in France (1815), Russia (1838) and Britain (1876), and the translation of a number of important Taoist texts, by amongst others Stanislas Julien, Edouard Chavannes, James Legge, and Samuel Johnson (the American orientalist), did serious interest arise. James Legge, holder of the first chair of Chinese Studies at Oxford, in particular, played a leading role in defining Taoism for the West, creating a vocabulary and way of speaking about it which remained authoritative for some years, while in America Samuel Johnson included a sensitive analysis of Taoism in his *Oriental Religions and Their Relation to Universal Religion: China* (1877).

ORIENTAL INFLUENCES

The difference in academic opinion, between those who take it for granted that European thinkers were frequently influenced by Oriental ideas in the modern period, and those who either doubt the possibility of Oriental influence or, whilst for the most part admitting the possibility of Oriental influence, find the concept of influence in one way or another problematic, finds no clear reflection in the articles contained in this collection. But a distinction, of sorts, can be made between those whose authors seek to discover a more or less specific Oriental influence (or lack of influence) on a European (Western) thinker (Cook and Rosemont, Jacobson, Nicholls, Riepe, Albert, Coward, May) and those who tend to concentrate on the engagement of a European thinker with Oriental ideas, and the use that thinker made of those ideas (Mungello, Lach, Guy, Taylor, Halbfass, Raghavan and Wood, Sprung, Brobjer, Eber). That is not to suggest that the more problematic aspects of the question of influence – a concept which it may be assumed implies also engagement and use, just as engagement and use imply influence – are ignored in the collection, as a number of the articles selected (Mungello, Guy, Taylor, Halbfass, Riepe, Brobjer) show. Thus David Mungello, in 'Malebranche and Chinese Philosophy' (Chapter 1) – an account of an imaginary conversation regarding the nature of matter (chi), spirit (li) and the infinite (God), held between a Chinese and a Christian philosopher, composed by Malebranche, the French philosopher, in the context of the Chinese Rites Controversy – finds that in his *Conversation* (1708), Malebranche displays an insular Eurocentricism, typical of his period. Far from responding directly to the particular version of Chinese philosophy – the neo-Confucian school of Chu Hsi – popular in China at the time, Malebranche, according to Mungello, tended to universalise a distinctly European standard of truth, assume that European culture had a universal validity, interpret *chi* merely as matter – a distinctly European concept – rather than as 'matter-energy' or 'material force', project a Christian view of God onto the Chinese concept of *li* (principle, organising element), and display an overriding pre-occupation with the debate then taking place in Europe between the defenders of Christian orthodoxy and the freethinkers – a category assumed by Mungello and others to include the followers of Spinoza. Malebranche, in other words, like many other thinkers of his time, some markedly more cosmopolitan than he – these according to Mungello included Leibniz, Wolff, Tindal, Voltaire and Quesnay – in interpreting Chinese thought almost invariably employed ideas and beliefs firmly anchored in the European tradition.

Daniel Cook and Henry Rosemont, in 'The Pre-Established Harmony Between Leibniz and Chinese Thought' (Chapter 2), similarly conclude that, contrary to the view expressed by Joseph Needham, in *Science and Civilisation in China* (1954), Chinese thought had no significant influence on the development of Leibniz's nature philosophy. Leibniz may have taken a great interest in Chinese philosophy, but he was not particularly well informed about it. In *Discourse on the Natural Theology of the Chinese*, – a long letter, of over 14,000 words, written in 1716, designed in part at least to support the Jesuit view in the Chinese Rites Controversy – for instance, Leibniz displays little or no real knowledge or understanding of Chinese thought. On the contrary, drawing mainly on Longobardi, *Traité sur quelques points de la religion des Chinois* (1701), and Antonio Cabellero a Santa Maria, *Traité sur quelques points importants de la Mission de la Chine* (1701) – whose numerous mistakes, with regard to names, places, dates, chronologies and philosophical terms he was evidently in no position to detect – he displayed merely a limited knowledge of Chinese thought, hardly sufficient to warrant the supposition that he was influenced philosophically by it, a naivety with respect to Chinese history, and a subdued but nonetheless 'clear Christian and Western bias' – all of which in Cook and Rosemont's opinion would seem to tilt the scales decisively against the possibility of an East-to-West metaphysical influence. Throughout the *Discourse*, particularly in the closing section, Leibniz was primarily concerned to use what little knowledge of Chinese he thought he had, not to rethink his own position, but to defend the accommodation approach adopted by the Jesuits, which he generally supported.

Cook and Rosemont's conclusion, that Oriental (Chinese) thought had little or no philosophical influence on Leibniz, finds support in Donald Lach, 'Leibniz and China', in Julia Ching and Willard Oxtoby, *Discovering China* (1992) (not included in this collection). Leibniz may in his various writings have used facts about China to corroborate his theory of universal culture, and frequently referred to the superiority of China's social and political system. But in his analysis of Chinese philosophy, he merely developed a system agreeable to his own precepts. That is to say, for Leibniz the concept of *li* served merely to confirm his own definition of the monad, which asserts that 'all simple substances or created monads may be called entelechies'. His refusal to acknowledge individual objects as miniatures of *li* and his insistence on the ego of every substance may be seen as reminders that 'each monad must be different from every other, for there are never in nature two beings which are exactly alike'. Finally, his identification of *li* with Christian divinity served merely as a stepping stone to the concept of *li* as 'the ultimate reason of all things'.

Not that the conclusions drawn by Cook, Rosemont and Lach have gone uncontested. J. J. Clarke, in *Oriental Enlightenment* (pp. 46–7), finds that remarkably close parallels exist between Leibniz's theory of monads, in which all aspects of the universe mirror all others and act together harmoniously, and the Chinese system of correlative thinking in which all parts of nature cohere and co-operate spontaneously without external direction. The possibility remains, therefore, that, as James Needham put it, Leibniz's monadology was indeed given an important stimulus by Neo-Confucian metaphysics, and that this way of thinking in its turn led to a counter-cultural organicist tradition in the West, one associated, in Needham's judgement, with a line of thinkers stretching from Schelling through Bergson to Whitehead and beyond. Hence, 'since the [Western] philosophy of organism owes a great deal to Leibniz', it owes something to Chinese scientific thinking as well, and since according to Needham, an organicist model has begun to replace the Newtonian mechanistic model in recent times, the organic outlook of the Chinese thinkers 'may turn out to have been a necessary element in the formation of a perfected world-view of natural science'. (See, J. Needham, *Science and Civilisation in China*, 2, 1956, pp. 292, 339. See also J. J. Clarke, *The Tao of the West*, 2000, pp. 40–1, and Yu Liu, 'From Christian Platonism to Organism: The Two Chinas of Leibniz', *International Philosophical Quarterly*, 41, 4, issue no. 164, December 2001.)

In 'The Sinophilism of Christian Wolff' (Chapter 3), Donald Lach finds that Christian Wolff, the noted eighteenth-century German philosopher and mathematician – whose rational and secular teaching led to his dismissal from his post at the University of Halle and his expulsion from Brandenburg-Prussia – throughout the greater part of his career took a profound interest in the new learning coming from the East, mainly China, the virtues of which he never failed to promote. In 1711, for instance, he favourably reviewed Father Francisco Noël's *Obervationes Mathematicae et Physicae in India et China factoe ab anno 1684 usque ad annum 1708* (Prague, 1710); and in 1721 he delivered a lecture, entitled *De Sinarum Philosophia*, before an audience of over a thousand persons, made up for the most part of the combined faculty and student bodies of the University of Halle. Nevertheless, though immensely impressed by the Chinese system of government – which he saw as an outstanding working example of enlightened despotism – the Chinese doctrine of natural morality, and the Chinese educational system, Wolff yet found that Chinese philosophy laboured under a considerable imperfection. The notions employed by the Chinese, that is to say, though determinate, were not distinct enough to bring them to determinate propositions and 'reduce them when demonstrated to System'. Moreover, according to Lach, examination of *Philosophia moralis sive Ethica, methodo scientifica pertractata*, Wolff's last major work, published in 1750–3, reveals no direct indebtedness to Confucian philosophy; though in a letter, relating to the *Philosophia moralis*, written to the President of the St Petersburg Academy in 1752, Wolff did reiterate his belief in the correspondence between his own moral teachings and those of Confucius.

Of all the European thinkers of the early modern period, Voltaire was probably the best informed regarding Chinese civilisation, and the most responsive to the implications – political, religious, philosophical, and historical – for Europe of its discovery. Nevertheless, as Basil Guy, *The French Image of China Before and After Voltaire* (1963) (Chapter 4), makes clear, in his early works, in particular *Orphelin de la Chine, Zadig* and a series of essays on politics and religion, Voltaire frequently used the material he had collected concerning China from a variety of sources, including the *Lettres edifiantes*, Father Lecomte, *Nouveaux Mémoires*, and Father Duhalde, *Description de l' Empire de la Chine*, merely to create local colour and illustrate ideas, regarding the defeat of irrationalism and intolerance, he wished to promote. Only in the *Essai sur les mœurs* (1756) – a major historical work, including sections on China, India and Arabia – did he fully exploit the potential of the subject. In the *Essai*, according to Guy, Voltaire created for the first time a truly universal history, incorporating many subjects, such as commercial revolution, the development of the human mind, astronomy and mathematics, seldom previously touched on. Yet even there – again according to Guy – he frequently prosecuted private quarrels, he interpreted (or misinterpreted) evidence in order to support a particular case, usually involving a veiled attack on the Christian religion, he suppressed evidence incompatible with his case, and he sacrificed truth on the altar of dramatic verisimilitude. In particular, Voltaire frequently ignored facts that would challenge the unity of his concept of a Chinese utopia, necessary to the prosecution of his case against intolerance and abuse. In the end, therefore, in the *Essai*, as elsewhere in his writings, Voltaire more often than not used the Chinese ideal as one more weapon with which to tilt at '*l'infâme*' (the Catholic Church).

In 'The Possibility of Oriental Influence in Hume's Philosophy' (Chapter 5), on the other hand, Nolan Pliny Jacobson concludes that Oriental ideas were in Hume's time so pervasive that neither he nor any of his contemporaries could have escaped their influence. Asia, that is to say, played a prominent role in eighteenth-century thinking, especially that part of it that was, in the future, to prove most influential in promoting secularisation; and it played a dominant role in the shaping of Hume's thought, particularly those parts which were concerned with notions of substance, causality and self – none of which could, in Hume's opinion, be logically inferred from matters of fact, found in our sense impressions. In particular, according to Jacobson, numerous similarities could be found between the thoughts of the Gotama Buddha on these issues and the thoughts of Hume. Not that the views expressed by Buddha and Hume were identical. The chief aim of the Buddha's thought was, according to Jacobson, the discovery of a route to salvation, while the chief aim of Hume's was the discovery of faulty reasoning. Buddha's thought implies a loosening of the individual's social involvement, while Hume's implies a deepening of social interchange. Such differences were to be expected, for they were the product of different times and different cultural traditions. But whence arose the similarities? According to Jacobson, they were the products of Oriental influence, exercised both directly and indirectly, on Hume and his contemporaries. Evidence cited by Jacobson in support of his contention, entirely circumstantial – Hume, according to Jacobson, makes no mention of the Orient in any of his writings* – includes the fact that for almost two centuries, prior to Hume's undertaking the writing of *A Treatise of Human Nature* (1739–40), Europe had been thoroughly exposed to Oriental influence, mainly by way of China; that Leibniz had studied the thought of Chu Hsi – the great synthesiser of Confucian, Taoist and Buddhist thought – accounts of which were supplied to him by the Jesuits; that many of Hume's contemporaries, including Montesquieu, Voltaire, Adam Smith, Quesnay and Hutcheson, were significantly influenced by Oriental ideas; and that at the Jesuit College at La Flèche, where Hume wrote his *Treatise*, the Jesuits had assembled a library of some 40,000 volumes, many concerning the Orient. Efforts to seek out the sources of Hume's thought must, therefore, acknowledge the 'wide range of influences, both Western and Oriental in origin' to which Hume was deliberately, and no doubt in part unconsciously, subjected.

Jacobson's conjecture – that Hume's thought was radically affected by Oriental influence – is clearly of the greatest importance, for if true it would mean that European thought thereafter was equally affected. For as Robert P. Wolff makes clear, in 'Kant's Debt to Hume via Beattie', *Journal of the History of Ideas* (1960), Kant owed an immense debt to Hume – a debt almost as great as that owed, in turn, by many nineteenth-century German philosophers, including Herder, Fichte, Hegel, Schelling, Schopenhauer and Nietzsche, to Kant, whose doctrine of transcendental idealism helped shape the course of European thought in that period.

In his chapter on 'The East and German Romanticism', in Raghavan Iyer (ed.), *The Glass Curtain* (1965) (Chapter 6), Ronald Taylor concludes that Herder – generally seen as a pioneer of German interest in the Orient, mainly India – though fascinated by the culture and civilisation of India, as revealed in

---

* Hume did in fact mention the Orient in his writings. In *Essays, Moral and Political* (1742), p. 151, he remarked that the Quakers were, perhaps, the 'only regular body of *Deists* in the universe, except the *Literati*, or Disciples of *Confucius* in China'.

translations of *Shakuntala*, the *Bhagavad Gita* and other Indian works made available in Germany in the 1780s and 1790s, yet remained in his dealings with the East essentially Western. True, in *Über den Ursprung der Sprache* (On the Origin of Language) (1772), Herder had pointed to the East as the original source of language; in *Auch eine Philosophie der Geschichte zur Bildung der Menschheit* (A Philosophy of History concerning the Formation of Mankind) (1774), waxed lyrical about India's contribution to the development of culture; and in *Ideen zur Philosophie der Geschichte der Menschheit* (Ideas for the Philosophy of the History of Mankind) (1784–91), extolled its moral excellencies. Nevertheless, throughout this period he looked to India not so much for original ideas as for ethical values which might be enlisted in the struggle to secure the achievement of his own didactic purposes. This, according to Taylor, was because Herder and the generation of German thinkers to which he belonged were inclined to look to the outside world primarily for a sense of direction – an inclination which led them to idealise the stimuli they received, magnify the qualities they felt most pertinent to their situation and ignore those that appeared to lie outside their pertinence.

In his chapter on Hegel, in *India and Europe* (1988) (Chapter 7), Wilhelm Halbfass finds that Hegel's interpretation of Indian thought, as found in his *Lectures on the Philosophy of Religion*, *Lectures on the Philosophy of World History* and many other works, was 'insufficient in various respects', lacking in accuracy, leaving 'much to be desired'. A 'son of his time', who had 'no adequate knowledge' of the systematic complexity and historical variability of classical Indian thought, Hegel, whose work should not be measured by abstract standards of scholarly objectivity, tended to deal with Indian ideas as a philosopher, whose philosophy committed him to 'not being neutral'. In his early writings, Hegel had largely ignored India and China, but in his later years he had studied numerous publications concerned with the Orient – these included F. Buchanan, 'On the Religion and Literature of the Burmas' (1801), published in *Asiatic Researches*, Henry Thomas Colebrooke, 'On the Philosophy of the Hindus' (1824), published in *Transactions of the Royal Asiatic Society*, and a series of essays by W. von Humboldt, on the *Bhagavad Gita* – and incorporated the results of his studies into his lectures on the history of philosophy, the philosophy of world history, the philosophy of religion and aesthetics. Not that Hegel's incorporation of new material, coming from the East, significantly affected the philosophical stance he adopted. According to Halbfass, Hegel remained a 'philosophical advocate and herald of . . . European self-representation', surveying Indian thought only from the peak of his own time and his own philosophical system. Asian thought, for Hegel, that is to say, was comprehensible and interpretable only as a preliminary form or presupposition of European thought, in which it remained inherent. Nor, given Hegel's concept of history, as the working out of thought (spirit) could it be otherwise. For according to Hegel's system, Indian thought consisted merely of a stage in the evolution of thought, which reached its fulfilment in Europe. Thus superseded by the Occident, Indian thought remained, therefore, static, trapped in a 'religion of substance', and incapable of further development.

Halbfass's view of Hegel, as a 'philosophical advocate and herald ... of European self-representation', finds substantial support in Dorothy M. Figueira, *The Exotic: A Decadent Quest* (1994). According to Figueira, Hegel, whose understanding of Indian philosophy was based mainly on W. Schlegel's translation of the *Bhagavad Gita* (1823) and Henry Thomas Colebrooke's essay, 'On the Philosophy of the Hindus' (1824), was not adequately informed regarding the true nature of Indian philosophy; and he frequently selected from the material available to him only those parts that suited his preconceived argument. To a certain degree, therefore, Schopenhauer's assessment, that Hegel's attempt to understand world history was naïve and trivial, 'would not be a gratuitous dismissal if it were based on Hegel's interpretation of Indian philosophy' (p. 85).

Schelling appears to have responded more positively to Oriental, mainly Indian, ideas, than Hegel; but in the end, like Hegel, he remained Eurocentric in his approach. In *Philosophie der Mythologie* (Philosophy of Mythology, published posthumously in 1856–7), for instance, he included lengthy sections on India and a number of other Oriental countries, and borrowed numerous Hindu ideas in shaping his own concepts of ultimate identity, difference, the return of the Absolute, pantheism and the 'world soul'. In *Darstellung meines Systems der Philosophie* (Presentation of My System of Philosophy) (1801), he proclaimed the 'point of indifference', which made the absolute accessible as 'undivided' or 'absolute' identity. In *Philosophie und Religion* (Philosophy and Religion) (1804), he referred to the absolute as the one true reality, from which finite things can only be a falling off. Nevertheless, according to Wilhelm Halbfass, 'Schelling and Schopenhauer', *India and Europe* (Chapter 8), Schelling retained throughout his career a clear commitment to Christian revelation; and remained critical of the Romantic glorification of India, as the source of all true religion and philosophy. Schelling's *Philosophie der Mythlogie* may well have represented an 'event in the history of intercultural and interreligious encounters', but it remained an attempt to 'subsume' the Indian phenomena under a 'systematic and fundamentally Christian scheme of a world history of mythology'.

Schopenhauer, according to Halbfass, 'Schelling and Schopenhauer' (Chapter 8), acquired in the course of his life an extensive knowledge of Hinduism and Buddhism; and in his numerous works, particularly the later ones, he made extensive reference to them. His interest in Oriental ideas was first aroused by the Orientalist F. Majer, and in 1813–14, whilst writing *The World As Will and Representation* (1818, second volume 1844), he read Anquetil-Duperron's Latin translation of a Persian version of the *Upanishads*, a work which he later described as 'the most rewarding and edifying reading (with the exception of the original text) that could be possible in this world; it has been the solace of my life, and will be the solace of my death'. Later he read the works of Henry Thomas Colebrooke, H. E. Röer and Rammohan Roy (an influential Indian reformer) on

Hinduism, and Spence Hardy, C. F. Koeppen and E. Burnouf on Buddhism. Yet, surprisingly, Halbfass finds that the question as to how far Schopenhauer's knowledge of Indian material was related to the genesis of his own system cannot be answered with complete clarity and certainty. Schopenhauer may have been exposed to the impression of Indian thought since 1813–14; admitted in 1816, during the production of his main work, that he could not have formulated his doctrine until the 'Upanishads, Plato and Kant were able to all cast their light simultaneously onto a human mind'; and included numerous Indological additions and emendations in the second edition of *The World As Will and Representation* and other, later works. But he nevertheless considered his own thought to be the 'perfection of the Kantian system', from the heights of which one could survey, ponder and assess the contributions to philosophy made by his predecessors and contemporaries. He rejected the Hegelian integration of the Kantian system and the history of philosophy, and he saw no scheme of reflection according to which a succession of cultural traditions and philosophical theories could be construed, and following which Indian and European thought could legitimately be co-ordinated with or subordinated to one another. His approach to Indian philosophy was, so to speak, that of a 'recognitive historiography of philosophy', which remained open to the possibility of finding the same insights in the most diverse historical contexts. Schopenhauer, that is to say, felt that the basic ideas of his philosophy, namely the doctrine of the world as 'will and representation', of a fundamental unity of reality and an apparent projection into spatiotemporal multiplicity, could be found among the Indians, and not just in the form of historical antecedents, but in a sense of truth which knows no historical and geographical restrictions. He may have found exemplary expressions of the 'metaphysical urge', to pierce the veil of spatiotemporal multiplicity and provide liberation from the cycle of life and suffering, in the Indian concept of *māyā*, in the *tat tvam asi* ('that art thou') of the *Upanishads* and the Buddhist goal of *nirvana*, but he considered the concept of *māyā* to be the equivalent of his notion of *principium individuationis*, the 'principle of individuation'. In his view, the *māyā* of the Vedas and the 'appearance' of Kant were identical. They were 'the world in which we live', or ' We ourselves, to the extent that we belong to this world'. He was convinced that both the Indian concept of *māyā* and Kant's 'appearance' were included in his own concept of the objectification of the will, i.e., the realm of validity of the principle of sufficient reason, and that it was here that their true meaning and identity was made manifest.

In 'Schopenhauer: Was India Really a Starting Point?' a chapter in *German Pessimism and Indian Philosophy* (1986) (not included in this collection), Johann Joachim Gesterling comes to a similar, if somewhat cruder, conclusion, namely that Schopenhauer, though fascinated by the Orient, remained essentially uninfluenced by it. Like Hegel, Schopenhauer remained throughout his life Eurocentric in attitude, largely 'unaware of the mechanics of the fundamentally different Indian tradition'. Indian thought he looked on as a practical source of knowledge, that might be exploited to provide support for his anti-Hegelian, non-historical view of time, according to which time is a physiognomic aspect of the will. True, certain aspects of Indian thought, such as the Vedantic *māyā*, are exchangeable and therefore valid as potential influences on Schopenhauer, but hermeneutically his appropriation of Indian thought, in an attempt to support, justify and prove his stance, remains problematic. India, in short, was 'no departure point for Schopenhauer, nor could it strengthen the conceptual content of his philosophy, although it obviously had a very stimulating influence on its form' (Gestering, 1986, pp. 34, 49, 59–60).

Moira Nicholls, on the other hand, in 'The Influences of Eastern Thought on Schopenhauer's Doctrine of the Thing-in-Itself', *The Cambridge Companion to Schopenhauer* (1999) (Chapter 9), concludes that, despite his many assertions to the contrary, Schopenhauer, in the four- or five-year period in which he wrote the first volume of *The World as Will and Representation* (1818), was significantly influenced by the knowledge of Hinduism he acquired from Anquetil-Duperron's retranslation of the *Upanishads* and articles published in *Asiatic Researches* and the *Asiatisches Magazin*; and that, in the years following publication, further knowledge, regarding Hinduism and Buddhism, acquired from such works as Remusat's translation of *The Foe Koue Ki*, Burnouf's *Introduction à l'Histoire du Buddhisme indien* and Spence Hardy's *Eastern Monachism* and *Manual of Buddhism*, persuaded him to shift his position significantly on three issues: the knowability of the thing-in-itself, the nature of the thing-in-itself and the possibility of describing the thing-in-itself. In short, Nicholls concludes, it is plausible to argue that, in the later period at least, the influence of Eastern thought accounts for Schopenhauer's shift from a 'post-Kantian position regarding the thing-in-itself' to one more philosophically aligned with what he took to be the essential tenets of Buddhism and Hinduism.

No such doubt appears to apply in the case of Ralph Waldo Emerson, the noted New England Transcendentalist. According to William Torrey Harris, quoted by Dale Riepe, in 'Emerson and Indian Philosophy' (Chapter 10), Emerson delighted in the 'all-absorbing unity' of the Brahman, the 'all-renouncing ethics' of the Chinese and the Persian, and the 'measureless images of the Arabian and Hindoo poets'. Inspired by Hindu ideas, concerning the nature of absolute being, *maya*, karma and the Oversoul, gleaned from articles published in the *Edinburgh Review*, Wilkin's translation of the *Bhagavad Gita*, Victor Cousin's *Course of the History of Modern Philosophy* (1852), Müller's *A History of Sanskrit Literature* (1860), and the collected works of Sir William Jones, Emerson, according to Riepe, was so deeply influenced by Indian thought that had he not come into contact with it, his writings would have been radically different – a conclusion confirmed by Carl T. Jackson, in his account of 'Oriental Ideas in American Thought', published in the *Dictionary of the History of Ideas* (1973). According to Jackson, Emerson was strongly influenced by his aunt, Mary Moody Emerson, who introduced him to the writings of the brilliant Indian reformer, Rammohan Roy, whose movement, the

Brahmo Samaj, exercised a 'magnetic attraction upon American and English Unitarians throughout the century'. His interest in Oriental thought, which 'blossomed rapidly' after 1837, led to the composition of two major poems, 'Brahma' and 'Hamatreya', and the publication of a selection of Oriental classics in *The Dial* (1842–3). Not that the influence exercised by Indian thought on Emerson – he showed little interest in Buddhism, which he associated with quietism and pessimism – was unlimited. Already, according to Jackson, before he came into contact with Hindu ideas – of Brahman, karma and *māyā* – Emerson had formulated his own ideas – of 'Over-Soul', 'Compensation' and 'Illusions'. Indian thought, that is to say, did not so much shape Emerson's thought as widen and deepen it.

Similarly influenced by Oriental, mainly Indian, thought, was Henry David Thoreau, also a New England Transcendentalist. According to David Albert, 'Thoreau's India: The Impact of Reading in a Crisis' (Chapter 11), Thoreau first made contact with India in 1837, when, at a critical point in his life, he read Hugh Murray, *A Historical and Descriptive Account of British India* (1843) (an encyclopaedic compendium of information about India, compiled by a team of British historians, scholars, travellers and statesmen), extracts from which he copied into his journal. It may be assumed, Albert concludes, that descriptions of Indian mystics, ideas concerning man's relationship with nature and suggestions regarding the possibility of social reform contained in this work, played a significant, possibly even a decisive, part in implanting in Thoreau's mind ideas concerning the role of the recluse in society, the quest for spiritual knowledge and the contribution the recluse might make to the process of social reform and regeneration – ideas which were to play an important part in his thinking for the rest of his life.

The important part that Indian (Hindu) ideas played in Thoreau's work is confirmed by Ellen M. Raghavan and Barry Wood, in 'Thoreau's Indian Quotations in *A Week*' (Chapter 12). This article contains a detailed list of all the Hindu quotations found in Thoreau's *A Week on the Concord and Merrimak Rivers* (1849). Some forty or so in number, the quotations are taken mainly from Wilkin's translations of the *Hitopadesa* and the *Bhagavad Gita*, Rajah Rammohan Roy's translation of *The Veds*, Colebrooke's edition of *The Sankhya Karika*, and the collected works of Sir William Jones. In Raghavan and Wood's opinion, these quotations show that, while writing *A Week*, Thoreau looked on his own activities as a form of Hindu 'discipline' and 'action'.

Several scholars (Glasnapp, Alsdorf, Ôkôchi) have suggested that Nietzsche took a serious interest in Indian thought. But Mervyn Sprung, 'Nietzsche's Trans-European Eye' (Chapter 13), argues that this was not the case. Nietzsche may have been introduced to Indian (mainly Buddhist) thought by Schopenhauer's *The World As Will and Representation*, frequently quoted (and misquoted) Hindu and Buddhist works, and numbered Paul Deusson, a leading orientalist (Sanskritist), among his closest friends, but, according to Sprung, a close examination of his personal library, his correspondence, and the recollections of a number of his closest friends suggests that Nietzsche's interest in Indian thought remained superficial. A copy of Oldenberg's *Buddha: Sein Leben, Seine Lehre, Seine Gemeinde,* for instance, found in his library following his death, had never been opened. His quotations from Hindu and Buddhist texts, seldom precise, presuppose merely knowledge of the *Ṛg Veda,* Deussen's *Das System des Vedanta,* Duperron's Latin version of the *Upanishads* and a French translation of the *Laws of Manu.* Nietzsche, according to Sprung, may have shown great perspicacity in sensing the Buddha's freedom from moral self-deception, but he betrayed little or no awareness of Buddhist philosophy, beyond the doctrine of release from suffering. His reading of Schopenhauer's *The World As Will and Representation* – as revealed in the prolific marginal markings and underlining of the 1873 edition – betrays an interest, not in Indian ideas, but in the 'travail and death of the genius', and certain questions concerning biology. In his correspondence with Deussen, Nietzsche never once, in twenty-four years, broached the subject of India; and he never asked a single question about Indian philosophy. Nietzsche's Trans-European Eye, in short, was more European than 'trans'. Indian ideas made little or no impression on him. They penetrated his mind about as much as 'drops of water penetrate a goose's feathers'.

Robert G. Morrison, in *Nietzsche and Buddhism* (1997) (not included in this collection) similarly finds that, given the amount of information about Buddhism, particularly the Mahāyāna version, available at the time, Nietzsche's response to the more philosophical aspects of the subject was distinctly limited. Nevertheless, Morrison concludes that Buddhism – seen by Nietzsche as an example of passive nihilism – played a central part in Nietzsche's analysis of the evolution of European culture – an evolution which, in Nietzsche's opinion, was likely in the near future to arrive at a crisis point, similar to the one that had afflicted India shortly before the coming of the Buddha. Not that Nietzsche necessarily had a profound understanding of the history of Buddhism. On the contrary, his knowledge of the subject appears to have been acquired almost entirely from the writings of Schopenhauer, Oldenburg's *Buddha,* Müller's *Selected Essays* and Koeppen's *Die Religion des Buddha*; and some doubt even remains about how far he actually read these works. A more likely source of Nietzsche's understanding of Buddhism might be found in the works of a number of contemporary British anthropologists, in particular Edward Tyler, Walter Bagehot and Sir John Lubbock, writing at the time.

Nietzsche's interest in Indian thought may well, as Sprung and Morrison suggest, have remained for the most part limited. But as Thomas H. Brobjer, 'The Absence of Political Ideals in Nietzsche's Writings: The Case of the Laws of Manu and the Associated Caste-Society' (Chapter 14) – an article mainly designed to show that Nietzsche did not find in the Laws of Manu the model of an ideal political system – shows, such was not always the case. In his article, Brobjer draws attention to the fact that, in May 1888, shortly before beginning *The Anti-Christ,* Nietzsche read and carefully annotated Louis Jacolliot's French translation of the Laws of Manu – a collection of Hindu laws dating from about the first century BC – published in *Les legislateurs religieux* (1876), a copy of which remains in his library. It is not known where Nietzsche acquired a copy of Jacolliot's translation, but he may well have seen it mentioned in Elizabeth Robins, 'Maenadism in Religion', an article published in the *Atlantic Weekly* some years earlier. Not that Nietzsche's reading of the Laws of Manu, as reflected in *The Antichrist* (sections 56–8) and *The Twilight of the Idols* ('The Improvers of Mankind'), led him radically to alter his political opinions. On the contrary, according to Brobjer, he merely cited the society of Manu as an example of a type of society/value system that was designed primarily not to promote creativity (Hellas, the Renaissance), or tame the animal (Christianity), but to preserve order and stability (Rome). Nietzsche used the Laws of Manu, in other words, not to promote some kind of political ideal, but to criticise Christianity and modernity, seen as being unhealthy and degenerate.

Finally, Barbara Spannhake, 'Umwertung einer Quelle', *Nietzsche Studien* (1999) (not included in this collection) – a re-evaluation of Carl Friedrich Koeppen's *Die Religion des Buddha und ihre Entstehung* (1857) as a source of Nietzsche's *The Birth of Tragedy* – agrees with Sprung and Morrison that Nietzsche's understanding of Buddhism was inadequate; and that he may have acquired the limited understanding he had from Schopenhauer, Oldenberg, Müller and Koeppen. But she suggests that Morrison, like many other students of Nietzsche, including Arifuku, Dumoulin, Ôkôchi, Brusotti and Hay, failed to make adequate allowance for the possibility that Koeppen's work, a copy of which Nietzsche borrowed from the University of Basel library in October 1870 – *The Birth of Tragedy* was published in 1872 – may have provided a significant source of Nietzsche's understanding of Buddhism, as reflected in his first major work. Though Nietzsche refers to Buddhism only three times in *The Birth of Tragedy*, as an example of a negation of the will, an example of a tragic culture and an example of escape from Dionysian orgy, Spannhake finds that the ideas reflected in these references, which may in part at least be derived from Koeppen, are to some extent central to the construction of *The Birth of Tragedy*. As she puts it in the concluding paragraph of her article:

> Beiden Darstellungen, der Koeppens ebenso wie der Nietzsches, liegt also ein emanzipatorisch-aufklärerischer Anspruch zugrunde. Im Unterschied zu Schopenhauer, dem philosophisches Erkennen Aufklärung über falschen Schein, folglich negative Ausfklärung ist, aus der er eine Ethik der Willensverneinung ableitet, eignet sowohl der Koeppenschen als auch der Nietzscheschen Vorstellung grundsätzlich ein welt- und lebensbejahendes Element. Während Koeppen jedoch Emanzipation aus sozial-politischer Perspektive propagiert, erkennt Nietzsche in der Theorie der ästhetischen Rechtfertigung eine Möglichkeit, sich aus der Abhängigkeit vom metaphysischen Willen, dessen Instrument der Mensch ist, zu befreien, indem er in der Kunst das Wesen der Welt zu erkennen und die aus dieser Erkenntnis resultierende nihilistische Folgerung zu überwinden vermag.

Readers interested in Nietzsche's use of the Laws of Manu in *The Antichrist* might also like to read Andreas Urs Sommer, 'Ex Oriente Lux? Zur Ermeintlichen "Ostorientierung" in Nietzsche's *Antichrist*', *Nietzsche Studien* (1999) (not included in this collection), in which Sommer comes to more or less the same conclusion as Brobjer.

In 'Taoism and Jung: Synchronicity and the Self', *Philosophy East and West* (1996) (Chapter 15), Harold Coward explains that in his book, *Jung and Eastern Thought* (1985), he had already explored the influence of Indian concepts, such as *karma*, *citta*, *buddhitattva*, *tapas*, and *mandala*, on the development of Carl Jung's notions of 'archetype', 'psyche', the 'collective unconscious', 'active imagination' and 'circumambulation'. But the question of Eastern influence on Jung's most complex concept, 'the self', was there given very sketchy treatment. At that time he had supposed that the notion of *atman*, as found in the Hindu *Upanishads*, was the major Eastern formative influence on Jung's concept of 'the self'. But additional research led him to conclude that Chinese Taoism, rather than Hinduism, provided the formative influence on Jung's concept. This Taoist influence, Coward concludes, came to Jung's 'self' concept not directly, but by the way of another of Jung's ideas, namely synchronicity – an idea, which depends directly on the Taoist Chinese text *I Ching*, with which Jung experimented for a whole summer in 1920. Failure to recognise this accounts for the fact that Jung is frequently accused of being 'simply a gnostic in modern psychological dress'.

As Irene Eber, 'Martin Buber and Taoism', *Monumenta Serica* (1994) (Chapter 16), shows, Martin Buber, like Jung was fascinated by Taoism, and like Jung he incorporated many Taoist concepts into his work. Buber approached Taoism by way of translations of three Chinese works, the *Chuang-tzu*, P'u Sung-ling's *Liao-chai chih-i*, and the *Tao-te-ching*, selections from which, in collaboration with Wang Ching-t'ao, a lecturer at the Seminar for Oriental Languages, Berlin, he published in 1910 and 1911. About the same time he wrote an essay, mainly concerned with the *Tao-te-ching*, which he regarded as the fountain head of Taoism, later appended, as an 'Afterword' to the 1910 publication; and in 1942 he published a translation, probably prepared earlier, of eight of its chapters. But, according to Eber, Buber did not engage in a sustained exploration of Taoist ideas, as represented in these and other Taoist works. What he did was to select and appropriate ideas, mainly from the *Tao-te-ching*, that at various times corresponded to his own ideas, retranslating them into his philosophical discourse. Taoist ideas that he appropriated, employed in his definition of the *tzaddick* (sage, genuine person), his attempts to overcome duality and his engagement with the problems of state and society, include those of oneness, duality and non-acting. Buber, that is to say, created for the *Tao-te-ching* a place in his own philosophical and religious discourse. In so doing, he may have been the 'first among Jewish philosophers who appropriated ideas of Taoism and integrated these into a specifically Jewish philosophical discourse'.

Finally, Reinhard May, in his conclusion to *Heidegger's Hidden Sources* (Chapter 17), an astonishing piece of research, concludes that Heidegger's thought was to a remarkable extent influenced by East Asian ideas. In a number of important cases, that is to say, Heidegger may, without citing any of his sources, have appropriated ideas germane to his work from German translations of Daoist, Zen Buddhist and other East Asian classics, in particular the *Zhuangzi* and the *Laozi*. As May remarks, in a footnote to his conclusion (note 153), and in the conclusion itself, it is now possible to surmise that Heidegger received the 'essential' impetus of his 'new' poetic thinking not from pre-Socratic thought, Western (Theo-) mystical thinking, Nietzsche's political thinking and Hölderlin's poetry, but from ancient Chinese thought, in which, according to May, metaphysics was never developed.

The conclusions drawn by Reinhard May, in *Heidegger's Hidden Sources*, appear all the more remarkable in view of the fact that, according to May, with the exception of Otto Pöggeler, Heidegger scholars have failed to take the possibility of Oriental influence on Heidegger seriously, even when reliable evidence to the contrary was made available.

CONCLUSION

Three reasonable conclusions can be drawn from the articles contained in this collection: that many European (Western) thinkers, operating at the cutting edge of European thought in the modern period, took a significant, and at times even a profound, interest in Oriental ideas (a conclusion which would seem to challenge Iyer's thesis regarding the existence of a 'glass curtain' dividing Asia and Europe); that European thinkers, inevitably perhaps, in their engagement with the Orient, all too often tended to subsume Oriental ideas into a European schema, submit them to distinctly European standards of truth, and enrol them as instances in strictly European debates (a conclusion which would seem to lend support to Iyer's thesis); and that Oriental influence on European thought tended to be cumulative and progressive, albeit intermittent, eventually resulting, in the twentieth century, in a ready willingness, on the part of many European thinkers, such as Jung, Buber and Heidegger, to exploit the rich resources made available to them (a conclusion which would seem to suggest that Iyer's glass curtain, if it ever existed, has been finally smashed).

There was, it may be noted, nothing unusual in the Eurocentric response to foreign cultures and ideas, displayed by many European thinkers in the period of the European Renaissance/Enlightenment. Throughout their history the Chinese remained largely indifferent to the existence of alien cultures, quite impervious to their influence. And though Chinese literati did at time display a willingness to discuss European (Christian) ideas with Jesuit missionaries, genuine interest remained limited. In 1770 the Chinese Emperor ordered the expulsion of the Jesuit and other Christian missionaries from China. Similarly in India the Hindus, until the beginning of the nineteenth century at least, showed no interest whatsoever in foreign cultures. And even when foreign (mainly British) conquest did enforce a response, the response elicited remained Hindu. Western ideas, that is to say, were simply comprehended and assimilated within the framework of Hindu tradition. As J. L. Mehta remarks, in *India and the West* (1985), at no time has traditional Hinduism 'defined itself in relation to the other, nor acknowledged the other in its unassimilable otherness' (quoted in W. Halbfass, *India and Europe*, p. 172).

The question arises as to whether the European (Western) thinkers cited in this collection contributed to the creation of the type of orientalist discourse or prejudice identified by Said, in *Orientalism*. Given the degree of Eurocentrism discovered in their work, it might be expected that they would have done so. Yet, with the single glaring exception of Hegel – who might with some justification be described as the founding father of modern orientalism – the contrary appears to be the case. That is not to suggest that they were not occasionally guilty of perpetuating orientalist images: of India and China as countries whose cultures were static, incapable of change, or in decline, from a once great classical civilisation (Leibniz, Herder, Hegel, Schelling); of India as the cradle of the human race – a concept which might seem to imply that the Indian peoples and their cultures were in some way childish and immature (Herder, Hegel, Schopenhauer); and of the Indian and Chinese people as gentle (effeminate) and lethargic – characteristics to be explained by the nature of their vegetarian diet (Herder, Nietzsche). But such occasional – very occasional – orientalisms are in no way characteristic of the approach adopted by virtually all of the major European thinkers concerned. Malebranche, for instance in his *Note on the Conversation*, and in the *Conversation* itself, gives the impression that he considered Chinese philosophy to be pre-eminently rational, worthy of the highest consideration. Leibniz, in his *Novissima Sinica*, praised the Chinese people for their 'precepts of ethics and politics, adapted to the present life and use of mortals'. For Leibniz, China, far from being inferior, was an 'Anti-Europe', an Oriental Europe, possibly excelling Europe in the refinement of its culture. Wolff was immensely impressed with the Chinese political and educational systems. For him, China was a country where 'Kings were Philosophers' and 'Philosophers Kings'. Schelling considered Indian ideas, with which he felt a great affinity, more advanced than those of Hegel, his great contemporary. Schopenhauer found Anquetil-Duperron's translation of the *Upanishads* to be 'the most rewarding and edifying reading (with the exception of the original text) that could be possible in this world'. They were the 'solace of his life', and would be the 'solace of his death'. Emerson and Thoreau found in Hindu philosophy, in particular the *Bhagavad Gita*, the Vedānta and the *Sankhya Karika*, an escape from the narrow confines of New England Puritanism. Nietzsche looked on Indian philosophy as the only major parallel to European philosophy. Jung found in Taoism the basic building blocks of his concept of self. Buber maintained a steady interest in the *Tao-te-ching* throughout his life. Finally, Heidegger so admired East Asian thought that he appears to have engaged at times in what might, in other circumstances, have been described as plagiarism. Yet the possibility remains that, in projecting images of Asia as a continent, inhabited by peoples who believed variously that the world was essentially fixed and unchanging, insubstantial (*māyā*, a dream), uncreated, unknowable and unworthy of value, European (Western) thinkers such as Malebranche (Mungello), Hegel (Halbfass), Schopenhauer (Halbfass and Nicholls), Emerson (Riepe), Thoreau (Albert) and Nietzsche (Sprung and Brobjer), may have inadvertently promoted images of the Orient, already well entrenched in the European imagination, as timeless, unchanging, irrational, effeminate and inferior.

I

MALEBRANCHE AND CHINESE PHILOSOPHY

David E. Mungello

This paper was delivered in slightly altered form at the opening session of the Special Seminar on China and the European Enlightenment at Yale University on 8 October 1976. I am indebted to Julia Ching, Daniel J. Cook, and Young-kun Kim for their critiques of this paper.

In the first half of the eighteenth century, the dominant cultural viewpoint of northwestern Europe was shifting from an insular to a cosmopolitan Euro-centrism.[1] As a result, European interpretations of philosophies from the other side of the world became less superficial, but remained centripetal and were limited by distinctly European concerns. The significance as well as the limits of this shift in perspective is important to an understanding of the European Enlightenment's interest in Chinese philosophy. One of the ingredients of this cosmopolitan Eurocentrism was an interest in China. In contrast, Nicolas Malebranche (1638–1715) did not have a compelling interest in China. Nevertheless, his concern with metaphysical demonstration of his faith drew him into the Chinese Rites Controversy, and he responded by composing, late in life, a hypothetical conversation between a Chinese philosopher and a Christian philosopher. From Malebranche's *Conversation* (1708) one finds a thread in intellectual history running to Leibniz and his composition of the 'Discours sur la théologie naturelle des Chinois' (1716) – more familiarly known as the 'Lettre sur la philosophie chinoise à M. de Rémond'. Both

David E. Mungello, 'Malebranche and Chinese Philosophy', *Journal of the History of Ideas*, 41: 4, 1980, pp. 551–78.

Leibniz and his discourse foreshadow many of the cosmopolitan Eurocentric attitudes toward China which become so prominent in the eighteenth-century European Enlightenment.

Malebranche (1638–1715) was the youngest son of a secretary to Louis XIII. His education at the college of La Marche and the Sorbonne left him with little interest in scholastic Aristotelianism. He became a novice in the French Congregation of the Oratory in 1660 and was ordained in 1664. In the same year of his ordination, he read Descartes' 'Traité de l'homme ou de la formation du foetus', a physiological treatise, and thereafter became a Cartesian. Malebranche had all the interests appropriate to the modern Cartesian spirit. As a scientist and mathematician, he made detailed observations of insects and was one of the earliest to analyze colors in terms of frequencies of vibration. He also had a mystical side and sought to combine the 'spiritualist' element in Descartes with the Platonic-Augustinian tradition. Yet he transcended both traditions to become a creative thinker on his own.

Philosophy and theology tended to become merged in Malebranche in a way which made his philosophy very controversial. He was a mild-mannered man who was drawn into polemical debate throughout his life. Unlike Leibniz, Malebranche had little interest in China or Chinese philosophy until late in life. His composition of the *Entretien d'un philosophe chrétien et d'un philosophe chinois sur l'existence et la nature de Dieu* came after his philosophy was fully developed. In fact, without his renowned reputation, it is unlikely that the forces which led to his somewhat reluctant composition of the *Conversation* would have urged him down this path. Foremost among these forces was Artus de Lionne.

I. MALEBRANCHE'S SOURCES ON CHINESE PHILOSOPHY

A. *Artus de Lionne as a stimulus and interpreter*

Artus de Lionne (Liang Huang-jen, 1655–1713), Bishop of Rosalie, had a much greater interest in China than Malebranche had. De Lionne was one of the early participants in the Society of Foreign Missions (Société des Missions étrangères) and his service first took him to Siam. There he met and clashed with the more established representatives of the Society of Jesus. While the Jesuits stressed the adaptation and assimilation of Christianity to the local culture, the members of the Society of Foreign Missions were resistant to de-Europeanizing the Christianity that they propagated.

In 1689, De Lionne entered Kwangtung province in China. Later he traveled to Fukien province to join Charles Maigrot (Yen Tang, d. 1730), a fellow member of the Society of Foreign Missions. Maigrot stood in absolute opposition to most of the Jesuits on interpreting the Chinese rites, and when De Lionne supported Maigrot, he was clearly aligning himself against the Jesuits. In 1693, Maigrot was made vicar-apostolic of Fukien[2] and issued a mandate which proscribed in the region of his vicariate certain missionary practices which had attempted to accommodate Christianity to certain Chinese, particularly

Confucian, religious practices. Maigrot condemned the Jesuit tendency to reconcile certain teachings in ancient Chinese classics with Christianity and specifically forbade Christian neophytes to participate in ceremonies to honor either Confucius or their ancestors. He further prohibited the words *ching t'ien* (revere Heaven) from being placed on tablets in Christian churches and, finally, he proscribed the use of the indigenous Chinese terms *shang-ti* (King-on-high) and *t'ien* (Heaven) and insisted on the newer *t'ien-chu* (Lord of Heaven) for referring to the Christian God. The evidence would indicate that De Lionne strongly supported Maigrot's mandate.[3]

Maigrot acquired particular notoriety from an embarrassing interview that took place when he accompanied the papal legate Charles de Tournon (1668–1710) to an audience with the K'ang-hsi emperor in 1706. In this interview, Maigrot's ignorance of the Chinese language, the Confucian literature, and even details of Christian missionary history in China was exposed so that the K'ang-hsi emperor formed a strong prejudice against him.[4] De Lionne's close identification with the methods of Maigrot does not lend any confidence to relying on De Lionne's interpretations of Chinese philosophy.

After leaving Fukien, De Lionne went to Szechwan where he was named vicar apostolic of the province of Szechwan.[5] De Lionne publicly entered the Rites Controversy with his *Lettre de M. l'Abbé de Lionne ... à M. Charmot, Directeur du Séminaire des Missions Etrangères de Paris*, November 14, 1693, at Canton and published in 1700 at Rome.[6] This work is extremely partisan in tone and was composed in rebuttal to Michel le Tellier's widely read apologia of Jesuit missionary methods entitled *Défense des nouveaux chrétiens et des missionaires de la Chine, du Japon et des Indes ...* (Paris, 1696). De Lionne also wrote the *Lettre à Madame de Lionne, sur la libelle des Jésuites contre l'Evêque de Rosalie, son Fils*[7] (Rome, 1701) and *Observationes in quaesita Sinarum imperatori a patribus S. J. proposita et illius ad ea responsionem circa Coeli, Avorum et Confucii Cultum, S. D. N. Papae Clementi XI ab episcopo Rosaliensi ...* (Rome, 1704).[8]

These publications would have given De Lionne a considerable reputation in Europe. The sympathetic biography of Malebranche by Yves Marie André, S. J. (1675–1764) claims that De Lionne's 'inflexible zeal against Chinese superstitions' caused him to be banished from China along with other uncompromising Christians.[9] He returned to France in 1702 after thirteen years of residence in China.[10]

De Lionne applied his knowledge of China to the cause of the Society of Foreign Missions in the Rites Controversy which was then at its peak in Europe. De Lionne seems to have spent hours conversing with eminent men of letters who were or might be persuaded to support the cause against the Jesuits. He visited Jacques Bossuet (1627–1704), Bishop of Meaux and a leading theologian of his age, and helped bring Bossuet into the Society of Foreign Mission's offensive against the Jesuit position on the Chinese rites.[11]

Malebranche stood especially high on De Lionne's list of eminent figures to be visited. To begin with, De Lionne is said to have used Malebranche's philosophy in teaching Christianity in China and was eager to express his gratitude to the master in person. But De Lionne also had the aim of persuading Malebranche to write a piece which could become a weapon in the rites debate. Malebranche's present status in studies of seventeenth-century philosophy is lower than in his own age. To his contemporaries, Malebranche was one of the most respected minds of the seventeenth century, and they visited him in droves at the Oratory house on Rue Saint-Honoré or in the salons sponsored by his socially eminent Parisian associates.[12] Given Malebranche's eminence, one can understand De Lionne's urgency in attempting to win the reluctant Malebranche over to the need for writing such a treatise.[13]

Without De Lionne, it is unlikely that Malebranche's *Conversation between a Christian Philosopher and Chinese philosopher* ever would have been written. Unlike his contemporary Leibniz, whose interest in China took the form of inquiry, one imagines Malebranche as a predominantly passive listener to De Lionne's many discussions of China and Chinese philosophy. Malebranche was in his sixties and not in the best of health. Furthermore, he did not share the intensity of De Lionne's anti-Jesuit obsessions. Nevertheless, Malebranche was a man who had committed much of his life to combatting idolatry and irreligion, and as he heard De Lionne discuss the 'erroneous' Chinese conceptions of the Deity, Malebranche responded to the need for a treatise rectifying what he regarded as mistaken views on the nature of God.[14]

De Lionne was not only the prime motivator of Malebranche's composition of the *Conversation*, he was also Malebranche's primary source of information on Chinese philosophy. Consequently, much of the validity of Malebranche's work will depend upon the accuracy of De Lionne's interpretation. In his later *Note on the Conversation*, in which he explains the genesis of the *Conversation*, Malebranche summarizes in six points the views of Chinese literati or, as Malebranche qualifies, '. . . at least those with whom the person who has instructed me in their beliefs has conversed.'[15] This person is De Lionne, and the statement indicates that De Lionne's sources were oral rather than textual. The nature of his sources would help explain De Lionne's, and consequently, Malebranche's emphasis on the currently prominent School of *li*, to the neglect of other currents of Chinese thought.

The six points in Malebranche's summary are:

1st. That there are only two types of being to know – *li* (or supreme Reason, Order, Wisdom, Justice) and matter [*ch'i*].
2nd. That *li* and matter are eternal beings.
3rd. That *li* does not subsist by itself and independently of matter. Apparently, they regard it as form or as a quality distributed in matter.

4th.   That *li* is neither wise nor intelligent although it is supreme wisdom and intelligence.

5th.   That *li* is not free and that it acts only by means of the necessity of its nature without knowing or wishing anything of what it makes.

6th.   That it renders intelligent, wise, and just the portions of matter disposed to receive intelligence, wisdom, and justice. For according to the literati of whom I speak, the mind of man is only purified matter, or disposed to be informed by means of *li*, and by it rendered intelligent or capable of thinking. This is apparently why they agree that the *li* is the light which illuminates all men and that it is in it that we see all things.[16]

In these six points, Malebranche misleadingly implies that all Chinese literati (i.e. Confucianists) make a fundamental distinction between *li* and 'matter' (i.e. *ch'i*) when, in fact, the distinction belongs mainly to the School of *li* Neo-Confucianism. The stress upon *li* and matter as well as the specific issues discussed in the six points strongly indicate that the ultimate source of Malebranche's interpretation of Chinese philosophy was the School of *li*. Although *li* has a long history of usage and considerable differences of interpretation in Chinese philosophy, its meaning within the School of *li* was fairly well established on the authority of Chu Hsi's writings.[17] Acceptance of an established meaning had become even more pronounced in the late seventeenth century because of the Ch'ing dynasty's official sponsorship of Chu Hsi's authority.

This does not mean that there was universal acceptance of Chu Hsi's interpretation of *li*. For example, in the sixteenth century Wang Yang-ming (1472–1529) and in the seventeenth century Wang Fu-chih (1619–92) differed with Chu Hsi's interpretation. However, the creative currents of Chinese culture were not very apparent to most of the missionaries who as foreigners were occupied with the difficulties of learning the Chinese language and reading the classical texts. As a result, most missionaries tended to perceive only the surface of contemporary Chinese culture.[18] Philosophically speaking, that surface was dominated by Chu Hsi's writings. For these reasons, the following evaluation of the accuracy of Malebranche's interpretation of Chinese philosophy is based upon the assumption that Chu Hsi's Neo-Confucianism was the ultimate source from which his interpreters drew.

Malebranche's reference in the first point to supreme Reason, Order, Wisdom, and Justice as synonyms for *li* implies a possible allusion to the four cardinal virtues of Confucianism. They are *jen* (Benevolence or Goodness), *li* (Propriety or Ritual Order), *chih* (Wisdom) and *i* (Righteousness or Justice). The four cardinal virtues were very prominent in the school of Chinese philosophy transmitted to Malebranche. While he consistently transliterates *li*, Malebranche refers to *ch'i* only in translated form as 'matter.' But speaking more precisely, *ch'i* means 'matter-energy' or 'material force.' As used by the School of *li*, *li* means principle in the sense of an organizing element. *Li* is sometimes referred to as 'infrastructure,' in contrast to 'superstructure' in order to highlight the contrast between inner organization versus surface manifestation. There are very strong organic connotations in *li*, as there are in many elements in Neo-Confucianism.

With reference to Malebranche's second point, it is misleading to say that *ch'i* (material force) is eternal. *Ch'i* is permanently present in the world but is in constant flux. On the third point, it is over-simplified to say that *li* cannot exist independently of matter. In one sense this is true, but there are two aspects to the relationship between *li* and *ch'i*. In the chronological dimension *li* is co-temporal with *ch'i* and cannot exist apart from *ch'i*, but in a second dimension *li* has a logical priority over *ch'i*.[19]

The fourth point presents a superficial conception of *li*. While it is true that *li* is not regarded as wise or intelligent, the philosophy of Chu Hsi regards *li* as but one of three manifestations of Heaven. Chu Hsi states that in the Chinese classics, Heaven (*t'ien*) '... sometimes designates the blue sky (*ts'angts'ang*), sometimes it signifies the sovereign lord (*chu-tsai*) and sometimes it denotes principle (*li*) alone.'[20] Chu Hsi also states 'Heaven is principle (*li*) but the blue sky is also Heaven, and the sovereign lord (*chu-tsai*) above is also Heaven.'[21]

The criticism applied to the fourth point also applies to the fifth point. To say that *li* is neither conscious nor wills anything of its creation is, in one sense, accurate. Chu Hsi himself says something similar.[22] However, to refer to *li* as neither conscious nor willful in the way that Malebranche does is meaningless if one realizes that Chu Hsi used *li* to designate specifically that part of Heaven which is neither conscious nor willful. Malebranche overextends this one aspect because he fails to realize that there is another dimension of Heaven which Chu Hsi designated as *chu-tsai* (sovereign worker) and which is conscious and wills things. In the sixth point, to say that the mind consists only of purified matter is to overemphasize the material aspect in the School of *li* Neo-Confucianism.

B. Longobardi's treatise on Chinese philosophy as a possible source

In his letter to Charmot, director of the Society of Foreign Missions, De Lionne makes no reference to Chinese texts nor does he show any evidence of familiarity with the literature of Chinese philosophy. This omission is not necessarily typical of those who oppose an accommodating interpretation of Chinese rites. For example, the Jesuit Nicholas Longobardi (1565–1655) and the Franciscan Antoine de Sainte-Marie (alias Antonio Caballero a Santa Maria, Li An-tang; 1602–69) both wrote treatises which include extensive quotations from Chinese classical and other philosophic texts in arguing against the accommodating interpretation of Chinese rites.[23]

The extent to which Malebranche might draw from Longobardi's *Traité sur quelques points de la religion des Chinois* is difficult to determine. He makes only one explicit reference to Longobardi's treatise; the reference comes in an appendix to the *Note on the Conversation* entitled 'Testimonies of Several Jesuits Regarding the Atheism of the Chinese.'[24] But the reference is brief and gives no indication of specific borrowing. One modern scholar has argued that Longobardi's treatise is an important link between the Chinese concept *li* and Malebranche's treatment of *li* in his *Conversation*.[25] Leibniz's correspondent Nicolas Rémond felt that Malebranche's *Conversation* made profitable use of Longobardi's treatise.[26] However, neither of these men nor any others have yet made specific connections between Longobardi's treatise and Malebranche's *Conversation*.

Nevertheless, there may be some basis to the claim that Malebranche relied on Longobardi's treatise. For example, Malebranche's Chinese philosopher states: '... what we call spirit or soul, is according to our Chinese doctors only organic and subtle matter.'[27] A similar interpretation of the Chinese spirit or soul as a rarified form of matter is found in Longobardi's treatise:

> I say, first, that the Chinese regard the life of man to consist of the narrow union of the parts which are in him, which they call the entities of heaven and earth. The entity of heaven is an air very pure, very light and of the nature of fire, which forms the soul or the vital and animal spirits, which they call *hun*, that is, soul. The entity of the earth is a grosser air, heavy and of a terrestrial nature, in which it forms a body with all the humors. This is what they call *po*, that is, the human body or cadaver.
>
> I say, secondly, that the death of a man is only the separation of the parts of which he is composed, and after this separation they return to the places which are appropriate to them. It is necessary to note that the Chinese give the name of air to the soul in several books, so that they conceive it like a corporeal thing, although very subtle.[28]

There is also evidence of Malebranche's borrowing from Longobardi in one of the few passages from the Chinese philosopher which distinguishes between the beliefs of the savant sect (i.e. Confucianism) and the beliefs of other segments of the population.[29] Malebranche's reference to the gods of stone and wood may have been derived from a passage in Longobardi's treatise on Chinese religion which refers to the very similar 'idols of the woods and earth.' The significance of this possible borrowing is that it is one of the few interpretations of Chinese philosophy by Malebranche that can be traced, through Longobardi, to a specific Chinese source.[30]

Longobardi's treatise was translated into French and published by the Society of Foreign Missions at Paris in 1701, the approximate time of De Lionne's return from China. The work was controversial and was doubtless discussed by intellectual circles in Paris interested in the Chinese rites question. Circumstances are favorable to support Malebranche's use of Longobardi's treatise in composing his *Conversation*, and yet the evidence needs to be more substantiated before a firm claim can be made.

It is also significant that Malebranche makes no reference to Sainte-Marie's *Traité sur quelques points importants de la mission de la Chine* although this work would have supported several of his arguments in the *Conversation*. It is not clear that Malebranche even read this work, although it had also been published at Paris in 1701 and, with the Longobardi treatise, was commonly familiar to those interested in China. In contrast, Leibniz was to rely heavily upon Longobardi's and Sainte-Marie's treatises for his information on Chinese philosophy in composing his *Discours sur la théologie naturelle des Chinois* (1716). Leibniz was able to include extensive quotations and specific citations from Chinese texts which may be traced back to the Chinese originals for an assessment of the accuracy of interpretation.[31] Malebranche's sources of information on Chinese philosophy in the *Conversation* are of a far more amorphous substance.

Since De Lionne showed little inclination toward citing from Chinese texts in making his arguments, he did not provide Malebranche with specific sources. Though Malebranche had access to specific sources through European-language works on China (see below), he made minimal use of them. Consequently, he is not absolved from the responsibility for using questionable source material. The methods of De Lionne's writing were primarily those of the polemicist while Malebranche's methods were more those of a philosopher. In the *Conversation*, Malebranche was more concerned with the logical validity of the argument itself than with the accuracy of his sources. But, of course, the argument becomes dubious if the sources are inaccurate. I would suggest that Malebranche's lack of attention to the validity of his sources derives in part from the insular Eurocentrism of his day.

C. Spinozism as a possible source and motivation

In this context of insular Eurocentrism, Malebranche may have been motivated to write the *Conversation* more because he recognized signs of the Spinozistic enemy in Chinese philosophy than because of any great interest in China. In his letter of June 1713 to Fénelon, Malebranche complains that his composition of the *Conversation* was not based on any desire to participate in the Chinese Rites Controversy and in the debate between the Jesuits and the Society of Foreign Missions, but simply to satisfy the repeated requests of De Lionne. Malebranche states that he had permitted the *Conversation* to be published because he believed he could use it to make clear that he had written not against the Jesuits but against Spinozists in disguise.[32] Furthermore, at the beginning of the *Note on the Conversation*, Malebranche concedes that his initial disinclination to publish the *Conversation* gave way under the urgings of his friends in order to combat seventeenth and eighteenth century libertinism or freethinking which rejected religious tradition and authority. Secondly, he sought to combat the rumored charge of anti-Jesuitism that had arisen while the *Conversation* circulated in manuscript.

To many Christian thinkers of the late seventeenth and early eighteenth centuries, libertinism was a far more serious problem than questions involving the Chinese rites. For these defenders of the faith, the Chinese Rites Controversy was important only as it related to their battles with Benedict

Spinoza (1632–77) and certain followers of Descartes who carried Cartesian principles in freethinking directions. Spinoza, in particular, was regarded as a deadly enemy of the Christian faith.

There was a tendency in seventeenth- and eighteenth-century Europe to connect Spinoza's philosophy with Chinese philosophy. The perception of similarities between the two philosophies is not without some basis, but it was carried to extremes by the inability of Christian thinkers to distinguish differences between philosophies outside of the orthodox Christian line. Spinozism was heterodox because it was monist philosophy, that is, reality is reducible to one substance, whereas for Christianity there are two fundamental and irreconcilable substances – matter and spirit. Spinoza called this one substance God or Nature (*Deus sive Natura*) which is infinite and has infinite attributes each with infinite modes.[33] Spinozism was also heterodox because of its alleged pantheism, thus obliterating the fundamental Christian distinction between God as creator and the world as creation. Spinoza also denied any sense of conscious personality to God. In addition, Spinoza's alleged pantheism eliminated the Christian sense of free will by making God responsible for all actions and denying personal choice to the individual.

Chinese philosophy was linked to Spinozism because certain interpreters of Chinese philosophy had held that the Chinese recognized only one substance which consists of matter in degrees ranging between gross and rarified. These interpreters held that the two basic Chinese states of being, *li*, and *ch'i*, were not really separate substances. For example, Longobardi had argued that *li* was not regarded by the Chinese as a spiritual substance, but only as rarified matter. In De Lionne's view, *li* is not sufficiently independent, intelligent, nor free to be regarded as a spiritual substance. Neither Longobardi nor De Lionne saw the *li* as having any features of personality. Of course, there were other interpreters, particularly the Jesuits, who disagreed with these views and argued not only that these interpretations of *li* and *ch'i* were inaccurate but that they were limited to only one school of Chinese philosophy and were therefore based on an incomplete survey of Chinese philosophy.

The intriguing claim has been made that Spinoza was influenced by Chinese philosophy.[34] While the claim of influence of Chinese philosophy upon Spinoza has not been supported with substantial evidence, the claim of similarity between Chu Hsi's School of *li* philosophy and Spinoza's philosophy has been argued more convincingly.[35]

Before concluding the discussion of Malebranche's sources on China, reference should be made to those European authors of books on China which Malebranche cites in his appendix to the *Note on the Conversation* entitled 'Testimony of Several Jesuits concerning the Atheism of the Chinese.' Although one can presume a familiarity on Malebranche's part with each of these books, at no point in the *Conversation* does he refer to any of these works, and, aside from the Longobardi treatise, one can assume that their influence on the *Conversation* was minor. In addition to the Longobardi text already discussed, these authors and books are: Ricci-Trigault, *Expédition chrétienne en la Chine*; Martin Martini, *Histoire* [*Histoire de la guerre des Tartares contre la Chine* (Paris, 1654 & 1657: Lyons, 1667)?]; Alvares Semedo, *Relation de la Chine* (1645); Charles le Gobien, *Histoire de l'Edit de l'Empereur de la Chine en faveur de la Religion chrétienne* (Paris, 1698); Le Favre, *Apologie pour la Société* (French translation of *De Sinensium ritibus politicis acta*. Paris, 1700); Louis Lecomte, *Nouveaux Mémoires sur l'état présent de la Chine* (Paris, 1696).

This attitude of insular Eurocentrism bestowed a certain universality upon European knowledge and philosophy which later ages would regard as unjustified. This universalizing tendency would fall under particular scrutiny in years following when the Enlightenment placed a concern with empirical knowledge above that of abstract or speculative metaphysics. A concern with investigating diversity of phenomena would clash with the mind-oriented preoccupation with reducing multiplicity to unity. The encyclopedic mind reaching outward toward the world would compete with the metaphysical mind moving inward toward the still point.

II. THE CONTENT OF THE *CONVERSATION*

Malebranche probably wrote the *Conversation* in 1707 and consented, with some reluctance, to its publication in February, 1708. He is said to have been shocked and completely unprepared for the intensity of the response. He was no novice to polemics, and yet he seems to have underestimated the intensity of feeling found on both sides of the Chinese Rites Controversy. He was soon to discover his error.

The first published reaction came in a critical review in the July 1708 issue of the prominent Jesuit journal, *Mémoires de Trévoux pour servir a l'histoire des sciences et des beaux-arts* (also known as the *Journal de Trévoux*). The review was unsigned but later identified as the work of Louis Marquet, S. J. (ca. 1650–1725), a professor of theology at Paris. Malebranche responded with a point-by-point rebuttal published in August 1708 as *Avis touchant l'Entretien d'un Philosophe chrétien avec un philosophe chinois* (referred to herein as *Note on the Conversation*). The second response from the *Mémoires de Trévoux* (December 1708) was less critical of Malebranche than the first response and, in fact, criticized the unnamed author of the first response (i.e. Marquet).

Malebranche made no further direct response to Jesuit criticisms, though his biographer André feels that Malebranche was indirectly responding to the Jesuit criticism when he reassembled his earlier responses to Arnauld into a single work published in 1709.[36] There were further countercharges of Spinozism and atheism against Malebranche by the Jesuits Jean Hardouin (1646–1729) and Joseph René Tournemine (1661–1739),[37] both of whom were closely associated with the *Mémoires de Trévoux*.

Although the title of the *Conversation* indicates that it is a dialogue, it is actually a one-sided exchange in which the position of the Chinese philosopher is not very developed. This, of course, was standard practice in traditional dialogues in both China and the West, although modern times have brought attempts at more two-sided philosophical dialogues.[38] Consequently, it is necessary to scrutinize the words of the Chinese philosopher, which amount to less than one-fourth of the total of the *Conversation*, in order to put together Malebranche's interpretation of Chinese philosophy. The Chinese philosopher has the opening word:

> What is the Lord of Heaven [i.e. *t'ien-chu*] that you have come from so far away to proclaim to us? We do not understand it, and we wish to believe what the evidence obliges us to believe. That is why we admit only matter and *li*, this supreme Truth, Wisdom, Justice, which subsists eternally in matter, which forms it and arranges it in the good order that we see, and which also elucidates this portion of pure and organized matter, of which we are all composed. For it is necessarily in this supreme Truth, to which all men are united, some more, others less, that they see the eternal truths and laws that are the bonds between all societies.[39]

The probable reference to *t'ien-chu* in the first sentence indicates that he is following the De Lionne-Maigrot preference for *t'ien-chu* (Lord of Heaven) rather than the Jesuit preference for *shang-ti* (King-on-high) and *t'ien* (Heaven) as names for God.

Although Malebranche does not indicate here or elsewhere in the *Conversation* that the primary elements 'matter and *li*' are limited to only one of several schools of Chinese philosophy, it is clear from his citations in the 'Testimony of Jesuit Authors' that this information was available to him. For example, the Ricci-Trigault Journal discusses the Buddhist and Taoist sects which competed with Confucianism. The preface of Charles le Gobien's *Histoire de l'Edit de l'Empereur de la Chine*[40] distinguishes not only the Buddhist and Taoist sects from the Confucianist sect, but further distinguishes Confucianism into ancient and modern sects. Malebranche even refers to this distinction to support his contention that the Jesuits themselves say the Chinese are atheistic. (The point which Le Gobien is trying to make, and which Malebranche completely misses, is that though the modern Confucianist sect is atheistic, the ancient Confucianist sect, of which few vestiges remain, was *not* atheistic.) It is true that Longobardi's treatise places a misleading emphasis on *li* and *ch'i*, but even Longobardi makes some distinction between the various schools. To the extent that Malebranche builds his argument in the *Conversation* upon the School of *li* alone, he misrepresents Chinese philosophy and severely limits the validity of his argument.

A. Malebranche's proofs for the existence of God

The Christian philosopher's response to the Chinese philosopher's first statement is also instructive:

> The God which we proclaim to you is the same one whose idea is engraved in you and all men. But it is necessary to devote attention to this because they do not understand what it is, and they strangely disfigure it. That is why God, in order to renew in us his idea, has spoken to us by means of his Prophet [i.e. Moses] that he is *He who is*,[41] that is, the Being who includes in his essence all there is of reality or of perfection in all beings, the infinite Being in its complete meaning and the word Being.

Malebranche distinguishes here between natural and revealed theology. The idea engraved in all men refers to the knowledge of God obtained through our created natures. Reason permits all men to form some idea of a divine being, and this is the basis of natural theology.

However, in the Christian viewpoint, reason is insufficient to establish supernatural truths so that some form of divine revelation is necessary. Therefore, natural theology must be supplemented by revealed theology, and it is to this revealed theology that Malebranche refers when he speaks of God renewing this idea of Him through one of his Old Testament prophets. The Christian philosopher goes on to say that the Chinese misconceive the Lord of Heaven (*t'ien-chu*) as a great and powerful emperor, that is, very powerful in a finite sense.[42] The Christian philosopher answers that *t'ien-chu* is powerful in an infinite sense and that the Chinese conception of *li* as sovereign justice comes much closer to the mark.

The Chinese responds by conceding the excellence of this divinity as infinite, but states that the Chinese deny that infinity exists. Malebranche's characterization of the Chinese view is not completely accurate since the Chinese had developed a view of infinity in the *hsüan yeh* (infinite empty space) theory of astronomy. This theory, which dates from at least the second century AD and probably earlier, taught that the heavens were empty and void of substance. Joseph Needham points out that this version of infinite space with celestial bodies floating in it at rare intervals had a far less rigidifying effect upon Chinese astronomy than the Aristotelian-Ptolemaic conception of fixed concentric crystalline spheres had upon European astronomy. Of particular significance to Malebranche's presentation of Chinese philosophy is the fact that the *hsüan yeh* theory was very influential on Neo-Confucian philosophers such as Chang Tsai and Chu Hsi who shaped the school of philosophy with which Malebranche mainly deals.[43]

Nevertheless, the Christian responds to the Chinese's skepticism about the existence of infinity with the first of his proofs for the existence of God. It consists of a variation of the ontological argument, which happens to be the principal argument in Malebranche's philosophy for the proof of God's existence. The ontological argument originated with Anselm of Canterbury (1033–1109) and was used by Descartes (1596–1650) whose version of it was adapted by Malebranche.

Stated briefly, the ontological argument holds that the idea of an infinite being implies its existence. In Malebranche's formulation of this argument, the idea of a mere finite thing does not imply its existence because finite things have ideas to represent them, i.e. the thing is separate from the idea. But infinity is inseparable from the idea of infinity. One cannot perceive being without perceiving the idea of being. One cannot perceive the essence of infinity without perceiving infinity. Admittedly, one's perception of the infinite is limited, because one's mind is finite, but that which is perceived as infinity is infinite. The idea of the infinite is the idea of infinitely perfect being, which is equivalent to the idea of God. God so defined Himself in *Exodus* 3:14 when he answered Moses' question by saying 'I am that I am,' that is, unlimited or infinite being. The Christian is saying to the Chinese that if he can have an idea of infinity, then he has an idea of God, and the mere possibility of this idea guarantees its existence. It is in this light that we are to interpret the theme reiterated in the *Conversation* that thinking of nothing and not thinking are really the same thing: therefore, when one thinks of infinity, he is really thinking of *something*.

B. Malebranche's reformulation and application of the Cartesian theory of perception

The Cartesian element in Malebranche's thinking becomes apparent when the dialogue discusses perception. Malebranche adopts Descartes' separation of mind and extension. There is no interaction between thought and extension, except through God who contains the idea of extension which our minds perceive. God has facilitated this interaction between thought and extension through his establishment of general laws of the union of the body and mind.[44] Ideas act on the human mind which is a passive faculty. The mind does not produce but receives ideas. How then do we acquire ideas?

At this point in his theory of perception, Malebranche parts with Descartes' conception of ideas or, more specifically, the category of clear and distinct ideas which are innate or placed in the human mind by God. Rather, Malebranche uses the Platonic sense of ideas as archetypes or models. Ideas are not produced by the mind because only God – not man – has the power to create. Ideas are more real than the material things they represent. Ideas are neither created by the mind nor innately present in the soul but are present within God. God contains within himself the ideas of all beings that he has created. Consequently, we arrive at Malebranche's famous statement 'we see all things in God'. Yet, we do not perceive in God separate ideas of individual material things but only the pure idea of intelligible extension which is the archetype of the material world. This archetype contains in ideal form the possibilities of relations which are manifested in concrete form in the material world.[45] This famous theory of vision in God, which Malebranche claimed to have derived from St Augustine, made Malebranche's philosophy far more theocentric than the philosophy of Descartes.

Armed with these ingredients of Malebranche's philosophy, we can better understand the Christian philosopher of the *Conversation* when he says

'... one cannot perceive all things in *li* if it does not eminently contain all beings. If the *li* is not the infinitely perfect Being, who is the God whom we adore?'[46] Malebranche makes it quite clear that to be regarded as the equivalent of the Christian God, *li* must be infinite in the extent of its being.

The Chinese philosopher responds that while he has no criticism of the Christian's demonstration of the existence of infinity, he remains unconvinced because it seems to him that conceiving of infinity is equivalent to conceiving of nothing.[47] The Christian counters by arguing against the popular belief that the reality of a thing is in direct proportion to the strength of the perception of it. On the contrary, the greater an idea is, the less acute the perception of it should be. Applying this standard, the Christian argues that the perception of infinitely perfect Being is that of infinite light. It is possible, though not at all certain, that Malebranche is addressing himself here to the Chinese tendency to associate their deity with the perception of an overarching domain of greatest extent, i.e. with *t'ien* (Heaven) or *shang-ti* (Lord-on-high).

The Chinese philosopher concedes the point but then raises a different objection which the Christian philosopher proceeds to answer. In such a manner, the Chinese philosopher yields ground throughout the *Conversation* until at the end he has fairly much conceded the Malebranchian position in obviously a very one-sided debate. The remaining dialogue reveals glimpses of authentic Chinese philosophy filtered through missionary minds prejudiced by intramural arguments and through Malebranche's preoccupation with Euro-Christian concerns.

C. Malebranche's projection of Cartesian criteria into Chinese philosophy

After the Chinese philosopher has accepted the notion of infinity, he still expresses considerable difficulty with the abstractness of the Christian philosopher's argument. In response to the former's request for a demonstration of God's existence as a particular being, the Christian philosopher responds that a particular God is too limited and would contradict God's infinite nature. Rather, God includes in the simplicity of his essence all reality or perfection of beings. The human mind, being finite, cannot completely grasp infinity, but it can deduce it from the idea of infinitely perfect being. The Christian then claims that this is similar to the Chinese conception of *li* because he has heard that most Chinese savants believe that one can see all things in *li*.[48] The Chinese philosopher responds: 'We find in *li* many things which we are unable to understand, among other things, the alliance of its simplicity with its multiplicity.'[49]

That response reveals the very mixed accuracy of Malebranche's interpretation of Chinese philosophy. The Christian philosopher correctly speaks of the simple and multiple aspect of *li*. Every given thing in the universe has its own *li*, i.e. its particular or multiple aspect. But all these particular aspects of *li* are interrelated to create a supreme or absolute *li*, which represents the simple aspect of *li*, and is a basically accurate characterization of an important element in the school of *li* Neo-Confucianism. However, when Malebranche has the

Chinese refer to the simplicity of the proof, Malebranche is unjustifiably projecting into Chinese philosophy the Cartesian assumption of clear and distinct ideas as the criteria of truth.[50] What we have here is an example of Malebranche's tendency to universalize a distinctly European standard of truth. His unjustifiable universalizing tendency weakens his argument as much as his incomplete understanding of Chinese philosophy.[51]

D. Li and ch'i used to define the nature of God

The second part of the *Conversation* attempts to define the nature of God. It begins with the Christian philosopher attempting to extend *li* from its nature as supreme truth into an infinitely perfect Being which contains in itself all reality or perfection.[52] In short, *li* becomes the equivalent of the Christian God. However, there are obstacles to this interpretive extension. In Malebranchian philosophy, truth consists of the correspondences between our ideas and the truth. Man cannot arrive at an understanding of such correspondences by himself, but needs God as the source of his illumination. We see eternal truths in God indirectly by means of ideas which correspond to these truths.[53] Malebranche concludes that *li* can be supreme truth only because, being infinitely perfect, it contains in the simplicity of its essence, the ideas of all the things that it has created and that it can create. This, of course, represents a projection of Malebranche's definition of God onto the Chinese *li*. We should not be surprised to find that *li* fails to satisfy some of these criteria.

Li fails to satisfy Malebranche's criteria of its association with matter. Drawing upon a view of matter traceable to Plato, the Christian philosopher speaks of matter as 'the lowest and most contemptible of substances.' (I again make note of the fact that the Chinese *ch'i* was not simply matter, but material force.) In order to satisfy Malebranche's idea of God, *li* must be more exclusively linked with the substance of infinitely perfect Being. The Chinese philosopher responds by saying that *li* includes not only the notion of the arrangement of matter, but also the sovereign wisdom which orders matter.[54] The Christian concedes that *li* accords with the Christian God in so far as it is seen as a supreme wisdom which arranges and regulates matter, but when the Chinese philosopher insists that *li* cannot subsist by itself without matter and that *li* is not consciously intelligent, the Christian philosopher argues that *li* is thereby deficient as an equivalent of God.[55]

Though Malebranche makes no mention of borrowing the interpretation of these deficiencies of *li* from Longobardi, the latter's treatise does state that *li* is unable to subsist without *ch'i* ('primary air') which is the equivalent of Malebranche's 'matter,' and that *li* is not intelligent in a conscious sense. Thus both of the deficiencies of *li* which Malebranche cites may be found in the following passage from Longobardi's treatise:

> They say then that it [i.e. *li*] is unable to subsist by itself, but has need of primary air [i.e. *ch'i*] ... Secondly, when considered in itself, it is

inanimate, without life, without determination and without intelligence. Thirdly, that it can make nothing without the air, without the properties which randomly emanate from it. Fourthly, that it is the cause of all generation and of all corruption, taking and abandoning diverse properties, which accidental forms give the being of things, and distinguish the one from the other. Fifthly, that all the things of the world are necessarily material, and that there is nothing at all truly spiritual in them. One can see this in books twenty-six and thirty-four of their *Hsing-li ta-ch'üan.*[56]

Malebranche resolves the deficiency of *li* being unable to subsist without matter when he claims that while the arrangements of matter may change and perish, *li* itself is eternal and immutable: thus, the Chinese philosopher is able to conclude that *li* really would subsist by itself.[57] The second deficiency proves to be more difficult to resolve, and an interesting debate ensues over whether *li* manifests Wisdom and Justice as abstract qualities or whether *li* is consciously wise and just. The Christian argues that *li* should manifest both, whereas the Chinese, perhaps reflecting less of a tendency toward anthropomorphizing divine forces, argues that *li* is Wisdom and Justice but not wise and just because the abstract qualities of Wisdom and Justice are greater than their human manifestation. Put somewhat differently, the Chinese argues that forms and qualities are different from subjects.[58]

This debate draws out further differences between the Christian and the Chinese on the power of their conceptions of deity. The Christian stresses that God as infinitely perfect being acts of his own volition and draws consequences from himself alone, that is, his power is unlimited. In contrast, the Chinese philosopher tends to see certain limitations on the power of *li*.[59] It is interesting to note that Leibniz saw similarities between the Chinese limits on the power of *li* and his own monadically-based limitations on God's power to intervene actively in the world.[60]

E. Malebranche's attempt to equate li with God

Eventually, the Chinese philosopher concedes that it is not contradictory to say that God who is Wisdom and Justice is also wise and just. However, he is unwilling to apply these same attributes to *li* and so demonstrates the distance that separates the Christian God from the Chinese *li*. The remainder of the *Conversation* attempts to bring God and *li* closer together. Malebranche has the Christian distinguish between material (i.e. finite) space and infinite space. To be equivalent to God, *li* would have to contain infinite space. More specifically, *li* would have to contain – Malebranche implies that the Chinese concedes it does – all the objects of our understanding as infinitely perfect and maintain a correspondence between the perfect simplicity of its essence and the reality of all finite beings.[61]

The Christian philosopher questions how *li* can guide and order the universe if it is acting out of blind impetuosity, though with a beneficent nature. The

Chinese responds that it is inconceivable that *li* be intelligent or conscious for if it were, its beneficent nature would not permit disorder and ugliness in the world. In his view, the existence of contradictions in the world confirms that *li* is neither wise nor intelligent. The Christian responds by saying that because man's mind is finite, he does not grasp the infinite element of God (or *li*). He holds that it is wrong to conclude from the existence of apparent contradictions in the universe that God or *li* is not all-wise.[62] Though men's finite minds make them unable to see God's plan, God consistently follows laws based on the dual criteria of simplicity and fecundity. These laws seek to maximize simplicity and fecundity in the world.[63]

In response to the question of why God allows evil to happen even though He is a loving God, the Christian philosopher answers that God's laws, although maximizing simplicity and generality, permit certain evils but that these abuses will be rectified on the day of 'his vengeance', i.e. Judgment Day. In spite of these evils, the world could not be a better place than God has made it in terms of simplicity and wisdom.[64] The similarity between this part of Malebranche's philosophy and Leibniz' view of this world as the best of all possible worlds is striking.

In spite of the persistence of Eurocentric preoccupations throughout the work, Malebranche concludes the *Conversation* without making any outright accusation of atheism against the Chinese philosopher. Rather, he seems to be endeavoring to have the Chinese redefine *li* in order to bring it into greater accord with his conception of the divinity. If this can be done, the Chinese, or at least those Chinese who embrace the philosophy of *li*, escape atheism. But if this accord cannot be established – and one must note that the terms for establishing it are overwhelmingly European – the charge of atheism against the Chinese is implicit.

III. CONTENT OF THE NOTE ON THE CONVERSATION

After the appearance of the highly critical review of his *Conversation* in the *Mémoires de Trévoux* of July 1708, Malebranche felt obliged to defend himself against the charges of atheism and Spinozism. These charges clearly pricked the sensitivities of a man who had spent his life combatting just such forces and consequently the tone of the *Note* is less restrained than that of the *Conversation*. Malebranche was probably extra-sensitive to the charge of Spinozism because his tendency to merge philosophy with religion had given some grounds for making the charge.[65]

In the opening lines of the *Note*, Malebranche remains reticent about his sources. The only interpreter of Chinese philosophy mentioned is De Lionne, and even he is referred to anonymously as a 'person very respectable and worthy of trust.' Malebranche does mention corroborative support for his ideas in a letter from a Jesuit father to French members of his company. The contemporary Malebranche scholar André Robinet identifies the author of this letter as Joachim Bouvet, S. J. (1653–1730).[66] Bouvet's views on Chinese philosophy were accommodationist and largely antithetical to those of

Malebranche; nevertheless, Malebranche interprets Bouvet's letter to be saying to his European confreres: 'Do not send us your savants in philosophy, but those who know mathematics and the works of Fr. Malebranche.'[67] Bouvet did have a great interest in applying Western mathematics in China and, in 1700–2, corresponded with Leibniz on this subject.[68] At any rate, Malebranche clearly regards Bouvet's letter as supportive of his approach.

Much of the July 1708 review in the *Mémoires de Trévoux* and of Malebranche's *Note* has very little to do with Chinese philosophy. This fact simply reminds us that the attitudes which shaped the two main sides in the Chinese Rites Controversy had European roots and involved distinctly European issues. My concern here will be with those issues raised in the *Mémoires de Trévoux* review and the *Note* which are more directly concerned with Chinese philosophy.

In response to the reviewer's charges that Malebranche should take great care not to interpret Chinese philosophy with terms carrying the 'evil meaning' (i.e. negative connotations) of Spinozism,[69] Malebranche claims that there is sufficient similarity between the impieties of Spinoza and those of 'le philosophe chinois' to justify the charge of atheism against the latter.[70] In linking the Chinese philosopher with Spinoza, Malebranche reveals his tendency as a metaphysician to argue philosophical principles without regard to the cultural context. Malebranche is able to disregard distinctively Chinese culture only because he is assuming that European culture has a universal validity. Enlightenment philosophers would begin to challenge this assumption.

In his *Note*, Malebranche states that although *t'ien-chu* (Lord of Heaven) would not be equivalent to the Christian God, terms such as the 'Lord of Heaven' and 'Heaven' can be used in speaking of God to 'revive in the mind the notion of the true God, in regard to those who may already understand it.'[71] However, it would appear that those who already understand God would refer only to Christians, and that this would exclude the Chinese. In sum, it appears that Malebranche's attitude toward Chinese philosophy in the *Note* became even more rigid and Eurocentric than it was in the *Conversation*. Viewed in this light, Malebranche, too, was a victim of the Rites Controversy.

Malebranche concludes his *Note* by rebutting Marquet's claim for China 'that the philosophy of the Nation condemns Atheism, and teaches the existence of a Creator God, and King of Heaven and Earth,'[72] Malebranche doubts this claim and concludes by manifesting his preoccupation with the struggle in Europe of Christian thinkers against Spinozism.[73] One sees that Malebranche's mind has not transcended Europe.

IV. MALEBRANCHE'S *CONVERSATION* AS A STIMULUS FOR LEIBNIZ

In relative influence, Malebranche's *Conversation* did not have extensive impact upon his contemporaries or later philosophers. Recent scholars have tended to regard Malebranche's *Conversation* as inferior to other pieces in a similar genre, such as Longobardi's treatise or Leibniz' *Discourse on the*

Natural theology of the Chinese.[74] However, Malebranche's *Conversation* is significant not only because it gives a clear insight into the attitude toward Chinese philosophy of a major European philosopher of his day, but also because Malebranche's work was an important stimulus for Leibniz' composition of his discourse on the Chinese.

The composition of their works on Chinese philosophy came at the end of a forty-year association between Malebranche and Leibniz, a predominantly cordial relationship which began about 1675.[75] Much of their contact was indirect and conducted through intermediaries such as the young philosophers and savants Michel de l'Hospital, Lelong, and Nicolas Rémond who had been frequent visitors to the Paris Oratory. A number of Malebranche's works had had a direct influence upon Leibniz' writings.[76] Malebranche's *Traité de la Nature et de la Grace* (1680) influenced the small but extremely significant *Discours de métaphysique* (1686) of Leibniz. Malebranche's *Entretiens sur la Métaphysique* (1688) influenced the obscure *Entretien de Philarète et d'Ariste* of Leibniz. But it is the effect of Malebranche's *Entretien d'un Philosophe Chrétien et d'un Philosophe Chinois* (1708) on Leibniz' *Discours sur la théologie naturelle des Chinois* (1716) which most concerns us here.

The intermediary most instrumental to the influence of Malebranche's *Conversation* upon Leibniz was Rémond, chief counsel to the duke of Orleans. Rémond appeared late in the association between Malebranche and Leibniz. After the death of l'Hospital, Leibniz no longer had a contact who was close to Malebranche. Rémond filled this gap. He initiated contact with Leibniz in a letter of June 2, 1713, after having read Leibniz' *Theodicy*. Over the next three years, there followed frequent exchanges which ended with Leibniz' letter to Rémond of October 19, 1716, just one month prior to Leibniz' death.[77]

Rémond first broaches the subject of Malebranche's *Conversation* in his letter to Leibniz of October 12, 1714 and asks for an opinion on Longobardi's treatise and Malebranche's dialogue between a Christian philosopher and a Chinese philosopher.[78] Six months later, Rémond again refers to the writings by Longobardi and Malebranche, and repeats his request for Leibniz' judgment on Longobardi's treatise.[79] Leibniz replies by saying that he has not yet seen these works by Longobardi and Malebranche.[80] Consequently, with his letter to Leibniz of September 4, 1715, Rémond sent copies of Malebranche's *Conversation* and the treatises by Longobardi and Sainte-Marie. These were the ingredients which stimulated Leibniz to compose his *Discourse on the Natural Theology of the Chinese*.[81] There is no doubt that Leibniz was greatly stimulated by the contents of this packet. In November 1715, Leibniz read Malebranche's *Conversation*, underlined passages and made a number of marginal notations.[82] There are also some brief marginalia on Malebranche's *Note*. (The *Note* was probably also included in the Rémond packet.) These marginalia, along with a very brief draft of a letter of November or December 1715 – possibly to Rémond – concerning the *Conversation*, combined with references by Leibniz in correspondence with Rémond, Lelong, and others give us pieces from which to draw together Leibniz' judgment of Malebranche's *Conversation*. Leibniz' assessment combines mild praise with criticism.[83]

Speaking more directly to the Chinese aspect of the *Conversation*, Leibniz is quite excited over the possibility that the Chinese do view *li*, or what he called 'the principle of order', in the way that Malebranche claims.[84] Furthermore, he feels that the method which Malebranche uses in the *Conversation* for leading the Chinese to the idea of infinity is a very good one. On the other hand, it is clear that Leibniz is not moved to an in-depth response to the points that Malebranche makes. On the contrary, Leibniz seems so dissatisfied with Malebranche's presentation that he was stimulated by him to try to improve on Malebranche's work. This is apparent in his letter to Rémond of January 17, 1716 in which Leibniz notes that since Malebranche's *Conversation* does not sufficiently suit the characters of the Chinese and Christian philosophers, he has been led to compose a 'complete discourse on their theology, dealing with God, spirits and the soul.' Furthermore, Leibniz believes that one can give a very reasonable interpretation of the ancient Chinese authors.[85] The implication here is that Malebranche's interpretation of Chinese philosophy was not as reasonable as it could have been.

Leibniz makes far more extensive use of the Longobardi and Sainte-Marie treatises than of Malebranche's *Conversation* in composing his *Discourse on the Natural Theology of the Chinese*. This neglect of Malebranche would be in part due to the greater suitability of the Longobardi and Sainte-Marie treatises as source material. Unlike Malebranche's *Conversation*, both the Longobardi and Sainte-Marie treatises contain lengthy quotations from specifically cited Chinese works.[86] Nevertheless, it is also clear that Leibniz did not push Malebranche's *Conversation* from his mind. When in his letter to Rémond of January 27, 1716, Leibniz wrote that he compared the length of his finished *Discourse* to that of Malebranche's *Conversation*, it is clear that Leibniz saw himself creating a treatise similar in type to that of Malebranche.

Leibniz' close association with certain Jesuits, developed through years of correspondence, did not prevent him from being extremely critical of the July 1708 review of Malebranche's *Conversations* in the Jesuit-controlled *Mémoires de Trévoux*.[87] Nevertheless, Leibniz' differences with Malebranche in regard to China are clear. There can be no doubt that Leibniz' attitude toward Chinese philosophy was more accommodationist and sympathetic than that of Malebranche.

Leibniz' sympathetic attitude is much closer to the Englightenment than is Malebranche's. And yet insular Eurocentrism is not completely different from cosmopolitan Eurocentrism. The extent of the difference centers on the varying degree of interest in China. The forces which influenced the different attitudes were in all cases firmly anchored in Europe. In opposition to the claims that Leibniz was significantly influenced by Chinese philosophy,[88] it is my contention that a close examination of Leibniz' relationship with China shows that China interested him more because it corroborated the universality of his own ideas than because he gathered new ideas from China. Unlike Malebranche, whose insular Eurocentrism gave him minimal interest in learning about China, Leibniz' enormous fascination with China continued over many years of his life. Yet, because Leibniz' cosmopolitan interest was not motivated by a need to borrow Chinese ideas so much as it was to confirm ideas developed in a European context, his interest remained Eurocentric.[89]

The Enlightenment attitude of other thinkers toward China was cosmopolitan because it was greatly interested in learning about China. It recognized that Chinese civilization possessed knowledge that Europe lacked. But it was also Eurocentric because, as with Leibniz, it sought essentially to corroborate its most fundamental ideas and beliefs historically derived from the European cultural background. Enlightenment thinkers, represented by Christian Wolff in Germany, Matthew Tindal in England, Voltaire and François Quesnay in France, extolled China's antiquity, glorified Confucius' teachings for their rationality and lack of superstition, and praised Chinese government by enlightened rulers and sage officials. Dissenters were notable, but few in number.[90]

Whatever these Enlightenment thinkers chose to emphasize in their reports of Chinese philosophy was determined by predisposing ideas and beliefs wholly anchored in Europe and European tradition. The same may be said of the ideas and beliefs which led Malebranche to focus on these elements emphasized in his *Conversation*. Viewed in this light, the Enlightenment attitude toward China shares much more with Malebranche's attitude toward China than superficially appears.

NOTES

1. My thesis concerns the general shift in perspective rather than the exact timing of the shift. One could find exceptions to dating the shift from 1700. For example, English Sinophilism could be traced to William Temple's writings in the late seventeenth century. See William W. Appleton, *A Cycle of Cathay* (New York, 1951), 42f.

2. The vicariates apostolic were bishoprics created in 1696 by Pope Innocent XII in order to circumvent the Portuguese crown's monopoly over missionary activity in China. The three dioceses of Peking, Nanking, and Macao remained under Portuguese authority, but the rest of China was divided into regions under the authority of individual vicars apostolic who were appointed from Rome by the Congregation, acting by the authority of the pope.

3. The agreement between De Lionne and Maigrot on the Chinese rites question is supported by the letter which Maigrot addressed to De Lionne in Europe from Fuchou on October 15, 1703 (Bibliothèque Nationale, Fr. 14687). The letter attacks the Jesuit theories which have claimed great antiquity for the Chinese nation. The contents of the letter are described in Virgile Pinot, *La Chine et la formation de l'esprit philosophique en France* (1640–1740) (Paris, 1932), 224–6.

4. Arnold H. Rowbotham, *Missionary and Mandarin* (Berkeley, 1942), 155–8. Voltaire refers to Maigrot's ignorance of the Chinese language in his *Essai sur les mœurs*, 2 vols. (1756; reprinted Paris, 1963), I, 70.

5. *Catholic Encyclopedia* (New York, 1909), III, 675, places De Lionne in Szechwan during 1697–1713. This dating is obviously inaccurate as De Lionne returned to France in 1702 or shortly thereafter.

6. According to Henri Cordier, *Bibliotheca Sinica* (Paris, 1905–6), 880, De Lionne's letter to Charmot was first published in 173 pages and then republished in a 257-page edition, both of which are dated 1700. My access was to the second edition.

7. According to Cordier, 890, this letter to Madame de Lionne was published with a number of other letters involving De Lionne. They include a letter from De Lionne to the Jesuit Claudio Grimaldi, February 3, 1699 at Nanking, and a letter from De Lionne to certain unnamed French Jesuits in China, January 7, 1699 at Nanking.

8. In his generally reliable comparative study of Malebranche and Chu Hsi, Pang Ching-jen makes the puzzling claim that De Lionne left no written record of his views on Chinese philosophy: Pang Ching-jen, *L'idée de dieu chez Tchou Hi* (Paris, 1942), 11–13. Furthermore, Pang omits any reference to De Lionne's written works in his bibliography. Yet, the works by De Lionne cited in this text deal with Chinese philosophy at least indirectly in terms of its connection to the Rites Controversy.

9. Yves Marie André, *Vie du Père Malebranche*, excerpted in André Robinet's edition of *Malebranche: Œuvres Complètes*, (Paris, 1958), XV, vi–vii.

10. There are conflicting claims for the number of years De Lionne spent in China. André's biography of Malebranche (Robinet, XV, vi–vii) claims that De Lionne spent twenty years there, but according to the more reliable *Mémorial de la Société de Missions étrangères*, cited in Pang, 12, De Lionne spent thirteen years in China.

11. Paul Hazard, *The European Mind 1680–1715*, trans. J. L. May (Cleveland, 1963), 209.

12. Henri Daniel-Rops, *The Church in the Eighteenth Century*, trans. John Warrington (Garden City, New York, 1966), 209.

13. André, *Vie du Père Malebranche*, excerpted in Robinet, *op. cit.*, XV:VII.

14. In discussing the origin of the *Conversation*, I am relying heavily on the sequence of events as presented in André's biography of Malebranche and excerpted in Robinet, *op. cit.*, XV, viii–ix.

15. Malebranche, *Avis touchant l'Entretien d'un Philosophe chrétien avec un Philosophe chinois*, hereafter *Note on the Conversation*, ed. A. Le Moine (Paris, 1708; reprinted Marseille, 1936), 96. I have chosen to cite from the Le Moine edition of the *Conversation* and the *Note on the Conversation* because it appears to be the edition most commonly used when referring to these works. The most comprehensive edition of these works appears in vol. XV of Robinet's edition of *Malebranche: Œuvres Complètes*. Through the kindness of Daniel J. Cook, I have had the benefit of comparing my translation of Malebranche's *Conversation* and the *Note on the Conversation* with an English translation in manuscript by George L. Stengren. In regard to De Lionne's *Observations*, I have been unable to secure a copy. However, Robinet states that the six points with which Malebranche summarized the beliefs of the Chinese literati at the beginning of his *Note on the Conversation* recapitulates De Lionne's position in the *Observations*, (Robinet, XV, xxi–xxxii.)

16. *Note on the Conversation*, 96–7.

17. For information on the involved development of *li*, see T'ang Chün-i, *Chung-kuo je-hsüeh yüan-lun* (A discussion of the fundamentals of Chinese Philosophy) 2 vols (Hong Kong, 1966–8), I, 1–69. T'ang classifies and discusses in detail six essential meanings of *li* which encompass the Taoist and Buddhist, in addition to the Confucian, traditions. For a useful article in English on the development of *li*, see Wing-tsit Chan, 'The evolution of the Neo-Confucian concept *li* as Principle,' *Tsing Hua Journal of Chinese Studies*, new series IV (2), (1964), 123–48.

18. Two missionaries who I believe saw below the surface of contemporary Chinese culture were Matteo Ricci, S. J. (Li Ma-t'ou, 1552–1610) and Joseph de Prémare, S. J. (Ma Jo-se, 1666–1736). See my *Leibniz and Confucianism: the search for accord* (Honolulu, 1977), 18–26, and 'The reconciliation of Neo-Confucianism with Christianity in the Writings of Joseph de Prémare,' *Philosophy East and West* XXVI (4), (1976), 389–410.

19. Chu Hsi makes this distinction in the *Hsing-li ta-ch'üan* (Great Compendium of Sung Neo-Confucianism), 26:3b.
20. *Chu-tzu ch'üan-shu* (Collected works of Master Chu), 49:25a. Thanks to Wingtsit Chan's 'The study of Chu Hsi in the West,' *Journal of Asian Studies* XXXV, (1976): 561n, I can note that the source of this passage is Chu Hsi's *Chu-tzu yü-lei* (reprinted Taipei, 1968), 1:4a–4b.
21. *Chu-tsu ch'üan-shu* 34:17a.
22. Chu Hsi states: '*Li* (principle) really lacks feeling and ideas, it lacks the ability to estimate and plan and it lacks the ability to create. But when *ch'i* (material force) is congealed, then *li* is present in its midst,' *Chu-tzu ch'üan-shu* 26:2b.
23. Around 1623, Nicolo Longobardi expressed some of his differences with his fellow Jesuit Matteo Ricci on accommodation with Chinese religion and philosophy in an unpublished Latin manuscript 'De Confucio ejusque doctrina tractatus' (A Treatise on Confucius and his Doctrine). The work first appeared in print in Spanish translation in Dominique Navarrete's *Tratados históricos, políticos, éticos y religiosos de la monarquía de Chine* (Madrid, 1676). The work was later translated into French and published as *Traité sur quelques points de la religion des Chinois* (Paris, 1701). Antonio Caballero a Santa Maria completed his manuscript critical of the Chinese rites in December 1668. The work was translated from Spanish into French and published as *Traité sur points importants de la mission de la Chine* (Paris, 1701). In the process, the author's name was Gallicized as Antoine de Sainte-Marie.
24. *Note on the Conversation*, 117.
25. René Etiemble, *L'Orient Philosophique an XVIIIᵉ siècle*. (Paris: cours professé à la Faculté des Lettres de Paris, 1957–8), II, 118–21.
26. Rémond, letter to Leibniz, April 1, 1715, *Die philosophischen Schriften von G. W. Leibniz*, ed. C. I. Gerhardt, 7 vols. (Berlin, 1875–90), III, 640.
27. *Conversation*, 59 (21). All citations from Malebranche's *Conversation* will include initial page references to the Le Moine edition followed by page references, in parentheses, to the original edition of 1708.
28. Longobardi, *Traité sur quelques points de la religion des Chinois*, reprinted with Leibniz marginalia in *Leibnitii epistolae ad diversos*, edited by Christian Kortholt, 4 vols. (Leipzig, 1738) II, 247–8 (#15, par. 3–4) or in *Leibnitii opera omnia*, Ed. L. Dutens, 6 vols. (Geneva, 1768) IV, 134 (#15:3–4).
29. *Conversation*, 68 (35–6).
30. The pertinent passage by Longobardi in Kortholt, II, 225–6 (#12, par. 3) or in Dutens, IV, 123 (#12:3) reads: This savant [i.e. Ch'eng I] in the *Hsing-li ta-ch'üan*, book 28, page 27b is asked what is the mist and rain, and answers 'that these are the effects of the steam and of the vapor of the air. Having assumed this as a basis, he concludes that when men sacrifice to the spirit of the rain, they sacrifice only to that in the air which is the cause and, by means of a second consequence, that this is a great stupidity to go to the idols of the woods and earth, who are in the temples, to ask for rain, while one neglects the mountains and water, which have nothing in common with all these laws. One could see clearly by means of this passage, that this author would not recognize spirits of the mountains and streams other than the air which is the basis.'
31. The Longobardi Treatise includes numerous quotations and citations from the following Chinese texts (in order of frequency): *Hsing-li ta-ch'üan* (Great Compendium of Sung Neo-Confucianism), *Chung yung* (Doctrine of the Mean) and *Shu ching* (Book of History). The Treatise includes less frequent reference to the *Lun yü* (Analects), the *Shih ching* (Book of Odes), the *Li chi* (Record of Rites) and the *T'ung chien* (Comprehensive Mirror). The emphasis is on works authored or favored by School of *li* Neo-Confucianism. These citations are discussed in detail, in terms of Leibniz' use of them, in my *Leibniz and Confucianism*, 69–115.
32. Robinet, *Malebranche: Oeuvres Complètes*, XIX, 843.

33. Spinoza said, 'By God I understand a Being absolutely infinite, that is to say, substance consisting of infinite attributes, each of which expresses eternal and infinite essence.' *Ethics*, trans. James Gutmann (New York, 1957), 41 (#1:6).

34. Lewis A. Maverick claims there is a good chance that Spinoza's philosophic doctrine, especially his pantheism, was influenced by the Chinese. Maverick cites no direct evidence for such an influence, but refers to circumstantial evidence such as (1) the publication of books in Amsterdam on Chinese philosophy which drew from the Ricci-Trigault *Journals*, (2) the influence of Spinoza's Latin tutor and friend, the former Jesuit Van den Ende, who as a freethinker may have had an interest in Chinese philosophy and may have communicated this to Spinoza, perhaps through the use of Trigault's Latin translation in the tutoring sessions, and (3) the active interest of the Jewish community in Amsterdam in Dutch commercial activity in the Far East, which was considerable and made Amsterdam a recipient of considerable news from China. See Lewis A. Maverick, 'A Possible Chinese Source of Spinoza's Doctrine.' *Revue de Littérature comparée*. XIX. (1939), 417–28.

35. The first Western scholar to have noted the similarities seems to have been J. Percy Bruce in his *Chu Hsi and His Masters* (London, 1923), 148 and 241. The claim of similarities is argued in some depth by Olaf Graf. S. J. in *Dschu Hsi, Djin si lu, die sunkonfuzianische summa mit dem Kommentar des Yä Tsai* (Tokyo, 1953). See in particular the chapter 'Chu Hsi and Spinoza's Monism', 278–97.

36. André, *Vie du Père Malebranche*, excerpted in Robinet, *op. cit.*, XV, xxii.

37. *Catholic Encyclopedia*, IX, 569. I have been unable to locate the exact sources of the charges against Malebranche made by Tournamine and Hardouin.

38. Pang Ching-jen's *L'idée de Dieu* (*op. cit.*, n. 8 above) attempts to correct some of the errors of Malebranche's *Conversation* by composing a new hypothetical dialogue between a Christian philosopher named Philalèthe and a Chinese philosopher named Ching-tao. This dialogue is much more two-sided than Malebranche's *Conversation*.

39. *Conversation*, 47 (1–2).

40. Charles le Gobien, *op. cit.*, préface, 1–16.

41. The reference is to *Exodus* III, 14.

42. *Conversation*, 48 (2–3).

43. See the discussion of the *Hsüan yeh* theory in Joseph Needham, *Science and Civilisation in China*, III, 210 and 219–24. Needham notes (*ibid.*, III, 438) the ironic opposition of certain Jesuit missionaries to the infinite empty space theory and their defense of the far more closed Aristotelian-Ptolemaic geocentric universe of solid crystalline spheres at a time when Europe was just breaking out of this rigid mold. This Jesuit opposition would have occurred in the seventeenth century or at approximately the same time when Malebranche's interpreters, Longobardi and De Lionne, were in China.

44. See the *Conversation*, 45 (16) and 62 (25).

45. The theory that we see all things in God dates from Malebranche's first work. *De la recherche de la vérité* (1674–5) 3, 2, 6. My explanation of this theory of vision in God draws from Emile Bréhier, *The History of Philosophy: The Seventeenth Century*, trans. by Wade Baskin (Chicago, 1966), 211–13, and Copelston, IV, 200–02.

46. *Conversation*, 53 (10).

47. *Ibid.*, 53 (11).

48. *Ibid.*, 56–7 (17–18).

49. *Ibid.*, 56–7 (17–18).

50. The Christian philosopher reinforces this observation when he refers to 'distinctly conceive,' 58 (19), and 'conceive clearly,' *ibid.*, 61 (24).

51. The tendency to universalize Cartesian criteria is continued by Malebranche when he has the Christian philosopher argue that our perception depends on God having established general laws involving geometry and optics. *Ibid.*, 64 (29) and 66 (32–34).

52. *Conversation*, 68 (36–7).
53. *Ibid.*, 69 (37–38).
54. *Ibid.*, 70 (39).
55. *Ibid.*, 70–71 (39–40).
56. Longobardi, in Dutens, 133 (#14:19)
57. *Conversation*, 71 (40–41).
58. *Ibid.*, 71–72 (41–3).
59. *Ibid.*, 73–74 (44–5).
60. See chapters 4 and 5 which deal with Leibniz' *Discourse on the Natural Theology of the Chinese* in Mungello, *Leibniz and Confucianism.*
61. *Conversation*, 80 (43–4).
62. *Ibid.*, 81–2 (56–7).
63. *Ibid.*, 83–4 (59–60).
64. *Ibid.*, 85 (61–2).
65. In the last polemic of his life, Malebranche engaged Dortous de Mairan (1678–1771) in correspondence (1713–14) over the charge of Spinozism. See Emile Bréhier, *The History of Philosophy: The Seventeenth Century*, 218: also the discussion of Spinozism in Malebranche, in particular, the tendency of Malebranche to place infinite 'intelligible extension' in God, in F. Copelston, S. J., *A History of Philosophy: Descartes to Leibniz*, (Garden City, NY, 1963), 207–8.
66. Robinet, *Malebranche: Oeuvres Completes*, XV, xxiv.
67. *Note on the Conversation*, 95.
68. Bouvet felt that Leibniz' binary system of arithmetic was a key to explaining the organization of the diagrams in the Chinese classic, the *I Ching* (Book of Changes). See Bouvet's letters to Leibniz of Nov. 4, 1700, Nov. 8, 1701 and Nov. 8, 1702, in Kortholt, III, 5–22, or in Dutens, IV, 146–68.
69. *Mémoires de Trévoux* (July 1708), 1136; *Note on the Conversation*, 100.
70. *Note on the Conversation*, 98.
71. *Ibid.*, 101.
72. *Mémoires de Trévoux* (July 1708), 1143.
73. *Note on the Conversation*, 116.
74. I agree with Demiéville's statement that Leibniz 'showed himself very superior ... in his Lettre à M. de Rémond [i.e. *Discourse on the Natural Theology of the Chinese*] to his Cartesian contemporary Malebranche.' However, I believe Malebranche's *Conversation* deserves to be regarded as more significant than 'only a diatribe against the pantheism of Spinoza.' See Paul Demiéville, 'The First Philosophic Contacts Between Europe and China', *Diogenes*, LVII (Summer 1967), 95–96.
75. The relationship between Malebranche and Leibniz has been extensively examined and documented by André Robinet, *Malebranche et Leibniz: relations personnells* (Paris, 1955).
76. Robinet, *Malebranche et Leibniz*, 467–8.
77. The Leibniz-Rémond correspondence is in Gerhardt, III, 597–678.
78. Rémond to Leibniz, October 12, 1714; Gerhardt, III, 630.
79. Rémond to Leibniz, April 1, 1713; Gerhardt, III, 640.
80. Leibniz to Rémond, June 22, 1715; Gerhardt, III, 644.
81. The packet which Rémond sent to Leibniz with his letter of 4 Sept. 1715 seems to have contained a number of works, including one by the Jesuit Du Tertre critical of Malebranche's philosophy. See Rémond to Leibniz, Gerhardt, III, 651.
82. Leibniz' marginalia on Malebranche's *Conversation* and *Note on the Conversation*, November 1715, Leibniz MS, IV, 308b, Niedersächsische Landesbibliothek, Hanover. Leibniz' underlined passages and marginal notations in the *Conversation* and *Note on the Conversation* are reproduced in Robinet, *Malebranche et Leibniz*, 483–9.

83. E.g., Leibniz disagrees with Malebranche's Cartesian criteria of substance as applied to extension. Malebranche had maintained that substance is what we can perceive in itself without thinking of any other thing and that this applies to matter or created extension: *Conversation*, 60 (22). In his marginalia, Leibniz responds that extension is never alone and cannot be considered alone. (See Leibniz' marginalia on the *Conversation* in Robinet, *Malebranche et Leibniz*, 484.) Also, the Chinese philosopher's claim that God rather than the human mind is the cause of our different perceptions is regarded by Leibniz as directed against his system of preestablished harmony. *Conversation*, 62 (25–6) and Leibniz' marginalia, in Robinet, *Malebranche et Leibniz*, 484.

84. Leibniz' draft of a letter on the *Conversation*, to Rémond (?), November or December 1715. *Leibniz Handschriften*, IV, VIII, 3, 29. Niedersächsische Landesbibliothek, Hanover, reproduced in Robinet, *Malebranche et Leibniz*, 490.

85. Leibniz to Rémond, January 17, 1716; Gerhardt, III, 665.

86. Though Leibniz used the Longobardi and Sainte-Marie treatises as source material for the composition of his discourse on Chinese philosophy, he disagreed with the anti-accommodationist positions of Longobardi and Sainte-Marie toward Chinese philosophy and religion.

87. Leibniz felt the author of the *Mémoires de Trévoux* review of July 1708 was guilty of twisting Malebranche's words and of quibbling. See Leibniz to Lelong, May 11, 1716, Leibniz-Lelong correspondence, *Leibniz-Briefwechsel*, 102, excerpted in Robinet, *Malebranche et Leibniz*, 492.

88. E. R. Hughes and Joseph Needham have both argued that Leibniz was influenced by the School of *li* Neo-Confucianism. See E. R. Hughes, *The Great Learning and the Mean in Action* (New York, 1942), 12–18, and Joseph Needham, *Science and Civilisation in China*, II, 504.

89. See chapters 1 and 5 in Mungello, *Leibniz and Confucianism*.

90. Some of the foremost dissenters of the eighteenth-century Sinophile movement in northwestern Europe were Defoe in England and Rousseau and Diderot in France. Defoe and Rousseau, as advocates of primitivism, opposed the antiquity and concomitant social and political refinements ascribed to China. Diderot, whose work on the *Encyclopedia* enshrined the idea of advancement of human knowledge, faulted China for its lack of belief in progress. A somewhat milder dissent came from Montesquieu who became involved in a polemical debate with Voltaire over the question of despotism in Chinese government. In *L'Esprit des Lois* (1748), Montesquieu argued that China was a despotic state governed by fear. See *The Spirit of the Laws*, trans. T. Nugent (New York, 1949) 122–5 (#8:21). Voltaire denied Montesquieu's charge in the opening chapter of his *Essai sur les mœurs* and held that China's government was enlightened and humane.

2

THE PRE-ESTABLISHED HARMONY BETWEEN LEIBNIZ AND CHINESE THOUGHT

Daniel J. Cook and Henry Rosemont

The lifelong interest of Gottfried Wilhelm Leibniz (1646–1716) in things Chinese has been largely ignored by later philosophers. His two most well-known philosophical biographers of the early twentieth century, Russell[1] and Couturat,[2] make only desultory references to China in their works. The more recent eight-volume *Encyclopaedia of Philosophy*[3] contains an entry on Leibniz over 10,000 words long without ever mentioning China either in the text or in the bibliography. And although Leibniz's fascination with the Chinese written language is amply documented and linked time and again with his famous search for a 'universal characteristic' or symbolic system for a calculus of reasoning (*calculus ratiocinator*), a recent philosophical commentary entitled *Leibniz's Philosophy of Logic and Language*[4] does not discuss China or the Chinese language even in passing.

Historians and sinologists have been more attentive to this short but significant chapter in the history of ideas, with scholars such as Franz Merkel, E. R. Hughes, Donald Lach, Hellmut Wilhelm, Arthur Waley, David Mungello, and Oliver Roy[5] alike raising the question of whether or not Leibniz's mature philosophy, especially his metaphysics, was indebted to Chinese thought in general, and to the Neo-Confucianism of the Sung Dynasty (960–1279) in particular. This question has, however, been most directly put – and answered affirmatively, albeit tentatively – by Joseph Needham's major study.[6] In addition to its importance for Leibniz scholarship and for philosophy, Needham's

Daniel J. Cook and Henry Rosemont, Jr., 'The Pre-Established Harmony Between Leibniz and Chinese Thought', *Journal of the History of Ideas*, 42: 2, 1981, pp. 253–67.

interpretation has implications for the history of science and for cross-cultural studies as well.

Briefly stated, Needham maintains that the old sinological riddle of 'Why didn't China develop science?' is poorly conceived because it suggests that the development of modern science is uniquely Western, which, according to him, it is not. Many rivers have emptied into the sea of science, with one of the major tributaries originating in China, bringing with it many artifacts and technologies that provided some of the necessary wherewithal for the successful voyages of the Age of Discovery, and the concomitant rise of modern science. But Needham goes much farther in challenging a monocultural focus for the history of science: in addition to objects and practices, the Chinese may well have contributed to theory too, especially the 'philosophy of organism', which Needham says is 'characteristically Chinese'.[7] This metaphysical system seems to arrive on the European intellectual scene fully mature in the philosophy of Leibniz, with few if any Western philosophical or religious antecedents. And Leibniz was the first major Western thinker to devote himself seriously to the study of China.

To be sure, Needham in elaborating his position does not confine himself to Leibniz; other scientific personalities and scholars of the sixteenth and seventeenth centuries (e.g., Robert Boyle, the Cambridge Platonists, etc.) also figure in his broader claims of the influence of Chinese thought on Europeans during this period. That Leibniz is central for Needham, however, is seen when he asks whether the philosopher's metaphysics was not 'strongly stimulated by, if not derived from, the organic world-outlook which we have found to be characteristically Chinese.'[8] The concern here is with Leibniz's mature views as expressed in the *Monadology* (1714) and not with his earlier, though systematic, writings such as the *Discourse on Metaphysics*. Needham accepts the view, common in Leibniz scholarship, that 'all the essentials of his system were worked out in the *Discourse on Metaphysics* (written in the winter of 1685–86), the terminology of monads alone being missing.'[9] For Needham the proviso about monads is crucial because it is basically on the monads and the consequent organic model of the world they imply that he builds his thesis: 'It might almost be said that the monads were the first appearance of organisms upon the stage of occidental philosophy.'[10]

Furthermore, another key term in Leibniz's metaphysics, 'pre-established harmony', is also not found in the early writings. The coining of that term (in 1695) is considered by Needham to be another piece of evidence to show a change of direction or emphasis in Leibniz's views in his later years, a change that came about at least in part because of his exposure to certain streams in Chinese thought. Thus Needham says:

> The hierarchy of monads and their 'pre-established harmony' resembled the innumerable individual manifestations of the Neo-Confucian Li in every pattern and organism. Each monad mirrored the universe like the nodes in Indra's net.[11]

He of course allows that many of Leibniz's distinctive organic notions could have been developed from such Western sources as Giordano Bruno or Nicholas Cusanus and through them (and others) from the hermetic tradition[12]; but in a later footnote he says: 'The assessment of the extent to which Neo-Confucian philosophy directly influenced Leibniz will involve detailed bibliographical references ...'[13] The question, then, for Needham, is not *whether* Chinese thought influenced Leibniz, but *how much* it did; his conclusion, though qualified, is that Leibniz 'derived a great deal more than simply a conviction of [his system's] congruency with Chinese philosophy.'[14]

Unlike his manifold and fully documented arguments that modern science owes much to Chinese efforts,[15] Needham's claim of a philosophical influence rests solely on circumstantial evidence. This evidence is by no means inconsequential: Leibniz *did* have a sustained interest in things Chinese; his metaphysics *did* contain many ideas novel in the West; and his metaphysics *does* bear a resemblance in places to Neo-Confucian speculative philosophy. Nevertheless, while research on the 'detailed bibliographical references' to which Needham alludes has not yet been undertaken (and will not soon be forthcoming, because a comprehensive and accurate inventory of Leibniz's voluminous writings is still several decades in the future), a close reading of the more accessible documents suggests strongly that his view of Leibniz as the, or a, theoretical link between West and East will not be sustained; the quality and quantity of Chinese thought clearly interested and impressed Leibniz, but there is to date no direct evidence to show that its content had any great influence on the development of his mature philosophical system.

First, there is the important matter of chronology. Leibniz mentions Chinese thought briefly in his correspondence as early as 1670 – sixteen years before writing the *Discourse on Metaphysics* – in a letter to the German Jesuit Athanasius Kircher. However, the letter merely evinces an interest in the latter's writings on China[16]; it does not show that Leibniz knew anything first hand about the subject at this time. From 1672 to 1676 Leibniz was in Paris, and a recent scholar has said that during this period Leibniz was exposed to Chinese materials in a 'massive way'; but he does not cite any textual evidence at all to support the claim, nor has any appeared to come to light from other scholars who have studied this period of Leibniz's life.[17]

By 1679 it is clear that Leibniz had some knowledge of the structure of the Chinese written language. In January of that year he learned of the efforts of Andreas Müller to work out a 'key' to written Chinese, and in June wrote a letter to Müller asking a number of sophisticated questions about the Chinese language and the latter's work on it.[18] Similarly we know that Leibniz was aware at this time of the view of the Dutch scholar Jacob Gohl that written Chinese had been invented all at one time.[19] Leibniz was also probably familiar with the work of the Englishman John Webb who had published a book in 1667 (a copy of which is still in Leibniz's library) and in it attempted to show that Chinese was the 'primitive language' of the human race.[20] Leibniz never abandoned his interest in the Chinese script, but already in this same year he indicates that he knew enough about it to doubt that it could serve as the basis for his 'universal characteristic'. In a letter to Duke John Frederick written in April he said:

> If you know Chinese characters, I believe that you will find a little more harmony in them, but basically they are indubitably far removed from that analysis of thought which comprises the essence of my plan, as they are apparently content to give several connotations.[21]

It must be noted, however, that to whatever extent these works provided Leibniz with his information about the Chinese language, they could not have provided him with metaphysical inspiration because they do not contain any substantive discussion of Neo-Confucian thought. (They could, and did, on the other hand, make available to him a fair amount of misinformation about Chinese history.)[22]

The beginning of Leibniz's mature study of China seems best to be dated in 1689, when he was in Rome. There he met and visited with the Italian Jesuit missionary Claudio Grimaldi who had recently returned from a seventeen-year stay in China, much of it spent at the court in Peking. The two men maintained a correspondence for some time thereafter, initiated by Leibniz with a letter written in July, asking thirty questions about China.[23] The questions ranged from topics in plant classification to Chinese armaments, and while taken collectively they are a good index of Leibniz's encyclopaedic mind, they also show that at the time of writing he was not well versed in Chinese geography, history, or culture, and not fundamentally concerned with Chinese metaphysics.

The next important document on China written by Leibniz was his 'Preface' to the *Novissima Sinica (Recent News from China)*, one of the relatively few of his works (on any subject) published during his lifetime, issued in 1697 and again in 1699.[24] Although the work contains very brief passages on Chinese philosophy and religion – including a reference to the 'accursed idol Buddha'[25] – the bulk of the *Novissima Sinica* is basically a catalog of current events dealing with China and the opening of trade routes (a subject which deeply concerned Leibniz); it is not at all a treatise on Chinese thought.

As late as 1710, in the preface to his *Theodicy*,[26] Leibniz discusses the doctrines of many non-Christian religions but makes no mention of Chinese thought as a bearer of a natural theology consonant with his own. It was not until the last year of his life, in 1716, that Leibniz wrote at length on Chinese thought and religion,[27] and it is to an examination of this document that we must now turn in our consideration of the question of the influence of Chinese thought on Leibniz. In a long letter (over 14,000 words) to Nicholas Remond de Montmart, a French Platonist and head of the councils of the Duke of Orleans, Leibniz set down his views on Chinese philosophy and religion, referring to his work as a 'Discours sur la Théologie naturelle des Chinois'.[28]

Remond – to whom Leibniz had addressed the *Monadology* two years earlier – had sent Leibniz two hostile works on Chinese religion written by Catholic missionaries and had asked the philosopher's opinion of them. The two books were the *Religion Treatise*, by the Italian Jesuit Nicholas Longobardi (the successor to Matteo Ricci as the head of the China Mission),[29] and the *Mission Treatise*, by the Spanish Franciscan Antonio Caballero a Santa Maria.[30] Both of these missionaries made basically the same claims about Chinese speculative thought, namely, that resemblances between Chinese and Christian concepts were only superficial, that the ancient Chinese thinkers were at best materialists and their modern counterparts out-and-out atheists, and, therefore, that conversion could only proceed by having the Chinese abandon altogether their intellectual and cultural heritage in favor of Revealed Christian Truth.

Leibniz's reply is the *Discourse on the Natural Theology of the Chinese*, an attempted rebuttal of the missionaries' views in which he discusses the Chinese conception of God, universal principles, spiritual substance(s), souls, immortality, and the correlations between his binary arithmetical notation and the ancient Chinese book of divination, the *I Ching*. In describing his position he employs many of his own key philosophical terms such as 'pre-established harmony', 'primary' (and 'secondary') matter, and 'entelechies' (the term 'monads' does not occur in the text). There are also repeated references in the *Discourse* to Greek philosophy, the early church fathers, and to history, both Western and Chinese. The length and contents of the work thus make it an important piece in the Leibniz corpus, especially when it is remembered that he wrote it in his seventieth and last year; it follows that the *Discourse* should shed light on the question of Chinese philosophical influences on Leibniz's own views, especially on his metaphysics.

The text of the *Discourse* is divisible into four sections. In the first, Leibniz argues, *contra* Longobardi and Santa Maria, that the Chinese do indeed have a conceptual analogue to the Christian concept of God and spiritual substance. In the next section (almost half the manuscript) he maintains that spirits and matter are treated very nearly the same in China and Europe. And the third section is devoted to making a similar case for the compatibility of the Chinese and Christian concepts of the human soul and its immortality.

Throughout these three sections (the fourth will be taken up below), Leibniz employs three distinct, but closely related, general forms of argument. First, he claims that Chinese thought is compatible with his own philosophy and his own philosophy is compatible with Christianity; therefore, Chinese thought is compatible with Christianity. Second, when confronted with a Chinese passage from the missionaries which appears to be clearly in conflict with Christian theology, Leibniz attempts to show that similar 'errors' had been made by the Greeks or the early church fathers, scholastics, etc., without destroying Christianity, or indeed, without diminishing the respect with which such persons were treated in the Western tradition. And third, when rebutting a specific charge of Longobardi and/or Santa Maria against the 'ancients', Leibniz would point out whenever possible that the ancient texts, as cited by the missionaries, did not explicitly state the heresy charged by them. (Whatever the persuasiveness of this latter form of argument from negative evidence may have been in his own day, it cannot be given credence today because most of the 'heresies' charged by the missionaries deal with metaphysical and/or theological issues which were not discussed in the ancient Chinese writings at all. There being no statements about prime matter in the classical texts, for example, it follows logically, but trivially, that there cannot be any statements in the classical texts which contradict Christian statements about prime matter.)

To anyone reading the *Discourse* from beginning to end it will be fairly clear that the work is not so much a treatise on philosophy *per se*, comparative or otherwise, as it is a sophisticated effort to provide an intellectual framework on behalf of the Riccian 'accommodationist' position in the Rites Controversy so that the ecumenical movement could go forward and China could be brought more closely into the family of Christian nations. His Protestantism notwithstanding, Leibniz had a deep and abiding sympathy for the (majority) Jesuit position on the nature of Confucianism, shown consistently not only in the *Discourse* but in earlier writings as well: 'In the Chinese controversy which is raging in Rome today, I favor the Jesuits and have for a long time. . . .'[31] In short, while the themes are often philosophically abstract, the overall tone of the *Discourse* is not basically philosophical; it is, in the broad sense, political.

But there are more positive indications in this work that Leibniz owed little to Chinese thought in regard to his own philosophical development. In the first instance, it is generally assumed that Leibniz not only had access to but read carefully early Chinese philosophical and religious texts, such as Father Couplet's *Confucius Sinarum Philosophus* (Paris, 1687). Perhaps so – because he had written *De cultu Confucii civili* in 1700[32] – but there is no evidence for it in the *Discourse*; every single Chinese passage discussed by Leibniz is taken *verbatim* either from the text of Longobardi or Santa Maria. Indeed, *no* other sinological study is cited in the *Discourse*, although Leibniz regularly sprinkles his text with references to Plato, Aristotle, Descartes, the Bible, Spinoza, and many other Western sources (some of which are also cited by Longobardi and/or Santa Maria).

Equally significant is the fact that Leibniz accepts in the *Discourse* without question every mistake made by Longobardi and Santa Maria with reference to Chinese names, places, dates, chronology, or terms.[33] Moreover, Leibniz regularly analyzes passages from the writings of the two missionaries in which Chinese terms figure prominently, in such a way as to suggest that because each missionary used a different system of Romanized transliteration for Chinese characters, he was unaware of when and where the two missionaries were discussing the same or different persons, places, things, or ideas.[34] In summary, and somewhat surprisingly, there is not a single indication in the whole of the *Discourse* that Leibniz thought he knew enough about Chinese philosophy independently of what was contained in the *Religion Treatise* and the *Mission Treatise* to challenge either of their authors on any point of fact. We can find, in other words, no documentary evidence from the *Discourse* to show that Leibniz had, before reading Longobardi and Santa Maria, immersed himself studiously in works and/or translations dealing with Chinese thought – which reduces markedly the possibility that evidence will be forthcoming that he was influenced philosophically by it.

Not altogether tangentially, it is worth noting that however much in his later years Leibniz applauded the Chinese for their 'precepts of ethics and politics adapted to the present life and use of mortals',[35] it is clear that he believed that those precepts were not original with them: Leibniz's ecumenism was not purchased at the expense of European or Christian chauvinism. To appreciate this point it must be seen that in the *Discourse* (and elsewhere), Leibniz accords his highest praise for the Chinese not to Confucius but to the very shadowy Fu Hsi whom Leibniz believed to have ruled China ca. 3000 BC This legendary emperor is the purported inventor of the trigrams which comprise the basic structure of the *I Ching*, and he figured prominently in the correspondence between Leibniz and the French Jesuit Joachim Bouvet, a contributor to the second edition of the *Novissima Sinica* and author of a number of letters to Leibniz from China in 1700–1703 (one of which described for the first time the now celebrated isomorphism between the *I Ching* hexagrams – two joined trigrams – and Leibniz's system of binary arithmetic).[36] In one of his letters Bouvet described Fu Hsi as the 'prince of all philosophers', but he then went on immediately to add that his commendation was not 'an atrocious offense against Europe' because Fu Hsi was not Chinese at all; he was either Zoroaster, Hermes Trismigestus, or Enoch. Longobardi held a similar view, and so did Santa Maria who believed that the Chinese were descendants of Noah. Leibniz approvingly cites these related views in the *Discourse*:

> And there are those who believe that because the beginnings of the Chinese empire occurred during the time of the Patriarchs, they could have learned about the creation of the world from them.[37] ... There is a great likelihood that these [Chinese] expressions, so close to the great truths of our tradition, have come to the Chinese through the tradition of the ancient Patriarchs.[38] ... Since, however, the Chinese have been fortunate enough to come by this wisdom without sufficient warrant for it, it may be that they learned part of it from the tradition of the Patriarchs.[39]

To recapitulate, the chronological evidence and an analysis of the *Discourse* together weigh heavily against any claim that Leibniz drew inspiration from Chinese thought in general, or from Neo-Confucianism in particular, in developing his own philosophical views. Chronologically, the available evidence shows no influence at all; the *Discourse* displays (a) a deep indebtedness to the Greeks and to Scholasticism, (b) a naiveté with respect to Chinese history and thought, (c) many mistakes and misunderstandings about that history and thought, (d) a subdued but nevertheless clear Christian and Western bias – all of which seem to tilt the scales decisively against any East-to-West metaphysical influence.

But what of Leibniz's interest in the *I Ching*, especially the hexagrams which appeared to be conceptual analogues to his new mathematical notation? It is obvious that this interest was not due to any corroborative evidence the *I Ching* might provide for the efficacy of binary arithmetic. Unlike most endeavors in the physical and biological sciences, mathematical work is not in general logically established more firmly by having one's research replicated by others. Colleagues may check one's proofs with care and/or suggest notational variants, but neither the proofs nor the worth of proffered variants are enhanced by the fact that someone else arrived at them independently. Thus, Leibniz could not have felt vindicated, except psychologically, for proposing a notation of 0 and 1 for arithmetic operations by learning that the Chinese arrived at a similar conclusion forty-seven centuries earlier. The same is true about Leibniz's infinitesimal calculus with respect to the knowledge that Newton had developed essentially the same system shortly before.

When Leibniz learned about the isomorphism (up to a point) of his binary notation with *I Ching* hexagrams, it may well be that his excitement was less philosophical or scientific than it was political, for the discovery of the similarity could serve to advance his avowedly ecumenical ends.[40] Such an interpretation comes from a consideration of that fourth section of the *Discourse* in which the isomorphism is discussed. The first three parts together make up more than nine-tenths of the text, leading most readers to take the final segment as more or less an appendix to the work. However, this latter section can be seen in another way, as an essential ingredient of Leibniz's overall argument against the missionaries Longobardi and Santa Maria, which in turn illuminates his overall view of the nature, history, and development of Chinese thought, and of the way he hoped to convince both Chinese and Europeans that Confucian views were compatible with Christian doctrine.

Leibniz accepts, for the most part, the claims of Longobardi and Santa Maria that many educated Chinese of his own time were atheists, but, he insisted, these moderns have 'strayed from their own antiquity.'[41] If we focus instead on the classical texts, he said, 'I find them quite excellent, and quite in accord with natural theology . . . . It is pure Christianity, insofar as it renews the natural law inscribed in our hearts.'[42]

To be sure, there are important theological issues on which the classical texts are silent, and even the most famous of Chinese philosophers, Confucius, is occasionally in error. But this only showed, Leibniz believed, that we have not gone back far enough in the relevant cases. If we would return to the era of Fu Hsi and the other sage-kings, 'we could uncover in the Chinese writings of the remotest antiquity many things unknown to modern Chinese and even to those commentators thought to be classical.'[43] The *I Ching* is one such work, according to Leibniz, and if we read it carefully, we will uncover the fact that the 'ancient Chinese have surpassed the modern ones in the extreme, not only in piety ... but in science as well.'[44]

The term 'science' may seem odd here, but Leibniz surely intended it, and it is crucial for understanding why Part IV of the *Discourse* is not merely an appendix: 'it concerns justification of the doctrines of the ancient Chinese and their superiority over the moderns.'[45] Leibniz acknowledged the theological weaknesses of modern Chinese thinkers, but he maintained that the ancient texts strongly suggested a natural theology consonant with Christianity and were thereby worthy of European respect. What better way to establish that respect than to show that the most ancient writers of those texts not only had theological ideas similar to Christian ideas but had also developed pure mathematics to a point which had only been reached in Europe during his own lifetime? Leibniz believed that while binary arithmetic was not his 'universal characteristic', it was nevertheless a possible foundation for the natural sciences. If he could show, therefore, to post-Galilean Europe that his new notation had been prefigured 4,700 years earlier in China, Leibniz would have a very strong case, founded on the principles of reason, for denying the conclusions of Fathers Longobardi and Santa Maria and for advancing his own view of the proper method for engaging the Chinese in ecumenical dialogue: show them the truth, but not simply by quoting from the Bible and giving them telescopes: show them also how both theological and *scientific* truth could be read in their own most ancient writings.[46]

Seen in this light, the closing section of the *Discourse* can be read as an intellectual *coup de grâce* to the anti-accommodationist position with respect to China. The text breaks off abruptly, and although Leibniz continued to write for the remaining months of his life, he never returned to the work to finish it. The evidence suggests, however, that conceptually the manuscript was complete and that Leibniz had accomplished what he had set out to do: provide a sophisticated philosophical, historical, and theological framework in which the ecumenical movement and missionary work in China could go forward.

For all of these reasons the conclusion seems compelling that Needham and other scholars who have urged a Neo-Confucian influence on Leibniz's philosophy will not be borne out in their interpretations, the circumstantial evidence notwithstanding: materials thus far analyzed provide little warrant for such interpretations: on the contrary, they go some way toward establishing the originality of Leibniz's metaphysics of monads and pre-established harmony – with an occasional salute to Western antecedents such as Bruno's organic ideas. But this conclusion does not entail that China and Chinese thought did not influence Leibniz at all: the whole of a person's views are not to be found in his or her metaphysics. The fact that Leibniz was interested in things Chinese for an extended period of time, and not merely for exotic or diversionary reasons, must be faced by serious Leibniz scholars: the bibliographic evidence indicates that he mentioned China more often in his writings than all other non-Western cultures put together. Why China? Why not Muslim culture(s) to which he refers on occasion? Or India? Or the Indians of the New World about whom books were being written and circulated in Europe while Leibniz was still a relatively young man?[47]

To answer these questions, even in outline form, we must appreciate Leibniz's geopolitical perception of China. He regularly called China an 'Anti-Europe', the antipodes which he sometimes also described as an 'oriental Europe'.[48] Between these two great centers of 'human culture and refinement', as he called them,[49] all other cultures and systems of thought find their place, theologically as well as geographically. Leibniz came to believe that if he could successfully demonstrate to both the Chinese and the Europeans – at opposite ends of the cultural spectrum in so many ways – the close resemblances between their theological beliefs, then it would follow *a fortiori* that every other religious tradition, no matter how different from Christianity, would be amenable to the same consideration and thus increase the chances for universal understanding and peace. Furthermore, demonstrating the similarities between Chinese and Christian thought would be an excellent way to prepare the Chinese for conversion to Christianity, which Leibniz always proclaimed was the true religion for all peoples. At the same time he often cited this historic opportunity for 'European piety' in order to make the public aware of the importance of a proper understanding of, and appreciation for, Chinese culture and thought.

As Merkel has pointed out, Leibniz consistently, in his correspondence, discusses 'European piety' and the civilizing aspects of missions despite the fact that 'the missionary idea in the awakening Pietistic movement . . . rested on a strictly Biblical and religious basis.'[50] But this idea does not condemn Leibniz to Europeocentrism because piety for him was not simply acceptance of revelation and/or surrender to God's will; rather the chief requirement for religion was a *rational* knowledge of the Divine Being since, in Leibniz's view, the knowledge of God and His perfections must be present before one could love Him. Merkel quotes Leibniz's optimistic ideas of civilization, proclaiming 'science and true evangelical religion as twin sisters who must ever serve each other', and again, that 'scientific enlightenment must bring even the heathen to the true Christian religion.'[51]

But if, as Leibniz believed, the fundamental religious idea of God was a demonstrable truth grounded in reason, it would follow that those 'heathen' who displayed the greatest employment of reason in their culture were *eo ipso* closer, or at least capable of being brought much closer, to the true Christian religion than those who did not. Again, Leibniz's interest in Fu Hsi is almost certainly less a function of the latter's stature as a pure mathematician than that the legendary ruler was a *rational* man who had attempted to pass down his legacy to later Chinese thinkers.[52]

To be sure, Leibniz admitted that 'the Chinese are seen to be ignorant of that great light of the mind, the art of demonstration, and they have remained content with a sort of empirical geometry, which our artisans universally possess.'[53] But although they had not fully developed any laws of deduction, it was clear to Leibniz that the Chinese regularly employed reason: 'Who would have believed that there is on earth a people who, though we are in our own view so very advanced in every branch of behavior, still surpass us in comprehending the precepts of civil life?'[54] Similarly, Leibniz's long-term interest in Chinese technology suggests an appreciation for, if not a full understanding of, the rational philosophical framework of the culture which had produced that technology.

In sum, it seems plausible to maintain that the civilization of China – not merely its size, population, location, specific inventions, or philosophy – had a significant impact on Leibniz because it displayed a very high level of rationality, making the rational Chinese people the most likely non-Christian candidates for true Christian conversion without any missionary compromises with irrational paganism or barbarism, nor even a reliance on Revelation. His seriousness of purpose in this regard is illustrated in a letter written to the Russian Tsar Peter shortly before Leibniz died. If we do not actively promote understanding, exchange and communication between the Chinese and ourselves, he said, 'it will follow that when the Chinese will have learnt from us what they wish to know they will then close their doors to us.'[55]

The prophetic nature of this remark underscores the way in which Leibniz's studies of China should be seen: not as philosophically seminal but as the sustained efforts of a gifted man to keep a Western foot in the door, to open the door wider, and then, perhaps, in concert with the Chinese themselves, to tear down the door altogether. Two and a half centuries of hindsight allow us to see that Leibniz did not transcend his own cultural heritage as much as he may have thought he did, but the list of major Western thinkers who have done better, or tried harder, is a very short list indeed.[56]

NOTES

1. Bertrand Russell, *The Philosophy of Leibniz* (Cambridge, 1900).
2. Louis Couturat, *La Logique de Leibniz* (Paris, 1901).
3. Paul Edwards, Editor-in-Chief (New York, 1967).
4. By Hide Ishiguro (Ithaca, NY, 1972).
5. Franz Merkel, *G. W. Leibniz und die China Mission* (Leipzig, 1920). E. R. Hughes, *The Great Learning and the Mean-in-Action* (London, 1942). Donald Lach, 'Leibniz and China', in the *Journal of the History of Ideas*, 6 (1945). Hellmut Wilhelm, 'Leibniz and the *I Ching*', in *Collectanea Commissiones Synodalis* no. 16 (1943). Arthur Waley, 'Leibniz and Fu Hsi', *Bulletin of the London School of Oriental Studies*. II (1921). Oliver Roy, *Leibniz et la Chine* (Paris 1972). David Mungello, *Leibniz and Confucianism: The Search for Accord* (Honolulu, 1977). The list is by no means exhaustive, and other relevant works are cited below.
6. J. Needham, *Science and Civilisation in China* (Cambridge, 1954–), Vol. II.
7. *Ibid.*, 498.
8. *Ibid.*
9. *Ibid.*, 504, fn. g.
10. *Ibid.*, 499.
11. *Ibid.*

12. *Ibid.*, 296.
13. *Ibid.*, 504, fn. g.
14. *Ibid.*, 501.
15. Indeed, the entire *Science and Civilisation* project bears on this issue, and the work must certainly rank as one of the scholarly monuments of the second half of the twentieth century. Perhaps the best testimony to its greatness is that other scholars are already going beyond it. Thus, while fully supportive of Needham's claims of the world-wide stimuli for science in the modern sense, Nathan Sivin goes on to question, on the basis of his own detailed researches in Chinese materials, what it is to be a science. If, as he argues, a science is a circumscribed body of empirical data linked by a testable theory, then there is no reason, *a priori*, why Chinese work in, say, astronomy should command our scholarly attention more than their work in geomancy. It is tempting to say that the former is truly a science whereas the latter is occult; Sivin, however, argues well that this dichotomy may be no less a Western conceit than the monocultural view of the development of science that Needham has laid to rest. See, for example, Sivin's 'Chinese Alchemy and the Manipulation of Time', in *Science and Technology in East Asia*, ed. Nathan Sivin (New York, 1977); 'Ailment and Cure in Traditional China' and 'Why the Scientific Revolution Did Not Take Place in China – Or Didn't It?', manuscripts soon to be published and kindly lent to us by the author.
16. *China monumentis qua sacris qua profanis ...* (Amsterdam, 1667) and *La Chine illustrée ...* (Amsterdam, 1670). The earliest mention of China we have come across is in 1668, when Leibniz compares Chinese medicine favorably with Europe's: 'No matter how foolish and paradoxical the Chinese ordinarily appear to be in *remedica*, nevertheless, theirs is better than ours' (Lach's translation). Preussiche Akademie der Wissenschaften, editors, *Gottfried Wilhelm Leibniz: Politische Schriften*, in G. W. Leibniz, *Sämtliche Schriften und Briefe* (Darmstadt, 1931), Series IV, I, 552; quoted in Lach, 'Leibniz and China', *op. cit.*, 436.
17. Tilemann Grimm, 'China und das Chinabild von Leibniz', in *Systemprinzip und Vielheit der Wissenschaften*, ed. U. W. Bargenda and Jürgen Blühdorn (Wiesbaden, 1969), xv, 167. For detailed studies of Leibniz's Paris years see supplements XVII and XVIII of *Studia Leibnitiana*, and Joseph E. Hoffman, *Leibniz in Paris, 1672–76* (Cambridge, 1974).
18. See Donald Lach, 'The Chinese Studies of Andreas Müller', *Journal of the American Oriental Society*, 60 (1940); see also P. Cornelius, *Languages in 17th and Early 18th Century Imaginary Voyages* (Geneva, 1965), esp. 98–101.
19. Lach, 'Leibniz and China', *op. cit.*, 437.
20. John Webb, *An Historical Essay Endeavoring A Probability that the Language of the Empire of China is Like Primitive Language* (London, 1669).
21. Lach, 'Leibniz and China', *op. cit.*, 437. Leibniz did, however, maintain his interest in the Chinese script, and thought well of it. In a letter of 1703 to father Joachim Bouvet, for example, he said, 'I cannot say of the Egyptian hieroglyphs ... that they have any agreement with the Chinese characters ... which are perhaps more philosophical and appeared to be built on more intellectual considerations such as are given by numbers, order, and relations.' Quoted in Philip P. Wiener, 'On Philosophical Synthesis,' *Philosophy East and West*, 12, no. 3 (October, 1963), 200.
22. This theme is developed more fully in our Introduction to Leibniz's *Discourse on the Natural Theology of the Chinese*, translated with an Introduction, Notes, and Commentary by Henry Rosemont, Jr, and Daniel J. Cook (Honolulu, 1977); hereafter cited as *Discourse*.
23. The Grimaldi-Leibniz file, *Leibnizbriefe*, 330, no. 3–5, in the Niedersächsische Landesbibliothek, 19 July 1689. A fuller discussion is found in Donald Lach, *The Preface to Leibniz's Novissima Sinica* (Honolulu, 1957), 3–4, 13–14, and in David Mungello, *Leibniz and Confucianism*, *op. cit.*, 32–6.

24. Lach's translation, *op. cit.*, is based on the 1699 edition.
25. *Ibid.*, 76.
26. Leibniz, *Theodicy*, ed. Austin Farrer (London, 1952).
27. *Discourse, op. cit.*
28. *Ibid.* The material which follows for the next three paragraphs is taken from our Introduction which contains the relevant citations.
29. *De Confucio Ejusque Doctrina Tractatus* (Paris, 1701). Published, with Leibniz's marginalia, in *Leibnitii Epistolae and diversos* (Leipzig, 1735), ed. Christian Kortholt.
30. *Traité sur quelques points importants de la Mission de la Chine* (Paris, 1701); also in Kortholt, *op. cit.* Leibniz also mentions receiving from Remond the essay by Nicholas Malebranche, 'A Dialogue Between A Christian Philosopher and A Chinese Philosopher: On the Nature and Existence of God', but does not refer to it in the *Discourse*, nor was there much reason for him to do so because Malebranche mentions only one Chinese philosophical term – *Li* – in the whole of his essay, and not with much understanding or sympathy. This essay has been translated by George Stengren of Central Michigan University (manuscript).
31. Carl Gerhardt, editor, *Die philosophischen Schriften von G. W. Leibniz*, 7 vols. (Berlin, 1875–90), III, 549.
32. A brief work no more sophisticated in its analysis of Chinese thought than his 'Preface' to the *Novissima Sinica* published three years earlier. See also Lach, 'Leibniz and China,' *op. cit.*, 448, and F. Merkel, *Leibniz und die China-Mission, op. cit.*, 99–101. Cf. also fn. 47 below.
33. See the Introduction to the *Discourse*, 5–6 and 34–43.
34. *Ibid.*, 5–6. In commenting on the *Discourse*, Paul Demiéville has come to a similar conclusion: 'When it came to details, Leibniz did not understand much about Chinese philosophy and its history. He was too poorly informed.' ['The First Philosophical Contacts between Europe and China', *Diogenes*, 58 (1967), 95.]
35. Lach, *The Preface to Leibniz' Novissima Sinica, op. cit.*, 69.
36. Introduction to the *Discourse*, 13–16. Several scholars have suggested that the isomorphism of his binary arithmetic and the hexagrams of the *I Ching* were discovered by Leibniz himself. Thus Lach, in 'Leibniz and China', *op. cit.*, 446, says: 'By his analysis of Fu Hsi's trigrams. Leibniz hoped to strengthen Father Bouvet's theory that the *I Ching* was a key to all the sciences.' And E. R. Hughes in *The Great Learning and the Mean-In-Action, op. cit.*, 20, notes: 'The inference is that Leibniz owed his inspiration for his *Arithmétique Binaire* [to Bouvet].' The latter is simply anachronistic, and the former is also in error because Bouvet's letter to Leibniz of 4 November 1701 shows clearly that Leibniz provided the missionary with an outline of his binary system and that Bouvet provided the hypothesis of the isomorphism of it with the symbols of the *I Ching*. At times Leibniz acknowledges Bouvet's efforts in this regard, as in a paper published in 1703: 'Explication de l'Arithmétique Binaire' *Histoire de l'Académie Royale des Sciences*, Année, 1703, (Paris, 1705), 85–9.
37. *Discourse*, 94.
38. *Ibid.*, 166.
39. *Ibid.*, 197.
40. For the arguments which follow on Part IV of the *Discourse*, see *ibid.*, 34–8, from which they were taken.
41. *Ibid.*, 54.
42. *Ibid.*, 107.
43. *Ibid.*, 157.
44. *Ibid.*, 159.
45. *Ibid.*, 160.
46. See also Merkel, *Leibniz und die China-Mission, op. cit.*, 19.

47. The number of such books to which Leibniz had access is not known. David Mungello has compiled a bibliography of seventy-one books on China preserved in the Niedersächsische Landesbibliothek in Hanover which were available to the philosopher. How many he read is in question; only four contain his marginalia. (We are grateful to Dr Mungello for sharing his bibliographical research with us.) Similarly, in 'Leibniz and China', *op. cit.*, 436, Lach says: 'There were available to [Leibniz] in the libraries at Vienna, Hanover, Munich and Berlin a number of studies concerning China and eastern Asia, most of which were Jesuit letters and books concerning missionary enterprises.' But Lach does not specify which materials Leibniz actually read, or when; indeed, later on the same page he goes on to say: 'From this analysis it is not to be assumed that Leibniz's work on things Chinese was systematized. It was not.'

48. Cited by C. A. van Peursen, *Leibniz* (New York, 1970), 26, and by C. Zangger. *Welt und Konversation: Die theologische Begründung der Mission bei G. W. Leibniz* (Zurich, 1973), 190. See also Jean Baruzi, *Leibniz et l'Organisation Religieuse de la Terre* (Paris, 1907), 147–8. The original source of 'anti-Europe' is in a letter by Leibniz (May 25, 1700) in O. Klopp. ed., *Die Werke von Leibniz* (Hanover, 1877), X, 309. Leibniz uses 'Oriental Europe' in a letter of January 3, 1708, in V. I. Guerrier, *Leibniz in seinem Beziehungen zu Russland und Peter der Grosse* (St Petersburg, 1873), Appendix, 76.

49. Lach, *Preface to the Novissima Sinica, op. cit.*, 68.

50. 'The Missionary Attitude of the Philosopher G. W. Leibniz'. *International Review of Missions* (1920), 399. It has been suggested that Leibniz's piety was grounded in political rather than religious concerns. In *Early German Philosophy* (Cambridge, MA, 1969), Lewis White Beck disputes this charge, saying: 'There is no decisive reason to discount the constantly repeated strains of baroque piety in his letters and publications, as if they were merely expressions of his diplomatic and not his religious make-up' (240).

51. Merkel, 'The Missionary Attitude of the Philosopher G. W. Leibniz', *op. cit.*, 402.

52. See fn. 37 above, and also Hans Zacher, *Die Hauptschriften zur Dyadik von Leibniz* (Frankfurt, 1973), 116ff.

53. Lach, *Preface to the Novissima Sinica, op. cit.*, 69.

54. *Ibid.*, 77.

55. Philip P. Wiener, *Leibniz: Selections* (New York, 1951), 598.

56. Portions of this paper were read by Cook at the Third International Leibniz Congress at Hanover (1977); drafts were read by Rosemont at the Columbia University Seminar on Oriental Thought and Religion (1978) and at the School of Oriental and African Studies of the University of London (1979). We are grateful to the participants for their comments and encouragement.

3

THE SINOPHILISM OF
CHRISTIAN WOLFF (1679–1754)[1]

Donald F. Lach

As one of the foremost architects of German rationalism, Christian Wolff was known to many of his contemporaries as 'our German Newton'. Like his master Leibniz, Wolff had catholic interests; unlike his great forerunner, Wolff sought to organize and present his thought systematically by publication of German and Latin works ranging over numerous aspects of philosophy. Like many of their contemporaries in various parts of Europe, the two German philosophers were admirers of China and its civilization. Leibniz's interests in the 'Middle Kingdom' were religious and intellectual, and they have already been explored by a number of interested scholars.[2] So far as is known, no detailed examination of Wolff's Sinophilism has hitherto been undertaken.

Very early in his academic career Wolff was in correspondence with Leibniz. In a letter of August 20, 1705, Leibniz discussed with Wolff his interest in the Chinese language as a possible philosophical language.[3] Though Wolff's reply to this letter is not known, it is clear that he probably did not commence at such an early date his study of China. Having taken up a new post as Professor of Mathematics and Natural Philosophy at the University of Halle in 1706, Wolff spent his first years at the great Pietist university writing his mathematical treatises and establishing himself among his colleagues and students. Three years after his arrival at Halle, however, Wolff turned his attention away from mathematics and towards philosophy.[4] In this new phase of his activities, Wolff began to study Chinese thought as well as western philosophy.

Donald F. Lach, 'The Sinophilism of Christian Wolff (1679–1754)', *Journal of the History of Ideas*, 14: 4, 1953, pp. 561–74.

The *Acta eruditorum* for 1711 carries a lengthy review by Wolff of Father Francisco Noël's *Observationes Mathematicæ et Physicæ in India et China factæ ab anno 1684 usque ad annum 1708* (Prague, 1710). Noël was one of the numerous Jesuits who had been dispatched to the Far East in the late seventeenth century. Like many of his colleagues, he wrote extensively of his travels in eastern Asia, and defended in his writings the religious policies of his order.[5] Though hardly of special importance to Wolff's thought, Noël's *Observationes* provided the philosopher with an excellent background of concrete details regarding Chinese history, chronology, geography, and communications. Of far greater significance to Wolff's understanding of Confucian philosophy was his examination of Noël's translations and résumés of the 'six Chinese classics'.[6] According to Noël these included the *Ta hsüeh* (*Great Learning*), *Chung Yung* (*Doctrine of the Mean*), *Lun Yü* (*Analects*), *Meng-tzü* (*Book of Mencius*), *Hsiao ching* (*Classic of Filial Piety*), and the *Hsiao hsüeh* (*Moral Philosophy for Youth*) of Chu Hsi (1130–1200),[7] a small work of interpretation used in pre-Republican China for instruction of young people in the classical writings. Wolff's lengthy review of Noël's version of these Chinese writings may be found in the *Acta eruditorum* for 1712.[8]

The influence of the Confucian teachings upon Wolff's thought did not immediately become apparent in his writings. Confronted from the outset of his career by theological hostility to his rationalist and secular philosophy, much of Wolff's time in his earlier years was spent in controversy with his Pietistic colleagues.[9] Fearful that he was teaching the students a pernicious doctrine leading only to atheism, the theological faculty of Halle became increasingly hostile to the mathematician who had become a philosopher. Though hostile to Wolff, the Halle theologians, particularly August Hermann Francke, shared Wolff's interest in China. Francke, however, was not particularly interested in Confucian thought. From his correspondence with Leibniz, Francke was stimulated rather by the prospect of sending a Protestant mission to China to compete with the Jesuits.[10]

Not particularly adept at smoothing ruffled feathers, Wolff antagonized his theological opponents further by his popularity with the students and by his open references to the bigoted character of his colleagues' lectures. Nor were the German theologians soothed by Wolff's open admiration for the thought of the French Descartes, as well as for the Chinese Confucius. In the preface dated April 18, 1721, to his famous metaphysical work, *Vernünftige Gedanken von dem gesellschaftlichen Leben der Menschen . . .*, Wolff remarked:

> From the most ancient times the Chinese have devoted great energy to the art of ruling: however, what I have managed to determine by examining their writings now and then is that their teachings are in harmony with my own . . . Perhaps I shall one of these days find the opportunity to organize the moral and political teachings of the Chinese into a scientific form which will show clearly their harmony with my teachings.

Wolff was not long in finding such an opportunity. On July 12, 1721, he delivered his famous lecture entitled *De Sinarum Philosophia practica*. This lecture was delivered on the occasion when Wolff formally handed over the prorectorate of the university to Joachim Lange, a Pietist theologian and one of his bitterest enemies.[11] Before the combined faculty and student bodies of over one thousand persons, Wolff proclaimed the virtues of the Chinese and the harmony of the Confucian teachings with his own moral philosophy. Wolff pointed out that China, the nation with the longest continuous historical record, enjoying in eighteenth-century Europe a brilliant reputation for intellectual and cultural achievements, possessed in the Confucian tradition a non-Christian philosophical system based on human reason and the example of nature. Wolff looked upon the rational Confucian system as practical substantiation of his own teachings regarding the efficacy of human reason in meeting the problems of daily life. He emphasized especially that the Chinese learned of duty and virtue from nature rather than revelation, and that they depended upon reason rather than divine guidance in discerning between good and evil, particularly at the personal level. Like a number of his philosophical contemporaries, Wolff was impressed by the doctrine of natural morality, or the belief that reasonable men everywhere have an inborn inclination for right action, and hence do not absolutely require the discipline of religious faith to live moral lives.[12]

In the prorectorate oration, as well as in other works of this period, Wolff was dependent upon Noël's description of the Chinese system of education. Hence his understanding of that system was far from accurate. What he learned of it, however, induced him to believe that the Chinese educational system also was in harmony with his own ideas concerning right education. Under their early emperors, Wolff asserted, the Chinese established two types of schools. In the *schola parvulorum* practical education was given to youths between eight and fifteen and was directed to the inferior or non-rational part of the human soul. In the *schola adultorum* a select group of aristocratic youths, capable of being governed by reason, were taught to develop their minds rather than practical skills.[13] The fundamental objective of the Chinese system of education, Wolff thought, was the better government of the state through the classification and training of people according to their abilities. Those who never advanced beyond the lower school were trained as good subjects; those who received training in the upper school were prepared to act as good leaders. The exemplary leader, whether the father of a family or the emperor of the state, Wolff looked upon as the cornerstone of Chinese society. He extended these ideas in his later studies on political philosophy.

Although Wolff explained repeatedly in his lecture that he saw no essential conflict between Confucian moral doctrine and Christian teachings, his colleagues pounced upon his speech as definitive proof of his heretical beliefs. His clear inference that atheists and pagans could be just as moral in their daily lives as practicing Christians was viewed as revolutionary. On the day after

Wolff delivered the lecture, Joachim Justus Breithaupt, the dean of the Halle theological faculty, preached openly against him and called upon the philosopher to turn his manuscript over to his colleagues for examination. His colleagues, moreover, insisted that the lecture should not be published without their consent and approval. When he refused to comply with their demands, the irate theologians began to publish tracts attacking him personally and his rational system of philosophy.

The controversy at Halle raged for almost two years with the tide slowly turning against Wolff. The Protestant theologians of many of the major German universities quickly supported their colleagues at Halle in asserting that Wolff was guilty of teaching a subversive doctrine.[14] Joachim Lange expressed in 1721 what was to become the general feeling in theological circles about Wolff:

> It is a poor philosophy for a Christian thinker to hold which has nothing more to recommend it than that it displays a certain similarity to the teachings of a heathen philosopher.[15]

Christian Thomasius, who was also outraged by Wolff's secular moral philosophy, remarked with particular bitterness: 'He [Wolff] censures our philosophers that he may publicly acclaim the philosophy of Confucius, and thereby make friends with the Jesuits.'[16]

Nor was Thomasius' reference to the Jesuits without point. Almost immediately after the delivery of his lecture, the Jesuits had taken up the cudgels for Wolff. In the *Journal de Trévoux* for 1722 they congratulated him on his understanding of Confucian moral philosophy. For a time it appeared as if Wolff might consent to have them publish his controversial speech. Wolff was angered, however, when a partial version of it was printed at Rome in 1722 without his permission and with the approbation of the Inquisition.[17] Thereafter he apparently turned his back upon association with the Jesuits.

Unable to defeat Wolff by their barrage of defamatory tracts, his colleagues at Halle finally appealed for help directly to King Frederick William I of Brandenburg-Prussia. This orthodox monarch, who resented all attacks upon established authority, took the matter under advisement and then acted swiftly, apparently on the advice of Paul Gündling, President of the Royal Society. By a secret royal edict of November 8, 1723, Wolff was formally accused of having advocated 'in public writings and lectures a doctrine contrary to the religion which had been revealed by God's own words', and was given but forty-eight hours to leave Halle and Prussian territory. Even Lange was shocked by the severity of this sentence.[18]

Though Wolff immediately left Halle and shortly took up a new post at the University of Marburg in more tolerant Hesse, the controversy continued to rage. From Germany, particularly after Frederick William's action in exiling the philosopher, the dispute spread to many other parts of Europe. The theologians of the University of Upsala attacked his position, but the Swedish Royal Academy and King Frederick I, who founded the Swedish East India Company in 1731, supported Wolff's contentions about Chinese philosophy.[19]

The universities of Leyden and Bologna also came to his defense, and Tsar Peter the Great of Russia showed his approval of Wolff's ideas by offering him the vice-Presidency of the St Petersburg Academy. Though he refused the tsar's offer, Wolff, nevertheless, in 1725 received a pension from Peter and an honorary professorship from the University of St Petersburg.[20] Perhaps Wolff's flattering description of Peter as a philosophical monarch enhanced his merit in the eyes of the tsar.[21]

While corresponding with his friends and answering the attacks of his enemies, Wolff apparently had undertaken further study of Confucian thought and Chinese history before publishing his lecture. His hesitation about having it appear in print was broken in 1725 when the unauthorized Roman version of 1722 was reprinted at Trévoux with notes written by Jesuit commentators.[22] Wolff thereafter published in 1726 at Frankfurt-am-Main the assertedly full and authentic version in Latin with an explanatory preface and copious notes.[23] This was entitled *Oratio de Sinarum Philosophia Practica, In Solemni Panegyri Recitata Cum In Ipso Academiae Hallensis Natali XXVIII. d. XII Julii A.O.R. 1721. Fasces Prorectorales Successori Traderet, Notis Uberioribus Illustrata.* In the notes especially, he reveals a much more thorough knowledge of the available Western literature on China than he had possessed five years earlier when his provocative speech had been delivered.[24] Realizing that publication of his own version would revive controversy, Wolff sent a copy of it off to Russia with the warning that it would probably provoke dispute in St Petersburg philosophical circles.[25]

In response to Wolff's publication of the *Oratio*, the various learned journals published lengthy reviews, apologias, and critiques.[26] Lange also prepared a rebuttal designed to answer the copious notes added by Wolff to his published version of the lecture.[27] Fear of the spread of Wolff's influence at this time was perhaps responsible for King Frederick William's decision in 1728 to require all students at the University of Halle to study at least two years of theology, and to turn their attention away from rational philosophy. It has been estimated that Wolff's dismissal from Halle inspired the writing of two hundred polemical tracts, one hundred and thirty against Wolff and seventy for him.[28]

The controversy provoked others to examine Chinese philosophy seriously. One of Wolff's earlier students at Halle, Georg Bernhard Bilfinger (1693–1750), published in 1724 his *Specimen Doctrinae Veterum Sinarum Moralis et Politicae* (Frankfurt-am-Main) in which he defended the position taken by Wolff but pointed out the importance of revelation in ascertaining truth and showed 'in what ways Confucian philosophy lacks the perfection of Christianity.'[29] In the following year with Wolff's help, Bilfinger received an appointment to the St Petersburg Academy. At Jena the attack upon Wolff's philosophy was led by Johann Franciscus Buddeus (1667–1729), a long-time opponent of the Jesuits, who roundly criticized Wolff's deference to their interpretations of Confucian thought. In 1724–5 a number of tracts were written by Bilfinger and Buddeus attacking the position taken by the other.[30]

This interchange was followed in 1727 by the *Historia philosophiæ Sinensis nova methodo tradita* ... (Brunswick) of Jakob Friedrich Reimmann (1668–1743). Though not actively taking sides in the Wolff-Lange dispute, Reimmann lists the polemical tracts and comments upon them. His *Historia* first appeared without his name, perhaps indicating the tension surrounding any discussion of Chinese thought. Reimmann's listing in Chapter IV of the thirty most important works known to him about Chinese thought throws great light on the quantity and quality of the information on China available to Wolff and his contemporaries.[31]

Meanwhile, at Marburg Wolff continued to elaborate his rational system and to attract to his lectures students from all over Germany and Europe. The records of the University of Marburg indicate also that a Moslem student from 'the East Indies',[32] and a Greek scholar[33] were among Wolff's disciples. In his Latin works of these years, Wolff continued regularly to quote the Chinese example on problems relating to lay morality and statecraft. Practically all of his major Latin works include allusions to aspects of Chinese thought and history.

Moreover, in the autumn term of 1750 Wolff delivered a lengthy lecture at Marburg entitled *De rege philosophante et philosopho regnante*,[34] in which he held up China as the outstanding working example of enlightened despotism. The following illustrations of Wolff's understanding of Chinese government are excerpted from the English translation of this lecture published in 1750 and entitled *The Real Happiness of a People under a Philosophical King Demonstrated; Not only from the Nature of Things, but from the undoubted Experience of the Chinese under their first Founder Fohi, and his Illustrious Successors, Hoam Ti, and Xin Num* (London).[35] Asserting, as Plato did, that a community will be happy when 'either philosophers rule, or they that rule are philosophers', Wolff developed the following thesis regarding statecraft in China:

> Let no one presume to judge contemptuously of the Chinese emperors, as if their Form of Government would lose in the Comparison with that of other Kings and Princes in the World. 'Tis a thing well known that the Empire of China is of a vast extent, divided into fifteen very large provinces, each of which are unanimously agreed by all Travellers into China, to deserve the Name of large kingdoms rather than Provinces.
>
> The three first Emperors, settled that Model of Government, wherein it now excels all other Models in the World, and which has for so many thousand years back flourished, and still continues to flourish at this Day, whilst other Monarchies and Kingdoms have had their final Period and Dissolution .... Should it be objected that a Ruler, can not possibly be supposed Master of the Time and Opportunity requisite for the Business of Invention, and of philosophical Reasonings, without neglecting the affairs of a vast Empire; the Example of these great Men, who never

suffered themselves to fail in any Thing, that seemed to have the least Relation to the Business of Rulers, is a sufficient Refutation . . . . This is the case of the Chinese, among whom Kings were Philosophers, and Philosophers Kings . . . . The Chinese Emperors . . . were furnished with a Stock of Philosophy, and by its Means they modelled their Government; and not having any Model of Government to copy after, not any compleat System of civil or political Philosophy to apply, they were by Dint of Genius carried . . . to reduce the Notion of a Commonwealth to that of a House or Family, and under the Person of the Head of the Family . . . . Nor are we to imagine that the Empire of China was constituted by any premature or precipitate Measures. Before even they thought of so arduous an Affair, they first applied themselves duly to form their own Conduct and Actions . . . . Again the Chinese had a Custom, as appears from the Works of Confucius and Mencius, in Things of an arduous Nature to consult the Philosophers, who were of the Council of the petty Princes . . . . For the philosophers excelled, and far surpassed all others in political knowledge. . . . What the Love of Truth, which Philosophy itself inspires, can effect in Rulers, the Chinese Emperors . . . are pregnant Instances . . . . For Yao turning his whole Attention to the Miscarriages of his People, and to the public Calamities, did by his great Penetration inquire into the Reasons of both, and wholly bent upon finishing the Form of Government, he principally applied his Attention whether by prudent Laws, and by his own Example he might not prevent any Misconduct of the Subjects, and by a better Method of Government obviate public calamities . . . .

Despite his fervent admiration for the political philosophy of China, as he understood it, Wolff warns that philosophy by itself cannot always master events, and that the Chinese example falls 'far short of that Perfection which we should attentively eye, to be thoroughly apprised of the Connexion of Civil Happiness with the Government of a Philosopher.' 'The Chinese Philosophy,' he believes, 'labours under a considerable Imperfection . . . . The Notions of the Chinese were, indeed, determinate, but not distinct enough, and hence their Incapacity to bring them to determinate Propositions, and to reduce them when demonstrated to System.' Wolff's belief in the promotion of civil happiness through a rational and enlightened system of government was thus not completely realized even in China. Nevertheless he candidly admitted that no more 'illustrious Example' of government by philosophy 'can anywhere be found.'

Among the most devoted of Wolff's students was Jean Deschamps (1709–69), who studied at Marburg in 1727–9, and became in 1737 the court almoner and tutor to Crown Prince Frederick of Prussia.[36] Deschamps and the influential Saxons, Count Ernst Christoph van Manteuffel and Ulrich Friedrich von Suhm, brought the writings of Wolff directly to the attention of Crown Prince Frederick (later Frederick the Great). With Frederick's prestige behind him, Manteuffel succeeded, too, in persuading the king in 1736 to permit a reëxamination of Wolff's case. Since Frederick William I was no longer under Gündling's influence, and since he had evidently been greatly distressed by the European reaction to Wolff's dismissal, he agreed to set up a commission of investigation.

Joachim Lange had meanwhile become disturbed by the revival of interest in Wolff's philosophy at the University of Halle and by the philosopher's popularity in court circles. On April 11, 1736, the queen wrote to Crown Prince Frederick a report of a visit by Lange to the court of Berlin and of his speeches against Wolff.[37] In response to Lange's warnings about the dangers of permitting a revival of interest in Wolff's 'errors', the king asked the Halle theologian to submit a written statement of his charges. On May 10, Lange sent to Berlin his *Kurzer Bericht derjenigen Lehrsätze, welche in der Wolffischen Philosophie der Natürlichen und Geoffenbarten nachtheilig sind ....* This work evidently made a strong impression upon the king. Seventeen days later, however, Wolff's reply in German arrived, and, along with Lange's attack, this was quickly translated into French for the benefit of the crown prince, who used French more readily than German. On June 5, 1736, Frederick William summoned a commission composed of Samuel Cocceji, minister of state for the department of ecclesiastical affairs, Jablonski and Noltenius, two reformed pastors, and Reinbeck and Carstedt, two Lutheran pastors.[38] Within three weeks the commission had agreed that there was nothing dangerous to the state in Wolff's writings or teachings. Thereafter Wolff's favor mounted swiftly in Prussia, even with the king himself. By 1739, Frederick William was reading Wolff's works and urging others to do likewise.

Among the materials reviewed by the commission was Lange's 'exposé'. In this he contended that Wolff's *Oratio* could be summarized in three points as follows:

1. The Chinese are the most grossly atheistic people under the sun.
2. The Chinese are the wisest and most virtuous of all mankind, and they should serve as a model to the other nations.
3. The author [Wolff] developed his philosophy along Chinese principles, and hence it is an erroneous and scandalous philosophy.[39]

In replying to Lange's imputations Wolff categorically denied that he had referred to the Chinese as 'grossly atheistic'. He insisted that he had stated merely that 'they have never had a distinct conception of God'.[40] Nor would Wolff accept responsibility for the full import of Lange's other assertions about his interpretation of Chinese moral philosophy. In fact, he vehemently inveighed against Lange's irresponsible distortion of his ideas through indiscriminate quotation from his writings. Hoping to bring this point home and to repudiate Lange, Wolff requested his readers to imagine the following situation:

Let us suppose . . . that Mr. Lange has been sent as a missionary to China in order to convert the Chinese . . .

Let us suppose again that some Chinese philosopher should rise against Lange, and denounce him to the emperor by presenting a Short Exposé of the Fundamental Errors of Mr. Lange. It seems that the Chinese philosopher in imitation of Lange's own beautiful method would then launch an attack in something like the following vein . . ..

1. Fundamental Error

The Apostle of Halle, he would say, makes of God, the creator of the world, a simple human; because he attributes to him a body resembling ours, and he represents him as not seeing that which goes on under his eyes; as satisfying himself by harming whoever displeases him, by hating without reason; and consequently by encouraging sin in order to appear just in punishing it.

2. Demonstration (a random selection of Biblical quotations)

In the beginning God created the heavens and the earth (Gen. I: 1). And they [Adam and Eve] heard the voice of Jehovah God who was walking in the Garden in the cool of the day; and the man and the wife hid themselves from the presence of Jehovah God amongst the trees of the garden. And Jehovah God called unto the man and said unto him, Where art thou? (Gen. III: 8–9). And Jehovah said, Because the cry of Sodom and Gomorrah is great, and because their sin is very grievous; I will go down now and see whether they have done altogether according to the cry of it which is come unto me; and if not, I will know (Gen. XVIII: 20–1). And he said, I will make all my goodness pass before thee; and I will be gracious to whom I will be gracious, and will show mercy on whom I show mercy (Exodus XXXIII: 19). And I will harden Pharaoh's heart, and multiply my signs and my wonders in the land of Egypt (Exod. VIII: 3). I will raise up evil against thee out of thine own house; and I will take thy wives before thine eyes, and give them unto thy neighbor, and he shall lie with thy wives in the sight of the sun . . .. For thou didst it secretly: but I will do this thing before all Israel, and before the sun (II Samuel XII: 11–12).[41]

In the meantime at Frederick's retreat at Rheinsberg, the crown prince continued to study Wolff's philosophy while Deschamps prepared French translations of more of Wolff's works. As they were completed, copies of the translations were forwarded to Voltaire for his comments.[42] Meanwhile, Frederick was writing the famous *Anti-Machiavel* in which he spelled out his doctrine of enlightened despotism. In this work and in his correspondence the influence of Wolff on his political philosophy is clear.[43] Through both Wolff and Voltaire the young Frederick was exposed to the Sinophilism of his day as well as to the philosophers' conceptions of statecraft. Frederick wrote to Wolff in 1740: 'It is up to the philosophers to be the preceptors of the universe and the tutors of its princes.'[44]

Though Frederick William in 1739 had sought to recall Wolff to Prussia, the philosopher refused to leave Marburg at that time. It was not until Frederick became king in 1740 that Wolff could be enticed to return to the Hohenzollern domains.[45] Not wishing to take the post offered him by the Royal Academy in Berlin, Wolff returned in 1741 to Halle, the scene of his former defeat, as vice-chancellor of the university. Not long thereafter Lange left for Copenhagen where he died in 1744.

While Frederick displayed interest in Wolff's thought, Deschamps continued to play an important rôle in court circles. After Frederick's accession to the throne, Deschamps was appointed tutor to Princes Henry and Ferdinand, the king's brothers. Charged with instructing the young princes in Wolff's philosophy, Deschamps continued to prepare French translations of Wolff's works. A number of these were published at Amsterdam between 1743 and 1746 in three volumes as the *Cours abrégé de la philosophie Wolffienne*.[46] However, Deschamps' translation of Wolff's lecture at Marburg of 1730 under the French title *Le philosophe-roi et la roi-philosophe* was published separately in 1740. There is no evidence, however, that Frederick either read or commented upon it. Though it might be concluded that these translations were prepared for Frederick as well as the young princes, the Prussian ruler after 1740 under Voltaire's influence gradually lost his enthusiasms for Wolff's rationalism. A practical result of Frederick's change of heart was the fact that Deschamps lost his position as tutor in 1746 and left shortly thereafter for England.

Though not enjoying the king's favor, Wolff during the last fourteen years of his life in Prussia rounded out his system of rationalism. Through his published writings, correspondence, and personal influence he also continued to spread the popularity of Chinese moral and political philosophy to his contemporaries. After 1740, he was particularly interested in clarifying for Europeans the rationale, as he understood it, of China's international practices. In his *Jus Gentium* (1740–48) especially, Wolff explains the Chinese practice of refusing to conduct international relations on a basis of equality by reference to China's unique degree of economic self-sufficiency.[47] In this connection it should be recalled that Wolff lived in the era when mercantilism was at its height in Europe and when self-sufficiency was the major objective of state economic planning, particularly in Prussia. Wolff also accounts for China's isolationism by reference to the 'Middle Kingdom's' assumption of superiority and its desire to protect the morals of the nation from foreign corruption.[48] Finally, he comments favorably upon the practice of the Chinese emperors who relieve famine among their subjects, not by expropriating grain from their neighbors, but by gifts from their own granaries.[49] Although he recognized the great benefits of Chinese civilization, Wolff retained sufficient objectivity to deplore the fact that 'almost none of them have made advances in metaphysics or physics, much less have they acquired the fame of Europeans in mathematics.'[50]

The last of Wolff's major works was his five-volume *Philosophia moralis sive Ethica, methodo scientifica pertractata* (Halle, 1750–3). Examination of this study reveals no direct indebtedness of the author to Confucian philosophy. However, in a letter relating to the *Philosophia moralis* written in 1752 to Count Cyrillus Rasumowski, President of the St Petersburg Academy, Wolff reiterated his belief in the correspondence between his own moral teachings and those of Confucius.[51]

Like Voltaire's in France, Wolff's Sinophilism exerted a continuous and impressive influence upon the thought and activities of his contemporaries. Although some followed him unquestioningly in his admiration for China, others challenged him and scoffed at his willingness to rely upon the Jesuit translations and interpretations of the Chinese classics. As in France (and also in Holland), the intellectuals of Germany differed seriously in their reactions to China. Nevertheless, the subject was kept alive and continued in academic and nonacademic circles to stimulate controversy until the last two decades of the eighteenth century.

NOTES

1. Presented in summary before the Philadelphia meeting of the Far Eastern Association, March 28, 1951.
2. See especially F. R. Merkel, *Leibniz und die China-Mission* (Leipzig, 1920); and D. F. Lach, 'Leibniz and China', this *Journal* VI (1945), 436–55.
3. C. I. Gerhardt (ed.), *Briefwechsel zwischen Leibniz und Christian Wolff aus den Handschriften der königlichen Bibliothek zu Hannover* (Halle, 1860), 32.
4. Consult H. Wuttke (ed.), *Christian Wolffs eigene Lebensbeschreibung* (Leipzig, 1841), 4–6.
5. L. Pfister, *Notices biographiques et bibliographiques sur les Jésuites de l'Ancienne Mission de Chine* (Shanghai, 1932), I, 414–19.
6. Francisco Noël, *Sinensis imperii libri classici sex, nimirum adultorum schola, immortabile medium, liber sententiarum, Mencius, filialis observantia, parvulorum schola, e sinico idiomate in latinum traducti* ... (Prague, 1711).
7. This was but a fragmentary translation and résumé of the Chinese work even though Noël speaks of it as a literal translation. For a criticism of Noël's work see C. de Harlez, *Le Siao Hio, ou Morale de la Jeunesse avec le commentaire de Tcheu-Siueu*, Vol. XV of the *Annales du Musée Guimet* (Paris, 1889), 6–8. A number of commentators (for example, A. Reichwein, *China and Europe* [London, 1925], p. 162, n. 34), have incorrectly identified this sixth 'classic' as a translation of the *San tzü ching* of Wang Yang-lin.
8. Pp. 123–8 and 224–9.
9. See Wuttke (ed.), *op. cit.*, 189–95; Eduard Zeller, '*Wolffs Vertreibung aus Halle: der Kampf des Pietismus mit der Philosophie*', *Preussische Jahrbücher*, X, 47–72; Gustav V. Herzberg, *Geschichte der Stadt Halle an der Saale* (Halle, 1891), III, 98–9; J. C. Gottsched, *Vita, fata et scripta Christiani Wolfii, Philosophi* (Leipzig, 1739), 76–7.
10. Merkel, *op. cit.*, 214–24, prints relevant correspondence of Leibniz and Francke. See also G. Kramer, *August Hermann Francke* (Halle, 1880), 333–35.
11. Details of this incident in C. G. Ludovici, *Ausführlicher Entwurf einer vollständigen Historie der Wolffischen Philosophie* (Leipzig, 1737), I, 8–9, and Wuttke (ed.), *op. cit.*, 19–26.

12. For an excellent discussion of this work in relation to the totality of Wolff's philosophy see Mariano Campo, *Christiano Wolff e il razionalismo precritico* (Milan, 1939), II, 516–46.

13. In Noël's translation the *Ta hsüeh* (*Great Learning*) was rendered *schola adultorum*; the *Hsiao hsüeh* (*Moral Philosophy for the Young*) was rendered *schola parvulorum*. According to Wolff's own testimony, he was influenced also by Aristotle's divisions of the *appetitus* into two categories: *sensitivus et rationalis*. See Wolff, *Venünftige Gedanken von Gott, der Welt, und der Seele der Menschen* (Frankfurt-am-Main, 1733), 227.

14. The major attacks were written and circulated by Joachim Lange. See especially his *Ausführliche Recension der wider die Wolfianische Metaphysik auf 9 Universitäten und 26 Schriften, mit dem Erweise, dass Wolff sich gegen die Vorwürfe bisher keinesweges gerettet habe* (Halle, 1725).

15. As quoted in Ludovici, *op. cit.*, II, 92.

16. As quoted in *ibid.*, I, 269.

17. This work has not been available. Reprinted in Jesuit edition of 1725 (see n. 22).

18. Text of the decree in Wuttke, *op. cit.*, 28; see also Ludovici, *op. cit.*, I, 57–9.

19. Christian Bartholmess, *Histoire philosophique de l'Academie de Prusse depuis Leibniz jusqu'à Schelling* (Paris, 1850), I, 96–7; H. Cordier, *Bibliotheca Sinica* (Paris, 1907–8), col. 1410, cites a Swedish dissertation entitled *Dissertatio Sententiam Wolfii de philosophia Sinarum Confuciana examinans, Praesidé Nicol. Lagerlöf publ. exam. subjicit Carolus Gust. Schröder* (Lund, 1737). See also Osvald Sirén, 'Kina och den Kinesiska Tanken I Sverige pa 1700-Talet', *Lychnos* (1948–9), p. 12, n. 1.

20. Consult [E. M.] Kunik (ed.), *Briefe von [and to] Christian Wolff aus den Jahren 1719–1753. Ein Beitrag zur Geschichte der Kaiserlichen Akademie zu St. Petersburg* (St Petersburg, 1860), 70–2.

21. *Ibid.*, 11.

22. It was entitled: *Pomum Eridis: hoc est, de Sapientia Sinensium Oratio in solemni Panegyri, quum fasces Prorectorales Successori traderet in ipso Fridericianae natali XXIIX die XII Julii A.R.S. MDCCXXI recitata a Christ. Wolfio, Potent, Reg. Bor. Consil. Aul. Mathem. et Natur, P.P.O. Societ. Reg. Brit. et Bor. Sodali. Romae cum Censura et Approbatione S. Officia Inquisitorii A.O.R. MDCCXXII: recusa Trevoltii cum cons. Societ. Jesu ap. Jo. Boudot, Bibliop. reg. et Acad. Scient, Reg Ordinar. An. 1725 in 4.*

23. In 1740, G. F. Hagen published a German translation of the *Oratio* in volume six of his compendium of Wolff's works entitled, *Kleine philosophische Schriften*. This translation has ben reprinted in part in Fritz Brüggemann (ed.), *Das Weltbild der deutschen Aufklärung* (Leipzig, 1930), 174–95. A French translation of the *Oratio* is included in Part II of J. H. Formey, *La Belle Wolfienne* (The Hague, 1746).

24. Wolff refers to the following works *inter alia*: Martin Martini, *Novus Atlas Sinensis* (Amsterdam, 1655); Philippe Couplet, *Tabula Chronologica monarchiae Sinicae juxta cyclos annorum LX ab anno ante Christum ad annum post Christum 1683* (Paris, 1686); J. H. Schall, *Historia relatio de ortu et progressu fidei orthodoxae in regno Chinensi per Missionarios Societatis Jesu ab A. 1581 usque ad A. 1669 collecta ex literis eorundem Patrum Societatis Jesu ...* (Ratisbon, 1672).

25. Kunik (ed.), *op. cit.*, 72.

26. For example, the *Acta eruditorum* (1726), *Journal des Şavans* (1727), and *Histoire littéraire* de l'Europe (1727).

27. This was entitled *Nova Anatome seu idea analytica systematis metaphysici Wolfiani, qua illud ... denuo resolutum ... exhibetur : cui ... praemittitur oratio de sapientia Sinarum Confuciana ... notis ... instructa, ac subjungitur ... in notas istius orationis Wolfianas* (Frankfurt and Leipzig, 1726).

28. Bartholmess, *op. cit.*, 96; see also the compendium of C. G. Ludovici, *Sammlung und Auszüge der sämtlichen Streitschriften wegen der Wolfianischen Philosophie* (Leipzig, 1737–8).

29. For Wolff's commentary on Bilfinger's work see the *Oratio*, n. 208.
30. Consult A. F. Stolzenburg, *Die Theologie des Jo. Franc. Buddeus und des Chr. Matth. Pfaff* (Berlin, 1926), 286–8; also Ludovici, *op. cit.*, I, 53–5.
31. Pp. 28–9. For further details on Reimmann's position see his *Eigene Lebensbeschreibung* ... (Brunswick, 1745), 131. In the first three chapters of the *Historia* he presents an outline of the definitions, divisions, and objectives required for a systematic study of Chinese philosophy. The fourth chapter lists and comments on possible sources of information among which he includes the translations of Intorcetta *et al.* and Noël, the major missionary accounts, and the works of the German scholars, such as Andreas Müller. Of particular interest is his item no. 10 of anonymous authorship and entitled *Artificiosa Hominum, miranda, naturae in Sina et Europa* (Frankfurt-am-Main, 1655). Another interesting work on Chinese philosophy based mainly upon Noël's account of Mencius is Johann Benedict Carpzov's *Memcius sive Mentius Sinensium Post Confucium Philosophus* (Leipzig, 1743). Carpzov also comments (p. 35, n. m) on Wolff's *Oratio*.
32. J. Cäsar, *Christian Wolff in Marburg* (Marburg, 1879), 18.
33. *Bibliothèque Germanique*, XVIII (1729), 210.
34. Published in the *Horae subsecivae Marburgenses, quibus philosophia ad publicam privatamque utilitatem aptatur* (Frankfurt and Leipzig, 1732).
35. Numerous commentators on this work have confused it with Wolff's *Oratio* (for example, A. H. Rowbotham, *Missionary and Mandarin* [Berkeley, 1942], p. 331, n. 20). Textual comparison shows this identification to be incorrect. This mistake may arise from a note to this effect in the British Museum *Catalogue of Printed Books* (Vol. LVIII). The catalogue of the British Museum also states incorrectly, as does that of the Library of Congress, that *The Real Happiness* was translated from Jean Deschamps' abridgement of Wolff's philosophy. These catalogues do not indicate the English translator. From internal evidence it is clear that Deschamps actually did not prepare the English translation, though he was in London at this time. A note in the *Journal Britannique* by M. Maty (1750), p. 88, indicates that the translator was 'Mr. Santhoroc, Gentilhomme Allemande'. Though no further reference to the identity of the translator has been discovered, it would appear that he was probably a relative of Johann Caspar Santoroc (1682–1745), a colleague of Wolff's at the University of Marburg, and possibly a friend of Deschamps.
36. See for further discussion of Deschamps' career, Andrew Hamilton, *Rheinsberg: Memorials of Frederick the Great and Prince Henry of Prussia* (London, 1880), I, 64–9.
37. See H. A. Droysen, 'Friedrich Wilhelm I, Friedrich der Grosse und der Philosoph Christian Wolff', *Forschungen zur Brandenburgischen und Preussischen Geschichte* XXIII (1910), 3.
38. See Formey's account of the reopening of Wolff's case in *Bibliothèque Germanique* XXXVI (1736), 1–34.
39. J. Lange, *Court exposé des Maximes de la Philosophie de Mr. Wolff, qui sont prejudiciables à la religion naturelle, et à la revelation* ..., 36–7, in *Recueil de nouvelles pièces philosophiques ... entre messieurs Lange et Wolff* ... ([Leipzig], 1737), as translated by the Count von Manteuffel.
40. See *ibidem, Réponse de M. Chretien Wolf, aux accusations mal fondées, que Mons. Lange a mises par écrit par ordre de Sa Maj. Prussienne*, 136; also see the *Oratio*, n. 54.
41. *Ibid.*, 191–4.
42. R. Koser, *Friedrich der Grosse als Kronprinz* (Stuttgart, 1886), 148. See also H. Droysen, 'Die Marquise du Châtelet, Voltaire und der Philosoph Christian Wolff', *Zeitschrift für französische Sprache und Literatur*, XXXV (1910), 226–48; Walter Engemann, *Voltaire und China. Ein Beitrag zur Geschichte der Völkerkunde und zur Geschichte der Geschichtsschreibung sowie zu ihren gegenseitigen Beziehungen* (Leipzig, 1932), 89–97.

43. See Eduard Zeller, *Friedrich der Grosse als Philosoph* (Berlin, 1886), 6–7; W. Frauendienst, *Christian Wolff als Staatsdenker* (Berlin, 1926), 17–22.

44. J. D. E. Preuss (ed.), *Oeuvres de Frederic le Grand* (Berlin, 1850), XVI, 179.

45. For Pastor Reinbeck's rôle in negotiating with Wolff for Frederick II see Anton Friedrich Büsching, *Beyträge zu der Lebensgeschichte denkenwürdiger Personen, insonderheit gelehrter Männer* (Halle, 1783), Vol. I, Part I.

46. Cf. *supra*, n. 35.

47. The *Jus gentium methodo scientifica pertractatum* was first published in eight volumes in the years 1740–8. The 1764 edition has been translated into English by Joseph H. Drake and comprises, along with a one-volume reproduction of the original Latin text and notes, Vol. XIII of the *Classics of International Law* (Oxford, 1934), 44.

48. *Ibid.*, 98.

49. *Ibid.*, 174.

50. *Ibid.*, 36.

51. Kunik (ed.), *op. cit.*, 151–2.

4

VOLTAIRE, SINOPHILE[1]

Basil Guy

On leaving the Jesuit 'college' of Louis-le-Grand and even into the heat of the fray which accompanied publication of the *Encyclopédie*, Voltaire's relations with the Jesuits were scarcely ever cool.[2] On the one hand, the latter never did completely despair of winning to their way of thinking this clever mind, whose cleverness was a prize example of the excellence of their teaching. And on the other, Voltaire always felt indebted to such masters, however slight his real obligation. In 1739 he wrote to Thieriot: 'Assurez les de mon attachement inviolable pour eux; je le leur dois; ils m'ont élevé; c'est être un monstre que de ne pas aimer ceux qui ont cultivé notre âme' (Best, 1676).[3] In spite of everything which separated him from them, in spite of his distaste for the politics and doctrine of the Company, he kept a pleasant memory of certain teachers and a lively appreciation of the way in which they taught. Whence certain other remarks showing his kindly disposition in the *Correspondence* (Best, 14239) and in the *Temple du goût* (M.viii.593). Yet the influence of his former professors extended to other fields, where, unconsciously, Voltaire was guided by them in the choice of his ideas, just as he was when it came to illustrating those ideas by example. This inspiration is perhaps difficult to discern, but it is, we believe, the case for China.

At the turn of the eighteenth century and for some time thereafter the Rites Controversy would occupy almost every Jesuit mind in seeking to exonerate the Company's good name. It was but natural that much of this effort be

Basil Guy, *The French Image of China Before and After Voltaire* (Geneva: Institut et Musée Voltaire, 1963), chap. 5, pp. 214–18, 243–76.

communicated to the youth entrusted to their care at one and another of their schools, not least of which was Louis-le-Grand, and that their teaching reflect their preoccupation with China, where the apology of civilization followed and depended upon the apology of human nature. Did our pupil of the Jesuits read at this time the *Nouveaux Mémoires* of Father Lecomte and the continuation published by Father Le Gobien, along with that almost interminable vehicle of Jesuit defense, the *Lettrés édifiantes*? Although at this distance it is impossible to decide with any surety, there is some likelihood that Voltaire, ever the avid reader, did peruse a few of these tracts. What is indubitable is the fact that he could not help but have some acquaintance with the oral propaganda of the Jesuits on behalf of their Chinese missions. Indeed, such can only have been the case, when we learn that the 'scriptor' at Louis-le-Grand from 1705–8 and from 1710–11 was none other than Etienne Souciet, a not inconsiderable mathematician who corresponded with missionaries in the Far East for the exchange of scientific and other knowledge.

Despite their censure by the Sorbonne, the Jesuits had not renounced their opinions on Chinese religion. Proof of this, if proof were wanting, could be found most easily in the fact that Father Le Gobien, one of those condemned specifically for his recalcitrant attitude, was charged in 1703 with editing the *Lettres édifiantes*. In effect, the decree of Clement XI did not solve the Rites Controversy, any more than would successive briefs and bulls issued by the Papacy in 1713, 1715, 1742, or yet in 1744. Thus, in 1708 the Company could go one step further in antagonizing its enemies by printing in the *Journal de Trévoux* for July (p. 1134) a defense of Confucianism against the attack of 'atheism' imputed to that doctrine by Malebranche earlier in the year; and in 1715 Father Tournemine, in his preface to an edition of Fénelon's *Démonstration de l'existence de Dieu* (p. xi). was able to invoke the pure theism of the Chinese as witness to the existence and validity of universal consent.

Although René-Joseph de Tournemine is perhaps best known to moderns as one of the editors of the *Journal de Trévoux*, his name is important to us here because, more than Souciet, he was able to play the rôle of catalyst between China and the young Voltaire. When still the latter's professor of rhetoric, he had become interested in Chinese science thanks to Father Bouvet, one of the mathematicians at the imperial court in Peking. Several letters from Bouvet to Tournemine, written in 1725–9, tell of sending a number of documents (treatises on Chinese algebra and similar topics) to the Jesuits in France. Voltaire could not help but be touched by his professor's enthusiasm for China and things Chinese, despite the fact that he did not include Father Tournemine's name in the 'Catalogue' appended to the *Siècle de Louis XIV* (1751) and that later he went so far as to pillory him in the following distich: 'C'est notre père Tournemine/Qui croit tout ce qu'il imagine' (Best.9694). Father Tournemine's imaginings were not so ridiculous, however, for the learned Jesuit and his correspondents (including Leibnitz) were all very much interested in the figurists and their theories. In 1702 he went so far as to write a treatise, wherein the ideas of this coterie were prominent, and in November, 1710, a note in the *Journal de Trévoux* announced other dissertations in which he pretended to show that 'l'histoire de Saturne est copiée sur celle d'Adam ... que Typhon, Moloch, Mars, Roumen, Ariman et Odin sont le même dieu' (p. 2017). Young as he was, Voltaire could not have helped knowing something of these endeavours, since there is later comment on this work in a letter to Thieriot, dated 7 February 1738, where Voltaire says: 'Je compte n'y point trouver que Cham est l'Ammon des Egyptiens, que Loth est l'Erichtée, qu'Hercule est copié de Samson, que Philémon et Baucis sont imités d'Abraham et de Sara' (Best.1386). Such were the flights of fancy when beset by the temptations of figurism! We might be surprised at this extravaganza if the *Journal de Trévoux* had not published in November 1702 (p. 89) an attempt to verify historically the idea that religion is at first but a simple experience among all peoples, that all religions stem from but one source, natural religion, and if we did not already have some acquaintance with these ideas in the work of Father Foucquet. And to his knowledge of figurist theory it is not therefore untoward that Voltaire, some years after leaving Louis-le-Grand, should add a personal touch with his introduction to Foucquet himself. We do not know whether the two men ever did meet. It is highly probable, however, given the confidential tone in which Voltaire speaks of him, saying: 'Le P. Foucquet, Jésuite, ... m'a dit plusieurs fois qu'il y avait à la Chine très peu de philosophes athées' (M.xi.180), and given the fact that Foucquet was for a short time in Paris, on his way to Rome in 1722, when Voltaire was likewise in the capital. Thus, once again the Jesuits were important to our purpose in that, after introducing Voltaire to the Middle Kingdom, they also contributed to his deformation of such facts as their teaching had included.

We might then conclude that the relations Voltaire maintained with the Order served only to confirm those impressions which meanwhile he had received from Jesuit works themselves. As we shall see, he knew this literature rather well, especially the works of Fathers Semedo, Martini and Kircher; he also appears to have read the translations from the Chinese classics prepared by a little group of Jesuits at Hangchow under Father Intorcetta during the previous century. Moreover, there is proof that later, as the volume of their propaganda increased, Voltaire managed to keep pace with their efforts, doing more than leaf through the volumes of those important sources, the *Mémoires* of Father Lecomte, the numerous volumes of the *Lettres édifiantes*, and Father Du Halde's *Description geographique, historique, chronologique, politique et physique de l'Empire de la Chine et de la Tartarie chinoise, 1735*. At the same time as he evinces a more than cursory interest in travel literature or in the relations of embassies to the Dragon Throne (all of which he would ultimately seek to discredit), there is a sure knowledge and grasp of Navarrete's work, the source of much anti-Jesuit literature on China. All of these works – and more like them which have been included in the list of books from Voltaire's library by Professors Havens and Torrey – contributed most certainly to the elaboration of Voltaire's Chinese ideal.[4] But the lion's share in this honour belongs to the Jesuits, if only because of the abundance of their propaganda. A study like Professor Rowbotham's *Missionary and Mandarin* (1942) proves that in his enthusiasm, Voltaire added very little indeed to what the missionaries had already said, whether in matters religious or political.[5] And insofar as these two poles of his interest were concerned, Voltaire was still indebted to his formation at Louis-le-Grand, where both were first impressed upon his alert, receptive mind. But how they would develop in later years!

[…]

In estimating the rôle China played in Voltaire's work before 1756, we have noted that until that date, the Middle Kingdom did not attract too much of his attention, and that even as an element of local colour it did not have his complete approval, that in working with China and Chinese motifs Voltaire was, as it were, constrained, ill at ease. And this, because he was more interested in developing his own thought, seeking in China merely an exemplification of certain interests that were uppermost in his mind. Until the *Essai sur les mœurs* (1761–63), Voltaire was not truly curious about the Middle Kingdom for its own sake, with the result that most of his attempts to work with Chinese material ended, for better or for worse, in 'chinoiseries'.[6] There was no concerted and objective adaptation of information then currently available, not even in the *Orphelin*, where this procedure would have been eminently practicable. No analysis of Chinese ideas or Chinese modes, either. No criticism, no 'philosophie' in the sense of a rational synthesis. We might conclude, therefore, that despite one or two rare instances, despite Voltaire's own pretensions, China in this first period of his creativity did nothing but accentuate his penchant for the more obvious and superficial side of one of the many passing expressions of the Rococo.

These 'chinoiseries' represent only the knowing use of a theme which could not help but arouse a certain interest on Voltaire's part, but it was the very example of China which would help him to abandon this false track and set out upon a task which would be most important for himself and for his age. This task would be the *Essai sur les mœurs*.[7] Necessary to the understanding of a more serious and imposing Voltaire after 1756, date of the authorized edition, the *Essai* would likewise witness the conscientious and full expansion of China's rôle in all his later work. This is not to say that China made Voltaire a 'philosophe' – we have just pointed out a few considerations that would lead to a quite contrary conclusion – but simply that without the Chinese example, Voltaire would not have become the 'philosophe' which today we recognize in him. And something would be lacking to complete that picture, if we did not try to grasp the full meaning of the contribution made by China, especially to the first two chapters of the *Essai*.

The gestation of the *Siècle de Louis XIV* had lasted for fifteen years, during which Voltaire's documentation had increased and his researches multiplied, with the result that anecdotes, chronologies, tables, and even extracts from the great poets and writers of all countries were accumulated, sometimes communicated by friends or benevolent correspondents, along with more usual facts relating to historical backgrounds. In the long run, Voltaire thought more and more of having this 'essay' as he called it form but the conclusion of another, more ambitious, undertaking, l'*Essai sur les mœurs*. The approach would be the same as for the *Siècle*, and, on occasion, the same documentation, researches, and inspiration might also serve, since the two works were written in the first place for one person only, Madame Du Châtelet, the bluestocking who protected him and who had collaborated in a number of his physical experiments, but who was completely discouraged by history as it was written in the eighteenth century (M.xxiv.546). In this manner was Voltaire led to become the lady's teacher and to undertake a history suited to her taste and intelligence. Like any good professor, he was also led to appeal at the same time to a wider public. But in his plan, he seems to have paid little attention to Thomas Salmon's *Modern History*, of which a French translation was begun in 1730, or to the British edition of a universal history which had appeared in 1736. At the same time he openly attacked the universal history of Bossuet, re-edited in 1738 in four volumes and quite popular, pretending to present merely his own views on history and the result of his own research. We shall soon see whether this was the case. Meanwhile, he prepared a *Discours sur l'histoire universelle*, an *Abrégé* and even an *Histoire générale* which would all contribute to and be included in the complete edition of the *Essai sur les mœurs* of 1756.[8]

So many sketches, so many steps in the elaboration of this work, were necessary to Voltaire, who devoted himself almost exclusively to this task for some twenty years, but twenty years during which he reached the prime of life and was carried along by enthusiasm for his work. There is no need therefore to be surprised as was Villemain when discussing the corrections and changes by which Voltaire sought to improve his creation, saying that they are to be found 'presque partout à la correction précise et à l'élégance animée du style. ... Cet ornement jusque-là si négligé dans l'histoire était un des traits de la physionomie nouvelle que Voltaire donnait à cette grande étude' (M.xi.v). Nor is it astonishing that imitators flocked to the press, attempting to derive their share of glory from the aura of success surrounding Voltaire's achievement. Most of them, however, never could and never would find in so apparently banal a theme as the progress of the arts and sciences Voltaire's historic sense. Because in this so-called 'abrégé' Voltaire knew how to collect anecdotes, knew how to select the contrast between cause and effect, knew how to write clearly, even wittily, about complicated matters to which, despite all, he accorded their natural depth through his keen perception and created as a result a true historic panorama. But there is more.[9] Thanks to this technical or stylistic success, the whole presentation is illuminated from many new angles. Especially in the first chapters on China, India, Arabia, novelty served to create a truly universal history, which proposed to continue or, rather, to refute the work of Bossuet. In his history 'Ad usum Delphini' the illustrious prelate had stopped with the reign of Charlemagne, after having limited the field of his inquiry to the Judaeo-Roman tradition in the West. If France recognized the historic genius of this work, it is also true that Bossuet had had his story begin with the Bible and had explained history in the light of Providence, instead of analyzing it as the result of human thought and activity. Such was Voltaire's early judgment which would remain unchanged from 1738, date of the following excerpt, until publication of his own enterprise, because he believed that limiting history to Western culture and its origins was falsifying history.

> [Un] Chinois qui parlait un peu hollandais, se trouva dans une boutique de librairie avec quelques savants; il demanda un livre; on lui proposa l'*Histoire universelle* de Bossuet, mal traduite. A ce beau mot d'histoire universelle: 'Je suis, dit-il, trop heureux; je vais voir ce qu'on dit de notre grand empire, de notre nation qui subsiste en corps de peuple depuis plus de cinquante mille ans, de cette suite d'empereurs qui nous ont gouvernés tant de siècles; je vais voir ce qu'on pense de la religion des lettrés, de ce culte simple que nous rendons à l'Etre suprême. Quel plaisir de voir ce qu'on pense de la religion des lettrés comme on parle en Europe de nos arts, dont plusieurs sont plus anciens chez nous que tous les royaumes européens! – Hélas! lui dit un des savants, on ne parle pas seulement de vous dans ce livre; vous êtes trop peu de chose; presque tout roule sur la première nation du monde, l'unique nation, le grand peuple juif.' (M.xix.267)

Such would be Voltaire's starting-point in the *Essai*, such, in short, would ever be his conception of history. Such were also the arguments he most frequently invoked in favour of Oriental nations, and especially of the one so worthily represented by the Chinese merchant.

Obviously, such an undertaking is deserving of praise, and [Gustave] Lanson did not say all that he might, when recognizing merely the advance it marks in the development of modern historiography.[10] At the same time, however, we cannot ignore its more glaring defects and especially the deficiencies of Voltaire's method, which we can perceive in most of the corrections and additions. Generally these changes are the result of more recent studies on the part of the author, sometimes resulting from new documents he had received or had himself discovered, if only to reply to his critics. A certain number are philosophical reflections which came to mind as he reread his work or which cropped up on the occasion of various quarrels he was prosecuting at the time of publication. Whatever their origin, these reflections contribute to the partisan tone of the text and give rise to specific criticisms on the way in which the eighteenth century and Voltaire envisaged the writing of history. On the other hand, we should note that Voltaire is never completely detached from his work and never did consider it completed, while his mind remained ever alert to many of the problems he had encountered in writing it.

The nature of those problems, so closely linked together, pushed Voltaire to greater daring and perhaps to greater truths than he had known or suspected until then. But since he pretended to be all-inclusive and to shed some light on every part of the world as it was known in his day, it is natural that his curiosity touch on many disparate topics. It matters little whether this was the result of doctrinal conviction or the simple desire to be up to date, the fact remains that he was indeed conscious that his universality was one of the great features of this work. And he insisted on this from the very beginning.

> Il y a quelques années que j'ai commencé une espèce d'histoire philoso-phique . . .; tout ce qui peut paraître important à la postérité doit y trouver place; tout ce qui n'a été important qu'en passant y sera omis. Le progrès des arts et de l'esprit humain tiendront dans cet ouvrage la place la plus honorable; tout ce qui regarde la religion y sera traité sans controverse et ce que le droit public a de plus intéressant pour la société s'y trouvera. Une loi utile y sera préférée à des villes prises et rendues, à des batailles qui n'ont décidé de rien. On verra dans tout l'ouvrage le caractère d'un homme qui fait plus de cas d'un ministre qui fait croître deux épis de blé là où la terre n'en portait qu'un, que d'un roi qui achète ou saccage une province. (Best.1558; cf. 4600).

Declarations like this have naturally attracted the attention of the critics and of none more astute than Raymond Naves.[11] When evaluating the rôle played by Voltaire in the development of modern historiography Naves writes in *Le goût de Voltaire*:

> Il a élargi le champ de l'histoire et fondé en même temps l'histoire de la civilisation, l'histoire ecclésiastique et l'histoire générale, ce qui est très considérable. Mais le plus étonnant dans tout cela, c'est qu'il y est arrivé comme par surcroît et sans en faire le but précis de son œuvre; le but réel est philosophique et moral. (p. 309)

In this rapid and changing panorama Voltaire the dramatist has condensed and frequently deformed the facts as his imagination saw fit. Even when he is carefully documented, he does not always profit by the expended effort and honesty of his approach. Instead of the savant we might have expected to discover in him, we find a proselyte who thinks only of destroying those doctrines he detests. Sometimes his attacks were suggested by material that was incidental to any given passage. The stories of Abraham and Moses furnish him with just so many opportunities for reasoning and for refuting by a *reductio ad absurdam* many a sacred text. China and her philosophers were no exception to this procedure. They serve him only as an excuse for taunting the atheists, since more than sacred texts, more than the Holy Land or other exotic countries, Voltaire wanted to know that China whose antiquity enchanted him because it brought into question certain theological calculations which founded world history on the authority of the Bible. At the same time this knowledge would give Europeans, so proud of their civilization, a precious lesson in humility.

> Leur vaste et populeux empire était déjà gouverné comme une famille dont le monarque était le père et dont quarante tribunaux de législation étaient regardés comme les frères aînés quand nous étions errants en petit nombre dans la forêt des Ardennes. ... Leur religion était simple, sage, auguste, libre de toute superstition et de toute barbarie quand nous n'avions pas même encore des Teutatès à qui les druides sacri-fiaient les enfants de nos ancêtres dans de grandes mannes d'osier. (M.xi.57)

Chinese wisdom, un-Christian and so different from that of the West, appeared to Voltaire as more elevated and more pure because of the novelty of the revelation of that difference, except perhaps insofar as everything but war was concerned. The greatest resemblance Voltaire could note, therefore, was this very negative one, this spirit of carnage and lust which has always devastated the earth, even though 'cette fureur entre bien moins dans le caractère des peuples de la Chine que dans le nôtre' (M.xiii.180). And here Voltaire remarked the existence in its innumerable mutations throughout the world of the fundamental oneness of mankind.

> Tout ce qui tient intimement à la nature humaine se ressemble d'un bout de l'univers à l'autre; tout ce qui peut dépendre de la costume est différent, et c'est un hasard s'il se ressemble. L'empire de la coutume est bien plus vaste que celui de la nature; il s'étend sur les mœurs et sur tous les usages; il répand la variété sur la scène de l'univers; la nature y répand l'unité; elle établit partout un petit nombre de principes invariables; ainsi le fonds est partout le même et la culture produit des fruits divers. (M.xiii.182)

Such, generally, was the development Voltaire presented of his ideas in the *Essai*.[12] Such, also, are three essential ideas of his conception of historial writing, with two of which we are already familiar, thanks to the example of the *Siècle*. First of all, there is that of writing a history of the human mind, of civilization as a whole and not merely as that of kings and emperors. Secondly, there is the intention of adjoining the history of commercial revolutions and developments in the arts and sciences, and not merely of detailing the barren facts of dates, places, and names relating to wars and treaties. The third, finally, is that of writing a truly universal history, a history of the world and not of Europe only. These three ideas form the frame of reference and govern the development of the *Essai*. Of 197 chapters, Voltaire devotes 90 to tableaux of customs, institutions, arts, and to the spirit of peoples and periods; and even in those chapters where the relation of wars and political developments is upper-most, he chooses the most significant facts. At last, in the *Essai*, Voltaire puts China in the vanguard of universal civilization. He assigns the most flattering rôle in his history to this empire of the Far East by having it begin and end with

China because that country represented to him the most ancient nation, the best ordered and the home of true wisdom.

In order for Voltaire to write the first sentences of the *Essai* or at least in order for him to write them without arousing the protest of his readers, the public would have had to set about studying those ancient chronicles of which Voltaire was so proud.[13] Furthermore, this task would have had to accustom the French mind to the very idea of Chinese antiquity, despite the dangers such knowledge represented for the establishment. Voltaire did not risk much in denying the universality of the Flood *à propos* of China. He was able to profit by the evolution of ideas. The discovery of Chinese antiquity contributed to the formation of the philosophic spirit but was also favoured by such a development. For as much as it profited by this progress, the idea of Chinese antiquity likewise profited by the weakening of people's faith in the value of the Bible as an historic document. National antiquity, aside from its importance for historical knowledge, was perhaps a greater claim to fame than national virtue in the eighteenth century. If, for individuals, nobility consists in having ancestors who participated in the Crusades, for a nation, nobility consists in having as founders people who lived prior to the Flood. Now China had just such pretensions. She even tried to justify them. She not only affirmed her antiquity, she thought it was possible to prove that antiquity. As witness, each government had contributed to a series of annals which had the advantage of having been composed from day to day by eyewitnesses and checked by professional historians. In this manner, the idea of partiality, error and inconsequence was avoided. Until further studies of historiography in eighteenth-century France are available it is impossible to say just how great a seduction these concepts exercised over the mind of Voltaire's audience, for if Chinese antiquity were adopted as a fact, universal history would have to be modified in the extreme. Furthermore, the antiquity of Chinese chronology posed another, still greater, problem regarding the location of the cradle of humanity. In what country or region was civilization first formed? For the eighteenth century, for Voltaire, and even for us moderns, universal history is then seen to be modified both in time and in space. Even if, toward 1740, the argument in favour of Chinese antiquity had often been invoked, no serious study of China was yet generally available in Europe. Like those arguments revolving around the colour of races and the inhabiting of America, this one too came from the arsenal which furnished arms against the Bible and revealed religion. Part of Voltaire's great originality in dealing with the problem was that he took facts and dates proving Chinese antiquity from the Jesuits, and from the libertines' analyses which made that antiquity much greater than did their common source. Any reconciliation between sacred chronology and that of the Chinese then being impossible, China assumed for Voltaire the rôle to which it was entitled by reason of its antiquity.

Voltaire's very first sentence is proof of this interpretation, especially when he says: 'Il est évident que l'empire de la Chine était formé il y a plus de 4.000 ans'

(M.xi.55). The assurance and the firmness of tone can allow no further doubt on this point. The statement is treated as purely factual and we are led to accept it as 'evident' on the faith of the author. Despite a grain or two of scepticism on our part because we know the author too well, despite later vacillations in his own point of view, the idea contained in such a beginning is not only one of Voltaire's main arguments on behalf of the distant nation, but is indeed fundamental to his 'philosophic' understanding of the Middle Kingdom. This is borne out when, in the following paragraph, he continues: 'Si quelques annales portent un caractère de certitude, ce sont celles des Chinois, qui ont joint . . . l'histoire du ciel à celle de la terre. . . . Les autres nations inventèrent des fables allégoriques; et les Chinois écrivirent leur histoire, la plume et l'astrolabe à la main, avec une simplicité dont on ne trouve point d'exemple dans le reste de l'Asie' (M.xi.55). Voltaire continues by subtly mocking Western erudition which has had the misfortune of stumbling upon the supposedly 'innate' wisdom of the Far Eastern peoples. For the authenticity of his Jesuitico-Chinese sources seems to him to be assured by the fact that they are free from all prophetic or miraculous sullying. In the *Essai* he repeats the charges we have seen in an article where a Chinese merchant is shocked to find the views of his Dutch hosts so picayune and their culture so limited, and he repeats these charges unceasingly (M.xi.55, 166 etc.).

Since Voltaire wished to synthesize history and wished, so to speak, to renew it, it is not surprising that he considers but few facts relating to politics taken by itself. In deviating from traditional historiography, he goes so far as to interest himself in anthropology and statistics, two new fields for the eighteenth century. When he treats of the size and greatness of the country (M.xi.165), he is led to conclude that since China is as large as formerly, its laws, its customs, its languages, and even the way in which its inhabitants dress cannot have undergone much change. For this reason, therefore, Voltaire states that he will limit himself to depicting the most important, the most 'creative' epochs of Chinese history.

> Il vous est fort inutile sans doute de savoir que dans la dynastie chinoise qui régnait après la dynastie des Tartares de Gengis-kan, l'empereur Quamkum succéda à Kincum et Kicum à Quankum. Il est bon que ces noms se trouvent dans les tables chronologiques; mais vous attachant toujours aux événements et aux mœurs, vous franchissez ces espaces vides pour venir aux temps marqués par de grandes choses. (M.xiii.162)

At this point, he at last begins to treat of Chinese history as such, and dwells briefly on the reign of Fu-hsi, who is supposed to have lived some three thousand years before Christ and assumed the government of the fifteen kingdoms (M.xi.166). In passing, Voltaire then mentions other monarchs, the burning of the books, and the development of judicial procedure under the so-called First Emperor being especially noteworthy for him.[14] Although he mentions the Roman embassy of 165 AD and the voyage of two Mohammedans which had earlier led Renaudot to criticize the sinophile movement, Voltaire pays neither more than token credence, since it is too difficult to control the documents on which these relations are based (M.xxiv.549). (And since, we might add, they might have disproved some of Voltaire's own theories.) He then spends a little more time and effort in analyzing, in its proper place, the material he would use for the *Orphelin*, the advent of the Mongol dynasty under Jenghis Khan (M.xii.433), after which he skips to the Manchu dynasty where he is particularly attracted to his contemporaries, the Yung Chêng and Ch'ien Lung Emperors (M.xiii.162). As earlier, when treating of the former's exile of the Jesuits in the *Siècle*, Voltaire utilizes the same materials to describe the details of their situation, especially when he has the Yung Chêng Emperor declare: 'Que diriez-vous si j'envoyais une troupe de bonzes et de lamas dans votre pays? Comment les recevriez-vous? Si vous avez su tromper mon père, n'espérez pas me tromper de même. Vous voulez que les Chinois embrassent votre loi. Votre culte n'en tolère point d'autre, je le sais; en ce cas que deviendrions-nous?' (M.xiii.168).

Thus did Voltaire, ever the same, attempt to formulate as religious criticism the historic sense of his development.[15] In this way he opposed those histories written in the manner of Bossuet, refusing to see in the history of the world a subject to be shaped by the hands of Providence, refusing also to decipher in Holy Writ the grand design of a God who hitherto had not been interested in China. Voltaire hoped to underline the fact that his history was as objective as possible, considered only humanity, and not the movements of God's 'mysterious ways'. Both his protestations of good faith and his prejudiced examples are vaunted rather too much to be believed implicitly. Contrary to those principles he so early and so eagerly professed, we feel that in composing this history, Voltaire did nought but adapt to his needs such guides as were most to be trusted in his time, that he relied on them to inform him about facts and details. And we are not wholly mistaken. For his errors, whether of fact or interpretation, are those of his guides, or even, those of his contemporaries. Seen in this light, we must admit with Lanson (*Voltaire*, p. 123), George Ascoli ('Voltaire', *Revue des cours et conférences*, xxvi, 511), and Bourgeois (*Siècle*, p. xxiv) that they are also kept to a respectable minimum.[16] If we wish to know more exactly the works consulted and used by Voltaire when treating of China, we must, for want of a complete work or critical edition, take a few examples which can only be incomplete but which might indicate the road to follow in a more exhaustive study than this.

From the first lines Voltaire devoted to China until the conclusion of the chapter wherein he speaks of the moral qualities of the Chinese, we may (rightly) suspect that such diverse observations could come only from a sort of encyclopaedia, if they come from a single source. Now the encyclopaedias Voltaire might have used during the period in which this chapter was composed (1745–68) are three in number: d'Herbelot's *Bibliothèque orientale* (1697), the *Lettres édifiantes*, whose publication continued until 1773, and Du Halde's

Description, which appeared in 1735. If the ordering of ideas is to be counted in Voltaire's presentation, we must also admit of other possible sources for the arrangement of the chapter as a whole. In this way, we shall eliminate one of the works just mentioned as a source of organization, the *Bibliothèque orientale*, since it is but an alphabetical catalogue of references to the Near East as well as to China. Meanwhile the contribution of the *Lettres édifiantes* and Du Halde's *Description* to the elaboration of the *Essai* is no more to be neglected than that of a few other works mentioned by Voltaire, such as Navarrete's *Tratados*, Lecomte's *Nouveaux mémoires*, Pétis's *Histoire de Genghizkan* and Anson's *Voyage* (c.f. *Notebooks*, ed. Theodore Besterman, Geneva, 1952, 2 vols, ii, 392). All explain in some measure why and how this brilliant effort to synthesize history marks the apogee of the sinophile movement for Voltaire and for his century. All attest to the fact that Voltaire accepted in a curious and uncritical manner only the testimony of documents available to him. That most of these sources were Jesuit writings should not surprise us, after we have seen the considerable influence they exerted in their time, especially those two massive and important compilations, the *Lettres édifiantes* and the *Description ... de la Chine*.

Already in the first chapter of the *Essai* Voltaire unwittingly helps us in our quest when he mentions the name of Father Gaubil (M.xi.165). This important Jesuit figure was a frequent contributer to the *Lettres édifiantes* and was probably the most intelligent of his Company to be stationed in the Empire. Yet after studying the *Traité de l'astronomie chinoise* which the learned Father published in 1732, we are convinced that Voltaire did not know this work. And that, despite so cautious a critic as Lanson.[17] For although most of the details related by Voltaire are to be found among the minute observations of Father Gaubil, the passage where he mentions them has nothing in common with the text he is reportedly quoting. If Voltaire thought merely to use a by now familiar device to distract the authorities (after all he was implicitly condemning Western science and Biblical chronology) there is also here the possibility that he was simply confused because of the extent of his documentation. This last hypothesis is strengthened when we consider that elsewhere he quotes almost verbatim from other sources like Du Halde when borrowing the translation of a Chinese inscription (M.xi.58; xxiv.552) and, in the first chapter, the spelling of the name of the K'ang Hsi Emperor (M.xi.169). The form of the name 'Kang-Hi' is to be found in the very first volume of the *Description*, but it seems that Voltaire did not utilize it until he revised the *Essai* in 1763. Despite the usual attention to detail that we note elsewhere, there are still places in the *Essai* where the form is given as 'Cam-Hi' (M.xi.55), a form Voltaire found in earlier Jesuit writings as well as in d'Herbelot. But thanks to the abundance of references to the *Description*, we can find in the work of Du Halde a relation of Chinese eclipses similar to Voltaire's. The reference and the subsequent filiation of ideas are easy to establish once we arrive at volume III, page 271 of the *Description*.

Nonetheless this is but an isolated example in a chapter where there is far more than a simple discussion of Chinese astronomy. And Du Halde's treatment is not Voltaire's. By means of a procedure similar to that we have just employed, we shall see that later in the first chapter, the name of Father Parrenin, another Jesuit, recurs with some frequency, enough in any case, to merit close attention. In the *Lettres édifiantes*, there was one letter from this Father which Voltaire had already used for the last chapter of the *Siècle*. As later the first chapter of the *Essai*, Parrenin's letter contains remarks on Chinese antiquity and Chinese astronomy, and ends with an exposé of the foibles of Chinese character. What is lacking notably from the good Father's contribution are those figures, for instance about the population of the Empire, its flora and its industries, which interested and intrigued Voltaire. This information can be readily recognized, however, in another letter of the collection, published in the same volume as Father Parrenin's (xxi.186), and which Voltaire could have readily encountered when consulting the latter for this section of his work. And when further along, it is a question of treating of the Rites Controversy in somewhat more detail than in the *Siècle*, most of Voltaire's information can be found, again in the third volume of Du Halde. Yet, were it not for the passages which mention the contradictions of Maigrot (M.xii.157), we might suspect that Voltaire had consulted an *Eclaircissement sur les honneurs* of Father Le Gobien which had been appended as a third volume to Lecomte's *Nouveaux Mémoires*. Of course, Du Halde had noted this information, but in not quite the same way as Le Gobien. But Voltaire needed neither one nor the other. Like the end of the *Siècle*, these details all came from a source he had consulted for the earlier work, the *Mémoires chronologiques* of Father d'Avrigny (cf. iv.165, *passim*). There remains but one further difficulty deserving our attention in the first chapter – the religious rôle played by the Emperor as sovereign pontiff when he sacrifices to 'Tien, au souverain du ciel et de la terre' (M.xi.175). The addition of the earth to the dominions of the Supreme Being is an error committed long since by d'Herbelot (p. 549b) when, in speaking of Chinese manicheans, he linked the translation of the name of God, *T'ien* (heaven) and that of the word explaining this concept, which specifies the honour to be rendered to God, *Li*. This assimilation is further complicated when the compiler spoke of Confucianism in the article 'Sin' of the *Bibliothèque orientale*. But what is perhaps most important to us in all this is that Du Halde did not commit this error. In spite of numerous changes he introduced into the letters from his correspondents, the wily Jesuit did not touch one of these sources where it was exactly a question of *T'ien* and *Li*. As Pinot has shown in his thesis,[18] sometimes the corrections of the *Description* are more important for the form than for the meaning of different contributions, even when they detract from the greater glory of the Society. Thus, in the third volume, pages 31 to 33, we find an explanation of just those aspects of Chinese religion which Voltaire would (for once) refuse in his interpretation.

Yet it is in such personal interpretations that Voltaire expresses himself best and reveals himself most intimately. In the last analysis, what creates his originality as an historian is not his manner of writing and teaching, nor the broadening of his own horizons when speaking of Chinese antiquity, nor even the pre-eminently religious sources he follows almost blindly. It is rather, the idea he has in the back of his mind and which guides him until the propitious moment for revealing it arrives. Thus, after having noted different facts relative to Chinese history and civilization, he inserts at the end of the first chapter, thanks to the inspiration furnished by the almost incidental mention of *T'ien*, a series of general remarks on toleration.[19] The conclusion seems indicated neither by the previous development nor by the needs of his theme. As in the case of the last chapter of the *Siècle*, it is the lesson of the chapter which here serves a dual purpose. On the one hand, it presents us with an important idea which will be explained ultimately by the complete work; on the other, it sets the stage for the opening of the next chapter where it will be uniquely a question of Chinese religion.

Such as they were known to the eighteenth century, Chinese ideas on religion and politics allowed Voltaire to reach important conclusions. We cannot, however, expect that his interpretations were in accord with reality, for where religion was concerned those interpretations either modified radically his former conceptions or broadened them until they became so unrecognizable as to be considered new. As for politics, Voltaire sought a program which might allow the monarchy a continuing existence, but without those abuses which were the bane of the French system. Only that, and little more, as Henri Sée long since pointed out.[20]

The most important element in his political program was naturally the monarch. The Jesuit relations were filled with facts and details relating to the emperors, their history, their rôle, and their duties. Yet the missionaries had had the enormous advantage of visiting the Empire at a time when the glory and the popularity of the Manchus were at their height. The monarchs then had been youthful and vigorous. Under the K'ang Hsi Emperor the monarchy as an institution was very strong, and foreigners had many occasions for admiring its undeniable merits (cf. Charles Commeaux, *De K'ang-Hi à K'ien-Long. L'Age d'or des Ts'ing: 1662–1796*, Paris, 1957). They spread far and wide their interpretations of Chinese greatness and the ruler's personal excellence, and Voltaire eagerly repeated their praises, whether of K'ang Hsi or Yung Chêng, in whom he hailed the very model of a monarch according to his desires. The missionaries had also vaunted the more practical aspects and serious nature of the Chinese institution of kingship. They praised unduly the emperor's constant care for his people's well-being and, to prove their point, adapted a multitude of picturesque details to their needs, for example: the Son of Heaven ploughing the field with his own hands in the spring rituals; rewarding husbandmen; holding himself responsible for those catastrophes which the vengeful justice of nature inflicted on his people from time to time; venerating in an almost superstitious manner both chastity and age; protecting the life of all, even of those accused of crimes; etc. Some of these illustrations were indeed founded on first-hand observation, but most came from Chinese texts where rules of virtue and examples of imperial wisdom abound. Nonetheless, Voltaire never seems to tire of accepting these examples on faith and repeating them *in extenso*. Perhaps he did have a quasi-superstitious veneration for both the institution and the person. In any event, he inserts little of his own commentary when writing about these matters of Chinese politics in the *Essai*.

> Il est impossible que dans une telle administration, l'empereur exerce un pouvoir arbitraire. Les lois générales émanent de lui; mais pour la constitution du gouvernement, il ne peut rien faire, sans avoir consulté des hommes élevés dans les lois et élus par les suffrages. Que l'on se prosterne devant l'empereur comme devant un dieu, que le moindre manque de respect à sa personne soit puni selon la loi comme un sacrilège, cela ne prouve certainement pas un gouvernement despotique et arbitraire. (M.xiii.162)

As in the last phrase or two, Voltaire even goes so far as to insist upon the beneficence of this absolutism, and especially on that aspect of it which had so impressed the Jesuit Fathers – its paternalism.[21] Here, as before, he admits that China is a despotism if we examine only the form of its government; but he also repeats, as before, that its constitution is the only one he knows of which is founded on paternalistic powers. In this system, the emperor is as the father, the tribunals as brothers, and the people as children. We must add that for Voltaire these children are very undisciplined, however, since the weakness of his interpretation lies in the subservient rôle he attributes, here as elsewhere, to the man in the street (M.xi.57, 173).

It had become impossible for Voltaire to find in Europe the example of a practising – and reigning – 'philosophe' that was to his liking. He extended the field of his investigation and found at the other end of the world where it was impossible to separate truth from fiction, desire from reality, an idol almost without fault, the Ch'ien Lung Emperor (1736–96). The praise which until the end of his life Voltaire did not cease showering on the head of this unwitting accomplice, derived in great measure from the idea he had created uniquely for the needs of his propaganda. We might also imagine that his judgment on the Chinese monarch had been influenced by that sententious element in imperial bureaucracy which found expression in the long resounding phrases of edicts voicing an irreproachable morality. This interpretation seems to be confirmed by a paragraph of the *Essai* where Voltaire does nothing but transcribe a letter from Father Attiret that had appeared in the *Lettres édifiantes* of 1749 (M.xii.433, *Lettres* xxii.490). Yet in the Chinese political system, what seems to have made the most profound impression on Voltaire, as might even be surmised from our last quotation, was the rôle of the tribunals.[22] The Jesuits, and notably Father Contancin, had nothing but the highest praise for most of these courts, from the *Liu Pu*, or Six Councils of Peking, forming the central body of the imperial government, to the viceroys and petty functionaries in the provinces (*Lettres* xxii.371). These councils consisted for the most part in Confucian mandarins, and in this respect we might say that Confucianism was closely allied to the governmental system of the China that was.[23]

Now Voltaire saw in that system two principal merits: on the one hand, the cult of justice; on the other, the absence of fanaticism or religious prejudice. Thus, when speaking of them, their task, and their successful accomplishment of that task, Voltaire's enthusiasm knows no bounds. '*L'esprit humain ne peut certainement imaginer un gouvernement meilleur que celui où tout se décide par de grands tribunaux*' (M.xiii.162). His extravagance is due in part to the fact that the functionaries played a rôle which, to his eyes, full of 'philosophic' prejudices, was very much like the one he had envisaged in his own political ideals. Among all the uncertainties of his theories on this subject, it would appear that Voltaire favoured an absolute monarchy where the judgments of the sovereign might be guided and controlled by incorruptible advisers. Nothing in all his writings approaches this ideal like his interpretation of the reciprocal action of the Chinese emperors and the Chinese courts.[24] Although Voltaire does not always distinguish between various administrative functions, and though he does not realize the serious temptation to corruption engendered by the system in China, it is true that he did realize or guess their essential character: the government by a monarch with almost unlimited powers and by an official body, chosen according to merit and intellectual formation, remarkable in effect by its incorruptibility as well as by its complete and perfect religious toleration (M.xi.58; xiii.163).

Nor is it any the less true that Voltaire seems to be impressed by the alliance of the administrative and judiciary powers.[25] Of all these ideas, none is perhaps so clear as that pertaining to the administration of justice. Here Voltaire the utopian reformer is on more solid ground than before, adapting his ideals to the exigencies not only of the times, but of human nature. In looking ahead, he foretells the day when the accused can demand guarantees for his own safety, when he will be sheltered from ills resulting from religious tyranny, when he will be able to defend himself before a judge, when he will be judged without prejudice because 'les lois sont toujours uniformes' (M.xi.174), and condemned, if guilty, to a punishment befitting his crime. Voltaire early thought he had found all these articles of belief exemplified and practised in the Chinese system where everything seemed not only to proclaim the dignity of man but also to prove the intrinsic value of human life. This opinion was held by those writers on whom Voltaire relied almost exclusively for his information of this nature, the Jesuit missionaries, one of whom underlined in a brief phrase from 1735 their general attitude, saying: 'Vous seriez surpris M. R. P., si vous étiez témoin de l'attention scrupuleuse qu'on apporte à la Chine quand il s'agit de condamner un homme à la mort' (*Lettres* xx.378). In turn, Voltaire declaims like a madman against contemporary European tribunals, and his indignation is almost boundless when Montesquieu suggests 'C'est le bâton qui gouverne la Chine' (cf. M.xxx.405).

At the beginning of his career, Voltaire had praised the English parliamentary system.[26] It is surprising to note, however, that never did he champion its adoption in France. Perhaps this was because the monarch would have been relieved of an essential part of his power. Thanks to the Chinese system the problem seemed to be resolved, since, there, the monarch, while retaining those qualities necessary to his absolutism, is guided and controlled by the most intelligent of his subjects. As we read in the *Notebooks*: 'Le meilleur gouvernement n'est ni le républicain ni le monarchique, mais celui qui est le mieux administré' (ii.465). Thus the Chinese system combined those qualities of absolute monarchy as it was known in France during the eighteenth century with those of the parliamentary government of England. This desire on the part of Voltaire is perhaps one of the most convincing reasons for his admiration of China. Despite the fact that they are as bad physicists as the French of 1300 or the Greeks and Romans, 'ils ont perfectionné la morale qui est la première des sciences' (M.xi.57). Such being the case, it sufficed to determine the rôle played by the nation in the development of this morality and the rôle of their leaders or best representatives in this field. Who had been their greatest moralist, who, by virtue of his own example, had most excelled as a moralist, if not Confucius?[27] In thinking beyond the Sage, in attempting to profit by his teachings personally, perhaps in hoping to see someday those lessons of Confucian morality adopted in Europe with himself as interpreter, guide, and councillor to kings and rulers of new, Chinese-inspired governments, Voltaire became ever more enthusiastic about the teachings of Confucius.

The absolutist doctrines of the eighteenth century all recognized the authority of a religious body in matters of morality because, for the absolutist state, the Church was a force in favour of the existence of that state. Voltaire did not wish to abolish this situation as did some of the more radical philosophers of his time. He belonged to the liberal circle of an enlightened bourgeoisie which did not cease to grow, and he desired at the outset but the reform of the existing political structure. As religious groups and even individuals attempted to control affairs of state, however, Voltaire's ideas became more radical, especially when he saw, or thought he did, how poorly they were acquitting themselves of this all-important task. The circumstances presiding over these failures did more, however, than merely incite his antagonism toward religion in general. They made him seek a remedy and the example of a remedy. Frequently, in this search, his attention was drawn to China and ultimately came to rest there, where he believed he had found the ideal of the absolutist state. This example was far more to Voltaire than an ideal. It existed. His sources said so. And he believed his sources to the point where, as we have seen in political matters, he did little but adapt their attitude. The same was true, but to a lesser degree where religion was concerned. But in the beginning, since his sources claimed that the absolute government of China was founded on Confucian ethics, Voltaire repeated that judgment, believed it, and sat down to study this country where no religious dogma, no government by a priestly association, was sanctioned by the political authorities. 'Dans la secte des lettrés la probité règne. Chez le peuple il y a des vices. C'est qu'ils sont gouvernés par les bonzes' (M.xxxii.578).

Confucius had founded neither a new religion nor a new Church.[28] On the contrary, he had merely taught a traditional morality which had but fallen into disuse and in which there was no trace of dogmatism. His teaching was in conformity with common sense, and was eminently reasonable. His morality proclaimed that virtue is supreme and just, necessary to the peace and happiness of men. According to Voltaire, Confucius had already interpreted this morality in such a way that it could easily be applied to reality; to his strong personality and innate wisdom, the Chinese owe their political perfection. And Voltaire began that hymn to the Sage which would hadly ever fail him when discussing religion, politics, and morality in the Middle Kingdom. 'Le temps le plus heureux et le plus respectable qui fût jamais sur la terre ... celui où l'on suivait ses lois' (M.xi.176). Still more, he could then conveniently make the Sage the Messiah of his own century which in itself was neither creative nor critical enough to discover a new form of government. And his example was the more welcome as Confucius's morality announced that of Voltaire himself. But Voltaire tells us very little about the life of the Sage.

For Voltaire, Confucius represented the perfect 'philosophe', he who had found a solution to the problems of revealed religion, who in a word was the ideal deist. The lack of dogma in the formalities of the Confucian cult was for Voltaire a quality, or, rather, a virtue; for among other things, the religion which lacks a rigid form allows the free development of toleration. And it was in toleration as taught and practiced by Confucius that Voltaire thought he had noted the essential characteristic of the Chinese people. In this perhaps unconscious deformation of the truth, Voltaire grasped at least a part of the spirit of the Sage's teaching and the humanitarian wisdom which was at the root of his religious precepts. For as his life proved, Confucius was primarily a teacher of ancient laws and preferred to exert his influence through the example of his teaching rather than through the government of human affairs.

> Leur Confutzée, que nous appelons Confucius, n'imagina ni nouvelles opinions, ni nouvelles rites; il ne fit ni l'inspiré ni le prophète; c'était un sage magistrat qui enseignait les anciennes lois. Nous disons quelquefois et bien mal à propos: la religion de Confucius. Il n'en avait point d'autre que celle de tous les empereurs et de tous les tribunaux, point d'autre que celle des premiers sages. Il ne recommande que la vertu; il ne prêche aucun mystère. (M.xi.57)

Yet there is here a curious contradiction, especially when we consider that despite the factitious link established by Voltaire between primitive monotheism and Confucius, the Sage had ever admitted his scepticism when faced with problems of a religious nature. But we must not forget either that Confucius was the one to preserve in all its purity ancient Chinese religion,[29] which explains in part why the Golden Age in China coincided with that period when his teachings and precepts were most closely followed. Moreover, this idea of a Golden Age is also in contradiction with the idea of progress, so widespread and esteemed in the eighteenth century. It is obvious that, when faced with the proofs, Voltaire could not afford not to accept the doctrine of the perfectibility of human nature (at least where China was concerned) and tried to turn the difficulty with such utterances as the following: 'Moïse, Numa, Confucius, et Zoroastre ont donné des lois sans être métaphysiciens' (*Notebooks* ii, 391).

Despite the fact that Confucianism had been praised for its moral values and not for its religious teachings, Voltaire persisted in repeating that since the beginning of their history the Chinese had possessed 'le culte simple du maître du Ciel' (M.xix.409). Because he was led to consider their system admirable and worthy of imitation, Voltaire believed he had found in the Middle Kingdom the flower of a tolerant religion, without dogma and without priests, in a word, pure deism. 'Le [déisme] est une religion répandue dans toutes les religions; c'est un métal qui s'allie avec tous les autres et dont les veines s'étendent sous terre aux quatre coins du monde. Cette mine est plus à découvert, plus travaillée à la Chine; partout ailleurs elle est cachée et le secret n'est que dans les mains des adeptes' (M.xx.505).

The missionaries had already made nicer distinctions in their panegyric to Confucius which, in their exclusivity, condemned all the rest. Voltaire once more repeats their song and blackens the priests of Fo or Buddha as well as that other Wise Man from the East, Lao Tzu.[30] The cult inaugurated by the latter, says Voltaire, is tolerated in China only through the good will of the government which admits that the people might need a religion different from that of the state-officials. His class prejudices are so strong as not to be denied, while the battle he was fighting can now be fairly said to have been in his own interests, where much of the pretended populism of Voltaire in preparing the Revolution is seen to be nonexistent. For according to him, the ignorant and stupid masses always demand a less refined spiritual nourishment than their betters. The case of Taoism in China is but one example of this, although there, through the wisdom of the government, the priests have been constrained by the laws and the fundamental toleration of the Confucians (cf.M.xi.58; xxv.34). Every Chinese doctrine and every Chinese cult thus receives its share of petty criticism in this clever, practical, and cunning attack. For Voltaire utilizes the Jesuits' dualism to distinguish between a religion for the aristocrats of the earth, cultivated and refined, and another for the poor, both in spirit and in goods.[31] There is no doubt as to the one he prefers personally. In his eyes the more important of the two is the first which closely resembles the deism of the Confucian literati. 'Les magistrats et les lettrés séparés en tout du peuple, se nourrissent d'une substance plus pure. ... Beaucoup de lettrés sont à la vérité tombés dans le matérialisme; mais leur morale n'en a point été altérée. Ils pensent que la vertu est si nécessaire aux hommes et si aimable par elle-même, qu'on n'a pas même besoin de la connaissance d'un dieu pour la suivre' (M.xi.179).

During the years which followed the preparation of the *Essai*, Voltaire seems to have associated the terms 'China' and 'deism' so that both became synonymous for certain needs of his propaganda.[32] But it goes without saying that Voltaire was not unaware of other aspects of Chinese life, or especially of Chinese religion, which contradicted his welcoming attitude toward Chinese toleration or the lack of superstitious beliefs in the religion of the Empire (M.xi.55; xiii.167). Nevertheless, he forced himself to ignore them, because otherwise the unity of his concept of a Chinese utopia would have been destroyed and all his nice arguments too easily controverted. This point of view is in conformity with his general attitude toward the institutions of his day, and it was in great measure for this reason that the Chinese ideal became for him simply one more weapon with which to tilt at 'l'infâme.'[33] As he grew older, his taste for things Chinese, whether materialistic or ideal, was useful to him only insofar as he could criticize with it contemporary abuse.

But if Voltaire turned the Jesuits' misfortunes to his own advantage in attacking their cause, he did not hesitate to suppress their ideas when convenient.[34] In general the missionaries had nothing but scorn for Buddhism, and Voltaire employs both their information and their arguments in his castigation of the sect. But Buddhist doctrines had been so well assimilated to Taoist or even to Confucian teaching in the years since the sect had been introduced into China, that for centuries the Three Rules, or *ju ch'iao*, had constituted a doctrinaire body of religious precepts.[35] In the *ju ch'iao* were to be found the principles of ethical or moral doctrines which satisfied the spiritual need of all classes of Chinese society in any circumstance. 'Within such a framework it was possible for one person to believe quite honestly in one or two or all three of the teachings of these principal Chinese sects. Nonetheless, under the influence of Confucian mandarins who had remained hostile to the mystic doctrines of the Buddha and Lao Tzu, the missionaries had formulated their concept of Chinese religion as being one, rationalistic, and non-transcendental (cf. Lecomte, ii.93; *Lettres*, xxv.iii; Du Halde, iii.2). Added to this was a tendency to consider that, aside from the cult rendered to Confucius, there was nothing. And Voltaire follows blindly, pretending that only Confucianism ruled in China and that it was a reasonable, natural religion.'[36] The two other sects represented in his eyes a revealed religion whose basis is superstition, the tyranny of priests and ignorance. Hence it is obvious that when Voltaire speaks of Buddhism at this time, he means Christianity, with which, to be sure, Buddhism does have certain superficial resemblances. Thus, one revealed religion was to be attacked in Voltaire's program by noting the similarities between it and its rivals. And when Voltaire reveals the ignorance, the rapacity, and the tyranny of the priests of Fo or the bonzes, he merely resorts to those procedures which had frequently served before his time and which Bayle and Fontenelle had made famous: indirect attack, by analogy, and against Christianity. At the very moment he was at work on the *Essai*, here is what he has to say in the *Notebooks*: 'Les lettrés chinois ont la plus pure et la plus ancienne religion selon le P. Lecomte; la populace chinoise n'a ni la même langue ni les mêmes mœurs, ni la même religion que les lettrés. Au fond il en est ainsi partout. ... La religion de l'honnête homme en tout pays n'est point celle d'une vieille du peuple' (ii.392).

Among thinking people morality is universally the same. Had not the Chinese example proved this sufficiently? The lack of morality in the Old Testament merely underlined the ignorance and superstition of the Jews.[37] Their God was far from being the Supreme Deity of the Chinese, and the idea of a particular Providence was only a vestige of tribal beliefs founded on ignorance. In several articles of the *Dictionnaire philosophique* ('Ana, Anecdote,' 'Anthropophages,' 'Genèse,' 'Job', etc.) Voltaire attempts to show the decadence of Hebrew monotheism as seen in the facile acceptance of dogmas which were prejudicial to the primitive spirit of Judaism. It seems that this was the method he wished to apply to Chinese religion. At the same time as he affirms the purity of the ancient Chinese cult in such a manner as to contrast it with more recent developments in their religion, Voltaire never denounces these modern forms explicitly. It is true that he prefers the Chinese formula to others, but even when he praises Confucius, as we have seen, it is only as the example of a wise interpreter of this cult. Nowhere in the history of thought can he find a better expression of what constitutes for him true religion. Here we may note the vital relation between his sinomania and his deism[38]

But if these religious and critical ideas are well defined, there are others which are less exact in Voltaire's mind, at least if we can believe those cases where he sidesteps certain details and begs the question. These ideas are none the less important for all that. Despite what Pinot has said about them in his thesis, one of the fundamental ones concerning China and Chinese religion involves the problem of Chinese atheism. About 1740, at a time when he was gathering information for the *Essai* and when he took a particular interest in China, Voltaire found himself faced by the problem of two religious currents which were not complementary (in spite of what he or even others may have said then or later), which were in effect contradictory: Chinese deism and Chinese atheism. And he would have to choose between them.[39]

At the beginning of the second chapter of the *Essai*, he admits the problem is complex, saying that Renaudot 'l'ennemi des gens de lettres, poussait la contradiction jusqu'à feindre de mépriser les Chinois et jusqu'à les calomnier' (M.xi.176). As for himself, the 'philosophe' of a more enlightened day, he would try to avoid the excesses of a Renaudot or even of a Father Lecomte who had written the following eulogy of the Chinese in which he attributes to them a knowledge of the one true God, pretending 'quand les autres peuples étaient idolâtres [ils] lui ont sacrifié dans le plus ancien temple de l'univers' (M.xi.177). And Voltaire continues by discussing theocracy, the worst form of tyranny he can imagine. He even goes so far as to repeat what he had written in the Introduction when he proclaimed that 'la Chine est le seul des anciens Etats connus qui n'ait pas été soumis au sacerdoce' (M.xi.27). Because he did not wish to follow the excesses of a Renaudot he cannot help but take a position exactly opposite that of the bilious abbé, uniquely because 'non seulement la théocratie a longtemps régné, mais elle a poussé la tyrannie aux plus horribles excès où la démence humaine puisse parvenir' (M.xi.27). Thus, if the Chinese have never known a theocratic government, they are nonetheless not atheists. Here we may note the ferocity of Voltaire's methods, for he immediately launches into an elaborate defense of this people against the reproaches which some of his contemporaries heaped upon them. Chapter II of the *Essai* bears even as its title: 'De la religion de la Chine. Que le gouvernement n'est point athée.' So we are led to realize that Voltaire could not, could never bear to be in the wrong – and to be found out. At the risk of appearing paradoxical, at the risk of ruining a good cause in his benighted obstinacy, he would re-affirm as true and good, facts and details which were patently false, thinking to overcome the opposition if only by the volume and the iteration of his rebuttal. 'Les reproches d'athéisme dont on charge si libéralement dans notre occident quiconque ne pense pas comme nous, ont été prodigués aux Chinois. Il faut être aussi inconsidérés que nous le sommes dans toutes nos disputes pour avoir osé traiter d'athée un gouvernement dont presque tous les édits parlent d'un "Etre suprême"' (M.xi.177). Furthermore, 'imputant l'athéisme au gouvernement de ce vaste empire, nous avons eu la légèreté de lui attribuer l'idolâtrie par une accusation qui se contredit ainsi ellemême ... c'est ainsi que nous jugeons de tout' (M.xi.178). For such are the Chinese, neither atheists nor idolaters. They follow a broad middle way which, assumes Voltaire, is that of Voltaire himself. This being the case, it was only natural that Confucius, as we have seen him treated by his eighteenth-century emulator, should be painted in the rosiest colours. Obviously, the 'philosophe' insists on representing a China scaled to his own image, and he is more than happy to have found a people who justify his theories. This whole development is aimed therefore at Christianity and intentionally highlights its inferiority in relation to the Chinese – wise, 'philosophical,' almost eighteenth-century enough to have never known fables, to have been spared persecutions and religious wars, and to have always practiced the broadest religious toleration, the proper study of unprejudiced minds. 'Nous insultons tous les jours les nations étrangères sans songer combien nos usages peuvent leur paraître extravagants. Nous osons nous moquer d'un peuple qui professait la religion et la morale la plus pure plus de 2.000 ans avant que nous eussions commencé à sortir de notre état de sauvages, et dont les mœurs et les coutumes n'ont offert aucune altération, tandis que tout a changé parmi nous' (M.xxiv.553).

But what was Voltaire's real intent? How did he feel about this problem himself? The question is a very delicate one and extremely difficult to resolve with any certainty.[40] If the Chinese were atheists, they furnished the most striking proof of the existence and of the excellence of a moral code divested of any relationship with political or social morality, or even with religion. Bayle had already said as much in his *Pensées ... sur la comète*, and although his attitude won some support, it served rather as an arm in the hands of those avowed enemies of religion, the libertines. Despite some critics, Voltaire was not one of them – at least not as we have understood them and him. Late in his life, when he was convinced of the social value of religion, he would refuse to admit the validity of atheism and would have recourse to the Jesuit argument. Yet on the other hand, earlier in his career, at a time when his ideas on natural religion were developing, Voltaire failed to use both Jesuit arguments and the Chinese example. For the *Abrégé* of 1753 is lacking in the attack against those who believed in Chinese atheism which we have quoted above in its different parts. The text must, however, have reflected some of Voltaire's innermost thoughts on the subject, since he added to it the 1756 edition where it stands to this day. Now in 1756 or shortly before, Voltaire passed through a rather startling crisis, provoked not only by his quarrel and rupture with Frederick, but also by his quarrel with Jean Jacques, the difficulties he encountered along the way leading him in search of a resting place from France to Switzerland, and finally by the Lisbon earthquake (cf. *Candide* and his *Lettres d'Alsace*). As Sir Thomas Kendrick has amply proved, the last-named catastrophe had shaken more than the capital of Portugal.[41] With many of his contemporaries, Voltaire was disturbed to the very core of his being by so untoward an attack on his most cherished, or, at least, on his most elementary, beliefs. In his need for 'moral support' he could think of no better solace than was to be found in the Chinese example. The number of references to China, Chinese religion and government begin in the interval to assume considerable proportions, as Voltaire sought more and more that stabilizing element to his thought which only China seemed to offer. Thus he was led to deny his charges of Chinese materialism and those of Chinese atheism to which those contemptuous of China now paid undue attention. On several occasions, Voltaire felt impelled even to declare that the religion of the literati was nothing but a spiritualism devoid of any confessional adherence (M.xvii.172; xviii.60, 154; etc.). In his newly opened eyes, atheism and fanaticism were the two unmistakable results of superstition. Despite his repugnance for atheism, it was of course preferable to fanaticism; and both remained in his sight as two monsters ready to devour and destroy society. Yet the atheist is still reasonable in his error, although it is reason which dulls his claws; the fanatic, however, is attacked by an unreasonable madness which merely sharpens his. This attitude in Voltaire at a critical period of his life may indeed be more significant than has been believed heretofore, and it would seem that the inquiring reader would not be wrong in seeking a more detailed explanation in that development of his thought which was the direct result of his study of China for the *Essai*.[42]

Insofar as his Chinese inspiration was concerned, however, we must note that the Chinese people were no exception to the common laws of humanity. Their religious and philosophic thought had evolved in the same way as that of other nations. Their books tell us so, and their institutions were available until only recently to show us how great was the error of the French 'philosophe.' For official Chinese doctrine was not atheistic. On the other hand, it was even farther from the likeable 'philosophic' deism which Voltaire had imagined. Like many another religion, it had its intransigent dogma, its condemnations of heresy, its prayers, its victims, its sacramental liturgy. The emperor in the great temples of Peking, the magistrates in the pagodas of local gods, fathers in front of the ancestral tablets, all were to celebrate a sacrifice which in many respects resembles the ritual of the mass, and all were to obey precepts whose value was thus salutarily increased. As for the gods of this religion which has been combined in a curious and almost undecipherable way with two others for several centuries – Taoism and Buddhism – they are practically the same as those who were once revered in Greece and Rome.

In the course of time, Chinese philosophers had added to this religious base explanations which were analogous to those of the most subtle Church Fathers. The grandiose spiritual deism of Voltaire was ever unknown to them, however, and they remained in an undoubtedly interesting stage of pantheism, but nothing more. The greatest of their books were moreover termed 'canonical', they had their saints and their explanations which constituted intellectual orthodoxy for them, as did the Roman Catholic Church for some of Voltaire's contemporaries. Works containing opinions contrary to theirs were to be destroyed by the civil authorities, and edicts ordering their destruction are not wanting either.

Once more, it is obvious that Voltaire appropriated Jesuit arguments which led him astray merely because he wanted support for 'philosophical' theses. Yet, here as elsewhere, nothing would let us call into question his own good faith, concerning which he himself does not hesitate to make a witty sally already noted in chapter 195 of the *Essai*, where he quotes the words of the Yung Chêng Emperor. This is, as it were, an attack against the Sorbonne, which dared to contradict the opinions of his favourite sources, the Jesuits. Yet as so often happens in quarrels like that over the Chinese Rites, the Jesuits' adversaries took a completely different viewpoint. They saw around them the Chinese plunged into a religion similar to Greek paganism, they had witnesses to the superstitious manifestations which formed the rite of their cult. To consider this idolatrous rite to be inoffensive before the celebrants had had time to clarify the notion of a divinity it was said to conceal beneath its outer crust of animistic imaginings was, for these enemies, to favour real idolatry in view of a distant and purely hypothetical conversion. The Jesuits might object in vain that prominent Chinese, including no less a personage than the Emperor, had allowed of the interpretation of Chinese books. But all was for naught. Jesuit efforts were futile because the mass of the people, superstitious, vain, and significant if only because of their numbers, proved the contrary opinion. And Rome, when at last embroiled in this disturbance which was as great in its day as the quarrel over the Bull *Unigenitus* in its (and the two were not without influencing one another), Rome could only decide in favour of those who feared lest such a complicated interpretation as the Jesuits' weaken the integrity of Catholic doctrine.

This last was perhaps not one of the least reasons for which Voltaire took the side of the Jesuits against the Law of the Church and painted the Chinese in glowing terms.[43] His lively imagination pictured them as an almost perfect people, in any case, superior to those in whose midst he dwelled and where wit, intelligence, and learning counted for little. Were not the Chinese, like the 'philosophes', enemies of dogmatic superstition? Were they not like Father Ricci, and Defoe's Father Simon, 'Gentlemen first . . . and Christians at the last'? This distant people, Voltaire firmly believed, had no priests like those who wore down his fighting spirit, none of those gross superstitions which inspired such rites as were practiced in his time. Respect for the aged and worship of a philosophic deity were their religion. They were possessed in consequence of a paternalistic government which for centuries had been in the hands of wise princes. Reason alone guided these men, and they had no need to base their morality on those mysterious dogmas which reason cannot explain. It was thus that Voltaire fell into error for attempting to fight alongside those Jesuits against whom he directed so many bitter and virulent attacks for the sake of China and her example.

As we have seen, toward 1740 Voltaire felt the need of seeking in history a buttress and a confirmation of his ideas. The *Essai* which he began to compose almost simultaneously would furnish him with desired support, especially those chapters dealing with China and the Chinese in which his thought may be said to have found an almost definitive form that could be applied not inappropriately to the past. Meanwhile, even the abuses Voltaire thought to correct in his criticism had their title to fame and an historic background as much as did 'philosophy'. After all, Error and Evil had their roots in certain representations of human development which still had to be replaced. And in order to assure the ultimate victory of his point of view over the forces of 'l'infâme', Voltaire, in those now-famous writings from the period following the *Essai* – opuscules, novels, dialogues, sermons, jokes, or treatises – completed his attack insofar as contemporary events were concerned and enlarged the field of his enlightened 'philosophy.'[44] And the rôle of China in this period of his development, or rather, of his maturity, was considerable because of the mastery he had finally achieved over himself, his ideas, and his material in the preparation of the *Essai*, the veritable turning-point of his career. Only through such an effort could Voltaire hope to educate the public of his day, accustom it to demand, as he, proofs from those who would make affirmations contrary to the laws of nature, reason, or conscience, and refuse their adhesion to those who could not provide such proof. In this sense, Voltaire's work represents a positive achievement. He succeeded in constructing a frame of reference destined to replace the mistaken representations of his time.

The greater part of his achievement had been realized or, at least, consecrated with the first chapters of the *Essai*, on Chinese history and antiquity, where Voltaire had obviously been carried along by certain ideas and tastes current among his contemporaries and which he knowingly sensed. The fact nonetheless remains that he was the first to profit by the Chinese vogue and saw that one of the earliest types of civilization in the world had been China with her theocratic society under dynasties sprung from the gods (not to mention her true religion, theism, the worship of a single deity, all the fruits of reason as cultivated by sages of old), and that in China were born science, astronomy, and mathematics. For 'c'est dans la morale et dans l'économie politique, dans l'agriculture et dans les arts nécessaires que les Chinois se sont perfectionnés. Nous leur avons enseigné tout le reste; mais dans cette partie, nous devrions être leurs disciples' (M.xviii.151).

NOTES

1. This chapter title was suggested by my late colleague and friend, Professor Arnold Rowbotham.
2. Cf. Rowbotham, Arnold, *Missionary and Mandarin* (Berkeley, 1942).
3. 'Best,' followed by a number refers to the first edition of *Voltaire's Correspondence* by T. Besterman (107 vols, Geneva, 1953–65), always in the text, as also 'M' (the Moland edition of Voltaire – 52 vols, Paris, 1877–85) and other important works, easily identified.
4. Havens, George and Norman Torrey, 'Voltaire's Catalogue of his Books', *Studies on Voltaire and the Eighteenth Century*, 9, 1959.
5. Rowbotham, *op. cit., passim.*
6. Honour, Hugh, *Chinoiserie* (London, 1961).
7. Cf. the edition by René Pomeau in Voltaire's *Œuvres historiques* (Paris, 1978).
8. Pomeau, review of *The French Image of China* (*Revue d'histoire littéraire de la France*, hereinafter cited as RHLF, 64, 1964), pp. 308–9.
9. Pomeau and Ch. Mervaud, *De la Cour au Jardin* (Oxford, 1991), pp. 196–201 and 298–300.
10. Lanson, Gustave, *Voltaire* (Paris, rev. ed. 1960), p. 131.
11. Naves, Raymond, *Le Goût de Voltaire* (Paris, 1938), p. 38.
12. Brumfitt, John, *Voltaire, Historian* (Oxford, 1954), p. 61–70.
13. *Id.*, pp. 76–84.
14. Rowbotham, 'Voltaire, Sinophile', (*Publications of the Modern Language Association of America*, 47, 1932), p. 1053. Further transcriptions from this seminal article are duly noted hereafter.
15. *Id.*, pp. 1063–4.
16. Lanson, *op. cit.*, p. 123; Ascoli, Georges, 'Voltaire', (*Revue des cours et conférences*, 26, 1925), p. 511; Voltaire, *Le Siècle de Louis XIV* (E. Bourgeois, ed.), (Paris, 1910), xxiv.
17. Lanson, review of Pierre Martino (*RHLF* 13, 1906), p. 546.
18. Pinot, Virgile, *La Chine et la formation de l'esprit philosophique* (Paris, 1932), p. 179.
19. Rowbotham, *art. cit.*, p. 1062.
20. Sée, Henri, 'Les Idées politiques de Voltaire', *Revue historique*, 98, 1908, pp. 255–93.
21. Rowbotham, *art. cit.*, p. 1054.
22. *Id.*, p. 1055.
23. Granet, Marcel, *La Religion des Chinois* (Paris, 1922), ix.
24. Rowbotham, *art. cit.*, p. 1056.
25. *Ibid.*
26. Torrey, Norman, *The Spirit of Voltaire* (New York, 1938), pp. 227–82.
27. Rowbotham, *art. cit.*, p. 1057.
28. *Ibid.*

29. *Ibid.*
30. *Id.*, p. 1058.
31. *Ibid.*
32. Carré, Jean-Marie, *Consistence de Voltaire* (Paris, 1938), pp. 60–84.
33. Rowbotham, *art. cit.*, p. 1064.
34. *Id.*, p. 1062.
35. *Id.*, p. 1064.
36. *Ibid.*
37. *Id.*, p. 1059.
38. Torrey, *op. cit.*, pp. 236–8.
39. Rowbotham, *art. cit.*, pp. 1057–8.
40. *Id.*, p. 1059.
41. Kendrick, Thomas, *The Lisbon Earthquake* (London, 1956).
42. Voltaire, *Essai* (ed. *cit.*), p. 1104, note.
43. Rowbotham, *art. cit.*, p. 1065.
44. *Id.*, p. 1060.

5

THE POSSIBILITY OF ORIENTAL
INFLUENCE IN HUME'S PHILOSOPHY

Nolan Pliny Jacobson

It might be easier for Asia and the West to understand their different religious and social philosophies if they knew how deeply these philosophies had affected one another in the past. European thought from 1600 to 1789 is especially important in this connection, for these are the years when the Orient contributed most to Western thought, and they are the years when the very foundations of modern philosophy in the West were being laid.

The conceptual links between the Buddha and David Hume have been observed by numerous scholars East and West, such as Murti and White-head, to mention only two who may be nearest to our time. Writing fifty years ago, La Vallée Poussin may have been the first to express surprise that 'the yellow-garbed monks of yore' propounded essentially the same theory of the self 'found in Hume or Taine and many scientists.'[1]

As far as I know, however, no one has ever investigated the other side of the problem, the possibility that Buddhist thought may have played a major role in the initial formulation of Hume's *Treatise*. If the venture seems slightly absurd, it may be worth remembering that almost any result from such a venture, even the most negligible, could have more than ordinary significance, considering the fact that it is the founder of modern philosophy of science, on the one hand, and a major philosophic tradition of Asia, on the other hand, with which we have to do.

Nolan Pliny Jacobson, 'The Possibility of Oriental Influence in Hume's Philosophy', *Philosophy East and West*, 19: 1, 1969, pp. 17–37.

SIMILARITIES IN HUME AND THE BUDDHA

In depriving the concepts of substance and causality of all rational justification, by showing that they rest upon the fictitious substitution of ideas that arise in the mind rather than from 'matters of fact and existence', David Hume attacked the fundamental conceptions around which seventeenth-century metaphysics had largely revolved. Locke's 'unknown substratum', Berkeley's spiritual substances, and the *res cogitans* which rescued Descartes in his sea of doubt – all are called in question as the mere customary conjunction of ideas upon the stage of experience, a stage which itself is only a 'bundle of perceptions'.

As Murti observes in his recent study of the Mādhyamika, 'Denial of substance is the foundation of Buddhism down the ages.'[2] We have before us here a very strange agreement between Hume and Gotama Buddha. 'The whole history of Buddhist philosophy,' Stcherbatsky says, 'can be described as a series of attempts to penetrate more deeply into this original intuition of Buddha, what he himself believed to be his great discovery.'[3] The Belgian Buddhist scholar whose writings were being read and published at Cambridge fifty years ago puts it this way:

> According to the Buddhists, no Self, that is, no unitary, permanent feeling or thinking entity, comes into the field of inquiry. We know only the body, which is visibly a composite, growing and decaying thing, and a number of phenomena, feelings, perceptions, wishes or wills, cognitions – in philosophic language, a number of states of consciousness. That these states of consciousness depend upon a Self, are the product of a Self or arise in a Self, is only a surmise, since there is no consciousness of a Self outside these states of consciousness . . . . 'There are perceptions, but we do not know a perceiver.'[4]

There is no thinker but the thoughts, no perceiver but the perceptions, no craver but the cravings. The conclusion was explicitly drawn by the Buddha that there is suffering but none who suffers.

The similarity here with Hume is striking. 'There are some philosophers,' Hume says,

> who imagine we are every moment intimately conscious of what we call our *self*; that we feel its existence and its continuance in existence; and are certain, beyond the evidence of a demonstration, both of its perfect identity and simplicity. ... For my part, when I enter most intimately into what I call *myself*, I always stumble on some particular perception or other, of heat or cold, light or shade, love or hatred, pain or pleasure. I never can catch *myself* at any time without a perception, and never can observe anything but the perception. ... I may venture to affirm of the rest of mankind, that they are nothing but a bundle or collection of different perceptions, which succeed each other with an inconceivable rapidity, and are in a perpetual flux and movement.[5]

For Hume, too, the only thinker is the thought, the only perceiver the perception, the only craver the craving.

There are Buddhist scholars, such as Nyanatiloka of Ceylon, who contend that the Buddhist concept of self 'has been clearly and unreservedly taught only by the Buddha.'[6] This, however, is not true. Both Hume and the Buddha insist that it is wrong-headed to call some enduring, ever-identical self more real than our changing states. Both insist that the experiences themselves are spread upon no substance and upon no substantial self but constitute a process in and for themselves. Both affirm that whatever self is conceived will be less concrete than the experiences themselves. Both see in other concepts of the self the propensity, widespread in the human community, for attributing ultimacy to the wrong things.

The Buddhist position is that there is no self-identical self, only 'the perpetual flux and movement', the abiding flow, but that each of us is 'a numerically new actuality every moment', as Hartshorne has put it. Hartshorne presents what he calls 'the Buddhist-Whiteheadian doctrine' as a 'radical pluralism' that takes its stand with our 'successive experiences' or 'successive actualities', arguing that these are 'the primary units of the plurality' constituted by 'the momentary experiences or selves'. Hartshorne applauds both Hume and the Buddha for returning us to an honest empiricism in which 'the concrete subjects are the momentary actualities'.[7] Existence is momentary in the Buddha's thought; at no two moments is a thing identical; thus things are different every moment.[8] This is the way Murti puts it.

This radical pluralism is offered by Hartshorne as a far more acceptable account of 'matters of fact and existence' than two other views of the self or soul, the superficial and unclear conventional pluralism which has been 'standard in most Western thought for over two thousand years', and the doctrine of Hindu monism that holds plurality of selves to be only appearance relative to the primary reality of Brahman, which is beyond all numerical diversity. He credits India with first producing the genius required 'to make us aware of the limitations' of these two non-Buddhist views, and he blames Western philosophy and religion prior to Hume, 'and in large part since Hume', for having 'failed to grasp these limitations'.[9]

Professor David Richardson of Utah State University was moved to explore the remarkable similarities between Western philosophy and Buddhist thought in its Indian background by Babbitt's study of Rousseau and Romanticism, which compares the Romantic movement to Taoism in China. Following this trail through Taoism backward into Buddhism, Richardson concludes that the doctrine of momentary actualities out of which all things are made, a doctrine involved in the Occasionalism of Malebranche, points to Hindu and Buddhist origins. The ancient Buddhist theory of causation, like that of Leibniz, Richardson observes, is a theory of 'the functional dependency of all point-instants on their preceding points.' A thing is not a cause 'producing' something; rather, 'the whole universe of point-instants immediately brings about the result in a functional dependence.' The same relation of causality is stated as follows: 'a thing is truly defined by its relations to *all* the other things of the entire universe.' Thus it is, Richardson writes, for early Buddhist philosophy, for Leibniz, and for Hegel [and the writer would add, for Whitehead and Hartshorne as well, with fewer reservations for these two than with respect, perhaps, to early Buddhism]. The literature and ideas encountered by Leibniz, Richardson concludes, must have included Buddhist and Indian modes of thought, and he is persuaded that even the metaphor of the monad mirroring the entire universe of monads from its own concreteness is a metaphor that made its way into Western Europe from Buddhist and Indian origins.[10]

For Hume, however, unlike Leibniz, there can be no thought of events being related to all the other things of the entire universe. The more primitive teaching of the Buddha is closer to Hume in the Whiteheadian sense indicated by Hartshorne above, accepting events and objects in their momentariness. This is what we find in the early Pāli texts.[11] Only the momentary event itself, co-present with others, is what we perceive. Events contiguous in time and place, Hume observed, can be and are considered in terms of cause and effect, but this is chiefly a way of thinking, a manner of speaking, a cultural habit which leads us to look at one event as cause, the other as effect, and the bond between them as the 'supposititious cause'. When we really analyze our experience, all we find is the momentariness of events and the cultural habit or 'propensity to feign' supposititious causes, which habit or propensity deadens our sensitivity to the sheer momentariness and co-arising (dependent origination) of the events.

Buddhist meditation and analysis is a process of heightening awareness of the momentariness of events, wherein all conditions are combined in a simultaneous correlation, as Govinda puts it; it is precisely because of this living juxtaposition and succession of the events in their momentariness that 'the possibility of becoming free is conceivable.'[12] 'Life knows no absolute units but only centres of relation, continuous processes of unification, because reality cannot be broken up into bits; therefore each of its phases is related to the others, thus excluding the extremes of complete identity or non-identity.'[13]

Murti formulates the Abhidhamma's position as follows: 'The Buddhist view ... reduces change to a series of entities emerging and perishing; each entity however rises and perishes in entirety; it does not become another. Movement for the Buddhist is not the passage of an entity from one point to another; it is the emergence, at appropriate intervals, of a series of entities, like the individual pictures of a movie show; it is a series of full-stops.'[14]

Buddhist schools of philosophy wrestled for centuries with these questions, and the results by 1700 were as much a part of Chinese as of Indian thought. Our inability to find anything more substantial than a 'supposititious cause' drives us 'logically', according to Murti, into occasionalism,[15] which is what Richardson has in mind in linking these Buddhist reflections with Malebranche. Since we are interested here in relations between Hume and the Buddha, we will want to reserve judgment for the time being on the comparison with Malebranche, and especially on Murti's conviction that the Mādhyamika moves the Buddhist denial of substance closer to Kant than to Hume. There are many alternatives, the present one between viewing the conceptual link between cause and effect in the framework of a transcendental psychology, as in Kant, and viewing it more simply as a mere social convention, as in Hume.

As with the substantial self and with causality, so likewise with substance in the broadest philosophical sense. Whitehead used to say that most modern forms of immorality are traceable to the Christian-Aristotelian concept of substance. The issue, therefore, is hardly insignificant. Just as 'we have no idea of external substance, distinct from the ideas of particular qualities', so likewise 'we have no notion of it [the mind or self], distinct from the particular perceptions.'[16] The unauthorized roving of thought beyond its proper territory, as in the case of the quail in the Buddhist parable,[17] results in the misuse of the mind, populating it with diversionary entities which mislead the human adventure. In actuality, we do not and cannot go behind the phenomena of matters of fact and existence. 'Did our perceptions either inhere in something simple and individual, or did the mind perceive some real connexion among them, there would be no difficulty in the case.'[18]

Infer an entity behind an individual man, and you will logically infer it behind every individual thing; and so the mishandling of sensory experience creates the suppositious ghost-world of metaphysical entities beyond our own. Plato accepts both worlds and tries unsuccessfully to account for their participation. Buddha and Hume reject both, seeing everywhere only those functional unities that spring into being and pass away, arising and ceasing. 'The mind,' Hume says, 'is a kind of theater, where several perceptions successively make their appearance, pass, re-pass, glide away, and mingle in an infinite variety of postures and situations. There is no *simplicity* in it at one time, nor *identity* in different [times].'[19] We invent the links we seem to need to hold our world together – Self, Cause, Substance, God. None of these can be logically inferred from matters of fact found in our sense impressions. In this way Hume attacked the fundamental conceptions around which the formative centuries of modern philosophy revolved.

According to Ramanan, this is the full force of Nāgārjuna's philosophy as well, not to weave the tangled web of our experience into a unitary all-embracing view of the world, but to become mature in the realization that the world can be formulated in many different ways with unique value to each different perceiver, provided only the false sense of the real can be overcome and the error of misplaced absoluteness avoided.[20]

Malalasekera attributes the notion of a permanent self to the impurity of conventional language, an explanation also proposed by the Buddha, such that we are in the habit of saying that 'it rains' and 'I think' when we should say merely that 'there is rain' and 'there is thinking'.[21] This is what Descartes would have said if he had had the analytic habit of mind found in Hume and the Buddha. The

Buddha, indeed, anticipates by twenty-five centuries Wittgenstein's struggle to overcome the bewitchment of the intellect by language. In both there is the same meticulous handling of small items of consciousness, in themselves often of no apparent significance, until as a final cumulative impact of the analysis one is struck silent, as silent as the Buddha, instead of running out on all sides in fragments of discursive thought. Through analysis we penetrate each matrix of meaning, until clarification leaves nothing on which to cling.[22]

No one has ever exposed more relentlessly than Hume our illogical tendencies to leap from causal sequences to a First Cause, from history to super-history, from nature to supernature, from species of goodness to Perfect Being, from the inexplicable to a divine miracle-worker. Logic and science require us to stop where our evidence runs out; beyond this point the Buddha referred to what he called the 'indeterminables'. The Buddha stopped all these speculations because they leave us in the grip of our compulsive drives, which function in the Buddha's thinking as a sort of original sin tearing the aboriginal harmony of existence asunder. In this way, Gotama Buddha discouraged belief in God without denying his existence; Hume did the same.

There are other similarities between Hume and the Buddha, such as their belief in the natural anthropocentric character of all knowledge, the belief that man's own nature is implicated in everything he knows, and the conviction held vigorously by both that reason is the slave of the passions,[23] that man's intellect but carries out what it is bidden by the sensitive side of our nature to do. This is what the Buddha calls *taṇhā*.[24] In reversing the role previously ascribed to the rational and the passionate sides of man's nature, both the Buddha and Hume shift mankind away from reliance upon established beliefs as a guide and directive for behavior. They are for this reason major turning points of history.

THE PHILOSOPHER AND THE RELIGIOUS LEADER OF MANKIND

The similarities mentioned above are more than remarkable when one remembers that Hume and the Buddha were separated by 2,300 years and by different cultural traditions. There are reason why Hume and the Buddha have been linked together more frequently than any other representatives of Eastern and Western thought. To avoid being entirely misleading, however, the major differences, at least, should be mentioned along with the emphasis that the differences certainly outweigh the similarities.[25]

The chief aim of the Buddha's thought is to distinguish sharply a path of salvation, a way of extricating the individual from the suffering which is the dominant feature of human living. The Buddha wishes to lead men to a supernormal type of vision and experience which can become the ballast and underpinning of man's life. In Hume there is nothing comparable to the concept of *Nibbāna*, and Hume is not trying to distinguish a path of salvation. He is not tortured with any fundamental wrongness in the way man lives; he is almost exclusively preoccupied with faulty reasoning and with certain steps which he believes may be taken to throw more light upon the sources of error in the way men use their minds. Although he was concerned with moral problems and with the grounds upon which men make judgments of value,[26] his chief aim was to analyze various ways of knowing and to discover principles which would stand up under critical examination. It is for this reason that Hume is everywhere viewed as the founder of the analytic movement in modern thought.

Hume is a philosopher pure and simple; the Buddha is a philosopher with few peers and also a religious leader of mankind. Hume considers honest skepticism a natural accompaniment of a good life, and to the very end viewed himself as an inquiet skeptic. Buddha's analysis of experience is undertaken to achieve a life centered in tranquility, like a flame in a windless place.

Even in their similar conclusions about the self, their differences stand out. The fact that the self as unitary and persisting is not found in the Buddha's analysis of experience comes as the solution of a problem and not as an enigma. Hume experiments with the possibility of explaining the self as a bundle of sensations held together with a sort of psychological gravity, after the manner of Newton's great discovery in the world of nature, while the Buddha finds man's freedom assured partly in the fact that this inner monitor which men everywhere accept as the governing principle of life turns out to be an illusion. Hume's rejection of the conventional view of the self follows upon his method of rejecting all concepts about the world which are not based in some sensory perception. For the Buddha, however, discovery of the illusory nature of the self represents a victory over the predicament of man.

The Buddha finds man's freedom also assured in the fact that the constituents of personality, like all other entities in nature, are a series of entities constantly emerging and perishing in the momentariness of *anicca*. His view of 'dependent origination', therefore, is inseparable from his confidence in the extinction of suffering, since what has no independent existence loses its grip upon the individual who is oriented toward *Nibbāna*. Life is constituted by neither rigid necessity nor blind chance, but only by centers of relation. Any sequence of events and their possibilities can be removed. These views are bound together in the very heart of the *dhamma*. The tendency to cling to the relative as a substantial entity, and to the fragmentary, vanishes when their impermanence has been disclosed.[27]

Unlike Hume, the Buddha considered it possible to destroy the hold of unconscious motivations and the whole passional side of man's nature, 'to transcend the experience of this conditioned world'; indeed, to achieve clarity of mind in what is called 'supernormal perception'.[28]

Hume, on the contrary, held the view that clarity of mind was at the sensory level and that ideas about the world (as distinct from mathematical concepts) grow increasingly confused the farther sense impressions are left behind. While he recognized with the Buddha that man 'must strive against the current of nature'[29] if he is to loosen the shackles that bind him to an ignorant enactment of whatever uncriticized convention and personal bias dictate, Hume in no sense of the word *knows* a reality beyond transitory sense data and their combinations. Most people have concluded that Hume defended the principle of continuity in human experience and inquiry, though the nature of this continuity remained in doubt. The Buddha, however, testified to a depth-dimension in experience that defies naming and conceptual thought, yet yields more certitude than either sense impression or theoretical construct. His analytic leads into this dimension by way of meditation.

What distinguishes Hume most sharply from the Buddha, particularly as he is interpreted in the Theravāda tradition, is the fact that their philosophies lead in opposite directions. Hume leads the individual, chastened and enlightened, back to the social interchange in which he believed the 'ultimate propensities' of human nature to be rooted. The Buddha's thought leads to a loosening of the individual's social involvement, at least in the conventional sense, into a type of metalingual meditation which frees the individual from ego-centered and social drives, freeing from all coercions, so that the outline of a fundamentally more humane social order may arise spontaneously from the activity of the liberated man.

Buddha sees into the solitariness of man, into the inexpressible and unshareable dimensions where one must walk alone; Hume sees man as a social being from first to last. This is a side of Hume's philosophy which has been neglected and distorted by English philosophers beginning with Moore, who misconstrued the role of sympathy and saw only the epistemology in Hume. We shall have occasion to wonder how much he drank at the well of Mencius' concept of universal sympathy, and how deeply it may have affected both Hume and Adam Smith. The capacity of man to project himself into the experiences of his fellow man was one of the world's marvels to David Hume.

Both Hume and the Buddha underwent a conversion and 'enlightment' in which they were redirected in their basic commitments. The Buddha's analysis led him to the basic problem of man in society, which is not why he has the habits he has but why he refuses to change them even when it is transparently clear to everyone else that continuance in his present style of life may wreck his entire civilization. For the answer to this problem we are directed to *Nibbāna*. Hume's conversion led him into a deep appreciation of bio-social interchange as the natural element of human living.

Both Hume and Buddha sought to lead men away from egotism and from rule by logic and doctrine. 'What peculiar privilege has this little agitation of the brain which we call thought, that we must thus make it the model of the whole universe?'[30] In a world which both Buddha and Hume view as transient, man seeks to hold on to the tangibles which sooner or later slip away like sand between his fingers. The usual reaction to this is to make everything center in and around the self. Both Hume and Buddha contend that the self is a false center around which to organize life. Buddha offers *Nibbāna*, which is not a social experience in any sense of the term. Hume offers as the alternative a kind of natural, sub-verbal communication, a sub-rational matrix in which the sources of mentality and meaning lie hidden. Just because of this, Hume is able to burrow beneath reason, loosening the shackles of concepts and language, not unlike the Buddhist analytic here, to arrive, not in *Nibbāna*, but in the sympathetic communication which is the fundamental bonding agent of human society and in which Hume found 'the ultimate propensities of human nature'. As I have attempted elsewhere to show, 'spiritual, non-verbal communication of this sort is possible, and according to Hume constitutes the reality 'beyond which we cannot hope to find any principle more general' or more basic. It is the ultimate and irreducible fact. To stand upon this ground, in Hume's own words, is 'to stand with security'.[31] This is what sympathy means in Hume, not a feeling or a 'moral sense', but fellow-feeling; not an emotion or intuition, but the non-verbal matrix of interpersonal relations to which Hume fled whenever he became 'afrighted' at the solvent power of his philosophy.

HOW TO ACCOUNT FOR THE SIMILARITY?

The differences between the teachings of the Buddha and the philosophy of David Hume will surprise no one, for they are what anyone would expect in the light of different cultural traditions and periods in history. But what about the similarities? How can the remarkable similarities be explained? In their rejection of traditional concepts of substance and causality, and in their view of the self, they are in closer agreement with one another than with people antecedent to them in their own tradition.

There are three possible explanations. First, the amazing convergence may be one of those rare parallel discoveries, like that of the zero in the subcontinent of India and in the Central American culture of the Mayas at approximately the same time, without any discoverable cultural influence (unless the Kon-Tiki expedition provides a clue). Second, there may be cultural diffusion at work from East to West, providing Hume and the entire eighteenth century in Western Europe with an intellectual environment unimaginably rich in Oriental ideas, whose influence upon Western philosophy has not yet been acknowledged by authors who write our histories of philosophy. Third, it could be a case of sheer historical miracle, so that there were no historical circumstances functioning in the elaborating of either of the philosophies, Hume's or the Buddha's. We might even follow Hume's famous criterion of a miracle here, holding that falsification of the case in favor of the miracle would itself be more miraculous than the miracle itself.

As indicated in the title of this essay, it is the second alternative that seems the most plausible when all the known facts are taken into consideration. This becomes increasingly clear when we consider the relevant features of Oriental influence which come directly to bear upon Hume's favorite authors, his closest friends, and his most provocative themes. Since Hume mentions no Asian materials of any kind in his writing, while many of those closest to him do, we are forced to build our case upon evidence wholly circumstantial in nature. However, two considerations support us at this point: (1) Circumstantial evidence is sometimes even more compelling than direct evidence in a court of law. As a precedent here, Carter's history of early European typography may be mentioned, in which the case for Asian models for early European playing cards and religious drawings is said to rest 'on such strong circumstantial evidence as to be accepted with a reasonable degree of certainty.'[32] (2) A very special circumstance giving powerful support to the case for Oriental influence is provided in the fact that Hume and the intellectuals of his time felt themselves under no obligation whatsoever to document the source of their ideas, and the evidence for this is boundless. The philosophical fraternity today follows such strict practices in this respect that it is easy to forget how largely if not exclusively this is a twentieth-century custom.

One of the major sources of Oriental thought for Hume is Pierre Bayle, as we shall indicate in some detail below; yet Hume mentions him only once by name in the *Treatise* (I. iv. 5 [243 n.]), and only once in the *Enquiries* (I. 12 [155 n.]). Kemp Smith and Richard Popkin have given us lengthy discourses on the uses Hume made of Bayle's treatment of identity and substance. Bayle's essay on Spinoza was a major influence upon Hume in many respects such as these, and Hume follows Bayle almost slavishly in discussions of these subjects, simply repeating Bayle's arguments in many places as though they were his own. *Yet no credit is given.* 'The fact that Hume does not mention Bayle by name, and gives no reference to the *Zeno* article,' Smith says in one connection, 'and follows him with almost verbal consistency, is but one illustration of how different from our own was the practice in this regard at the time when Hume was writing.'[33] 'All too often,' Popkin says, 'the presentation of the problems, the terminology, and the ideas at issue derive directly from Bayle.'[34]

In the light of these facts, Hume's failure to say anything about Oriental sources in both Bayle's and his own philosophy is worth nothing whatsoever, and we are left with circumstantial evidence developed from the massive Oriental influence in the intellectual climate of the time and from the remarkable similarity of some of these ideas with Hume's. We have already indicated the striking similarity between the central concepts of Hume and the Buddha. It remains for us to see how this Oriental influence is a major feature of the total intellectual climate of Western Europe at the time, and a philosophical influence Hume could not escape. In some ways, as we shall see, and especially in the areas of ethics, political thought, and philosophy of science, Europe during the seventeenth and eighteenth centuries was more interested in Oriental ideas than in its own classical background.

ASIAN INFLUENCE IN EIGHTEENTH-CENTURY EUROPE

By the time Hume arrived in France to begin writing the *Treatise*, Europe had been in the orbit of Oriental influence for two centuries and more, and in his own century was experiencing what has been called a 'craze' for everything Chinese.

China by this time had become a repository for all the major ideas of the entire continent of Asia, and far too much coalescence of Hindu, Buddhist, and Chinese philosophy had occurred over the centuries to permit any dissociation for our purposes here between the influence of Chinese thought, on the one hand, and the influence of Buddhist and other Indian ideas, on the other.

Buddhism had made its way into China during the first century AD. The Mādhyamika was introduced to the Chinese by Kumoārajīva shortly after 400 AD. It is also unnecessary for our purposes to decide the precise nature of the influence these Buddhist inroads each had had in China.[35] From the first to the fifth centuries a general homogenizing of Taoist, Confucian, and Buddhist concepts had occurred. Between the ninth and the fifteenth centuries this coalescence had been carried much further, so that among Chinese intellectual historians today this condition is taken for granted. This is not to deny that certain types or schools of Buddhism confined themselves rather successfully to Indian traditions and, while in China, managed to keep the original Indian tradition intact. Fung Yu-lan calls this 'Buddhism in China' to distinguish it from the 'Chinese Buddhism' which made contact with Chinese thought and had far-reaching influence on Chinese philosophy, literature, and art. Buddhist and Taoist ideas, especially, were blended together, one outcome being the Ch'an school (the Japanese 'Zen'). Taoist terminology was used to explain Buddhist ideas, *Yu* as Being, *Wu* as Non-Being, *Yu-wei* as action, *Wu-wei* as non-action.

Thus a synthesis took place during these centuries, 'a synthesis of Indian Buddhism with Taoism, leading to the foundation of a Chinese form of Buddhism.'[36] The culmination of this synthesis during the twelfth century is suggested by Fung Yu-lan, with remarkable grasp of the deepest meaning of Buddhism, when he quotes Wang Shou-jen saying, 'The claim of the Buddhists that they have no attachment to phenomena shows that they do have attachment to them. . . . They are forced to escape because they are already attached to them.' To which Fung adds that this is an instance of a Neo-Confucian being 'more Buddhistic than Buddhists'.[37] One is reminded of numerous Buddhist warnings against becoming attached to the yearning for *Nibbāna*.

In his discussion of the Sung Neo-Confucians, Needham says that 'they accomplished their great synthesis of Confucian, Taoist and Buddhist elements just before the greatest synthesiser of European scholastic Christian-Aristotelian thinking entered upon his career. [Chu Hsi died in 1200; Aquinas was born in 1225.] If the contemporaneity of these two synthetic enterprises is but a coincidence, it is a rather remarkable one.'[38] Passing over Needham's belief that Oriental influence upon European philosophy came much earlier than the period we are discussing, and that it entered Europe through such philosophers as the Moslem Averroes and the Jew Maimonides, let us note that Chu Hsi, whom Needham considers 'the greatest of all Chinese thinkers', the great synthesizer of Confucian, Taoist, and Buddhist elements as indicated above, had been studied by Leibniz through the good offices of the Jesuits, who transmitted Chu Hsi in 'translations and despatches'.[39] Of Leibniz' concept of pre-established harmony, Needham suggests that this was 'the first appearance of organisms upon the stage of occidental theorising. . . . That things should not react upon one another but all work together by a harmony of wills was no new idea for the Chinese; it was the foundation of their correlative thinking.'[40]

The role of Leibniz as a major vehicle for bringing Taoist, Confucian, and Buddhist ideas into the intellectual climate of Europe has already given rise to an extensive literature into which we need not go, except to indicate two trails leading out of the Orient into the very heart of Hume's philosophy; one leading from Leibniz to Bayle to Hume, the other from Quesnay to Adam Smith to Hume.

Leibniz learned his Chinese thought from Jesuit missionaries, who had kept up a running battle with rival monastic orders and incurred their hostility century after century by insisting upon probing deeply into the thought world of those to whom the Christian faith was to be brought. We are working here with philosophical resources that testify to the value of this Jesuit struggle which in every century risked the disfavor of Rome.[41] After Leibniz, Oriental philosophy was a major feature of European thought.

We may conclude, then, that Indian, Buddhist, and traditional Chinese ideas, in process of synthesis over more than a thousand years in China, came into Europe with powerful impact upon the intellectual climate from before Leibniz to the French Revolution.

The China 'craze' lasted too long to be called a fad, and it penetrated far beyond the preoccupations of philosophy into all the major areas of culture. Admiration for Chinese rationality, virtue, and art was especially prevalent in England and on the Continent. Houses had Chinese rooms; the Duke of Kent had a beautiful Chinese garden created, complete with the pagoda; Chippendale had designed a Chinese bedstead for a room with Chinese wallpaper, mirrors, and chairs. Porcelain, lacquer, silks, and Chinese landscape painting are part of the substance of this learning from the East.

Everything Chinese was in fashion and indiscriminately admired in the French coffeehouse and salon of the mid-eighteenth century where Hume was a frequent celebrity. The Chinese were admired chiefly for their achievement in education, for their thinking about the nature of man, the reliability of his natural interests, his perfectibility, the idea that virtue can be taught and that the ethical is the highest level of human fulfillment, the doctrine of universal sympathy found in Mencius, which came to figure in the reflections of both Hume and Adam Smith, and in all this the complete absence of any need for a religious metaphysics, or even for bringing religious doctrines into accord with reason. This was the century that saw in China, as Hudson puts it, 'the religion of the philosopher enlarged to the status of a national cult.'[42] Are there any ideas in Hume more central to his philosophy than these? Is it likely that books and discussions of issues such as these would have completely escaped his attention?

To look a bit more at the broad scope of the impact of the Far East, the Oriental source of Europe's movable block printing is well known, as is the case of gunpowder, the mechanical clock, the equine harness, the stirrup, and the wheelbarrow. Less well known is the case of the magnetic compass, known in China from about 300 BC. There is every likelihood that the Vikings, who were in contact with Asia through their colonies in Moscow and Kiev, acquired by the ninth century the compass they must have had to cross the Atlantic and sail up the Saint Lawrence five hundred years before Columbus.

One can hardly imagine a more substantial and many-sided influence than the impact China was having upon seventeenth-and eighteenth-century Europe. 'The spread of knowledge about Asian beliefs, institutions, arts, and crafts was of genuine and serious interest,' Lach's recent work observes, 'to European rulers, Humanists, churchmen, governmental reformers, religious thinkers, geographers, philosophers, collectors of curios, artists, craftsmen and the general public. . . .'[43]

Except for the authors of our histories of philosophy, the influence of the Orient upon western European thought, and particularly upon the following major figures, is so generally known by historians as to be assumed. In France those chiefly influenced include Pierre Bayle, Malebranche, Fénelon,[44] Montesquieu, Voltaire, and Quesnay. In Germany they include Leibniz and Christian Wolff, who had to leave Halle and Prussia briefly because of a lecture given in 1721 in which he praised Confucian morality and placed it on the same level as Christian morality.[45] In England, Anthony Ashley Cooper (Lord Shaftesbury) and Alexander Pope stand out in this connection, Shaftesbury having founded the so-called 'moral sense' school worked out in systematic form by Hutcheson and considered by some (erroneously, I am sure) to find its clearest formulation in Hume. In Scotland the major figure for our purposes is Adam Smith, whose doctrine of the 'invisible hand' and concept of sympathy bear too close resemblance to Taoism's idea of the rational adjustment of all interests to one another in human society to let us think that the influence of the Orient could have been less than prominent. It can hardly be accidental that one of the concepts most central to Hume, the doctrine of universal sympathy, originates in Mencius and underlies the ethics of several European contemporaries of Hume, the chief one being Adam Smith. Maverick writes that Mencius' doctrine of sympathy was probably a major influence in both Adam Smith's *Theory of Moral Sentiments* (1759) and the work of a French public servant named Silhouette, also well known to Quesnay.[46] This is where Hume went beyond the 'moral sense' concept of Shaftesbury and Hutcheson.

All of these people were in more or less close communication, reading each other's books and discussing one another's ideas, so that the implications of Oriental ideas in such a community of scholars would have been in a continuous process of unfolding. A group of Chinese studying theology at the Jesuit college in Naples kept up a lengthy correspondence after returning to China and seem to have had a profound influence in shaping the theories of the physiocrats, the leading one being Quesnay, with whom Hume talked at length on numerous occasions, and to whom Hume's closest friend, Adam Smith, had intended to dedicate *The Wealth of Nations*, but for Quesnay's unexpected death. The dependence of Quesnay's political and economic theories upon the Chinese, a dependence Quesnay gladly and frequently confessed, is, as one writer puts it, 'astonishingly clear'.[47] One idea which is central to the Enlightenment, the idea that virtue can be taught, was thought by Quesnay to have been universally neglected except among the Chinese.[48] The school program of Turgot, another member of Hume's French community, was based upon the same ideas.

Bayle was also a friend of Leibniz, with whom he debated their different philosophies at length, to the profit of everyone who heard these two eminent minds come to grips with the philosophical issues of the time. Leibniz, indeed, was the first eminent European to recognize the great intellectual importance of Chinese culture for the development of the West. More circumspect in public pronouncements than his fellow countryman, Christian Wolff, and capable of misleading us regarding his high estimate of Chinese thought with remarks unfavorable to features of Chinese behavior which his readers might be expected to find objectionable, Leibniz seems actually to have done more than anyone to interest serious European students in the subtleties of Chinese philosophy. 'The influence of Leibniz,' Lach says, 'upon his contemporaries and upon his successors was just as important in the field of Chinese studies as it was in general philosophy and mathematics.'[49] Lach goes further to affirm that Leibniz considered Chinese philosophy 'not a foreign system of thought, but simply an alien counterpart of his own monadology and the Christian religion. . . . His was not a mystical longing for union with the "enchanting" Orient; his was a carefully outlined plan to bring together in intellectual harmony the East and West which Kipling later contended would never meet.'[50] It is beyond believing that Leibniz would have failed to exert this kind of influence upon Bayle, who as we shall see was the major philosophical influence upon Hume's life.

This is the natural scene of Europe going to school to civilizations of great antiquity. Voltaire speaks in the tempo of the period as follows: 'If as a philosopher one wishes to instruct oneself about what has taken place on the globe, one must first of all turn one's eyes towards the East, the cradle of all arts, to which the West owes everything.'[51]

This intellectual atmosphere, moreover, is the natural fruition of communication with the East, which had been going on for a very long time. Jesuits had been in the Far East for over two hundred years, and in Burma since 1600. Franciscans had been throughout the East as early as the thirteenth and fourteenth centuries, and a Franciscan, Jean de Montecorvin, had actually built a church in Peking by 1369.[52] The 'first European to gain any insight into the doctrines of the Buddhists of Burma was the Franciscan friar, Pierre Bonifer, a Frenchman and a doctor of the University of Paris.'[53] This is the mid-sixteenth century.

Jesuits had acquired some 40,000 volumes in their college at La Flèche, where Hume wrote his famous *Treatise* and, according to Mossner, spent three years, 1734–7, reading French works which 'seem so astonishing for a foreigner to have consulted.'[54] Hume not only made full use of the library; he also refers to his Jesuit acquaintances there as men 'of some parts and learning'.

The first ambassador Louis XIV had ever received from the Far East was from Siam; 'the same ship taking this ambassador home also had on board M. Vachet from the Society for Foreign Missions in Paris, who was returning to his mission in Siam, bringing with him three priests of his Society, after having accompanied the Siamese ambassador to Paris. There were several Jesuits traveling aboard the same ship bound for Siam and other nations of the Far East.'[55] Only the person who has never been to Thailand could believe that Europeans could live there without coming face to face with Buddhist forms of beauty and authentic Buddhist attitudes and viewpoints toward life. Dominicans and Benedictines add to the lines of communication.

Considering the amount of Asian influence that had been present in Europe, particularly in the eighteenth century and in France in a special way since before 1600, and considering both the nature of David Hume and the kind of ideas he spent his life writing and discussing, his exposure to major concepts of Asian civilizations would appear to have been unavoidable. Hume would seem to have been reading Asian materials which passed out of print and into discard with the French Revolution, when Europe's attraction with the East came to an abrupt end under the mounting pressures of the new age of science and industry. According to Lach, 'by 1776 the variety and wealth of materials available to any European scholar such as Hume was overwhelming'; and 'no systematic analysis of these materials has so far been undertaken.'[56] It is more than tempting to conclude, therefore, that Hume's cultural matrix included a great deal of Chinese, Hindu, and Buddhist thinking, some of it but poorly understood, but nonetheless provocative for all that. Hume lived in a flood of Oriental ideas that had been around for so long that people more often than not would have become unconscious of its source.

We can sharpen the focus of Oriental influence upon Hume by choosing Bayle as the specific vehicle for ideas that are central in Hume, particularly his treatment of causality, his refutation of all rational arguments for God, and the solvent he applied to the philosophic concepts of substance and the substantial self. Among the people Hume was reading intently, the man most likely to have grasped the significance of ideas in full flood from the Far East would have been Bayle, who Popkin contends was '*the* major intellectual figure of the early 18th century'.[57] Hume, moreover, Popkin says, 'is more Bayle's successor than any French Enlightenment figure can claim to be.'[58]

Leibniz, Bayle, and Shaftesbury all died within a single decade, the decade in which Hume was born. The influence of Oriental philosophy is an established fact, and an acknowledged fact, in all three. Popkin believes that Hume received the most from Bayle. As early as 1732 he was avidly reading Bayle, and as we noted above there is a great deal of Hume's writing which follows Bayle even slavishly without any acknowledgement of the origin of his ideas. This reading of Bayle occurred, it should be emphasized, during Hume's deepest and most formative reflections and particularly during the writing of the *Treatise*. He picks up the battle against efforts to give religious doctrines rational justification. It had been Bayle's labor to show that all dogmatic doctrines, all knowledge which carries us beyond the senses, is contrary to reason. Arguments for the existence of God and for the immortality of the soul lose their cogency with Bayle. Everything we find in the *Dialogues Concerning Natural Religion* had been anticipated in Bayle.

Bayle's skepticism has two major philosophical sources, however, one being his frank admiration for China, where men seemed to understand that religion succumbs to intolerance only at the cost of losing its soul. Bayle wrote admiringly of the tolerance of the Chinese emperor for Jesuit missions. He writes with understanding of the 'real nothingness' of Buddhism as 'that which has no properties of sensible matter'.[59]

The other source of Bayle's skepticism reaches back to Pyrrho, who accompanied Alexander to India, and who in Greece subsequently established Skepticism, a doctrine which confers freedom upon man in the Hindu-Buddhist style by detachment and disentanglement from knowledge-claims regarding the true constitution of things.

Efforts to seek out the sources of Hume's major ideas must soon come to acknowledge the wide range of influences, both Western and Oriental in origin, to which Hume was part deliberately, part unconsciously subjected. Ideas propounded by 'the yellow-garbed monks of yore' climbed the Himalayas, and were linked with an unexpected destiny by being synthesized and sharpened in a thousand years of Chinese philosophic discourse, whence they traveled the Old Silk Road and ocean trade routes to make a major contribution to the struggle of Western man to wriggle free from the fading philosophic tapestry of the ancient world.

It is worth wondering whether western Europe, without this unconfessed assistance from the East, could have succeeded in the secularization and desacralization of life which is now the dominant feature of that great venture in civilization whose headwaters lie around the Mediterranean, and whose values, until the quiet invasion of the East, were enshrouded in the authoritarianism of a divinely instituted church and a supernaturally revealed scripture.

If the history of philosophy is to be written at all, it ought to be written in the light of the East-West encounter which has really been going on now for a very long time. Nowhere is provincialism and cultural hypnotism more disastrous, perhaps, and linked more intimately with continued ignorance, mutual suspicion, and hostility between the various fragments of the emerging world civilization, than in our ethnocentric histories and conferences of philosophy. The present essay has selected one major Western figure, David Hume, in order to attempt to discover whether and how far the similarities between him and the dominant philosophic figure of the East, Gotama Buddha, point to the East-to-West influence which one might immediately suspect. We have found that the trails are many, but that the direction points ever Eastward. One of the most convincing results, however tangential it may be to the main line of the inquiry, is this, that in the only really significant gulf that opens between Hume and the Buddha, the non-verbal communication which Hume views as the fundamental bonding agent of human life and the ultimate ground of human nature, the philosophic trail leads, not backward into the Mediterranean, but to another major Asian tradition that rises in the concept of universal sympathy in Mencius.

To put it with the utmost brevity, it appears that Oriental influences were so much a part of the intellectual climate in which Hume moved that neither he nor anyone of comparable prominence in the debates of the time could have formulated his thoughts apart from these influences. Asia played a dominant role in the thinking of the eighteenth century, especially in that thinking which had the largest future to play in the secularization of modern life; it played a prominent role in the shaping of Hume's thought, particularly in his working over of the notions of causality, substance, the role of reason in religion, and the enduring, ever-identical self. Hume's position in the history of philosophy belongs, not to the West alone, but to the world of man; and his great eminence as a founder of modern philosophy rests, not on the originality of his conceptual tools, but on the fact that he developed the implications of these ideas with a rigor and thoroughness probably unmatched in the history of thought.

NOTES

1. L. de la Vallée Poussin, *The Way to Nirvana* (Cambridge: Cambridge University Press, 1917), pp. 38–9.
2. T. R. V. Murti, *The Central Philosophy of Buddhism* (London: George Allen & Unwin Ltd, 1960), pp. 26–7.
3. T. I. Stcherbatsky, 'The Soul Theory of the Buddhists', *Bulletin of the Academy of Sciences, U.S.S.R.*, (1919), pp. 824–5.
4. La Vallée Poussin, *op. cit.*, pp. 38–9.
5. David Hume, *A Treatise of Human Nature*, ed. Selby-Bigge (Oxford: Clarendon Press, 1896), II. ii. 5 (363).
6. Nyanatiloka, *Buddhist Dictionary* (Colombo: Frewin & Co., Ltd, 1956), pp. 11–12. ' "Non-Ego, Not-Self" (*anattā*), i.e. the fact that neither within these bodily and mental phenomena of existence, nor outside of them, can be found anything that in the ultimate sense could be regarded as a self-reliant real Ego-entity, personality, or any other abiding substance. ... All the remaining Buddhist doctrine may, more or less, be found in other philosophic systems and religions, but the Anattā-Doctrine has been clearly and unreservedly taught only by the Buddha.'
7. Charles Hartshorne, 'The Buddhist-Whiteheadian View of the Self and the Religious Traditions', *Proceedings of the 9th International Congress for the History of Religions* (Tokyo, 1960), pp. 298–302.
8. Murti, *op. cit.*, pp. 174–8, 121–3. 'All theories of causation are conceptual devices and make-shifts.'
9. Hartshorne, *op. cit.*, p. 301. This radical pluralism, as Masson-Oursel writes in *Comparative Philosophy* (London: Kegan Paul, 1936), received its earliest expression in Indian Buddhism, whence it passed naturally into Chinese Buddhism beginning with the first century AD, viz., 'the antisubstantialism of Hume ... is only equalled by the antisubstantialism of the Buddhists which likewise only acknowledges phenomena linked together by causality, and which exorcises the phantom of the object as object and teaches a phenomenology including a psychology "without a psyche" ' (p. 159).

10. D. B. Richardson, 'The Leibnizian Reason of "Matter-of-fact"', *Scientia: Revue Internationale de synthese scientifique* [Como, Italie], 6th ser. (1965), pp. 11 and 13.
11. E. R. Sarathchandra, *Buddhist Psychology of Perception* (Colombo: Ceylon University Press, 1958), p. 42.
12. Lama Anagarika Govinda, *The Psychological Attitude of Early Buddhist Philosophy* (London: Rider & Co., 1961), p. 56.
13. *Ibid.*, p. 57.
14. Murti, *op. cit.*, p. 75. Cf. pp. 121, 175, 177.
15. *Ibid.*, p. 175.
16. Hume, *op. cit.*, p. 635.
17. *Samyutta Nikāya*, V. 146 (PTS V. 125–6).
18. Hume, *op. cit.*, p. 636.
19. *Ibid.*, I. iv. 6 (253).
20. K. Venkata Ramanan, *Nāgārjuna's Philosophy* (Tokyo: Charles E. Tuttle Co., Inc., 1966), pp. 320–1.
21. G. P. Malalasekera, 'Some Aspects of Reality as Taught by Theravāda Buddhism', *Essays in East-West Philosophy*, ed. C. A. Moore (Honolulu: University of Hawaii Press, 1951), p. 185.
22. Nolan Pliny Jacobson, *Buddhism: The Religion of Analysis* (London: George Allen & Unwin Ltd, 1966), chaps 3 and 4.
23. Hume, *op. cit.*, II. iii. 3 (415).
24. Jacobson, *op. cit.*, pp. 57 ff., 72 ff.
25. Nolan Pliny Jacobson, 'Gotama Buddha et David Hume', *Revue Philosophique de la France et de l' Étranger* (1964), pp. 145–63.
26. Hume, *op. cit.*, I. iv. 7 (271). Cf. Norman Kemp Smith, *The Philosophy of David Hume* (London: Macmillan & Co., Ltd., 1960), p. 12.
27. Ramanan, *op. cit.*, p. 48. Cf. Govinda, *op. cit.*, pp. 56–9.
28. Shwe Zan Aung, *Compendium of Philosophy* (London: Luzac & Co., Ltd., 1956), pp. 55 and 60.
29. Hume, *op. cit.*, I. iv. 7 (269).
30. David Hume, *Dialogues Concerning Natural Religion*, ed. H. D. Aiken (New York: Hafner Publishing Co., 1951), p. 22.
31. Nolan Pliny Jacobson, 'The Uses of Reason in Religion: A Note on David Hume', *Journal of Religion*, XXXIX (Apr., 1959), p. 104.
32. T. F. Carter, *The Invention of Printing in China and its Spread Westward* (New York: Columbia University Press, 1925).
33. Kemp Smith, *op. cit.*, pp. 43 n., 284 n., 514–15.
34. Richard H. Popkin, 'Bayle and Hume', *Communicaciones Libres* (Memorias del XIII Congreso International de Filosofia, Mexico, 1963), IX, 318.
35. Richard H. Robinson, *Early Mādhyamika in India and China* (Madison: University of Wisconsin Press, 1967), chaps 3–7. This is a study of the interpretation of the Mādhyamika by Kumārajīva and three of his Chinese contemporaries, Hui-yüan, Seng-jui, and Seng-chao.
36. Fung Yu-lan, *A Short History of Chinese Philosophy*, trans. Derk Bodde (New York: The Macmillan Co., 1948), p. 242, chaps 21–6.
37. *Ibid.*, pp. 318–19.
38. Joseph Needham, *Science and Civilization in China* (Cambridge: Cambridge University Press, 1956), II, 457.
39. *Ibid.*, p. 291.
40. *Ibid.*, p. 292.
41. *Ibid.*, pp. 496–505.
42. G. F. Hudson, *Europe and China* (London: E. Arnold & Co., 1931), pp. 287 and 328. Cf. Beacon Press edition, p. 319.
43. Donald Lach, *Asia in the Making of Europe* (Chicago: University of Chicago Press, 1965), I, xx.

44. Fénelon is one of the French authors with whom Hume was making a conscious effort to come to terms while at La Flèche. Archbishop of Cambray and philosopher of Quietism, Fénelon had acquired one of Hume's countrymen, Chevalier Ramsay, as an ardent disciple. Ramsay was awarded an honorary degree of LL.D. at Oxford University and was a well-known man of letters. Dr John Stevenson, an eminent Edinburgh physician, recommended David Hume as a possible translator for some 'Chinese Letters' that Ramsay was writing. The arrangement was never consummated, but it is another indication of the proximity of China to the French intellectual climate in which Hume was living. See E. C. Mossner, *The Life of David Hume* (Austin: University of Texas Press, 1954), pp. 79 f., 93–6.

45. Wolfgang Franke, *China and the West: The Cultural Encounter, 13th to 20th Centuries* (New York: Harper & Row, 1967), p. 63. Better fortune attended Tindal in England, who saw no difference in the 'simple maxims' of Confucius and Christ except that the former helped to illuminate the 'more obscure ones of the latter'. *Christianity As Old As Creation* (2nd ed.; London, 1731), p. 314. Father Lecomte, member of the French Jesuit mission, who went to China in 1685, was less fortunate than either Wolff or Tindal, his writings being condemned by the Theological Faculty of the University of Paris because he praised the morality of the Chinese and the beneficent philosophy of Confucius. See p. 177 of Arnold H. Rowbotham's article, 'China and the Age of Enlightenment in Europe', *The Chinese Social and Political Review*, 19 (July, 1935), 176–201.

46. Lewis A. Maverick, *China: A Model for Europe* (San Antonio: Paul Anderson Co., 1946), p. 32. One paragraph of Silhouette's work calls to mind the subsequent work of Adam Smith in *Moral Sentiments*: 'The good man has for the basis of all his virtues, humanity. The love which one man should feel for all men is not a thing foreign to man; it is the man himself . . . it is the quality that distinguishes him from other creatures; and it is the basis of all his laws' (quoted by Maverick, p. 32).

Cf. Lewis A. Maverick, 'Chinese Influences upon the Physiocrats', *Economic History*, III, nos. 13–5 (Feb., 1938), 54–67; and 'The Chinese and the Physiocrats: a Supplement', *Economic History*, IV, no. 15 (Feb., 1940), 312–18.

Consider the following striking similarity between Hume and Mencius. ' 'Tis certain, that sympathy is not always limited to the present moment, but that we often feel by communication the pains and pleasures of others, which are not in being, and which we only anticipate by the force of imagination. For supposing I saw a person perfectly unknown to me, who, while asleep in the fields, was in danger of being trod under foot by horses, I shou'd immediately run to his assistance; and in this I shou'd be actuated by the same principle of sympathy, which makes me concern'd for the present sorrows of a stranger.' Hume, *op. cit.*, II. ii. 9 (385). Mencius puts it this way: 'When I say that all men have a mind which cannot bear to see the sufferings of others, my meaning may be illustrated thus: – nowadays, if men suddenly see a child about to fall into a well, they will without exception experience a feeling of alarm and distress. They will feel so, not as a ground on which they may gain the favor of the child's parents, nor as a ground on which they may seek the praise of their neighbors and friends, nor from a dislike to the reputations of having been unmoved by such a thing.' *The Works of Mencius* (trans. James Legge), II. i. 6 (3).

47. Adolf Reichwein, *China and Europe* (New York: A. A. Knopf, 1925), p. 107.

48. *Ibid.*, p. 108. Quesnay asserts that the government of the Middle Kingdom is 'the most ancient, the most humane, the most widely extended and the most flourishing which has ever existed.' Auguste Oncken, *Oeuvres économiques et philosophiques de F. Quesnay* (Paris, 1888), p. 627.

49. Donald Lach, 'Leibniz and China', *Journal of the History of Ideas*, VI, no. 4 (Oct., 1945), 453.

50. *Ibid.*, p. 455.

51. Reichwein, *op. cit.*, p. 90.
52. Virgile Pinot, *La Chine et la Formation de l'Esprit Philosophique en France, 1640–1740* (Paris: P. Geuthner, 1932), pp. 17–18.
53. Lach, *Asia in the Making of Europe*, I, bk. II, *op. cit.*, p. 557.
54. E. C. Mossner, *The Life of David Hume* (Austin: University of Texas Press, 1954), p. 102. This is the college that had educated Descartes.
55. Pinot, *op. cit.*, p. 15.
56. Donald F. Lach, personal correspondence with the author, March 30, 1966.
57. Popkin, *op. cit.*, p. 318.
58. *Ibid.*, p. 319.
59. Pierre Bayle, *Historical and Critical Dictionary*, trans. R. H. Popkin (Indianapolis: Bobbs-Merrill Co., Inc., 1965), pp. 290–4.

6

HERDER AND GERMAN ROMANTICISM

Ronald Taylor

In 1789 the remarkable Sir William Jones – jurist, Oriental scholar and founder of the Bengal Asiatic Society – published an English translation of *Shakuntala*, a play by the fourth-century Indian dramatist Kalidasa. The work caught the imagination of European writers, among them the author and traveller Johann Georg Forster, who at once set to work on a German version of Jones's translation, adding his own commentary on the philosophy and mythology which underlies the drama. Forster's work appeared in 1791, and in May of that year he sent a copy to Johann Friedrich Herder.

For Herder, who had long devoted himself with characteristic fervour to the dissemination of foreign literatures, this was a moment of triumph. Over twenty years earlier, in his essay *Über den Ursprung der Sprache*, he had pointed to the East as the original source of language and claimed Oriental alphabets as the prototypes of those in the West; in his *Auch eine Philosophie der Geschichte zur Bildung der Menschheit* of 1774 his zeal had led him to an even more embracing expression of his convictions: 'Behold the East – the cradle of the human race, of human emotions, of all religion!'[1] But all that Herder knew of the East at that time was derived from travel-books and essays. Later Forster drew his attention to Charles Wilkins's translations of the Hindu *Bhagavadgita* (1785) and *Hitopadesa* (1787); and now, a few years later, came the full vindication of his faith – an authentic work of Sanskrit literature accessible in his mother tongue, a work which revealed with

Ronald Taylor, 'The East and German Romanticism', in Raghavan Iyer (ed.), *The Glass Curtain Between Asia and Europe* (London: Oxford University Press, 1965), chap. 12, pp. 188–200.

unmistakable immediacy those noble human qualities which he had proclaimed as expressive of Indian civilization:

> Where Shakuntala dwelt with her once lost scion, Where Dushyanta
> welcomed her back from the realm of the Gods – O Holy Land, I salute
> thee, thou Source of all Music, Thou voice of the Heart – O raise me aloft
> to thy spheres![2]

It was this temper of reverence, this commitment to an idealization, which set
the tone for the German Romantics' view of the East – and when they talked of
the East, their thoughts were almost invariably of India. Here was a world of
new treasures, a world not buried in the past but accessible and, above all,
relevant, to the present. Cultural history had been seen in terms of simple linear
evolution: from the Orient via the civilizations of the Old Testament to Greece,
Rome, and modern Europe, each absorbing and transmuting the inherited
values of its predecessor. Now came a direct confrontation with the oldest of
Aryan cultures, and with it the discovery that characteristic European literary
genres such as drama and religious epic, gnomic poetry and fable, had already
flourished in classical Sanskrit literature.

The realization of this fact of literary and cultural history, however, striking
as it was, would hardly of itself have stimulated the Indophile emotions
expressed by so many German poets and thinkers in the last decades of the
eighteenth century and in the early nineteenth. Nor was there anything
historically new in the claim that India was the fountain-head of wisdom. Its
effect was made possible by the desire – a desire itself the product of differing
and sometimes conflicting casts of mind – for a rallying-point towards which
men's minds could be turned and from which new inspiration for dealing with
human affairs could be drawn. At this time, as at others in the history of their
country, many German intellectuals were looking to the outside world for a
sense of direction, and were thus peculiarly susceptible to the attractions of a
doctrine, be it metaphysical, political, or aesthetic, which seemed to promise a
fulfilment of their needs. Indeed, the Germans were disposed to idealize the
stimuli which they received, magnifying those qualities which they felt most
pertinent to their situation and ignoring what appeared to lie outside this
pertinence.

Thus thinkers such as Herder and his spiritual mentor Johann Georg Hamann
remained essentially 'Western' in their dealings with the East. Herder looked
above all for ethical values which could be employed to his own didactic
purpose, and even before coming upon Wilkins's and Jones's translations, he
extolled the moral excellencies which travelogues had attributed to Indian
civilization:

> The Hindus are the gentlest race on earth. They dislike causing pain; they
> respect all living creatures, drawing their sustenance from milk, rice, fruit
> and health-giving herbs – the pure, undefiled food which Nature offers.[3]

It was not surprising that Herder, in this Rousseauesque frame of mind, should turn a blind eye to the aggressive exploits of the Mahratta cavalry, the cult of military bravery and personal glory among the Rajputs, and the set caste-structure which was principally responsible for sustaining the qualities he so enthusiastically greeted.

The nebulous ideal of human progress which Herder called *Humanität* gained stature from the discovered relevance to it – even if a less complete relevance than Herder believed – of values from the Indian world. 'Humanity', which was later to be re-interpreted in the context of the philosophy of German Romanticism, was a dynamic, if unprecise, evocative concept of the latent perfectibility of man, a quasi-religious persuasion that the hope of immortality contains the seed of the supreme ethical and cultural achievements of the human race. 'The highest form of "Humanity" is religion', he declared.[4] And as the attainment of 'Humanity' challenged man at his most profoundly human, so religion was one of man's imperative, most elemental needs, a religion to be made manifest through the facts of human experience and in the language of human life; Nature was ruled by a Universal Spirit, and all knowledge existed within a harmonious framework, a Providential Plan.

In Kalidasa's drama *Shakuntala* Herder found the imminent, all-embracing spirit – the presence which Friedrich Schlegel was to call the *Allheit* – in whose shadow he believed his ideal could be nurtured. 'I doubt', he wrote in his preface to the second edition of Forster's translation of the play, 'whether one could imagine any more refined, more sublime conceits in the whole of our universe than this regal dignity, this sense of nature, this love – India's divine possessions.'[5] But there is a *caveat*: this is not a book to be read 'in the European spirit, that is to say, with a fleeting curiosity, just for the sake of finding out how it ends; but in the Indian spirit – attentively, in tranquillity, and in deep meditation.'[6] One will see in *Shakuntala*, not sententious idealizations of desirable qualities, not elaborate allegorizations of the human condition, but the portrayal of real human virtue in real human circumstances, a microcosm of authentic experience.

Even more significant for Herder, in *Shakuntala* the Gods are directly involved in human events, not figures standing above and aloof from the world. Mythology is woven into the fabric of man's affairs; the real and the supernatural unite in a single, multi-dimensional context within which the story of the drama is played out. Divine revelation, the source of all knowledge, thus penetrates the very core of human existence, and in the society which is sustained by this faith there prevail those values of which man stands in the greatest need.

So we return to Herder's starting-point, the contemporary situation from which the trail of his moral argument has proceeded. The nobility of Hindu culture puts to shame those European colonizers, missionaries, and would-be educators who, through their misunderstanding of the forms of the Hindu religion and their lack of sympathy for the manifestations of Hindu civilization, betray a false pride and an unforgivable condescension: 'Christians, you have a great deal to atone for, a great deal to make good'.[7]

Of the artistic qualities of *Shakuntala*, the *Bhagavadgita* and other works of Sanskrit, Persian, and Arabic literature with which he became familiar in English or German translations, Herder has, not surprisingly, little to say. As his attitudes hardened, and notwithstanding his claims to the contrary, his didactic purposes made him largely indifferent to the aesthetic values of art, and he drew the moralist's line between ethical good and sensuous beauty. In his rhymeless adaptations of William Jones's translations from the Persian, for example, a language in whose poetry rhyme plays an integral part, his lack of regard for purely poetic values left a fundamental aspect of the original untouched and uncommunicated. It is wholly in character that he should prefer the moralizing of Sadi to the hedonism of Hafiz: 'We are almost satiated with Hafiz' odes; Sadi has proved more edifying'[8]

In his stimulation of interest in the East, as in many others of his spheres of activity and influence, Herder's true spiritual inheritors were the philosophers and poets of the German Romantic movement. To be sure, others were also to feel the attraction of the Orient. In his hymn *At the Source of the Danube*, Hölderlin invokes a shadowy image of Mother Asia, whose mighty patriarchs and prophets were

> The first who understood
> How to speak alone
> To God.

Wilhelm von Humboldt devoted three essays to the *Bhagavadgita*, declaring it 'the most beautiful, perhaps even the only truly philosophical poem to be found in all the literatures known to us'.[9] Goethe, too, who in his early career had owed much to Herder, received *Shakuntala* with great enthusiasm, and subsequently professed a scholarly interest in the embryonic academic discipline of Indology, even making attempts to write in Devanagari characters (they can still be seen in the Goethe-Archiv at Weimar). But Goethe's was not the mind to surrender its supremely 'European' quality to the attractions of the East, and close as the religion of Hinduism came in some respects to the pantheism of his own beliefs, he rejected Indian mythology as an unnatural and unhealthy world peopled by creatures half-human, half-beast, the utter antithesis of those ideals, both in human and divine shape, which were embodied in the noble myths of Greece. 'That modicum of serenity for whose existence the Greeks ... may be said to be responsible, will be completely obscured by these dark and dismal fantasies of Indian and Egyptian provenance.'[10] The only traces of Indian themes in his work are the two poems *Gott und die Bajadere* and *Der Paria* – neither of them taken directly from Sanskrit literature but from a travel-book – and the 'Vorspiel auf dem Theater' in *Faust*, which is usually held to be modelled on the prologue to *Shakuntala*. Later his encounter with Josef

Hammer-Purgstall's German translation of the odes of the fourteenth-century Persian poet Hafiz was to lead to *Der West-östliche Divan*, but here again he shows himself, in letter and in spirit, in form, attitude, and manner, to be a poet of the West.

To Friedrich and August Wilhelm Schlegel, however, as to Novalis, Tieck, Schleiermacher, Görres, and the other early Romantics, Herder's revelations took on a prophetic quality, and his enthusiasms assumed the power of commands. Vagueness, lack of personal knowledge, an uncritical *Schwärmerei* for things Oriental conditioned the first thoughts of the young Romantics as they looked towards the East for the divine revelation of the Golden Age in which Herder had taught them to believe. The aura which surrounded the Indian world became one of the symbols by which they expressed their visions of life and their yearnings for happiness, a symbol to serve the ideals of Love and Art. 'Under the spell of music', wrote Novalis, 'the spirit, stirred by vague desires, is set free; everything appears familiar to it in the happiness so redolent of its native clime, and for these fleeting moments it lives in its Indian motherland.'[11] But it was not the current moral values of the 'Indian motherland' which moved him, not the Hindu's dedication to the conquest of the objective world and its illusoriness, but the perfection of the illusion, the transcendence of its purely temporal manifestations, the creation of a new world of the spirit.

The Romantic philosophy of passivity, the cult of aimlessness in life, found what appeared to be an echo in the religion of India, in the mode of existence of her people, in her art. Here was an ideal, it seemed, of being rather than of becoming; here, in a civilization of great antiquity, lay the cultural values to which the Romantics sought to convert the Europe of their own day. The need was for receptivity; the task was one of communication. 'It is to the East that we must look for the supreme ideals of Romanticism', wrote Friedrich Schlegel in his *Rede über die Mythologie*. 'If only the treasures of the Orient were as accessible to us as those of Classical Antiquity!'[12] And it is in the writings of Friedrich Schlegel, above all in the treatise *Über die Sprache und Weisheit der Indier*, that the Romantic view of the East, in both its philosophical and practical aspects, finds its most significant expression.

Friedrich Schlegel was a man of impulses, of sudden conversions to new ideas. As in his early career he had immersed himself in the study of Classical literature; had then, in the novel *Lucinde*, given unbridled expression to the Romantic demand for the liberation of human passion from the false restrictions of social convention; had, under the influence, and partly in emulation, of his elder brother August Wilhelm, half turned back to the Classics and then begun to formulate in the *Athenaeum* the new aesthetic doctrines of Romanticism; and was a few years later to become a convert to Roman Catholicism; so now, at the opening of the nineteenth century, he was gripped by the desire to experience directly, through the medium of the original language, those values of Indian culture which had hitherto been communicated in translation and paraphrase. In India, he wrote to Tieck, lay 'the real source of all tongues, of all thoughts and utterances of the human mind ... everything – yes, everything without exception – has its origin in India'.[13] The religion of Buddha had spread from India to the remainder of Asia; China had become what he later called, in the language of Indian sources themselves, 'a colony of the Indian warrior caste', while Egypt had become 'a colony of the Indian priest caste'.[14] When he wrote 'Orient', he thought only of India.

The Germans, contended Friedrich Schlegel, were of all European peoples spiritually the closest to Asia, and therefore had not only a unique opportunity but also an unequivocal responsibility to understand and reveal the nature of the Asiatic world. His own course was clear. The European centre of Oriental studies was Paris, and in 1802 he joined Fauriel, Chézy, Langlès, and other scholars there. In the following year the group studied Sanskrit under the tutelage of the only man in Continental Europe at that time who was known to be able to teach it – the Englishman Alexander Hamilton, who had been captured by the French in India and brought to Paris as a prisoner of war.

For Schlegel, as for Herder before him, the discovery of the East held an immediate meaning, spiritual and practical, for the development of German literature and thought, a meaning which derived from the informing power of the mythology that was embedded in the heart of Indian life. In their quest for a science of life the Romantics asserted the equality of faith and knowledge, believing that from the supreme moments of spiritual and intellectual achievement a religion might be distilled, the purest formulation of human virtue, the quintessential expression of the meaning of nature. Philosophical support for the quest came from Schelling's assertion that the evolution of nature and the evolution of the human mind were one and the same. The need now was for a new mythology in which the truths of this religion could be clothed, in and through which its beauties could be symbolized. Ancient mythologies appeared as interpreted nature; the prescience and premonitions characteristic of the mythological imagination were seen as the oldest sources of knowledge. In the modern context myths became what Schleiermacher called 'abbreviatures of the universe', finite forms of an infinite Christianity.

Friedrich Schlegel's pursuit of the new Romantic mythology involved every aspect of the human mind and implied a synthesis of all intellectual activities. Science would join with art, philosophy with poetry; the world of the spirit would merge with the world of nature, the antithesis of real and ideal would melt away, and the rule of transcendental unity, of *Allheit*, would prevail. This unity he saw in the luxuriant mythology of Sanskrit literature. Here was the divine revelation of *Allheit*, the new religion, which, like all true religions, 'has as its sole aim the reunion of fallen man with the Divinity'.[15] The history of the human race emerges as a theodicy.

And as art and life are one, and as the world is an aesthetic phenomenon, it is above all to the artist that this revelation will be made. Philosophy at one with religion; poetry infused into human wisdom; the supernatural woven into the events of the everyday: from this vision of aesthetic perfection the Romantics evolved their mythical image of India, an image which could serve as a symbol of their aspirations and longings. In so doing, they passed over the ethical content of Indian mythology as Herder had passed over its aesthetic content, and their pronouncements on the East, as on other objects of their enthusiasm, have the unsubstantial quality of an idealization rather than the solid ring of comprehensive and considered knowledge.

There was also a political aspect to this activity. In 1803, while in Paris, Friedrich Schlegel founded and edited a short-lived journal called *Europa*, devoted in the main to interpreting the achievements of French culture to the German public. On the basis of a Franco-German *rapprochement*, he believed, a unified Europe could be built, a Europe which was needed if the characteristic culture of the West was to be preserved in a condition worthy to exist alongside – indeed, eventually to merge with – the parent culture of India. To a nationally divided Germany and a politically divided Europe the apparent unity and contentment of the world portrayed in Hindu legend possessed the quality of an ideal: all activity in this ideal life, personal, social, and political, was directed from a single, central point by a single, central inspiration, fostering not only the purity and nobility of personal character but also the serenity and wisdom of the Hindus as a people.

Europe, wrote Novalis in his essay *Die Christenheit oder Europa*, seemed intent on destroying itself: 'Only religion can rouse Europe and protect the nations, openly raising Christendom to a renewed glory in its ancient role of peacemaker'.[16] Friedrich Schlegel, writing in the first number of his *Europa*, found the source of the disintegration of Europe in the atomization of its culture, the separation of the arts and the sciences, the growth of ever more, ever lesser autonomies: 'What grandeur and beauty there once was has been so utterly destroyed that I do not know how one can possibly claim that Europe still exists as an entity'.[17] And when followed to its roots in the individual consciousness, the decay, diagnosed by Schlegel in terms indistinguishable from those of Novalis, was seen to proceed from an 'incapacity for religion, the complete numbness of the higher organs. There are no lower depths to which man can sink.'[18]

The culmination of Friedrich Schlegel's Sanskrit studies came with the publication in 1808 of *Über die Sprache und Weisheit der Indier*. This consists of a technical investigation into the character of the Sanskrit language, its development and its historical relationship to other languages (he believed it to be the *fons et origo* of all tongues, European and Asian); an exegesis of Hindu philosophy, including such subjects as metempsychosis and astrology; and a sketch of the historical circumstances from which the language and philosophy of Sanskrit emerged, concluding with a group of observations on social and political institutions and on the nature of Oriental studies in general.

Two ironies attended the publication of this epoch-making book. Even before he had finished writing it, Schlegel was turning his eyes away from the East and towards the architecture and literature of medieval Europe, towards the writings of the Church fathers, towards – Roman Catholicism. One creed of universality began to yield to another, one mythology to be edged out by another, one set of symbolic meanings to be superseded by another. And in the same year that *Über die Sprache und Weisheit der Indier* appeared, he underwent the last of his conversions: in the company of his wife Dorothea, daughter of Moses Mendelssohn, the apostle of German Enlightenment, he entered the Roman Catholic Church. From this moment until his death twenty-one years later, the Orient was reduced to a mere historical concept, devoid of its one-time power to command enthusiasm, worship, and love.

The other irony lies in the nature of the influence which the book was to exert on German intellectual life. For Friedrich Schlegel himself the study of Sanskrit was a means to an aesthetico-philosophical end, a duty attendant upon the exposition of Indian culture; moreover, through his insistence on the organic nature of nationality and culture, of which purely physical factors such as climate and land-formations were an intrinsic part, he had thought to offer a model for the study of the history of civilization in relation to the ideals of Romanticism. But these ideals were fading. And in the records of history his work is accorded its chief significance in the realm of the comparative study of language, the dispassionate, analytical investigation of words, not as vehicles of thought but as units of sound – in short, it stands as an exercise in the establishment of cold historical 'facts'. Grammarians such as Jakob Grimm and Franz Bopp owed much to it; above all, his brother August Wilhelm, already established as an aesthetician and a critic of European literature, was stimulated to learn Sanskrit, becoming in 1818 the first professor of Indology in Germany and publishing the first critical editions of original Sanskrit texts.

In this growing activity Friedrich Schlegel took no part. He had left the world of Asia behind – if, indeed, for all his knowledge and apparent former passion, he had ever really been part of it. Here, perfectly expressed in the career of this one man, lies the crux of the Romantics' relationship with the East. Novalis, in *Die Lehrlinge zu Sais*, might equate Sanskrit with Holy Writ;[19] the Orientalist Friedrich Majer, contributing to Tieck's *Poetisches Journal* of 1800, might enthuse over ancient Indian mythological poems as 'dreams from the dawn of the human race';[20] Friedrich Schlegel might proclaim, at the moment when the tide of Romantic theory was at its flood: 'It is to the East that we must look for the supreme ideals of Romanticism'.[21] In reality the Romantics were not seeking their ideal in the Orient. They were not seeking an external ideal at all. They were seeking themselves. Like the hero of Novalis' fragmentary novel *Die Lehrlinge zu Sais*, they set out on the quest for understanding, for knowledge; like him, they found no satisfaction in the sciences and philosophies of man, in the achievements of history, in the ideals of society and nation, in the promises of religion; like him, they ended the search where they had begun it – in their own selves.

> In the temple at Sais, a man once lifted the veil of the goddess,
> And found – O wonder of wonders! – and found concealed there –
>   himself.[22]

So, in their individual ways and from individual motives, the Romantics left behind their ideal conception of the East as a fructifying power for the philosophy and art of their day. Specific motifs drawn from the Orient, whether poetic or philosophic in character, lingered on as colourful souvenirs, but the central spell was broken. Heine, who, as a student in Bonn, had heard lectures on Indian literature from August Wilhelm Schlegel, imported into his poetry a number of the decorative commonplaces of Sanskrit literature and gave them symbolic status – the love of flowers and animals, the cult of lotus blossom, the sacred mystery of the Ganges. The character of the magician in Romantic tales – the agent of the supernatural and the miraculous – is also Eastern in inspiration. Similarly, certain Oriental poetic forms found their way into German verse as first-hand knowledge of the original languages spread. Friedrich Rückert and August Graf von Platen-Hallermünde, for example, following the lead given by Friedrich Schlegel, exploited the Persian *ghazal* – a highly stylized poetic form 'closely akin', in Friedrich Schlegel's description, 'to the gloss, the sestina and the sonnet'[23] – the former translating widely, not only from the Persian, but also from the Arabic and the Sanskrit.

There remains, finally, the influence of the moral philosophy embedded in Sanskrit literature, which from the days of the early translations by Wilkins and Jones had been shown to underlie the spiritual and intellectual history of the Indian peoples. Neither Kant nor Hegel knew anything of the Indian philosophers – although a parallel has been traced between Hegel's *Negativität* and the Buddhist concept of *sunyata* – but Fichte and, to a greater degree, Schelling, the two philosophers most closely linked with the German Romantic movement, both showed affinities with certain concepts of Hindu thought. The latter considered the Upanishads to be the oldest source of human wisdom, and accorded them a higher importance in his ethical canon than the Biblical writings.

But it is above all, perhaps, in Schopenhauer that the strictly religio-philosophical virtues of Indian civilization find a European echo. Already as a student he had come under the influence of the Romantic poets' enthusiasm for India. While maintaining that the seemingly Indian elements in *Die Welt als Wille und Vorstellung* – his pessimistic view of the world, derived from his postulate that the Will is ethically evil; his advocacy of asceticism; his statement of an ideal course for European civilization which, seen as a doctrine of salvation without God, is virtually that of the Buddhist *nirvana* – were the products of his own European thought-processes, he admitted at the same time to a sense of satisfaction at discovering their relatedness to such noble predecessors:

> If I were to take the conclusions of my philosophy as the criteria of truth, I would have to accord Buddhism pride of place among religions. In any case I cannot but be gratified to find that my teaching agrees in such large

measure with the religion which, of all world-religions, has the greatest number of adherents. This agreement is all the more gratifying since, in the course of my own philosophical activity, I was certainly not influenced by it.[24]

One should learn to see the world as a 'place of penance', as a 'penal colony':

> This view finds theoretical and objective justification, not only in my philosophy, but in the wisdom of all ages, in Brahmanism, in Buddhism, in Empedocles and Pythagoras ... even in authentic Christianity our existence is clearly depicted as the consequence of Sin, of the Fall.[25]

And in his *Kritik der Kantischen Philosophie* he specifically acknowledges his debt to Hindu philosophy as, together with Kant and Plato, the main formative influence on his thought.[26]

Plato, Kant, India – much of the history of German Romanticism could be written from these three points. – Platonic idealism: utopian, metaphorical and allusive, introspective, Orphicmystical. – Kant: the appeal to the heart, the challenge to the supremacy of reason, the opposition to utilitarianism. – And India? *Ex Oriente lux.* Friedrich Schlegel wrote:

> The primary source of all ideas and all intellectual development – in a word, of the whole of human culture – is unquestionably to be found in the traditions of the East.[27]

The light of this knowledge, he believed, would reveal to man the essential unity of the human race and of its seemingly divergent, irreconcilable civilizations. And – to think with the Romantics – if man is to understand what unity means, and where the path of true progress, political as well as spiritual, lies, he must be guided by a vision of the ultimate fusion of East and West in the realization of this higher unity.

Let the final expression of the ideal be Friedrich Schlegel's:

> As therefore Asiatics and Europeans form a single great family; as Asia and Europe together make up a single indivisible whole; so we should strive the more to see the literatures of all cultured peoples as one continuous development, as a single closely-knit structure, as a unique entity. In this light certain ignorant and prejudiced attitudes will automatically disappear; much will become intelligible for the first time in this universal context; and everything – everything – will take on a new meaning.[28]

NOTES

1. *Sämtliche Werke*, ed. B. Suphan (Berlin, 1877 ff) vol. v, p. 562.
2. *Ed. cit.*, vol. xxix, p. 665.
3. *Ideen zur Philosophie der Geschichte der Menschheit* vi, 3, *ed. cit.*, vol. xiii, p. 222.

4. *Ideen* ... iv, 6, *ed. cit.*, vol. xiii, p. 161.
5. *Ed. cit.*, vol. xxiv, p. 578.
6. *Ed. cit.*, vol. xvi, p. 88.
7. *Ed. cit.*, vol. xxiii, p. 505.
8. *Ed. cit.*, vol. xxiv, p. 356.
9. *Gesammelte Schriften*, ed. A. Leitzmann, vol. v, 1906, p. 59.
10. Letter to J. H. Meyer, August 25, 1819.
11. *Fragmente*, vol. i, ed. E. Wasmuth (Heidelberg, 1957), p. 134.
12. *Athenaeum*, iii (1800), p. 103.
13. *Ludwig Tieck und die Brüder Schlegel, Briefe*, ed. H. Ludeke (Frankfurt-am-Main, 1930), p. 140.
14. *Friedrich Schlegel, Kritische Ausgabe seiner Werke*, 1958 ff., vol. xiv, p. 30.
15. *Kritische Ausgabe*, vol. xi, p. 9.
16. *Schriften*, ed. J. Minor (Jena, 1907), vol. ii, p. 43.
17. *Europa*, i (1803), p. 32.
18. *Ibid.*, ii, p. 292.
19. *Ed. cit.*, vol. iv, pp. 3–4.
20. *Poetisches Journal*, ed. L. Tieck (Jena, 1800), p. 176.
21. *Athenaeum*, iii, p. 103.
22. Novalis, *ed. cit.*, vol. i, p. 259.
23. Letter to A. W. Schlegel, January 15, 1803.
24. *Die Welt als Wille und Vorstellung (Grossherzog Wilhelm Ernst Ausgabe)*, vol. ii, 888.
25. *Ed. cit.*, vol. v, pp. 328–9.
26. *Ed. cit.*, vol. i, p. 543.
27. *Vorlesungen über Universalgeschichte, Kritische Ausgabe*, vol. xiv, p. 167.
28. *Über die Sprache und Weisheit der Indier. Sämtliche Werke* (Vienna, 1846), vol. viii, p. 381.

7

HEGEL

Wilhelm Halbfass

1.

The first results of modern Indological research became available during one of the most creative and dynamic periods in the history of European philosophy – a period of unprecedented globalization of European thought and science. New standards for the exploration of Indian philosophy and science were set by the works of H. Th. Colebrooke (1765–1837). His presentation of the classical systems of Indian philosophy remained unsurpassed for the better part of the nineteenth century.[1] G. W. F. Hegel (1770–1831), one of the quintessential European thinkers, was not only Colebrooke's contemporary; he was also one of his readers – and his response to Indian thought illustrates some of the most fundamental problems of the encounter and 'dialogue' between India and Europe.[2]

Hegel's presentation and interpretation of Indian thought has not met with much interest, not to mention approval, from the side of Indological scholars. According to H. von Glasenapp, Hegel was a 'bookman', living in a world of abstractions and speculations, unwilling and unable to adjust his conceptual schemes to empirical evidence. Moreover, he was the 'prototype of a Westerner', who saw Western thought as the measure of all things: 'Therefore, whatever he knew to say about the Indian world, turned out to be very insufficient; and the result was a caricature which shows – regardless of the fact that he had a correct understanding of certain details – that he ventured on a task for which he was not qualified . . .'[3]

Wilhelm Halbfass, *India and Europe: An Essay in Understanding* (New York: State University of New York Press, 1988), chap. 6, pp. 84–99.

Hegel's statements about India are indeed insufficient in various respects. As far as historical and philological accuracy and objectivity are concerned, they leave much to be desired. But they cannot be measured by the standards of scholarly objectivity alone. Hegel deals with India as a European philosopher whose philosophy commits him to not being neutral.[4] He is not just part of the European philosophical tradition, but makes a conscious effort to comprehend and fulfill it in his own thought. He is one-sided, but his one-sidedness is not a simple bias: It is a matter of intense historical and systematic reflection, and a challenge to the very idea of objective intercultural 'understanding'.

2.

Hegel's interest in India is inseparable from that of the Romantics: He was one of the heirs, but also the most rigorous critic of the Romantic conception of India. What distinguishes his approach above all from that of the Romantics is his commitment to the present, and his sense of an irreversible direction of history. He does not glorify origins and early stages. The spirit of world history progresses to greater richness and complexity. What has been in the beginning cannot be richer and more perfect. It may be true that India, as part of the Orient, is a land of 'sunrise', of early origins and 'childhood'. But this does not justify nostalgia and contempt of the European present. We cannot and need not return to the Orient: It is a matter of the past.[5] Unlike the Schlegel brothers, Hegel was not an Indologist, and he made no attempt to learn Sanskrit or another Indian language. Yet, his judgements on India are not as unfounded and irresponsible as it appears in von Glasenapp's presentation. Hegel made full use of the translations, reports and investigations concerning India which were available to him. His knowledge of Asian, specifically Indian matters was as broad and comprehensive as one could expect in his days. In this respect, he can certainly bear comparison with A. Schopenhauer, who survived him, however, by almost thirty years and gained access to materials on India, especially Buddhism, which were not available to Hegel.[6]

In Hegel's early writings and lectures, India and China play no significant role whatsoever. Only the Near East, Turkey in particular, was always within his historical horizon.[7] Occasional references to India do not demonstrate any specific interest, nor a level of information which would be in any sense remarkable. However, from an early time on, we notice a negative attitude to Romanticism, and this includes a negative response to the Romantic glorification and mystification of the Orient. The anti-Romantic perspective provides the background and an important point of departure for Hegel's approach to India.[8] His initial response to the Indian tradition is an expression and continuation of his response to the contemporary Western phenomena of Romanticism and 'Orientalism'.

However, with the growth of his knowledge, and with the publication of new and more reliable sources, his understanding and evaluation became more differentiated and balanced – though never really impartial. A period of very intense study of the traditions of China and India began in 1822.[9]

3.

In 1818, the year when the University of Bonn established the first chair for Indology in Germany, Hegel assumed his responsibilities as professor of philosophy at the University of Berlin. This was the beginning of a period of very successful and influential teaching; it lasted up to his death in 1831. During these culminating years of his academic life, he kept studying new publications on India, and he sought advice and information from his colleague at the University of Berlin, the pioneer Sanskritist and linguist F. Bopp.[10] He incorporated the results of his studies into his great lectures on the history of philosophy, the philosophy of world history, aesthetics and the philosophy of religion. The presentation of India became more and more detailed and comprehensive in the later versions of these periodically repeated lectures.[11] The fact that he did not publish his lectures, and that they have to be reconstructed from his own sketches and the notes taken by his students, leads to complex philological and editorial problems.

In 1824, H. Th. Colebrooke's first two essays 'On the Philosophy of the Hindus' were published in the *Transactions of the Royal Asiatic Society*.[12] Hegel welcomed these essays, which deal with the systems of Sāṃkhya and Nyāya-Vaiśeṣika, as a new basis for the Western understanding of Indian thought. In his view, they exemplified that type of thorough, sober and sensitive research which he regarded as an indispensable prerequisite of philosophical interpretation and evaluation.[13] He referred to them extensively in his lectures on the history of philosophy. However, he did not utilize Colebrooke's later studies of Indian philosophy, specifically those on Vedānta and the 'sectarian' philosophies (including Buddhism and *Cārvāka*), which were also published in the *Transactions of the Royal Asiatic Society*.

Hegel's basis for Buddhism was in general rather narrow. To a considerable extent, he had to rely on older missionary reports from East Asia. For Theravāda Buddhism, F. Buchanan's long article 'On the Religion and Literature of the Burmas' was one of the major sources.[14] The pioneering contributions of E. Burnouf (1801–52) came too late to be utilized for his lectures.[15]

Hegel also praised and studied W. von Humboldt's essays on the *Bhagavadgītā*, and he responded to them in 1827 in an extensive review article. Its two parts fill almost a hundred pages in the *Jahrbücher für wissenschaftliche Kritik*. In his review, Hegel deals not just with von Humboldt's interpretation, but much more with the world-view of the *Bhagavadgītā* itself and with what he sees as the role of Yoga and meditation in the Indian tradition. In a sense, this is Hegel's testament, as far as his understanding of India is concerned.[16]

Although von Glasenapp's statement that Hegel does not mention Anquetil Duperron's *Oupnek'hat* is not correct, references to it are, indeed, casual and perhaps indirect.[17] Unlike Schopenhauer, Hegel did not fulfill Anquetil's explicit hope that German philosophers, specifically followers of Kant, would read and respond to his translation. However, Anquetil receives more attention as pioneer investigator of the *Zend Avesta*.[18]

The Abbé J. A. Dubois, whose influential *Hindu Manners, Customs and Ceremonies* would seem to be more commensurate with Hegel's own critical attitude, appears only in casual and inconspicuous references.[19] In general, British sources, including the writings of W. Jones, F. Wilford and J. Mill, were most important for Hegel.

4.

Before we discuss in greater detail Hegel's interpretation of Indian thought, we have to refer briefly to the systematic context of his philosophy, in which his observation on India have their peculiar role and meaning.

In Hegel's thought, system and history are combined, even integrated, in an unprecedented manner. The history of philosophy is the unfolding of philosophy itself, and Hegel's own system is designed as the consummation of the historical development of philosophy. System and history are the two sides of the self-manifestation of the spirit. We are what we have become in and through history. History shows us the genesis and evolution of our present state of being and knowing: '... it is the course of history which shows us not the genesis of alien things, but our very own genesis or becoming, the genesis of our science.'[20] Historical understanding explicates and objectifies what is implicit in, and presupposed by, the current conditions of our existence. In particular, the history of philosophy aims at comprehending the fundamental constituents and the inner structure of our present existence and self-awareness.

In and by the process and progress of historical development, what is prior is integrated in what is posterior. It is – in Hegel's suggestive and ambiguous terminology – 'aufgehoben', i.e., cancelled, suspended, preserved and moved upward all at once. According to one of the central and most controversial principles of Hegel's philosophy and historiography, this implies 'that the sequence of the systems of philosophy in history is the same as the sequence in the logical deduction of the conceptual determination of the idea', and that consequently 'the study of the history of philosophy is a study of philosophy itself.'[21] – 'Just as in the logical system of thought each of its formations has its position, at which alone it has its validity ..., so every philosophy is a particular stage of development in the whole process, and it has its specified position at which it has its true value and meaning.'[22]

The philosophy of the present comprehends the philosophy of the past, which is contained in it, by recollecting it. It cannot return to it; there is no way back in history. 'Therefore, there cannot be Platonists, Aristotelians, Stoics, Epicureans in our days.'[23] The superior 'height' of the present which gives us the freedom of viewing and comprehending the past also prevents us from returning to it and from thinking the thought of the past in the same way in which it was thought in the past. The fact itself that we reflect and look back upon the thought of the past, that we comprehend it as something prior to, and presupposed by, our own thought, shows that it is no longer what it was at its own stage: It is now included in and superseded by a new, more developed and comprehensive context. Insofar, it does not provide a real, actual alternative for us, nor should we expect from it solutions to problems which have emerged only with our own, richer and more complex, stage of development. The 'reassignment of the developed, enriched spirit to such simplicity' would be nothing but 'the refuge of impotence', an attempted, but futile withdrawal from 'the rich material of development' into sheer 'indigence'.[24]

5.

Hegel's scheme of the history of philosophy is primarily designed to deal with the history of European thought from Thales to Kant and Hegel himself. However, this is not just one line of development among others. Hegel's conception of 'Weltgeist' ('world spirit'), and the corresponding unity of the world-historical process, leaves no room for the assumption of other, independent or parallel streams of historical development.[25] Where in this scheme does Asia, and India in particular, have its place?

According to Hegel, the Orient is essentially beginning, introduction, preparation. The way of the 'Weltgeist' leads from the East to the West. The Occident supersedes the Orient, and in dealing with the Oriental traditions, it faces, in a sense, its own petrified past. Compared to Europe, Asia, and India in particular, is 'static', i.e., without the dynamics of progress which characterizes European history. Those tensions and dynamic forces which have driven European thought from its Greek beginnings through the unfolding of the ideas of the subject, of human freedom, and of 'being-for-itself' to the social and political ideologies of the period of the French Revolution have been absent in India. Although the exploration of India is part of the Western historical self-exploration, it is thus also reflection upon a level of existence and awareness which is essentially different from, and incompatible with, the modern Western level.

The inherent and distinctive principle of the Oriental, and specifically the Indian, stage of thought is, according to Hegel, the principle of 'substantiality' or 'substanceness' ('Substantialität'), i.e., of the unity and ultimacy of one underlying 'substance'. The religions of India are basically 'religions of substance'. They see God as ultimate 'substance', pure, abstract being-in-itself, which contains all finite and particular beings as non-essential modifications, leaving them without any identity and dignity of their own.[26]

6.

In his *Lectures on the Philosophy of Religion*, Hegel discusses Hinduism – referring also to what he considers as Buddhism – in accordance with his conception of 'religion of substance'. We may even say that Hinduism appears as the prototype of a 'religion of substance'.[27] In this discussion, Hegel refers to phenomena in which he sees the potential for further developments, but no actual transcendence of the underlying 'substantiality' of Hinduism. In particular, he deals with the idea of *trimūrti*, the trinity of Śiva, Viṣṇu and Brahman,[28] with the 'superficial personification' of the neutral *brahman* (nominative: *brahma*) through the corresponding masculine form *brahmā*,[29] and with the interpenetration of polytheism and underlying pantheism. We cannot enlarge on these speculative and idiosyncratic, yet challenging comments. Instead, we will focus on what Hegel himself presents as the philosophical quintessence of Hinduism and the central target of his response as a philosopher.

In Hegel's view, Indian philosophy is inseparable from religion,[30] and the fundamental role of 'substantiality' applies to philosophy as well as religion. Pure 'substance' means indeterminate being-in-itself. It has no differentiation either within or outside of itself. It is the One out of which everything arises, and in which it vanishes again; and it is ultimately nothing but abstract unity. And exactly this is what Hegel finds in the Indian conception of *brahman* ('Brahm'): It is formless and indeterminate, unspeakable and unthinkable. Any attempt to describe or think it would lead away from it to the particular and non-essential. *Brahman* as such is 'abstract unity without determination' ('abstrakte Einheit ohne Bestimmung'), 'unity as nothing but abstract universality, as indeterminate substance' ('die Einheit nur als die abstrakte Allgemeinheit, als bestimmungslose Substanz'), 'substance without subjectivity' ('Substanz ohne Subjektivität'), 'pure being, without any concrete determination in itself' ('das reine Sein, ohne alle konkrete Bestimmung in sich'),[31] 'eternal rest of being-in-itself' ('die ewige Ruhe des Insichseins'),[32] 'spiritless substance' ('geistlose Substanz').[33]

7.

The Indian mind has thus found its way to the One and the Universal which Hegel, too, sees as the true ground of religion and philosophy. But it has not found its way back to the concrete particularity of the world. It has not brought about a mediation and reconcilation of the universal and the particular, the one and the many. The finite is lost in the infinite; the world is lost in *brahman* which is the 'naught of all that is finite' ('das Nichts alles Endlichen').[34] The undivided unity of *brahman* and the multiplicity of the world do not and cannot affect or permeate each other. Regardless of all abstract assertions to the contrary, they are related to one another in unreconciled negation and exclusion: '... the One, just because it is entirely contentless and abstract, because it has not its particularizations in itself, lets them fall outside it, lets them escape in uncontrolled confusion.'[35] This leads to the other extreme of Indian thought – its 'wild excesses of fantasy' ('wilde Ausschweifung der Phantasie'), an 'unrestrained frenzy' ('haltungsloser Taumel') of particulars,[36] a rampant chaos of mythological and iconographic details. The Indian religion is not only 'religion of substance', it is also 'religion of fantasy' ('Religion der Phantasie').[37]

According to Hegel, such constant oscillation between the 'supersensuous' and 'wildest sensuality' finds its most visible and striking expression in Indian art, and he refers to it repeatedly in his *Lectures on Aesthetics*.[38] In this work, he also proposes his curious yet challenging thesis that the Indian way of thinking leaves no room for 'symbols' in the true and full sense of the word.[39]

Hegel reiterates and illustrates his interpretation in his critique of the concept of *māyā* and above all, the role of Kṛṣṇa in the *Bhagavadgītā*. The Indian absolute, regardless whether it is called Brahman or Kṛṣṇa, is either principle of an abstract negation of the finite or – as in the Gītā – principle of an abstract combination of negation and identification. The divine being of the *Bhagavadgītā* is discovered in all finite beings. It permeates them – but only as their abstract indeterminate self-identity, as the 'being of their existence' ('Sein ihres Daseins').[40] It does not secure them in their finite individuality, nor is the finite a real factor in or for the infinite. On the contrary, the abstract self-identity of the finite existences, which identifies them with the abstract absolute, is incompatible with their concrete individual identity. Absolute abstract identity of God and the world thus coincides with unreconciled and equally abstract difference and mutual exclusion.[41]

There is, in short, a lack of dialectical mediation: The absolute and infinite is not put to work in and for the finite and relative; and the relative and finite does not affect the infinite. Accordingly, there is no historical progress towards the enhancement of man and the world.

8.

What appears as the ultimate depth of Indian thought, is at the same time its essential defect: The finite and particular has not been transcended; rather, it has not been discovered and posited as such. According to Hegel, this discovery has been accomplished only by the 'hard European intellect'.[42]

The full scope and concrete relevance of these observations becomes manifest in their application to the themes of human individuality and freedom. 'World history ... shows the development of the spirit's consciousness of its freedom, and of the actualization which is brought about by such consciousness.'[43] Philosophy reflects this development. It is inseparable from the unfolding of the idea of human freedom, as well as from its social and political actualizations. Human freedom is autonomy of the person. In order for it to be real, the individual subject, the concrete ego, has to accept its particularity and to affirm itself, its 'being-*for*-itself' ('Fürsichsein'), against the 'being-*in*-itself' ('Ansichsein') of the ultimate substance.

Hegel does not find such self-affirmation of the free and unique individual in India. Here, the individual in its subjective freedom 'has no value in itself'. It is part of a world which is a 'transitory manifestation of the One. . . . Man has not been posited.'[44] Instead of affirming and unfolding its individuality and particularity, the individual tries to subdue and suspend it. The aim of philosophical thought and religious practice is self-identification with *brahman*, return to 'substantiality' and 'being-in-itself'. This requires extinguishing all contents of awareness, creating an 'emotionless, will-less, deedless pure abstraction of mind, in which all positive content of consciousness is superseded'.[45] 'The ascent to Brahman is brought about by utter stupefaction and insensibility.'[46] 'The abstract unity with God is brought into being in this abstraction of man.'[47] 'Pure egoity' ('reine Ichheit'),[48] i.e., pure, abstract subjectivity, coincides with pure, abstract substanceness. Contrary to what we might expect, Hegel does not cite the correlation and identification of *ātman* and *brahman* in this connection; in general, the concept of *ātman* is conspicuously absent in his presentation.

9.

Just like W. von Humboldt, Hegel sees the *Bhagavadgītā* as a most representative, quintessential Indian religious poem; and he believes that Yoga is its central teaching. He thanks von Humboldt for his rich background of scholarly information and analysis concerning the Yoga tradition in general. He also refers to other studies and translations, such as A. W. Schlegel's Latin translation and H. Th. Colebrooke's survey of Sāṃkhya and Yoga. Supplementing his observations on the Gītā with references to other texts and traditions, he concludes: 'Therefore we may legitimately consider what is called Yoga as the general center of Indian religion and philosophy.'[49] Hegel discusses various attempts to translate the word *yoga* into European languages, primarily Latin, English, German, and he finds von Humboldt's expression 'Vertiefung' ('absorption,' 'immersion') most appropriate. However, he adds that this yogic absorption is neither immersion into an object, such as a piece of art or an object of scholarly investigation, nor immersion into one's own concrete personal subjectivity. Rather, it is absorption, immersion without content or object. Hegel suggests that it could be called 'abstract devotion', and he says that it aims at complete contentlessness of the subject as well as the object.[50] Its ultimate goal is isolation from the world and withdrawal into the empty unity of *brahman*.

Yoga exemplifies a 'negative attitude' of the mind[51] and the 'negative nature of what is the highest in Indian religion'.[52] It negates what Hegel calls 'mediation' ('Vermittlung'), the dialectical interplay of subject and object, and the creative self-explication of man in history. It aims at immediacy, 'pure unity of thought in itself',[53] involution instead of evolution, return to pure indefinite being which is identical with pure nothingness. It represents 'quietism', 'mysticism' and 'meditative' withdrawal in a sense which is diametrically opposed to Hegel's orientation.

Hegel refers to 'contemplation' and 'meditation' in his *Bhagavadgītā* review.[54] He also uses the word 'meditation' in two sections of his *Lectures on the Philosophy of World History*, of which he delivered five versions between 1822/23 and 1830/31. In a somewhat casual usage, we find the expression 'silent meditation' ('schweigende Meditation') in a section which summarizes and paraphrases a report by Col. F. Wilford and which has parallels in the *Lectures on the Philosophy of Religion*.[55] The more significant usages occur in the chapter on 'The Mongolian Principle' ('Das mongolische Prinzip'), which precedes the chapter on India. Hegel first introduced this chapter, which replaces a similar, though much shorter appendix to the chapter on India in the version of 1822/23, in the second version of his *Lectures on the Philosophy of World History* (1824/25). He presented it again, with additions and revisions, in 1826/27 and 1828/29, i.e., approximately at the time of the composition and publication of the *Bhagavadgītā* review, which contains a number of literal parallels. However, he did not include it in the last presentation of these *Lectures* before his death, i.e., the winter of 1830/31.[56]

In this chapter, Hegel speaks about Buddhism, which represents for him, perhaps in an even more radical manner, the same basic orientation as the Yogic tradition of Hinduism. In Buddhism, or the 'religion of Fo', nothingness – which he finds in the notion of *nirvāṇa* – is the principle, 'the ultimate goal, the highest point'.[57] Man should try deliberately and methodically to identify himself with it, to produce such emptiness within himself through 'constant meditation' ('beständige Meditation'); and that means, according to Hegel, 'mental abstraction' ('Abstraktion des Geistes'), getting used to 'being nothing, feeling nothing, desiring nothing'.[58]

In making these statements about Buddhism and Yoga, Hegel continues and summarizes a tradition of European speculation about and criticism of Eastern 'quietism' and obsession with voidness and nothingness, which had its origins in seventeenth-century missionary reports from China and received wide publicity through P. Bayle's *Dictionnaire historique et critique* and the *Encyclopédie* of Diderot and d'Alembert.[59]

10.

What the Indians call *mokṣa* is, according to Hegel, only an abstract and negative liberation. It precludes that very context of 'mediation' which is the condition of the possibility of concrete human, i.e., personal freedom. And without the explicit recognition of the subject as person, there is, in Hegel's view, no real basis for philosophy in its full sense. 'The real philosophy begins only in the Occident. Here the spirit goes down into itself, immerses itself into itself, posits itself as free, is free for itself. Philosophy can exist only here; and hence we have free constitutions only in the Occident.'[60] Philosophical thought and social and political reality are inseparable; again and again, Hegel refers to those features of Indian society which he considers to be incompatible with the spirit of philosophy.

The development of Occidental history, from the Greek and early Christian world to the age of the French Revolution, is the development and self-organization of the substance as *subject*, descent and unfolding of the absolute and divine into the finite and human world, self-discovery and self-affirmation of the autonomous person. The 'phenomenology' or self-manifestation of the absolute merges into man's work in history, into human self-fulfillment. Man becomes 'present God' ('präsenter Gott')[61] and continues the divine process in his own worldly presence, in taking charge of his world and discovering the dignity of the absolute *in* it. Philosophy has to deal with the present, with *this* world. 'Hic Rhodus, hic saltus ...' ('Here is Rhodes, here is your jump').[62] Philosophy cannot escape from the historical process; it is its mirror as well as its motor.

11.

Consciousness of individual freedom, concrete evolution of human autonomy – this is the fundamental criterion which distinguishes the Occident from the Orient and accounts for the fact that the Orient has been 'superseded'. If we apply this standard, some apparent parallels between Eastern and Western thought turn out to be utterly superficial and irrelevant. But if we neglect 'the difference which is related to the self-awareness of freedom' and refer to such 'abstract categories' as unity, universality and substance, it is easy to find similarities everywhere. Indeed, 'Chinese and Indian philosophy, as well as Eleatic, Pythagorean, Spinozistic and even all modern metaphysics can be paralleled insofar as all of them are based upon the one or unity, upon abstract universality ... However, such equating proves that it knows only of abstract unity, and in so judging of philosophies is ignorant of what constitutes the interest of philosophy.'[63] – 'Regarding what is entirely abstract one can find similarities everywhere. But since this is so, such comparison is superficial; it disregards what is peculiar, for instance the peculiarity of what is Greek against what is Oriental, to which it owes its value.'[64] In general, Hegel characterizes comparison as a superficial and abstract intellectual activity:[65] It is a co-ordinating procedure, and as such, it is inappropriate for historical understanding, which is guided by the notions of dialectical progression and subordination.

The relationship between Orient and Occident is a relationship of subordination; the Orient has been superseded by the Occident. Yet, it is not simply an obsolete matter of the past. Hegel's view is more ambiguous and complex than we might conclude from some of his explicit statements. The Orient, India is a preliminary stage – yet it can function as a corrective and antidote. It can remind us of aberrations in the modern Western orientation; it can help to supplement and rectify deficiencies and one-sided developments. According to Hegel, a major aberration of modern Western thought is its excessive subjectivism and anthropocentrism, its tendency to isolate itself from any firm ground and context, to display its own peculiarity to itself, and to lose itself in sheer narcissism. 'The extreme, the one-sidedness of European thought comprises all the fortuitousness of will, imagination and thought. Insofar, it is the extreme of vanity. Contrary to this vanity, this one-sided subjectivity, solid unity prevails in the Orient. In it, there is no vanity. It is the ground in which all vanity is consumed.'[66] It is important for us to know of this unitary ground, of which the Indian tradition keeps reminding us, to 'bathe the spirit in this unity which is eternal and restful', 'to assert the substantiality of the Orientals, and to drown in it that vanity with all its cleverness.'[67] To be sure, the Indian past has been superseded by the European present; nevertheless, or rather therefore, it is to be preserved and recalled.

12.

Hegel finds prime examples of bad and abstract subjectivity in the thought of F. Schlegel and his Romantic contemporaries, and specifically in the notion of Romantic irony. Here he sees 'infinite absolute negativity' ('unendliche absolute Negativität'), 'vanity' ('Eitelkeit'), 'shallow, arbitrariness' ('hohle Willkür'), and even 'what is quite generally evil in itself' ('das in sich ganz allgemeine Böse').[68] Hegel's recommendation to 'drown' the vanity of European subjectivity in the Oriental unity may certainly be associated with the Romantics. On the other hand, he is sharply critical of the Romantic fascination with ancient India, and with the 'Oriental principle' in general. Does this mean that he criticizes the Romantics for something which he also recommends to them? We may indeed assume that Hegel's argumentation is to a certain extent *ad hominem* and not entirely consistent. Yet, we may also find a peculiar dialectical turn in this apparent inconsistency: It suggests that the 'Orientalizing' attitude, which seems to be a potential remedy for the Romantic disease of 'subjectivism', only aggravates the condition. In Hegel's view, Romantic subjectivity, this 'yearning of the heart' ('Sehnsüchtigkeit des Gemüts') and 'consumption of the spirit' ('Schwindsucht des Geistes'),[69] does not really 'bathe' or 'drown' itself in the Orient; rather, it finds itself reflected in, and confirmed by it. The Romantic correlation of European 'subjectivism' and Oriental 'substantialism' does not bring about a concrete mediation and reconciliation: An empty and abstract subjectivity relates itself to an empty and abstract substantiality; and instead of finding fulfilment it rediscovers its voidness. More than once, Hegel associates the modern European 'vanity' of subjective reflection with the 'abstractness' of the Indian absolute, most explicitly in his *Lectures on the Philosophy of Religion*: here he parallels the modern 'faith in reflection' ('Reflexionsglaube'), which recognizes the ego alone as a positive and universal element, as 'the exclusive affirmative point' ('der ausschliessende affirmative Punkt'), with the Indian self-identification with the absolute *brahman*.[70]

13.

As we have indicated, Hegel's interest in India is inseparable from his anti-Romantic attitude and his criticism of the Romantic glorification of India. However, F. Schlegel himself subsequently revised and modified his evaluation of the Indian tradition, and he distanced himself from the unqualified enthusiasm of his earlier statements.[71] As a matter of fact, his critique of the abstract One and absolute of Indian 'pantheism', which in his view leaves no room for the individual and its particularity, seems to concur with Hegel's characterization of the 'substantiality' of Indian thought. Furthermore, Schlegel's criticism of Hegel sometimes reminds us of, and even seems to echo, Hegel's own polemics against Schlegel. While Hegel finds 'infinite absolute negativity' in Schlegel's thought, Schlegel in turn finds 'the evil spirit of negation and contradiction' in Hegel; both accuse each other of abstractness.[72] – Yet, in spite of all parallels, Hegel's and Schlegel's approaches are fundamentally different; Hegel's sense of legitimacy of the present, his belief in the irreversibility of history and the self-perfection of reason in history are incompatible with Schlegel's philosophy.

At this point, we may also recall the name of Schelling, whom we mentioned as an advocate of pantheism against Schlegel. Schelling's philosophy, too, is included in Hegel's criticism of India, although in a different sense than that of Schlegel. It seems that key terms of Hegel's interpretation of India, such as 'substantiality', the abstract 'One', the empty absolute, were first developed or employed in Hegel's critique of Schelling. In his *Phenomenology of the Spirit* (1807), i.e., at a time when he had no particular interest in India, Hegel says, with an apparent implicit reference to Schelling: 'To pit this single assertion, that "in the Absolute all is one," against the organized whole of determinate and complex knowledge, or of knowledge which at least aims at and demands complete development – to give out its absolute as the night in which, as we say, all cows are black – that is the very *naiveté* of emptiness of knowledge.'[73]

14.

Hegel's critique of the 'extreme of vanity' and other aberrations of modern European thought does not imply any basic doubts concerning the direction of the Occidental development and the destiny of Western philosophy in general. Hegel never loses his Occidental and anthropocentric self-confidence. Such self-confidence reflects Europe's historical position at the beginning of the nineteenth century. Europe appears as the peak of progress. It claims intellectual, moral and religious superiority over the rest of the world, and it attempts to demonstrate and establish its superiority in its colonial expansion. Hegel himself is a philosophical advocate and herald of this European self-presentation; and occasionally, he even tries to justify the historical necessity of Europe's colonial activities.[74]

Hegel is a fully conscious European of the early nineteenth century; and his motto that everybody is a 'son of his time'[75] has to be applied to him, too. In all his statements about India, he presents himself as a European and a 'son of his time'. He sees Indian thought from the peak of his own time and his philosophical system, which is meant to summarize and consummate the history of European thought. Hegel is fully aware of his position and the historical conditions of his thought. But this clear and explicit awareness of his historical position and his European identity appears itself as a manifestation of superior reflexivity; and it adds to his historical and cultural self-assurance and the confidence in the hermeneutic potential of his level and context of thought. In his view, his European horizon transcends all Asian horizons. Asian thought is comprehensible and interpretable within European thought, but not vice versa. The question of an adequate standpoint for the evaluation and comparison of different cultural traditions has been decided by the course of history itself, and it has been decided in favor of Europe. European thought has to provide the context and categories for the exploration of all traditions of thought.

15.

That Hegel was a 'son of his time' has the obvious implication that he had to depend on the amount of information concerning India which was available to him in his time. This information was not sufficient. Hegel had no adequate knowledge of the systematic complexity and historical variability of classical Indian thought. He was not sufficiently aware of its high level of argumentation and reflection, of its deep and pervasive tensions and antagonisms. He knew virtually nothing about the great debates between Hindu and Buddhist philosophy. He tended to reduce what he found in his sources to a few basic ideas, to elements of a 'prehistory' of philosophy, to abstract patterns of thinking which occur again and again in more or less insignificant variations.

However, Colebrooke's articles on Sāṃkhya and Nyāya-Vaiśeṣika introduced him at least to some of the technical details of Indian philosophy, and he referred to them in his *Lectures on the History of Philosophy* since 1825/26. He appreciates the 'high standard of intellectuality' in these systems, emphasizes the explicit development of 'logical forms' in Nyāya and discusses the significance of the Sāṃkhya theory of three *guṇas*.[76] More than once, specifically in his *Bhagavadgītā* review, he cautions against unwarranted generalizations and comparisons, and against an uncritical 'application of the next best categories of our culture on the one hand, and of a European philosophy, which is itself often confused, on the other hand', and he advocates an impartial documentation of the 'peculiarity of the Indian spirit'.[77] There are signs of change, of a process of learning in Hegel's later and latest statements on Indian thought; there is an increasing readiness to differentiate, to await the results of further research, and perhaps even to reconsider some of his own earlier generalizations.[78]

16.

As a result of his study of Colebrooke's essays, Hegel seems to be less reluctant to treat Indian philosophy as philosophy. In his earlier statements, he takes it for granted that India and the Orient in general have to be 'excluded from the history of philosophy', and that 'real philosophy' begins only in Europe.[79] However, Colebrooke's account leads him to the explicit conclusion that there is 'real philosophy' ('eigentliche Philosophie'), and 'truly philosophical systems' ('wirklich philosophische Systeme'), in India; he adds that these systems were previously unknown in Europe, and that they had been confused with 'religious ideas.' The 'real philosophy' of the Indians is to be distinguished from their cults, their tradition of Yoga, and so forth. It is 'the way, the movement through the developed and determinate thought. Of this (real philosophy), little was known to us so far.'[80] While the 'ultimate goal' of Indian philosophy is the same as that of religion, its form and method have been developed in such a manner, that it is clearly distinguishable from the 'religious form', and 'that it deserves indeed the name of philosophy' ('... dass sie sehr wohl den Namen der Philosophie verdient').[81] Even in Hegel's own thought, the ultimate goal and essence of philosophy is the same as that of religion. Philosophy itself is 'worship of God' ('Gottesdienst')[82] or cultivation of the absolute. What distinguishes it from religion is its intellectual and conceptual development and 'form.'

Hegel's oral and written statements are quite unambiguous: He does find philosophy in the true and proper sense in India. Yet, he returns again and again to his assumption that the Indian orientation was basically incompatible with philosophy as a concrete historical process. It is and remains dominated by the principle of 'substance'; it has failed to unfold the idea of the person, the autonomous individual subject. In this connection, he takes notice of the doctrine of the plurality of 'souls' (*ātman, puruṣa*) in Nyāya-Vaiśeṣika and Sāṃkhya; but in his view, this should not be confused with the true concept of the person or the free, self-affirming individual. Such plurality is ultimately nothing more than a particular application, a multiplication as it were, of the principle of substance.[83] The following passage, which Hegel added to his *Lectures on the History of Philosophy* in the version of 1829/30, may be taken as his final, somewhat ambiguous word: 'First of all, we meet with Oriental philosophy. We may regard it as the first part, thus as real philosophy; but we may also see it as preliminary, as a presupposition of philosophy, and we begin only with Greek philosophy ... In the formation of the Oriental world, we do find philosophizing, too – indeed, the most profound philosophizing. ... But insofar as it remains the most profound, it remains also abstract ... For us, the real philosophy begins only in Greece. Measure and clarity begin here.'[84]

17.

Already in his earliest philosophical publication, *Differenz des Fichteschen und Schellingschen Systems der Philosophie* ('Difference between Fichte's and Schelling's Systems of Philosophy', 1801), Hegel refers to some fundamental problems of his own historical period, which has 'such a multitude of philosophical systems as its past' and is thus led towards 'indifference'. While it accumulates information, the 'living spirit' of philosophy 'slips from its hands', and it cannot find any other meaning in philosophical systems, 'than that they are opinions' ('Meinungen'): 'The urge towards totality manifests itself only as urge towards the completeness of information, once the ossified individuality no longer ventures into life. By the variety of what it has, it tries to give an appearance of what it is not.'[85] At the time of this statement, Hegel was referring only to the multitude of European systems; he was not thinking of the wider multitude of non-European systems of which he caught a glimpse in his later years. But the problem remains relevant in this wider application.

While it is true that Hegel did not do justice to Indian philosophy, he certainly did not treat what he knew about it as mere 'information' or 'opinions'. He dealt with it in a subordinating and, at times, pejorative manner, but he did not forget that 'it has an impact upon the highest notions of our understanding'.[86] Hegel was not a neutral scholar and expert. He was a philosopher par excellence, representing like few others the glory and greatness as well as the futility and arrogance of philosophy. His system is one of the most intense and spectacular efforts to think reality, to comprehend it, to subdue it to the power of the concept, and it is instructive even in its failures and excesses. And while Hegel was one of the greatest systematizers and universalizers, he was also one of the most deliberately European thinkers. He tried to demonstrate in concrete terms the universalistic potential of European thought, its conceptual power to cope with all other traditions, and to show that these traditions are in fact superseded by it. His approach exemplifies once and for all one basic possibility of dealing with a foreign tradition.[87]

18.

Hegel's influence in the history and historiography of philosophy has been far-reaching and complex. However, his reception has often been one-sided and selective. Among the historians of philosophy in the nineteenth century, Hegel's negative statements on India and the Orient in general, and his pronouncement that 'real philosophy' begins only in Greece, found wide acceptance, and they were taken as a justification to dismiss Indian thought entirely from the historiography of philosophy, or to relegate it to a preliminary stage.[88] The later statements that there is philosophy in the true and proper sense in India had virtually no impact; they were hardly ever noticed.[89]

In spite of his negative and condescending attitude, and regardless of his basic scheme of historical subordination, Hegel was genuinely fascinated by Asian, specifically Indian thought. As a European philosopher of the early nineteenth century, he considered it an essential responsibility to deal with the newly discovered non-European traditions of thought. As we have seen, he was a careful observer of the beginnings of Indological research, and he continued to refer to it in his lectures on the history of philosophy, the philosophy of world history, aesthetics and the philosophy of religion. This puts him apart from most of his academic followers in the nineteenth century, who secluded themselves in the tradition of Western thought.

Hegel tries to comprehend Indian thought as something that is superseded by, and contained in, modern Western thought. This is obviously incompatible with the neutrality and openness which the advocates of the 'comparative method' – Comparative Religion, Comparative Philosophy, and so forth – postulate. However, it is also a challenge to some of the unquestioned hermeneutic assumptions of the 'comparative' and 'coordinating' disciplines: It challenges the very ideas of 'comparison' and neutral 'understanding'.

Hegel's influence is not confined to Europe. There is also a significant tradition of 'Hegelianism', 'Neo-Hegelianism' and 'Anti-Hegelianism'[90] in India, i.e., reception of, critical response to, and comparison with, Hegel's philosophy in general. There has, however, been much less response to his specific arguments concerning Indian philosophy and religion.

NOTES

1. Colebrooke's essays on Indian philosophy were republished in: *Miscellaneous Essays*. Vol. I. London, 1837 (several reprints).
2. The following presentation uses sections of W. Halbfass, 'Hegel on the Philosophy of the Hindus', in: *German Scholars on India*. Vol. I, ed. by the Embassy of the Federal Republic of Germany (New Delhi). Benares, 1973, 107–22. Some passages (specifically §9) are borrowed from: W. Halbfass, 'Hegel on Meditation and Yoga', in: *Zen Buddhism Today, Annual Report of the Kyoto Zen Symposium* 3 (Kyoto, 1985), 72–84.
3. See H. von Glasenapp, *Indienbild*, 39f.; 59. A more favorable assessment is found in H. Zimmer, *Philosophies of India*, (New York, 1951). See also, for instance, the references to Hegel in L. Dumont, *Homo Hierarchicus*, (Paris, 1966), 63 (cf. revised English translation, (Chicago 1980), 42; 355: Hegel on the caste system).
4. See his critique of the 'platitude . . . to face the facts without bias' in: G. W. F. Hegel, *Vorlesungen über die geschichte der Philosophie*, ed. J. Hoffmeister, Leipzig, second edition, 1944, hereinafter cited as *G.d.Ph.* (I, 8)
5. For Hegel's criticism of the speculations on 'origins' by F. Schlegel and other catholic (or 'catholicizing') Orientalists, cf. G. W. F. Hegel, *Vorlesungen über die Philosophie der Weltgeschichte*, ed. Hoffmeister, Hamburg, 1955–68, hereinafter cited as *Ph.d.W.* I, 158ff.; *G.d.Ph.* I, 263f.
6. On Hegel's interest in the Orient in general, see E. Schulin, *Die weltgeschichtliche Erschliessung des Orients bei Hegel und Ranke*, (Göttingen, 1958); M. Hulin, *Hegel et l'Orient*, (Paris, 1979). On non-Christian religions: R. Leuze, *Die ausserchristlichen Religionen bei Hegel*, (Göttingen, 1975) (not always adequate; see the review by H. Schneider, *Hegel-Studien* 13, 1978, 319–23). On India: F. Kreis, 'Hegel's Interpretation der indischen Geisteswelt', *Zeitschrift für deutsche Kulturphilosophie* 7/2 (1941), 133–45 (inadequate); on Indian philosophy: W. Ruben, 'Hegel über die Philosophie der Inder', in: *Asiatica, Festschrift F. Weller*, (Leipzig, 1954), 553–69 (very superficial); I. Viyagappa, *G. W. F. Hegel's Concept of Indian Philosophy*, (Rome, 1980).
7. On an early essay on the 'Spirit of the Orientals' ('Geist der Orientalen,' probably written in 1797), see E. Schulin (see above, note 6), 18.
8. See J. Hoffmeister, 'Hegel und Creuzer', *Deutsche Vierteljahrsschrift für Literaturwissenschaft und Geistesgeschichte* 8 (1930), 260–82; esp. 262f.
9. See E. Schulin (note 6), 40; on Hegel's treatment of Chinese philosophy, cf. Young Kun Kim, 'Hegel's Criticism of Chinese Philosophy', *Philosophy East and West* 28 (1978), 173–180.
10. See I. Viyagappa (note 6), 57ff.
11. A special section on Indian and Oriental philosophy was first added to the *Lectures on the History of Philosophy* in the version of 1825/26; cf. J. Hoffmeister, Introduction to *G.d.Ph.* I, XXXII.
12. *Transactions of the Royal Asiatic Society* 1 (1824), 19–43 (part I, read June 21, 1823); 92–118 (part II, read February 21, 1824).
13. Cf. *G.d.Ph.* I, 293ff.
14. *Asiatic Researches* 6 (1801), 163–308; on *nirvāṇa* ('nieban'), cf. 180; 266ff.; Buchanan used Latin translations of Burmese texts by the Italian missionary V. Sangermano. See also I. Viyagappa (see above, note 6), 229ff.

15. However, it would have been theoretically possible for him to consult Burnouf's early 'Sketch of Buddhism Derived from the Bauddha Scriptures of Nipal', *Transactions of the Royal Asiatic Society* 2 (1829), 222–57.

16. This review has not found the attention which it deserves. It was never translated into English. A French translation is found in M. Hulin, *Hegel et l'Orient*, (Paris, 1979).

17. See G. W. F. Hegel, *Berliner Schriften*, 1818–31, (Frankfurt, 1970), hereinafter cited as *Berl. Schr.*, 193: a reference to *Oupnek'hat* IX (i.e. the *Atharvaśiras Upaniṣad*, which is dedicated to Rudra-Śiva); Hegel may be following Th. A. Rixner in this reference. On Hegel and the *Oupnek'hat*, see also I. Viyagappa (note 6), 24ff.

18. See *Ph.d.W.* II, 420. Hegel read Anquetil's *Zend Avesta* in Kleuker's German version. For an indirect quote from Anquetil, see *G.d.Ph.* I, 264 (following Abel Rémusat and added to the version of 1829/30).

19. See H. Schneider, 'Unveröffentlichte Vorlesungsmanuskripte Hegels', *Hegel-Studien* 7 (1972), 28; I. Viyagappa (note 6), 28ff. H. J. Schoeps, 'Die ausserchristlichen Religionen bei Hegel', *Zeitschrift für Religions-und Geistesgeschichte* I (1955), 1–34.

20. *G.d.Ph.* I, 14 (following the Heidelberg version). Apart from the translation of the *Lectures on the History of Philosophy* by E. S. Haldane and F. H. Simson (London, 1892; many reprints), there are two recent translations of the 'Introduction' to these *Lectures* (both more or less abridged): Q. Lauer, *Hegel's Idea of Philosophy*, (New York, 1971); *Introduction to the Lectures on the History of Philosophy*, trans. T. M. Knox and A. V. Miller, Oxford, 1985.

21. *G.d.Ph.* I, 34f.

22. *G.d.Ph.* I, 71f.: 'Wie nun im logischen System des Denkens jede Gestaltung desselben seine Stelle hat, auf der es allein Gültigkeit hat …, so ist auch jede Philosophie im Ganzen des Ganges eine besondere Entwicklungsstufe und hat ihre bestimmte Stelle, auf der sie ihren wahrhaften Wert und Bedeutung hat.'

23. *G.d.Ph.* I, 72.

24. Cf. *G.d.Ph.* I, 74; see also 69: 'What is in the beginning, is the most abstract, because it is in the beginning' ('Das Anfängliche ist das Abstrakteste, weil es das Anfängliche ist').

25. Cf. *G.d.Ph.* I, 124: 'The history of philosophy considers only *one* philosophy, *one* process, which is, however, divided into different stages' ('Die Geschichte der Philosophie betrachtet nur *eine* Philosophie, nur *eine* Handlung, die aber in verschiedene Stufen abgeteilt ist').

26. On 'substantiality' and 'pantheism,' cf. G. W. F. Hegel, *Vorlesungen über die Philosophie der Religion*, ed. G. Lasson, Hamburg, second edition, 1966 (first edition: Leipzig, 1925–9), hereinafter cited as *Phil.d.Rel.* I/1, 195ff.

27. See specifically *Phil.d.Rel.* I/2, 119ff.

28. Cf. I. Viyagappa (note 6), 121f.

29. Hegel prefers 'Brahm' for the neuter and 'Brahma' for the masculine, but he also speaks in general about 'Brahman'.

30. See *G.d.Ph.* I, 289f.; but see his later qualification (below, §16).

31. Cf. *Berl. Schr.*, 185–8; according to Hegel's *Logic*, 'pure being' coincides with 'pure nothingness'.

32. *Phil.d.Rel.* I/2, 149.

33. *Ph.d.W.* II, 398.

34. *Berl. Schr.*, 190.

35. W. T. Stace, *The Philosophy of Hegel*, (London, 1924), 496.

36. See *Ph.d.W.* II, 400; *Berl. Schr.*, 193.

37. Cf. *Phil.d.Rel.* I/2, 137ff.; 149ff.; also *G.d.Ph.* I, 289ff.; 335.

38. See *Vorlesungen über die Ästhetik* I (Jubiläumsausgabe, ed. H. Glockner, vol. 12), 445ff.

39. *Vorlesungen über die Ästhetik* I, 451: The Indian 'religion of fantasy' does not distinguish between symbolic reference and identity. The 'ape, the cow, the

individual brahmin, etc. ... are not a related symbol of the divine, but the divine itself.'

40. *Berl. Schr.*, 190; 'being' in this sense is so abstract that it includes even 'nonentities'.
41. Cf. *Berl. Schr.*, 158; 184f.; 190ff.
42. *G.d.Ph.* I, 335; see also 332ff.
43. *Ph.d.W.* I, 167: 'die Weltgeschichte stellt ... die Entwicklung des Bewusstseins des Geistes von seiner Freiheit und der von solchem Bewusstsein hervorgebrachten Verwirklichung dar.'
44. *Ph.d.W.* II, 399; cf. also *G.d.Ph.* I, 267.
45. W. T. Stace, *The Philosophy of Hegel*, (London, 1924), 497.
46. *Ph.d.W.* II, 407: 'Die Erhebung zum Brahm wird durch höchste Abgestumpftheit und Bewusstlosigkeit bewirkt.' See also *Ph.d.W.* I, 176; *G.d.Ph.* I, 286 (associating the cynics and the gymnosophists); 293; 331.
47. *Ph.d.W.* II, 406; see also *Berl. Schr.*, 151, on the 'contentlessness of the subject' ('Inhaltslosigkeit des Subjekts').
48. *Phil.d.Rel.* 1/2, 166.
49. *Berl. Schr.*, 148: 'Wir dürfen daher mit Recht das, was Joga heisst, für den allgemeinen Mittelpunkt indischer Religion und Philosophie betrachten.'
50. See *Berl. Schr.*, 150f. See also W. von Humboldt, *Gesammelte Schriften* (Akademie-Ausgabe) 1/5 (Berlin, 1906; reprint 1968), 221: *yoga* as 'Vertiefung'; 164: *samādhi* as 'contemplation' (defending Schlegel's Latin 'contemplatio').
51. *Berl. Schr.*, 157.
52. *Berl. Schr.*, 163.
53. *Enzyklopädie der philosophischen Wissenschaften* (1830), ed. F. Nicolin and O. Pöggeler, (Hamburg, 1959), §573 (p. 455). The long note (pp. 451–61) in which this phrase ('reine Einheit des Gedankens in sich selbst') occurs is an addition to the revised third edition of 1830; the first edition was published in 1817.
54. The word 'Meditation' does not appear at all in H. Glockner's *Hegel-Lexikon*. But cf. *Berl. Schr.*, 195ff.
55. *Ph.d.W.* II, 403; see the parallel passage, *Phil.d.Rel.* II/1, 165.
56. See the introduction by G. Lasson, *Ph.d.W.* II, XI. Lasson refers to the testimony of E. Gans.
57. *Phil.d.Rel.* 1/2, 124.
58. *Ph.d.W.* II, 334f. See also *Phil.d.Rel* 1/2, 134: After mentioning the Buddhist 'Nirwana', Hegel refers to meditation and paraphrases it as 'going back into oneself' ('Zurückgehen in sich').
59. See above, ch. 4, §6; also H. de Lubac, *La rencontre du bouddhisme et de l'occident*, (Paris, 1952), 86ff. A. E. Gough, *The Philosophy of the Upanishads*, (London, 1882) (third ed.: 1903), claims: 'The Indian sages seek for participation in the divine life ... by the crushing out of every feeling and every thought, by vacuity, apathy, inertia and ecstasy.'
60. *G.d.Ph.* I, 232; but see below, §16.
61. *Phil.d.Rel.* II/2, 172, has the expression 'present spirit' ('präsenter Geist'); 'präsenter Gott' is found in the corresponding passage of the *Jubiläumsausgabe*, ed. H. Glockner, vol. 15, 307; see also *Werke, Vollständige Ausgabe*, vol. 12, Berlin 1832, 253: 'der Mensch' instead of 'das Menschliche.'
62. *Grundlinien der Philosophie des Rechts*, ed. J. Hoffmeister. Hamburg, fourth edition, 1955, 16.
63. *Ph.d.W.* I, 175.
64. *G.d.Ph.* I, 264 (addition to the version of 1829/30).
65. See *Wissenschaft der Logik*, ed. G. Lasson. Leipzig, 1951, II, 36f.
66. *G.d.Ph.* I, 287.
67. *G.d.Ph.* I, 287; 334. The metaphor of 'bathing' the spirit in the 'ether of the one substance' is also used with reference to Spinoza, whom Hegel calls an 'echo of the Orient' ('Nachklang des Morgenlandes'); see *G.d.Ph.* III, 368; 376.

68. See O. Pöggeler, *Hegels Kritik der Romantik*, (Bonn, 1956), 66ff; 263ff. Also E. Behler, 'Friedrich Schlegel und Hegel', *Hegel-Studien* 2 (1963), 203–50; specifically 208ff. (on Hegel's criticism of 'Romantic irony') and 212ff. (criticism of Schlegel's 'irony').
69. See E. Behler (note 68), 210.
70. *Phil.d.Rel.* 1/2, 168.
71. See above, ch. 5, §10f.
72. See E. Behler (note 68), 241ff; esp. 249: 'Ebenso wie Schlegels frühromantische Ironie Hegel als "unendliche absolute Negativität" erschienen war, wird also Hegels Dialektik von Schlegel als "böser Geist der Verneinung und des Widerspruchs" empfunden.'
73. *Phänomenologie des Geistes*, ed. J. Hoffmeister. Hamburg, sixth edition, 1952, 19. Quoted from the translation by J. B. Baillie, *The Phenomenology of Mind* (1910). New York, 1967, 79. On Hegel's notion of 'Orientalism', which seems to be implied in this passage, see *Dokumente zu Hegels Entwicklung*, ed. J. Hoffmeister, (Stuttgart, 1936), 338.
74. See, for instance, *Ph.d.W.* II, 365.
75. *Grundlinien der Philosophie des Rechts*, ed. J Hoffmeister, (Hamburg, fourth edition, 1955), 16.
76. Cf. *G.d.Ph.* 1, 330ff.; 312ff.
77. *Berl. Schr.*, 133; 203. Hegel concurs with W. von Humboldt's postulate that a detailed study of the sources should precede all further activities of interpretation, comparison, and so forth.
78. This applies, above all, to the versions of the *Lectures on the History of Philosophy* since 1825/26 and the *Bhagavadgītā* review (1827).
79. See *G.d.Ph.* I, 232.
80. *G.d.Ph.* I, 293ff. ('... der Weg, das Gehen durch den entwickelten, durch den bestimmten Gedanken ...'); these are additions to the versions since 1825/26; see also 288 (1827/28): 'abstract philosophies'. The aforementioned references to 'real philosophy' in India are not found in the edition of the *Lectures* by H. Glockner (*Jubiläumsausgabe*, vol. 17), which reproduces the first edition of the text by K. L. Michelet, published in 1833. Michelet's abbreviated second edition (1840–4) was used for the English translation by E. S. Haldane and F. H. Simson (1892). But even here, we hear about 'wirklich philosophische Werke' in India (*Jubiläumsausgabe*, vol. 17, 163; cf. Haldane/Simson, 127; 'real philosophic writings').
81. *Berl. Schr.*, 144.
82. *Phil.d.Rel.* I, 29.
83. *G.d.Ph.* I, 331ff. We need not discuss the factual accuracy of Hegel's statements; a somewhat naive and superficial attempt to assess such accuracy is made by R. Leuze, *Die ausserchristlichen Religionen bei Hegel*, (Göttingen, 1975), 112ff.
84. *G.d.Ph.* 1, 373f. (appendix; additions to the version of 1829/30). On further Hegelian reflections concerning the applicability of the concept of philosophy to Indian thought see *India and Europe*, ch. 9, §7.
85. *Differenz des Fichteschen und Schellingschen Systems der Philosophie*, (Hamburg, 1962), If. Hegel associates such accumulation of information with the 'collection of mummies'.
86. *Berl. Schr.*, 203 ('... weil sie in die höchsten Begriffe unseres Bewusstseins eingreift ...').
87. M. Hulin, *Hegel et l'Orient*, (Paris, 1979), 139, calls Hegel's interpretation of the Orient 'a unique enterprise in the history of ideas' ('une enterprise unique dans l'histoire des idées').
88. See *India and Europe*, ch. 9.
89. Among Hegel's direct disciples and successors, only E. Gans and K. Rosenkranz showed a noteworthy interest in India.

90. See, e.g., H. Haldar, *Neo-Hegelianism*, (London, 1928); P. T. Raju, *Thought and Reality*, (London, 1937); L. Saxena, *Neo-Hegelian and Neo-Advaitic Monism*, (Delhi, 1980); and numerous references in *Contemporary Indian Philosophy*, ed. S. Radhakrishnan and J. H. Muirhead, (London, 1936) (fourth edition, 1966).

8

SCHELLING AND SCHOPENHAUER

Wilhelm Halbfass

1.

F. W. J. Schelling (1775–1854) and A. Schopenhauer (1788–1860), Hegel's younger contemporaries, exemplify perspectives on Indian thought which are significantly different from, yet complementary to the Hegelian perspective. Together, Hegel, Schelling and Schopenhauer represent what is still the most memorable episode in the history of European philosophical responses to India.

Hegel and Schelling were fellow-students and roommates at the University of Tübingen,[1] and for a number of years, they remained close to each other. In his first philosophical publication, *Differenz des Fichteschen und Schellingschen Systems der Philosophie* ('Difference between Fichte's and Schelling's Systems of Philosophy,' 1801), Hegel dealt with the achievements of his prodigious younger friend. But when his masterpiece, *Phänomenologie des Geistes* ('Phenomenology of the Spirit') was completed in 1806, a process of personal and doctrinal estrangement had begun which turned out to be irreversible. In 1841, ten years after Hegel's death, Friedrich Wilhelm IV of Prussia called Schelling to the University of Berlin, to 'eradicate the dragon seed of Hegelianism'. However, after a few years, Schelling resigned from this prestigious position.

Among his last academic presentations, the lectures on the 'Philosophy of Mythology' (*Philosophie der Mythologie*) deserve special attention. Schelling had been lecturing on this topic since 1828; a final version was delivered in

Wilhelm Halbfass, *India and Europe: An Essay in Understanding* (New York: State University of New York Press, 1988), chap. 7, pp. 100–20.

1845/46. These lectures, which were published after Schelling's death, contain elaborate sections on India and other Eastern traditions, though in a distinctly critical perspective and with a clear commitment to the Christian revelation.[2]

2.

Already in Schelling's earlier works and letters, we find expressions of interest in and support for Indian and Oriental Studies, specifically in his correspondence with A. W. Schlegel.[3] A general openness for non-European and Indian thought is indicated by various statements, for instance in the *Vorlesungen über die Methode des akademischen Studiums* ('Lectures on the Method of Academic Studies', 1802). In these lectures, Schelling praises the 'sacred texts of the Indians' and suggests that they are superior to the Bible.[4]

However, specific references to Indian teachings are rare in Schelling's early works, and he did not take an active part in the Romantic glorification and exploration of India. In particular, his assessment of F. Schlegel's interpretations was very critical.[5] In his *Philosophy of Mythology*, Schelling notes that his criticism of the Romantic speculation on Indian origins of European developments started at a time when the polemical expression 'Indomania' ('Indomanie') had not yet been invented. As a documentation of his early critique, he mentions his work *Über die Gottheiten von Samothrake* ('On the Deities of Samothrake'), which was published in 1815.[6]

But regardless of what Schelling said or knew about India in his earlier years, his way of thinking suggested a certain affinity with Indian ideas, an element of 'Orientalism' which became a target of criticism as well as a source of inspiration for others.[7] In particular, Schelling's persistent fascination with ultimate identity and indifference, with a return to the Absolute, with pantheism and the 'world-soul', his readiness for a self-transcendence of philosophy, his references to 'intellectual intuition', etc. seemed to imply potential associations with India. As a further illustration, we may also quote the following definition of philosophy: 'Philosophy is the science which has for its subject, subjectively, the absolute harmony of mind with itself, objectively, the return of everything real to a common identity.'[8]

3.

Schelling develops his idea of a 'system of absolute identity' ('absolutes Identitätssystem') in his programmatic *Darstellung meines Systems der Philosophie* ('Presentation of My System of Philosophy', 1801), and as the ultimate goal of philosophy, he proclaims that 'point of indifference' which makes the absolute accessible as 'undivided' or 'absolute identity' ('ungeschiedene', 'absolute Identität').[9] 'This identity ... is not what is produced but what is original ... It is therefore already in everything which is. The power which flows forth in the mass of nature is essentially the same as that represented in the mental world.'[10] In another work, Schelling refers to such unity and identity as 'the holy abyss from which everything proceeds and into which everything returns'.[11]

Hegel criticized Schelling's notion of identity repeatedly. In the preface to his *Phenomenology of the Spirit*, he referred to 'the night in which all cows are black'.[12] Although Hegel tried to assure Schelling that this was a criticism directed against some of his followers, it was generally taken as a reference to Schelling himself.[13] Hegel also criticized Schelling's idea of the world as a 'falling off' or 'secession' ('Abfall') from the absolute, as presented, e.g., in the essay *Philosophie und Religion* ('Philosophy and Religion', 1804): 'The absolute is the only reality, the finite things are not real; therefore, their ground cannot be a transfer of reality ('Mitteilung von Realität') to them or their substrate – a transfer which would have proceeded from the absolute; it can only be a removal ('Entfernung'), a falling off ('Abfall') from the absolute ...'[14]

4.

When Schelling presented the final version of his *Philosophy of Mythology* at the University of Berlin in 1845/46, he still praised the theory of the illusory nature of the finite world, and of a 'falling off' from the absolute, as a superior idea. He now found it exemplified in the Vedānta system. Vedānta is 'nothing but the most exalted idealism or spiritualism'.[15] It sees the world as *māyā*, illusory being. In accordance with A. W. Schlegel and W. von Humboldt, Schelling postulates an etymological connection between *māyā* and *magia*, 'magic'; he also associates it with the German *Macht* ('power') and *Möglichkeit* ('potentiality'), and he explains it as 'the possibility of other-being, and thus of creating the world, as it presents itself to the creator' ('die dem Schöpfer sich selbst darstellende Möglichkeit des anders-Seins, und demnach der Welther-vorbringung') and as 'the whole essence of that capability which still rests in volition' ('das ganze Wesen jenes noch im Willen ruhenden Könnens'), i.e., the freedom of the absolute to transcend, even forget itself.[16] As 'primeval potentiality' ('Urmöglichkeit'), *māyā* is also a seductive principle, which may distract the absolute from its own timeless identity. 'The world comes into being because of a momentary self-forgetfulness ('augenblickliche Selbstvergessen-heit'), some sort of mere distraction on the part of the creator – unquestionably the highest point to which idealism, or the belief in the merely transitory and illusory reality of this world could rise without revelation in the proper sense.'[17]

However, the Upaniṣads, the authoritative basis of the Vedānta system, provide, in Schelling's words, only 'a very unsatisfactory reading'. There is, in his view, not enough theoretical clarification in these predominantly practical texts; their presentation of the unity of all reality in *brahman* is abstract. 'A positive explanation of the supreme unity is not found anywhere.'[18]

5.

Critical remarks, idiosyncratic evaluations and speculative interpretations are frequent in the more than one hundred pages of the *Philosophy of Mythology* which deal with India. But just as Hegel, Schelling does not claim to be a neutral scholar and 'expert'. His response to Indian thought and mythology is a philosophically and theologically committed response, and it cannot be measured in terms of factual accuracy alone. The *Philosophy of Mythology* is certainly not a reliable source of information about India but an event in the history of intercultural and interreligious encounters. Whatever its shortcomings may be, it is one of the great constructive attempts to deal with the spiritual history of mankind, and India holds an important position in its scheme.[19] This scheme is dominated by the idea that mythology is estranged, pagan, natural religion, yet a necessary prerequisite for true revelation. The gods of mythology are false gods: nevertheless, they express a genuine relationship to God. 'Mythology is natural religion, revelation is supernatural religion; the supernatural is not the negation of the natural, not the unnatural, but the correlate of the natural. In revelation, God is revealed to consciousness in the unity of his potencies, in the fullness of his being and in his freedom from it.'[20]

In Schelling's presentation, India (together with China) has its place between Egypt and Greece. This, however, does not imply any historical sequence or transition from one culture to the other.[21] As a profoundly mythological tradition, India is contrasted with Zoroastrian Persia, which Schelling sees as a basically unmythological tradition.[22]

The Indian mythological tradition reflects deep tensions, a process of decomposition, a yearning for unity, an initial loss of the 'truly religious principle' of monotheism.[23] Unlike many of his contemporaries, Schelling does not believe in an original monotheism, an originally pure notion of divine unity in ancient India. That tradition which is in a specific sense Indian or Hindu, was always dominated by the separation and tension of three principles or potencies, which find their expression in the *trimūrti* of Brahman (in the masculine form *brahmā*), Śiva and Viṣṇu.[24] Brahmā, the 'real God', is a God of the past, a lost and forgotten God without images and temples. Śiva dominates the Indian awareness. 'He is the destructive principle, but not in an evil sense: he destroys Brahma, who is the power of the real principle that keeps man in bondage.'[25] Viṣṇu seems to restore the lost and destroyed unity, but his concept and worship cannot recover the true sense of monotheism: Viṣṇu excludes Śiva and functions as a basically sectarian and divisive principle.

6.

Schelling discusses and rejects a view which was widely accepted in his days and had the support of authorities such as A. W. Schlegel – the theory that the neuter *brahman*, as found in the Upaniṣads and other ancient texts, represents the 'pure worship of the divine being'. According to Schelling, this abstract divine principle is not the God of monotheism, but a philosophical afterthought, a secondary, derivative phenomenon.[26] In this connection, he also criticizes the attempt of Rammohan Roy to uncover a 'pure theism' and a 'religion of reason' as the most ancient and original Indian religious teaching. In a sarcastic passage, he associates him with the rationalistic ministers of the Protestant Church who in his opinion were trying to do with the Bible what Rammohan did with the

Veda and who 'would have given him a truly brotherly reception' if he had visited Germany.[27]

In general, Schelling deplores that 'the concept of monotheism has not yet been properly defined'[28] and that it is commonly misunderstood and misused. As an example of such misuse, he cites Hegel's application of this concept to Spinoza's system.[29] According to Schelling, pantheism, abstract unitarian theism and other systems of 'rational religion' fail to recognize what is essential to monotheism: the 'factual uniqueness' ('faktische Einzigkeit') of God; such uniqueness is not a matter of abstract, ahistorical and ultimately 'negative' reasoning, but it has to be accepted as a 'positive' historical fact.[30]

7.

Against the background of Indian mythology, Schelling sees the mystical tendencies towards reunification with God, towards inclusion and extinction of the human individual as 'a natural phenomenon' ('eine natürliche Erscheinung'). 'Everything tends towards this reunification ... in which all striving, including all science is extinguished.'[31] Yoga, too, reflects this fascination with unity and union.[32] But such mystical yearning for absorption in absolute identity is itself a symptom of alienation from the God of monotheism, a response to the pervasive tension and disintegration which Schelling sees in the Indian mythological tradition. In spite of his persistent efforts to subsume the Indian phenomena under his systematic and fundamentally Christian scheme of a world history of mythology, Schelling is fully aware of the complexity of the Indian situation, as well as of uncertainties resulting from the state of research and the nature of the available sources. He refers to the fact that we know about the Indian religious and mythological ideas mainly from works produced 'by the higher, more educated castes of India.'[33] He discusses the tensions between Hinduism and Buddhism, which he calls 'the greatest riddle in the history of Indian culture';[34] but he also considers the possibility of deep and pervasive Buddhist influences on the Hindu tradition. Unlike Hegel, he is able to refer to E. Burnouf's pioneering *Introduction à l'histoire du buddhisme indien* ('Introduction to the History of Indian Buddhism', 1844).[35]

But it is not only the presence of Buddhism which accounts for the diversity of the Indian tradition: Hinduism itself, with its social stratification and its sectarian divisions, has its own inner differentiation and multiplicity. According to Schelling, one could say that 'there is not one single religion, or one single mythology in India, but rather really different religions and different mythologies.'[36] What is elsewhere divided among different nations and traditions, is in India only divided among different parts or 'organs' of one nation, one comprehensive tradition.

8.

Does Schelling's critique of the Indian tradition in the 'Philosophy of Mythology' amount to a critique or reversal of the implicitly 'orientalizing' tendencies of his own earlier thought? As we have seen, he is still fascinated with the Indian 'system of absolute identity', *Advaita Vedānta*. He calls it the 'highest point' to which idealism could rise 'without proper revelation', and we may assume that it exemplifies for him a 'higher' type of idealism than the system of his erstwhile friend Hegel.

According to Schelling, neither the Indians nor Hegel were able to grasp the truly 'positive', i.e., existence in its concreteness, the 'factuality' of the one God and of revelation.[37] Just like the Indians, Hegel was unable to comprehend the meaning of monotheism; and that his philosophy is historically more developed, more advanced in terms of reflexivity, does not mean that it is truly 'higher' than that of the Indians. On the contrary, that it is more developed means, in a sense, that it has fallen deeper into the arrogance of conceptuality and the negativity of mere reflection. Hegel's thought leaves itself to mere concepts, to thinking about thought; it posits itself as reflexivity. It is fundamentally negative, narcissistic, without 'true life':[38] 'Hegel and his followers call only that thought "pure thought" which has mere concepts as it content. This, however, one cannot call real thinking. Real thinking is such that it overcomes something that is opposed to thought.'[39]

The thinking of thinking, the unfolding of reflexivity, the attempt to supersede all presuppositions both historically and systematically – this is, in Hegel's view, the essence and direction of philosophy in the true sense, i.e., philosophy which is inseparable from the destiny of Europe. Schelling's critique of the Hegelian apotheosis of reflection is, implicitly at least, also a critique of fundamental premises of his Eurocentric universalism, or of his apotheosis of Europe.

In a curious, yet intriguing illustration of his critique, Schelling compares Hegel's conceptualism to Viṣṇu's incarnation as Vāmana, the dwarf.[40] This inconspicuous creature requests nothing more than a piece of land to be measured by three steps (Schelling says: 'feet'). Bali ('Mahabala'), the powerful demon king, grants the apparently innocent wish, and immediately finds himself deprived of his supremacy over the universe. Vāmana's 'three steps' (or 'feet') – that is Hegel's trinity of fundamental concepts 'being, nothing, becoming' ('Sein, Nichts, Werden'). Once a supposedly autonomous human reflection is allowed to claim these fundamental notions as its own categories, it will soon claim unlimited jurisdiction over the entire universe and, in a sense, devour heaven and earth.

9.

A. Schopenhauer's name is much more commonly associated with India than those of Hegel and Schelling. Indeed, it may even be said that no other Western philosopher so signalizes the turn towards India as does Schopenhauer. Within the history of philosophy, Hegel and Schopenhauer are among the notoriously contrastive figures, and this contrast, as will be demonstrated below, is quite clearly reflected in the relations between the two and India.

Whereas Hegel generally refrained from commenting on the eighteen-year younger Schopenhauer (1788–1860), Schopenhauer for his part treated his antipode Hegel to some of the sharpest invective that has been recorded in the annals of philosophy; his opposition to Schelling was equally intransigent, but more restrained.[41] He considered Hegel as having a 'completely worthless, indeed, thoroughly pernicious mind,' as being a 'crude and disgusting charlatan,' a 'scribbler of rubbish and a corrupter of minds'; his philosophy was 'confused, empty verbiage,' a 'philosophy of absolute nonsense'.[42] He did, however, not comment explicitly on Hegel's interpretation of Indian thought. It is obvious that personal elements were involved in Schopenhauer's criticism of Hegel. Nevertheless, there was also strain enough in the factual department; and in both what they shared and what kept them apart, and specifically in their relationships to India and the non-European world in general, the two reflect the ambivalence which typified nineteenth-century Europe. Both simultaneously stood in a peculiar and ambiguous relationship to the Romantic movement.

Yet it is not our intention to present a comprehensive comparison of Schopenhauer and Hegel, nor of Schopenhauer and Indian philosophy, nor shall we attempt to reconstruct an accurate developmental history of Schopenhauer's personal relationship to India.[43] Instead, we shall primarily concern ourselves with Schopenhauer's basic hermeneutical position vis-à-vis India and the role which Indian ideas played in his own philosophical thinking and self-understanding.

10.

Schopenhauer's interest in India was awakened early by the Orientalist F. Majer,[44] who was effective as a recruiter for India among the Romantics and was himself influenced by Herder. During the almost three decades in which Schopenhauer outlived Hegel, he became aware of material, especially in the area of Buddhism, to which Hegel could never have had access. Yet like Hegel, and unlike the Schlegel brothers or W. von Humboldt, Schopenhauer never made an effort ot learn Sanskrit, although he repeatedly glorified the excellence of this language and the rewards of mastering it.[45] As noted above, he became acquainted with the Upaniṣads through Anquetil Duperron's Latin translation (*Oupnek'hat*, 1801/1802) of the Persian version made under Dārā Shukōh.[46] Throughout his life, he clung to the belief that this was a definitive achievement and the key to a philosophical understanding of the Upaniṣads; it was 'the most rewarding and edifying reading (with the exception of the original text) that could be possible in this world; it has been the solace of my life and will be the solace of my death.'[47] He greeted the subsequent direct translations by H. Th. Colebrooke and H. E. Röer, and especially those of Rammohan Roy, with suspicion and dismissal.[48] He found theistic and Europeanizing corruptions in these works, and was not ready to accept them as a basis for reexamining or revising his own opinion of the Upaniṣads. In general, the Upaniṣads, together with the knowledge of Buddhism he later acquired, remained decisive for his views on the nature and value of the Indian tradition. While he did indeed make note of those works that appeared in European languages and which did not necessarily suit his enthusiasm, his interest and his esteem were nevertheless quite selective and generally limited to the literature on religion and philosophy, insofar as he was able to apply them to his own basic metaphysical doctrines.

11.

Schopenhauer exhibited little interest in Indian art, *belles-letters*, and so on.[49] He described the portions of the *Ṛgveda* and *Sāmaveda* which he knew from the translations by F. Rosen and J. Stevenson as 'completely insipid reading'.[50] While he generally noted attentively all publications on Indian philosophy, and was also acquainted with Colebrooke's treatises, such systems as the Nyāya and the Vaiśeṣika remained outside the circle of his interests, and he did not treat them in his writings.[51] Among the works on Buddhism with which he worked, those of I. J. Schmidt, Spence Hardy, C. F. Koeppen, and E. Burnouf should be mentioned.[52]

How his knowledge of the Indian material was related to the genesis of Schopenhauer's own system is a question which cannot be answered with complete clarity and certainty; his own explicit remarks, in any case, do not provide a sufficient basis for answering it. Yet one contradiction which he is often accused of in this regard vanishes when a distinction is made between the references Schopenhauer made to Buddhism and those he made to Hinduism. In 1856, referring to Spence Hardy's *Eastern Monachism* and *Manual of Buddhism*, he remarked to his disciple A. von Doss in the following fashion about the relationship of his philosophy to Buddhism: 'On the whole, the harmony with my teachings is wonderful, all the more so because I wrote the first volume (of *Die Welt als Wille und Vorstellung*) between 1814 and 1818 and did not, nor could not, have known of all that.'[53] Yet he did have contact with F. Majer and had been exposed to the impression of Indian thought since the turn of the year 1813–14. In 1816, in fact, he wrote during the production of the first volume of his main work: 'By the way, I admit that I do not believe that my doctrine could have ever been formulated before the Upaniṣads, Plato, and Kant were able to all cast their light simultaneously onto a human mind.'[54] Naturally, the second edition of *The World as Will and Representation*, published in 1844 in two volumes, contains numerous Indological additions and emendations. Schopenhauer notes the great advances of Buddhist studies between the two editions of his work. He is now aware that his original references to *nirvāṇa* (or 'nieban', according to Burmese sources) were inadequate, and he presents the following more differentiated statement on the 'denial' of the will and its correspondence with *nirvāṇa*: 'The Buddhists with complete frankness describe the matter negatively as *nirvāṇa*, which is the negation of this world or of *saṃsāra*. If *nirvāṇa* is defined as nothing, this means only that *saṃsāra* contains no single element that could serve to define or to construct *nirvāṇa*.'[55]

12.

Schopenhauer's concern with ancient Indian wisdom was also a concern with something incipient and pristine. This did not, to be sure, conform with the Romantic glorification of childhood and yearning for a lost home; even less did it have to do with the Hegelian retrospective attitude towards a supposedly undeveloped and static phase of historical inchoation. For Schopenhauer, there was no such thing as a lost paradise, nor did he recognize a Hegelian sense of direction in history. He saw no pure primal cause, and no lost or decayed totality or harmony. On the other hand, history could not be conceived of as an unfolding system exhibiting progress and structure, nor was there any teleology of ascending and self-surpassing phases in the phenomenology of the spirit. For Schopenhauer, history was ultimately meaningless, a 'farce' without aim or direction. Hegel's attempt 'to understand world history as a systematic whole' was, in Schopenhauer's eyes, the symptom of a naive and 'trivial' realism that was unable to see beyond the 'farce' of historical events and the coming and going of historical individuals, and unable to distinguish appearances or ideas from the true nature of the world, since it 'believed that history, its configurations and occurrences, were what counted'.[56]

In contrast to the Christian doctrine of salvation and, more generally, as opposed to linear views of time and history, he extolled the recurrent periods of the world which he found in the Buddhist teachings, the 'thousand Buddhas', and the possibility of a redemption that was not tied to a unique and non-recurrent event.[57] The world does indeed unfold, yet this unfolding has neither a determinable beginning nor a direction nor a purpose. Schopenhauer's central concept was that of the will, which evolves blindly and leaves thought no other goal than to deny and undo this evolution.

Whatever may come to pass in the world, its true cause is blind, its purpose merely a projection of this blindness, and its meaning and substance remain within the realm of appearance or representation. ' "The world is my idea." ... Thus, no truth is more certain and more independent of all the others and less in need of proof than this: that all that is available to knowledge, i.e., the entire world, is simply object in relation to subject ... Everything that does and can belong to the world in any way is inescapably tied to this conditionality through the subject and is therefore only for the subject. The world is idea.'[58] It is an idea for a subject which, for its part, is not objectifiable, i.e., is not in space and time and cannot be defined through such categories as unity, multiplicity, etc.

13.

As an idea, the world is subject to certain conditions which Schopenhauer found to have been fundamentally revealed in Kant's Transcendental Philosophy and which he traced back to the four-fold figure of the principle of sufficient reason.[59] This principle has a four-fold figure or 'root' insofar as it refers to four fundamental types of necessary relationships: 1. As the principle of sufficient reason for being, it is concerned with the perceptual forms of space and time. 2. As the principle of sufficient reason for becoming, it refers to the domain of physical causality. 3. As the principle of sufficient reason for knowledge, it has to do with the domains of the truth and falsity of propositions, with the connection between propositions and facts. 4. As the principle of sufficient reason for action, it refers to causality in the form of motivation. As a whole, the principle of sufficient reason describes the fundamental structure of our world as well as our cognitive abilities, and encompasses the domain of 'the context of experience', which, in the terms of Kant's Transcendental Philosophy, is determined *a priori* by forms of perception and categories, in other words, the domain of the possible objects of our empirical knowledge and our practical life.

As noted above, the world of objects, at least to the extent that they are subjected to this ordering principle, is mere appearance: it is a projection of the 'thing in itself', the metaphysical basis of the world, which Schopenhauer identified as blind will. The manner in which this absolute will, lying as it does beyond the jurisdiction of the principle of sufficient reason, objectifies itself in the forms of appearance of our world, receives its most thorough treatment in the second book of *Die Welt als Wille und Vorstellung*. The *one* will produces its effects through a succession or hierarchy of objectifications, of forms of spatiotemporal existence. Devoid of any kind of historical teleology, this hierarchy leads from the realm of the inorganic to the higher and more complex forms of organic conscious life, i.e., to increasingly higher and more complex forms of self-assertion and the struggle against others. Within this hierarchy, thought, 'the mental', retains an essentially instrumental role; whether implicitly or explicitly, it stands in the service of self-assertion, of the will to live.

14.

The will itself knows no purpose and no direction. Once the emptiness and aimlessness of its objectifications has been understood, there is no other meaningful and legitimate goal than to achieve their cancellation, and to destroy all forms of attachment to them. The drive of the will to live and to assert and preserve oneself has to be discontinued, so that it may withdraw itself, and its projections and objectifications collapse within themselves. In Schopenhauer's eyes, art and the aesthetic experience represent a temporary repose in this blind, egoistic drive. Moreover, the projections of egoism are also pierced by the phenomenon of compassion, which is in itself the key to ethics: through compassion, the multiplicity and variety of individuals become visible and transparent as being merely apparent, and the power of egoism wanes. The unity at the world's foundations reveals itself without, however, being understood and clearly seen as such. According to Schopenhauer, it is the task of philosophic thought, and especially his own definitive achievement, to clarify theoretically and explain metaphysically the actual phenomena of aesthetics and ethics, while simultaneously creating a comprehensive theoretical basis for soteriological praxis.

Schopenhauer saw his own philosophy as the perfection of Kantian thought. From its heights, one could survey, ponder, and assess what his predecessors as well as his contemporaries had brought to philosophy. Yet he rejected the Hegelian integration of the system and history of philosophy, and saw no scheme of reflection according to which a succession of cultural traditions and philosophical theories could be construed and following which Indian and European thought could legitimately be coordinated with or subordinated to one another. His approach to Indian philosophy was, so to speak, that of a 'recognitive historiography of philosophy' ('wiedererkennende Philosophiegeschichte')[60] which remained open to the possibility of finding the same insights in the most diverse historical contexts. Schopenhauer felt that the basic ideas of his philosophy viz., the doctrine of the 'world as will and representation', of a fundamental unity of reality and an apparent projection into spatiotemporal multiplicity, could be found among the Indians, and not just in the form of historical antecedents, but in a sense of truth which knows no historical and geographical restrictions.

15.

Schopenhauer's notion of philosophy is utterly incompatible with the characterization which Hegel presents in the introduction of his 'Philosophy of Right' (*Philosophie des Rechts*), i.e., 'its time comprised in thought' ('ihre Zeit in Gedanken erfasst'). The 'metaphysical urge' makes no reference to time, and its essential aim is everywhere the same: to pierce the veil of spatiotemporal multiplicity and to provide liberation from the cycle of life and suffering. The same motif is able to nourish religious aspirations for salvation just as it can affect philosophical thought; in Christianity, too, it played an important role, although often obscured and suppressed.

Schopenhauer found exemplary expressions of this motif in the Indian concept of *māyā*, in the *tat tvam asi* ('that art thou') of the Upaniṣads, and in the Buddhist goal of *nirvāṇa* – of peace without rebirth, a return into the state of non-becoming. He made repeated use of these concepts and formulas in order to illustrate and even to express his own thoughts. He considered the concept of *māyā* to be the equivalent of his notion of *principium individuationis*,[61] the 'principle of individuation'. In his view, 'the *māyā* of the Vedas ... and the "appearance" of Kant' were identical; they were 'the world in which we live', or 'we ourselves, to the extent that we belong to this world'.[62] He was convinced that both the Indian concept of *māyā* and Kant's 'appearance' were included in his own concept of the objectification of the will, i.e., the realm of validity of the principle of sufficient reason, and that it was here that their true meaning and identity was made manifest.[63]

Schopenhauer often invoked Indian thought when he wished to illustrate what he saw as the central relationship between ethics and metaphysics. As early as 1813, while working on his doctoral dissertation, he formulated his principle of a 'philosophy which should be at once ethics and metaphysics'.[64] He attempted to achieve such a unified system of thought by anchoring the fundamental ethical phenomenon of compassion in a metaphysics of identity which he found exemplified in the Vedānta. He repeatedly explained that for him, 'the foundation of morals ultimately rests upon that truth' which was expressed in the Upaniṣadic formula *tat tvam asi* ('that art thou').[65]

16.

Schopenhauer also repeatedly referred to the Buddhist concept of *nirvāṇa*, which he considered to be mainly a negative idea that agreed in essence with his own goal of liberation from the blind forces of will. Since *nirvāṇa*, the transcendence and denial of all worldly experience (*saṃsāra*), expresses a more radical sense of freedom and negation, he tended to prefer this concept to the metaphysical and soteriological terminology of Hinduism.[66] He found too much unnecessary mythological fiction in the Hindu concepts of *brahman*, *jīvātman*, *paramātman*, etc., and the doctrine of the reunion of the individual soul with *brahman* (which when referring to the neuter, he generally rendered as 'Brahm').[67] Still, he saw no reason to doubt that the Vedāntic idea of *brahman* also fundamentally corresponded to the theory of the cosmic will which he himself expounded, and he made repeated attempts to find a meaning for the word *brahman* that would approximate his own 'will'. In doing so, he referred to Max Müller's statement that *brahman* originally meant 'force, will, wish, and the propulsive power of creation'.[68] He greeted the translations of Tamil Vedāntic works published in K. Graul's 'Bibliotheca tamulica' with 'great joy and edification' because he saw his own teachings reflected in them 'as in a mirror'.[69] Time and again, he interpreted Buddhist concepts as precise analogies of his own teachings. Referring to Spence Hardy, for example, he declared that *upādāna* could be understood as the 'will to live,' and *karman* as 'empirical character.'[70]

Schopenhauer's basic position was: 'in general, the sages of all times have always said the same.'[71] Making explicit reference to his own thought, he stated that 'Buddha, Eckhardt, and I all teach essentially the same.'[72] And speaking of the results of his own thought, he explained that they corresponded 'with the most ancient of all world views, namely, the Vedas.'[73] In like manner, he found himself in agreement with what he called the 'majority' of religious humanity, i.e., the Buddhists; occasionally, he even referred to himself as a Buddhist.[74] In claiming these and other correspondences, he was not concerned with the external forms and specific historical manifestations of such teachings, but rather with their 'inner sense and spirit'.[75] Here again, Schopenhauer proved himself to be the antipode of Hegel, for Hegel, as we have already seen, considered any comparisons and parallelizations which disregarded historical particularities to be abstract and void. Yet even prior to this, I. Kant, whom Schopenhauer claimed as his own great predecessor, had stated that 'since human reason has been enraptured by innumerable objects in various ways for many centuries, it cannot easily fail that for everything new, something old can be found which has some kind of similarity to it.'[76]

17.

In spite of his penchant for fundamental parallelizations and for rediscovering his own philosophical convictions in ancient Indian thought, the manner in which Schopenhauer related his own philosophy and his own position as a nineteenth-century European to the Indian tradition remained ambivalent in many respects.

On the one hand, he found correspondences and parallels within what was essentially a timeless and non-historical frame and outside all questions concerning genesis and historical derivation. Ideas of progress or regress had no place here; for Schopenhauer, history was metaphysically irrelevant and without purpose. He could not concern himself with discovering an order or sense of direction while gathering together the metaphysical insights and the expressions of a 'metaphysical urge' that were scattered throughout the various cultures and historical epochs. On the other hand, Schopenhauer also viewed India in accordance with the Romantic speculations, as the land of the most ancient and most pristine wisdom, the place from which Europeans could trace their descent and the tradition by which they had been influenced in so many decisive ways, and yet behind which they had also fallen. He was convinced that Christianity had 'Indian blood in its veins',[77] especially insofar as it distinguished itself from the world-affirming tradition of Judaism, i.e., in its tendencies to denounce the world, in its asceticism and pessimism. 'In contrast, the New Testament (i.e., as compared to the Old Testament) must somehow be of Indian origin: this is attested to by its completely Indian ethics, which transforms morals into asceticism, its pessimism, and its *avatār* (i.e., the person of Christ).'[78]

Occasionally and somewhat ironically, Schopenhauer even claimed that his own philosophy could be called 'the truly Christian philosophy' ('die eigentliche christliche Philosophie').[79] Just as Sanskrit opens up a more basic understanding of Greek and Latin, in like manner is a knowledge of Brahmanism and Buddhism the prerequisite for any real understanding of Christianity. Schopenhauer also thought to have found Indian elements in Egyptian religion, in Neoplatonism, etc.[80] In accordance with the Romantic view of India, he characterized the Indians as the 'most noble and ancient people' and their wisdom as the 'original wisdom of the human race' ('Urweisheit des Menschengeschlechts').[81] He also spoke of the 'original religion of our race' ('Urreligion unseres Geschlechts') and 'the oldest of all world views'[82] as being native to India, and of India itself as the 'fatherland of mankind' ('Vaterland des Menschengeschlechts').[83] Moreover, it was his hope that the European 'peoples who stemmed from Asia ... would also reattain the holy religions of their home.'[84]

The signs of downfall and degeneration which he saw in the later Indian developments were, fully in accordance with Anquetil Duperron, blamed primarily upon the predominance of Islam.[85]

18.

Along with this historical assessment of the Indian tradition, certain problems and ambiguities arise with respect to the manner in which Schopenhauer assessed his own thought and his own philosophical achievements in relation to the wisdom of ancient India. On the one hand, he took the great age of Upaniṣadic thought (an age which he overestimated) as a sign of its special venerability, as justification of a superior claim to truth, and as indication of an immediacy and originality that was later lost. The Vedas – whereby he was, of course, primarily referring to the Upaniṣads – were the 'fruit of the most sublime human knowledge and wisdom' and documents of 'almost superhuman conception'. Their authors could 'hardly be thought of as mere mortals'.[86]

Instead, 'this direct enlightenment of their spirit' should perhaps 'be attributed to the fact . . . that these sages, standing as they did closer to the time of the origin of our race, comprehended the essence of things more clearly and profoundly than the already weakened stock, οιοι νυν βϱοτοι ειϭιν, was able to.'[87] The best that we, the later generations, could hope for was as complete a rediscovery of these origins as possible. Indeed, this seems to be implied in Schopenhauer's prediction that a new Renaissance would be inaugurated by the study of the Indian tradition. He expected the influx of Indian wisdom into Europe to bring about 'a fundamental change and reorientation of our thought'; the 'influence of Sanskrit literature' would, so he felt, impinge upon our lives in a way no less significant than the 'resuscitation of the Greek language during the fifteenth century'.[88] As a measure of the quality of his own philosophical work, he invoked, as we have seen, its special closeness to the age-old wisdom of the Indians.

19.

On the other hand, Schopenhauer also claimed to have made considerable progress with respect to the systematic coherence of his thought and the clarity of its presentation. Indeed, he was convinced that he had discovered and systematically unfolded the metaphysical principle that had remained hidden to the Vedic 'patriarchs' ('Urväter'), although it was implied in their teachings: 'the Vedas, or rather the Upaniṣads, . . . have no scientific form, no presentation that is systematic in any way . . . Yet when one has grasped the teachings which I have advanced, one may afterwards derive all of those most ancient Indian statements as conclusions and then recognize their truth, so that it must be assumed that what I have recognized to be the truth had also been grasped by those sages at the beginning of earthly time and uttered according to their fashion, even if it did not become clear to them in its unity.'[89] In the Upaniṣads we are faced with 'solitary and abstract statements', which may be explained through recourse to the basic concepts of *The World as Will and Representation*, 'although the reverse, that these could already be found there, by no means holds'.[90] He repeatedly accused the thinkers of ancient India of having deviated into 'myths and meaningless words'.[91] Thus, Schopenhauer did not try to validate his teachings by referring to the authority of the Indian sources; instead, he presented his own thought as the standard and fulfilment of the Indian teachings. Schopenhauer, too, saw himself as standing on a pinnacle of knowledge, albeit a different peak from Hegel's. From there, he tried to bring 'sense into the matter' ('Verstand in die Sache') of Indian thought[92] and uncover its true meaning and implications, which had been hidden to the Indians themselves. Accordingly, Indian philosophy appears not so much as a source of inspiration or revelation, but rather as a mirror and medium of self-representation and self-confirmation. In another context, Schopenhauer called it a general rule that anybody who establishes a 'new philosophical system', declares 'all previous attempts to have failed'.[93] Nevertheless, even if it did not attain complete clarity and perfect systematization, Indian thought, and especially Buddhism, was still superior to all that was possible within the framework of Christian religiousness. 'Buddha, Eckhardt, and I all teach essentially the same.' To this sentence, which we have already quoted above, Schopenhauer added the following words: 'Eckhardt within the bonds of his Christian mythology. In Buddhism, these ideas are not encumbered by any such mythology, and are thus simple and clear, to the extent that a religion can be clear. Complete clarity lies with me.'[94]

20.

Schopenhauer was deeply convinced of the originality and unprecedented explanatory power of his philosophical system: 'My work is a new philosophical system; but new in the full sense of the word: not a new presentation of something already existing, but rather a series of thoughts that are coherent to the highest degree and that have not entered any human head until now.'[95] Schopenhauer claimed that his philosophy did not merely explain natural phenomena by referring to *one* underlying principle, but also put the ideas of the past into place with respect to just *one* interpretive point of view. He was convinced that it provided what may be termed a metaphysical key to the full understanding of these ideas, moreover, an understanding which fulfilled their own intentions. Of course, this was not an Hegelian scheme of historical inclusion and subordination, yet it nonetheless provided a framework and context for exegesis and appropriation which countered the Hegelian procedure with a universalism of a different kind.

But in contrast to Hegel, and in spite of all the claims to originality which he made for himself, Schopenhauer did not consign Indian thought to an antecedent and subordinate position with respect to our own. Even when, as he was convinced, his own thought had given that of India its definitive clarification and completion (an achievement which Kant had helped prepare), in his mind,

Indian thought did not merely belong to the prehistory of Christian-European thought. For he saw it as a corrective and alternative that was in many ways superior to the one-sidedness and aberrations of the Western, i.e., primarily Judaeo-Christian tradition and its theistic and personalistic orientation. As an encouragement and stimulus for his own thought, which was incompatible with the spirit of his time and opposed to the ideas of the person and the personal God, Indian thought certainly had a significant impact upon Schopenhauer's personal development. In this sense, Indian thought was obviously 'more important' for him than for Hegel.

21.

Although it could not have brought Schopenhauer on to the path which was to lead him to his metaphysics of the *will*, and even though the essential points of his own thinking had probably been taking shape before he had ever even heard of the work, the *Oupnek'hat* nevertheless had an enduring and far-reaching effect upon Schopenhauer's life and thought. Yet all too frequently, the fact is overlooked that his encounter with the *Oupnek'hat* was by no means a purely 'Indian' encounter. It was also an encounter with Anquetil Duperron's own ways of thinking and interpreting, with his methods of comparing and paralle-lizing, and with the manner in which he incorporated the Upaniṣads into the context of contemporary European philosophy. Anquetil himself had repeat-edly asserted and attempted to demonstrate that the sages of all countries and all times have basically 'always said the same' or at least meant the same, and that the Upaniṣads in particular have parallels in European doctrines. It is especially remarkable that Kant was very explicitly cited in these comparisons, indeed, an entire 'Parergon' of the first volume was devoted to the relationship between Kantianism and the Upaniṣads.[96] There, Anquetil claimed that the two do not greatly differ with respect to their emphasis upon man's self-discovery and return to his own inner reality. This postulated affinity was significant not just for Schopenhauer alone, but also far beyond; we notice its echoes even in modern Indian thought. Of course, Anquetil could not have known of Schopenhauer when he drew up his list of German philosophers whom he hoped to see as students and interpreters of the *Oupnek'hat*. Schopenhauer's stubborn adherence to the *Oupnek'hat* in the face of all the European transla-tions of the Upaniṣads which he subsequently became aware of is certainly also an expression of approval for the very personal and explicitly philosophical approach of Anquetil.

While Schopenhauer proclaimed the concordance of his philosophy with the teachings of Vedānta and Buddhism, he also recognized, although less con-spicuously, its factual inseparability from the history of European philosophy: 'What I have to present agrees very precisely with the ancient Indain utterances. Yet it is also connected with the entire development of philosophy in the Occident; it is a continuation of its history; in a sense, it follows from it as its result.'[97] Indeed, Schopenhauer no less than Hegel is a European thinker of the nineteenth century. His critique of the European tradition, of the ideas of history and progress shows us the other side of the nineteenth century. It negates, but also supplements the Hegelian consummation of European thought. Schopenhauer, too, is 'a son of his time'.

22.

Is it true that Schopenhauer's thought, as has been claimed, represents an entirely new synthesis between East and West? Is it true that with him 'the stream of Indian thought flows into the spirit of Europe with an unprecedented force and depth'? Did he really show the way to the 'unfolding of a new Europe'?[98] And were the Orient and the Occident truly united in his thought?[99] Or was he in the end nothing but a 'crank' ('Querkopf') and 'querulous pessimist' ('Entrüstungspessimist')?[100] Is his alliance with the ancient Vedic past and with the Buddhist 'majority' of religious mankind a reflection of an anti-European, anti-Hegelian resentment and indignation? Does he use the Indian tradition as a mirror of his own, though negative, Eurocentrism? In what sense is his usage and interpretation of Indian concepts different from the abstract and evasive 'comparison' and 'equalization' of generalities which Hegel criticized?

In order to clarify these questions and to assess Schopenhauer's significance for the encounter between India and Europe, it is not sufficient to examine the philological 'correctness' of his usage of Indian terms, or to balance the 'Indian' against the 'non-Indian' elements of his thought. More or less successful attempts of this kind have been made by H. von Glasenapp, I. Vecchiotti and J. W. Sedlar.[101] Whatever the merits of these attempts may be, they cannot do justice to the philosophical and hermeneutical dimensions of Schopenhauer's response to India. Moreover, we should not only rely on Schopenhauer's own programmatic claims and statements, or on his explicit self-interpretation. In order to do justice to his historical and philosophical potential, it may occasionally be necessary to defend him not only against his successors and devotees, but also against his own idiosyncratic self-presentation.

23.

The concepts of *māyā*, *brahman* and *jīva*, *parkṛti* and *puruṣa*, *karman* and *upādāna*, *saṃsāra* and *nirvāṇa* are familiar to all serious students of Schopenhauer. Does his usage of these concepts contribute to a better understanding of their original Indian meaning? Does it, on the other hand, contribute to the clarification and better understanding of his own philosophy? What is the significance of these concepts for Schopenhauer's self-understanding and for the articulation of his metaphysical thinking?

Schopenhauer seems convinced that his own concepts and insights provide the definitive tools to explicate and clarify the true implications of the Indian teachings. For himself he claims that systematic clarity which he finds missing in the ancient Indian teachings. Does this mean that he always uses his own

European concepts as measures of truth, clarity and validity, and never considers the possibility of re-examining their meaning and validity in the light of Indian ideas? Numerous statements suggest a positive answer to this question; yet his approach is more ambiguous than his explicit self-representation seems to indicate. There is more openness; there is a certain cautious and implicit readiness to re-examine and re-articulate his own ideas, and perhaps even to 'bring sense into the matter' of his own thought, by referring to Indian concepts. Schopenhauer's central notion of the 'will', and his varying attempts to associate it with Indian ideas, may help us to illustrate this point.

24.

The problems inherent in this notion, in the relationship between 'will' and 'knowledge', and in the enigmatic possibility of a 'negation', i.e., self-negation of the will, have often been emphasized. To some extent, Schopenhauer's own statements have been conducive to misunderstandings and confusions, in particular to the familiar, yet inappropriate metaphysical equation of 'will' and 'absolute'.[102] Schopenhauer himself frequently characterizes the will as 'thing in itself'; he seems to claim that he has discovered the 'ultimate reality' behind all appearances, the unknown absolute which Kant failed to identify, the transcendent cause of the world. On several occasions, however, he sharply rejects this interpretation which his own formulations seem to suggest. He insists that his philosophy is immanent, not transcendent: 'It teaches what appearance is, and what the thing in itself is. But this is thing in itself only in a relative sense, i.e., in its relation to appearances . . . but I have never said what the thing in itself is apart from that relation, since I do not know it; but in it, it is the will to life.'[103]

In this sense, the 'will' is not a transcendent absolute, but the immanent principle of the world of objects and representations, its inner essence and most fundamental condition which we can experience in ourselves. We may even say that it is a new interpretation of the Kantian idea of the conditions of the possibility of experience. 'Everybody finds himself as this will, in which consists the inner essence of the world.'[104] The world is a constellation of causally interrelated representations, of means and ends, of more or less complex forms of power and domination. In it, the will is 'the most real entity which we know' ('das Allerrealste, was wir kennen').[105] It upholds and perpetuates this world of appearances by accepting and affirming it. It is not its absolute cause (which would be a contradiction in terms). Schopenhauer consistently uses the term 'absolute' in a pejorative sense.[106]

25.

The 'negation of the will' ('Verneinung des Willens') is not 'destruction of a substance' ('Vernichtung einer Substanz') but a subjective act, an event of self-transformation and of withdrawal from the world of experience and cognition: '. . . the same entity which has willed so far wills no more. Since we know this entity, the will, as thing in itself only in and through the act of willing, we are not able to say or grasp what it is and does after it has relinquished this act.'[107] 'The essence in itself which may or may not, at its own discretion, express itself as will and thereby as world – this essence in itself, seen in isolation (i.e., in an absolute sense; 'dieses Wesen an sich ausserdem betrachtet'), is not accessible to any possible cognition . . . since cognition is only in the world, just as the world is only in cognition.'[108]

We can transcend the world by withdrawing the will from it, i.e., in radical soteriological self-transformation. However, we cannot objectify or explain theoretically this practical, soteriological step. The will exists, insofar as we are attached to, and engaged in, the world of representations which is its projection. It is released from existence, insofar as we are no longer committed to the world, and disengage ourselves from the network of means and ends, as well as from all claims of theoretical, representational mastery and domination.

26.

'I have named the thing in itself, the inner essence of the world, in accordance with what we know best: as will. This, however, is an expression which has been chosen subjectively, i.e., with reference to the subject of cognition. But since we are dealing with cognition, this reference is essential. Thus it is infinitely better than calling it Brahm or Brahmā or world soul or whatever.'[109] In this statement, Schopenhauer counts *brahman* among those dogmatic and mythological conceptions of a first cause and absolute principle with which he contrasts his immanent will. Elsewhere, however, he states that 'Brahmaism and Buddhism' are free from the Jewish-Christian 'recourse to an unconditional cause'.[110] In general, he does not simply relegate the numerous Indian concepts with which he associates his doctrine of the will to a lower or more mythological level of understanding.

Among these concepts, we find the Vedic *asu* as well as the Nyāya-Vaiśeṣika notion of (*pra*) *yatna*, i.e., 'effort', 'initiative'.[111] In both concepts, he seeks support for his idea of a 'will' which expresses itself not only in deliberate actions, but also in unconscious physiological or biological processes. He sees the Buddhist concept of *upādāna*, i.e., attachment to the world and self-identification with worldly objects, as a precise equivalent of his 'will to life'. *Karman* is the 'individual will without the intellect', that which appears as 'empirical character'.[112] He is convinced that his 'will' corresponds to the true meaning of the Sāṃkhya concept of *prakṛti*, 'nature,' i.e., the blind cosmic energy which is contrasted with *puruṣa*, the pure spirit and 'witness.'[113] Occasionally, Schopenhauer also mentions the Vedānta concept of *māyā* as an equivalent of his will; later on he specifies that it is not so much the will itself, but rather its 'objectness' ('Objektität').[114]

27.

The concept of *brahman*, for which he postulates an etymological meaning 'force, will, wish',[115] is Schopenhauer's most important Indian point of reference. In particular, it illustrates the deeply problematic relationship between affirmation and negation of the will, and it plays a paradigmatic role in Schopenhauer's understanding of India. Just as we are the will, so *brahman* is ultimately identical with ourselves. The creation of the world, 'a sinful act of brahman', is ultimately nothing but our own worldly attitude, our commitment to the network of representations, causes, means and ends, which the Vedāntins associate with the concepts of *māyā* and *avidyā*.[116] However, the *brahman* which unfolds itself into the world is not the true and complete *brahman*. 'According to the doctrine of the Veda, only one quarter of *brahman* is incarnated in the world, and three quarters remain free from it, as blissful *brahman* ('seliges Brahm'). The visual representative of this latter *brahman*, or more properly speaking, of the negation of the will to life against its affirmation, is the infinite space against the finite world in which the affirmation objectifies itself, and which in spite of its dizzying size is infinitely small.'[117]

The variety of Indian concepts with which Schopenhauer associates his concept of will exemplifies not only the extent and limits of his understanding of Indian materials, specifically of Buddhism and Vedānta, but also the ambivalence and problematic nature of his concept of will itself. Insofar, it illustrates not only his awareness of India, but can also help to clarify his own philosophy. Schopenhauer's invocation of Vedānta and Buddhism is most genuine and significant in connection with his doctrine of the negation of the will, which even his devoted follower J. Frauenstädt called the 'Achilles heel' of the system.[118] More than other traditions the Indian tradition provides him with documents of an 'immediate experience' ('unmittelbare Erfahrung') of true resignation and 'releasement' ('Gelassenheit') to which he does not and cannot add any attempts of theoretical explanation. His own philosophical and theoretical approach to the 'negation of the will' is inevitably 'abstract', 'general' and 'cold'.[119] Those who understand its true and concrete meaning are the practitioners of detachment and self-liberation, i.e., the yogins and sannyāsins who forget the entire world 'and themselves with it'. What remains in their state of awareness or being is the 'primal essence' ('Urwesen') itself.[120]

28.

Regardless of the adequacy of Schopenhauer's interpretations and conceptual equations, he showed an unprecedented readiness to integrate Indian ideas into his own, European thinking and self-understanding, and to utilize them for the illustration, articulation and clarification of his own teachings and problems. With this, he combined a radical critique of some of the most fundamental presuppositions of the Judaeo-Christian tradition, such as the notions of a personal God, the uniqueness of the human individual and the meaning of history, as well as the modern Western belief in the powers of the intellect, rationality, planning and progress. The intellect is in the service of the will; rationality itself is blind. The intellect is committed to the world as representation. It functions in the context of means and ends, but it has no ultimate goal or direction. Schopenhauer's doctrine of the will implies a critique of the European tradition of representational and rational thinking, of calculation and planning, science and technology which foreshadows much more recent developments. In spite of Heidegger's emphatic dissociation from Schopenhauer, it may even remind us of the Heideggerian critique of European metaphysics.[121]

The familiar association of Schopenhauer's thought with 'pessimism' and 'irrationalism' has not been conducive to an appreciation of the more subtle and ambivalent elements of his approach to the Indian tradition. It is also one of the reasons why the response from the Indian side has in general been rather reserved and superficial. Modern Indian thinkers, such as Vivekananda and Radhakrishnan, have tried to free the Indian tradition from the 'stigma' of pessimism and escapism. Radhakrishnan defended the Upaniṣads and the Vedānta against the pessimistic and other-worldly interpretation which he associated with Schopenhauer. In his view, modern European pessimism, as exemplified by Schopenhauer and E. von Hartmann, is nothing but a vulgarized Buddhism.[122] An Indian scholar of the nineteenth century, the great Indologist Rajendralal Mitra, thought that Schopenhauer's doctrine of the will and Hartmann's concept of the unconscious had been anticipated by the classical Yoga system.[123]

Schopenhauer's influence on the development of 'comparative philosophy' has, at least indirectly, been considerable. However, the Indian advocates of this approach have generally paid much less attention to Schopenhauer than to Hegel, the great critic of transhistorical and cross-cultural comparison and equalization.

NOTES

1. The great poet F. Hölderlin was the third member of this group of friends.
2. They were published as volumes 1 and 2 of the 'second division' of Schelling's collected works, in the edition of his son, K. F. A. Schelling (i.e., *Sämmtliche Werke*, II/1–2, Stuttgart and Augsburg 1856–7, hereinafter cited as *S. W.*).
3. See, for instance, *Briefe und Dokumente*, ed. H. Fuhrmans, vol. 2, (Bonn 1962), 414. (letter to A. W. Schlegel); supporting the idea of 'a complete Oriental academy' ('eine ganze orientalische Akademie').
4. These lectures were first published in 1803; see also H. von Glasenapp, *Indienbild*, 34f.
5. See *Briefe und Dokumente*, ed. H. Fuhrmans, vol. 3, (Bonn 1975), 616f. (letter to Windischmann). See also J. W. Sedlar, *India in the Mind of Germany: Schelling, Schopenhauer and Their Times*, (Washington, DC, 1982).
6. Cf. *S. W.* II/1, 23, note 1; also II/2, 431ff. (criticism of the notion of an Indian 'Urvolk', or 'original', 'primeval nation', and specifically of the speculations of P. von Bohlen and A. H. L. Heeren concerning Indian influences on Egypt).
7. See W. Halbfass, *India and Europe*, ch. 8.
8. *Propädeutik der Philosophie* (1804); *S. W.* I/6, 78 (in the translation by F. de W. Bolman; see his introduction to: Schelling, *The Ages of the World*, (New York, 1942), repr. 1967, 18. See also Bolman's notes on Schelling's evaluation of 'traditional and mystical empiricism', 41ff.).
9. See *S. W.* I/4, 113.
10. *S. W.* I/4, 128; as translated by F. de W. Bolman (see above, n. 8), 16.

11. *Bruno oder über das göttliche und natürliche Princip der Dinge* (1802); *S. W.* I/4, 258.

12. See W. Halbfass, *India and Europe*, ch. 6, §13; cf. also *Wissenschaft der Logik*, ed. G. Lasson, I. (Leipzig, 1951), 59.

13. Cf. *Briefe von und an Hegel*, ed. J. Hoffmeister, vol. I. (Hamburg, 1952), 194 (Schelling's response to the preface).

14. *S. W.* 1/6, 38. Cf. Hegel, *Enzyklopädie der philosophischen Wissenschaften* (1830), ed. F. Nicolin and O. Pöggeler, (Hamburg, sixth ed., 1959), §248 (p. 201). Although Hegel uses the expression 'Abfall der Idee von sich selbst' ('secession of the idea from itself'), he does not accept the implications which this concept has in Schelling's thought.

15. *S. W.* II/2, 482.

16. See *S. W.* II/2, 148ff. Cf. Gauḍapāda, *Kārikā* II, 19, on divine 'self-delusion': *māyā-eṣā tasya devasya yayā saṃmohitaḥ svayam.*

17. *S. W.* II/2, 482.

18. *S. W.* II/2, 480. However, Max Müller claims that he translated several Upaniṣads for Schelling in 1845, and that Schelling considered the Upaniṣads as 'the original wisdom of the Indians and mankind' ('die Urweisheit der Inder und der Menschheit'; see 'Damals und jetzt', *Deutsche Rundschau* 41, 1884, 416; quoted by H. von Glasenapp, *Indienbild*, 35). This is hardly compatible with the statements in the *Philosophy of Mythology.*

19. J. W. Sedlar states in her aforementioned study (see above, n. 5), 130: 'A list of Schelling's errors on the subject of India – avoidable errors, for the most part – makes painful reading.' Unfortunately, Sedlar's own understanding of Schelling and his contemporaries is as superficial as her knowledge of the Indian tradition, and she does not even attempt to explore Schelling's hermeneutical situation and the philosophical and theological background of his statements on India. It is obvious that Schelling's approach to India and the Orient in general deserve a more competent and sympathetic exploration. W. Heinrich, *Verklärung und Erlösung im Vedānta, bei Meister Eckhart und bei Schelling*, (München, 1961), is an unsatisfactory 'comparative' study.

20. V. Nuovo, Introduction to his translation of: P. Tillich, *The Construction of the History of Religion in Schelling's Positive Philosophy*, (Lewisburg, 1974), 22. This is a translation of Tillich's first doctoral dissertation (*Die religionsgeschichtliche Konstruktion in Schellings positiver Philosophie*, Breslau, 1910), which continues to be one of the most valuable studies of Schelling's lectures on the *Philosophy of Mythology* and the *Philosophy of Revelation.* Tillich's philosophical dissertation was followed by a theological dissertation on Schelling: *Mystik und Schuldbewusstsein in Schellings philosophischer Entwicklung*: Halle, 1912 (published Gütersloh, 1912). On Schelling's interpretation of mythology and revelation, paganism and Christianity see also: C. M. Schröder, *Das Verhältnis von Heidentum und Christentum in Schellings Philosophie der Mythologie und Offenbarung*, (München, 1936). On Schelling's later philosophy in general: W. Schulz, *Die Vollendung des deutschen Idealismus in der Spätphilosophie Schellings*, (Stuttgart, 1955).

21. *S. W.* II/2, 577.

22. *S. W.* II/2, 509.

23. *S. W.* II/2, 441.

24. *S. W.* II/2, 472; according to Schelling, indications of a genuine sense of religious unity are not specifically Indian, but a heritage of mankind in general, of which India was a part (431ff.).

25. P. Tillich, *The Construction of the History of Religion* (see above, n. 20), 86; cf also *S. W.* II/2, 444f.

26. Cf. *S. W.* II/2, 447: 'das Nachempfundene einer Philosophie. . . .' Schelling does not trust the reports of Paulinus a S. Bartholomaeo concerning a 'highest God',

parabrahma, in Indian religion; he suspects that this could be an *ad hoc* invention of a modern 'brahmin or pandit'.

27. *S. W.* II/2, 476.
28. *S. W.* II/2, 24.
29. *S. W.* II/2, 40, note 1; on Spinoza and pantheism, see W. Halbfass, *India and Europe*, 68ff.
30. *S. W.* II/2, 26; elsewhere (*S. W.* II/1, 568), Schelling says that there cannot be any 'rational religion' ('Vernunftreligion'), since this would be a contradiction in terms.
31. *S. W.* II/2, 179; see also 574, on the meaning of *mokṣa*, 'final liberation'.
32. Cf. *S. W.* II/2, 488; 'Einheit ist auf jeden Fall das Vorherrschende im Begriff.' In this passage, Schelling discusses various attempts to translate the word *yoga*; without mentioning Hegel's name, he refers to his *Bhagavadgītā* review.
33. *S. W.* II/2, 457.
34. *S. W.* II/2, 466.
35. Cf. *S. W.* II/2, 519.
36. *S. W.* II/2, 455.
37. See above, notes 17; 28f.
38. Cf. *Zur Geschichte der neueren Philosophie* (Münchener Vorlesungen), *S. W.* I/10, 137f.; also 127f.: God himself as 'concept' ('Begriff').
39. *S. W.* I/10, 141.
40. *S. W.* I/10, 144f. Schelling introduces the dwarf, generally known as the fifth *avatāra*, as Viṣṇu's 'third incarnation'.
41. See, for instance, A. Schopenhauer, *Parerga und Paralipomena*; quoted from the edition of Schopenhauer's works begun by P. Deussen, (Munich, 1911–42); with additional references to the edition by A. Hübscher, (Wiesbaden, 1946–50), hereinafter cited as *PP*, I; Deussen IV, 32–42 (Hübscher V, 22–32). There is an English translation of *PP* by E. F. J. Payne; A. Schopenhauer's *Die Welt als Wille und Vorstellung* is available in two English versions (by R. B. Haldane/J. Kemp and E. F. J. Payne).
42. See *PP* I, 'Über die Universitäts-Philosophie', Deussen IV, 159–221, specifically 188; 190, 201 (Hübscher V, 178; 180; 191); also S. Hochfeld, *Das Künstlerische in der Sprache Schopenhauers*, (Leipzig, 1912), for an inventory of Schopenhauer's terminology of abuse.
43. Cf., for instance, F. Mockrauer, 'Schopenhauer und Indien', *Jahrbuch der Schopenhauer-Gesellschaft* 15 (1928), 3–26; M. F. Hecker, *Schopenhauer und die indische Philosophie*, (Köln, 1897); H. von Glasenapp, *Indienbild*, 68–101; P. Wörner, *Der Idealismus und das Ding an sich bei Schopenhauer und den Indern*, (Diss. Erlangen, 1914); D. W. Dauer, *Schopenhauer as Transmitter of Buddhist Ideas*, (Bern, 1969) (inadequate); A. Hübscher, 'Schopenhauer und die Religionen Asiens', *Jahrbuch der Schopenhauer-Gesellschaft* 60 (1979), 1–16 (unreliable); see below, n. 101.
44. On Majer, see R. F. Merkel, 'Schopenhauers Indien-Lehrer', *Jahrbuch der Schopenhauer-Gesellschaft* 32 (1945/48), 158–81.
45. Cf. *PP* II, §179 (Deussen V, 415; Hübscher VI, 406); §184 (Deussen V, 431f.; Hübscher VI, 421f.).
46. On Dārā Shukōh, see above, ch. 2: on Anquetil Duperron, W. Halbfass, *India and Europe*, ch. 4.
47. *PP* II, §184 (Deussen V 432; Hübscher VI, 422): 'Es ist die belohnendste und erhebendste Lektüre, die (den Urtext ausgenommen) auf der Welt möglich ist: sie ist der Trost meines Lebens gewesen und wird der meines Sterbens sein.'
48. *PP* II, §184; A. Schopenhauer, *Handschriftlicher Nachlass*, hereinafter cited as *HN*. ed. A. Hübscher, vol. 5, 324; 341ff. Schopenhauer does not tolerate any attempt to interpret the *Upaniṣads* in a theistic sense.
49. See *PP* II, ch. 16 (§183–90); the following statement introduces this chapter: 'Regardless of my admiration for the religious and philosophical works of Sanskrit

literature – I have rarely been able to appreciate its poetical works; at times it has even appeared to me that they are as tasteless and monstrous as the sculpture of the same peoples.' He adds, however, that this may be due to the problems of translating poetry.

50. *PP* II, §185 (Deussen V, 434; Hübscher VI, 423f.).
51. He deals somewhat more explicitly with the Sāṃkhya system, for which he relies not only on H. Th. Colebrooke, but also on F. H. H. Windischmann and Ch. Lassen; see *HN*, ed. A. Hübscher, vol. 5, 331ff; *PP* II, §187 (criticizing the fundamental dualism of the system).
52. For a survey of Oriental materials in Schopenhauer's library and a reproduction of his marginal notes, see *HN*, ed. A. Hübscher, vol. 5, 319–52.
53. *Briefe*, Deussen XV, 470.
54. *HN*, Deussen XI, 459.
55. A. Schopenhauer, *Die Welt als Wille und Vorstellung*, quoted from the edition of Schopenhauer's works begun by P. Deussen, Munich, 1911–42; with additional references to the edition of A. Hübscher, Wiesbaden, 1946–50, hereinafter cited as *WWV*, II, ch. 48 (Deussen II, 696; Hübscher III, 698): 'Die Buddhaisten aber bezeichnen, mit voller Redlichkeit, die Sache bloss negativ, durch Nirwana, welches die Negation dieser Welt, oder des Sansara ist. Wenn Nirwana als das Nichts definiert wird, so will dies nur sagen, dass der Sansara kein einziges Element enthält, welches zur Definition oder Konstruktion des Nirwana dienen könnte.' The translation follows E. F. J. Payne.
56. See *WWV* II, ch. 35; 'Über Geschichte' ('On History'). Schopenhauer argues against the 'Hegelians, who consider history as the main purpose of all philosophy'; in his view, they have not grasped the fundamental truth that 'at all times there is one and the same, that all becoming and origination are only apparent, ideas alone are permanent, time is ideal' ('. . . dass nämlich zu aller Zeit das Selbe ist, alles Werden und Entstehen nur scheinbar, die Ideen allein bleibend, die Zeit ideal').
57. *PP* II, §187: 'How wise is, by contrast, the assumption of the thousand Buddhas in Buddhism.'
58. *WWV* I, §1. In the second edition (1844), Schopenhauer added to his opening statements a reference to a 'fundamental proposition' ('Fundamentalsatz') of the Vedānta system, which he had found in W. Jones' article 'On the Philosophy of the Asiatics' (*Asiatic Researches* 4, 164) and in which he recognized his own doctrine of transcendental ideality.
59. Cf. Schopenhauer's doctoral dissertation of 1813: *Über die vierfache Wurzel des Satzes vom zureichenden Grunde* ('On the Fourfold Root of the Principle of Sufficient Reason').
60. We borrow the expression 'wiedererkennende Philosophiegeschichte' from G. Teichmüller without adopting its systematic implications.
61. Cf. *WWV* I, §68; 65; on the 'metaphysical urge' ('metaphysisches Bedürfnis'), cf. *WWV* II, ch. 17.
62. Cf. *HN*, Deussen XI, 410.
63. *HN*, Deussen XI, 323.
64. *HN*, Deussen XI, 46.
65. *PP* II, §115 (Deussen V, 240; Hübscher VI, 233); *Preisschrift über die Grundlage der Moral*, §22 (Deussen III, 741; Hübscher IV, 271); *WWV* I, §66 (Deussen I, Hübscher II, 440ff.). See also P. Hacker, 'Schopenhauer und die Ethik des Hinduismus', *Saeculum* 12 (1961), 366–99 (*Kl. Schr.*, 531–64).
66. Cf. *WWV* II, ch. 48 (Deussen II, 696; Hübscher III, 698); *PP* II, §189 (Deussen V, 436f.; Hübscher VI, 426f.); on the etymology of *nirvāṇa*, *WWV* II, ch. 41 (Deussen II, 581; Hübscher III, 583); *WWV* I, §71 (Deussen I, Hübscher II, 487) is more critical.
67. Cf. *PP* II, §189 (Deussen V, 436f.; Hübscher VI, 426f.).
68. See H. von Glasenapp, *Indienbild*, 85; *Briefe* II (Deussen XV), 522; 563.

69. *Briefe* II (Deussen XV), 359.
70. *Briefe* II (Deussen XV), 46 (letter to A. von Doss, Febr. 27, 1856).
71. *PP* I, Deussen IV, 348 (Hübscher V, 334).
72. *Senilia* (1858); see *HN*, ed. A. Hübscher, vol. 4/2, 29; cf. also *WWV* II, ch. 48 (Deussen II, 703; Hübscher III, 705).
73. *HN*, Deussen IX, 89.
74. *WWV* II, ch. 17 (Deussen II, Hübscher III, 186); also *Über die vierfache Wurzel des Satzes vom zureichenden Grunde* (revised version of 1847), §34 (Deussen III, 233; Hübscher I, 125); *Gespräche*, ed. A. Hübscher, (Stuttgart 1971), 244 (conversation with C. J. Bähr).
75. *WWV* II, ch. 48 (Deussen II, 702; Hübscher III, 705).
76. *Prolegomena zu einer jeden künftigen Metaphysik*, preface (1783).
77. *Über die vierfache Wurzel des Satzes vom zureichenden Grunde* (847), §34 (Deussen III, 236; Hübscher I, 128): 'Denn das Christentum … hat indisches Blut im Leibe und daher einen beständigen Hang, vom Judentume los zu kommen.'
78. *PP* II, §179 (Deussen V, 413; Hübscher VI, 404).
79. *PP* II, §163 (Deussen V, 341; Hübscher VI, 334).
80. Cf. *PP* II, §179 (Deussen V, 415; Hübscher VI, 406); §190 (connections with Egypt, etc.). For contemporary speculations concerning India and Egypt, see P. von Bohlen, *Das alte Indien, mit besonderer Rücksicht auf Ägypten*, (Königsberg, 1830).
81. *WWV* I, §63 (Deussen I, Hübscher II, 421).
82. *PP* II, §115 (Deussen V, 246; Hübscher VI, 239); *HN*, Deussen IX, 89.
83. *PP* II, §115 (Deussen V, 243; Hübscher VI, 236). Schopenhauer criticizes the activities of Christian missionaries in Asia, predicts their failure, and would like to see 'Buddhist priests' in Europe (Deussen V, 247f.; Hübscher VI, 240f.).
84. *PP* II, §115 (Deussen V, 248; Hübscher VI, 241).
85. See, e.g., *PP* II, §189 (Deussen V, 437; Hübscher VI, 427). His judgement on Islam is in general very harsh.
86. *WWV* I, §63 (Deussen I, Hübscher II, 419); II, ch. 17 (Deussen II, Hübscher III, 178); II, ch. 41 (Deussen II, 542, Hübscher III, 543).
87. *WWV* II, ch. 41 (Deussen II, 542; Hübscher III, 544); see also ch. 17 (Deussen II, Hübscher III, 178), where Schopenhauer refers to the 'greater energy of the intuitive cognitive powers' ('grössere Energie der intuitiven Erkenntniskräfte') of the ancient Vedic teachers.
88. *WWV* I, preface to the first edition (1818; Deussen I, XXIVf.; Hübscher II, XIIf.); cf. R. Schwab, *Oriental Renaissance*, 13 (on Anquetil Duperron's earlier reference to the Renaissance).
89. *HN*, Deussen IX, 89f.
90. *WWV* I, preface to the first edition (Deussen I, XXV; Hübscher II, XIII).
91. *WWV* I, §71 (Deussen I, Hübscher II, 487).
92. *PP* II, §187 (Deussen V, 435; Hübscher VI, 425; referring to the Sāṃkhya dualism).
93. *HN*, Deussen XI, 459; this passage is, however, not without a sense of irony.
94. See above, n. 72.
95. *Briefe*, Deussen XIV, 221 (letter to his publisher, F. A. Brockhaus; 1818). On the other hand, Schopenhauer often acknowledges his indebtedness to Kant.
96. *De Kantismo; Oupnek'hat* I, 711–24; see above, ch. 4.
97. *HN*, Deussen IX, 90f (from Schopenhauer's unsuccessful lectures at the University of Berlin, 1820; new edition by V. Spierling; *Theorie des gesammten Vorstellens, Denkens und Erkennens*, (München, 1986), 106).
98. See F. Mockrauer, 'Schopenhauer und Indien', *Jahrbuch der Schopenhauer-Gesellschaft* 15 (1928), 6; 26.
99. See R. Gérard, *L'Orient et la pensée romantique allemande*, (Paris, 1963), 220: 'Orient et Occident se rejoignent dans la pensée Schopenhauerienne'.

100. See M. Scheler, *Liebe und Erkenntnis*, (München, 1955), 55.
101. Cf. H. von Glasenapp, Indienbild, 68–101; I. Vecchiotti, *La dottrina di Scho-penhauer, Le teorie schopenhaueriane considerate nello loro genesi e nei loro rapporti con la filosofia indiana*, (Rome, 1969); J. W. Sedlar, *India in the Mind of Germany; Schelling, Schopenhauer and Their Times*, (Washington, DC, 1982).
102. Cf. *Materialien zu Schopenhauers 'Die Welt als Wille und Vorstellung'*, ed. V. Spierling, (Frankfurt, 1984), 328.
103. Letter to J. Frauenstädt, August 21, 1852; *Briefe*, Deussen XV, 155f.
104. *WWV* I, §29 (Deussen I, Hübscher II, 193).
105. *WWV* II, ch. 28 (Deussen II, 401; Hübscher III, 400).
106. See, for instance, *WWV* I, §7 (Deussen I, Hübscher II, 30f.); *WWV*. Appendix (Deussen I, Hübscher II, 574); *WWV* II, ch. 4 (Deussen II, Hübscher III, 50).
107. *PP* II, §161 (Deussen V, 338; Hübscher VI, 331).
108. *Metaphysik der Sitten*, ed. V. Spierling, (München, 1985), 272 (based upon *HN*, Deussen X, 364–584).
109. Cf. H. von Glasenapp, *Indienbild*, 85. Schopenhauer uses the form 'Brahm' to refer to *brahman/brahma* as neuter.
110. *WWV* I, Appendix (Deussen I, Hübscher II, 574).
111. *Über den Willen in der Natur*; Deussen III, 322; Hübscher IV, 30f.
112. *Briefe* II (Deussen XV), 46 (a letter to A. von Doss, Febr. 27, 1856).
113. *PP* II, §187 (Deussen V, 435; Hübscher VI, 425). WWV II, ch. 19 (Deussen II, Hübscher III, 233) uses the simile of the blind and the lame, which is familiar in Sāṃkhya (e.g., *Sāṃkhyakārikā*, v. 21).
114. *HN*, Deussen XI, 323 (§441; a note written in 1815).
115. See above, n. 68.
116. Cf. *PP* I, §9 (Deussen IV, 73f.; Hübscher V, 66).
117. Cf. *Indienbild*, 84.
118. Cf. *Metaphysik der Sitten*, ed. V. Spierling, (München, 1985), 39 (introduction).
119. Cf. *WWV*, §68 (Deussen I, Hübscher II, 448; 452f.; 460).
120. *PP* II, §189 (Deussen V, 436f.; Hübscher VI, 426f.). On 'quietism' in its connection with mysticism and asceticism, see also *WWV* II, ch. 48 (Deussen II, 702ff.; Hübscher III, 704ff.)
121. Cf. A. Diemer, 'Schopenhauer und die moderne Existenzphilosophie', *Schopenhauer*, ed. J. Salaquarda, (Darmstadt, 1985), 125, n. 3; M. Heidegger, *Nietzsche* I, (Pfullingen, 1961), 44. See, on the other hand, Heidegger's remarks on the relationship between 'will' and 'releasement' ('Gelassenheit') in: *Gelassenheit*, (Pfullingen, 1959), 30ff.; 57ff. (tr. J. M. Anderson and E. H. Freund: *Discourse on Thinking*, (New York, 1969), 59ff.; 79ff.).
122. Cf. I. Vecchiotti, 'Schopenhauer im Urteil der modernen Inder,' *Schopenhauer*, ed. J. Salaquarda, (Darmstadt, 1985), 185ff. (Italian original in I. Vecchiotti, *A. Schopenhauer*, (Florence, 1976), 108–17).
123. See R. L. Mitra's preface to: *The Yoga Aphorisms of Patanjali with the Commentary of Bhoja Rājā*, (Calcutta, 1883).

9

THE INFLUENCES OF EASTERN THOUGHT ON SCHOPENHAUER'S DOCTRINE OF THE THING-IN-ITSELF

Moira Nicholls

Many commentators accept Schopenhauer's claim that there are no significant changes in his thinking after 1818.[1] I, however, argue that there are good reasons for maintaining that there are significant developments in his thought after that date and that these concern his doctrine of the thing-in-itself. Furthermore, I contend that it is Schopenhauer's increasing knowledge of and admiration for Eastern thought which provided the impetus for the changes in doctrine that occurred. I begin by outlining three significant shifts that occurred in Schopenhauer's doctrine of the thing-in-itself after 1818. I then discuss his degree of acquaintance with Eastern thought, and I suggest various similarities to and differences between Eastern teaching and Schopenhauer's doctrine. Finally, I argue that the identified shifts in Schopenhauer's doctrine of the thing-in-itself can be plausibly explained, at least in part, by his increasing familiarity with and appreciation of Eastern thought.

I. SHIFTS IN DOCTRINE

Three identifiable shifts in Schopenhauer's doctrine of the thing-in-itself occur between the publication of the first volume of *The World as Will and Representation* in 1818 and his later works. The first shift concerns what he says about the knowability of the thing-in-itself; the second concerns what he says about the nature of the thing-in-itself; and the third concerns his explicit

Moira Nicholls, 'The Influences of Eastern Thought on Schopenhauer's Doctrine of the Thing-in-Itself', in Christopher Janaway (ed.), *The Cambridge Companion to Schopenhauer* (Cambridge: Cambridge University Press, 1999), pp. 171–212.

attempt to assimilate his own doctrines about what can be said of the thing-in-itself with Eastern doctrines.

The most important of these shifts is the first.[2] Schopenhauer asserts numerous times throughout his works that the thing-in-itself is will or 'will to life',[3] and he claims that we know this through direct intuition in self-consciousness. For example:

> The *thing-in-itself*, this substratum of all phenomena, and therefore of the whole of Nature, is nothing but what we know directly and intimately as *the will*.[4]

However, there are also passages in his later works in which he seems to withdraw the claim that in self-consciousness we are aware of the will as thing-in-itself, suggesting instead that in self-consciousness we are aware of no more than our phenomenal willings. For example:

> But this knowledge of the thing-in-itself is not wholly adequate. In the first place, such knowledge is tied to the form of the representation; it is perception or observation, and as such falls apart into subject and object.[5]

If we accept this latter suggestion, Schopenhauer's claim that the thing-in-itself is will seems either to be without foundation or to be a misleading way of making the much weaker claim that the thing-in-itself is called will because in introspective awareness we are closest to the thing-in-itself, and in introspection the object of our awareness is will. While some commentators endorse this interpretation of Schopenhauer's seminal claim that the thing-in-itself is will,[6] I believe that it is implausible for the following reasons. First, it is inconsistent with Schopenhauer's many assertions that the thing-in-itself *is* will and with his claim that metaphysics concerns the thing-in-itself.[7] Second, since these assertions are the principal ways in which Schopenhauer sees his own philosophy as an advance upon that of Kant's, their inconsistency with this interpretation is a major difficulty for it. Third, if Schopenhauer's claim that the thing-in-itself is will rests on the supposition that in introspective awareness of will there are fewer phenomenal forms standing between the thing-in-itself and the knowing subject, his argument is an extremely weak one. For, as both Janaway and Young point out, there are no grounds for believing that a smaller number of phenomenal forms will more truly reveal the nature of underlying reality than a larger number.[8] In light of the preceding considerations, it is more plausible to suggest that the passages in the later works, in which Schopenhauer apparently withdraws his claim of direct acquaintance with the thing-in-itself as will, indicate a shift in his thinking. While in the later works he continues to assert both that the thing-in-itself is will and that we are directly aware of it in self-consciousness, I suggest that the presence of the previously mentioned passages indicates that in the years following the publication of the first volume of *The World as Will and Representation* he became increasingly aware of the difficulties attending this claim.

Schopenhauer's use of the veil metaphor illustrates his uneasiness. For example:

> And though no one can recognise the thing-in-itself through the veil of the forms of perception, on the other hand everyone carries this within himself, in fact he himself is it; hence in self-consciousness it must be in some way accessible to him, although still only conditionally.[9]

Schopenhauer wants to claim that just as we both do and do not know an object that is concealed by a veil, so in introspective awareness we both do and do not know the thing-in-itself that is concealed behind the temporal form. Our *not* being able to know the thing-in-itself is consistent with Kant's teaching that introspection yields only knowledge of inner phenomena, and it may be the strong influence of Kant on Schopenhauer's thinking that prompts him to qualify his oft-repeated claim of direct awareness. However, as Schopenhauer holds that the Kantian influence on his thinking is strongest in his youth,[10] it may well be that other factors were also at work. Another explanation is put by Höffding, namely, that Schopenhauer modified his views in the later work after reflecting upon the critical reviews of his earlier work.[11] However, since Schopenhauer was generally disdainful of critics and their comments, it seems that this can be at best a partial explanation. While the influence of both Kant's epistemology and critical reviews may partly explain the previously mentioned passages, a more enduring influence is also called for in order to explain this change in his doctrine after 1818.

The second shift in Schopenhauer's doctrine of the thing-in-itself concerns what he asserts about its nature. The traditional interpretation of Schopenhauer's metaphysics is that the thing-in-itself is will or will to life. He makes this claim many times throughout his writings, and furthermore, as the title of his main work suggests, he also asserts that reality comprises just two aspects, will and representation. For example:

> This will alone constitutes the other aspect of the world, for this world is, one the one side, entirely *representation*, just as, on the other, it is entirely *will*.[12]

However, in his later works Schopenhauer introduces the idea that the thing-in-itself has multiple aspects, only one of which is will. Its other aspects are the objects of awareness of such persons as mystics, saints, and ascetics, who have denied the will.

> Accordingly, even after this last and extreme step, the question may still be raised what that will, which manifests itself in the world and as the world, is ultimately and absolutely in itself; in other words, what it is quite apart from the fact that it manifests itself as *will*, or in general *appears*, that is to say, is *known* in general.[13]

The third shift in Schopenhauer's doctrine of the thing-in-itself concerns his explicit attempt to assimilate his own views on what can be said about the thing-in-itself with Eastern doctrines. I have identified six passages in which Schopenhauer asserts that the thing-in-itself can be described as will, but only in a metaphorical sense. Of these, three are in his earlier and three in his later works.[14] However, in two of the later passages he explicitly assimilates his own views with what he sees as similar views expressed in Eastern thought, and this assimilation is in keeping with his increasing knowledge of and admiration for the East.

> The will as thing-in-itself is entire and undivided in every being; just as the centre is an integral part of every radius; whereas the peripheral end of this radius is in the most rapid revolution with the surface that represents time and its content, the other end at the centre where eternity lies, remains in profoundest peace, because the centre is the point whose rising half is no different from the sinking half. Therefore, it is also said in the Bhagavad-Gita: 'Undivided it dwells in beings, and yet as it were divided; it is to be known as the sustainer, annihilator, and producer of beings.' Here of course we fall into mystical and metaphorical language, but it is the only language in which anything can be said about this wholly transcendent theme.[15]

A further passage is worth mentioning. In the first edition of the first volume of *The World as Will and Representation* (1818), when discussing the state of denial of the will, Schopenhauer draws attention to the ways in which his doctrine and those of the East differ.

> We must not evade it, as the Indians do, by myths and meaningless words, such as reabsorption in *Brahman*, or the Nirvana of the Buddhists. On the contrary, we freely acknowledge that what remains after the complete abolition of the will is for all who are still full of the will, assuredly nothing. But also conversely, to those in whom the will has turned and denied itself, this very real world of ours with all its suns and galaxies, is – nothing.[16]

However, in the second edition of the first volume (1844), he adds the following footnote to the preceding passage:

> This is also the Prajna-Paramita of the Buddhists, the 'beyond all knowledge', in other words, the point where subject and object no longer exist. See I. J. Schmidt, *Über das Mahajana und Pradschna-Paramita*.

Since the work by Schmidt to which Schopenhauer refers was not published until 1836, it seems that between the publication of the first and second volumes of *The World as Will and Representation*, Schopenhauer's understanding of the Buddhist concept of Nirvana changes, and he sees parallels between his later understanding of that notion and his own doctrine of denial of the will. He suggests that what the two views have in common is the recognition that our ordinary ways of knowing and describing the phenomenal world are inapplicable to knowing and describing reality as it is experienced by saints and mystics.

The previously mentioned passages support the view that in the years following the publication of the first edition of the first volume of *The World as Will and Representation*, Schopenhauer increasingly sought to find parallels between his own and Eastern ideas on what can be said about the thing-in-itself. And this practice at least leaves open the possibility that his increasing knowledge of and admiration for Eastern thought actually influenced his thinking, giving rise to changes in his views concerning the knowability, nature, and ways of describing the thing-in-itself.

In summary, there are three identifiable shifts in Schopenhauer's doctrine of the thing-in-itself between the publication of the first volume of *The World as Will and Representation* and of his later works. They concern its knowability, its nature, and Schopenhauer's explicit attempt to assimilate his own doctrines concerning what can be said about the thing-in-itself with Eastern ideas. While the influence of Kant and of critical reviews may partly explain the first of these shifts, a more enduring influence is also called for to explain all three shifts. In support of my claim that it is Schopenhauer's increasing knowledge of and admiration for Eastern thought that fulfils this role, I next consider Schopenhauer's degree of acquaintance with Eastern thought.

II. THE EXTENT OF SCHOPENHAUER'S ACQUAINTANCE WITH EASTERN THOUGHT

Schopenhauer's introduction to the ideas of the Hindus and to Eastern ideas more generally is thought to have occurred in late 1813. He had moved to Weimar after submitting his doctoral thesis, *On the Fourfold Root of the Principle of Sufficient Reason*, and it was in his mother's Weimar salon that he met the orientalist Friedrich Majer. That he was unacquainted with Eastern thought prior to this time seems probable for several reasons. First, he makes no reference to Eastern thought in the 1813 version of his doctoral thesis;[17] second, in his *Manuscript Remains* all but one reference to it date from 1814 on (the one occurring in the period 1809 to 1813); and third, there were relatively few scholarly sources of information about Eastern thought available to Europeans in the early part of the nineteenth century.[18]

A study of Schopenhauer's *Manuscript Remains* suggests that he first becomes acquainted with Hindu thought around 1813–14 but that he did not acquire much knowledge of Buddhism until after 1818. The two earliest volumes of *Manuscript Remains*, dating from 1804 to 1818 and from 1809 to 1818, respectively, contain very few references to Buddhism (I counted two),[19] while there are at least twenty references to Hindu thought in these volumes after 1813, and only one of these was obviously added to the notes at a later date.[20] However, in the third volume of the *Manuscript Remains*, dating from 1818 to 1830, there are at least fifteen references to Buddhist thought and about thirty to Hinduism. In the final *Manuscript Remains*, covering the period 1830 to 1860, there are at least seven references to Buddhism and fifteen to Hindu thought. This means that in the period 1813 to 1818 the *Manuscript Remains* contain approximately two references to Buddhist thought compared to at least twenty references in the period 1818 to 1860, and that for the same periods there are at least twenty and forty-five references, respectively, to Hindu thought. The first volume of *The World as Will and Representation* contains about eight references to Buddhist thought, five of which are added in the later editions (1844 and 1859) of that volume.[21] By comparison, in the second volume, first published in 1844 with a second edition in 1859, there are at least thirty references to Buddhism. References to Hindu thought in the first volume number over fifty, seven of which are added in the later editions,[22] and in the second volume there are over forty-five references to Hinduism.[23] While these figures are only approximate, they indicate a marked rise in Schopenhauer's knowledge of and interest in Buddhist thought from 1818 on, and a strong and consistent interest in Hindu thought from 1813 until his death in 1860. That Schopenhauer was in the habit of adding references to his earlier works is clear from the following footnoted comment in the 1859 edition of the first volume:

> In the last forty years Indian literature has grown so much in Europe that if I now wished to complete this note to the first edition, it would fill several pages.[24]

Such comments indicate that Schopenhauer had an abiding interest in Eastern philosophy, and that he was keen to demonstrate parallels between his own doctrines and those of the East.

III. SOURCES OF ACQUAINTANCE OF EASTERN THOUGHT

As well as considering the number of references to Hindu and Buddhist thought in *The Manuscript Remains* and *The World as Will and Representation*, it is instructive to look at Schopenhauer's sources for these references.[25] It seems clear that his early sources of knowledge of Hinduism are the *Oupnek'hat*[26] and the Asiatic journals.[27] While throughout his works he also frequently refers to the *Vedas*, the *Puranas*,[28] and the *Bhagavadgita*, praising the ideas expressed in them and drawing parallels with his own doctrines, it seems that his early references to these primary texts originated from articles in the Asiatic journals rather than from an acquaintance with the texts themselves. It was not until 1838 that a translation of part of the *Vedas* first became available,[29] and the translation of the *Bhagavadgita* to which Schopenhauer makes reference in the second volume of *The World as Will and Representation* is that by A. G. Schlegel, which was not published until 1823.[30] Schopenhauer first acquired a copy of the *Oupnek'hat* from the orientalist Friedrich Majer in late 1813,[31] and its subsequent value to him is evident from his statement in *Parerga and Paralipomena* that 'it [the *Oupnek'hat*] is the most profitable and sublime reading that is possible in the world; it has been the consolation of my life and will be that of my death'.[32] He goes on to assert: 'I am firmly convinced that a real knowledge of the *Upanishads* and thus of the true and esoteric dogmas of the *Vedas* can at present be obtained only from the *Oupnek'hat*.[33] However, in addition to the *Oupnek'hat*, it is clear that Schopenhauer read any available secondary sources that he could find.[34] In the *Manuscript Remains*, in addition to the frequent references to the journals *Asiatic Researches*,[35] *Asiatisches Magazin*,[36] *Asiatick Researches*,[37] and *Asiatic Journal*,[38] Schopenhauer refers to books and articles by oriental scholars of the time. In *Parerga and Paralipomena*, under the title 'Some Remarks on Sanskrit Literature', Schopenhauer discusses the merits of various translations of sacred Hindu texts, and in the course of a discussion of Hindu ideas and the possibility that Indian mythology is remotely related to that of the Greeks, Romans, and Egyptians, he mentions additional texts on Hinduism. In both volumes of *The World as Will and Representation* and scattered throughout his other works, there are many further references to both primary and secondary sources. However, it is noteworthy that all but ten references (seven of which concern either the *Asiatic Researches* or *Asiatisches Magazin*) are to publications after 1818, confirming the view that until that date Schopenhauer's main sources of knowledge of Hindu thought were the *Oupnek'hat* and articles in the Asiatic journals.

Turning now to Schopenhauer's sources of Buddhist teaching, the entries in the first two volumes of the *Manuscript Remains* indicate that Schopenhauer's primary source prior to 1818 is the *Asiatic Researches*; there are only two references to Buddhism in these volumes, and they both refer to that journal as their source.[39] However, from 1818 on, Schopenhauer's sources become more diversified, a fact that he himself alludes to in the second volume of *The World as Will and Representation* when he states that 'up till 1818, when my work appeared, there were to be found in Europe only a very few accounts of Buddhism, and those extremely incomplete and inadequate, confined almost entirely to a few essays in the earlier volumes of the *Asiatic Researches*, and principally concerned with the Buddhism of the Burmese'.[40] The increased availability of information after 1818 is reflected in the *Manuscript Remains* for the later periods, 1818 to 1830, and 1830 to 1860, where he refers to journals and other secondary texts. Also, in the chapter entitled 'Sinology' in his essay *On the Will in Nature*, Schopenhauer recommends to his readers a list of twenty-six works on Buddhism of which he says, 'I can really recommend [them] for I possess them and know them well.' In both volumes of *The World as Will and Representation* and scattered throughout his other works there are many further references to both primary and secondary sources. Only two of these works were published prior to 1818. Finally, in both Grisebach's and Hübscher's listings of titles in Schopenhauer's posthumous library, only three of those that specifically refer to Buddhist thought have publication dates before 1818.

At his death, Schopenhauer had accumulated a library of at least 130 items of orientalia. Given this evidence, as well as the many references to Eastern thought that appear in his works, it seems reasonable to conclude that

Schopenhauer had an abiding interest in Hindu and Buddhist ideas throughout his life. In the next section I consider the extent to which these ideas may have exerted an influence on Schopenhauer's own doctrine of the thing-in-itself.

IV. LIKELY INFLUENCE OF EASTERN THOUGHT ON SCHOPENHAUER'S DOCTRINE OF THE THING-IN-ITSELF

Schopenhauer states: 'I owe what is best in my own development to the impression made by Kant's works, the sacred writings of the Hindus, and Plato'.[41] Writing in 1818 in the Preface to the first edition of *The World as Will and Representation*, he says that while Kant's philosophy is the only one with which a thorough acquaintance is positively assumed, a knowledge of Plato is also desirable. And regarding the Hindus, he states:

> But if he [the reader] has shared in the benefits of the *Vedas*, access to which, opened to us by the *Upanishads*, is in my view the greatest advantage which this still young century has to show over previous centuries, since I surmise that the influence of Sanskrit literature will penetrate no less deeply than did the revival of Greek literature in the fifteenth century; if, I say, the reader has also already received and assimilated the divine inspiration of ancient Indian wisdom, then he is best of all prepared to hear what I have to say to him. It will not speak to him, as to many others, in a strange and even hostile tongue; for, did it not sound too conceited, I might assert that each of the individual and disconnected utterances that make up the *Upanishads* could be derived as a consequence from the thought I am to impart, *although conversely my thought is by no means to be found in the Upanishads.*[42]

From the last sentence of this passage, it is clear that while Schopenhauer readily sees parallels between his own philosophy and that of Hindu thought, he does not believe that the development and expression of his own ideas is in any way dependent on the ideas expressed in the sacred Hindu texts. In the second volume of *The World as Will and Representation* he also disclaims direct influence of Buddhist ideas, maintaining that

> [in] any case, it must be a pleasure to me to see my doctrine in such close agreement with a religion that the majority of men on earth hold as their own, for this numbers far more followers than any other. And this agreement must be yet the more pleasing to me, *inasmuch as in my philosophising I have certainly not been under its influence.*[43]

However, this disavowal of influence needs to be balanced against both the developments in Schopenhauer's thought which I discussed earlier and other remarks that he makes.[44] With regard to the latter, the following passage written in 1816 is relevant.

Moreover, I confess that I do not believe my doctrine could have come about before the Upanishads, Plato and Kant could cast their rays simultaneously into the mind of one man.[45]

While in this passage he does not speak of direct influence, Schopenhauer nevertheless strongly suggests that his reading of the *Upanishads* is essential to the formulation of his own ideas. Also relevant here are his somewhat ambiguous comments regarding what he sees as the unchanging character of his philosophy. In the *Manuscript Remains* he states in a footnote dated 1849:

These sheets, written at Dresden in the years 1814–1818, show the fermentative process of my thinking, from which at that time my whole philosophy emerged, rising gradually like a beautiful landscape from the morning mist. *Here it is worth noting that even in 1814 (in my 27th year) all the dogmas of my system, even the unimportant ones, were established.*[46]

It seems that Schopenhauer became acquainted with oriental thought only in late 1813. Given the preceding two passages, it seems we must assume either that his reading of the *Upanishads* made such a dramatic and sudden impression on him that he could maintain that by 1814 all his ideas were settled, or that in this passage he means that while certain central ideas were formed by 1814, they subsequently developed over the next four years. The latter view is more plausible, particularly since in the immediately preceding passage he himself speaks of the 'fermentative process of my thinking' between 1814 and 1818, and since the previous passage was not written until 1816. Furthermore, given the numerous and varied references to the ideas of the Hindus in the first two volumes of *Manuscript Remains* (at least twenty) and in the first volume of *The World as Will and Representation* (at least fifty), it seems plausible to suppose that the degree of familiarity thus presupposed was acquired over a number of years, rather than all at once in late 1813 to 1814. The preceding passages and argument support the conclusion that Schopenhauer's acquaintance with Hinduism had a significant input into the formation of his own doctrines as they appeared in the first volume of *The World as Will and Representation*.

V. SCHOPENHAUER'S LIKELY UNDERSTANDING OF HINDUISM

To make clearer how Eastern ideas may account in part for the presence of passages in Schopenhauer's later works in which he seems to withdraw from his earlier claims concerning the thing-in-itself, it is worth looking at Schopenhauer's likely understanding of both Hindu and Buddhist teaching.

Orthodox Hindu religion recognises the validity of the *Vedas* as the authoritative scriptural texts. Of these texts, the *Upanishads* are the most metaphysical and systematic in style, although there are often seemingly conflicting strands of thought expressed in them, and these have given rise to a range of interpretations. The *Upanishads* represent the final stage in the tradition of the *Vedas*, and for this reason the teaching that is based on them is known as the Vedanta (Sanskrit: 'conclusion of the *Veda*'). Within the Vedanta there exist different sub-schools of thought, the most important of which are the school of Nondualism (Advaita, whose main exponent is the eighth-century philosopher Sankara), qualified Nondualism (Visistadvaita, which develops in the twelfth century), and Dualism (Dvaita, which develops in the thirteenth century). Frederick Copleston notes that Schopenhauer's philosophy bears some resemblance to the most prominent form of Vedanta, Advaita.[47] Although Schopenhauer writes only of the Vedanta and does not mention its various sub-schools, some of his most important doctrines are mirrored in those of the Advaita school. That he is acquainted with Advaita teaching seems clear from his reference in the *Manuscript Remains* to Windischmann's *Sancara sive de Theologia Vedanticorum*,[48] a book also listed by Grisebach in his catalogue of titles in Schopenhauer's posthumous library.

According to Advaita teaching as articulated by Sankara, Brahman, the Holy Power spoken of in the *Upanishads* and elsewhere referred to as the sustainer of the cosmos, is identical with Atman, the self. Consequently, since they are identical, there is only one Absolute, and similarly, there is only one Self, which is not to be identified with the empirical Ego which undergoes reincarnation. Further, given that Brahman alone is real, the world (together with empirical egos) considered as distinct from Brahman, is an illusion (maya). Sankara's monism not only claims to give a correct interpretation of central scriptural texts, but also claims to preserve simultaneously both the chief insights of the *Veda* and the common-sense attitudes that appear to be in conflict with this illusionist doctrine. He achieves this by introducing the notion of two levels of truth; the higher levels are expressed in the mystical experience of release and identification with Brahman, while the lower ones are expressed in both religious and common-sense descriptions of the world. For the person who has not attained the higher insight, spatio-temporal objects such as trees and rivers are real, but for the person who has attained the higher viewpoint, these objects are illusory, and reality is the undifferentiated 'one' of which the mystics speak.[49]

It is not difficult to see parallels between Advaita philosophy, as just outlined, and the following of Schopenhauer's own doctrines: his doctrine that the will as thing-in-itself is the sustainer of the world; his doctrine that the will as thing-in-itself is identical with the will that is objectified in individual phenomena, a view that he expresses by asserting the identity of the macrocosm and the micro-cosm;[50] his doctrine that there is only one will and only one knowing subject, in the sense that both lie outside the forms of differentiation, space and time;[51] his doctrine that our essential nature, the will as thing-in-itself, is not to be identified with empirical consciousness, since the former is a timeless One, while the latter is distinct and transient; his doctrine that the will as thing-in-itself alone is real, while the world (together with consciousness) considered as distinct from the will as thing-in-itself is an illusion; and his doctrine that there are two kinds of awareness of reality: perceptual awareness, which is the foundation of egoism, and mystical awareness, which is the foundation of moral goodness.[52]

Without dwelling on the closeness of these parallels, there are two striking instances in which Schopenhauer's doctrines do not find any agreement with the preceding outline of Advaita philosophy. The first is his doctrine that the thing-in-itself, or ultimate reality, is a will that is the source of immense suffering in the world. Such a view seems incompatible with the Advaita conception of Brahman as the Holy Power,[53] although it might be thought to have some similarity with the other conception of it as the sustainer of the cosmos.[54] Of Schopenhauer's references to Brahman or Brahm or Brahma in the first volume of *The World as Will and Representation*, all refer to it in its role as sustainer, creator, and originator. For example:

> Each day of the creator Brahma has a thousand such periods of four ages, and his night again has a thousand such periods. His year has 365 days and as many nights. He lives a hundred of his years, always creating; and when he dies a new Brahma is at once born, and so on from eternity to eternity.[55]

In Brahma's role of sustainer, one can see some parallel to Schopenhauer's thing-in-itself in its role as an endlessly striving will to life, the essence and explanation of all phenomenal reality. For example:

> Thus everywhere in nature we see contest, struggle, and the fluctuation of victory, and later on we shall recognise in this more distinctly that variance with itself essential to the will. Every grade of the will's objectification fights for the matter, the space, and the time of another. Persistent matter must constantly change the form, since, under the guidance of causality, mechanical, physical, chemical, and organic phenomena, eagerly striving to appear, snatch the matter from one another, for each wishes to reveal its own Idea. This contest can be followed through the whole of nature; indeed only through it does nature exist.[56]

That Schopenhauer himself interprets the Hindu conception of Brahma as parallel to his own conception of will is evident from the following passages:

> Brahma means originally force, will, wish, and the propulsive power of creation.[57]

> The origin of the world (this Samsara of the Buddhists) is itself based on evil, that is to say, it is a sinful act of Brahma, for Indian mythology is everywhere transparent.[58]

> The Vedas also teach no God creator, but a world-soul Brahm (in the neuter). Brahma, sprung from the naval of Vishnu with the four faces and as part of the Trimurti, is merely a popular personification of Brahm in the

extremely transparent Indian mythology. He obviously represents the generation, the origin, of beings just as Vishnu does their acme, and Shiva their destruction and extinction. Moreover, his production of the world is a sinful act, just as is the world incarnation of Brahm.[59]

The importance of these passages cannot be over-emphasised. For they illustrate Schopenhauer's desire to interpret the doctrine of the *Vedas* so that it accords with his own conception of the thing-in-itself as will. It is also worth emphasising that in the second of the preceding passages he acknowledges that his characterisation of Brahma as evil is an interpretation of Indian mythology rather than an actual statement of accepted Hindu doctrine. This is important since it is doubtful that the similarity between Brahma and the will is nearly as strong as Schopenhauer thinks. While Hindu doctrine asserts that Brahman is the sustainer of the world, it also maintains that Brahman is the ground of all value, the core of the true, the good, and the beautiful.[60] That Schopenhauer recognises that Brahma also has this role is suggested by the following passages:

> Just as when Vishnu, according to a beautiful Indian myth, incarnates himself as a hero, Brahma at the same time comes into the world as the minstrel of his deeds.[61]

> Therefore, what is moral is to be found between these two; it accompanies man as a light on his path from the affirmation to the denial of the will, or, mythically, from the entrance of original sin to salvation through faith in the mediation of the incarnate God (Avatar): or, according to the teaching of the *Veda*, through all the rebirths that are the consequences of the works in each case, until right knowledge appears, and with it salvation (final emancipation), *Moksha*, i.e., reunion with *Brahma*. But the Buddhists with complete frankness describe the matter only negatively as *Nirvana*, which is the negation of the world or of *Samsara*. If *Nirvana* is defined as nothing, this means only that *Samsara* contains no single element that could serve to define or construct *Nirvana*. For this reason the Jains, who differ from the Buddhists only in name, call the Brahmans who believe in the *Vedas*, Sabdapramans, a nickname supposed to signify that they believe on hearsay what cannot be known or proved.[62]

Such passages suggest that Schopenhauer sees Brahma as the source of good deeds and as the ultimate goal for those seeking salvation.

What then are we to make of Schopenhauer's interpretation of Brahma as something that is evil, and whose sinful act creates this world of suffering? I suggest that Schopenhauer is attempting to interpret Brahman's role as sustainer of the cosmos in a way which accords with his own doctrine of will. But such an interpretation seems forced and artificial, since it is clearly incompatible with the Advaita conception of Brahman that Schopenhauer endorses elsewhere. I suggest that the tension created by these opposing conceptions of the nature of ultimate reality provides a plausible explanation that in part may account for one of the identified shifts that occurred in his thinking between the publication of the first volume of *The World as Will and Representation* and of his later works. As I discussed earlier, whereas in the first volume Schopenhauer is emphatic that the thing-in-itself is exclusively will or will to life, in his later writings there are passages which suggest that the thing-in-itself is will in only one of its aspects, and that it has other aspects that are the focus of mystical awareness. Speculatively, this shift from a strict identity of the will with the thing-in-itself to the view that the will is just one aspect of the thing-in-itself suggests that had Schopenhauer lived longer, he may well have shifted his views even further so as to embrace the idea that the thing-in-itself is not will at all, but instead is solely the object of awareness of those who have achieved salvation. The will, on this view, becomes the esoteric but non-noumenal essence of the world.[63]

I stated earlier that there are two striking instances in which Schopenhauer's doctrines do not find any agreement with the Advaita teaching. The first is his doctrine that the thing-in-itself, or ultimate reality, is a will that is the source of immense suffering in the world, a doctrine that seems incompatible with the Advaita conception of Brahman as the Holy Power. The second point of difference is that for Schopenhauer the thing-in-itself is knowable to normal consciousness, whereas in Advaita teaching, awareness of the higher truth that concerns ultimate reality comes only to those who achieve the special consciousness or pattern of life that comes with the practice of yoga.[64] As I discussed in Section I, Schopenhauer claims numerous times throughout his works that the thing-in-itself is will or will to life and that we are directly aware of it in self-consciousness. Yet, in his later works there are passages in which he withdraws from this claim of direct acquaintance. Instead, he contends that introspective awareness is always temporal and that it conforms to the subject-object divide of phenomenal appearance. Accordingly, it seems that awareness of the thing-in-itself is limited to those who have denied the will and who attain mystical awareness. For example:

> Accordingly, at the end of my philosophy I have indicated the sphere of illuminism as something that exists but have guarded against setting even one foot thereon. For I have not undertaken to give an ultimate explanation of the world's existence, but have only gone as far as is possible on the objective path of rationalism. I have left the ground free for illuminism where, in its own way, it may arrive at a solution to all problems without obstructing my path or having to engage in polemic against me.[65]

Such passages are consistent with the Advaita teaching that only those who have attained a higher consciousness can be acquainted with ultimate reality, but they contrast sharply with passages such as the following one, in which Schopenhauer claims that we have a direct acquaintance with the thing-in-itself (or ultimate reality) in self-conscious awareness.

> By looking inwards, every individual recognises in his inner being, which is his will, the thing-in-itself, and hence that which alone is everywhere real.[66]

A plausible explanation that may account in part for this shift in Schopenhauer's ideas in the years following the publication of the first volume of *The World as Will and Representation* is the increasing influence of Hindu ideas on his own doctrine concerning the knowability of the thing-in-itself. Hence, in Schopenhauer's later works his views have changed to reflect a greater alignment with Hindu doctrine. Nevertheless, since he never gives up his doctrine that the thing-in-itself, in at least one of its aspects, is will, he also continues to assert in these later works that this claim is grounded in a direct awareness in self-consciousness of the will as thing-in-itself.

VI. SCHOPENHAUER'S LIKELY UNDERSTANDING OF BUDDHISM

To clarify how Eastern ideas might explain the shifts in Schopenhauer's doctrine of the thing-in-itself between the first and second volumes of *The World as Will and Representation*, it is useful to consider his understanding of both Hindu and Buddhist teaching. Having looked briefly at one school of Hindu thought with which it seems likely that Schopenhauer was acquainted, and having examined the similarities and differences that exist between it and Schopenhauer's doctrines, I now propose to consider Schopenhauer's understanding of Buddhist teaching.

It seems likely that with the increasing availability of literature on Buddhist teaching after 1818, Schopenhauer would have been aware of the distinction between the two principal branches of Buddhism, Theravada and Mahayana.[67] That he is acquainted with Mahayana seems clear from his reference to *The Foe Koue Ki*,[68] translated by A. Rémusat and published in 1836. Dauer states that this book, one of the earliest reliable documents on Buddhism known in Germany, is Mahayanist,[69] and she stresses the parallels between Schopenhauer's own doctrines and Mahayana teaching.[70] Copleston, however, restricts comparisons between Schopenhauer and Buddhism to themes common to all Buddhist thinking, such as compassion, the transitory nature of all phenomena, and atheism.[71] Kishan adopts a similar approach, asserting that 'Schopenhauer has no particular predilection for any school of Buddhism.'[72] Nanajivako, however, thinks that Schopenhauer is first acquainted with and influenced by the Theravada teaching of the Burmese, then in middle life becomes influenced by the Mahayana doctrine mainly through the writings on Tibetan Buddhism that were promoted by the Russian St Petersburg Academy, and finally that in the later phase of his life he is influenced by the Theravada Pali Buddhism of Ceylon.[73] Nanajivako bases this last claim on Schopenhauer's comment concerning two books on Buddhism written by Spence Hardy after his twenty-year stay in Ceylon. Schopenhauer says of these books that they 'have given me a deeper insight into the essence of the Buddhist dogma than any other work'.[74]

However, as they were not published until 1850 and 1853, respectively, it is difficult to agree with Nanajivako's claim that Schopenhauer's comment is evidence of the stronger Theravada influence at the time of his preparation of the second volume of *The World as Will and Representation*. While Schopenhauer refers to these books three times in the second volume, and also once in the first volume, these references must have been added only in the 1859 third editions of those volumes. Finally, Abelsen argues that Schopenhauer's conviction of being an original European Buddhist kept him from making a detailed philosophical comparison between his own system and those of the Buddhist schools with which he is acquainted. Consequently, contends Abelsen, the connections which Schopenhauer thinks are obvious remain a matter of atmosphere rather than content.[75] Given this diversity of opinion, my strategy in discussing the likely influence of Buddhism on Schopenhauer is to consider the general comparison between Schopenhauer's philosophy and what is commonly taken to be the essential teaching of Buddhism.[76]

The basic doctrine taught by the Buddha is summed up in the Four Noble Truths. That Schopenhauer is aware of this doctrine is clear from a passage in the second volume of *The World as Will and Representation* in which he lists the four truths.[77]

They affirm the following:

1. Life is permeated by suffering and dissatisfaction.
2. The origin of suffering lies in craving or thirst.
3. The cessation of suffering is possible through the cessation of craving.
4. The way to this cessation of suffering is through the Eightfold Path. This path is an ascending series of practices; the first two concern the right frame of mind of the aspirant, the next three concern ethical requirements, and the last three concern meditation techniques that bring serenity and release. The attainment of peace and insight is called *nirvana*, and upon its attainment the saint, at death, is not reborn.[78]

It is not difficult to find parallels between these truths and Schopenhauer's own doctrines. Corresponding to the first truth is Schopenhauer's pessimistic world-view, which derives from his conviction that the world is a wretched place, permeated by terrible, inescapable, and endless suffering.[79] Corresponding to the second truth is his doctrine that suffering results from the endless and ultimately aimless striving of all beings, a striving that is inevitable because all beings are manifestations of the metaphysical will, whose essence is to strive endlessly.[80] The Buddhist *samsara*, the empirical world permeated by thirst and craving, corresponds to Schopenhauer's world of representation, the phenomenal world. Furthermore, just as *samsara* is said to be governed by the causal nexus, so Schopenhauer's world of representation is governed by the four roots of the Principle of Sufficient Reason, one of which is the law of causality. Corresponding to the Buddhist doctrine of the impermanence of *samsara* is the conditioned nature of the world of representation in Schopenhauer's philosophy, that is, his doctrine that the formal features of the world of our everyday experience, such as its temporality, spatiality, and causal connectedness, are contributed by our minds, thereby making that world (the world of representation) one which is conditioned by us.

Corresponding to the third truth, namely, that cessation of suffering is possible by cessation of craving, is Schopenhauer's doctrine that salvation is possible by denial of the will.[81] Associated with this third truth is another doctrine that finds a parallel in Schopenhauer's philosophy. It is the Buddhist teaching of re-birth without continuation of individuality. The essential idea of the 'wheel of life' is that attachment to life (thirst) causes actions (karma), and karma conditions the next life. It is thus thirst that is the energy that drives the chain of re-births and karma that determines the conditions of the reborn. Consciousness and hence individuality spring from the karma of the previous life and are therefore derivative and fleeting. This idea is also expressed in the Buddhist doctrine of non-self (anatta), according to which there is no enduring self. Parallel to these ideas is Schopenhauer's doctrine that it is the will which endures through endless rounds of birth and death, consciousness, by contrast, is but a fleeting manifestation of will, and it perishes with the physical death of beings who possess it. Hence, corresponding to the Buddhist idea of thirst is Schopenhauer's idea that all forms of life are essentially will; corresponding to the Buddhist doctrine of non-self is Schopenhauer's doctrine that consciousness is fleeting; and corresponding to the Buddhist idea that with cessation of thirst release from suffering is possible is Schopenhauer's doctrine that with denial of all willing salvation is attainable.

The next comparison concerns the Buddhist concept of Nirvana and Schopenhauer's doctrine of denial of the will. What is Nirvana? Sri Rahula asserts:

> Volumes have been written in reply to this quite natural and simple question; they have, more and more, only confused the issue rather than clarified it. The only reasonable reply to give to the question is that it can never be answered completely and satisfactorily in words, because human language is too poor to express the real nature of the Absolute Truth or Ultimate Reality which is Nirvana.[82]

Despite this disclaimer, Sri Rahula is prepared to make the following remarks about Nirvana. He asserts that if Nirvana is expressed and explained in positive terms, this will inevitably create a false understanding since any positive terms will be tied in meaning to objects and ideas that pertain to experiences of the sense organs. Since a supramundane experience like that of the Absolute Truth is not of such a category, any literal application of ordinary language is bound to be misleading. He goes on to state that it is because of these difficulties that Nirvana is generally expressed in negative terms, such as 'Extinction of Thirst', 'Uncompounded', 'Unconditioned', 'Absence of desire', 'Cessation', 'Blowing out', or 'Extinction'.[83] However, Sri Rahula points out that the use of such negative terms has given rise to the flawed idea that Nirvana itself is negative, expressing self-annihilation. He stresses that Nirvana is definitely no annihilation of self because there is no self to annihilate. Rather, if anything is annihilated, it is the illusion that such a self exists. Furthermore, the notions of 'positive' and 'negative' are themselves misleading. For they belong to the realm of relativity, whereas Nirvana, or Absolute Truth, is beyond such relational categories.[84]

What then is Absolute Truth? It is the truth that there is nothing absolute in the world; that everything is relative, conditioned, and impermanent; and that there is no unchanging, everlasting, absolute substance like Self, Soul, or Atman within or without. To realise this truth is to see things as they are without illusion or ignorance, and this brings about extinction of craving 'thirst' and the cessation of suffering; this is Nirvana. Sri Rahula notes that according to Mahayana doctrine we should understand Nirvana as being no different from Samsara. The same thing is Samsara or Nirvana according to the way you look at it.[85]

Sri Rahula stresses that we must not understand Nirvana to be the natural result of the extinction of craving, since this would be to understand it as an effect produced by a cause. Nirvana cannot be described as 'produced' and 'conditioned', since it is beyond cause and effect; it is simply realised. It is also a mistake to reify Nirvana, as occurs when it is understood as a state or realm or position in which there is some sort of existence, imagined in terms of our ordinary understanding of sensory existence. This mistake is evident in the popular expression 'entering into Nirvana', an expression which, as Sri Rahula makes clear, has no equivalent in the original texts. A similar lack of understanding is evident in the question 'What happens to a Buddha after his death?' The question is ill-formed since Nirvana is realisable in this world and is not a state which one hopes to enter upon death.[86] Huntington elucidates this point in the following passage:

> Paradoxically, by stripping away the tendency to reify the screen of everyday affairs, this same recognition simultaneously lays bare the intrinsic nature of all things, which is their 'suchness' (*tathata*), their quality of being just as they are in reciprocal dependence. What is immediately given in everyday experience is indeed all that there is, for the inherently interdependent nature of the components of this experience is the truth of the highest meaning: both the means to the goal (*marga*; *upaya*) and the goal itself, (*nirvana*).[87]

In other words, the realisation of the highest truth, Nirvana, occurs with the recognition of the inherently interdependent nature of all phenomena in our world of everyday affairs.

In summary, the notion of Nirvana is not easy to explicate adequately. The limitations of language mean that any positive ascriptions may lead to the mistaken view that Nirvana is a state, realm, or position in which there is some kind of existence, imagined in terms of our ordinary sensory existence of subject-object duality. On the other hand, recourse to negative ascriptions may create the equally erroneous impression that Nirvana is an annihilation of Self, a doctrine that is inconsistent with the central Buddhist doctrine of non-self (anatta). Nirvana is often characterised as Absolute Truth, the truth that there is nothing absolute in the world, no substances such as Selves or Souls; instead, all is relative, conditioned, and impermanent. The realisation of this truth is accompanied by the extinction of craving and the cessation of suffering, though these must not be understood as the effects of a cause; rather, they are simply realised as both the means to the goal and the goal itself.

Having briefly outlined core elements of the Buddhist conception of Nirvana, I turn to its counterpart in Schopenhauer's philosophy, denial of the will. Schopenhauer likens denial of the will to the experiences had by mystics.[88] For both denial of the will and mystical experience are accompanied by the disappearance of the phenomenal forms of space, time, and subject-object duality.[89] Some critics argue that Schopenhauer's doctrine of denial of the will implies a 'dismal' nihilism – dismal because if the thing-in-itself is will, the will's destruction leaves only nothingness, and with it the denial of all possibility of value in existence.[90] However, such a conclusion overlooks the passages in Schopenhauer's writings where he talks of the *relative* nature of nothingness and refers to aspects of the thing-in-itself other than will. In the following passage, he draws parallels between his own doctrine of relative nothingness and Buddhist teaching.

> As a rule, the death of every good person is peaceful and gentle; but to die willingly, to die gladly, to die cheerfully, is the prerogative of the resigned, of him who gives up and denies the 'will to life'. . . . He willingly gives up the existence that we know; what comes to him instead of it is in our eyes nothing, because our existence in reference to that one is nothing. The Buddhist faith calls that existence Nirvana, that is to say, extinction.[91]

The relative nature of the nothingness as it pertains to denial of the will is again stressed by Schopenhauer in the following passage.

> Contrary to silly objections, I observe that the denial of the 'will to life' does not in any way assert the annihilation of a substance, but the mere act of not-willing, that which hitherto willed no longer wills. As we know this being, this essence, the will, as thing-in-itself merely in and through the act of willing, we are incapable of saying or comprehending what it still is or does after it has given up that act. And so for us who are the phenomenon of willing, this denial is a passing over into nothing.[92]

In the next passage the point is made yet again.

> That which in us *affirms itself as 'will to life'* is also that which *denies this will* and thereby becomes free from existence and the sufferings thereof. Now if we consider it in this latter capacity as different and separate from

us who are the self-affirming 'will to life'; and if from this point of view we wish to call '*God*' that which is opposed to the world (this being the affirmation of the 'will to life'), then this could be done for the benefit of those who do not want to drop the expression. Yet it would stand merely for an unknown x of which only the negation is known to us, namely that it denies the 'will to life' as we affirm it, and hence in so far as it is different from us and the world, but again is identical with both through its ability to be the affirmer as well as the denier, as soon as it *wants* to.[93]

The preceding passages reveal a number of similarities between the Buddhist doctrine of Nirvana, as outlined earlier, and Schopenhauer's doctrine of denial of the will. First, neither Nirvana nor denial of the will is amenable to adequate description in ordinary language. Second, neither Nirvana nor denial of the will entails nihilism; that is, neither entails the denial of all possibility of value in existence. Finally, both Nirvana and denial of the will signify the end of craving or willing and the cessation of suffering. However, alongside these similarities, it is arguable that there is also a significant difference. It is that whereas the Buddhists refuse to discuss Nirvana in terms of a substance ontology – that is, in terms of an enduring independent state or thing, which has identifiable properties that are at least conceptually distinct from the thing which owns them – Schopenhauer's discussion of denial of the will can be interpreted as assuming just such an ontology; that is, of assuming that the thing-in-itself is an enduring propertied thing. For example, he asserts that 'that which hitherto willed no longer wills' and 'what comes to him instead of it is in our eyes nothing, because our existence in reference to that one is nothing'. Arguably, both claims suggest that the thing-in-itself is an enduring independent thing-like entity which reveals other aspects or properties of its nature once it gives up the activity of willing. While the non-temporal and non-spatial character of the thing-in-itself necessarily make it unlike the things of our everyday physical world, it is nevertheless arguable, though not conclusive, that Schopenhauer thinks of the thing-in-itself as a substance-like thing, capable of possessing properties of various kinds.

What are we to make of this alleged difference between Buddhism and Schopenhauer's philosophy? Perhaps Schopenhauer did not grasp that Buddhism rejects substance ontology or perhaps the literature on Buddhism with which he was acquainted was ambivalent on this point. Given that contemporary Buddhist scholars recognise that within Buddhism itself there exists a rival school, the Yogacara, which, its critics argue, resurrects the Vedantic concept of a metaphysical substrate (substance) of all phenomenal appearance, clothing it in the guise of 'dependent nature',[94] each of the previously discussed alternatives has some plausibility. Furthermore, given that Schopenhauer's formative philosophical education was grounded in the Western tradition, a tradition which almost universally assumes a substance ontology,[95] it would hardly be surprising if he interpreted the available Buddhist literature in terms of the ontological assumptions with which he was familiar.

The alleged difference between Schopenhauer and Buddhism over their respective ontological presuppositions is, I believe, important in its own right. However, it is also important as background to the following point. Schopenhauer claims that denial of the will yields only a relative nothing; yet this claim seems to make sense only on the assumption that the thing-in-itself has aspects other than will. As I argued earlier, it is only in Schopenhauer's later work that he introduces a multiple-aspect notion of the thing-in-itself, and only in his later works that he sees parallels between the Buddhist notion of Nirvana and his own doctrine of denial of the will. My contention is that it is his increasing knowledge of and admiration for Buddhism, and in particular his realisation that Nirvana does not mean the end of all possibility of value in existence, that in part may explain this shift in his thinking concerning the nature of the thing-in-itself. This shift from a strict identity between the thing-in-itself and will to a multiple-aspect notion of the thing-in-itself allowed Schopenhauer to assimilate the Buddhist notion of Nirvana with his doctrine that denial of the will is the path to salvation. For just as Nirvana is not simply a negation of everything, but rather represents a way of experiencing the world such that it has positive rather than negative value, so denial of the will is a denial of that which is the source of negative value, making possible the experience of that which is of positive value. This assimilation may appear ill-judged if my earlier suggestion of fundamental ontological differences between Buddhism and Schopenhauer's philosophy is warranted. However, it is unlikely that it would have appeared ill-judged to Schopenhauer. For, as I discussed earlier, there are good reasons for believing that if such differences existed, Schopenhauer would not have been in a position to fully appreciate them.

Finally, there is the fourth truth of Buddha's teaching, which outlines the eight-fold way of attaining enlightenment through the adoption of the right view, the correct ethical practices, and the recommended ascetic and contemplative practices. Corresponding to these steps is Schopenhauer's view that denial of the will requires first of all that a person sees through the *principium individuationis* constituted by space and time. This insight is reflected in a shift from egoistic to altruistic behaviour, and finally to the practice of meditation and a complete withdrawal from the world.[96] However, alongside these similarities, a sharp contrast is also evident. Schopenhauer maintains that denial of the will is an exceptional human experience. However, as I mentioned in Section I, he also contends that awareness of the will as thing-in-itself comes about in ordinary introspective consciousness.[97] If it is the thing-in-itself, albeit in its other aspects, that for Schopenhauer is the object of awareness for those who have denied the will, then it would seem to follow that the thing-in-itself is the object not only of enlightened consciousness, but also of ordinary consciousness. This contention, however, finds no parallel in Buddhism. For in Buddhism, ordinary and enlightened consciousness are radically different from each other. I mentioned in both Sections I and V that there are passages in Schopenhauer's later works in which he appears to withdraw from his claim of direct awareness in ordinary consciousness of the will as thing-in-itself.[98] My hypothesis is that as Schopenhauer became increasingly aware of the epistemological differences between his philosophy and Buddhist teaching, he shifted his views to accord more readily with what he understood of theirs. Hence, in passages from his later works, a clear distinction is made between the objects of ordinary and enlightened consciousness.

VII. CONCLUSION

I have argued that a plausible case can be made for explaining shifts in Schopenhauer's doctrine of the thing-in-itself by suggesting that these changes occurred in response to his increasing knowledge of and admiration for the teachings of the Hindus and Buddhists. I have identified three such shifts; the first concerns the knowability of the thing-in-itself; the second concerns its nature; and the third concerns Schopenhauer's explicit attempt to assimilate his own views on what can be said about the thing-in-itself with Eastern teaching.

The influence of Hindu and Buddhist doctrines, according to which the possibility of enlightenment is restricted to persons who have achieved a refined state of consciousness, offers a plausible explanation that in part may account for the first shift. For in Schopenhauer's later works, while he still asserts that in ordinary introspective consciousness we have direct awareness of the will as thing-in-itself, there are also passages in which he withdraws from this claim. Instead he maintains that ordinary introspective consciousness yields knowledge of phenomena alone, and only mystics and those who have denied the will are aware of reality stripped of its phenomenal forms.

The impact on Schopenhauer of both the Hindu idea of ultimate reality as a Holy Power which is the source of value, and of the Buddhist notion of Nirvana, which can be described negatively as the extinction of suffering, suggests a way of at least partly explaining the second shift. For, in his later works, while he continues to maintain that the thing-in-itself is will or 'will to life' and the source of suffering, he also introduces the idea that the thing-in-itself has other aspects. Speculatively, this shift from a strict identity of the thing-in-itself with will to the view that the thing-in-itself has multiple aspects only one of which is will suggests that had Schopenhauer lived longer, he may well have embraced the view that the thing-in-itself is not will at all; rather it is the object of awareness of saints, mystics and those who have denied the will. The will, by contrast, is the esoteric but non-noumenal essence of the world.[99]

Schopenhauer's familiarity with the Buddhist doctrine which insists that no words can be used to describe Nirvana, offers a persuasive way of accounting in part for the third shift. For it is only in his later works and in later additions to his earlier works that he explicitly attempts to assimilate his own views on the limitations of language in describing the thing-in-itself with Eastern ideas.

In short, it is plausible that the influence of Eastern thought accounts for Schopenhauer's shift from an initial post-Kantian position concerning the thing-in-itself to one more philosophically aligned with what he takes to be the essential tenets of Buddhism and Hinduism.

APPENDIX: SCHOPENHAUER'S ORIENTAL SOURCES*

Listed here are references from Schopenhauer's works to literature on Hinduism and Buddhism. As he does not consistently provide full details in noting his references, I have made additions and standardised titles and spelling in accordance with the list of titles in Schopenhauer's posthumous library (see E. Grisebach, *Edita und Inedita Schopenhaueriana* [Leipzig: Brockhaus, 1888], 141–84, and A. Hübscher (ed.), *Der handschriftliche Nachlass*, Fünfter Band [Frankfurt a. M.: Verlag Waldemar Kramer, 1968], 319–52).

Grisebach's list of titles was compiled from the auction catalogues of 1869 and 1871, and from the warehouse catalogue of 1880, which had been prepared for the auction of the library that Schopenhauer had bequeathed to his executor, Wilhelm von Gwinner. While Grisebach's list is extensive, he states that it is incomplete, noting that some books were disposed of by Gwinner in other ways. Grisebach also states that it is only in the case of those books that he personally acquired that he can be certain of the bibliographic exactness of the entries on his list. For the sake of consistency, I have chosen to standardise titles in accordance with the details that he provides. However, in cases where these details differ from those provided by Hübscher, I have used the latter since it is the more recent work.

Grisebach lists about 130 items of orientalia in Schopenhauer's posthumous library, while Hübscher lists approximately 150. Whichever figure is more accurate, it represents a considerable collection, and suggests that Schopenhauer has a strong and abiding interest in Eastern ideas.

Hinduism

Manuscript Remains

Polier, *Mythologie des Indous, Roudolstadt*, 1809 (*MR* 1 515/Hn. 1, 465 [1817]); Rhode's *On Religion and Philosophy of the Hindus*, Leipzig, 1827 (*MR* 2 459 n/Hn. 2, 395 n. [1815–16], which must be a footnote added to the 1815–16 notes after the 1827 publication date of the book, *MR* 4 149/Hn. 4/i, 125 [1832]); *Desatir* of unknown author (*MR* 3 64/Hn. 3, 58 [1820]); Wilson, *Iswara Krishna Sankhya-Karica*, Oxford, 1837 (*MR* 3 137 n./Hn. 3, 126 n. [1820]); F. Schlegel, *Ueber die Sprache und Weisheit der Indier, nebst metrischen Uebersetzgungen indischer Gedichte*, Heidelberg, 1808 (*MR* 3 442/Hn. 3, 403 [1828–30]); Colebrooke, *On the Philosophy of the Hindous*, Transactions of the Asiatic London Society, vol. 1 (*MR* 3 682/Hn. 3, 627 [1828–30]); Max Müller, *Rig Veda, Text and Notes* Sanskrit, London, 1854 (*MR* 4 376/Hn. 4/ii, 17–18 [1852–60]); Max Müller, 'On the Veda and the Zend Avesta', in Bunsen, *Hippolytus and his age*, London, 1852 (*MR* 4 376/Hn. 4/ii, 18 [1852–60]).

Parerga and Paralipomena, Vol. 2

'Some Remarks on Sanskrit Literature', *P2* 395–402/Z. 10, 435–43. Obry, *Du Nirvana indien, ou de l'affranchissement de l'âme après la mort, selon les Brahmans et les Bouddhistes*, Amiens, 1856; the *Edinburgh Review*, 1858; Langlès, *Monuments anciens et modernes de l'Hindoustan*, Paris, 1821; Hardy, *Eastern Monachism*, London, 1850; the *Asiatic Researches*; and Schlegel's translation of the *Bhagavadgita*, Bonnae, 1823. Schopenhauer also refers the reader to his essay *On the Basis of Morality*, Section 22, where in a footnote discussion of the genuineness of the *Oupnek'hat* he mentions the secondary texts, F. Windischmann, ed., *Sancara, sive de theologumenis Vedanticorum*, Bonn, 1833; J. J. Bochinger, *Sur la connexion de la vie contemplative ascétic et monastique chez les Indous et chez les peuples boudhistes*, Strasbourg, 1831, and the recent (in his day) translations of the *Upanishads* by Rammohun Roy, Poley, Colebrooke, and Röer.

Other literature on Hinduism that Schopenhauer refers to in *P2* includes the following: *A Bengal officer, Vindication of the Hindoos from the aspersions of the Reverend Claudius Buchanan, with a refutation of his arguments in favour of an ecclesiastical establishment in British India: the whole tending to evince the excellence of the moral system of the Hindoos*, 1808 (*P2* 223/Z. 9, 243); *The Times*, 1849 (*P2* 223 n./Z. 9, 243 n.); *The Times*, 1858 (*P2* 226/Z. 9, 246); *Edinburgh Review*, 1858 (*P2* 401/Z. 10, 442).

The World as Will and Representation, Vol. 1

Asiatic Researches (see *W1* 4, 48, 381, 388 n./Z. 1, 30, 82; Z. 2, 471, 480 n.); *Oupnek'hat* (see *W1* 181, 283 n., 388 n./Z. 1, 235; Z. 2, 356 n., 480 n.); *Upanishads* (see *W1* xv, xvi, 181, 205, 355 n., 381/Z. 1, 11, 235, 264; Z. 2, 442 n., 471); *Bhagavad-Gita*, trans. A. Schlegel, Bonnae, 1823 (see *W1* 284, 388 n./ Z. 2, 358, 480 n.); *Veda* (see *W1* xv, 8, 17, 86, 181, 205, 283 n., 355–7, 374, 380, 388, 419, 495 n./Z. 1, 11, 34, 45, 128, 235, 264; Z. 2, 356, 442, 464, 471, 480, 516, 604 n.); Wilson, *Iswara Krishna Sánkhya Karika*, Oxford, 1837 (see *W1* 382 n./473 n.); Colebrooke, 'On the philosophy of the Hindus': *Miscellaneous Essays*, London, 1837 (see *W1* 382 n./Z. 2, 473 n.); Polier, *Mythologie des Indous*, Roudolstadt, 1809 (see *W1* 384, 388 n., 495 n./Z. 2, 475, 480 n., 604 n.); *Asiatisches Magazin* (see *W1* 388 n./Z. 2, 480 n.); *Puranas* (see *W1* 8, 17, 388, 419, 495 n./Z. 1, 34, 45; Z. 2, 480, 516, 473 n.

The World as Will and Representation, Vol. 2

Asiatic Researches (*W2* 169–70, 505, 608/Z. 3, 197–8; Z. 4, 592, 712); *Bhagavad-Gita*, trans. A. Schlegel, Bonnae, 1823 (see *W2* 326, 473/Z. 3, 381; Z 4, 555); *Oupnek'hat* (see *W2* 457, 607 n., 613/Z. 4, 538, 711 n., 718); *Veda* (see *W2* 162, 457, 475, 506, 508, 608, 613/Z. 3, 89; Z. 4, 538, 557, 592, 596, 712, 718); *Upanishads* (see *W2* 162, 457, 475, 609, 611 n./Z. 3, 189: Z. 4, 538, 557, 713, 715 n.); Colebooke, 'History of Indian Philosophy', in the *Transactions of the Asiatic London Society* (see *W2* 488/Z. 4, 572); F. Windischmann, ed., *Sankara, sive de theologumenis Vedanticorum*, Bonn, 1833 (see W2 508 n, 607 n./Z. 4, 596 n., 711 n.); Colebrooke, *Miscellaneous Essays*, London, 1837 (see W2 508 n./Z. 4, 596 n.).

On the Will in Nature

Colebrooke, 'Report on the Vedas', in the *Asiatic Researches*, vol. 8 (undated) (*WN* 45/Z. 5, 230); Bopp, 'Sundas and Upasunda', in *Ardschuna's Reise zu Indra's Himmel*, 1824 (*WN* 48/Z. 5, 234).

On the Basis of Morality

Bhagavadgita (*BM*, 213/Z. 6, 314–15).

Excluding the *Asiatiches Magazin* and *Asiatic Researches*, which are dated 1802 and 1806–12, respectively, Grisebach and Hübscher each list approximately forty other titles that specifically refer to Hinduism. While up to eighteen of these have publication dates earlier than 1818, only two (the works by Polier and F. Schlegel) are mentioned in the *Manuscript Remains* in the period before 1818. It therefore seems likely that it was not until after 1818 that Schopenhauer acquired the other works.

Buddhism

As Schopenhauer does not consistently provide full details in noting his references, I have, where appropriate, made amendments in accordance with the details provided in Grisebach's list. In cases where Schopenhauer refers to works which do not appear on this list, but which do appear in the bibliography that Schopenhauer himself provides in his chapter 'Sinology' in *On the Will in Nature*, I use the fuller details noted there.

Manuscript Remains, Vols. 3 and 4

Journal Asiatique (*MR* 3 66/Hn. 3, 60 [1820]; 336/Hn. 3, 305 [1825]); *Asiatic Journal* (*MR* 3 349/Hn. 3, 317 [1826]; 424/Hn. 3, 389 [1828]; 658/Hn. 3, 605 [1828–30]); Morrison, *Chinese Dictionary*, 1815 (*MR* 3 60/Hn. 3, 55 [1820]); *San-tsung fa sou*, the principal document of the Buddhist religion (*MR* 3 372/Hn. 3, 339 [1826]); Abel Rémusat, *Mélanges asiatiques*, 1825 (*MR* 3 372/Hn. 3, 339 [1826]; 37 n./Hn. 3, 306 n. [1826]); Upham, *The History and the Doctrine of Buddhism*, London, 1829 (*MR* 3 675/Hn. 3, 621 [1828–30]); I. J. Schmidt, *Geschichte der Ost-Mongolen und ihres Fürstenhauses*, St Petersburg, 1829 (*MR* 4 47/Hn. 4/i, 33 [1830–31]); B. Hodgson, descriptions of Buddhism in Nepal as recorded in the *Transactions of the Royal Asiatic Society of Great Britain and Ireland*, London, 1828, and as elucidated by I. J. Schmidt in his essay in *Mémoirs de l'Académie de St. Petersbourg* (*MR* 4 455/Hn. 4/ii, 91 [1852–60]).

On the Will in Nature

'Sinology', *WN* 130–1 n./Z. 6, 327 n. Schopenhauer lists the following works, whose details I amend according to Grisebach's list in cases where the works appear on both lists, but with slightly different details on each: 1. I. J. Schmidt, *Dsanglun oder der Weise und der Thor*, St Petersburg, 1843; 2. I. J. Schmidt, Several lectures delivered to the Academy of St Petersburg in 1829–32; Schopenhauer is probably referring to the following lectures listed by Grisebach: *Ueber einige Grundlehren des Buddhaismus*, 1929, *Ueber einige Grundlehren des Buddhaismus*, 1830, *Ueber die sogenannte dritte Welt der Buddhaisten als Forsetzung der Abhandlungen über die ihren des Buddhaismus*, 1831, *Ueber die tausend Buddhas einer Weltperiode der Einwohnung oder gleichmässigen Dauer*, 1832; 3. I. J. Schmidt, *Forschungen im Gebiete der älteren religiösen, politischen und litterarischen Bildungsgeschichte der Völker Mittelasiens, vorzüglich der Mongolen und Tibeter*, St. Petersburg, 1824; 4. I. J. Schmidt, *Ueber die Verwandtschaft der gnostisch-theosophischen Lehren mit den Religionssystemen des Orients, vorzüglich dem Buddhaismus*, Leipzig, 1828; 5. I. J. Schmidt, *Ssanang Ssetsen Chung-Taidschi, Geschichte der Mongolen und ihres Fürstenhauses*, St Petersburg, 1829; 6. Schniefer, two treatises in German in the 'Mélanges Asiatiques tirés du Bulletin Historico-Philol. de l'Acad. d. St. Petersburg', Tome 1, 1851; 7. Samuel Turner, *Gesandtschaftsreise an den Hof des Teshoo Lama*. Aus dem Englischen, 1801; 8. J. Bochinger, *Sur la connexion de la vie contemplative, ascétique et monastique chez les Indous et chez les peuples bouddhistes*, Strasbourg, 1831; 9. *Journal Asiatique*, vol. 7, 1825; 10. E. Burnouf, *Introduction à l'histoire du Buddhisme indien*, Paris, 1844; 11. *Rgya Tch'er Rol Pa*, trans. from Tibetan by Foucaux, 1848; 12. Chi Fa Hian, *Foe Koue Ki*, trans. from Chinese by Abel Rémusat, Paris, 1836; 13. *Description du Tibet*, trans. by Bitchourin and Klaproth, 1831; 14. Klaproth, *Fragments Bouddhiques*, 1831; 15. Spiegel, *Liber de officiis Sacerdotum Buddhicorum*, Bonnae, 1841; 16. Spiegel, *Anecdota Palica*, 1845; 17. Fausböll, *Dhammapadam*, Hovniae, 1855; 18. Buchanan, 'On the Religion of the Burmas', and C. Körösa, three articles, including 'Analyses of the Books of the Kandshur', *Asiatic Researches*; 1839; 19. Sangermano, *The Burmese Empire*, Rome, 1833; 20. Turnour, *The Mahawanzo; and a prefatory essay on Pali Buddhistical literature*, Ceylon, 1836; 21. Upham, *The Mahávansi: the Rájá Ratnácari and the Ráyá-vali*, London, 1833; 22. Upham, *The History and doctrine of Buddhism*, London, 1829; 23. Hardy, *Eastern Monachism*, London, 1850; 24. Hardy, *Manual of Buddhism in its modern development*, London, 1853; 25. C. F. Koeppen, *Die Religion des Buddha*, 1857; 26. 'The Life of Buddha' from the Chinese of Palladji in the *Archiv für wissenschaftliche Kunde von Russland*, ed. Erman, vol. xv, Heft 1, 1856.

Other works on Buddhism that Schopenhauer also refers to in 'Sinology' are: *Asiatic Journal*, 1826; Morrison, *Chinese Dictionary*, Macao, 1815; Neumann, 'Die Natur- und Religions-Philosophie der Chinesen, nach den Werken des Tchu-hi', an article in Illgen, *Periodical for Historical Theology*, vol. vii, 1837 (Grisebach lists only *Asiatische Studien*, Leipzig, 1837, against Neumann's name. However, given that the dates of the two titles are the same, they may refer to the same article).

The World as Will and Representation, Vol. 1
Chi Fa Hian, Foe Koue Ki, trans. from Chinese by Abel Rémusat, Paris, 1836
(see W1 381/Z. 2, 472); Upham, The History and Doctrine of Buddhism,
London, 1829 (see W1 484/Z. 2, 592).

The World as Will and Representation, Vol. 2
I. J. Schmidt, Uber das Mahâjâna and Pradchnâ-Pâramita der Bauddhen, 1836
(see W2 275/Z. 3, 321–2); Rgya Tch'er Rol Pa, trans. from Tibetan by Foucaux,
Paris, 1848 (see W2 400 n./Z. 4, 473 n.); Upham, The History and Doctrine of
Buddhism, London, 1829 (see W2 488/Z. 4, 572); Hardy, Manual of Buddhism
in its modern development, London, 1853; Taylor, Prabodha Chadro Daya,
London, 1812; Sangermano, The Burmese Empire, Rome, 1833; Asiatic
Researches, Köppen, Die Religion des Buddha, 1857; Obry, Du Nirvana indien,
Amiens, 1856; and T. Burnet, Histoire du Manichéisme (see W2 503–4/Z. 4,
592); Hardy, Eastern Monachism, London, 1850; I. J. Schmidt, Geschichte der
Mongolen und ihres Fürstenhauses, St Petersburg, 1829; Colebrooke in Transactions of the Royal Asiatic Society (see W2 508 n./Z. 4, 596 n.); Asiatic Researches
(see W2 608/Z. 4, 712); E. Burnouf, Introduction à l'histoire du Buddhism
Indien, Paris, 1844 (see W2 623/Z. 4, 730); I. J. Schmidt, Ueber die Verwandtschaft der gnostisch-theosophischen Lehren mit den Religionssystemen
des Orients, vorzüglich dem Buddhaismus, Leipzig, 1828 (see W2 624/Z. 4, 731).

On the Basis of Morality
Journal Asiatique; vol. ix, Meng-Tseu, ed. Stan. Julian, 1824; Livres sacrés de
l'orient, undated (BM 186 n./Z. 6, 132 n.).

Parerga and Paralipomena, Vols. 1 and 2
F. Buchanan, 'On the Religion of the Burmese', Asiatic Researches, vol. vi, 1839
(P1 116 n./Z. 7, 132 n.); I. J. Schmidt, Forschungen im Gebiete der älteren
religiösen, politischen und litterarischen Bildungsgeschichte der Völker Mitte-
lasiens, vorzüglich der Mongolen und Tibeter, St Petersburg, 1824 (P1 116 n.;
P2 153/Z. 7, 132 n.; Z. 9, 168); Sir G. Stanton, An Enquiry into the proper
mode of rendering the word of God in translating the Sacred Scriptures into the
Chinese Language, London, 1848 (P1 116 n./Z. 7, 132 n.); S. Hardy, Eastern
Monachism, London, 1850 (P2 84 n., 358/Z. 9, 95 n.; Z. 10, 395); S. Hardy,
Manual of Buddhism, London, 1853 (P2 84 n., 276/Z. 9, 95 n.; Z. 10, 300);
Klaproth, Fragmens Bouddhiques in the Nouveau Journal asiatique, 1831;
Koeppen, Die Lamaische Hierarchie, undated (P2 153/Z. 9, 168); I. J. Schmidt,
Sanang Ssetsen Chung-Taidschi, Geschichte der Mongolen und ihres Fürsten-
hauses, St Petersburg, 1839; Lettrés édifiantes et curieuses, 1819 (P2 203/Z. 9,
221); Sangermano, The Burmese Empire, Rome, 1833; Asiatic Researches, vol.
vi, ix (P2 276/Z. 9, 300); Obry, Du Nirvana indien, ou de l'affranchissement de
l'âme après la mort, selon les Brahmans et les Bouddhistes, Amiens, 1856 (P2
401/Z. 10, 441).

Only two of these works were published prior to 1818. These are: Morrison, *Chinese Dictionary*, Macao, 1815; and Samuel Turner, *Gesandtschaftsreise an den Hof des Teshoo Lama. Aus dem Englischen*, 1801.

Of the works listed in Schopenhauer's posthumous library which specifically refer to Buddhist thought, only three have publication dates earlier than 1818. These are: M. Ozeray, *Recherches sur Bouddhou*, Paris, 1817; Abel Rémusat, *Le livre des récompenses et des peines, traduit du chinois avec des notes et des éclaircissements*, Paris, 1816; and Samuel Turner, *Gesandtschaftsreise an den Hof des Teshoo Lama*, Aus dem Englischen, 1801. The total number of titles specifically referring to Buddhist thought is thirty-eight in Grisebach's list and forty-four in Hübscher's.

NOTES

1. See *W1* xiii–xiv, xxi–xxiii/Z. 1, 9–10; 18–20 for Schopenhauer's claim that there are no significant changes in his thinking after the publication in 1818 of *W1*[1].
2. See H. Höffding, *History of Modern Philosophy* (London: Macmillan and Co., 1915), 226; F. Copleston, *Arthur Schopenhauer: Philosopher of Pessimism* (London: Burns Oates & Washbourne, 1946), 65; P. Gardiner, *Schopenhauer* (Middlesex: Penguin Books, 1967), 173; D. Hamlyn, *Schopenhauer* (London: Routledge & Kegan Paul, 1980), 84–5; C. Janaway, *Self and World in Schopenhauer's Philosophy* (Oxford: Clarendon Press, 1989), 196.
3. See *W1* 110, 112, 113, 119, 120, 128, 181, 184, 275, 280, 282, 286, 287, 288, 289, 290, 292, 301, 328, 354, 366, 402, 421, 436, 474, 501, 503, 504–5, 506, 534; *W2* 14, 16, 18, 136, 174, 201, 206, 214, 239, 245, 259, 299, 307, 308, 309, 313, 320, 322, 335, 348, 443, 472, 484, 497, 501, 530, 579, 589, 600, 601; *WN* 20, 36, 47, 116; *P1* 20, 78, 229, 267, 299, 303, 305; *P2* 46, 48, 90, 94, 95, 176, 312, 313, 383, 599; *FW* 34, 97; *MR 1* 184, 205, 206, 319, 488, 491; *MR 2* 463, 485, 486; *MR 3* 84, 121, 164, 197, 227, 245, 247–8, 365, 572; *MR 4* 110, 139, 211, 217, 223/Z. 1, 155, 157, 158, 165, 166, 228, 235, 238, 347; Z. 2, 353, 356, 361, 363, 364, 365, 367, 378, 410, 441, 455, 497, 519, 536, 580, 612, 614, 615, 616, 618, 650; Z. 3, 23, 24, 27, 158–9, 203, 234, 240, 249, 280, 286, 302, 349, 359, 360, 361, 367, 374, 377, 393, 408; Z. 4, 521, 553, 568, 583, 587, 620, 678–90, 703, 705; Z. 5, 202, 220; Z. 6, 233, 310; Z. 7, 29, 92, 251, 290, 325, 328, 331; Z. 9, 55, 56, 102, 107, 192, 339, 340; Z. 10, 423, 651; Z. 6, 72, 137; Hn. 1, 169, 187, 188, 291, 440, 444; Hn. 2, 399, 419; Hn. 3, 75, 110, 149, 180, 207, 224, 226, 333, 525; Hn. 4/1, 88, 116, 184, 189, 194.
4. *WN*, trans. Hillebrand, 216/Z. 5, 202. Also see *W2* 600; *W1* 162, 436, 503, 504, 345/Z. 4, 703; Z. 1, 215; Z. 2, 536, 614, 615, 310. For less explicit references see *W2* 179, 195, 313, 364; *W2* 288, 290; *FR* 119–20/Z. 3, 209, 228, 367; Z. 4, 433; Z. 3, 363, 365; Z. 5, 99.
5. *W2* 196–7/Z. 3, 229–30. Also see *W2* 182, 185, 197–8, 318, 496, 612: *P1* 42; *MR 3* 40, 114, 171, 353, 472, 595, 713, 716; *MR 4* 296–7/Z. 3, 213, 216–17, 230, 231, 372; Z. 4, 581, 716; Z. 7, 54; Hn. 3, 36–7, 103, 155, 321–2, 432, 546, 657, 600; Hn. 4/i, 261.
6. See G. Simmel, *Schopenhauer and Nietzsche*, trans. Helmut Loiskandl, Deena Weinstein, and Michael Weinstein (Amherst: University of Massachusetts Press, 1986), 33–4; R. Tsanoff, *Schopenhauer's Criticism of Kant's Theory of Experience* (New York: Longman, Green & Company, 1911), 66–70; T. Whittaker, *Reason, A Philosophical Essay with Historical Illustrations* (Cambridge: Cambridge University Press, 1934), 8; A. Hübscher, *The Philosophy of Schopenhauer in Its Intellectual Context, Thinker Against the Tide*, trans. Joachim T. Baer and David Cartwright (Lewiston, NY: Edwin Mellen Press, 1989), 20.

7. *W1* 445/Z. 6, 546.
8. See J. Young, *Willing and Unwilling: A Study in the Philosophy of Arthur Scho-penhauer* (Dordrecht: Martinus Nijhoff, 1987), 30; Janaway, *Self and World*, 197.
9. *W2* 182/Z. 3, 213. Also see *W2* 197, 318/Z. 3, 230, 372.
10. See *W1* xiv/Z. 1, 9.
11. See Höffding, *History of Modern Philosophy*, 226 (n. 51).
12. *W1* 4/Z. 1, 31. Also see *W1* 125, 141, 153, 162, 502/Z. 1, 172–3, 191, 204–5, 215, 613.
13. *W2* 198/Z. 3, 231. Also see *W2* 560, 644; *P2* 312, *W2* 288, 294, 642; *MR* 3 79; *W1* 405, 411/Z. 4, 656, 754; Z. 9, 339; Z. 3, 338, 343; Z. 4, 753; Hn. 3, 70; Z. 2, 500, 507.
14. *W2* 325, 325–6; *MR* 1 36–7; *MR* 4 35; *W1* 110–12, 410/Z. 3, 380, 381; Hn. 1, 34–5; Hn. 4/i, 23; Z. 1, 155; Z. 2, 506.
15. *W2* 325–6/Z. 3, 381; relevant also to *W2* 325/Z. 3, 380.
16. *W1* 411–12/Z. 2, 508.
17. However, several references to both Hindu and Buddhist thought are added by Schopenhauer in the revised 1847 edition of *FR*. See *FR* 50, 184–8, 208/Z. 5, 47, 141–5, 158. In the third edition, published in 1864, the editor, Julius Frauenstädt, amends the 1847 text to include corrections and additions jotted down by Schopenhauer in an interleaved copy of the 1847 edition. In Frauenstädt's preface to the third edition he lists the principal passages that are new. Of the twenty-four listed, three concern references to Eastern thought and literature. (See *FR*, trans. Mme Karl. Hillebrand [London: G. Bell, 1889], xxvi–xxviii. The three passages in question are in section 34.)
18. See H. G. Rawlinson, 'India in European Literature and Thought', in *The Legacy of India*, ed. G. T. Garratt (Oxford: Clarendon Press, 1937), 35–6; H. G. Rawlinson, 'Indian Influence on the West', in *Modern India and the West*, ed. L. S. S. O'Malley (London: Oxford University Press, 1941), 546–7; L. S. S. O'Malley, 'General Survey', in *Modern India and the West*, 801–2; P. J. Marshall and G. Williams, *The Great Map of Mankind* (London: Dent, London, 1982), 111–12. See also Janaway, *Self and World*, 29.
19. See *MR* 1 456/Hn. 1, 412, and *MR* 2 477/Hn. 2, 412, where Schopenhauer refers to undated editions of the *Asiatic Researches* and *Asiatick Researches*, respec-tively. Because he does not give publication dates, it is possible that these references are added to his notes after 1818. However, since elsewhere he makes it clear that he has access to these journals prior to 1818 (see *W2* 169/Z. 3, 197, and *MR* 2 459–61/Hn. 2, 395–7), it seems probable that these references are not later additions.
20. I refer to Rhode's *On the Religion and Philosophy of the Hindus*, 1827, which Schopenhauer refers to in a footnote at *MR* 2 459/Hn. 2, 395. He also refers to undated editions of the *Asiatic Researches*, *MR* 1 286, 515/Hn. 1, 260, 465; the *Asiatick Researches*, *MR* 2 477/Hn. 2, 412; and the *Asiatic Magazine*, *MR* 2 262/ Hn. 2, 245 (Grisebach notes the correct spelling as *Asiatisches Magazin*). However, for the reasons outlined in note 19, these references are probably not later additions to Schopenhauer's notes.
21. I determined this figure by comparing all references to Buddhism in Payne's translation of the 1859 edition of *W1* to the 1819 first edition of that volume, *W1¹*, edited by R. Malter. The relevant page numbers in Payne's translation of *W1* are as follows: 381, 383, 384, 424, 484/Z. 2, 472, 474, 75, 521–2, 592. The corresponding page numbers in Malter's edition of *W1¹* are as follows: 548–9, 550, 552, 602, 665.
22. The relevant page numbers in Payne's translation of *W1* are as follows: 4, 181, 330, 382 n., 424, 436, 484/Z. 1, 30, 235, 412, 473 n., 521, 522, 592. The corresponding page numbers in Malter's edition of *W1¹* are as follows: 4, 260, 475, 549–50, 602, 617, 665.

23. To determine these approximate numbers, I noted and cross-checked all references in the index of Payne's translation of *The World as Will and Representation* that pertained to Buddhist and Hindu thought. For the *Manuscript Remains*, since there is no index, I scanned the text for similarly relevant references.

24. *W1* 388 n/*Z.* 2, 480 n.

25. See my appendix, 'Schopenhauer's Oriental Sources', for a listing of the literature on Hinduism and Buddhism referred to by Schopenhauer in his various works.

26. Schopenhauer's *Oupnek'hat* is an 1801 Latin version translated by Anquetil-Duperron of a Persian version translated by Sultan Mohammed Dara Shikoh (brother of Aurangzeb) of the Sanskrit original (see *P2* 396/*Z.* 10, 436).

27. In 1784 Sir William Jones established the Asiatic Society in Calcutta, the prototype of similar societies in Europe. The society published volumes of proceedings called *Asiatic Researches*, which attracted wide European readership and which were re-issued and translated into French and German. Marshall says that the translations of Sir Charles Wilkins, who made the first English translation of the *Bhagavadgita* in 1785, and who is said to be the first European to really understand Sanskrit, and the essays by Jones in the *Asiatic Researches* set standards that were not to be matched for a generation (Marshall, *The Great Map of Mankind*, 76). Furthermore, Rawlinson notes that in 1805 in the *Asiatic Researches*, H. T. Colebrooke, the greatest of the early orientalists, gave the world the first account of the *Vedas*, which hitherto had been jealously concealed from European eyes (Rawlinson, 'Indian Influence on the West', 546).

28. The *Puranas* consist of a collection of legends that are sometimes said to be part of the fifth *Veda* (*The New Encyclopaedia Britannica*, 15th ed., s.v. 'South Asian Arts', by Pramod Chandra).

29. Rosen published the first edition of some of the hymns of the *Rig-Veda* in 1838 (Rawlinson, 'India in European Thought', 36). At *MR* 4 376/Hn. 4/ii, 17–18, Schopenhauer also mentions the 1854 publication *Rig-Veda, Text and Notes Sanskrit*, by Max Müller. See also Rawlinson, 'Indian Influence on the West', 547–9, for a discussion of the outstanding pioneering achievements of Max Müller from 1845 on. In Rawlinson, 'India in European Literature and Thoughts', 36, the author says that 'the publication, in 1875, of the first of the great series of the *Sacred Books of the East*, under the editorship of Max Müller, made the Hindu scriptures available for the first time to the ordinary reader'.

30. In the two volumes of the *Manuscript Remains* up to 1818, there are three references to the *Bhagavadgita* (*MR* 1 452, 515; *MR* 2 262/Hn. 1, 409, 465; Hn. 2, 245). No details are given for the first two references, but the *Asiatiches Magazin* is given as the source of the third. In *W1* there are two references, one of which refers to the 1802 edition of the *Asiatisches Magazine* (*W1* 388 n./*Z.* 2, 480 n.). The other is not referenced (*W1* 284/*Z.* 2, 358). In *W1*, of the two references to the *Bhagavadgita*, one is not referenced (*W1* 473/*Z.* 2, 555), but the other gives as its source the translation by Schlegel (*W2* 326/*Z.* 3, 381).

31. See Hübscher, *The Philosophy of Schopenhauer in Its Intellectual Context*, 65–6.

32. *P2* 397/*Z.* 10, 437.

33. *P2* 398/*Z.* 10, 438.

34. See also R. K. Das Gupta, 'Schopenhauer and Indian Thought', *East and West* 13, 1 (1962), 32–40, who lists books on Hindu teaching with which Schopenhauer is likely to have been acquainted.

35. See *MR* 1 286, 456, 515; *MR* 2 459–61, 477/Hn. 1, 260 (1814), 412 (1816), 465–6 (1817); Hn. 2, 395–7 (1815–16), 412 (1816–18).

36. See *MR* 1 515/Hn. 1, 465 (1817).

37. See *MR* 2 262/Hn. 2, 245 (1809–13).

38. See *MR* 3 351, 658, 672, 691/Hn. 3, 319 (1826), 605 (1828–30), 618 (1828–30), 36 (1828–30).

39. *MR* 1 456; *MR* 2 477/Hn. 1, 412; Hn. 2, 12.

40. *W2* 169/Z. 3, 197.
41. *W1* 417/Z. 2, 513.
42. *W1* xv–xvi/Z. I, II (italics mine).
43. *W2* 169/Z. 3, 197 (italics mine). See also *W2* 508–9 n., *MR* 3 336/Z. 4, 96 n.; Hn. 3, 305.
44. See Dorothea W. Dauer, *Schopenhauer as Transmitter of Buddhist Ideas*, European University Papers, Series 1, vol. 15 (Berne: Herbert Lang, 1969), 6–9, who notes that while Schopenhauer claims that his own doctrines are independent of the influence of Hindu and Buddhist thought, he is probably much more indebted to them than he realises.
45. *MR* 1 467/Hn. 1, 422.
46. *MR* 1 122 n./Hn. 1, 113 n. (italics mine).
47. F. Copleston, 'Schopenhauer', in *The Great Philosophers* by Bryan Magee (Oxford: Oxford University Press, 1987), 215. While Schopenhauer does not mention the three sub-schools of the Vedanta system, it is clear that he is aware that the Vedanta is only one of several systems of Orthodox Hindu thought (see *MR* 3 442/Hn. 3, 403, where he refers to Schlegel's discussion of the six sects of the Hindus, and *MR* 3 701–4/Hn. 3, 646–8, where he goes on to discuss the merits of these various systems).
48. *MR* 3 701/Hn. 3, 646.
49. Ninian Smart, 'Indian Philosophy', in P. Edwards (ed.), *Encyclopedia of Philosophy* (New York: Macmillan and Free Press, 1967).
50. See *W1* 162, 332; *W2* 486, 591/Z. 1, 216; Z. 2, 414; Z. 4, 570, 692.
51. However, Schopenhauer's knowing self does not seem analogous to the Hindu Self that is identical with Brahman, since Schopenhauer says of the knowing self that it is a tertiary phenomenon. It is metaphysically dependent upon the presence of consciousness, and the latter is in turn an objectification of will (*W2* 278/Z. 3, 325). He also takes the 'I' to be a composite of the knowing and willing subjects, with the willing subject being the more fundamental. On this view, the 'I', or self, is the intelligible character. However, since Schopenhauer describes the latter as 'an act of will outside time' (*W1* 289/Z. 2, 364), it seems that it too is not identical with the will as thing-in-itself, but is instead a manifestation of it. See Janaway, *Self and World*, for a comprehensive discussion of the inherent tensions in Schopenhauer's philosophy that result from this twofold conception of the self. See also Richard E. Aquila, 'On the "Subjects" of Knowing and Willing and the "I" in Schopenhauer', *History of Philosophy Quarterly* 10, 3 (1993), 241–60. Aquila attempts to overcome the alleged difficulties in Schopenhauer's dual account of the self by interpreting the knowing self as 'the pure form of the directedness of consciousness itself'. As such, it is neither the material that constitutes the body nor the will that is manifest in it, but is rather an irreducible phenomenal 'projection' through those ingredients (248). However, since such a knowing self is clearly not identical with the will as thing-in-itself, there is no parallel with the Atman-Brahman identity of Hindu philosophy.
52. It is also possible to see resemblances between some of Schopenhauer's doctrines and those of the Samkyha school, another of the six main systems of Hindu thought. Resemblances between that school and Schopenhauer's doctrines include its atheism and its explanation of the perceptible world in terms of a single unitary substance, evolving according to rudimentary dynamics. However, there are distinct differences too in that it posits a plurality of eternal selves and a correspondence theory of perception. (See 'Indian Philosophy' in Edwards (ed.), *Encyclopedia of Philosophy*, 156–7.) That Schopenhauer is aware of both the resemblances and differences is clear from his discussion in the chapter 'Remarks on Sanskrit Literature' in *P2* 399/Z. 10, 439–40. There he makes it clear that he values the older Vedic formulation more highly than the Samkhya system.

53. See Helmuth von Glasenapp, 'The Influence of Indian Thought on German Philosophy and Literature', *Calcutta Review* 29 (1928), 203, who also notes this incompatibility. He says 'Whilst, however, for the Vedanta what exists is our eternally blessed spirituality, the Brahma, that is characterised by the attributes Sat, Cit, and Ananda, it is for Schopenhauer a blind and therefore unblessed will'.

54. Kaplan asserts that Brahman refers to the ultimate reality that transcends all differentiation and of which all else is only a manifestation. However, he also notes that the word has a number of other meanings. In its most literal sense it refers to certain rituals in the Vedas, but later it becomes the name of one of the deities, the king or ruler of all the gods, who still remains as the chief of the great trinity of Brahma, Vishnu, and Siva. In another usage it refers to the name of the priestly caste in the service of the deities (see Abraham Kaplan, *The New World of Philosophy* [London: Collins, 1962], 241). While Schopenhauer writes of Brahman as being 'the original being himself' (*W2* 463/Z. 4, 543), he also says of salvation that it is the 'reunion with Brahma' (*W2* 608/Z. 4, 712). It is clear that he knows that Brahma is one of the three deities and that these are popular personifications of the world-soul Brahm (*P1* 127/Z. 7, 144–5). Consequently, in the following discussion I include his references to all three terms: 'Brahma', 'Brahman', and 'Brahm'. While he refers to a belief in the Vedas as both Brahmanism and Hinduism, I use only the latter term. He also uses the term 'Brahmans' and 'Hindus' to refer to those who teach and practice the doctrine of the Vedas, but again I use only the latter term.

55. *W1* 495 n./Z. 2, 604–5 n. See also *W1* 276, 399/Z. 2, 348, 493, and in the second volume see *W2* 463, 489/Z. 4, 543, 574.

56. *W1* 146–7/Z. 1, 197.

57. *MR* 4 377/Hn.4/ii, 18. Schopenhauer attributes this derivation of the word 'Brahma' to Max Müller, and he believes that it appears in an essay that Müller contributed to *Hyppolytus*.

58. *P1* 62/Z. 7, 75. See also *FR* (1847), 184/Z. 5, 141–2, where Schopenhauer states, 'Brahma who is born and dies to make way for other Brahmas, and whose production of the world is regarded as sin and guilt'.

59. *P1* 127/Z. 7, 144–5.

60. Kaplan, *The New World of Philosophy*, 242. See also S. Radhakrishnan, 'Hinduism', in Garratt (ed.), *The Legacy of India*, 271, who says, 'The Beyond is Within. Brahman is Atman. He is the *antaryamin*, the inner controller. He is not only the incommunicable mystery standing for ever in his own perfect light, bliss, and peace but also is here in us, upholding, sustaining us.'

61. *P2* 472/Z. 10, 517.

62. *W2* 608/Z. 4, 712.

63. This is the interpretation of Schopenhauer's metaphysics favoured by Julian Young; see Young, *Willing and Unwilling*, ix; see also all of ch. 3. For a very useful discussion of Young's interpretation, see J. Atwell, *Schopenhauer on the Character of the World: The Metaphysics of Will* (Berkeley: University of California Press, 1995), 122–8.

64. See Kaplan, *The New World of Philosophy*, 327–49.

65. *P2* 10/Z. 9, 17.

66. *W2* 600/Z. 4, 703.

67. See Heinrich Dumoulin, 'Buddhism and Nineteenth-Century German Philosophy', *Journal of the History of Ideas* 42 (1981), 458, who says that all of the German philosophers, Kant, Hegel, Schopenhauer, and Nietzsche, knew, though not too clearly, that Buddhism was divided into two principal branches. That Schopenhauer had acquaintance with the teachings of both branches is evident from the bibliography he provides in his chapter 'Sinology' in *On The Will in Nature* and from his posthumous library. Included are books that refer to the Buddhism of the Ceylonese (Theravada) and to that of the Chinese (Mahayana).

68. *W1* 381/Z. 2, 472.

69. Dauer, *Schopenhauer as Transmitter of Buddhist Ideas*, 32.

70. *Ibid.*, 21.

71. Copleston, *Arthur Schopenhauer*, 227.

72. B. V. Kishan, 'Schopenhauer and Buddhism', in Michael Fox (ed.), *Schopenhauer: His Philosophical Achievement* (Sussex: Harvester Press, 1980), 255.

73. Bhikkhu Nanajivako, *Schopenhauer and Buddhism* (Sri Lanka: Buddhist Publication Society, 1970), 18–20.

74. See *WN*, trans. Hillebrand, 362 n/Z. 5, 327 n.

75. Peter Abelsen, 'Schopenhauer and Buddhism', *Philosophy East & West* 43, 2 (1993), 255.

76. Abelsen argues that any worthwhile comparison must involve the four basic forms of Buddhist philosophy in their own right rather than merely looking at Buddhism *as such* (see Abelsen, 'Schopenhauer and Buddhism', 256). I agree that this approach is desirable if we wish to determine actual correspondences between Schopenhauer's philosophy and Buddhism as currently understood. However, since I wish to look at the possible influence of Buddhist ideas on Schopenhauer's thought, and since we are not in a position to know with any certainty the extent and nature of his knowledge of Buddhism, it is legitimate in this case to restrict the comparison to those more general tenets of Buddhism with which Schopenhauer is likely to have been acquainted.

77. W2 623/Z. 4, 730. Schopenhauer refers to E. Burnouf, *Introduction à l'histoire du Buddhisme indien* (Paris, 1844), for an explanation of these truths.

78. Ninian Smart, 'Buddhism' in Edwards (ed.), *Encyclopedia of Philosophy*.

79. W2 309–10, 311–12, 322–23; W2 581–4; P2 293/Z. 3, 388, 390, 403–4; Z. 4, 680–4; Z. 9, 318.

80. W1 164, 196, 342–3, 351, 352–3, 363–4; W2 204, 580, 599; P1 303/Z. 1, 217, 52; Z. 2, 427, 438, 439, 451–2; Z. 3, 237–8; Z. 4, 679, 702–3; Z. 7, 328.

81. W1 379, 397, 405, 412; W2 609, 634–7/Z. 2, 469, 491, 500, 508; Z. 4, 713, 743–7.

82. W. Sri Rahula, *What the Buddha Taught* (New York: Grove Weidenfeld, 1959), 35.

83. *Ibid.*, 36.

84. *Ibid.*, 36–7.

85. *Ibid.*, 39–40.

86. *Ibid.*, 40–3.

87. C. W. Huntington, *The Emptiness of Emptiness: An Introduction to the Early Indian Madhyamika* (Honolulu: University of Hawaii Press, 1989), 40.

88. W1 410/Z. 2: 506 and W2 612/Z. 4, 716.

89. W. T. Stace, 'The Nature of Mysticism', in *Philosophy of Religion: Selected Readings*, ed. W. L. Rowe and W. J. Wainwright (New York: Harcourt Brace Jovanovich, 1973), 268–9.

90. As it is notoriously difficult to be precise in elucidating Schopenhauer's conception of 'denial of the will', my paraphrase 'the denial of all possibility of value in existence' can at best be an educated guess as to the meaning which Schopenhauer would have attached to the phrase. For commentary on the way in which one might interpret 'denial of the will', see L. Navia, 'Reflections on Schopenhauer's Pessimism', in Fox (ed.), *Schopenhauer: His Philosophical Achievement*, 178–81; E. Heller, *Thomas Mann: The Ironic German* (Cambridge: Cambridge University Press, 1958), 50–1; Bertrand Russell, *History of Western Philosophy* (London: Allen & Unwin, 1961), 726.

91. W2 508/Z. 4, 596. See also W2 608; W1 412 n./Z. 4, 712; Z. 2, 508 n.

92. P2 312/Z. 9, 339.

93. MR 3 376/Hn. 3, 343.

94. Huntington, *The Emptiness of Emptiness*, 63.

95. Consider, for example, the pervasive influence of the notion of 'substance' elaborated in Aristotle's *Metaphysics*. Not only did this notion perdure into the Middle

Ages and the writings of St. Thomas Aquinas, but it is also assumed in the *Meditations* of Descartes, often taken to be the founding figure of modern philosophy in the West.

96. *W1* 390, 391–3; *W2* 606/Z. 2, 483, 484–6; Z. 4, 709–10.
97. *WN* 20/Z. 5, 202. Also see *W2* 600; *W1* 162, 436, 503, 504, 345/Z. 4, 703; Z. 1, 215; Z. 2, 536, 614, 615, 310. For less explicit references, see *W2* 179, 195, 313, 364; *W1* 288, 290; *FR* 119–20/Z. 3, 209, 228, 367; Z. 4, 433; Z. 2, 363, 365; Z. 5, 99.
98. *W2* 196–7/Z. 3, 299–30. Also see *W2* 182, 185, 197–8, 318, 496, 612; *P1* 42; *MR* 3 40, 114, 171, 353, 472, 595, 713, 716; *MR* 4 296–7/Z. 3, 213, 216–17, 230, 231, 372; Z. 4, 581, 716; Z. 7, 54; Hn. 3, 36–7, 103, 155, 321–2, 432, 546, 657, 660; Hn. 4/i, 261.
99. See n. 63.

*REFERENCES TO SCHOPENHAUER'S WORKS

The following abbreviations are used for Schopenhauer's writings in the above appendix and notes.

BM	*On the Basis of Morality*, trans. E. F. J. Payne (Providence and Oxford: Berghahn Books, 1995).
FR	*On the Fourfold Root of the Principle of Sufficient Reason*, trans. E. F. J. Payne (La Salle, Ill: Open Court Press, 1974).
FR¹	*Schopenhauer's Early Fourfold Root* [1813 edition], trans. F. C. White (Aldershot, Avebury, 1997).
FW	*On the Freedom of the Will*, trans. Konstantin Kolenda (Oxford: Blackwell, 1985).
MR	*Manuscript Remains*, trans. E. F. J. Payne (Oxford: Berg, 1988), 4 vols.
P1, P2	*Parerga and Paralipomena*, trans. E. F. J. Payne (Oxford: Clarendon Press, 1974), vols. 1 and 2.
W1, W2	*The World as Will and Representation*, trans. E. F. J. Payne (New York: Dover, 1969), vols. 1 and 2.
W1¹	*Die Welt als Wille und Vorstellung*. 'Faksimiledruck der ersten Auflage 1819 1818 (Frankfurt: Insel Verlag, 1987).
WN	*On the Will in Nature*, trans. E. F. J. Payne (New York and Oxford: Berg, 1992).

Unless otherwise specified, the number immediately following the work's abbreviation gives a page reference to the translation or edition listed here. After an oblique stroke, corresponding passages from the standard German editions are cited.

H.	*Sämtliche Werke*, ed. Arthur Hübscher (3rd edn., Wiesbaden: Brockhaus, 1972; 4th edn., 1988), 7 vols.
Hn.	*Der handschriftliche Nachlass*, ed. Arthur Hübscher (Franfurt: Waldemar Kramer, 1966–75; repr. Munich: Deutscher Taschenbuch Verlag, 1985), 5 vols.
Z.	*Werke in zehn Bänden*, ed. Arthur Hübscher (Zurich: Diogenes Verlag, 1977), 10 vols.

For example, *W1* 272/H. 2, 320 refers to page 272 of Payne's translation of *The World as Will and Representation*, vol. 1, and to the corresponding passage on page 320 of Hübscher's *Sämtliche Werke*, vol. 2. Note that in volumes of H. which contain more than one of Schopenhauer's works, each work has its own pagination.

10

EMERSON AND INDIAN PHILOSOPHY

Dale Riepe

Two quite different American philosophers looked upon Emerson's concern with Indian philosophy as a kind of aberration: William Torrey Harris (1835–1909) and Charles Sanders Peirce (1839–1914). Peirce and Harris both wished to disassociate themselves from such concerns, but of the two, Peirce showed himself the more impatient. He says that:

> I was born and reared in the neighborhood of Concord – I mean in Cambridge – at the time when Emerson, Hedge,[1] and their friends were disseminating the ideas that they had caught from Schelling, and Schelling from Plotinus, from Boehm, or from God knows what minds stricken with the monstrous mysticism of the East.[2]

Ralph Waldo Emerson (1803–82), however, seemed of tougher stuff than his younger friend Charles S. Peirce, for he could read the works of the mystical East without annoyance, yet without devouring it all uncritically. Harris tried to explain Emerson's deviation in the following way: 'What Emerson says of Plato we may easily and properly apply to himself. But he goes farther than Plato towards the Orient, and his pendulum swings farther West into the Occident. He delights in the all-absorbing unity of the Brahman, in the all-renouncing ethics of the Chinese and Persian, in the measureless images of the Arabian and Hindoo poets. . . . It is the problem of evil that continually haunts him, and leads him to search its solution in the Oriental unity which is above all dualism of

Dale Riepe, 'Emerson and Indian Philosophy', *Journal of the History of Ideas*, 28: 1, 1967, pp. 115–122.

good and evil. . . . Finally, it is his love of beauty, which is the vision of freedom manifested in matter, that leads him to Oriental poetry.'[3]

Emerson became the leading exponent of Indian thought among the Transcendentalists, many of whom saw it as not only curious and interesting but also as an antidote to the rising American materialism. It had been hoped that New England would provide a kind of Christ's Kingdom in the Wilderness; instead rationalism, deism, and worldly concerns in Boston and elsewhere were setting a tone described at that time as 'low thinking and money-grubbing'.[4] That a number of Transcendentalists themselves were coupon-clippers was scarcely recognized as a serious consideration in rendering moral and economic judgments. Theodore Parker (1810–60), for example, who was certainly not much taken with Indian thought, finds it convenient to purge Christianity by reference to some of the sects commonly compared to it in the days of unitarian and transcendentalist influence.

> Of the five great world sects, the Brahmins, the Jews, the Buddhists, the Christians, and the Mohammedans, none started with such humane ideas, with such pious moral feelings in its originators, none had such a magnificent character in its founder, as the Christian sect, but no one has taught such absurd doctrines, none has practised such wanton and monstrous cruelty, and I think there is none at the present day in which so great a fraud is imposed upon the people by the priesthood.[5]

About 1836, several years after Emerson had begun reading the Indian classics,[6] and two years before he had read Heeren's *India*, a group of intellectuals 'with high moral aim' met together in Emerson's study in Concord to discuss new developments in philosophy, literature, and theology. At first called Mr. Hedge's Club[7] this association was born July 20, 1836. Thereafter known as the New English Transcendentalists, it was the first group in America, however loosely knit, to pay serious attention to Indian thought. Besides Emerson, the Transcendentalists included Theodore Parker, George Ripley, F. H. Hedge, Amos Bronson Alcott, Henry David Thoreau, William Ellery Channing, Margaret Fuller,[8] Elizabeth Peabody, Nathaniel Hawthorne, and Orestes W. Brownson. These New England spirits, with strong clerical backgrounds,[9] or fideist leanings, found in Indian thought not only ideas with which they agreed, but suggestions as to the possible shape future spiritual developments might take if they were to be universalistic in appeal.

Emerson and the other Transcendentalists found Indian wisdom attractive because it was profound without being gloomy. The 'Puritan's harsh insistence on the preeminent importance of salvation was suited to the exigencies of reform, or of revolution, or of migration and settlement'[10] but was simply not sufficient to appeal to the spiritual hunger of Emerson. Emerson, of all the Transcendentalists, rose above the melancholy of New England and its relative emptiness of sun and a warm sea. His valiant cry in 'The Method of Nature', read at Waterville College[11] in 1841 was that 'We ought to celebrate this hour by expression of manly joy. Not thanks, not prayer seem quite the highest or truest name of our communication with the infinite, – but glad and conspiring reception. . . . When all is said and done, the rapt saint is found the only logician. Nor exhortation, but argument becomes our lips, but peans of joy and praise.'[12]

It is worth noting that early Buddhist sculpture seemed to express most of the joy that was the heritage of Hinduism. Gradually the juice was wrung out of it until we end with the husk-like Bodhisattvas that frequently depress at least the non-believer. The Buddhist believer does not see with his eye, but with his dogma-center. Emerson's fondness for Persian wisdom and literature also attests to his almost pathetic drive towards sunlight and the joy that mankind derives from it, not bundled up in storm coats, but naked and stretching with bare feet planted on the warm sand or the cool grass. Such was the naturalistic aesthetic charm of Hinduism for the Transcendentalists who were often unaware of it, except for Thoreau who smelled it out. Thoreau's naturalist grasp was more scientific than Emerson's poetic and metaphysical embrace. Emerson's moral Hinduism consisted as much in his refusal to use the puritan homeopathy as it did in his delight in the emphasis upon *māyā*. His sense of depravity refused to bend to the ultimate depravity of man. Emerson was not morbid. His sense of realism gave him balance in the judgment of the human condition. Here he may be contrasted with Jonathan Edwards, America's foremost puritan philosopher. Edwards made a business of moral virtue and was a death's head at a naturalist feast. Buddhism has also this quality when it is not cajoled out of it by the Taoists in China and the Shintoists in Japan who bring it light, sunshine, and fresh air. Whenever a philosophy neglects external nature it is bound to become musty, taking to flexing a tenuous will to the embarrassment of its virile appetites. Brutality replaces skill and the ascetic jaw is substituted for intelligence, the seat of kindliness. Emerson could never tolerate fanaticism or obstinacy and it was this that led him to adhere to the teachings of the *Bhagavadgītā* rather than to a more ascetic call.

An unrecorded appeal of Indian philosophy is the feeling of sympathy Americans had with Indians who were still under the heavy hand of the English oppressor. This became more noticeable after the World Parliament of Religion, held in 1893 in Chicago, where the delegates from India were able in a personal yet unobtrusive way to gain sympathy for the cause of Indian independence. But much earlier, Americans had been delighted to observe that after his defeat in America in 1781, General Cornwallis was again beaten near Madras at the ancient city of Kanchi (Conjeeveram) by Dravidian soldiers.

> Philosophy for him [Emerson] was rather moral energy flowering into sprightliness of thought than a body of serious and defensible doctrines. In practicing transcendental speculation only in this poetic sporadic fashion, Emerson retained its true value and avoided its greatest danger.[13] [Comparing Emerson to the German system-makers, Santayana also says:] Emerson cannot rival them in the sustained effort of thought by

which they sought to reinterpret every sphere of being according to their chosen principles. But he surpassed them in an instinctive sense of what he was doing. He never represented his poetry as science, nor countenanced the formulation of a new sect that should nurse the sense of private and mysterious illumination.[14]

If we change 'sects' to 'academic schools' we might have the equivalent in Germany and the United States to what would readily come to mind when considering the growth of a spiritual school in India. In the one the ritual is highly circumscribed and unimaginative, appealing more to antagonism and a sense of virulent rightness than to the tinkle of bells and the gentle waving of incense smoke. In one passage in 'Compensation' Emerson refers to the incorporation of the divine: 'A plain confession of the in-working of the All, and of its moral aim. The Indian mythology ends in the same ethics.'[15] Emerson himself found in Vedānta[16] an answer to his quest for absolute being, as illustrated in the Chandogya-Upanishad by the dialogue on the soul (soul which is equal to Reality) between Svetaketu and his father. In his journal at this time Emerson records, 'Blessed is the day when the youth discovers that Within and Above are synonymous.'[17] Friendship and love are closely related in Emerson to Ātman, 'Every friend whom not thy fantastic will but the great and tender heart in thee craveth, shall lock thee in his embrace.'[18] Emerson's receptivity to non-dualistic Vedānta here is a remarkable testimony to the fact that even though men may be separated by a dozen cultures and ten thousand miles, yet strikingly similar thoughts and allegiances seem to penetrate them. And if it is the duty of intellect not only to analyze and dissect, but also to discover unity, parallelism, analogies, and similarities, then Emerson found these in Indian philosophy. Nevertheless, as Swami Paramananda has pointed out,

> ... this does not mean that Emerson borrowed. I believe that there cannot be any borrowing in the higher realms of knowledge. ... A gentleman once said to Emerson that he had studied all the different philosophies and religions of the world, and he was now convinced that Christianity was the only one; to which Emerson replied: 'That only shows, my friend, how narrowly you have read them.'[19]

According to Emerson, the intellect discovers behind polarity, behind the positive-negative, behind the laws on earth, the centrality of Truth, the centrality of mind. To Emerson 'My dreams are not me; they are not Nature, or the Not-me: they are both.'[20]

Besides being highly receptive to the Vedānta view of deity, Emerson was greatly influenced by the notions of *māyā* and *karma*, although transmigration seems to have left him a trifle chilled. Emerson's own understanding of *māyā* may best be shown by quoting his own short poem having that word as its title:

> *Maya*
> Illusions works impenetrable,
> Weaving webs innumerable,
> Her gay pictures never fail,
> Charmer who will be believed
> By man who thirsts to be deceived.
>
> Illusions like the tints of pearl,
> Or changing colors of the sky,
> Or ribbons of a dancing girl
> That mend her beauty to the eye.[21]

As Man Mohan Singh has reminded us, Emerson frequently used books for their quotations alone. If this is true, then the mass of quotations concerning *māyā* that he gathered is evidence of his preoccupation with *māyā* as interpreted by the ancient Indian philosophers. Some of these quotations carrying the kernel of Emerson's beliefs, include the following:

> Hindoo theology [teaches that the] . . . supreme good is to be attained . . . by perception of the real and unreal . . . and thus arriving at the contemplation of the one eternal Life.[22] Truth is the principle, and the moral of the Hindoo theology, – as against Maya.[23]

Emerson goes on to say that:

> The first illusion that is put upon us in the world is the amusing miscellany of colours, forms, and properties.[24] Our education is through surfaces and particulars . . . as infants are occupied wholly with surface-differences, so attitudes of adults remain in the infant or animal estate, and never see or know more.[25] . . . The world of the senses is a world of shows.[26]

If we think of a vast totality, Emerson thinks,

> In the kingdom of illusion life is a dream, in the language of the ancients – we change only from bed to bed.[27] . . . God is a reality and his method is illusion.[28]

After Emerson had composed 'hamatreya,'[29] according to Leyla Goren, he was still playing with the idea of illusions. In 1861 he wrote about the legends surrounding the successive *māyās* of Vishnu.[30]

Turning from Emerson's view of *māyā* to his view of *karma*, we again note his great perceptiveness. Writing in his journal, Emerson says:

> The Indian system is full of fate, the Greek not. The Greek uses the word, indeed, but in his mind the Fates are three respectable old women who spin and shear a symbolic thread, – so narrow, so limitary is the sphere allowed them, and it is with music. We are only at a more beautiful opera,

or a private reality, it is the cropping-out in our planted gardens of the core of the world: it is the abysmal Force, untameable and immense.[31]

For comparative philosophy here is a splendid example of what awareness of a philosophy from the other side of the globe can bring to understanding of a 'familiar' philosophy. Yet in his essay on 'Compensation', Emerson shows his nineteenth-century Yankeeism ordinarily contrasted with Indian self-immolation. 'You think me the child of my circumstances: I make my circumstances. ... As I am, so shall I associate, and so shall I act.'[32] Universal law is unconscious and inscrutable with no act of Grace possible on the part of God, since God for Emerson has been absorbed into Brahman. Universal law is both physical and moral; whatever will be, will be. Yet there are innate qualities in the individual waiting to be unfolded. Later, the pragmatists, first James, and then Dewey, were to give this innate unflowering a specifically biographical or biopsychological interpretation. For Emerson the individual seems to have more freedom to act than perhaps the Vedāntin will allow. And yet, having heard many pleas to the effect that Vedānta and other Indian outlooks are not fatalistic nor really pessimistic, I am possibly taking unwarranted liberties in holding that Emerson's notion of compensation here is more optimistic, as a child of American upward mobility, than is the Indian.

A fourth influence of Indian thought on Emerson is to be found in his doctrine of the Oversoul, certainly an atypical conception in the history of American thought.[33] Kurt Leidecker has examined Carpenter's belief that this notion was not based upon an Indian prototype. It was believed by William Torrey Harris and John Smith Harrison that *Bhagavadgītā*, 8.3, was the prototype Emerson used, in which *adhyātman* easily yields 'Oversoul'. That Emerson did not know Sanskrit is adduced by Leidecker to show the unlikelihood that Emerson did in fact borrow his notion from the *Gītā*. Various translations with which Emerson was familiar, such as Rammohun Roy's or Sir William Jones's might have stirred his imagination more, Leidecker believes, than the Neo-Platonic concept of emanation.[34] After scrutinizing the 'Self-Reliance' essay of Emerson, Leidecker concludes that no sense can be made of *it* without seeing it 'against the philosophical or metaphysical background of the "Indian Self"'.[35] Relevant to this discussion is Emerson's poem published in the *Dial* magazine called 'The Three Dimensions' in which he expresses an image of Creative Principle manifesting itself in diversity:

> Room room willed the opening mind,
> And found it in Variety.[36]

This aspect of vision is closer to Neo-Platonism than to Indian views. Still many have seen the Indian influence important in Emerson's Oversoul; and nearly all have found passages to substantiate plausibly that both Brahmanism and Neo-Platonism entered into Emerson's notion of Oversoul, and perhaps more beside.[37]

It is worthy of note that Emerson was much less influenced by Buddhism than Hinduism, although the reverse proved to be the case with Josiah Royce. Emerson first mentions Buddhism in a letter to Margaret Fuller September 8, 1841, in which he makes the cryptic remark that 'Buddhism cometh in like a flood. Sleep is better than waking: Death than life.'[38] It seems clear from his letters in 1835 that he is not certain as to the difference between Hinduism and Buddhism, or whether the *Bhagavadgītā* is Buddhistic in its message. By May 30, 1845 in a letter to John Chapman, Emerson seems to have cleared up this problem for he says:

> There is a book which I very much want of which this is the title. 'The Bhagavat Geeta, or Dialogues of Kreeshna & Arjoon; in eighteen lectures; with notes. Translated from the original in Sanskreet, or ancient language of the Brahmins, by *Charles Wilkins*; London: C. Nourse; 1835.'[39]

In the same volume of letters Emerson mentions that he read the Purana on a trip to Vermont[40] and that he thought of Thoreau as 'Our Spartan-Buddhist Henry'.[41] In 1843 Emerson asked the question, 'Buddhism or Occidentalism, which is best?'[42] Perhaps this would be tantamount to asking today 'Orientalism or Pragmatism, which is best?' Obviously neither pair expresses mutual exclusion.

It is curious that in 1835 when Emerson mentions 'Orientalism' he is speaking of the following: 'That "God is a petty Asiatic king" is obstinate Orientalism'.[43] Here by the oriental man he means Abraham, Seth, and Job.[44]

Emerson's knowledge of Indian and Buddhist philosophy came from a variety of sources, but he owed a major debt to Victor Cousin's *Course of the History of Modern Philosophy* in two volumes (1852). What Emerson thought of Cousin's opinion that 'The Vedan philosophy is the idealistic philosophy of India; it is therefore, the most obscure',[45] we can only guess. What was Cousin's source of information? He derived his knowledge from Colebrooke's work (London, 1837) in Volume I, consisting of around 75,000 words. Colebrooke's essays in eight volumes first appeared in the *Transactions of the Asiatic Society of London* (1824–28). It is interesting to note that Burnouf got his material from Houghton, an English resident in Nepal who communicated it to the Asiatic Society of Paris, having translated it from the Sanskrit. Cousin's roughly 14,000 words on Indian philosophy comprising Lectures V–VI of his *Course* also refers to the opinions of M. B. Saint-Hilaire concerning the Nyāya logic. But it must be conceded that the French Indianists were heavily indebted to Colebrooke.

The last known letter of Emerson to mention Indian thought was to Max Müller on August 4, 1873. It is of interest because it indicates the excellent mileage that Emerson had got out of his rather sparse sources. He says:

> All my interest in the Aryan is old reading of Marsh's Menus [there was no such work. Emerson probably confused it with Joshua Marshman, an editor of the work of Confucius], then Wilkin's Bhagavat Geeta;

Burnouf's Bhagavat Purana; & Wilson's Vishnu Purana – yes & few other translations.[46]

Emerson owned at least four of Müller's books, including *A History of Sanskrit Literature* (London, 1860, 2nd ed.), the *Works* of Sir William Jones (6 vols. 1799), Schlegel's *Lecture on the History of Literature* (2 vols. Edinburgh, 1818), and H. H. Wilson's translation of the Rig-veda-sanhitā (4 vols. London, 1850–66).[47]

That Emerson was deeply influenced by Indian thought cannot be doubted. Furthermore it must be said that his writing would have been different if he had not known it. And this is not meant in the trivial or obvious sense. Not only American scholars have been aware of this, but Indians have discovered in Emerson a kindred spirit to which a voluminous literature attests. Protap Chunder Mozoomdar in 'Emerson as Seen from India,' pointed out shortly after Emerson's death in 1882, that:

> Yes, Emerson had all the wisdom and spirituality of the Brahmans. . . . In whomsoever the eternal Brahma breathed his unquenchable fire, he was the Brahman. And in that sense Emerson was the best of Brahmans.[48]

Herambachandra Maitra has said that Emerson's writings represent a union of the modern spirit with what was noblest in ancient times.[49] And the literature on Emerson continues to be written as I sit here myself writing it. When Principal A. S. Narayana Pillai visited me in Grand Forks, North Dakota several winters ago (1962) he told me of a venerable scholar not far from Trivandrum who is in the process of writing a voluminous work on Emerson's philosophy in its relation to Indian thought; perhaps he is the same scholar of whom I heard when I lived in Mylapore, Madras in the early 1950s. It is difficult to assess just how much a man like Emerson is influenced by any thought, but surely no American philosopher ever found in Indian thought nuggets of wisdom and expanding horizons that Emerson did.

NOTES

1. Frederic Henry Hedge (1805–90) was a Unitarian minister and professor of ecclesiastical history at Harvard Divinity School.
2. Peirce, *Collected Papers*, ed. C. Hartshorne and Paul Weiss (Cambridge, MA, 1931–35), VI, 86, par. 102.
3. Harris, 'Emerson's Orientalism', *The Genius and Character of Emerson*, ed. F. B. Sanborn (Boston, 1885), 372–3.
4. George F. Whicher, ed., *The Transcendentalist Revolt Against Materialism* (Boston, 1940). Introduction, vi.
5. Parker, *Lessons from the World of Matter and the World of Man*, Selected by Rufus Leighton from notes of unpublished sermons (Chicago, © 1865), 400.
6. Emerson began reading borrowed copies of *The Edinburgh Review* between 1820–5 so that he could read its articles about India among other fascinating topics. He was between seventeen and twenty-two at this time, already a graduate of Harvard College. Emerson mentions 'tasting' the *Bhagavadgītā* in Victor Cousin's *Cours de philosophie* (1828) in a letter to his brother William (1831); cf. his *Letters*, ed. Ralph

L. Rusk (New York, 1939) I, 322; his reading after 1836 included Sir William Jones, To Nārāyena, 'Hindu Mythology and Mathematics,' in *The Edinburgh Review*, and Vyāsa's *Rāmāyana*. It is a curious note that the same Sir William Jones was unanimously elected a corresponding member of the Historical Society of Massachusetts in 1795 but 'the society had soon the mortification to learn that, nine months before the date of their votes the object of their intended distinction was no more', according to Lord Teignmouth, *The Life, Writings, and Correspondence of Sir William Jones* (Philadelphia, 1805), 416–17.

7. Emerson, *Letters*, I, 346.
8. Margaret Fuller, as editor of the *Dial* after 1850, published some translations of Indian classics.
9. Whicher, *The Transcendentalist Revolt . . .*, vii.
10. R. B. Perry, 'The Moral Athlete', *Puritanism in Early America* (Boston, 1950), 101.
11. Today Colby College.
12. Milton Konvitz and Stephen Whicher, *Emerson: A Collection of Critical Essays* (Englewood Cliffs, NJ, 1962), 59.
13. Santayana, *Interpretations of Poetry and Religion* (New York, 1911), 223.
14. *Ibid.*, 222.
15. Emerson, *The Works of R. W. Emerson* (New York, n.d.), 71.
16. This was the non-dualistic Advaita Vedānta of Guadapāda and Sāmkara.
17. Emerson, *Journals of Ralph Waldo Emerson*, ed. E. W. Emerson and W. E. Forbes (Boston, 1910), III, 399 (1833–5).
18. *Emerson*, Works, II, 294.
19. Paramananda, *Emerson and Vedanta* (Boston, 1918), 9.
20. Emerson, *Works*, X, 8.
21. Emerson, *Works*, IX, 348.
22. Emerson, *Journals*, X, 162.
23. *Ibid.*, X, 123–4.
24. See also Plato's *Symposium*: Socrates, Diotima, and the Ladder of Love.
25. Emerson, *Journals*, X, 123–4.
26. Emerson, 'Prudence' in *The Works of R. W. Emerson, op. cit.*
27. Emerson, *Journals*, VIII, 415.
28. Emerson, *Journals*, VII, 505.
29. A minor poem which includes a minor poem, called 'Earth-Song'.
30. See L. Goren, *Elements of Brahminism in the Transcendentalism of Emerson* (New York, 1959), 39.
31. Emerson, *Journals*, VII, 123.
32. Emerson, *Works*, I, 334–5.
33. Yet it did attract adherence even in Jacksonville (Illinois), Quincy, and other Platonic centers along the Mississippi. See Paul Russell Anderson, *Platonism in the Midwest* (New York, 1963).
34. See Goren, *Elements of Brahminism . . .*, 41.
35. Leidecker, 'Emerson and East-West Synthesis', *Philosophy East and West* (July 1951), 43.
36. Goren, *Elements of Brahminism . . .*, 42.
37. According to S. Radhakrishnan, for example, 'Emerson's Oversoul is the paramātman of the Upanishads', for which he produces no evidence. See his *Eastern Religions and Western Thought* (1959), 249.
38. Emerson, *Letters*, II, 445.
39. Emerson, *Letters*, III, 228., See also III, 290, 291n and *Journals* VII, 68.
40. Emerson, *Letters*, III, 293.
41. Emerson, *Letters*, III, 455.
42. Emerson, *Letters*, III, 153.
43. Emerson, *Journals*, III, 505–06.
44. *Ibid.*, III, 566.

45. Cousin, *Course of the History of Modern Philosophy*, trans. O. W. Wright, (New York, 1852) I, 387.
46. Emerson, *Letters*, VI, 246, 246*n*.
47. K. W. Cameron, *Ralph Waldo Emerson's Reading* (Raleigh, 1941).
48. Quoted by Goren, *Elements of Brahmanism* ..., 46.
49. *Ibid.*

11

THOREAU'S INDIA: THE IMPACT OF READING IN A CRISIS

David H. Albert

> Man's moral nature is a riddle which only eternity can solve.
> Henry David Thoreau, *Journal*, March 19, 1842.[1]

Literary historians have generally placed Thoreau's first acquaintance with works of Eastern literature and philosophy in 1841, at which time Thoreau was residing at the home of Ralph Waldo Emerson in Concord and would have had access to Emerson's well-stocked library. Indeed, 'It is a singular fact that not a single Oriental volume appeared on the record of Thoreau's reading as an undergraduate (1833–1837) at the Harvard College Library.'[2]

While we hope to touch upon the later period in Thoreau's creative life, it is the purpose of this paper to demonstrate that Thoreau's first confrontation with the literature, culture, and philosophy of India actually occurred four years earlier in the autumn of 1837, and that this confrontation represents a crucial though overlooked milestone in the development of his literary sensibilities.

Some background to Thoreau's own life and the parallel development of Transcendentalist thought is necessary to provide a context for the event. Thoreau graduated from Harvard College in August, 1837. His record was undistinguished, marked by periods of ill-health and indifferent disposition,[3] noteworthy perhaps only for the strong friendship he struck up with Emerson and the continued growth of his love for the woods of Massachusetts. Oddly enough, Thoreau did not attend Emerson's Harvard Phi Beta Kappa address,

David H. Albert, 'Thoreau's India: The Impact of Reading in a Crisis', *Proceedings of the American Philosophical Society*, 125: 2, 1981, pp. 104–9.

'The American Scholar', delivered the day after the former's graduation and now generally recognized as the crowning achievement of Emerson's prose.

Nonetheless, during his last three months at Harvard, Thoreau seems to have read Emerson's *Nature*, the 'testament of Transcendentalism' published in 1836, several times.[4] In it, Emerson confirms his faith in a doctrine of correspondences between the moral and ideal and the workings of nature.

Having formulated the philosophical underpinnings of Transcendentalism prior to 1836, Emerson spent the next several years pondering how the 'whole man' could adapt himself profitably to already existing social institutions by entering into a new creative relationship with nature, books, and the world of action. This 'whole man' would come to realize that, 'The one thing in the world of value is the active soul – the soul, free, sovereign, active.'[5] The 'educational agenda' of Transcendentalism thus became the subject of Emerson's two most celebrated prose works, *The American Scholar*, delivered in August, 1837, and the *Divinity School Address* of July, 1838.

We can speculate that the educational program of Transcendentalism was the primary subject of Emerson's intercourse with the young Thoreau during this period. In retrospect, it could be said that the contents of *The American Scholar* appear as a blueprint upon which Thoreau began to build his life.

Following graduation Thoreau returned to his native Concord full of these high-minded ideas with which he had been in contact in previous months. He now faced uncertain prospects for the future. The young man of twenty found himself confined to living at home with his parents and family. He taught at Concord's Center School for several weeks only to resign as a result of his refusal to administer corporal punishment. He changed the order of his names from David Henry to Henry David Thoreau, probably as a symbolic 'declaration of independence' from his family. Because of the severe economic conditions of 1837, he could not find another position. His family apparently is always apologizing for his 'strange' way of thinking. Thoreau wrote to his sister Helen on October 27, 1837:

> Please you, let the defendant say a few words in defense of his long silence. You know we have hardly done our own deeds, thought our own thoughts, or lived our own lives hitherto. For a man to act himself, he must be perfectly free; otherwise he is in danger of losing all sense of responsibility or of self-respect. Now when such a state of things exists, that the sacred opinions one advances are apologized for by his friends, before his face, lest his hearers receive a wrong impression of the man, – when such gross injustice is of frequent occurrence, where shall we look, and not look in vain, for men, deeds, thoughts? As well apologize for the grape that is sour, or the thunder that is noisy, or the lightning that it tarries not.[6]

Thoreau is now bitterly estranged from social life. But in the midst of this dark period there is a new source of enjoyment and haven of retreat, his journal. The first entry in a long sequence of journals kept by Thoreau for most of his life is dated October 22, 1837, just five days before the above letter.

The importance of Thoreau's *Journals* cannot be overestimated. All of his published writings are structured reworkings of material and reflections first recorded in the *Journals* over long periods of time. In a famous passage near the beginning of *Walden*, Thoreau, with characteristic irony, links the keeping of the journal with his observation of nature:

> So many autumn, ay, and winter days, spent outside the town, trying to hear what was in the wind, to hear and carry it express! I well-nigh sunk all my capital in it, and lost my own breath into the bargain, running in the face of it ....
>
> For a long time I was reporter to a journal, of no very wide circulation, whose editor has never yet seen fit to print the bulk of my contributions, and, as is too common with writers, I got only my labor for my pains. However, in this case my pains were their own reward.
>
> For many years I was self-appointed inspector of snow storms and rain storms, and did my duty faithfully; ...[7]

Serious writing for Thoreau did not begin as a result of any particular literary ambitions, but rather as an escape from a trying domestic situation and, in response to his own growing insecurity, as an escape from himself. The journal entry for October 22, the first day of journal entries, is significant for a display of inwardness unknown in Thoreau's Harvard writings:

> To be alone I find it necessary to escape the present, – I avoid myself. How could I be alone in the Roman emperor's chamber of mirrors? I seek a garret. The spiders must not be disturbed, nor the floor swept, nor the lumber arranged.
>
> The Germans say, 'Es ist alles wahr wodurch du besser wirst.'[8] [Everything is true which makes you better.]

Here we begin to witness the characteristic antithesis which was to become the true mark of his literary character: an escape from the mundane effected through withdrawal 'to the garret', and yet a continuing belief in the ability of each man to reform himself with the affirmation that the reformation of society would automatically follow.

But how was this inner reform to be accomplished? The path for Thoreau in the midst of this crisis of identity was murky, and he felt he had little control over his environment. During October, Thoreau read Goethe, and in his journal translated a passage from *Torquato Tasso* which perhaps best reflects his own feelings:

> *The Poet*
> He seems to avoid – even to flee from us, –
> To seek something which we know not,
> And perhaps he himself after all knows not.[9]

We see here the beginning of the cultivation of Thoreau's unique sensibility.

And it is only at this point that Thoreau, his sense of self-worth shaken, his domestic situation oppressive, his prospects at best doubtful, had his first recorded confrontation with the life and thought of India. It came about through a reading of *A Historical and Descriptive Account of British India*, an encyclopedic compendium produced by a team of British historians, scholars, travelers, and statesmen led by Hugh Murray.[10] The evidence points to Thoreau having borrowed the three volumes of the work from Emerson, as there is no evidence of a library borrowing, and having read it in the beginning of November, at the height of his inner turmoil.

The *Account of British India* was the most popular work of its genre written during the 1830s and 1840s. It is well over a thousand pages long, with sections on history, natural history and zoology, botany, climate, geology, minerology, medicine, astronomy and computation, religion, philosophy, literature, and sea travel. It betrays the usual Victorian and imperialist prejudices towards the 'natives', as can be illustrated through passages taken from the section on religion:

> The Hindoo is also much addicted to a worship which indicates the lowest degradation of the human mind, – that of the brute creation; and his most exalted deities, the creators and preservers of the world, scarcely command a reverence equal to that bestowed on the cow.[11]

> The worship and services paid to the Hindoo deities are generally speaking, irrational, unmeaning, and often immoral.[12]

The quotations taken from the *Account of British India* found in Thoreau's copybook are very sparse, but come from all three volumes, signifying perhaps that he read through the great body of the work. The passages that he did choose to copy, however, are pregnant with meaning for the maturing Thoreau and, as we shall indicate, seem to telescope most of his later development.[13]

The first quotation to appear in the copybook, from the section on history, is the only one taken from the first five hundred pages:

> The Macedonian [Alexander the Great] does not seem to have been himself inclined to enter into conversation with these uncouth sages; but he sent Onesicritus to endeavor to obtain some idea of their doctrines and principles. This envoy was accordingly guided to a solitary spot about two miles from the city, where a group of fifteen, braving the noonday heat, had placed themselves in the most painful and fantastic attitudes. The Greek accosted them, and made known the object of his visit; when one of their number, name Calanus, observed, that it little became them to reveal the mysteries of philosophy to one arrayed in the costume of a courtier and warrior: and required, as an indispensable [sic] preliminary to all communication, that he should throw himself naked on the same stones where they lay extended. As Onesicritus appeared to pause, Mandanis, another of the Indian group, condemned this harsh reply made to the

representative of a sovereign and conqueror, who deserves praise for such enlightened curiosity. Through the medium of an interpreter, he gave a summary of the leading tenets held by his fellow sages, inquiring if they bore any resemblance to the doctrines professed in Greece. Onesicritus assured him that Pythagoras, Socrates, and above all, Diogenes entertained many opinions similar. Mandanis admitted this to be in so far satisfactory, yet conceived that no one who wore clothes, or mingled in human society, could attain to that mysterious height of wisdom which distinguished the Indian philosophers.'[14]

We would do well not to underestimate the importance of this entry, given its sole selection for Thoreau's copybook from more than five hundred pages of text. Here, Thoreau was for the first time presented with the paradigm of the recluse, the man who does not 'mingle in human society', as one capable of advancing to 'mysterious heights of wisdom'. These ascetic notions are something Thoreau surely did not pick up from the urbane Emerson who was to remark of his reclusive friend later, 'Instead of engineering for all America, he was the captain of a huckle-berry party.'[15]

The satisfaction which Thoreau may have gained through identification with the Indian ascetics would of course have been purely emotional, but given the exigencies of Thoreau's domestic situation at the time, its importance is almost too obvious. Instead of attempting to come to terms with and deal forthrightly with his immediate circumstances, he displaces his anxiety, transferring it to a higher, almost transcendent realm. If we had to date the genesis of Thoreau's authentic 'voice' in his writing, we might well look to the *Journal* entries of November 12 and November 13, written only days after Thoreau's reading of Murray's *British India*:

Nov. 12

I yet lack discernment to distinguish the whole lesson of to-day; but it is not lost, – it will come to me at last. My desire is to know *what* I have lived that I may know *how* to live henceforth.

Nov. 13

This shall be the test of innocence – if I can bear a taunt, and look out on this friendly moon, pacing the heavens in queen-like majesty, with the accustomed yearning.

Truth is ever returning into herself. I glimpse one feature to-day, another to-morrow; and the next day they are blended.[16]

This singularity and stoicism, and the appeal to the benevolent forces of nature ('this friendly moon') in the face of his neighbors' and family's lack of appreciation for his solitary pursuit of truth, was to grow into a remarkable sense of self-deprecating irony which is the hallmark of *Walden*:

In short, I went on thus for a long time, I may say it without boasting, faithfully minding my business, till it became more and more evident that my townsmen would not after all admit me into the list of town officers, nor make my place a sinecure with moderate allowance . . . .

Finding that my fellow-citizens were not likely to offer me any room in the court house, or any curacy or living any where else, but I must shift for myself, I turned my face more exclusively than ever to the woods, where I was better known. . . . My purpose in going to Walden Pond was not to live cheaply nor to live dearly there, but to transact some private business with the fewest obstacles; to be hindered from accomplishing which for want of a little common sense, a little enterprise and business talent, appeared not so sad as foolish.[17]

But it was from this tale concerning the sage of India from which Thoreau originally received external validation for his withdrawal into solitude as a way of pursuing truth.

The second important passage that Thoreau chose to preserve is a passage from a newspaper entitled *The Reformer* quoted by Murray. It is of particular interest because the sections in *British India* on Hindu religion, literature, and philosophy contain great stores of quotations from classical texts. Yet, other than three epigrams from the *Panchatantra* and several short quotations from the Vedas, Thoreau made this passage from an English-language newspaper his eccentric choice for preservation:

Whatever may be the opinion of those who advocate the continuance of things as they are, there will come a time when prejudice, however deep and ramified its roots are reckoned to be, will droop, and eventually wither away before the benign radiance of liberty and truth. Our ideas do not now range on the surface of things. We have commenced probing, and will probe on, till we discover that which will make us feel that we are men in common with others. We cast off prejudice and all its concomitants, as objects abhorrent to the principles which are calculated to ennoble us before the world. Assisted by the light of reason, we have the gladdening prospect before us of soon coming to the standard of civilization, which has established the prosperity of the European nations. Let us then, my countrymen, pursue with diligence and care the track laid open by these glorious nations. Let us follow the ensign of liberty and truth, and, emulating their wisdom and their virtues, be in our own turn the guiding needle to those who are blinded by their own gloom and superstition.[18]

The broad nineteenth-century liberalism, with its appeal to the casting off of prejudices, 'gloom and superstition', and the call to range below the surface of things are certainly among the factors in the passage which recommended themselves to the young Thoreau. And yet one must conclude that Thoreau really did not appreciate its central thrust. The prejudices which were to be cast off are part of the dynamic complex of classical Indian culture which would not tend to 'ennoble the modern Hindu before the world'. The light of reason of which *The Reformer* speaks is a peculiarly European star, the 'standard of civilization' which was to drive Thoreau to Walden Pond eight years later. The wisdom and virtues were distinctly those of Imperial Victorian ideology, the 'benign radiance' not that on the face of the 'yogi', with whom, as already noted, Thoreau was to feel an uncommon affinity:

> Free in this world as the birds in the air, disengaged from every kind of chains, those who practice the *yoga* gather in Brahma [sic] the certain fruit of their works.
>
> Depend upon it that, rude and careless as I am, I would fain practice the *yoga* faithfully.
>
> The yogi, absorbed in contemplation, contributes in his degree to creation; he breathes a divine perfume, he hears wonderful things. Divine forms traverse him without tearing him, and united to the nature which is proper to him, he goes, he acts an animating original matter.
>
> To some extent, and at rare intervals, even I am a yogi.[19]

It is precisely the pre-modern India which *The Reformer* rejected which took hold of Thoreau's imagination.

Furthermore, any belief in the moderate progressivism exampled in *The Reformer*, also a major feature of most of Emerson's writings at least before 1840, was clearly foreign to Thoreau's emotional disposition. Thoreau, unlike Emerson or the Hindu reformers saw very few 'auspicious signs of the coming days'.[20] His overabiding egotism was of the grand Romantic cast, even in the pleasant surroundings of Concord; it is earthly transcendence which calls him. 'Why has man rooted himself thus firmly in the earth, but that he may rise in the same proportion into the heaven's above'.[21] Thoreau's primary interests as exhibited in the works of his maturity were in the potentialities of existence contrasted with the incapacities of men to recognize these potentialities because of the exigencies of everyday life. This is one of the great themes of *Walden*:

> But men labor under a mistake. The better part of the man is soon ploughed into the soil for compost. By a seeming fate, commonly called necessity, they are employed, as it says in an old book, laying up treasures which moth and rust will corrupt and thieves break through and steal . . . .
>
> Most men, even in this comparatively free country, through mere ignorance and mistake, are so occupied with the factitious cares and superfluously coarse labors of life that its finer fruits cannot be plucked by them. Their fingers, from excessive toil, are too clumsy and tremble too much for that. Actually, the laboring man has not leisure for a true integrity day by day; he cannot afford to sustain the manliest relations to men; his labor would be depreciated in the market. He has not time to be anything but a machine . . . .[22]

His wisdom here is of the homespun practical variety and contains the germ of a radical critique of the new Western industrialism; it contrasts sharply with the rhetorical flourishes of his older friend and those of *The Reformer*. Thoreau possesses none of what Westerners often consider to be the cosmic pessimism of the Hindu,[23] and yet little believed that an entire society, in this case American rather than Indian had any real prospect of a universal rise to true knowledge of liberty and truth. He is forever the outsider with an intensely personal vision, unconcerned with the consistent reconciling of discordant polarities.

A joint consideration of the two passages which Thoreau copied out of Murray's *British India*, one against the other, reveals the unique complexities of Thoreau's mind and art, the 'different drummer' marking time for him.[24] On the one hand there is the eccentric ascetic anticipating cosmic experiences, avoiding society (especially that of women), discounting human friendship for a deeper relationship with nature, fleeing perhaps even from himself, avoiding all entanglements, subscribing to a cult of simplicity and of self-discipline on all levels. On the other hand, Thoreau was profoundly concerned with the social consequences of his actions, in a way a yogi would never make explicit or accept. He believed wholeheartedly that reform must come from within, but he is extremely concerned with the social consequences of that reform. The Walden retreat was to become for Thoreau a paradigmatic gesture, a rite of passage, in much the same way that the eating of meat and the adoption of Western modes of dress might have been for the nineteenth-century Hindu rebelling against the general norms of Indian life. Neither would he have considered leaving the elimination of social ills to the operation of divine law.

As we noted earlier, this quest for spiritual self-knowledge and regeneration may have offered a new rationale, a new way of coping with the intimate personal trials and social conditions which the young Thoreau did not find himself capable of changing. They also provided a new tentative self-assurance which was to grow stronger as he grew older. The motif of withdrawal as a *positive social act* was to return again and again, gaining in intensity as Thoreau matured:

> How shall I help myself? By withdrawing into the garret, and associating with spiders and mice, determining to meet myself face to face sooner or later. Completely silent and attentive I will be this hour, and next, and forever. The most positive life that history notices has been a constant retiring out of life, a wiping one's hands of it, seeing how mean it is, and having nothing to do with it.[25]

This confused antithesis of the 'positive life' being a negation of action was not to be resolved, but to gain new power and clearer articulation in later years, in *Walden*, and most notably of all, in one of the most oft-quoted and influential passages in 'Civil Disobedience':

> I know this well, that if one thousand, if one hundred, if ten men whom I could name, – if ten *honest* men only, – ay, if *one* HONEST man, in this state of Massachusetts, *ceasing to hold slaves*, were actually to withdraw from this copartnership and be locked up in the county jail therefore, it would be the abolition of slavery in America. For it matters not how small the beginning may seem to be: what is well done is done forever.[26]

Finally, in a passage from Thoreau's essay 'Walking,' published posthumously in *The Atlantic Monthly*, all tinges of bitterness both about his own social situation and the social condition of America has disappeared, leaving behind a Sanskritic purity of expression which represents the contemplative at his best:

> Live free, child of the mist, – and with respect to knowledge we are children of the mist. The man who takes the liberty to live is superior to all the laws, by virtue of his relation to the lawmaker. 'That is active duty,' says the Vishnu Purana, 'which is not for our bondage; that is knowledge which is for liberation: all other duty is good only unto weariness; all other knowledge is the cleverness of the artist'.[27]

At once a unique combination of escapism and social responsibility, civic concern and cosmic eccentricity, practical knowledge of men and a quixotic vision of himself, we can see all of this in the above and its roots in Thoreau's personal plight and literary experience of India in 1837.

There is one more passage in Murray's *British India* which Thoreau thought worthy of copying that should be noted. In the section on philosophy, Murray spends several pages on Vedanta which Thoreau totally ignored. Instead, Thoreau abstracts a passage from the very small section on Sankhya philosophy:

> Kapila was an Indian metaphysician who wrote the Sanchye. He compares 'matter to a female dancer, exhibiting herself to the soul as a spectator; but considers the perfection of intellect as attainable only by an entire abstraction from material objects.' – But there is a slight connecting link between the soul and the body, consisting in a 'certain mysterious substance' which he calls 'the subtile person'.[28]

It is probable that Thoreau had heard much of this 'doctrine of correspondences' from Emerson, whose own work shows a deeper understanding of the original Hindu doctrine. Emerson thought of the 'material prima' as blind, but forever working to help man realize his full spiritual freedom. This, in a sense, is the 'telos' of Nature. For Emerson, Nature is never a symbol, or the raw material to be acted upon, but the 'dancer' herself.

Thoreau's own thought was to take a more 'romantic', though less philosophically coherent cast, as one can see from his characterization of the poet:

> He must be something more than natural, – even supernatural. Nature will not speak through but along with him. His voice will not proceed from her midst, but, breathing on her, will make her the expression of his

thought. He then poetizes when he takes a fact out of nature into spirit. ... He is another Nature, – Nature's brother. Kindly offices do they perform for one another. Each publishes the other's truth.[29]

Here, Thoreau does not distinguish between the poet's egotism and the transcendentalist ideal. As a 'poet' Thoreau finds that he must create his own 'symbols' by abstracting from nature, rather than allowing his mind to be a pure reflection of it. In this, *Walden* is one of the most 'artful' of books; it is the work of another Nature.

And yet, Thoreau's acquaintance with the philosophy of Sankhya is later to permeate his writings, particularly used to emphasize the possibility of a fully mystical knowledge grounded in nature. One of the best passages in Thoreau's 'A Week on the Concord and Merrimack Rivers', written about a trip he and his brother took more than two years later (in 1839) and published twelve years later (in 1849), utilizes the very passage on Sankhya Thoreau read and copied from Murray's *British India* in 1837:

> We need pray for no higher heaven than the pure senses can furnish, a purely sensuous life. Our present senses are but rudiments of what they are destined to become. We are comparatively deaf and dumb and blind, and without smell or taste or feeling. Every generation makes the discovery that its divine vigor has been dissipated, and each sense and faculty misapplied and debauched. The ears were made, but not for such trivial uses as men are wont to suppose, but to hear celestial sounds. The eyes were not made for such groveling uses as they are now put to and worn out by, but to behold beauty now invisible. May we not *see* God? Are we to be put off and amused in this life, as it were with a mere allegory? Is not Nature, rightly read, that of which she is commonly taken to be the symbol merely? Did not he that made that which is *within* make that which is *without* also? What is it, then, to educate but to develop these divine germs called the senses? for [sic] individuals and states to deal magnanimously with the rising generation, leading it not into temptation – not teach the eye to squint, nor attune the ear to profanity. But where is the instructed teacher? Where is the normal school?
>
> A Hindoo sage said, 'As a dancer, having exhibited herself to the spectator, desists from the dance, so does Nature desist, having manifested herself to the soul. Nothing, in my opinion, is more gentle than Nature; once aware of having been seen, she does not expose herself to the gaze of the soul.'[30]

And here is where Thoreau's own life comes to bear. Like the man he so profoundly influenced through his writings, Gandhi, Thoreau sees his own personal life as one broad 'experiment with truth', and yet the symbol of what the life of humanity could be. The senses cannot be washed free in society, so he will step outside of it. The Brahman ascetic and the Hindu reformer are one and the same. The pure egotist is purely passive, the hermit leads a purely sensuous life; he will cultivate the senses in order to transcend them.

Thoreau never outgrew the personal crisis of 1837. The disturbances and trials, conflicts and self-reflections, and above all, the new directions found during this time became the very stuff of his life work. He is a yogi, and the child of mist, the poet and crafter of his own pencils. He creates by the fact of his being. But it is the willingness to recognize and accept the ironies, passions, disappointments, and cosmic inconsistencies of life as a source of creativity which most identifies Thoreau with the India to which he was first introduced in 1837. For Thoreau, the introduction to India was to turn out to be no less than an introduction to himself.

NOTES

1. 'The Writings of Henry David Thoreau – Walden Edition,' edited by Bradford Torrey, (Cambridge, MA, 1906), *Journal* 1: p. 339. All further references to the *Journal* are to this edition unless otherwise noted.
2. Arthur Christy, *The Orient in American Transcendentalism*, (New York, 1932), p. 188.
3. Franklin E. Sanborn (*Henry D. Thoreau*, [Boston, 1882], pp. 53–4) notes that Emerson interceded with then Harvard President Quincy to have Thoreau awarded a twenty-five dollar exhibition, despite a mediocre record.
4. Kenneth Walter Cameron, 'Thoreau Discovers Emerson', *Bulletin of the New York Public Library* 57, No. 7, July 1953: pp. 319–34.
5. Ralph Waldo Emerson, *The American Scholar*, in *The Collected Works*, edited by Robert E. Spiller, 1: p. 56.
6. *The Correspondence of Henry David Thoreau*, edited by Walter Harding and Carl Bode, (New York, 1958), p. 14.
7. Henry David Thoreau, *Walden*, in 'The Writings of Henry David Thoreau', 1, edited by J. Lyndon Shanley, (Princeton, 1971), pp. 17–18.
8. Thoreau, *Journal* 1, October 22 1837: p. 3.
9. Thoreau, *Journal* 1, October 25 1837: p. 4.
10. Hugh Murray, James Wilson, R. K. Greville, Professor Jameson, Sir Whitelaw Ainslie, William Wallace, Capt. Clarence Dalrymple, *A Historical and Descriptive Account of British India*, 3v., (Edinburgh, 1843).
11. *Ibid.*, 2: p. 243.
12. *Ibid.*
13. The passages from Thoreau's copybooks are printed in Kenneth Walter Cameron, *Transcendentalists and Minerva* – Vol. 1, (Hartford, CT, 1958).
14. Quoted by Cameron, *Transcendentalists* 1: p. 239.
15. Quoted by Henry Seidel Canby, *Thoreau*, (Cambridge, MA, 1939), p. xv.
16. Thoreau, *Journal*, 1: p. 9.
17. Thoreau, *Walden*, pp. 18–20.
18. Quoted by Cameron, *Transcendentalists* 1: p. 240.
19. Henry David Thoreau, 'Letter to Harrison Blake, Nov. 20, 1849', in *Writings* 6, edited by Bradford Torrey, (Cambridge, MA, 1906): p. 175.
20. Emerson, *The American Scholar*, p. 67.
21. Thoreau, *Walden*, p. 15.
22. Thoreau, *Walden*, pp. 5–6.
23. See Walter Harding, *A Thoreau Factbook*, (New York, 1959), p. 99.
24. Thoreau, *Walden*, p. 326.
25. Thoreau, *Journal* 1: April 8, 1940: pp. 132–3.

26. Thoreau, 'Civil Disobedience', in *Walden and Other Writings*, edited by Brooks Atkinson, (New York, 1937), p. 646.
27. Thoreau, 'Walking', in *Writings* 5: pp. 240–1. (First published in 1862.)
28. Quoted by Cameron, *Transcendentalists* 1: p. 240.
29. Thoreau, *Journal*, 1: pp. 74–5.
30. Thoreau, 'A Week on the Concord and Merrimack Rivers', in *Writings*, pp. 408–9.

12

THOREAU'S HINDU QUOTATIONS
IN *A WEEK*

Ellen M. Raghavan and Barry Wood

Thoreau's first book, *A Week on the Concord and Merrimack Rivers* (1849), contains scores of direct quotations from the wealth of reading the author had done since his years at Harvard. A few quotations appear beside discussion of the author quoted – Homer, for instance – but most were not identified by Thoreau. Although an extended effort to identify them was made by the editors of the Walden or Manuscript Edition of Thoreau's works in 1906, the identifications, placed at the back, were limited to the names of authors, with no attempt to provide either title of the work or the edition Thoreau used. In the 1940s Ernest E. Leisy corrected a number of errors in this list, provided some titles, and added to the number of quotations identified.[1] But neither Leisy nor anyone since has published the sources of more than forty Hindu quotations in *A Week* taken from several books, even though Thoreau's indebtedness to the Orient has been noted repeatedly.[2]

One reason for the neglect of this important group of quotations stems from the unfamiliarity of the titles; a second is related to the variation between modern and nineteenth-century transliterations of foreign names, which poses recognition problems; while a third derives from the casual way in which Thoreau mentions Hindu works, usually without our modern signals to indicate that he is referring to a specific book. He did name six, which are listed here as he presented them to illustrate the difficulties described (pagination is to the Manuscript edition): (I) Veeshnoo Sarma (*Week*, p. 128), the Heetopades of

Ellen M. Raghavan and Barry Wood, 'Thoreau's Hindu Quotations in *A Week*', *American Literature*, 51: 1, 1979, pp. 94–8.

Veeshnoo Sarma (*Week*, p. 153); (2) Menu (*Week*, p. 140), the Laws of Menu (*Week*, p. 154), the Laws of Menu with the gloss of Culluca (*Week*, p. 157); (3) the Bhagvat-Geeta (*Week*, p. 140); (4) the Vedas (*Week*, pp. 160, 183); (5) the Sacontala by the Indian poet Calidas (*Week*, p. 183); and (6) the Vishnu Purana (*Week*, p. 302). It turns out that the quotation Thoreau says is from *The Vishnu Purana* does not appear in that popular volume, while another quotation (*Week*, p. 409) traces to a Hindu work called *Sankhya Karika*, which Thoreau nowhere mentions in *A Week* (though he does in his *Journal*, II, 192); he simply attributes the words to 'a Hindoo sage'.

These works were all available in New England in the years preceding publication of *A Week*. Charles Wilkins's 1787 translation of *The Heetopades of Veeshnoo Sarma*, a large collection of fables and aphorisms, had been excerpted by Emerson for the *Dial* (July, 1842). The writings of Rajah Rammohun Roy had been well known since the Indian Unitarian controversy, when *The Christian Register* (Dec. 7, 1821) had filled eight columns with his work. Thoreau's mention of the Vedas refers to Roy's 1832 translation of *The Veds*. Both have been reprinted with introductions by William Bysshe Stein.[3] Two other Hindu sources Thoreau mentions were available to him through the six-volume *Works* of Sir William Jones, 1799. What Thoreau describes as the Laws of Menu refers to *Institutes of Hindu Law; or, The Ordinances of Menu, According to the Gloss of Culluca*, which was translated in Volume 3 of Jones's *Works*; and the long play by Kalidasa called *Shakuntala* (c. fifth century AD) appeared in Volume 6.[4] The Charles Wilkins translation of *The Bhagvat-Geeta, or Dialogues of Kreeshna and Arjoon*, 1785, was well known in Concord from about 1845, and Thoreau read it with close attention.[5] Henry Thomas Colebrooke's 1837 edition of *The Sankhya Karika*, from which Thoreau quotes without naming his source, was also read in Concord in the late 1840s.[6]

The following list of quotations, like the lists published by Leisy, is keyed to the Manuscript edition of *A Week* (1906), which is still readily available in the Sentry paperback. A handful of these quotations have been identified before: Stein identified the only quotation from *The Veds* (*Week*, p. 68) and three quotations from the *Hitopadesa* (*Week*, pp. 220, 237, 301) in his introductions to the facsimile editions; Carl F. Hovde identified one quotation from the *Laws of Menu* (*Week*, p. 159) but referenced it to a later edition of Jones's *Works*;[7] and David G. Hoch identified the quotation from the *Sankhya Karika* (*Week*, p. 409).[8] The rest of the quotations have not previously been identified, including a large number from *The Bhagavad Gita* – the most accessible of Thoreau's Hindu sources. For convenience the entire list is provided, with pagination referring to the editions (or volumes of Jone's *Works*) which Thoreau used. Three quotations from the *Geeta* (*Week*, pp. 142–3) are taken from the introductory letter by Warren Hastings; in all the other quotations from the text of the *Geeta* itself chapter and verse references have been added in parentheses to aid in the study of this important source with the use of more accessible editions:

p. 68   'God is the letter ... Khu' *The Veds*, p. 12
p. 98   'There are the ... another?' *Geeta*, pp. 54–5 (IV, 28, 31)
p. 128 'Time drinketh up ... execution' *Heetopades*, p. 151
p. 140 'Immemorial custom ... law' *Menu*, p. 80
p. 140 'Perform the settled ... inaction' *Geeta*, p. 45 (III, 8)
p. 140 'A man's own ... smoke' *Geeta*, p. 131 (XVIII, 48)
p. 140 'The man who ... himself' *Geeta*, p. 48 (III, 26)
p. 140 'Wherefore, O Arjoon ... fight' *Geeta*, p. 36 (II, 37)
p. 142 'Of a sublimity ... unequalled' *Geeta*, p. 10
p. 142 'will survive when ... remembrance' *Geeta*, p. 13
p. 143 'To those who ... own' *Geeta*, p. 9
p. 144 'The forsaking of works ... lost' *Geeta*, p. 51 ('The forsaking of works' is a title added by Wilkins to Chapter 4 of the *Geeta*; the rest of the quotation is from IV, 2.)
p. 144 'In wisdom is ... exception' *Geeta*, p. 55 (IV, 33b)
p. 144 'Although thou wert ... wisdom' *Geeta*, p. 55 (IV, 36)
p. 144 'There is not ... purity' *Geeta*, p. 56 (IV, 38)
p. 144 'The action stands ... wisdom' *Geeta*, p. 40 (II, 49a)
p. 144 'is confirmed ... purposes' *Geeta*, p. 41 (II, 58)
p. 144 'Children only ... other' *Geeta*, p. 57 (V, 4–5)
p. 144 'The man enjoyeth ... event' *Geeta*, pp. 44–45 (III, 4–7)
p. 145 'Let the motive ... inaction' *Geeta*, p. 40 (II, 47)
p. 145 'For the man ... Supreme' *Geeta*, p. 46 (III, 19)
p. 145 'He who may ... nothing' *Geeta*, p. 53 (IV, 18–20)
p. 145 'He is both ... action' *Geeta*, p. 62 (VI, 1)
p. 145 'He who enjoyeth ... Supreme' *Geeta*, p. 55 (IV, 31)
p. 146 'I am the same ... hatred' *Geeta*, p. 81 (IX, 29)
p. 146 'formed upon the ... *Sastra*' *Geeta* (II, 39)
p. 146 'Seek an asylum ... alone' *Geeta*, p. 40 (II, 49b)
p. 146 'hath to do' *Geeta*, p. 46 (III, 19: see above, *Week*, 145)
p. 146 'action' *Geeta*, Chaps. II–VI. The place of 'action' or *karma* relative to 'discipline' or *yoga* is a central theme of the *Geeta*, expecially in these chapters from which most of Thoreau's are taken.
p. 146 'settled functions' *Geeta*, p. 45 (III, 8: see above, *Week*, p. 140)
p. 146 'a man's own religion' *Geeta*, p. 48 (III, 35)
p. 146 'a man's own particular calling' *Geeta*, p. 131 (XVIII, 47)
p. 146 'natural duty ... field' *Geeta*, pp. 56, 130 (IV, 42; XVIII, 43)
p. 147 'walketh but ... wake' *Geeta*, p. 43 (II, 69)
p. 147 'As, O mighty ... belief' *Geeta*, p. 135 (XVIII, 76–8)
p. 154 'Vyasa, the son ... human' *Menu*, p. 59
p. 154 'to have been ... beings' *Menu*, p. 54
p. 154 'taught his laws ... code' *Menu*, p. 59
p. 154 'A number of ... Law' *Menu*, p. 60
p. 159 'When that power ... away' *Menu*, p. 72

The implications of Thoreau's Hindu borrowings are yet to be fully worked out. It can be noted, however, that his accuracy in quotation suggests that he worked directly from the sources while writing *A Week*. Paul David Johnson has recently drawn our attention to the 'redemptive' qualities of *A Week*, reminding us of a fact which *Walden* does not emphasize: that 'much of the "private business" which Thoreau transacted at Walden was the writing of *A Week*.'[9] It seems clear from these quotations that Thoreau saw his own activities while writing *A Week* (although not necessarily during the actual river trip) and while staying at Walden Pond in terms of Hindu 'discipline' and 'action'. In this light the crucial importance for Thoreau of *The Bhagavad Gita*, especially Chapters 2 to 6, remains to be investigated. It may be noted, too, that the importance to Thoreau of Hinduism is not diminished by the fact that there are relatively few direct Hindu quotations in *Walden*. In the five years between the two books Thoreau had so completely integrated his Hindu perspective with his transcendental inheritance that quotation hardly seemed necessary. Thus the student of Indian thought can feel a distinctively Hindu quality coming through numerous passages in *Walden*, even where no specific Hindu references occur.

NOTES

1. Ernest E. Leisy, 'Sources of Thoreau's Borrowings in *A Week*', *American Literature*, XVIII (March, 1946), 37–44; 'Thoreau and Ossian', *New England Quarterly*, XVIII (March, 1945), 96–8; 'Francis Quarles and Henry D. Thoreau,' *Modern Language Notes*, LX, (May, 1945), 335–6.
2. See especially Arthur Christy. *The Orient in American Transcendentalism: A Study of Emerson, Thoreau, and Alcott* (1932; rpt. New York, 1963), pp. 185–233; and Dale Riepe, *The Philosophy of India and Its Impact on American Thought* (Springfield, Ill., 1970), pp. 39–45.
3. William Bysshe Stein, ed., *Hitopadesa: Fables and Proverbs from the Sanskrit*, trans. Charles Wilkins (1787; 1886: tpt. Gainesville, Fla., 1968); Rajah Rammohan Roy, *Translation of Several Principal Books, Passages, and Texts of the Veds ...*, (1832), in William Bysshe Stein, ed., *Two Brahman Sources of Emerson and Thoreau* (Gainesville, Fla., 1967).
4. Sir William Jones, *Works*, 6 vols. (London, 1799).
5. Charles Wilkins, trans., *The Bhagavat-Geeta, or Dialogues of Kreeshna and Arjoon* (1785; rpt.; Gainesville, Fla., 1959).
6. Henry Thomas Colebrooke, *The Sankhya Karika, or Memorial Verses on the Sankhya Philosophy by Iswara Krishna ...* trans. Horace Hayman Wilson (Oxford, 1837).
7. Carl F. Hovde, 'Literary Materials in Thoreau's *A Week*', *Publications of the Modern Language Association of America*, LXXX (March, 1965), 79.

8. David G. Hoch, 'Thoreau's Source for the Story of the King's Son', *Thoreau Journal Quarterly*, XCIX (April 15, 1970), II.
9. Paul David Johnson, 'Thoreau's Redemptive Week', *American Literature*, XLIX (March, 1977), 22.

13

NIETZSCHE'S TRANS-EUROPEAN EYE

Mervyn Sprung

According to a tenacious tradition, still apparently alive in our day – though Eastern allusions are not quite the popular fashion they were a few years ago – Nietzsche had a lifelong interest in Sanskrit philosophy and Indian thought. His early adoration of Schopenhauer, who *was* a serious student of Buddhism and the Upanishads, and his persistent, if broken, acquaintance with Paul Deussen, who *was* an academic sanskritist and comparative philosopher, from their schooldays until after Nietzsche's breakdown, have fed this tradition with plausibility. Most convincing, however, is Nietzsche's own use of passages and sayings from Sanskrit texts and his recurrent adductions, some repudiative, some grudgingly favourable, of Buddhism.

In a vivacious letter to Paul Deussen of 3 January 1888 Nietzsche speaks of his 'trans-European eye' which enables him to see that 'Indian philosophy is the only major parallel to our European philosophy.' Some thirteen years earlier (January 1875) he had assured Deussen of his 'eagerness, myself to drink from the spring of Indian philosophy which you will one day open up for all of us'. A normal reading of such passages would suggest a persistent concern for Indian philosophy on Nietzsche's part throughout this span of years, and most of those who have been aware of the question have indeed so inferred. Alsdorf[1] relied heavily on the widely held belief that Deussen and Nietzsche were 'life-long close friends' and yet offered Nietzsche's praise of the *Laws of Manu* (with which Deussen had nothing to do and which he must have found repugnant) as

Mervyn Sprung, 'Nietzsche's Trans-European Eye', in Graham Parkes (ed.), *Nietzsche and Asian Thought* (Chicago: University of Chicago Press, 1991), pp. 76–90.

evidence of his interest in India. Even Glasenapp, despite his straight-laced criticism of Nietzsche, found it encumbent to praise his serious and penetrating study of Indian thought: 'He penetrated deeply into its essence'; 'He reflected a great deal on Buddhism.'[2]

Quite recently the common presumption has been both tacitly and explicitly reinforced. Ryōgi Ôkōchi in *Nietzsche-Studien*,[3] though remarking on Nietzsche's limitations as a scholar of Buddhism, believes he was, through Deussen, in direct contact with the findings of German Sanskrit philosophy of his time and had a rather large number of books on Indian philosophy and Buddhism in his personal library (which is, regrettably, not the case: Hermann Oldenberg's *Buddha: Sein Leben, seine Lehre, seine Gemeinde*, the *only* book on Buddhism still there, appears never to have been opened). A current note[4] on Nietzsche and Deussen accepts the statements and protestations in letters and the use of Indian concepts in Nietzsche's published work at face value, and quite naturally concludes to a major impact of Indian thought on Nietzsche due to his 'life-long friendship' with Deussen.

When we recall that the rhetoric, if not the argument in *The Birth of Tragedy* virtually turns on the Sanskrit term *māyā* (world illusion), that the title page of *Daybreak* carries a line from the *Ṛg Veda*, and that, in a note to Rohde a few days after his final collapse, the underlayers of Nietzsche's mind could produce the sentence 'Taine composed the Vedas', the impression is virtually irresistible that Indian thought was formative in Nietzsche's intellectual destiny, although to a much lesser extent than Greek and German philosophy, Judaism, and Christianity. Sharing this impression, I thought it worthwhile to search out whatever might tell us more about this area of Nietzsche's thought. During a few weeks in Weimar, assisted invaluably by my wife, I worked through the dossiers of letters between Nietzsche and Deussen and searched Nietzsche's personal library for any trace of his interest in or knowledge of Indian thought. This included leafing through every relevant book to note marginal comments, underlinings, and any other indicator of interest or lack of it, such as uncut pages.

The reflections stimulated by this brief search easily broadened to form a set of related questions. It seems to me now that these questions have some interest for Nietzsche research in general.

1. What was the nature and extent of Nietzsche's interest in Indian thought?
2. What Indian texts did Nietzsche *know*?
3. How adequate was Nietzsche's understanding of Indian thought?
4. What importance did Indian thought have in the formation of Nietzsche's own thought?
5. What, if anything, has Nietzsche done for Western access to Indian thought (this not necessarily scaled to his knowledge of it)?

Such a wide-ranging questionnaire presupposes mastery both of the Nietzsche corpus and of the secondary literature, a mastery I would certainly not claim for myself. It is only the first two queries – those concerning Nietzsche's interest in and knowledge of Indian thought – which this brief report and discussion can deal with, and even so, in some points only partially. It is convenient to consider what might be called 'evidence' in these two matters according to the following grouping and sequence.

1. Nietzsche's own statements in the published works, including the notebooks.
2. Nietzsche's library.
3. Nietzsche's correspondence with Deussen.
4. Nietzsche's correspondence with others.
5. The correspondence of Nietzsche's friends among themselves.
6. The memories and observations of Nietzsche's friends expressed elsewhere than in letters to or about him.

As I proceed it will become clear which of these kinds of evidence I believe I have considered thoroughly and which only partially. In either case I shall proceed through these various types of evidence in the order given and begin with the published works, considering quotations first and afterwards references and allusions.

Though he speaks of or alludes to Indian thought frequently enough to arouse the presumption that it was alive in his mind, Nietzsche seldom quotes from an Indian text: I have found some nine or ten such quotations, though this is perhaps not exhaustive. Precise references are, of course, never given, and what Nietzsche puts between quotation marks is more often than not drawn from several points in the original text and composed by him into one quotation to intensify the power of his argument.

In his *Untimely Meditation* on Schopenhauer, Nietzsche introduced the Upanishadic sentence 'Men are born, in accordance with their deeds, stupid, dumb, deaf, misshapen'[5] (*UM* III, 8) to beat German academics with, but without a flicker of interest in the principle of *karma*, a *leitmotiv* of Indian philosophy. The title page of *Daybreak* carries the line 'There are so many days that have not broken' from the *Ṛg Veda*. This verse fragment is, I judge, drawn from *Ṛg Veda* VII 76, although Nietzsche's version of this obscure passage does not correspond to the interpretation of the German and English translators. Geldner and Griffith agree that the thought is rather 'There are so many dawns that have *already* dawned', a version not quite so appropriate to Nietzsche's mood of 1881. In the *The Gay Science* Nietzsche uses the mantras '*oṃ mane padme hum*' and '*Ram, Ram, Ram*', though they are hardly quotations, derisively, to belittle prayer (*GS* 128). With the approval often vouchsafed Buddha, the admonition 'Do not flatter your benefactor' (*GS* 142) is quoted in disparagement of Christian practice.

The only passage in which Nietzsche quotes substantially from Indian philosophy is in *On the Genealogy of Morals* during his discussion of asceticism. He first introduces a Buddhist statement 'Good and evil, both are fetters:

the Perfect One became master over both'; then the *Vedanta* believer is said to hold 'What is done and what is not done give him no pain; as a sage he shakes good and evil from himself; no deed can harm his kingdom; he has gone beyond both good and evil' (*GM* III, 17). This latter quotation is drawn from the *Kauṣītakī Upaniṣad* but is Nietzsche's own composition.

Immediately following this Nietzsche adduces three considerable 'quotations' from Deussen's *Das System des Vedanta*. They are all taken from Shankara's Commentary on the *Brahma Sūtras* and consist, in fact, of passages from the *Chāndogya Upaniṣad* (VIII 3, 4, 11, 12) with one sentence unidentified: 'For the man of knowledge there is no duty.' Nietzsche finds praise for the Indians' recognition that virtue does not suffice for redemption, but believes that their doctrine of release is at bottom Epicurean, a valuation of the hypnotic experience of nothingness as supreme. In this passage Nietzsche, uncharacteristically, names Deussen and praises his work.

In *Twilight of the Idols* Nietzsche reports on the *Laws of Manu* (which he had read in French translation) and composes a 'quotation' from it (*TI* VI, 3). He focuses exclusively on the genetic engineering (*Züchtung*) implicit in Manu's decrees casting out the *Chaṇḍālas* from normal communal life. Finally, in *Ecce Homo*, discussing *ressentiment* Nietzsche praises Buddha as the physiologist whose teachings are more a hygiene than a religion and quotes from the *Dhammapada*: 'Not by enmity is enmity ended; by friendliness enmity is ended' (*EH* I, 6).

Thus the meagre list of Nietzsche's quotations from Indian texts so far as I can find them. What do these quotations tell us about his reading? Excepting the three brief Buddhist quotes and the line from the *Ṛg Veda* in *Daybreak*, none presupposes more than Deussen's book *Das System des Vedanta* backed up by DuPerron's Latin version of the Upaniṣads, and a French translation of the *Laws of Manu*. Compared with the assiduous and persistent efforts of Schopenhauer to keep himself abreast of the lively Indian scholarship of the day, the evidence from quotations does not support the view that Nietzsche's 'trans-European eye' was scanning the Indian horizon with much interest.

But then Nietzsche *quotes* little from any source. It is the frequency, spontaneity, and unpredictability of his naming of ideas, philosophical schools, and religions of India, invariably with a strong argumentative twist, that persuades the casual reader that Nietzsche drew substantially on a strong, if nontechnical, sympathy with Indian thought. *The Birth of Tragedy*, studded as it is with 'the veil of Māyā' and 'Buddhistic denial of the will' and structured on the key concept of 'Buddhistic culture', reads as if the author were *approaching* the Greeks from a point of departure in classical India. This impression is, of course, not sustained in the pieces that followed. 'On Truth and Lie in the Extra-Moral Sense', the early piece which Nietzsche never published, though its theme longs for nurture and support from the skeptical epistemologies of India, is written as if classical Sanskrit did not exist. In his *Untimely Meditation* on Schopenhauer Nietzsche does of course have India in the background much of the time. He thinks Indian history is virtually the history of Indian philosophy; he beats at the German philologists for ignoring Indian philosophy 'as an animal [ignores] music'; he sees Schopenhauer as a hero of the spirit whose will should find its end in nirvana. The comment which, unwittingly, reveals most about Nietzsche himself is his opinion that Schopenhauer, in expounding his own philosophy, resorted to Buddhist and Christian mythology simply as 'an extraordinary rhetorical instrument' (*UM* III, 7).

Daybreak not only carries the *Ṛg Veda* quote mentioned earlier but has a fine passage (aph. 96) on the religious history of India, which praises a height of culture capable of abolishing gods and priests and of producing a religion of *self*-liberation (Buddhism), an achievement Nietzsche urges Europe to emulate. In *The Gay Science* it is clear that neither Buddhism nor Vedanta, however 'scientific', qualifies as 'gay'. Nirvana is 'The oriental nothing', 'rigid resignation ... self extinction' (*GS* Prologue, 3), which nevertheless can induce a new self-mastery and stronger will to live, and which is the condition of a higher humanity. Nietzsche seems to imply he has made this passage himself. A tendency to positivistic sociology and history is unmistakable in Nietzsche's use of the vegetarian diet to explain oriental lethargy and indulgence in opium, and in relating these to the spread of Buddhism (*GS* 145).

From *Beyond Good and Evil* on, the influence of Deussen's first major book, *Das System des Vedanta* (the copy in Nietzsche's library bears, in some sections, the marginal marks of his attentive reading) is quite unmistakable. Nietzsche recognizes that the liberated man of Vedanta is beyond good and evil, but regrets that he is still within the framework of morality; he finds Vedanta an example of the way dogmatic philosophy becomes 'a mask', as Platonism did in Europe (*BGE*, Preface); he believes that Europe is threatened by a softening of the mind, 'a new Buddhism' (*BGE* 202); he approves of the Brahmins using religion to win power over kings (*BGE* 61). In *On the Genealogy of Morals* Nietzsche continues his attack on nirvana as a 'nihilistic turning away from existence' which is creeping into Europe (*GM* II, 21); he writes vehemently against Vedanta asceticism, holding it to be Epicurean, 'a hypnotic feeling of nothingness', but again praises the Indian schools for going beyond good and evil (*GM* III, 17).

The last of Nietzsche's published works, including the notebooks, are dominated, so far as India is concerned, by his reading, in the spring of 1888, a French translation of the *Laws of Manu*. In *Twilight of the Idols* he says the Bible should not be mentioned in the same breath with it; it is '*vornehm*' (noble) and has a philosophy behind it; the caste system reflects the order of nature and excretes useless products; it is a 'holy lie'; 'the sun shines upon the entire book'. Only this once in all his writing does Nietzsche speak unreserved praise of anything Indian. He acquired the concept of *chaṇḍāla* – an outcast misbegotten – and uses it liberally during the last year of his work, even seeing himself as chaṇḍāla (*TI* VII, 2). In *The Antichrist* Nietzsche uses Buddhism to make disparaging comment on Christianity the easier. Buddhism is the only positivistic religion we know of; it ripens after a long tradition of philosophic thought; it has transcended the self-deception of morality: it is beyond good and evil; and all this in spite of its being a religion of decadence (*AC* 20). In *Ecce Homo* Buddha is praised as a great physiologist and Buddhism is said to be more a hygiene than a morality (*EH* I, 6). The notebooks of the last years contain a number of observations that emphasize much the same conclusions as we have already noted. Buddhism is more frequently taken up than Vedanta, and Nietzsche more than once draws a historical parallel between Buddha's position in Indian cultural history and his own position in Europe, implying that the doctrine of the eternal recurrence, in its negative aspect, is analogous to Buddhist nihilism (or perhaps vice versa) (*WP* 55).

This hasty scanning of Nietzsche's writings supports, in the main, the impressions gained from reviewing the quotations themselves. Noteworthy is the absence of India from the two works which are most spontaneous and least historically argumentative: *Human, All Too Human* and *Zarathustra*.[6] Nowhere are there references to Vedanta which imply wider reading than the quotations did: i.e., Deussen and at least two or three Upanishads. The case of Buddhism is slightly more complex. Though Nietzsche's grasp of Buddhism does not go beyond Schopenhauer, so that he betrays no awareness of a Buddhist philosophy beyond the doctrine of release from suffering, nonetheless the perspicacity he shows in sensing the freedom from moral self-deception in the words of Buddha suggest some reading of the original discourses, although there is no hint left us which ones, if any, he may have read. He quotes from the *Dhammapada* and quite conceivably knew nothing else.

The books still held in Weimar as Nietzsche's own library are a fascinating, if limited, further source of information about his knowledge of and, especially, interest in India. No volumes are presently held which offer evidence of any reading not apparent from Nietzsche's writings. Indeed, some precisely relevant books bear no sign of having been opened, e.g., Böhtlink's *Indische Sprüche*, Oldenberg's *Buddha*, Deussen's *Sutras des Vedanta*, and Max Müller's *Essays*, all published before his collapse. Even though one bears in mind the possibility that these copies are not the ones Nietzsche possessed, the consistency of the absence of evidence of reading together with the absence of reference to these works in Nietzsche's own writings cannot be dismissed. The volume which rivets one's attention is, of course, Schopenhauer's *The World as Will and Representation*. The extant copy is the fourth edition (1873), so that Nietzsche's student copy, in which he will have revealed his early reaction to the master, is not available. This makes the prolific marginal markings and underlinings in the 1873 edition all the more clearly the voice of Nietzsche's second and mature response to the Schopenhauerian *Weltbild*. This is, of course, a study in itself. For present purposes it is enough to note that Nietzsche's markings occur consistently in the passages dealing with the travail and death of the genius and with biological observations. Goethe is the person most frequently singled out. In spite of the rich sprinkling of allusions to Indian thought and mythology throughout Schopenhauer's pages, none catches Nietzsche's eye excepting only three: (1) 'The creators of the Vedas and Upanishads were scarcely human' (underlined); (2) 'Nirvana alone makes it possible to willingly surrender the will to live' (marginal comment: 'false'); (3) 'Death is *Schein*, as in the Bhagavad Gītā' (marginal strokes).

It is only too clear that even in these three instances Nietzsche was not interested in the ideas of the Indians but in the problems of the genius and of death. Taking the weight of evidence of the entire work, nothing could be more clear than that Nietzsche is quite insensitive to, indeed virtually deliberately ignores, the philosophical possibilities of the Indian material which Schopenhauer introduces. It is like a man striding through an exhibition of modern painting bent on finding the Greek sculpture. The conclusion from Nietzsche's copy of Schopenhauer, as from an examination of his library in general, for what these devices are worth, is quite unavoidable: Nietzsche's trans-European eye was more European than 'trans'. Or, one might say, his trans-European eye saw India through a powerful Nietzchean lens.

The outward signs of a 'life-long friendship' between Nietzsche and Deussen have been universally accepted as evidence of Nietzsche's life-long interest in Indian thought. However trustworthy these outward signs may prove to be, it is true that the acid test of Nietzsche's interest in Indian thought must be his relationship to Deussen. The long acquaintance of the two men, from schooldays to the years after Nietzsche's collapse, is a theme worthy of a monograph, and until that has been written perhaps the last word about the significance of India for Nietzsche cannot be spoken. Restricting my survey to the exchange of letters between the two, and drawing on Deussen's two autobiographical books[7] marginally, I find that the evidence here is not different from that so far noted, and indeed is surprisingly confirmatory.

The Weimar Archives hold twenty-seven letters and two postcards from Nietzsche to Deussen and thirty-two letters from Deussen to Nietzsche. The bulk of this correspondence dates from their *Studentenzeit* up to Deussen's disastrous visit to Nietzsche in Basel in July of 1871. During the next sixteen years – the creative period in the lives of both men – Nietzsche wrote Deussen four letters, two of which were gracious acknowledgements of the receipt of Deussens's first two books. In the last year of his activity, 1888, Nietzsche wrote Deussen four letters and one postcard, the fresh stimulus being Deussen's visit to Sils Maria the previous summer, the first meeting of the two since 1872, and his offer of an anonymous gift of two thousand Deutschmarks.

Apart from gracious and perspicacious words of recognition and praise on receipt of Deussen's books – followed of course immediately by a blunt rejection of their content for himself – Nietzsche never in the course of twenty-four years broaches the subject of India and never asks one question, nor ever solicits Deussen's opinion, about Indian philosophy. The two revert again and again to Schopenhauer, and Deussen reports from time to time on his progress in

Sanskrit studies, referring on one occasion to the 'clear, luminous Indo-German world' without touching a sympathetic nerve in his classical friend.[8] Nietzsche was quite aware of Deussen's eminence and unique ability to interpret Indian ideas in European terms, but never once bothered to seek information from or discuss issues with him. In short, the correspondence gives no evidence not available from his own writing of any reading Nietzsche may have done, and no indication of a more active or wider interest. The correspondence, indeed, does rather the reverse: it suggests a much lesser interest than the published writings do. Without the latter as corrective, one could study the letters of Nietzsche to Deussen and conclude that his interest was not so much in the subject matter of Deussen's work as it was in remaining loyal to an old school friend.

And indeed this is the final, if surprising, impression which Nietzsche's relation to Deussen makes on one. Nietzsche never takes Deussen seriously as a thinker; he often scolds him, lectures him on the elements of philosophy, sometimes barely, sometimes not at all, concealing his slight regard for, not to say scorn of Deussen's ideas. Nietzsche plays the part of the impatient teacher and imperious father. During a breathless midnight visit of Deussen to Basel in the summer of 1871, Nietzsche told him 'You are not gifted philosophically'.[9] Deussen, although himself a man of great ambition and self-esteem, never fights back; he humbles himself in front of his great friend and, when deeply hurt, suffers in prolonged, tortured silence.

It may, of course, have been precisely this unhappy lack of respect which made it impossible for Nietzsche to learn from Deussen; one cannot say. But the fact is that Nietzsche made no attempt to exploit his acquaintance with the most competent comparative philosopher of the time in order to study critically the ideas of the Sanskrit philosophers. Oddly, Deussen, who has generally been seen as concrete evidence of Nietzsche's 'trans-European vision', and whom I certainly so regarded before working through his correspondence with Nietzsche, turns out to be, as I now believe, the most crucial evidence we have of Nietzsche's lack of interest in trans-European ideas.

Nietzsche's letters to his other acquaintances – primarily Overbeck, Meysenbug, Rohde, Gast, von Gersdorff – present a mass of material with which I would make no claim to be critically familiar. Hasty scanning emboldens me to risk merely a few cautious generalizations. No aspect of Indian philosophy, excepting, of course, his loyal mention of Deussen's books, arises in Nietzsche's lively correspondence with precisely those fellow scholars with whom he would have discussed such matters had they been questions of genuine interest. He enthuses about the *Laws of Manu* to Peter Gast.[10] It appears that Nietzsche made no attempt to interest his friends in things Indian, with one further notable exception. In a letter to Gersdorff of 13 May 1875 he mentions borrowing an English translation of the *Sutta Nipāta*, a collection of early Buddhist poetry and anecdotes. At that time only fragments were available, I believe. Nietzsche mentions one poem, with the refrain, 'Let one wander alone like a Rhinoceros', and intimates he has taken it to heart. He quotes it 'I wander lonely as a Rhinoceros', a typical Nietzschean re-reading of a text. The idea of nirvana as 'clarity of mind' is drawn to Gersdorff's attention.[11] The passing mention of Deussen's *Elemente der Metaphysik* to Meysenbug, and of *Das System des Vedanta* to Overbeck and *Die Sutras des Vedanta* to Gast, Overbeck, Gersdorff, and sister Elizabeth, has more the character of a report to a small circle of friends of the noteworthy achievements of one of its members. Nietzsche does not appear to have gone even this far in his letters to Rohde: in the twenty years of their correspondence not one mention of Indian philosophy has come to my attention.

From correspondence with his closest friends I move to the last source of evidence available to us: reports on Nietzsche's conversations and activities by these same friends in letters to one another or in their own publications. Of Deussen we have said enough already; Franz Overbeck must be the most fruitful remaining source and Malwida von Meysenbug close after him. These two should suffice to contradict or confirm what has already been said.

Bernoulli's wonderful book[12] allows us to picture Nietzsche in the circle of the Overbecks, light-heartedly improvising on the piano, relating lively episodes from his reading, discussing Byron, Shelley, Hobbes, and Hume as well as Goethe and Schiller, arguing repeatedly about music and language though never about sculpture, architecture, or painting, and from time to time declaiming principles of his own philosophy (e.g., 'to be able to amalgamate one's Yes and one's No').

In all the close and loving documentation from the years of this lively friendship, even in Overbeck's expansive and moving letters to Nietzsche's family and friends, there appears not one mention of books or ideas concerning India. Overbeck's historical and religious interests would have been receptive to a trans-European turn in the discussions and his personal tolerance would have invited it, yet there is no indication, that I am aware of, that Nietzsche and the Overbecks ever betrayed the slightest suspicion that outside of the Greek-Christian tradition there might be other worlds of ideas and culture from which Europeans could learn anything seriously relevant to their own problems and from which might come fresh critical perspectives.

Malwida von Meysenbug's reminiscences[13] permit essentially the same conclusion, but add more incisive evidence. Meysenbug recounts, fascinatingly, some weeks she passed together with Nietzsche in Sorrento in the autumn of 1877 after the Bayreuth season had concluded. The Wagners had left, as had Paul Rée, leaving Nietzsche alone with the woman he had once said should be his mother. Large portions of *Human, All Too Human* were in draft and Meysenbug was shocked at their tone and content; she thought Nietzsche was much too much under the influence of Rée and of the exclusive claims of the natural sciences; she urged the wisdom of the Upanishadic *tat tvam asi* against Nietzsche's one-dimensional historicism. At one point, after much talk about Goethe, Schiller, and Cervantes, she gave Nietzsche a copy of Kālidāsa's play

Śakuntalā and requested his response to it. Nietzsche read it and his subsequent comments, as recounted by Meysenbug, are, for myself, the single most revealing episode in the entire documentary evidence available to us concerning his stance in matters of European and trans-European philosophy and culture. For one thing, Meysenbug says Nietzsche had never read the play, *the* play which German poets and scholars had enthused over from the times of Schlegel and Goethe onward. He refused to concede much worth to it because it violated European dramatic rules of plot, motivation, and temporal unity. He was incapable, in spite of Meysenbug's urging, of sensing the irrelevance of the European canons in the face of the quite different Indian mythological background, lyrical freedom, ethical presuppositions, and, above all, in the face of the Indian treatment of time as dream time. Even allowing for a certain reluctance on Nietzsche's part to concede a point in argument, it seems bluntly true that in this episode he disclosed no sensitivity to aesthetic and philosophic values lying outside his classical European upbringing. This is, as far as I know, the one passage in Meysenbug's writings where Nietzsche and India are brought together in more than a casual way.

And with this Sorrento episode, Nietzsche being thirty-three years old, I will close this brief report on Nietzsche's interest in and knowledge of Indian thought.

There may well be much more to say than this sketchy survey of the complex material has turned up; and I may have too easily inferred an absence of interest from an absence of documentary evidence; again my initial assumption of a substantial, if minor, concern with Indian thought on Nietzsche's part may have led me to undervalue or overlook anything less than this. However this may be, a summing up of my impressions from the sources used turns out something like this.

We can conveniently name four areas of Nietzsche's interest – Buddhism, Vedanta, *Laws of Manu*, historical parallels – in descending order of frequency of reference.

Buddhism means to Nietzsche essentially what it meant to Schopenhauer, though his appreciation is more superficial: a religion of release from the inevitable suffering of human existence; a religion of pity based on the refined hedonism of the experience of nothingness. Nietzsche praises Buddhism for showing no trace of Semitic *ressentiment*, for being more a hygiene than a morality, and for rejecting the ultimacy of good and evil (though he quite fails to grasp the radical nature of this rejection). Often the word Buddhism can be read as a synonym for pessimism and this in turn as shorthand for Schopenhauer. One can apply Nietzsche's comment on Schopenhauer, that he used Buddhist mythology as a 'rhetorical instrument', to himself. The term 'Buddhism' functions most frequently as a focus of Nietzsche's abuse, as a counterpole to his own Dionysian ideas, as a device for saying succinctly what it is he disapproves of and thinks must be overcome ('European Buddhism'). That

Buddhism is so often a scapegoat derives perhaps from Nietzsche's tendency to attack most relentlessly what he most feared as his own weakness.

Vedanta served Nietzsche as the perfect model of a world-denying way of thought. It was conveniently remote, and the swift perusal of two of Deussen's books confirmed his suspicion that Schopenhauer's pessimism was rooted in such philosophy. He made little attempt to grapple with the mysteries of negation as a strong form of affirmation, the 'pivotal point' of Indian philosophy. He found the asceticism of Vedanta too extreme; in denying the body as well as subject and object, it was guilty of an 'assault on reason'. Its rejection of good and evil as ultimates was however a saving mark of its realism, Nietzsche thought. Here, too, as in the case of Buddhism, one must conclude from Nietzsche's disinclination to penetrate the issues raised by Vedanta, that the term served him more as a shibboleth, useful for denouncing what he believed to be his arch-enemy.

Little can be added to what has already been said about the *Laws of Manu*: Nietzsche seized on it as a happy and unexpected confirmation of an aspect of his own thinking. It was the radical hierarchy of human worth that aroused his enthusiasm; one has to admire Nietzsche's sensitive 'nose', when he says 'Plato reads like one who had been well instructed by a Brahmin'.

The explicit references to Indian history attempt either to apply a blunt materialist theory or to draw parallels with the Europe of Nietzsche's own time. Both Buddhism and Vedanta as historical phenomena are accounted for by the rice and vegetarian diet of the Indians, which so enfeebles that it exposes those who follow it to the temptations of opium, and thus to a withdrawal from life. Such comments are, however, merely thrown off in passing. More than once Nietzsche sees in the rise of atheistic, amoral Buddhism, at a time of crumbling Vedic religions, a parallel to his efforts to create a new basis for humans in the face of the collapse of Christian culture in Europe, a parallel which does not quite extend to the philosophic content of the two doctrines. That Nietzsche accorded Indian history and ideas so much importance that he found it worthwhile to draw them into his own thinking, even if only in an impressionistic way, is perhaps the appropriate concluding observation on the nature and extent of his interest in these matters.

This perhaps somewhat pedantic exposure of Nietzsche's acquaintance with Indian philosophical literature leaves the remaining questions, stated at the beginning of this paper, for further and more probing consideration: (1) The adequacy of Nietzsche's grasp of Indian thinking; (2) the nature and importance of any influence Indian thinking may have had on Nietzsche's own work; (3) the extent to which, or at least the possibility that Nietzsche, in spite of his fragmentary and second-hand knowledge of the Sanskrit texts, has made Western access to them easier. These questions demand a fully-rounded grasp of Nietzsche's own life-long thought struggles, no less than a careful study of the reluctant rapprochement of Western thought since Nietzsche, and the available texts from India's classical age. Indeed they demand a sure grasp of the volcanic changes in Western thought itself since Nietzsche. There can be no question of these matters being discussed here. If I can give a useful edge to the questions themselves, based on the limited research of this paper, that will be all.

1. Nietzsche's conceptions were probably not greatly different from those prevailing in his time, or at least not greatly less adequate. After all, Max Müller argued that nirvana did not exclude the possibility of personal immortality in heaven! Nietzsche's hard and courageous comments have the merit of silhouetting the contrast between the European Faustian man and the Indian liberated man. At the same time they reveal the inadequacy of setting up an absolute polarity between yes and no in philosophical thought. The Indians are wary of this and would remind us that Nietzsche's enthused yes-saying Dionysian is suppressing human capacities no less, perhaps more, than the composed Bodhisattva who is master of his enthusiasms. No injunction is more common in Buddhist literature than to summon the courage and the virility to make passions one's servants, not one's master. Nietzsche's repudiation of Buddhism and Hinduism as 'life-denying' is hardly adequate to the Indian conception.

2. How important was Nietzsche's knowledge of Indian thought for the development of his own thought? This must remain a problem for a full-length study of the growth of Nietzsche's thought from Röcken to Sils Maria. However, the first impression one has is that ideas from India penetrated Nietzsche as little as drops of water penetrate a goose's feathers. Certainly the conclusions of this study appear to support that impression. When one re-reads the *The Birth of Tragedy*, however, one can be struck by the force of Nietzsche's conviction that the person conventionally understood as *das Ich* (the 'I') – the free agent of thinking and of action – was purely phenomenal, a part of *māyā*, and was not a metaphysical absolute. This conviction never weakened, I believe, in spite of the primary place he accords the individual. Nietzsche tried to be sceptical toward all Greek-European categories, but the one he attacks most vehemently and which he appears to regard as the key is the Cartesian and Kantian *ich*, the grammatical subject of the *cogito*. The hallowed concepts 'being', 'knowledge,' and many others are equally repudiated. Could it be that Nietzsche was sustained in these heresies by knowing that Indian thinkers shared them with him? Perhaps, but I would not hazard an opinion.

3. Finally, has Nietzsche, in spite of his inadequacies or even misconceptions, made Western access to Indian thought any easier? It is difficult to believe that he understood himself in this way, but often enough a thinker's influence is quite other than his intentions. Nietzsche was the first European to sweep through the inherited systems of Greek categories with a disconcerting, disintegrating scepsis. Being, truth, causality, person, whatever he found in use, he rejects as 'fictions, unusable'. This is a striking parallel to the Vedantist and Buddhist treatment of concepts, a treatment which Westerners, almost without exception, take to be irresponsible or eccentric, and at the very least irrelevant. That a great Western thinker has been driven to this conclusion must shake our complacency somewhat and alert us to the odd fact that in some matters

Nietzsche is in substantial agreement with thinkers from another, remote, tradition. Ironically, he denied this throughout, with vehemence. Is it possible that Nietzsche's historical sense was acute when he surmised that Europe might now be in a cultural phase comparable to India at the time of the Upanishads and Buddha, a phase in which a radically altered self-understanding is needed if humans are to continue to believe in themselves?

NOTES

1. Ludwig Alsdorf, *Deutsch-Indisch Geistesbeziehungen* (Heidelberg, 1944).
2. H. Von Glasenapp, *Das Indienbild Deutscher Denker* (Stuttgart, 1960), pp. 102, 106.
3. Ryōgi Ôkōchi, 'Nietzsches Amor Fati im Lichte von Karma des Buddhismus', *Nietzsche-Studien* 1, 1972, pp. 36–94.
4. Hans Rollmann, 'Deussen, Nietzsche and Vedanta', *Journal of the History of Ideas* 39, 1, 1978, pp. 125–32.
5. I cannot locate this precise sentence, but it reminds one of the *Kauṣītakī Upaniṣad* I, 2.
6. Freny Mistry, *Nietzsche and Buddhism* (Berlin, 1981), p. 142, note 9, draws attention to an entry in the note books from the time of *Zarathustra – Sämtliche Werke: Kritisheausgabe* (Munich, 1980), 11, 26 [220]. Nietzsche mentions pages in Oldenberg's *Buddha* which deal with the Upanishadic problem of suffering, infinite rebirth, and freedom, in connection with his own thinking about the eternal return.
7. Paul Deussen, *Erinnerungen an Friedrich Nietzsche* (Leipzig, 1901); *Mein Leben* (Leipzig, 1922).
8. Deussen to Nietzsche, 6 January 1867.
9. Deussen to Nietzsche, 5 January 1872.
10. Nietzsche to Peter Gast, 5 May 1888.
11. I owe the details of this letter to Mistry, *Nietzsche and Buddhism*, p. 17.
12. Carl Albrecht Bernoulli, *Franz Overbeck und Friedrich Nietzsche: Eine Freundschaft* (Jena, 1908).
13. Malwida von Meysenbug, *Individualitäten* (Berlin, 1902).

14

NIETZSCHE AND THE LAWS OF MANU

Thomas H. Brobjer

Nietzsche very rarely speaks explicitly of politics and even less often, if ever, of a future ideal society. One possible and apparent exception is in sections 56–8 of *The Antichrist* (hereinafter cited as *AC*) and the chapter 'The "Improvers" of Mankind' in *Twilight of the Idols* where Nietzsche describes Manu's society with much apparent appreciation. In *The Antichrist* he writes:

> *Not* forgetting the main thing [in the Lawbook of Manu], *the* basic difference from any sort of Bible: it is the means by which the *noble* orders, the philosophers and the warriors, keep the mob under control; noble values everywhere, a feeling of perfection, an affirmation of life, a triumphant feeling of well-being in oneself and of goodwill towards life – the *sun* shines on the entire book. (*AC*, 56) [...] The *order of castes*, the supreme, the dominating law, is only the sanctioning of a *natural order*, a natural law of the first rank over which no arbitrary caprice, no 'modern idea' has any power [...] The order of castes, *order of rank*, only formulates the supreme law of life itself; the separation of the three types is necessary for the preservation of society, for making possible higher and higher types – *inequality* of rights is the condition for the existence of rights at all. – A right is a privilege. (*AC*, 57) [...] If we have just now examined a religious legislation the purpose of which was to 'eternalize' a grand organization of society, the supreme condition for the *prosperity* of

Thomas H. Brobjer, 'The Absence of Political Ideals in Nietzsche's Writings: The Case of the Laws of Manu and the Associated Caste-Society', *Nietzsche-Studien*, 27, 1998, pp. 300–18.

life – Christianity discovered its mission in making an end of just such an organization *because life prospered within it*. There the revenue of reason from long ages of experimentation and uncertainty was to be employed for the benefit of the most distant future and the biggest, richest, most complete harvest possible brought home: here, on the contrary, the harvest was *poisoned* overnight. (*AC*, 58)[1]

In *Twilight of the Idols* the discussion is more limited but apparently also in favour of Manu's laws and society:

> Let us take the other aspect of so-called morality, the breeding of a definite race and species. The most grandiose example of this is provided by Indian morality, sanctioned, as the 'Law of Manu', into religion. [...] Here we are manifestly no longer among animal-tamers: a species of human being a hundred times more gentle and rational is presupposed even to conceive the plan of such a breeding. One draws a breath of relief when coming out of the Christian sick-house and dungeon atmosphere into this healthier, higher, *wider* world. How paltry the 'New Testament' is compared with Manu, how ill it smells![2]

Nietzsche's affinitive statements here, together with his elitism and antidemocratic values in general, seem to make it almost impossible to deny that this, or something akin to it, constitutes a political ideal for him. This is also how most commentators have interpreted it.

Hunt, in his otherwise excellent study, *Nietzsche and the Origin of Virtue* (1991), understands Nietzsche's words about the society of Manu literally (and this colours important parts of the book). He refers to *The Antichrist* and claims: 'there he describes his ideal of a "healthy society" which embodies "the order of castes"' and then discusses it on the following pages (pp. 98–100). Later he refers to 'the pyramid-shaped utopia he describes in section 57 of *The Antichrist*' and to Nietzsche's words of the society of Manu as 'a description of a utopia written at the end of his career' (p. 141, compare also p. 168).[3]

Bruce Detwiler, in his *Nietzsche and the Politics of Aristocratic Radicalism* (1990), uses Nietzsche's words about Manu in *The Antichrist* as an argument in favour of the view that Nietzsche's antipolitical stance is limited (p. 63), later he claims that Nietzsche's 'ideal order appears to resemble Plato's' (p. 111). Detwiler hence seems to see these sections as affirmative political statements made by Nietzsche.

Ofelia Schutte argues in *Beyond Nihilism: Nietzsche without Masks* (1984), that from Nietzsche's words about the Tschandalas he 'would want to see all human beings bred for a specific function – as in the castes celebrated by him' (p. 156).

Mark Warren, like most commentators, says very little about Nietzsche's views about the laws of Manu in his *Nietzsche and Political Thought* (1988), but at least once he accepts the text in *The Antichrist* literally: 'A case in point is Nietzsche's praise of the Hindu's Law of Manu, with its order of castes sanctioned by God. [...] With unsettling clarity, he analyzes and cites with approval the social psychology of traditional political culture: [he then quotes a longer section from *The Antichrist*] [...]. Why Nietzsche defends this conception of political culture will become clear' (p. 69).

Henning Ottmann, in his detailed and interesting study *Philosophie und Politik bei Nietzsche* (1987) also says relatively little about Nietzsche and Manu, but nonetheless clearly sees it as an ideal for Nietzsche: 'Der ältere Nietzsche kehrt zurück zum politischen Platonismus seiner Jugend. Das Ideal der "Nomoi" wird ersetzt durch das der "Politeia"'. He then comments on the similarity between 'der altindischen Kastenordnung' which Nietzsche and Plato discuss – and argues that neither means caste in a biological sense (pp. 276–7). He notes that 'Nietzsche hat sie [die Dreiteilung der Stände] nur ein einziges Mal platonisierend dargestellt' and that a dualism is much more typical for his thinking (p. 278).

Also Giorgio Colli in the 'Nachwort' to the last volume of *Friedrich Nietzsche: Sämtliche Werke: Kritische Studienausgabe* (1980), seems to have understood Nietzsche's words in this sense:

> Auch seine übliche Suche nach Anregung durch die Lektüre scheint in dieser Epoche zurückzugehen. Nur das Buch von Jacolliot über das indische *Gesetz des Manu* macht einen großen, ja übertriebenen Eindruck auf ihn. Die Spuren dieser Lektüre finden sich häufig in den Heften und gehen dann auch in die *Götzen-Dämmerung* ein. Angesichts der vergrößernden Perspektive, unter der Nietzsche diesen Kodex hier betrachtet, kann man gar nicht anders, als an die Übersteigerung von Dingen und Personen zu denken, die die letzte Turiner Periode kennzeichnen wird. In dieser Lage wurde alles von der Zufälligkeit einer einzelnen Lektüre bestimmt. (*KSA* 13, p. 667–8)

Eric Blondel has recently in his commentary to his translation of *The Antichrist* into French, *L'Antéchrist* (Paris, 1994) claimed in a note to section 57 that we see here Nietzsche's affirmative morality:

> Dans tout ce paragraphe, étonnamment long, Nietzsche, à travers une sorte de réexposition résumée du code de Manou, va indiquer en filigrane sa propre conception morale positive. [...] Il tire ici, sous le masque, des conclusions assez radicales de sa critique du christianisme, jusqu'à frôler d'ailleurs une cynisme pagano-aryen qui annonce (ou reprend) certains thèmes de l'extrême droit préfascisante de son temps. [...] Reste qu'ici parle, aussi et surtout à son propre compte, un Nietzsche enfin positif, affirmatif et pas seulement critique.

Most recently Hubert Cancik has in his *Nietzsches Antike: Vorlesung* (1995) understood the society of Manu as a sort of Nietzsche utopia:

Nietzsche hat im Antichrist sein antisemitisches System durch den Einbau von arischen Traditionen komplettiert. [...] Das Gesetz des Manu war Nietzsche lieb, weil es die Kasten-Ordnung als Naturordnung sanktioniert. [...] Die Entlarvung von Socialisten als Juden, von Christen als Anarchisten ist der negative Beitrag Nietzsches zur Lösung der Probleme von 1888, der positive: dorischer Staat, Sklaverei oder Kastenordnung. [...] Das hyperboreische Credo zu Beginn entspricht der ultrakonservativen Utopie am Ende des Antichrist, dem Gesetz des Manu. (p. 147–8)

I have chosen to discuss Nietzsche's statements about the laws of Manu because they seem to be perhaps the most compromising and most evidently problematic of all of Nietzsche's 'political' statements. Though there is less discussion and emphasis on Nietzsche's relation to the laws of Manu than one perhaps would have expected – perhaps because most Nietzsche-scholars do not wish to bring to light a side of Nietzsche they disprove of and find embarrassing – I have found none who deny Nietzsche's affinity to the laws of Manu.

However, there exist important reasons to question such an interpretation. The alternative interpretation I propose here is carried out on several levels, descending deeper and deeper into Nietzsche's thinking. It uses, respectively, textual criticism, contextual reading, comparative reading (compares Nietzsche's statements here with his view of other cultures and caste-societies), study of Nietzsche's notes and early drafts for the texts in *The Antichrist* and *Twilight of the Idols* and finally political philosophical considerations.

The Manu whom Nietzsche praises is in the mythology of India the first man and the legendary author of an important Sanskrit code of law, the *Manu-smrti*. This code of law, or lawbook, is one of the most authoritative of the books of the Hindu code in India. In its present form it dates back to about the first century BC. The book contains twelve chapters dealing with such themes as initiation, marriage, hospitality, dietary restrictions, pollution, the conduct of women and the law of kings. Its influence has been monumental, and it has provided justification and a practical morality for the Hindu Caste system.

The direct reason why Nietzsche does, and is able to, discuss Manu and the society and laws of Manu is his reading of Louis Jacolliot's *Les legislateurs religieux: Manou-Moise-Mahomet* (Paris, 1876) which is a 480-page translation of a version of the *Manu-smrti*. The French title is somewhat misleading for it refers to a series of books which Jacolliot planned to write, each only dealing with one religious legislator – thus, this work is only a translation of the laws of Manu, with some commentaries in footnotes.

Nietzsche read the work in May 1888 and his copy of the book, with annotations, is still in his library. The reading resulted in a fairly large number of notes, discussions of Manu in *Twilight of the Idols* and *The Antichrist*, discussion of it in one letter to Gast and relatively infrequent annotations in Nietzsche's copy of the book (in the form of underlinings, marginal lines and a few minor corrections of spelling throughout).

Jacolliot's book is essentially a translation of one version of the laws of Manu with occasional discussions and comments in the brief preface and in footnotes. Annemarie Etter has examined and discussed the reliability of Jacolliot's text and has characterized him as someone who knew India well but his work as pseudo-scientific.[4] Jacolliot was an India-fanatic who believed that all of human culture literally had its origin in India, everything from Greek and Roman Law to weights. He also believed that most peoples were originally Indians, like Arabs, Semitics, Babylonians, etc. He combined this belief with an anti-semitism, but also with a still stronger antichristianism, especially directed against Catholicism. The reading of this book may have influenced Nietzsche's decision to write *The Antichrist*, which he had not planned before May 1888, but in general Nietzsche probably was very little influenced by the comments in the footnotes.

It is not known when Nietzsche acquired Jacolliot's book, but a possible source of knowledge of him, and interest in him, could come from Nietzsche's reading in 1884 of the article 'Maenadism in Religion' by Elizabeth Robins in the *Atlantic Monthly*.[5] She there writes: 'There was, unfortunately, no Louis Jacolliot in ancient times to watch unseen the sacred midnight revels, and then give a glowing description of them to the unilluminated' (p. 498).

Nietzsche's words in *Twilight of the Idols* are less evaluative and explicit than his statements in *The Antichrist* and will therefore here only briefly be discussed. The main thrust of the chapter 'The "Improvers" of Mankind' is against morality. But beyond or behind morality two realities exists – it is either of a taming nature or of a breeding one.[6] Nietzsche exemplifies the former with Christianity and the latter with the laws of Manu. It seems very probable that in the choice between the two alternatives, Nietzsche would choose the latter[7] – but, in fact, although he speaks better of breeding than taming, he does not here actually choose one or the other. Instead, he not only emphasizes their differences (where he seems to favour breeding), but also their similarity (where he rejects both). In the title of this chapter in *Twilight of the Idols* the word 'Improvers' has been placed in quotation marks – implying a scepsis with regard to *both* alternatives. He begins the chapter with a critique of morality which is aimed at *both* alternatives and in the last section he writes: 'The morality of *breeding* and the morality of *taming* are, in the means they employ to attain their ends, entirely worthy of one another'. The chapter ends with an explicit critique of both Manu and Christianity, and in emphasizing an 'inconsistency', or paradox, which they both share: 'Neither Manu nor Plato, neither Confucius nor the Jewish and Christian teachers, ever doubted their *right* to tell lies. Nor did they doubt their possession of *other rights*. ... Expressed in a formula one might say: *every* means hitherto employed with the intention of making mankind moral has been thoroughly *immoral.* –' Nietzsche does not choose one alternative, he rejects both.

1. With regard to the longer and more explicit discussion of Manu in *The Antichrist*, the first and perhaps most obvious reason to be careful to see sections 56–8 as expressing Nietzsche's political ideal is that the theme of these sections is introduced at the end of section 55 as being priestly structures based on the 'holy lie'. Nietzsche explicitly states that, among others, Christianity, the laws of Manu and Plato's political thinking belong to these. One would normally not expect that what comes after such an introduction would be Nietzsche's ideal.

2. If one ignores the rhetoric and examines Nietzsche's description of the Lawbook of Manu in *The Antichrist*, one will discover that the most fundamental aspect of it is that it is based on a lie and that it 'brings to a close, it creates nothing new' and it is based on the view that 'what, consequently, is to be prevented above all is the continuation of experimenting, the perpetuation in *infinitum* of the fluid condition of values, tests, choices, criticizing of values' (*AC*, 57). Nietzsche's ideal is more like the opposite of this, a continual striving and competition (*agon*), selfovercoming, will to power and a striving to become a human being of higher value (*Übermensch*). When Nietzsche in *Beyond Good and Evil* (1886) described his ideal, the philosophers of the future, he did so with the words: 'they will certainly be experimentors. Through the name with which I have ventured to baptize them ["attempters"] I have already expressly emphasized experiment and the delight in experiment' (*BGE*, 42).

In regard to Nietzsche's view of the 'holy lie' it is difficult to believe that he would accept it, considering that he has written in the preface to *The Antichrist* that: 'one must have become indifferent, one must never ask whether truth is useful or a fatality' and in the section before the ones about the laws of Manu, section 54, he has praised scepticism which is characterized precisely by the fact that it does not accept lies and holy lies. In the third section of the preface to his autobiography, *Ecce Homo*, he uses as his criteria for the value of a man how much truth he can endure: 'How much truth can a spirit *bear*, how much truth can a spirit *dare*? That became for me more and more the real measure of value.'

The virtue of the laws of Manu is that they attempt to stabilize society and prevent decline and degeneration. Nietzsche, however, does not emphasize stability and attempts to save what can be saved, but instead continually refers to the future and the possibility of a higher future. His *Beyond Good and Evil* has as subtitle: 'Prelude to a Philosophy of the Future' and in *The Antichrist*, section 3, he states that what interests him is the human being which is 'more valuable, more worthy of life, more certain of the future'. In *Ecce Homo*, 'Why I am a Destiny', 4, he discusses 'the *most harmful species of man*' which 'preserves its existence as much at the expense of *truth* as at the expense of the *future*' and he then quotes from his own *Thus Spoke Zarathustra*:

The good – cannot *create*, they are always the beginning of the end – – they crucify him who writes *new* values on new law-tables, they sacrifice the future *to themselves*, they crucify the whole human future!
The good – have always been the beginning of the end …
And whatever harm the world-calumniators may do, the *harm the good do is the most harmful harm.*

Nietzsche's critique of the state – prominent, for example in *Thus Spoke Zarathustra*, I, 'The New Idol' and in *Twilight of the Idols*, 'What the Germans Lack' – as a new idol and thus regarded as a value in itself, when it ought to be human beings and culture which constitute the goal and final value. With such a view it is difficult to believe that Nietzsche would genuinely accept and praise the strong emphasis on the state (and on religion) which the society of Manu requires. To give such powers to the state also constitute a contradiction to Nietzsche's 'individualism' and belief in self-development (compare his harsh critique of all forms of morality which 'depersonalize'). In Nietzsche's critique of socialism and Plato in the first volume of *Human, All Too Human*, section 473 in the chapter 'A Glance at the State', he claims that they are reactionary in their will to give total power to the state, a power so great that the individual will degenerate and be transformed into merely a useful organ for the state.

The laws of Manu also, more generally, imply a monolithic way of thinking, valuing and viewing society and humanity – which Nietzsche, at least sometimes, claims to be 'the opposite of *my* tendency'.[8]

3. That the laws and the society of Manu do not constitute Nietzsche's highest historical ideal is clear from the discussion in section 58 of *The Antichrist* where he clearly places Rome higher than Manu and claims that the Roman Empire constitutes 'the most grandiose form of organization [...] which has hitherto been achieved'. The Roman Empire has the advantage of not being built on a 'holy lie' and of not being coloured by priest-values and priestly ideologies. Nietzsche's choice of Rome here is determined by his aim of criticizing and constructing contrasts to Christianity (compare the comments on the next level). Rome may have created the greatest organization in history, but there can be no doubt that on a more general level Nietzsche regarded the Renaissance as a higher epoch than Rome and that of ancient Greece as still higher. If the society of Manu is an ideal for Nietzsche, it is so only to a very limited extent and as ideal it stands *below* the other alternatives mentioned here. This surely robs it of the right to the name of Nietzsche's 'ideal' or 'utopia'.

4. On the contextual level one ought to take note of the fact that Nietzsche's main purpose in this work is a critique of Christianity, that is, his own and his readers own tradition. When he compares Christianity negatively with other alternatives (here the laws of Manu) this does not necessarily mean that these constitute Nietzsche's ideal, or even that his view of them are as positive as it

might appear. The rhetoric in such a situation exaggerates the positive sides of the alternatives. That the purpose of introducing the discussion of Manu here was part of Nietzsche's critique of Christianity is apparent in a note from this time. 'A comparison of the Indian lawbook with the Christian cannot be avoided; there exist no better means to make visible the immature and dilettantish nature of the whole Christian attempt.' (*KSA* 13, 15 [24]).

That the alternatives appear more positive than they really are is clear in the sections in *The Antichrist* about Buddhism (sections 20–3) which could also have appeared as an ideal for Nietzsche if it were not for a sentence early in the discussion in which Nietzsche clearly states that Christianity and Buddhism both 'belong together as nihilistic religions – they are *décadence* religions'. With the exception of this sentence Nietzsche's discussion appears highly positive although we know from this sentence and from other references – for example, 'the tired nihilism, which no longer attacks: its most well-known form Buddhism: as nihilism which makes passive' (*KSA* 12, 9 [35]) – that Buddhism is more of a counter-ideal than an ideal for Nietzsche.

The perhaps strongest individual textual argument for believing that the basis of Manu represents Nietzsche's ideal is his use of the word noble [*vornehm*] in his description of it – 'the *noble* orders, the philosophers and the warriors, keep the mob under control; noble values everywhere' (*AC*, 56) – for with the word *noble* Nietzsche usually designates that which he regards as highly valuable. Also because Nietzsche regards the values of the privileged as more valuable and healthy than those of the lower classes. The contrast to Christianity, which Nietzsche sees as the ideology and value of the lowest classes, is evident. However, also in regarded to Buddhism (and Plato's philosophy), which is far from Nietzsche's ideal, he has in his notes made similar claims: 'Origins in the highest castes' (*KSA* 13, 14[91]). That something has its origin in the values of the higher classes, or in the elite, is for Nietzsche better than if the origin is with the values of the lower classes, but the difference of origin is not sufficient to make the former an ideal for him.

There is a direct parallel between Nietzsche's contrast of Christianity with the laws of Manu and the contrast with Buddhism (in sections 20–3) and with Islam (in sections 59 and 60). In comparison to Christianity Nietzsche praises all three – but in reality none of them is close to his ideal.

5. On a comparative level Nietzsche's statements about the society implied by the laws of Manu can be compared with his statements of other similar caste-societies (for Sparta and Plato's ideal state, see below). If Manu's society was Nietzsche's ideal society, or akin to it, it is surprising how little interest he shows in such and similar societies. The absence of interest in such societies constitutes a clear indication that this is not Nietzsche's political ideal.

The feudal Middle Ages is the period in the history of Western civilization which has most similarity with Manu's society. Nietzsche sees this similarity and writes in his letter to Peter Gast, 31 May 1888, in which he tells about his reading of Jacolliot and the laws of Manu: 'The form of organization during the Middle Ages appears as a strange key for regaining all of the ideas on which the ancient Indian-Aryan society rested'.[9] But the Middle Ages is precisely the epoch in European history which Nietzsche shows least interest in and least sympathy for.

6. Ancient Sparta could, and has, to a large extent been described in a manner similar to how Nietzsche describes Manu's society, while Athens, on the contrary, can reasonably be described as dynamic and experimenting. When asked which state and culture Nietzsche sympathizes most with between Athens and Sparta, many would guess that the answer is Sparta, but this answer is incorrect.[10] Such a view lacks support in Nietzsche's texts and is not based on what Nietzsche has said about these two city states and their cultures, but more likely on an erroneous conclusion of the sort: Nietzsche was positive about hierarchy and the laws of Manu, Sparta is similar to Manu, thus Nietzsche is positive about Sparta.

However, a study of what Nietzsche actually writes shows that his interest and sympathy is wholly directed at Athens – which is not surprising considering his cultural interests. In contrast to the common belief that Nietzsche sympathized with Sparta, his actual position was a mixture of disinterest and critique. 'As a whole their state is a caricature of a city state and the ruin of Hellas. The forthbringing of the complete Spartan – but what sort of greatness does he represent when it requires such a brutal state to create him!'[11] And 'To be a philhellene means to be the enemy of raw power and muddled thinking. Sparta was the ruin of Hellas in the sense that it forced Athens into a league of city states and to concern itself exclusively with politics'.[12] Both of these statements were written in 1875, under the influence of Burckhardt's *Griechische Culturgeschichte* (which, however, also had more positive things to say about the Spartans which Nietzsche did not pick up) which he read at this time. Thereafter there is hardly a single reference to Sparta in Nietzsche's writings. This, if anything, shows his indifference to Sparta.

A similar contrast can be set up between Nietzsche's view of Hellas and Rome, where Rome has more similarity to the laws of Manu than Hellas. Nietzsche was always much more influenced by ancient Greece and his sympathy and interest more directed towards ancient Greece than towards Rome. He wrote, for example: 'one must first learn to make distinctions: *for* the Greeks, *against* the Romans – *that* is what I call *ancient Bildung*'[13] and just a month before he wrote *The Antichrist* he wrote: 'the Greeks remain the *supreme cultural event* of history'.[14]

7. Nietzsche's description of a caste-society in section 58 of *The Antichrist* has much similarity to Plato's description of the ideal state in *The Republic*. This fact alone ought to make the reader who understands Manu as Nietzsche's ideal surprised and wary. Nietzsche describes his philosophy as 'reversed Platonism'

and sees Plato as one of his main enemies (although at the same time retaining a large amount of respect for the person Plato). In spite of the fact that Plato is one of the persons Nietzsche most frequently mentions and discusses in his writings, he almost never mentions Plato's political utopia and *The Republic* after the middle of the 1870s. If what Nietzsche describes in sections 58 is his ideal or near to it, this lack of reference to Plato's 'utopia' is highly surprising. This lack of reference to Plato's political thinking is consistent with the interpretation of Nietzsche as an in the main a- and anti-political thinker, as he himself claims,[15] but those who interpret Nietzsche more politically have a case to answer.

That Nietzsche also considered Plato's *Republic* when he speaks of Manu in these sections is undeniable. Not only is Plato explicitly mentioned at the end of section 55 which introduced this discussion, he is also mentioned in a number of notes relating to Manu, and in the letter Nietzsche wrote to Peter Gast discussing his reading of Jacolliot: 'and even Plato appears to me in all the main points only to have been well educated by a Brahman'.[16] In several notes written in early 1888 while reading Jacolliot,[17] Nietzsche emphasizes not only that 'Plato is completely in the spirit of Manu', but also that Plato in Egypt had been directly influenced by this manner of thinking. He mentions explicitly that Plato copied 'the castes' and 'the caste-morality' from this sort of thinking. In another note, with the title 'Toward a Critique of the laws of Manu',[18] he again associates Plato with Manu and expresses strong critique:

> The whole book rests on the holy lie; [...] The most cold-blooded self-control has here been effective, the same sort of self-control which Plato had when he thought out his 'Republic'.
> 'One must want the means when one wants the end' – all law-givers have realized this politician-insight.

> The classical pattern of thought here is specifically *Aryan*: we must thus make the most well-constituted and self-controlled sort of human being responsible for the most fundamental lie that has ever been created . . . One has copied it almost everywhere: the *Aryan influence* [i.e. the pattern of the laws of Manu] has ruined the whole world . . .

The association of Plato with Manu in these sections is not an indication of Nietzsche's approval of Manu, but rather part of his critique of Plato, who, according to Nietzsche, also based this thinking on priest morality and priestly structures. Still more evident is that Nietzsche's limited interest in Plato's political thinking (including the *Republic*), in spite of this great concern with other aspects of Plato's thinking, indicates that this is not Nietzsche's ideal and that Nietzsche is not particularly interested in political questions.

8. The Lawbook of Manu, or rather the *Manu-smrti*, is a central Hindu text. One would expect that Nietzsche's view of Manu would, at least partially, correlate with his view of Hinduism. In fact, Nietzsche never refers to, or

mentions, the word Hinduism explicitly at all, either in his books, notes or letters. However, after having received and read his friend Paul Deussen's *Das System des Vedânta* (Leipzig, 1883) he writes:

> Much must come together in a human being, for him to be able to reveal such a Vedanta-teaching to us Europeans [...] It is a great pleasure for me to learn to know the classic expression of the for me most alien way of thinking: your book gives me this opportunity. Everything which I have suspected in regard to this way of thinking comes in it in the most naive way to light: I read page for page with complete 'malice' – you cannot desire a more *grateful* reader, my friend!
>
> As it happens, a *manifesto* of mine is at this moment being printed [i.e. *Thus Spoke Zarathustra*, book I], which, with approximately the same eloquence, says Yes! where your book says No![19]

Thus, at least in 1883 Nietzsche regarded important parts of Hinduism as being the opposite to his own philosophy. In a note from 1885/86 (*KSA* 12, 2 [100]) in which he describes the planned content of book two of *The Will to Power* he writes: 'Critique of the Indian and Chinese way of thinking, likewise the Christian (as preparing the way for a *nihilistic* –) The danger of dangers: Nothing has any meaning.' In the preface to *Beyond Good and Evil* (1886) he refers to dogmatism as 'a monstrous and frightening grimace [Fratze]' and examplifies with 'the Vedanta doctrine in Asia'. In the letter to Gast where he speaks of his reading of Jacolliot, he refers to the laws of Manu as 'a priestly code of morality based on the Veda'.[20] In *Ecce Homo*, 'Zarathustra', 6, written immediately after *The Antichrist*, Nietzsche says: 'the poets of the Veda are priests and are not even worthy to unloose the latchet of the shoes of a Zarathustra'.

9. That the view expressed by Nietzsche in sections 56 to 58 in *The Antichrist* does not constitute Nietzsche's political ideal is most clearly seen in the notes which he wrote while reading Jacolliot, and thereafter, on this theme, and which constitute the material out of which the content of these sections has grown.[21] The context and the rhetoric in these notes are not as clearly determined by the intention of constructing a contrast to Christianity as is the case in the finished *The Antichrist* text and it is therefore easier there to see Nietzsche's views and values (which is often the case with his notes).

In the note *KSA* 13, 14 [195] Nietzsche constructs a scheme of five religions and places Manu, Islam and the *Old Testament* in the same group. Nietzsche held these as higher than Christianity, but few would believe that they constitute his ideal. In the long note, *KSA* 13, 14 [199], with the title 'The Origin of Morality', Nietzsche critically discusses how the priests make themselves into the highest caste, that which he on several occasions claims to be typical of the spirit of Manu.

Most distinctly, three notes from early 1888 have variants of 'A Critique of Manu' as title.[22] In these notes the laws of Manu are strongly criticized for being built on a lie, for the fact that they only use obedience and punishment as means, for only using metaphysical motivations (the 'beyond') and for making people and society numb and dumb. In the first of these notes he writes: '*Nature* is reduced down to morality: a state of human punishment: there are no natural effects – the cause is the Brahman. [...] It is a school *which blunts the intellect* [...] Including the *in-breeding* within the castes ... Here nature, method, history, art, science – is lacking'. This note is immediately followed by one in which Nietzsche claims that the spirit of the priest is worse in the book of Manu than anywhere else.

In the second of these notes, Nietzsche among other things writes: 'For this purpose the whole life is set in the perspective of a beyond, so that it in the most horrible manner is seen as *rich in consequences ...*', i.e. in imaginary consequences.

In many other notes from this time the laws of Manu are also criticized for similar reasons.[23] In *KSA* 13, 15 [44] with the title *The Reversal of the Order of Rank*, Nietzsche claims that 'among us', the opposite of what was characteristic of the society of Manu would be the case: 'the pious counterfeiters, the priests, will among us become tschandala [...] we are proud that we no longer need to be liars, slanderers, or belong to those who arouse distrust of life ...'. Immediately after this note comes the third note with critique of Manu in the title – 'Toward a Critique of the Lawbook of Manu' – and it contains harsh expressions like: 'The whole book rests on the holy lie: [...] – we [there] find a sort of human being, the *priestly sort*, which regards itself as norm, as peak, as the highest expression of man: from themselves they take their view of "improving".' This note ends with the already quoted words: 'the *Aryan influence* [i.e. the pattern of the laws of Manu] has ruined the whole world ...'.

What is then the reason why Nietzsche expresses himself in the published text of *The Antichrist* in such a manner that it can easily be misunderstood as his ideal? The main reason, as I see it, is that the purpose here is to make the contrast with Christianity as strong as possible, to provoke the reader, to make the reader 'realize' that even the laws of Manu – about which he in *Twilight of the Idols* had said: 'perhaps there is nothing which outrages our feelings more than *these* protective measures of Indian morality' – are higher and more humane than Christianity. Where Christianity destroys, the intention at least of the laws of Manu was to save and protect. The task of *The Antichrist*, as the first volume of four in the projected *Revaluation of All Values*, was to be critical – to free us from Christianity in the widest sense of that word – and therefore it was of secondary importance what took its place temporarily and if the constructive counter-ideal was not yet apparent. Nietzsche had intended to present and discuss this in detail in later volumes of *The Revaluation of All Values*, especially in the fourth, with the title *Dionysos Philosophos*.

A reason why it is so easy to misread Nietzsche's description of the laws of Manu as his ideal, is that one does not take note of his main intention, which is the critique of Christianity. Secondly, it is true that Nietzsche's view of man (and society) was hierarchical, elitist and antidemocratic, and it is therefore, apparently, not wholly incompatible with a caste-society *à la* Manu or Plato. Nietzsche referred to the concept and word caste relatively often long before he read Jacolliot's description and translation of the laws of Manu, but then in the more general sense of hierarchy. He also writes in a draft of a letter to Georg Brandes, early December 1888, and thus denies every form of caste-society: '*If we will win*, then we will have the world government in our hands – including world peace ... We have overcome [*überwunden*] the absurd boundaries between race, nations and class [*Stände*]: there exist from now on only order of rank between human beings, and, in fact, a tremendously long ladder of rank'.

10. A more important and fundamental reason for the misreading of the laws of Manu as Nietzsche's political ideal is of a political, and political philosophical, nature. Politics has more and more taken over the role religion had earlier as the dominant perspective on all questions. Politics has become the opium of the people, and still more of the elite. This politicizing 'Weltanschauung' makes it difficult to understand Nietzsche who, for us, to a surprising degree was a- and anti-political and called himself: 'I, the last *antipolitical* German'.[24] Nietzsche's perspective was always personal, philosophical and cultural, and never, or very rarely, political in any ordinary sense of that word.[25]

Nietzsche was most politically interested and involved during the wars and crises 1866 and 1870/71, at the time when an almost feverish political excitement caught hold of the German-speaking part of Europe. In the notes to his 'Rückblick auf meine zwei Leipziger Jahre 17 Oktober 1865–10 August 1867' he describes the period between Easter and October 1866 with the words 'Politische Aufregung'.[26] But even at these times, Nietzsche's interest was much less intensive than that of most of his compatriots. To his friend Wilhelm Pinder he appeared remarkably calm and unmoved in the midst of the political and military upheaval. In a letter to Nietzsche he writes: 'Bewunderungswürdig ist mir Deine Seelenruhe in jetziger Zeit. Also Du kannst wirklich codices kollationiren und – verzeih mir den Ausdruck – mit dem abstrusen Gegenstand theognischer Reliquien Dich befassen? Meine wissenschaftliche Thätigkeit ist seit Wochen – schlafen gegangen.'[27]

The picture of the young Nietzsche as having a very limited interest in political questions is confirmed by Ritschl's letter to Wilhelm Vischer-Bilfinger in Basel, who was responsible for the appointment of the new professor in philology there. In his letter Ritschl wrote: 'N. possesses in no way an especially political nature, but has, I suppose, in general, on the whole, sympathies with the growing greatness of Germany, but – as little as I do – an especial liking for *das Preußenthum*'.[28] That Ritschl was right is shown by the ease with which

Nietzsche voluntarily gave up his Prussian citizenship before he left for Basel so that, in Nietzsche's words, the university there could trust that he would do his duty towards it independently of war and peace in Germany.[29] Nietzsche never applied for a new citizenship and remained stateless for the rest of his life.

Nietzsche wrote *The Birth of Tragedy* (1872) at a time when he was probably more politically involved than at any other time in his adult life – and under the influence of Wagner, a much more political man than Nietzsche. In spite of this the book is remarkably unpolitical[30] while at the same time being culturally, philosophically and philologically committed and radical.

Political indifference and even hostility towards politics was a major motive for his choice of label when he shortly thereafter began to refer to himself as 'untimely' and wrote his *Untimely Meditations*.[31] In the fifth section of the second *Untimely Meditation* he claimed that 'all modern philosophizing is political' and this was something he wanted to avoid. In the fourth section of the third *Untimely Meditation* he wrote that 'any philosophy founded on the belief that the problem of existence has been changed or solved by a political event is a parody of philosophy and a sham' and in section 7 he claimed that 'the man with the furor philosophicus will have no time for the furor politicus'. The latter is a claim that echos throughout most of his writings and which he later will further radicalize.

After the early 1870s Nietzsche became still less politically interested and involved. One of the ten commandments of the free spirit was: 'Du sollst keine Politik treiben',[32] and in a note from 1879 entitled 'Die Lehre von den *nächsten Dingen*' in which he foreshadows much of the content of *Ecce Homo* he writes in the form of an imperative: 'Zurückgezogenheit von der Politik'.[33] Two years later he writes: 'Der politische Wahn, über den ich eben so lächle, wie die Zeitgenossen über den religiösen Wahn früherer Zeiten, ist vor allem *Verweltlichung*, Glaube an die *Welt* und Aus-dem-Sinn-Schlagen von "Jenseits" und "Hinterwelt". Sein Ziel ist das Wohlbefinden des flüchtigen Individuums [. . .] Meine Lehre sagt: *so* leben, daß du *wünschen* mußt, wieder zu leben ist die Aufgabe'.[34]

Thus Spoke Zarathustra is a supremely apolitical book, but it nonetheless contains several more specific expressions of critique of nationalism and politics – the new idol and the flies of the market-place – and a major leitmotive in it is that the greatest events are not our noisiest but our stillest hours.

His comments about nationalism and politics in *Beyond Good and Evil*, 251 are typical for the late Nietzsche's view of politics. His statement here is especially interesting for he also alludes to his own former youthful sympathies with Sybel, Treitschke and German nationalism:

> If a people is suffering and *wants* to suffer from nationalistic nervous fever and political ambition, it must be expected that all sorts of clouds and disturbances – in short, little attacks of stupidity – will pass over its spirit into the bargain: among present-day Germans, for example, now the

anti-French stupidity, now the anti-Jewish, now the anti-Polish, now the Christian-romantic, now the Wagnerian, now the Teutonic, now the Prussian (just look at those miserable historians, those Sybels and Treitschkes, with their thickly bandaged heads –), and whatever else these little obfuscations of the German spirit and conscience may be called. May it be forgiven me that I too, during a daring brief sojourn in a highly infected area, did not remain wholly free of the disease and began, like the rest of the world, to entertain ideas about things that were none of my business: first symptom of the political infection.

In a note from this time he further distances himself from all contemporary politics: 'Es gibt viele Dinge, gegen welche ich nicht nöthig gefunden habe, zu reden: es versteht sich von selbst, [...] daß mir alle politischen Parteien von heute widerlich sind.'[35]

In *On the Genealogy of Morals*, III, 26 he claims that the cause of 'the undeniable and palpable stagnation of the German spirit' is 'a too exclusive diet of newspapers, politics, beer and Wagnerian music'. His objection to, and contempt for, the reading of newspapers, expressed throughout his writings, is to a large extent due to the fact that they are superficial and political. In a note from the same year in which he wrote *On the Genealogy of Morals* Nietzsche recommends 'die Vorherrschaft der *Physiologie* über Theologie, Moralistik, Ökonomie und Politik' as a remedy against modernity.[36] In *Twilight of the Idols* he claims that 'politics devours all seriousness for really intellectual things',[37] and in the short preface to *The Antichrist*: 'One must be accustomed to living on mountains – to seeing the wretched ephemeral chatter of politics and national egoism *beneath* one'.

If one examines Nietzsche's reading and library one finds that he did read some political books, or books about political themes and questions, such as, for example, several volumes of Bismarck's *Speeches*, but, all in all, he read remarkably few such books and texts.[38]

This does not mean that he never said things which are politically interesting or which have political consequences, but this is not Nietzsche's main interest or motive.

> After all, no one can spend more than he has – that is true of individuals, it is also true of nations. If one spends oneself on power, grand politics, economic affairs, world commerce, parliamentary institutions, military interests – if one expends in *this* direction the quantum of reason, seriousness, will, selfovercoming that one is, then there will be a shortage in the other direction [i.e. in regard to culture]. Culture and the state – one should not deceive oneself over this – are antagonists: the 'cultural state' is merely a modern idea. The one lives off the other, the one thrives at the expense of the other. All great cultural epochs are epochs of political decline: that which is great in the cultural sense has been unpolitical, even *anti-political*. [...] the main thing – and that is still culture [...] The

essential thing has gone out of the entire system of higher education in Germany: the *end*, as well as the *means* to the end. That education, *culture*, itself is the end – and *not* 'the Reich' – [...] has been forgotten.[39]

When Nietzsche-scholars attempt to interpret his thinking politically it almost inevitably leads to distortions of it beyond recognition. Too many commentators today, not to speak of the lay reader, more or less consciously, in a manner similar to that of the sixteenth century when it was almost impossible to interpret a thinker in other than religious ways, claim that it is impossible to be apolitical, and use political perspectives as their first approach to understanding Nietzsche's thinking. Thus they encourage and justify distortions in the interpretation of Nietzsche's philosophy.

Nietzsche was not primarily a political thinker and it is not as a political thinker he is interesting and profound. On the contrary, Nietzsche almost never speaks of contemporary political persons or events, and when he speaks of more generally 'political' persons such as Napoleon and Caesar, it is *not* as politicians or because of their political significance he speaks of them. An examination of the persons Nietzsche most often refers to and discusses shows that 'political' persons came way down the list.[40] The misinterpretation of the laws of Manu as Nietzsche's political ideal is to a large extent the consequence of a politicising attempt to force Nietzsche's thinking into categories into which it does not fit.

A division of values, human beings and societies which Nietzsche implies is to divide them into three groups.[41] Firstly, the downwardmoving, or degenerating, values and lifeforms. Christianity and Buddhism belongs to this group. Secondly, those which emphasize stability. To these belong the conservative man, the 'camel', stoicism, the laws of Manu and the Roman Empire. These are, according to Nietzsche, generally better than the first group, but far from his ideal. Thirdly, the ascending values and lifeforms. Those which are creative, experimenting, affirmative and promising for the future. To these belong the philosophers as law-givers and creators of new values, 'the child'[42] and, according to Nietzsche, historical examples of such cultures are the Renaissance and ancient Hellas.

A more correct interpretation of sections 56 to 58 in *The Antichrist* than to see them as expressing Nietzsche's political ideal, is to see them as part of his critique of Christianity and modernity. He makes the contrast to provoke and to show a 'related' ideology (which is still built on priest-values) but which is nonetheless much better and more healthy. If we seek for more explicit political and social ideals in the writings of the late Nietzsche we will not find them – for they do not exist.[43] However, if we seek after more concrete and historical examples of Nietzsche's ideal in a wider sense, philosophically, culturally, and in relation to values and individuals, we will to a large extent find them in his view of the Renaissance, and, still more, in his view of ancient Greece.

NOTES

1. I quote *The Antichrist, Twilight of the Idols* and *Ecce Homo* from the translations of Hollingdale, but sometimes make minor changes to the translation where I find that appropriate. The quotations from notes and letters have been translated by me.
2. *Twilight of the Idols*, 'The "Improvers" of Mankind', 3.
3. Hunt admits that this is 'surprising' and that it is a 'significant shift' in regard to his earlier position, but nonetheless this is the interpretation he uses.
4. A. Etter, 'Nietzsche und das Gesetzbuch des Manu' in *Nietzsche-Studien* 16 (1987), p. 340–52. This interesting article contains much information about Jacolliot and Hinduism, but says little about Nietzsche. It would more aptly be entitled 'Jacolliot und das Gesetzbuch des Manu'.
5. This issue of the *Atlantic Monthly* is still in Nietzsche's library, with annotations. For a discussion of Nietzsche's reading of it, see S. L. Gilman, 'Nietzsche's Reading on the Dionysian: From Nietzsche's Library', *Nietzsche-Studien* 6 (1977), p. 292–4, and S. L. Gilman, 'Nietzsches Emerson-Lektüre: Eine unbekannte Quelle', *Nietzsche-Studien* 9 (1980), pp. 406–31.
6. It should be noted that although the emphasis in the discussion appears to be on biological breeding, the German words *Zucht* and *Züchtung* can also have a substantial social and cultural component.
7. In *The Antichrist*, 3, written less than a month later, Nietzsche says that: 'The problem I raise here is not what ought to succeed mankind in the sequence of species (– the human being is an *end* –): but what type of human being one ought to *breed*, ought to *will*, as more valuable, more worthy of life, more certain of the future.' This implies that Nietzsche's emphasis in his own use of *Züchtung* is *not* the biological, at least not a strongly or exclusively biological one. This is made still more clear in an early version of this text, *KSA* 13, 15 [120], and in *KSA* 13, 14 [133].
8. 'Aus dem Geiste der Funktion heraus denken jetzt die Philosophen darüber nach, die Menschheit in Einen Organism zu verwandeln – er ist der Gegensatz *meiner* Tendenz. Sondern *möglichst viele wechselnde verschiedenartige Organismen*'. KSA 9, 11[222].
9. Compare *KSA* 13, 14 [204] where Nietzsche says about the same thing as in the letter about Manu and the Middle Ages.
10. Hubert Cancik, for one, has recently claimed that Nietzsche's ideal in 1888 was 'the dorian state [which essentially means the Spartan state], slavery and caste-society'. Hubert Cancik, *Nietzsches Antike. Vorlesung* (1995), p. 147.
11. *KSA* 8, 5 [71].
12. *KSA* 8, 5 [91].
13. *KSA* 11, 25 [344].
14. *Twilight of the Idols*, 'Expeditions', 47.
15. See section 10 below, and especially footnotes 24 and 25.
16. Letter to Peter Gast, 31 May 1888.
17. KSA 13, 14[175 + 191 + 204 + 213].
18. KSA 13, 14[45].
19. Letter to Paul Deussen, 16 March 1883. Compare also Nietzsche's letter to Overbeck, 6 March 1883: 'Deussens Vedanta-Werk ist *ausgezeichnet*. Übrigens bin ich für *diese* Philosophie beinahe das böse Princip'.
20. Letter to Peter Gast, 31 May 1888. Compare also *KSA* 13, 11 [228] and 14 [25] where Nietzsche speaks of the Vedanta-philosophy and Brahmanism as nihilistic and as phenomena of decline.
21. Nietzsche's reading of Jacolliot is reflected in a large number of notes, for example: *KSA* 13, 14 [106 + 175–8 + 189 + 190–1 + 193 + 195 + 196 + 198–204 + 212–18 + 220 + 221 + 223 + 224 + 225], 15 [21 + 24 + 42 + 44 + 45 + 47 + 62 + 109], 16 [53 + 60], 18[3] and 22 [10].

22. *KSA* 13, 14 [203], with the title 'Critique of Manu', *KSA* 13, 14 [216], with the title 'Critique of the laws' and *KSA* 13, 15 [45], with the title 'Toward a Critique of the Lawbook of Manu'.

23. For example, in *KSA* 13, 14 [199 + 204 + 221].

24. Nietzsche says this in a text which was long regarded as part of *Ecce Homo*, 'Why I Am so Wise', 3, and as such published in earlier versions of that text and in the English translations of that work, but which now in the critical edition of Nietzsche's works (*KGW* and *KSA*) has been replaced by another text and instead placed in the commentary volume, *KSA* 14, p. 472.

25. In a letter to Erwin Rohde, 27 Oct. 1868, Nietzsche speaks of the Biedermann family, from whom he rents a room in Leipzig and with whom he eats dinner, and says that they are politically interested: 'to my consolation, however, there is *hardly* any talk of politics, since I am no *zoon politikon* [written in Greek letters], and against such things [politics] have a porcupine nature'.

   In a letter to Malwida von Meysenbug, 25 Oct. 1874, Nietzsche writes in regard to his writing, especially the *Untimely Meditations*: 'Luckily, I lack every form of political and social ambition, so that I do not have to fear danger from that direction, no restrictions, no need for transactions or considerations'.

   In a letter to Louise Ott in Paris, from 7 Nov. 1882 he asks: 'Or do you advise me against coming to Paris? Is it not a place for hermits, for human beings who want to calmly walk around with a lifetask and absolutely not worry about politics and the present age?'.

   In a letter to Ferdinand Avenarius, ca. 20 July 1888: 'I cannot persuade myself to read journals regularly. My whole task demands, my taste insists on my alienation, becoming indifferent, forgetting the *present* . . .'

   And finally, Nietzsche repeats about the same sentiment – and again refers to himself as an 'Eremit' – in a letter to Emily Fynn, 11 Aug. 1888, when discussing his plans to visit Corsika, but not Ajaccio, for the following winter: 'I need such a profound selfcontrol [Selbstbesinnung] that I find no place quiet, no place *anti-modern* enough.'

26. *BAW* 3, 313. It is not clear if these words refer to Nietzsche's own political excitement or to a general one at this time.

   A little earlier in this text, pages 300–1, Nietzsche refers to his friendship with Gottfried Kinkel, in 1867/68, who was highly politically involved 'während ich nach meiner Art die selbstlose Würde der Wissenschaft vertrat. Plötzlich war er umgestimmt, erhob sich, erfaßte meine Rechte und schwur von jetzt ab nach meinen Grundsätze(n) zu leben.'

27. Letter from Pinder to Nietzsche, 9 July 1866 (*KGB* I.3, p. 114).

28. *KGB* I.4, p. 548.

29. Letter to Wilhelm Vischer-Bilfinger, 7 March 1869.

30. This is also Nietzsche's own view 16 years later, in *Ecce Homo*, 'GT', 1: 'It is politically indifferent – "un-German" one would say today'.

31. At about this time he also wrote in a letter to Rohde, 15 Feb. 1874: 'Ich löcke jetzt sehr stark wider den Stachel der politischen und Bürgertugend-Pflichten und habe gelegentlich selbst über das "Nationale" hinausgeschwiffen'.

32. *KSA* 8, 19 [77].

33. *KSA* 8, 40 [16].

34. *KSA* 9, 11 [163].

35. *KSA* 12, 2 [180].

36. *KSA* 12, 9 [165].

37. *Twilight of the Idols*, 'What the Germans Lack', 1 and KSA 13, 19 [1].

38. For a detailed examination of the late Nietzsche's reading, see my 'Nietzsche's Reading and Private Library, 1885–1889' in *Journal of the History of Ideas* 58 (1997), 663–93.

39. *Twilight of the Idols*, 'What the Germans Lack', 4–5.

40. The persons Nietzsche most frequently refers to in his published writings are, in descending order: Wagner, Goethe, Schopenhauer, Plato, Kant, Socrates, Homer, Luther, Schiller, Shakespeare, Epicurus, Beethoven, Hegel, Napoleon, Voltaire, Spinoza, Rousseau, Pascal, Sophocles, Aeschylus and Aristotle. This list is taken from the chapter 'The Place and Status of Persons in Nietzsche's Philosophy' in Thomas H. Brobjer's *Nietzsche's Ethics of Character: A Study of Nietzsche's Ethics and its Place in the History of Moral Thinking* (Uppsala, 1995).

41. This is, for example, the case in the notes *KSA* 13, 11 [138 + 143] and 12 [1] (372). It is also expressed in the chapter 'The Problem of Socrates' in *Twilight of the Idols*.

42. The 'lion' in the section 'The three metamorphoses' in the first book of *Thus Spoke Zarathustra* constitutes a transition-state between stability (the camel) and creativity (the child).

43. In a letter to Theodor Curti, from July/August 1882 Nietzsche writes: 'No man can in regard to *these* things [political-social questions] live *more* 'in a corner' than I: I never speak about them, I do not know the most well-known events and do not even read newspapers – I have even made a privilege out of all this!'

15

TAOISM AND JUNG:
SYNCHRONICITY AND THE SELF

Harold Coward

In my book *Jung and Eastern Thought*,[1] I explored the influence of Indian concepts such as *karma, citta, buddhitattva, tapas*, and *maṇḍala* on the development of Carl Jung's notions of 'archetype,' 'psyche,' the 'collective unconscious,' 'active imagination,' and 'circumambulation.' But the question of Eastern influence on Jung's most complex concept, 'the Self', was given only very sketchy treatment. Following the lead of one of Jung's senior North American students, Joseph Henderson of Stanford University, I suggested that the notion of *ātman*, as found in the Hindu Upaniṣads, was the major Eastern formative influence in Jung's concept of 'the Self'.[2] Additional research, however, has led me to conclude that Chinese Taoism, rather than Hinduism, provided the fundamental formative influence in Jung's developing notion of 'the Self'. This Taoist influence, I will argue, came to Jung's 'Self' concept not directly, but by way of another of Jung's ideas, namely synchronicity. 'Synchronicity', it will be shown, depends directly on the Taoist Chinese text the *I Ching*, with which Jung experimented for a whole summer in 1920.[3] His experiments demonstrated to Jung that there are meaningful connections between the inner psychic realm and the external physical world. In his autobiography Jung says, 'Time and time again I encountered amazing coincidences which seemed to suggest the idea of an acausal parallelism (a synchronicity, as I later called it).'[4]

It is this notion of correlative parallels between the inner and the outer realms of experience that is fundamental for understanding Jung's complex notion of

Harold Coward, 'Taoism and Jung: Synchronicity and the Self', *Philosophy East and West*, 46: 4, 1996, pp. 477–95.

the 'Self'. Failure to recognize the Taoist background to Jung's thinking has, I will argue, resulted in the mistaken charge that Jung is simply a gnostic in modern psychological dress. This mistake is made when the external half of the correlation of the outer world with the inner psyche in Jung's individuated Self is ignored. By highlighting the Taoist context of Jung's thinking, this error, common among Jungians, is avoided.

In addition, the analysis offered will show that in the case of Eastern influence on his notion of the Self, Jung rejects some aspects of the Hindu *ātman*, but fully accepts Taoist thinking. This article is divided into three sections: (1) The Taoist Background of Jung's Thinking, (2) Synchronicity and Individuation of Archetypes, and (3) Tao and the Self. In this essay I am explicitly concerned with Jung's own reading, not the Chinese texts themselves.

THE TAOIST BACKGROUND OF JUNG'S THINKING

Jung was led to Taoist and Indian thought in the period 1915–20, while he was doing the research for his book *Psychological Types*.[5] Of this book Jung says:

> This work sprang originally from my need to define the ways in which my outlook differed from Freud's and Adler's. In attempting to answer this question, I came across the problem of types; for it is one's psychological type which from the outset determines and limits a person's judgement. My book, therefore, was an effort to deal with the relationship of the individual to the world, to people and things.[6]

Already we see here Jung's interest in correlating the inner psyche with the external world. The identification of opposite personality types (e.g., introversion versus extroversion) gave Jung the insight that every judgment made by an individual is conditioned by how his or her personality type relates to the surrounding world. Extreme introverts or extroverts suffered from a very limited experience of their world or themselves. This insight raised for Jung the question of how one could find a unity in which these opposite personality types would be balanced and their narrowness transcended. The search for an answer, said Jung, led him directly to the Chinese concept of *Tao*,[7] the idea of a middle way between the opposites.[8]

John Henderson has recently demonstrated that Taoism, along with most other traditional forms of Chinese thinking, is rooted in 'correlative thinking', a sort of perennial philosophy of Chinese civilization.[9] Correlative thinking draws systematic correspondences between various orders of reality such as the human, the world of nature, and the divine. 'It assumes that these related orders as a whole are homologous, that they correspond with one another in some basic respect, even in some cases that their identities are contained one within the other.'[10] Underlying 'correlative thinking' is the notion of cosmological resonance (*kan-ying*). Correlations, it is held, can interact at a distance by virtue of a mutual sympathy, an idea based on music theory or harmonics.[11] In Chinese thought, this notion of resonance is applied even in social relations, as, for example, in the Confucian concept of filial piety. In its most general form the theory of resonance is stated as 'the principles of the cosmos are the same as the principles of my mind'.[12]

Much of the groundwork for this theory of resonance or correlative thinking was established by the classical Taoists, especially Lao Tzu in his proposal that humans pattern themselves after heaven and earth.[13] While Lao Tzu's idea did not lead directly to the pairing of the human with the cosmic, it did much to create a context in which correlative thought could develop. What caught Jung's attention in his *Psychological Types* was Lao Tzu's discussion of *Tao* as the middle way between opposites such as man-and-nature and heaven-and-earth, as well as being the source of all arisings and the receiver of all subsiding. Jung quotes from the *Tao Te Ching*:

> One may think of it as the mother of all things under heaven.
> Its true name we do not know;
> 'Way' is the name that we give it.[14]

There was also the central Taoist teaching that the *Tao* manifests in creation as a fundamental pair of opposites, *yang* and *yin*. Jung summarizes as follows:

> *Yang* signifies warmth, light, maleness; *yin* is cold, darkness, femaleness. *Yang* is also heaven, *yin* earth. From the *yang* force arises *shen*, the celestial portion of the human soul, and from *yin* force comes *kuei*, the earthly part. As a microcosm, man is a reconciler of the opposites.[15]

The aim of the Taoist sage is to live in harmony with the *Tao* and thereby avoid falling into one extreme or the other, neither introvert nor extrovert, to use Jung's terms, but striking a balance between the two. Specific guidance toward that end is provided by the *I Ching*, which Jung tried out on himself with convincing results.[16] A few years later, Jung read Richard Wilhelm's translation of the *I Ching* and invited Wilhelm to Zurich. From Wilhelm Jung learned a great deal about Chinese thought. This friendship led Jung to write commentaries on two of Wilhelm's translations: first *The Secret of the Golden Flower*, and later the *I Ching* itself.

In his Foreword to the *I Ching*, Jung notes that the coincidence or correlation between the opposites is the chief concern of the work.[17] To enter into the 'Chinese mind' of the text requires that modern Westerners drop for the moment their fixation on rational and causal thought as the only valid thinking. This is why Jung refers to the meaningful correlations of the *I Ching* not as chance but 'acausal'[18] and why W. A. Callahan, in a recent article, refers to Taoist thought not as irrational but 'arational'.[19] Both agree that the acausal, arational, relational experience described in Taoist texts like the *I Ching* is a direct reflection of natural reality. All of this confirmed Jung's intuition of a connection that is potentially present in each of us between our inner psychic realm and the external cosmos. Jung coined the term 'synchronicity' to describe this correlation between inside and outside events.[20] The *I Ching* offered a traditional Chinese technique for reflecting on these correlations. Jung felt that his method of active imagination would achieve the same goal and was more appropriate for the modern Westerner. But Jung was convinced that the goal of the *I Ching*, namely a reestablishing of balance between the *yang* and *yin* in the *Tao*, and the goal of his psychotherapy, namely a balancing of the psychic opposites in the experience of the Self, were parallel processes. Let us now examine in depth the way in which Taoism and the *I Ching* influenced Jung's notions of 'synchronicity' and its crucial role in the realization of the 'Self'.

SYNCHRONICITY

Although one of his earliest notions, 'synchronicity' was a concept that Jung struggled to express adequately throughout his life. When in 1960 he finally produced a little monograph on the subject, containing an extended discussion of astrology, it was generally assumed that this was simply Jung's attempt to explain odd psychic events such as a table splitting in half, a steel knife shattering, or seances for communicating with the dead. Indeed, in his 'Editorial Preface' to the volume, Michael Fordham largely consigns synchronicity to Jung's attempts to deal with the occult.[21] It is not surprising, therefore, that synchronicity has not been seen as a key concept in Jung's psychology. Jolande Jacobi, for example, in her authoritative presentation of Jung's psychology, does not even treat it as a separate concept and offers only one rather weak paragraph under the heading 'archetype'.[22] This consigning of 'synchronicity' to Jung's offbeat interest in things occult has helped to create a serious misperception of Jung's theory as being almost totally inward, focused on the collective unconscious and the archetypes. It has led to a misunderstanding of the process of individuation, with external factors being given short shrift. And it has paved the way for the charge to be leveled that Jung is nothing more than a modern-day gnostic who does not take the external world seriously. In what follows we will show that all of these errors are corrected if 'synchronicity' is approached from Chinese Taoism rather than from modern parapsychology. The difference this makes for one's estimate of Jung's thought and the understanding of his concept of 'the Self' is enormous.

Jung's earliest thinking on synchronicity was prompted by a conversation over dinner with Albert Einstein sometime between 1909 and 1913. Einstein was developing his first theory of relativity and this started Jung thinking about the relativity of time and space 'and their psychic conditionality'.[23] But it is in the 'Chinese orientation' of a 1930 memorial address for sinologist Richard Wilhelm that Jung first clearly speaks about synchronicity:

> The science of the *I Ching* is not based on the causality principle, but on a principle (hitherto unnamed because not met with among us) which I have tentatively called the *synchronistic* principle. My occupation with the psychology of unconscious processes long ago necessitated my looking for

another principle of explanation. ... Thus I found that there are psychic parallelisms which cannot be related to each other causally ....[24]

Jung's sense of the existence of psychic parallelism or correlations between inner and outer events was strongly nourished as a result of reading Wilhelm's translations of the *I Ching* and a book on Taoist Yoga, *The Secret of the Golden Flower*, for which he wrote a psychological commentary.

To understand the importance of this notion of synchronicity for Jung's psychology, it is useful to remind ourselves of the main constructs of his theory. It is Jung's view that each of us shares in three different levels of consciousness: the conscious level of the ego; the dreams, memories, and repressions that comprise the personal unconscious; and the predispositions to universal human reactions, the archetypes, that compose the collective unconscious. It is, of course, the notion of the archetypes and the collective unconscious that is the trademark of Jung's thought. It is in the raising of the archetypes to the conscious level and in the shifting of the center of gravity of the personality from the ego to the Self that synchronicity plays a vital role. Without synchronicity both of these processes could not take place, for Jung's psychology would be encapsulated within the inner psyche and out of touch with the external world. Then the charge against Jung of gnosticism or mere idealism could be made to stick.

Although Jung's synchronicity concept saved him from falling into the gnostic trap, Jung never developed a theoretical framework that would enable him to discuss this concept systematically. About this failing of Jung, Ira Progoff says: 'His vision was so rich and essentially valid, yet he could not reduce it to a form that he could communicate ...'.[25] It remains for us, then, to reread Jung's notion of 'synchronicity' through his references to the Chinese texts so that the meaning intended by Jung will be understood.

To be clear about the archetype and its creative individuation through the use of materials of the external world, one needs to know the Chinese doctrine *T'ien-jen chih chi* ('the interrelation of heaven and man'). In English we might use the term 'correlative anthropocosmology'.[26] This is what underlies Jung's notion that an archetype includes not only psychic equivalences but psycho-physical equivalences too.[27] Like the Chinese doctrine of the interrelation of the individual with the cosmos, Jung conceived of the archetype as interrelating the meaning content of the inner psyche with the meaning content of the external cosmos. When the two connected, an experience of synchronicity took place. The deeper meaning within one's psyche was experienced in relation to a corresponding meaning in the external reality. Jung said, the 'archetype has a tendency to behave as though it were not localized in one person but were active in the whole environment.'[28] Or, as he put it in a letter dated August 1951, the archetype is an 'arranger' of psychic forms inside and outside the psyche into meaningful patterns.[29] When this occurs one is taken out of one's small ego consciousness by experiencing contact with the larger meaning-whole of oneself within the cosmos. As is the case in Chinese thought, this notion of Jung's is not allegorical or prelogical, but is based on the idea of an ordered universe into which everything fits harmoniously.

In a letter to Pastor Bernet, Jung indicates that the archetype mediating the phenomena of synchronicity is embedded in the brain structure and is physiologically verifiable through electrical stimulation of certain areas of the brain stem that produce *maṇḍala* visions.[30] But in a letter to Walter Schmid, Jung warns that even though the archetype and synchronicity are rooted in the psychic realm, we should not take them to be only psychic. 'In so far ... as synchronistic events include not only psychic but also physical forms of manifestation, the conclusion is justified that both modalities transcend the realm of the psychic and somehow belong to the physical realm.'[31] The inherent patterning activity by the archetype is not only present at the level of the collective unconscious but, under Chinese influence, came to be regarded by Jung as a psychophysical continuum present throughout the cosmos. Thus the deepest levels of the collective unconscious were seen to participate in the underlying patterns of the external world of nature. When the two are brought together a significant moment of synchronicity is experienced, and the archetypal meaning is revealed. In Eastern religion this is the revelation of the divine.

In summary, then, Jung's 'synchronicity' is the idea that a person is a participant in and meaningfully related to the acausal patterning of events in nature.[32] The weakness in Jung's theory is that he does not consistently demonstrate how the synchronistic event and its meaning are clearly related to the depth psychology of the individual.[33] What is clear is that Jung became quite sure that the multiplicity of the empirical world rests on an underlying unity. It is this underlying unity that gives opposites such as inner versus outer, psychic versus physical, and spiritual versus worldly the potential to become linked in meaningful acausal synchronistic experiences. It is the Chinese worldview that started Jung in this direction, and it is Jung's reading of Chinese thought that can render his thought more systematic in relation to synchronicity.

In his discussion of the forerunners of the idea of synchronicity Jung points strongly to Chinese thought.[34] There nature constitutes a dynamic, organic whole. The individual participates in the whole in accordance with its comprehensive pattern (the *Tao*). When we think of the unfolding of events in this interaction between humans and nature, Western ideas of cause and effect are replaced in Chinese thought by notions of interdependence. This interdependence is based on the idea of a simultaneous resonance between otherwise independent entities.[35] As mentioned earlier it is more like a music theory of resonance than Newtonian physics. According to Joseph Needham, the key word in the Chinese worldview is 'pattern': 'The symbolic correlations or correspondences all formed part of one colossal pattern.'[36] Things behave as they do not because of cause-effect relationships with other things but because of their intrinsic interdependent relationship with the existential pattern of all life. Jung quotes Chuang Tzu saying the *Tao* (the whole) is obscured when one fixes one's eye on little segments of existence only.[37] Limitations are not grounded in the pattern of the whole of life. Thus the vision of the successful artist is of one who 'can follow Nature's spontaneity and be aware of the subtlety of things, and his mind will be absorbed by them. His brush will secretly be in harmony with movement and quiescence and all forms will issue forth.'[38] One who is not in tune with the harmonics of reality 'becomes a slave of passion and his nature will be distorted by externalities.'

From the viewer's perspective, when a Chinese artist is successful, the painting is said to reveal the potentialities of the 'spiritual court', a term first used by Chuang Tzu to mean what Jung calls the depth of the unconscious. So, when Fu Tsai saw Chang Tsao's paintings of pines and rocks, he said: 'When I sense the vigor of Chang Tsao's painting, I no longer see a painting, I see *Tao*. . . . [T]hings brought out are not from consciousness of the eye and ear, but from the Spiritual Court.'[39] In Jung's view this is also what happens in the making of the best *maṇḍalas*.[40] The potentialities within and without come together according to the divine pattern, and synchronicity is complete. The *Tao* is revealed.[41] In other places Jung describes this as the mystery of the coniunctio, in which the extreme opposites unite, night is wedded with day, outside with inside, and male with female. There is a universal validity, he observes, from the *Tao* of Lao-Tzu to the *coincidentia oppositorum* of Cusanus.[42]

The Taoist approach is the synchronistic way. As in the *I Ching*, it involves the study and classification of events wherein meaningful interdependence transcends space, time, and causality as the determining factor. The archetype contains the meaningful pattern that waits to resonate sympathetically with events sharing the same pattern in the external world. News of the external world is first taken into the psyche by the sensing function and then taken deep within the psyche by the intuiting function. There, under the influence of the archetype, contact is made between the inner and outer forms of the pattern. The work of individuation or symbol formation involves the creative working together of the archetypal forms with the interiorized contents of the psychical world until a 'synchronous fit' is achieved and the interdependent meaning revealed (usually in a series of dreams ending finally in a conscious experience). While in Chinese culture the throwing of the yarrow stalks in accordance with the *I Ching* helps the process of seeing the *Tao* along, in the West Jung felt that his practice of 'Active Imagination' played a parallel role in a way more suited to the modern Western mind. In both cases the end result was an experience of the inner psyche and the external world coming together synchronistically in a meaningful whole.

SELF

Jung typically describes spiritual maturity and psychological integration as the shifting of the center of gravity of the personality from the ego to the self.[43] Jung's discovery of the self as the goal of psychic development occurred as a result of his study of Taoism in 1918 while writing *Psychological Types* and in

1927 while writing a commentary for Wilhelm's translation of *The Secret of the Golden Flower*. These Chinese texts taught Jung that in the development of the self there is no linear evolution; there is only a circumambulation in which everything is related to the center.[44] And this circumambulation process of the self includes materials from both the inner psyche and the external world in ever widening circles. The equal inclusion of the external world is of crucial importance, in Jung's view, for it saves one from falling into the theosophical trap of much Hindu thought, namely that the external world is mere *māyā* and ultimately disappears, leaving a pure, universal consciousness.[45] Jung makes it clear that his concept of the self is not that kind of 'universal consciousness', which he says is simply another name for the unconscious. The Taoist insistence on a balance between inner and outer, between *yin* and *yang*, confirmed in Jung's mind that both sides were essential for the development of the self. As Frieda Fordham puts it: '[The self] consists . . . in the awareness on the one hand of our unique natures, and on the other of our intimate relationship with all of life, not only human, but animal and plant, and even that of inorganic matter and the cosmos itself. It brings a feeling of "oneness" and of reconciliation with life . . .'[46] The two Chinese notions of correlation between the inner and outer (synchronicity) and a balanced center that expands or circumambulates so as to include both the inner and the outer are fundamental to Jung's notion of the self.

In explaining his concept of self, Jung points to the Hindu Upaniṣadic teaching that it is not the individual ego that speaks, thinks, and acts. Rather it is the universal *Brahman*, which speaks through the individual and so uses the individual as a means of expression.[47] But the danger in Hindu thought is that *Brahman* becomes one-sidedly identified as pure consciousness and, as such, is no longer in dynamic interrelation with the physical world. This is exactly Śaṅkara's notion of *nirguṇa Brahman*, Brahman without qualities.[48] From Jung's perspective, as soon as one gets out of dynamic interrelation with the empirical world, one is either unconscious or out of life altogether. On the other extreme is the modern Western mind, which is overbalanced on the external empirical consciousness and virtually cut off from the internal unconscious. Because it balanced both extremes, Jung found his reading of Chinese thought, and Taoism in particular, to offer a better clue to the self. Taoism is structured such that an overbalance on one side is necessarily compensated by a stress on the other so that within the personality the two sides are always seeking to be in balance. In the Taoist book, *The Secret of the Golden Flower*, Jung found for the first time an outline for the development of a balanced self.

In his Introduction to the Causeway Edition of *The Secret of the Golden Flower*, Charles San states that the aim is 'an enrichment of consciousness which will unite the inner and outer worlds of reality'.[49] The translator, Richard Wilhelm, adds that the book teaches a correlation of the inner spiritual principle with the psychogenic forces of the cosmos so as to prepare for the possibility of life after death in a transfigured bodily form.[50] In the text, Master Lu teaches that the one primordial whole is the *Tao*. The *Tao* phenomenalizes into a multiplicity of individuals in the form of *hun* and *p'o*. *Hun* dwells in the eyes and is bright and active. It is identified with *yang* and associated with the lighter, higher spirit, which after death rises in the air and flows back into the reservoir of life. *P'o* dwells in the abdomen and is dark and earthbound. It is identified with *yin* and associated with the body and its sexual energy. At death it decays and returns to the earth whence it continually begets.[51] The goal of the yoga as taught in the text is to arouse the sexual energy of the *yin* or *p'o* and convert it into the lighter spiritual energy of *yang* or *hun* until a balance is achieved.[52]

What struck Jung about this Taoist model for the development of the self was that it never attempted to force the pairs of opposites so far apart that all connection between them is lost. Yet the Taoist Yoga of the text sought out a point of balance or freedom that would take one beyond the clash of opposites without becoming one-sided or overbalanced.[53] The self, said Jung, is the midpoint of the opposites. It is equivalent to the *Tao*.[54] Problems caused by being overbalanced on one side or the other can never be solved but only outgrown. To remain overbalanced and caught up in a conflict between the opposites is pathological. Growth into the self, however, is normal. Jung comments:

> When I examined the way of development of those persons who, quietly, and as if unconsciously, grew beyond themselves, I saw that their fates had something in common. Whether arising from without or within, the new thing came to all those persons from a dark field of possibilities; they accepted it and developed further by means of it. It seemed to me typical that, in some cases, the new thing was found outside themselves, and in others within; or rather, that it grew into some persons from without, and into others from within. But it was never something that came exclusively either from within or from without. . . . [I]n no case was it conjured into existence through purpose and conscious willing, but rather seemed to flow out of the stream of time.[55]

This new thing, the developing self, Jung goes on to say, seldom corresponds to conscious expectation, does not permit mechanical duplication, contradicts deeply rooted instincts, and yet is 'a singularly appropriate expression of the total personality, an expression that one could not imagine in a more complete form.'[56] All this was accomplished by doing nothing, or, as Master Lu Tzu said, by *wu wei* (actionless action). This art of letting things happen – action in nonaction, letting go of oneself – became for Jung the key to opening the door to the development of the self. Later he was technically to designate the process as 'active imagination'. In fact, at this point in his Commentary, Jung provides one of his clearest descriptions of 'active imagination' as inspired by his reading of the Taoist notion of *wu wei*.[57]

As the Taoist text makes clear, said Jung, some have to enlarge their personality into a self by taking from without, others by expanding within. It depends on their starting personality type – introvert or extrovert. Either way, an enlargement into a self occurs by making present parts of one's inner or outer world that one had previously blocked out. The process involves an enlargement of consciousness through a uniting or correlating of what was separated. In Chinese terms, says Jung, this is the bringing about of *Tao*. In Western terms this making the opposites consciously in harmony with the larger pattern of life is 'conversion' – conversion from the ego as the center of the personality to the self as center.[58]

This expansion of the personality and the union of the opposites through the process of letting go of the ego expresses itself in symbols. Such symbols are *maṇḍalas*. The term implies a circular nature. *Maṇḍalas* pictorially represent the harmonious inclusion of both the inner and outer realms within the self. In Jung's view, finding one's own *maṇḍala* symbol is crucial for the development of the self. Earlier (1918–20), says Jung, 'I had a dream about the center and the self which I represented in a *maṇḍala* painting called "Window on Eternity".' A year later Jung painted a second picture, likewise a *maṇḍala*, that was very Chinese in character, with a golden castle at the center. Some years later, in 1927, when Jung read *The Secret of the Golden Flower*, he found confirmation of his ideas about the self, the *maṇḍala*, and the circumambulation (the circling around) of the center.[59] In the Taoist text, the Golden Flower of Heavenly Light is the *maṇḍala*. As was the case with Jung, the *maṇḍala* of the text, the Golden Flower, symbolizes the self in which the unconscious has become conscious in a harmonious union with all of life. The union of these two, life and consciousness, is the *Tao*.[60] In a later article, Jung comments that *ātman*, *Tao*, and Christ are different cultural symbols for wholeness that correlate the inner self with the animating principle of the cosmos.[61]

> Behind the opposites and in the opposites is true reality, which sees and comprehends the whole. ... We use the word 'self' for this contrasting it with the little ego. ... [T]his self is not just a rather more conscious or intensified ego, as the words 'self-conscious', 'self-satisfied,' etc. might lead one to suppose. What is meant by the self is not only in me but in all beings, like the ātman, like Tao. It is psychic totality.[62]

In *The Secret of the Golden Flower* Jung was particularly struck by a drawing of a yogi with five human figures growing out of the top of his head and five more figures growing out of the top of each of their heads. The picture, thought Jung, portrays the spiritual state of the yogi who is about to rid himself of his many small egos and pass over into the more complete objective state of the self.[63]

Jung found the process of circumambulation, by which the self is built up, fully represented in the *maṇḍala* and text of *The Secret of the Golden Flower*. A *circumambulatio* or circular course of development is prescribed. Through meditation, claims Jung, the *Tao* begins to take leadership. Action is submerged into nonaction, and everything peripheral is subjected to the command of the center. Psychologically, says Jung, the turning in ever widening circles about oneself engages all sides of the personality.

Thus the circular movement has also the moral significance of activating all the light and dark forces of human nature, and with them, all the psychological opposites of whatever kind they may be. That means nothing else than self-knowledge by means of self-incubation (Hindi, *tapas*).[64]

For this circular movement to take place, a symbol such as the sun, a castle, or, as in this text, a golden flower is necessary. The symbol is a visual image of the divine pattern, which gathers up and integrates materials from the unconscious with those of the external world received through the senses. As such the symbol is a manifestation of the God or self archetype. As it refocuses one's psychic energy from the ego to the self, there is felt a heightening and clearness of consciousness, a freeing of oneself from emotional or sensory entanglements, and a deepening sense of unity of being.[65]

Jung observes that the Taoist text is aware of certain dangers that arise when such an expansion of consciousness is taking place. Newly activated unconscious contents are frequently projected upon the outside world. The text offers visual representations of such projections and describes them as 'thought-fragments' that are empty colors and shapes possessing no being in and of themselves. Jung comments that such psychic partial systems are common in mental illnesses (like schizophrenia), mediumistic phenomena, and religious phenomena (in which the thought-fragments may be personified as spirits or gods). The beginning formation of a self gives one a center from which to recognize these partial psychic systems for what they are and, in turn, makes possible their depotentialization and assimilation by the center.[66] Again the circular movement dominates the process.

This is not an easy or quick process but, as the Tibetan Book of the Dead (the *Bardo Thödol*) makes clear, one that may engage one even beyond one's death.[67] The assimilation of such psychic projections through the process of circumambulation is an essential part of the individuation of the self from its entrapment in either the inner unconscious or the external world. The instructions in *The Secret of the Golden Flower*, thought Jung, teach the pupil how to free himself or herself from inner or outer bondage. The unconscious is not projected any more; therefore, the *participation mystique*, the primordial interweaving of consciousness with the world, has been disentangled. Levy Bruhl defines *participation mystique* as 'the indefinitely large remnant of non-differentiation between subject and object'.[68] In primitive peoples this non-differentiation takes the form of plants and animals behaving like humans and vice versa. In modern people this nondifferentiation takes another form. As Jung puts it, one is identified with one's parents or with one's affects, or one accuses others of things one does not see in oneself. In both kinds of non-differentiation, people feel themselves to be magically influenced by things, circumstances, and other people. But when these unconscious projections are made conscious, the *participation mystique* is transcended and the center of gravity of the personality shifts its position. 'It ceases to be the ego, which is merely the center of consciousness, and is located instead in what might be called a virtual point between the conscious and the unconscious. This new center might be called the self.'[69] This is what is meant by the text, says Jung, when it speaks of 'the diamond body'. Such an expression symbolizes a psychological attitude that is invulnerable to entanglements in the outer or inner world. Jung agrees with the text that the time for this process to take place is in the second half of life as a preparation for death. This naturally follows the focus of the first half of life on 'begetting and reproduction'.[70] In the second half of life, one's sexual energy is transmuted, through yoga practice, into the universal spiritual energy of the self.

Jung's reading of the Taoist text highlighted another important aspect, namely the text's emphasis on direct experience and the refusal to attempt a metaphysical description. Whereas in Taoism any metaphysical description is negated (e.g., Lao Tzu: 'The Tao that can be told of is not the eternal Tao.'[71]), in Western religion metaphysics has become the norm and, Jung thinks, an obstacle to direct experience of the divine. Jung's following of Taoism on this point has led to charges of 'psychologism.' If by 'psychologism' is meant the bringing of 'metaphysics' within the range of experience, then Jung says he pleads guilty and is flattered, for that indeed is the aim: 'To understand metaphysically is impossible; it can only be done psychologically.'[72] The Taoists, says Jung, understand this well. They are really symbolical psychologists. When the text speaks of the 'diamond body', the indestructible spirit body that develops in the Golden Flower, it is describing not a dogma but a real experience, which Master Lu Tzu has had and expects his pupil to have. Nor do the Taoists make the mistake of taking this breath or spirit 'diamond body' to be separated from the physical. There is no dualism here. What is experienced is a purifying and correlating of the physical and the mental into a balanced self symbolized by the 'diamond body'.[73] This ultimate experience can only be hinted at in words such as 'It is not I who live, it lives me', or, to use the Christian context, 'No longer do I live, but Christ lives in me'.[74] Jung adds: 'In a certain sense, the thing we are trying to express is the feeling of having been "replaced", but without the connotation of having been "deposed". It is as if the leadership of the affairs of life had gone over to an invisible center.'[75]

The experience of this new center is the *Tao* or, in Jung's terms, the self. It is not skepticism or agnosticism but, says Jung, an experience of Kant's *Ding-an-sich*, the thing in itself. This is why, when asked, in an interview with the BBC, 'Do you believe in God?' Jung paused and responded, 'I do not believe, I know!'[76] This direct knowledge, says Jung, brings with it a release from the compulsion and impossible responsibility that are the inevitable results of dogmatism and the *participation mystique*. Instead, there is a feeling of reconciliation with oneself and with what is happening in the world. One is released to live in *wu-wei*, spontaneous action centered not in the ego but in the self, the *Tao*.[77] Jung concludes his Commentary on *The Secret of the Golden Flower* with the following words: 'It is . . . the atmosphere of suffering, seeking, and striving common to all civilized peoples; it is the tremendous experiment of becoming conscious, which nature has imposed on mankind, uniting the most diverse cultures in a common task.'[78] In his reading of Taoism, Jung found not only an adequate expression of synchronicity but also a trustworthy guide to the experience of the self as the spiritual center.

CONCLUSION

This study has shown that two of Jung's central and often misunderstood concepts, 'synchronicity' and 'the self', were strongly influenced in their initial formulation by his reading of Taoist thought. When placed against the background of Chinese correlational cosmology, synchronicity is seen as primarily concerned with the inherent interrelation of the inner psyche with the external world, and only secondarily as an explanation of occult events. When examined in relation to the *I Ching*, synchronicity is understood to be a fundamental principle underlying the archetypes and the way in which the opposites within and without the psyche interact. As such it becomes a basic building block for Jung's concept of self. First encountered in his dreams and later confirmed and explained in *The Secret of the Golden Flower*, Jung developed his notion of the self in a detailed reflection on the *Tao*. Of central importance here is the idea that the contents of the inner psyche and those of the external world must be assimilated and balanced to approximate the *Tao*. Following the lead of *The Secret of the Golden Flower*, Jung finds that the self evolves by a process of circumambulation around the center in ever expanding circles. When a sufficient number of projections has been made conscious and archetypes individuated through this process, a self symbol, usually in the form of a *maṇḍala*, will be born. This is not a process of the conscious ego, however, but, again following his reading of Taoism, a letting go of ego in *wu-wei* or spontaneous action. The evolving self is not something that can be described, metaphysically or otherwise, but simply experienced.

All of this is important not just for our understanding of how Jung developed his basic ideas, but because it corrects some major misunderstandings. The first is that Jung's psychology is so dominantly intra-psychic or inwardly focused that for him everything comes out of the collective unconscious. The Taoist background helps us to see that throughout there is a balance between inner and outer in Jung's thinking, that the physical world is as important as the inner archetypes, and that both are expressions of the same fundamental pattern or whole, the *Tao*.

The second misunderstanding relates to the same basic problem. Commentators who have not seen Jung through his reading of Taoism have frequently charged him with being a gnostic – Maurice Freedman[79] and R. C. Zaehner[80] have branded Jung as 'a modern gnostic'. Gnosticism places a one-sided emphasis on the subjective, the unconscious as the source of knowledge, a fact that Jung himself recognizes in *Aion*.[81] The part of gnosticism that Jung accepted was that there was knowledge to be found within the psyche. But this was immediately balanced by his Taoist insight that any inner knowledge must be interrelated with a corresponding knowledge of the external world. This insight is basic to Jung's concepts of synchronicity and the self and effectively safeguarded Jung from becoming a gnostic. For Jung, the inner, though real, is always in tension with the outer, which is equally real. Jung's psychology requires that we expand our personality types of introvert and extrovert in ever widening circles until the opposite aspect is assimilated and made conscious in the new whole of the self, the *Tao*.

The third misunderstanding relates to suspicions, usually voiced by ministers or theologians, that Jung is a skeptic or agnostic, that he has done away with God by psychologizing God into an archetype. That this charge bothered Jung a great deal is evident from the attention it receives in his Commentary on *The Secret of the Golden Flower*.[82] Basing himself on Lao Tzu's teaching, 'The Name that can be spoken or described is not the true Name', Jung seeks to demonstrate that he is neither a skeptic nor an agnostic but a direct experiencer of the divine. Following his reading of Taoism, Jung rejects metaphysics as having any grip on reality. All dogma, all theology, is necessarily one-sided because it engages in making distinctions. The divine, the underlying whole, which gives birth to, supports, and receives back all of existence, provides the cosmic pattern in which all distinctions inhere. To know God, the *Tao*, the *ātman*, requires not metaphysics but a direct experience of the whole – and that, Jung maintains, is available to us all through the Self.

It is not likely that theologians or metaphysicians will be happy with Jung's Taoist experience of the divine. But it is something quite different from skepticism or gnosticism. If it is to hit the mark, any discussion of Jung's religion would be advised to begin with the Taoist background and then to grapple with his contention that in Paul's *experience* of Christ 'the deepest religious experience of the West and the East meet'.[83] Jung seems to have been convinced that in Pauline theology Taoist and Christian thought coalesce.

NOTES

1. Harold Coward, *Jung and Eastern Thought* (Albany: State University of New York Press, 1985).
2. *Ibid.*, pp. 52–5.
3. C. G. Jung, *Memories, Dreams, Reflections*, ed. Aniela Jaffe, trans. Richard and Clara Winston (New York: Vintage Books, 1965), p. 373.
4. *Ibid.*, p. 374.
5. C. G. Jung, *Psychological Types*, in *The Collected Works of C. G. Jung*, vol. 6 (Princeton: Princeton University Press, 1971).
6. Jung, *Memories, Dreams, Reflections*, p. 207.
7. *Ibid.*, p. 208.
8. Jung, *Psychological Types*, p. 214.
9. John B. Henderson, *The Development and Decline of Chinese Cosmology* (New York: Columbia University Press, 1984), p. xv. In an even more recent book, Benjamin Schwartz suggests the term 'correlative anthropocosmology' as a more exact translation of the Chinese principle (*The World of Thought in Ancient China* [Cambridge: Harvard University Press, 1985]).

10. *Ibid.*, p. 1.
11. *Ibid.*, p. 22.
12. *Ibid.*, pp. 154–5.
13. *The Tao Te Ching of Lao Tzu*, Chapter 25, trans. James Legge, in *The Texts of Taoism* (New York: Dover Publications, 1962), pt. 1, p. 68.
14. As quoted by Jung from Waley's translation; see Jung, *Psychological Types*, in *Collected Works*, 6:214.
15. *Ibid.*, pp. 216–17.
16. Jung, *Memories, Dreams, Reflections*, p. 374.
17. C. G. Jung, Foreword to *The I Ching or Book of Changes*, trans. Richard Wilhelm (Princeton: Princeton University Press, 1950), p. xxii.
18. *Ibid.*, p. xxiv.
19. W. A. Callahan, 'Discourse and Perspective in Daoism: A Linguistic Interpretation of *Ziran*', *Philosophy East and West*, 39, 1989, p. 171.
20. Jung, Foreword to *The I Ching*, p. xxiv.
21. C. G. Jung, *Synchronicity: An Acausal Connecting Principle* (Princeton: Princeton University Press, 1973) (see *Collected Works*, vol. 8), pp. v–vi.
22. Jolande Jacobi, *The Psychology of C. G. Jung* (New Haven: Yale University Press, 1973), pp. 49–50.
23. Jung, *Synchronicity*, p. vi.
24. *The Secret of the Golden Flower*, trans. Richard Wilhelm with Commentary by C. G. Jung (New York: Causeway Books, 1975), p. 142.
25. Ira Progoff, *Jung, Synchronicity and Human Destiny* (New York: Dell, 1973), p. 158.
26. Schwartz, *The World of Thought in Ancient China*, p. 350.
27. Jung, *Synchronicity*, p. 99.
28. C. G. Jung, *Civilization in Transition*, in *Collected Works*, 10:451–2.
29. *C. G. Jung: Letters*, vol. 2, ed. Gerhard Adler and Aniela Jaffé (Princeton: Princeton University Press), p. 22.
30. *Ibid.*, pp. 258–9.
31. *Ibid.*, p. 447.
32. As Robert Aziz has demonstrated, the 'meaningfulness' Jung associates with synchronistic events consists in four interrelated layers of deepening significance: (a) the intrapsychic state and the objective event as 'meaningful parallels', (b) the numinous charge associated with the synchronistic experience (from R. Otto, a feeling of 'grace' is conveyed), (c) the import of the subjective level of interpretation, and (d) the archetypal level of meaning (Robert Aziz, Ph.D. thesis, *C. G. Jung's Psychology of Religion and Synchronicity*, pp. 98–9; subsequently published by State University of New York Press, 1990).
33. *Ibid.*, p. 110.
34. Jung, *Synchronicity*, pp. 69 ff.
35. Nathan Sivin, *Chinese Alchemy: Preliminary Studies* (Cambridge: Harvard University Press, 1968), p. 5.
36. Joseph Needham, *Science and Civilisation in China* (Cambridge: Cambridge University Press, 1956), 2:281.
37. Jung, *Synchronicity*, in *Collected Works*, 8:488.
38. Chang Huai's 'Treatise on Painting' as quoted in *Creativity and Taoism*, by Chang Chung-yuan (New York: Harper Colophon, 1963), p. 206.
39. *Ibid.*, p. 207.
40. Jung, Commentary on *The Secret of the Golden Flower*, p. 137.
41. C. G. Jung, *The Symbolic Life*, in *Collected Works*, 18: 68–9.
42. C. G. Jung, *Mysterium Coniunctionis*, in *Collected Works*, 14:166.
43. C. G. Jung, *The Holy Men of India*, in *Collected Works*, 11:576–86.
44. Jung, *Memories, Dreams, Reflections*, pp. 196–7.
45. Jung, Commentary on *The Secret of the Golden Flower*, in *Collected Works*, 13:6–7.

46. Frieda Fordham, *An Introduction to Jung's Psychology* (Harmondsworth, England: Penguin, 1957), p. 63.
47. See, e.g., *Chandogya Upaniṣad* 6.12.1–3.
48. See Karl H. Potter, *Advaita Vedanta Up to Samkara and His Pupils* (Princeton: Princeton University Press, 1981), pp. 76ff. It should, however, be noted that Hindu Tantric systems share with Taoism a balanced emphasis on the inner and outer worlds. It just happens that Jung found his help in this regard from Chinese Taoist texts.
49. Charles San, Introduction to *The Secret of the Golden Flower*, trans. Richard Wilhelm (New York: Causeway Books, 1975), p. xii. The book is said to go back in oral form to Lu Yen, an eighth-century Taoist adept.
50. *Ibid.*, p. 4. It would be interesting to compare this Taoist notion of the transfigured body-spirit personality that survives death with the Christian doctrine of a resurrected transfigured body-spirit entity.
51. *Ibid.*, pp. 14 ff.
52. *Ibid.*, p. xi.
53. *Ibid.*, p. 87.
54. C. G. Jung, *Two Essays on Analytical Psychology*, in *Collected Works*, 7:221.
55. Jung, Commentary on *The Secret of the Golden Flower*, p. 89.
56. *Ibid.*, p. 90.
57. *Ibid.*, pp. 90–2.
58. *Ibid.*, p. 96. This is one of the few times Jung uses the term 'conversion'.
59. Jung, *Memories, Dreams, Reflections*, p. 197.
60. Jung, Commentary on *The Secret of the Golden Flower*, p. 100.
61. C. G. Jung, *A Psychological Approach to the Trinity*, in *Collected Works*, 11:156.
62. C. G. Jung, *Good and Evil in Analytical Psychology*, in *Collected Works*, 10:463.
63. C. G. Jung, *'Ulysses': A Monologue*, in *Collected Works*, 15:126. Jung sees the many figures in James Joyce's *Ulysses* as many small egos, like the many small egos of the drawing from *The Secret of the Golden Flower*. There is no one character or figure in the novel to represent the self.
64. Jung, Commentary on *The Secret of the Golden Flower*, pp. 101–2. As a modern parallel to this description from the ancient Taoist text, Jung quotes from an experience of Edward Maitland: 'Once started on my quest, I found myself traversing a succession of spheres or belts … the impression produced being that of mounting a vast ladder stretching from the circumference toward the center of a system, which was at once my own system, the solar system, and the universal system, the three systems being at once diverse and identical …' (p. 102).
65. *Ibid.*, p. 104.
66. *Ibid.*, pp. 106–13.
67. Jung, of course, usually rejected the Eastern notion of individual rebirth, although toward the end of his life he came close to accepting it. In *Memories, Dreams, Reflections*, he toys with the idea that rebirth might be conceived as a psychic projection and offers evidence from his own dreams (pp. 322–3).
68. *The Secret of the Golden Flower*, p. 123.
69. *Ibid.*
70. *Ibid.*, p. 124.
71. Lao Tzu, *Tao-Te Ching*, in *A Source Book in Chinese Philosophy*, trans. Wing-tsit Chan (Princeton: Princeton University Press, 1969), p. 139.
72. Jung, Commentary on *The Secret of the Golden Flower*, pp. 128–9.
73. *Ibid.*, p. 131 n. 1.
74. *Ibid.*, pp. 131–2.
75. *Ibid.*, p. 132.
76. 'The Story of Carl Gustav Jung', interview, BBC TV, 1972.
77. Jung, Commentary on *The Secret of the Golden Flower*, pp. 133–4.
78. *Ibid.*, p. 136.

79. Maurice Friedman, *To Deny our Nothingness* (New York: Delta, 1967), pt. vi.
80. R. C. Zaehner, 'A New Buddha and a New Tao', in *A Concise Encyclopedia of Living Faiths*, ed. R. C. Zaehner (New York: Hawthorn Books, 1959). Zaehner represents Jung as identifying God and the self with the collective unconscious (p. 404).
81. C. G. Jung, *Aion*, in *Collected Works*, vol. 9, pt. 2, p. 223.
82. Jung, Commentary on *The Secret of the Golden Flower*, pp. 128–35.
83. Ibid., p. 133. Jung frequently quotes from Paul, 'No longer do I live, but Christ liveth in me', as a manifestation of the self within a Christian context (e.g., p. 132).

16

MARTIN BUBER AND TAOISM

Irene Eber

At various times during his life Martin Buber had a considerable interest in Taoist thought.[1] In 1910 and 1911 this led to the publication of two small volumes of translations, the first, selections from the *Chuang-tzu* 莊子, and the second, the following year, consisted of a number of stories from P'u Sung-ling's 蒲松齡 *Liao-chai chih-i* 聊齋志異 (Liao-chai Tales).[2] In later years he occasionally commented in lectures or essays on Taoist ideas, specifically those of the *Tao-te-ching* 道德經 (*TTC*), and in 1942 he translated into Hebrew a number of the *TTC*'s chapters.[3] Throughout these decades Buber's interest was, however, confined to certain selected concepts, chosen in accordance with his philosophical concerns. This essay will not explore whether Taoism had a lasting impact on Buber's philosophical work.[4] Rather, the object here is to outline the background that led Buber at various times to occupy himself with Taoist concepts and then inquire more specifically how he understood these and which concepts he considered significant to his philosophical enterprise.

THE BACKGROUND OF BUBER'S CONCERN WITH MATTERS CHINESE

Buber's initial concern with matters Chinese occurred against the background of a wider German interest in China which began in 1897 with Germany's occupation of Chiao-chou Bay and the port of Tsingtao. But German interest in Chinese culture went well beyond purely practical matters of the military or

Irene Eber, 'Martin Buber and Taoism', *Monumenta Serica*, 42, 1994, pp. 445–64.

trade. German writers after the turn of the century enviously eyed the accomplishments of English sinology and the work of such translators as James Legge.[5] But even if German scholars considered themselves initially to lag behind the British, modern Chinese studies, including Sino-German scholarly contacts, developed rapidly.

In the first decade of the twentieth century, the Berlin University's Seminar for Oriental Languages grew in importance and its offerings included, in addition to language instruction, practical knowledge on Asia. After 1912, generous budgets leading to the substantial growth of its Chinese library holdings together with the presence of the outstanding Dutch scholar, J. J. M. de Groot (d. 1921) established, furthermore, Berlin's Sinological Seminar as a leading academic center for Chinese studies.[6] At the same time numerous Chinese students began to study at Western universities. Some also came to German institutions and, as a result, Chinese intellectuals, too, began to show an interest in German thought and literature.

Buber's encounter with China took place against this larger background and it coincided with his preoccupation with Hasidic materials and his interest in questions of myths and culture. He may also have come across materials on China when he was a reader for the publisher Rütten und Loening in 1905 and later. With Rütten und Loening he published his own works as well as a series called 'Society' (between 1906 and 1912), which consisted of socio-psychological monographs.[7] At about this time Buber became acquainted with Wang Ching-t'ao 王警濤 who in 1907 was a lecturer, or Chinese language instructor, at the Seminar for Oriental Languages.

Wang remained in Germany until 1911, but little is known about him. He translated several Chinese short stories into German (no doubt, to earn extra cash) and he introduced Buber to P'u Sung-ling's stories.[8] But Wang's scholarly interests seem to have been more political than literary as is apparent from the one or two publications he has to his credit. After his return to China he held some kind of official position in the newly established Republican government.[9] Buber and Wang collaborated on the translation of a number of stories from the *Liao-chai chih-i* collection, Buber translating from the English version by Herbert A. Giles, and Wang translating several from the Chinese original. Most of the *Chuang-tzu* portions were also prepared from Giles' English version. In the preface Buber acknowledged the aid of Chinese colleagues without, however, mentioning Wang or anyone else by name.[10]

Enthusiastic reviews in the German language press greeted the appearance of both volumes. Buber was praised for making these works available to German readers and for thus furnishing evidence of the universality of ideas. The poetic content of the *Liao-chai chih-i* was highly praised by Hermann Hesse.[11] Considering the paucity of translated works from Chinese in the early decades of the twentieth century, the widespread response is not surprising. Except for the *TTC*, German speaking readers had few translations from Chinese available to them and even fewer critical works. The *Lun-yü* 論語 could be read only in a very dated edition, and Chinese poetry translations, aside from the *Shih-ching* 詩經, were still in the future.[12] Buber's collection of P'u Sung-ling's stories was the first selection of Chinese fiction in German and thus deserved the well-earned praise it received.

Although Buber published no further books on Chinese subjects, his interest in Taoist ideas did not cease in 1911. In 1924 he subjected the *TTC* to a fairly systematic study when asked to give a series of privately arranged lectures to a lay group. These lectures, not recorded by Buber himself but probably by one of the participants, were neither revised nor published, and exist today only as a typewritten manuscript entitled, 'Talks with Martin Buber in Ascona, August 1924, about Lao-tzu's Tao Te Ching'.[13]

In 1924 Buber was living in Heppenheim, coming regularly to the University of Frankfurt where he lectured on the history of religions. Although the majority of the courses which he offered between 1924 and 1933 were clearly on Jewish topics, some course titles suggest that he included also other subjects and that he probably discussed Taoist concepts also.[14] In 1924, Richard Wilhelm (1873–1930) joined the faculty, beginning a distinguished albeit shortlived career in Chinese studies. Hermann Hesse (1877–1962) whose friendship with Buber was of some years' standing, also visited the university and was there, for example, at the end of 1926, to read from his works. Wilhelm's close friendship with Hesse dated from 1897.[15] In addition, a rare personal relationship existed between Wilhelm and Carl Gustav Jung (1875–1961) who was brought into this charmed circle for a time due to Wilhelm and Jung's mutual interest in Chinese thought, especially Taoism and the *I-ching*.

Wilhelm had gone to Tsingtao in 1899 as a missionary for the Weimar Mission, two years after Germany occupied the Shantung peninsula. His missionary career was soon diverted, however, into other channels. He acquired remarkable expertise in Chinese and Chinese classical literature, and from 1910 on, he published a series of outstanding translations and beautifully crafted books about China. In 1924, when he joined the philosophical faculty of the University of Frankfurt, he also founded the China-Institut which became a focal point for a variety of China-oriented cultural activities. The institute attracted visiting sinological luminaries from other European universities, as well as major Chinese literary and religious figures, among them the ever popular Hu Shih 胡適 (1891–1962).[16]

But Wilhelm's hopes for the institute transcended the mere staging of cultural activities: the institute was to be a beacon for the culture of the future when, he believed, East and West would at last meet. Both parts of the world had elements to contribute to this future culture which like *yin* 陰 and *yang* 陽, Wilhelm argued, complemented each other. The institute's function, said Wilhelm at its opening in 1924, was to promote this aim.[17] To what extent Buber subscribed to similar views is uncertain. Nor do we know how active a participant he was in the institute's many events. Did Buber, Wilhelm, Hesse, and Jung engage in discussions and did they share thoughts on Chinese philosophy? Unfortunately, concrete evidence for Buber's involvement in the institute's activities and in an ongoing dialogue is meager. Apparently Wilhelm kept Buber informed on matters of interest to him,[18] and Buber (together with Jung) participated as discussants in the institute's 1928 fall lectures delivered by Wilhelm.[19]

Buber, however, had still other contacts. Between 1927 and 1931 Buber corresponded with Willy Tonn (d. 1957) about the latter's Chinese interests and work. Tonn pursued Chinese studies in Berlin in the late twenties and early thirties, but seems not to have earned a doctorate.[20] He was at the time translating a brief, esoteric Taoist text and the 1512 stele inscription of the K'aifeng Jews.[21]

Tonn, who in the 1950s assisted Buber with the *Chuang-tzu* revisions, had fled to Shanghai in 1938, shortly after the *Kristallnacht*, where he devoted himself to educating his fellow refugees about China. His many publications in the refugee press of the 1940s include translations from Chinese prose and poetry as well as critical articles on a variety of Chinese subjects. During that decade he also established an Asia Seminar where he lectured to the German-speaking refugees on Chinese history and culture. After Tonn came to Tel Aviv in 1948 or 1949, contact between the two men was resumed. But Tonn in Tel Aviv, like Buber in Jerusalem, found little interest then in China, her history and civilization.

Buber continued a slight but steady interest in the *TTC* in the 1940s while teaching at the Hebrew University in Jerusalem. Among his notes from those years there are several translated chapters from the *TTC*, notations on Chinese classical grammar, and several translated passages from the *Lun-yü* (Analects), suggesting that he included materials on Chinese thought in his lectures.[22] In 1942 he published the translation of eight *TTC* chapters, mentioned earlier. Finally, in the 1950s, he revised the *Chuang-tzu*, enlisting Tonn's help on points of transliteration and translation.[23] Still, for both men this must have been lonely work. Jerusalem's Hebrew University had then neither a department of East Asian Studies nor did its library contain even the most basic works on China and Chinese philosophy.

These, briefly, are the years and circumstances of Buber's interest in Taoist ideas. Clearly the *TTC* occupied him more than the *Chuang-tzu* and, except for work on the *Chuang-tzu* revisions, he returned time and again to concepts expressed in that brief, enigmatic work. The two questions this raises are, which Taoist concepts did he consider significant, and how did he understand and use them. In what follows, some answers will be attempted.

Buber recorded his initial reflections on Taoist thought in a brief essay which he later appended as an 'Afterword' to the 1910 translations from the *Chuang-tzu*.[24] Whereas the *Chuang-tzu* text was twice revised for the 1918 and the 1951 editions, the essay has remained in its original form. In later years Buber distanced himself from this essay, describing it as belonging '... to a stage that I had to pass through before I could enter into an independent relationship with being. One may call it the "mystical" phase ....'[25]

The essay discussed ideas found in both the *Chuang-tzu* and the *TTC*, however, relatively more space is devoted to the latter, thus only loosely connecting the 'Afterword' with the translated text. In this essay Buber regarded the *TTC* as the fountainhead of Taoism following which no further original contributions were made. Indeed, he assigned to Chuang-tzu the subordinate position of 'apostle', stating that 'Chuang Tzu was a poet ... who did not "continue to develop" the teachings of Laozi (Lao-tzu) from the words in which they have come down to us, but he shaped them into poetry.'[26] According to Buber, therefore, Chuang-tzu was not an independent philosopher, and he ignored or glossed over Chuang-tzu's innovative and original contribution to Chinese thought as well as some of the important differences between the *Chuang-tzu* and the *TTC*.

TAO, WU-WEI, I, CHIH

The Taoist concepts that Buber sought to explain in this essay are the meaning of *Tao* 道 and those which he considered associated with *Tao*: non-acting, *wu-wei* 無爲, the One (unity or oneness), *i* 一, and knowledge (understanding), *chih* 知. In Buber's view an inherent interrelationship exists between the four concepts. He recognized philosophical Taoism's claim that at the basis of genuine existence is an unknowable of which nothing can be predicated. *Tao* cannot be named and it cannot be investigated for it has no attributes. The presence of *Tao* in the phenomenal world, stated Buber, is as oneness where it is neither recognized nor known; *Tao* is lived, *Tao* is acting; *Tao* manifests itself in the genuine existence of the sage. Knowledge consists in being, not in the knowledge of external matters or objects. But knowledge is also acting. It is the deed. Yet genuine acting is non-acting because it originates in 'a gathered unity', or oneness. To experience *Tao* directly means being one with *Tao* and means also being unified within oneself:

> ... the unified [geeint] person is described as one who lives and experiences Dao [*Tao*] directly. He perceives unity in the world. But that does not mean that the world is a closed thing outside himself, whose unity he penetrates. Rather, the unity of the world is only a reflection of his unity ...

Tao in relationship to the human being is what interested Buber, not *Tao* as an abstract idea, and it is, no doubt, for this reason that he chose to discuss the interrelationship of these particular concepts.[27] For this reason he also apparently ignored the cosmogonic implications of the One, expressed, for example, in chapter 42 of the *TTC*.

Knowledge and non-acting were assigned an important place in this essay because it is, after all, the living person who knows and acts. Acquiring and storing knowledge is, however, not the goal,[28] nor is it the 'emptying' stressed by the *TTC*. Buber argued that knowledge acquired in non-acting – knowledge that is not in knowing but in being – leads to a different way of existing, the way of the 'perfected person'. Buber did not differentiate between the *TTC* and the *Chuang-tzu*'s ideas here. Both texts give different names and attributes to this kind of person. In the former, he is the sage, *sheng-jen* 聖人, who still exercises his calling toward practical ends, though he is like the newborn child, unsullied by the dross and artificiality of civilization. In the latter, he is the genuine person, *chen-jen* 真人, to whom practical ends are a matter of indifference. He is someone who has shed all learned and acquired preconceptions, who regards his individual existence as having merged with everything there is, who is one with cosmic being.

That Buber did not sort out these differences was not due to his having misunderstood them. Rather, he was after something else, more concrete, on the one hand, but also more related to his own interpretations of mysticism, on the other. As pointed out by Benjamin Schwartz, common to all mysticism is the ineffable ground of reality which is accessible only to a higher kind of knowledge (gnosis), beyond commonly used language. Also commonly held is the assumption that only some human beings (perfected in their essence) can attain to oneness with the ultimate source.[29] Buber's concept of the *tzaddik*, developed in his works on Hasidism at that time, was thus not only the result of his reflections concerning mysticism, it was also indebted to how he interpreted the significance of the sage and the genuine person in Taoist thought. According to Hans Kohn, Europe's philosophical discourse was undergoing changes in the first decade of the twentieth century, precisely when Martin Buber had his fateful encounter with both Hasidism and Taoism. By means of Hasidism, writes Kohn, Buber found and developed his own teaching, while Taoism (Kohn does not specify which ideas of Taoism) left a lasting imprint on his theories.[30] Buber's study of Hasidism between 1904 and 1909 which resulted in two books, *Tales of Rabbi Nahman* (1906) and *The Legend of the Baal Shem* (1907), dealt with the men, the *tzaddikim*, the 'righteous' or 'the proven', who exemplify the teaching in their own lives. Although called by different names, *tzaddik*, sage, or genuine person, the attributes by which they are known are essentially the same as far as Buber was concerned. Therefore, his description of the *tzaddik* does not differ greatly from that of the Chinese sage: for the *tzaddik*, too, thinking (knowing) is being; outer and inner are one; he who has attained wisdom will not lose himself; evil is a lack rather than something in itself and is also worthy of love.[31]

Buber's interest in P'u Sung-ling's stories at that time was similarly related to his preoccupation with Hasidism. In these stories Buber saw the meeting of the divine and the human in mundane existence which he defined as the unity or oneness (*Einheit*), obvious in Taoism as well as in Hasidism.[32] Although, in his studies on Hasidim, Buber dwelled on the religious motif and the nearness of God, he seems to have perceived something not altogether dissimilar in the easy co-existence of spirits and humans in the *Liao-chai chi-i*. Today critics agree that P'u Sung-ling's deceptively simple stories possess a rare sophistication and, upon closer analysis, exhibit startling complexities. It is indeed remarkable that

Buber in his encounter with Chinese literature nearly a century ago and without the benefit of a critical apparatus to point the way, realized that these stories contain a philosophical substratum as well as important aspects of the Chinese worldview.

Buber was apparently little concerned with the divergence of his and the Chinese idea of unity. In Chinese thought the idea of unity is that of an all-embracing order which encompasses this and the world beyond. The two spheres, the socio-political order and the order of spirits and gods are not hermetically sealed off from one another. They interact in often strange and unexpected, though never chaotic, ways. Within this all-encompassing order, ancestor worship has a central function (as Buber was to point out in 1928) by assigning to ritual the continued maintenance of the human and cosmic order. But Buber's idea of unity developed from an entirely different basis and was motivated by his assumption of a dualism in Jewish existence. The Jew, he believed, forever vacillated between historical and existential contradictions. Therefore, the creative impulse of Judaism lies in the reconciliation of these contradictions and in the attempt to overcome the dualism and to achieve unity.[33] To Buber and a Chinese reader, P'u Sung-ling's stories certainly suggested multiple and different messages on the nature of unity and order, yet both would have agreed on the importance of unity and order.

The ideas which Buber had first developed in connection with the *Chuang-tzu* and the *Liao-chai chih-i* translations continued to recur in different contexts. He again raised the question of overcoming dualism in existence in a lecture some years later.[34] Entitled 'The Spirit of the Orient and Judaism', the lecture's message was that Judaism had closer affinities with Oriental (in his view, Indian, Near Eastern, and Chinese) thought and attitudes than with Occidental ones.[35] Especially remarkable for its day was Buber's assertion that men like the prophets, Lao-tzu, and the Upanishadic thinkers (Buber neglected to include the Buddha) shared a common mission to restore, to regenerate, and to announce a renewal.

Humanity in the West, said Buber, is caught in a dichotomous state. Westerners objectify the world and thus draw a distinction between themselves and the objects of the external world. This dichotomization (*Entzweiung*) of the self with the self of the world can be remedied only by reunifying the human personality and by entering into, what he calls, genuine existence. None of the great religious teachings had their source in the Occident, said Buber. These originated in the Orient and were received and adapted in the Occident. But as receptor, the Occident has been unable to construct a view of a seamless world together with a suprarational divine teaching. Lacking in the West, therefore, is 'the exclusiveness of the message about genuine existence'. In distinction to the West, the Orient considers genuine existence a fundamental metaphysical principle, conditioned by no other consideration.

By genuine existence Buber had in mind a non-bifurcated life, lived both in thought and in deed, in knowing and in acting. Once a person recognizes how the original oneness was severed and distorted, it is encumbent upon him – and this is his mission – to return to the original unity. Oriental thought significantly insists that such knowledge, such a realization, is a matter of life lived. The Taoist, said Buber, recognizes the duality of existence, but he knows that this duality is rooted in the One, the *Tao*. *Tao* assumes reality in the life of the sage by his acting and non-acting which, in turn, permits the emergence of the real significance of the world.

In this lecture Buber did not intend to establish general East-West considerations; he was concerned once more with the condition of the Jew and how to remedy dichotomous Jewish existence. The Jew, Buber declared, was and has remained an Oriental in spite of using Western languages, in spite of martyrdom and oppression. Buber defined the Jew's affinity with the Orient as follows:[36]

> Action is more vital to him than experience, or, more accurately, his experience is his acting. He experiences the world's objects less in their separate, multiple, singular existence than in their relationships, their mutuality ... The Greek considers the concept as the conclusion, the Jew considers it the beginning. Stronger than others, the Jew possesses the Oriental's elementary drive to unity (*Einheitstrieb*) ...

However, where the Chinese accepts the duality of existence by realizing its unity in *Tao*, the Jew consciously decides and engages in restoring unity and completeness. The Jewish belief that the deed's absolute value consists in the decision to act is, therefore, a distinguishing characteristic, according to Buber.

In this lecture Buber skillfully wove together strands of the *TTC*'s ideas with his own reflections on how to give meaning and substance to Judaism. The ideas he had deemed important in his earlier encounter with Taoism, oneness and duality, acting and non-acting, were translated in this lecture into coherent views on the meaning of Jewish existence. A mystical oneness continued to figure in his thought, but this unity was already more action-oriented and was combined with the conscious act of deciding. And decisions were based on knowing.

In 1928, Buber briefly returned to thoughts on *Tao* and non-acting. By then the 'mystic phase', as he had called it, was behind him, and his preoccupation with the Bible, his concerns with God, the life of dialogue, and the world, led him to locate spiritual endeavors in the 'living reality of every-day'.[37] *Tao*, he wrote, 'affirms the whole reality of the world'. In the world's separateness is embodied the working of *Tao*.[38] His discussion on non-acting also differed significantly from the 1910 essay and the lecture some five years later. Commenting on Richard Wilhelm's suggestion in his China-Institute lecture that Confucianism had something to offer a Europe in crisis, Buber expressed considerable pessimism. Defining Chinese culture as Confucian culture, Buber doubted that the West would find in it much that was congenial. For one, said Buber, Chinese people have a fundamentally different relationship to their dead, neither abhorring nor dreading them. A Chinese continues to maintain contact with his ancestors through ancestor worship and, therefore, Chinese culture conceives of generational continuity in entirely different terms than the West. Secondly, Chinese have a profound trust in a person's fundamental 'being'. This trust does not exist in the West.

For this reason, Taoism, stated Buber, and specifically Taoist non-acting as non-interference, striving for success by non-aggressive means, has something to offer to the West. In a radical departure from his views of sixteen years earlier, Buber's comments did not relate non-acting to either cognition or a special person; anyone can practice it, he implied, as long as the person realizes that short term success in the historic here and now is illusory. Non-acting is genuine acting, it has imperceptible effects, is long lasting, becoming 'a part of the life of mankind'.[39] Non-acting in this sense is concrete and takes place in the world's arena. *Wei wu-wei* 爲無爲, act by non-acting, which Buber apparently had in mind here, occurs twice in the *TTC*, in chapters three and sixty-three. The latter especially recommends to the sage (*sheng-jen*) a way of life in this world where goals must be achieved, but where the means for achieving them are supremely important and must be carefully chosen. Buber's intellectual concerns had changed and, perhaps as a result, he had reached a more profound understanding of some of the *TTC*'s ideas.

Buber had expressed similar views at greater length already in 1924, when invited to give a series of talks on the *TTC* in Ascona, Switzerland.[40] The talks consisted in a chapter by chapter exposition of the text, and he discussed altogether thirty-three of the book's eighty-one chapters. Broader religious and philosophical issues were also raised in conjunction with the text either by Buber or the participants. Buber's lectures are not preserved among his manuscripts (was there, in fact, a written text?), but their contents were recorded by one (or several) participant(s). It can be assumed that the typewritten manuscript conveys in abbreviated form the gist of his talks.[41]

Buber obviously was no longer interested in the *Chuang-tzu*. In part this may have been due to the *TTC*'s popularity as one of the most widely translated works of Chinese philosophy by then. In German, there were as many as half a dozen different translations by the second decade of the twentieth century, several of them in multiple editions. The *TTC* appealed to scholars and laymen alike, whereas the *Chuang-tzu*'s audience was much smaller. Unlike the *Chuang-tzu*, the *TTC* was not burdened with unpronounceable Chinese names, in fact, not a single proper name occurs in its eighty-one chapters. To its often cryptic sayings, many ascribed a universal sense, pregnant with meaning for all times and in all places. Hermann Hesse compared the book to the Bible, and C. G. Jung considered it a part of the world's literary heritage, a pillar in the '... bridge of the spirit which spans the morass of world history'.[42] Perhaps to the serious-minded, Chuang-tzu's humor seemed too frivolous; his strain of anarchism too daring in post-World War I Europe; his method of argumentation too pugnacious.

Buber's intellectual enterprise at the time was, no doubt, also important in how he interpreted the *TTC*. His major work, *I and Thou*, with its emphasis on the meeting of the human and the divine, was published in 1923, and the issues he had raised in the book continued to occupy him in subsequent years.[43] At that time, furthermore, Buber engaged in wider educational activities outside the university, among these his lectures at the Frankfurt Freies Jüdisches Lehrhaus, founded by Franz Rosenzweig in 1920.[44] Thus the 1924 'Ascona Talks' reflected a significantly different approach to the *TTC*'s ideas. Although caution is indicated since the talks were probably not recorded by Buber himself, the lectures reveal a new understanding of the *TTC*'s concepts. They also established a wider philosophical context for the text by comparing its ideas with Jewish, Christian, and Confucian thought. In these talks, Buber created for the *TTC* a place in his philosophical and religious discourse, and his explanations of the various chapters, now far less mystically interpreted, can be considered an attempt at a commentary on the *TTC*. Non-acting was no longer accorded a central position, and he was also not overly concerned with the role of the sage. On the other hand, issues related to society and the political state received more attention, and the *Tao* in the world (not as mystic oneness) was exhaustively discussed.

For their *TTC* text, Buber and his small band of devotees used the translation by Victor Friedrich von Strauß und Torney, *Lao-Tse's Tao Te King* (Leipzig, 1870).[45] That Buber preferred this translation to more recent ones (such as Wilhelm's translation, of 1910) can be attributed, no doubt, to his finding von Strauß's assumptions and most of his interpretations congenial to his own way of thinking. This will be obvious when we take a closer look at von Strauß's introduction to the text. Von Strauß assumed that there was a time before time, an 'Urzeit,' when all religions were one, out of which both Judaism and Taoism developed. In more historic times, but long before Lao-tzu, there must have been a Taoist community (perhaps with participants in mystery rites) from which Lao-tzu took the name *Tao* and the religious basis of his teaching. Thus the *TTC* is a religious text. Lao-tzu's basic ideas are theosophical, stated von Strauß, and he belongs, therefore, to that group of thinkers we call mystics. For these theosophical mystics, being (*Seyn* [Sein]) was their vital source, from which they intuitively drew.[46] Men turn to theosophy not by choice or influence, but by religiously motivated individual inclinations. Theosophical thought does not discover divine truth, but needs the religious heritage to test divine truth. Now, China does not have a body of religious literature referring to the existence and activities of the Highest Being in His relationship to man and history. Nonetheless, von Strauß believed, there are religious traditions, mentioned both in the *Shu-ching* 書經 and *Shih-ching* as well as in the *TTC*. In the latter, they appear as rhymed hymns and songs.[47] That so little of Taoist thought (or religious thought) remains in the *Shu-ching*, according to von Strauß, is because Confucius edited the text. Von Strauß was not overly fond of the sage, describing him as an immodest, ambitious man with high-flown plans, who opposed everything sacred and otherworldly.[48]

TAO AND GOD

After he established that the *TTC* is a basically religious text which reflects ancient religious traditions, von Strauß easily identified *Tao* with God. Lao-tzu, stated von Strauß, had a profound awareness of God (*Gottesbewußtsein*), comparable to the concept of revelation. Such an awareness existed only in China and among the people of Israel at the time. Therefore, when referring to the *Tao*, von Strauß consistently used the personal pronoun 'he', labelling *Tao* a being (*Wesen*). Other names in Chinese which can be translated as God, such as *ti* 帝, *shang-ti* 上帝, or *t'ien-ti* 天帝, did not worry von Strauß and he argued that in antiquity these, together with *Tao*, may have been simply different names for the one God. Not surprisingly, he concluded that the ancient Chinese were monotheists and not polytheists. Their worship of nature deities was not polytheism, but resembled the Catholic worship of saints and angels.[49]

If Taoism is in large part a religious system, what distinguishes it then from Western religious systems, according to von Strauß? Chinese religion of antiquity, he explained, was a-historical. It was neither mythology nor revelation. This religion was transmitted without manuscripts, without teachers, heroes, or writings about the faith. Thus no possibility existed for constant renewals of religious consciousness as in the West. With Lao-tzu, religious consciousness reached its apogee, but thereafter declined and deteriorated.[50]

The 'Ascona Talks' notes indicate that Buber accepted most of von Strauß's notions, building his interpretations in many parts on these. Buber, too, viewed the *TTC* as a religious text which, he apparently believed, must be interpreted in a religious spirit.[51] Although he never explicitly described *Tao* as synonymous with God, he attributed to *Tao* the quality of the divine (*das Göttliche*). Von Strauß's technical explanations – points of Chinese grammar, interpretations of Chinese characters according to the K'ang-hsi 康熙 dictionary, or von Strauß's frequent resort to Ho-shang kung's[52] 河上公 commentary to the *TTC* – were, however, not repeated in the notes. Possibly, some of Buber's Chinese acquaintances advised him on interpretations of Chinese terms, since there are occasional explanations of terminology other than those given by von Strauß.[53]

Buber's comments on chapters one and nineteen ascribe an ontology to the *TTC*. By stipulating both an eternal *Tao* and one that is manifested in the world, Lao-tzu established an ontological fact (p. 1). *Tao*, therefore, is not a law of nature, not abstraction, but being or substance. Two indivisible parts of the divine exist; one transcendent and unknowable, the other immanent and personal. Because the human being interacts with the immanent part, it can be termed the personal aspect of the divine (p. 14). Buber argued that the ineffable, the transcendent *Tao*, is not the beginning of existence, stipulating a difference between origin (*Ursprung*) and cause (*Ursache*). The origin which makes possible creation is the transcendent *Tao* and the cause that sets the process in motion is the immanent *Tao* (p. 2). Buber's comments to chapter seven stress two additional points: First, Lao-tzu was not interested in other-worldliness, his ideas deal with reality itself, and second, *Tao* manifests itself in multiplicity. But the idea of *Tao* must not be taken to mean that the One is real and the many an illuson (p. 7). Possibly, Buber aimed for consistency here for he did not comment on chapters forty-two and fifty-one, for example, where *Tao* is said to begin the process of creation.

In spite of stipulating transcendence and immanence, Buber did not want to suggest a dichotomizing of *Tao*. Hence his comments to chapter ten and twenty-two reiterated once more the *Tao*'s oneness (pp. 7, 17). But oneness that had been so important to him more than a decade earlier now had somewhat different implications. It was no longer only a mystic and difficult to explain concept. Oneness now signified to Buber completeness and he related it to the person who participates in the divine, who stands in proximity to God (p. 24), who exists in a higher sphere of undividedness (p. 7), or who has sought the divine and been united with it (p. 21). When such a person acts, the difference between acting in the name of man or in the name of God disappears. It is one and the same (p. 19).[54] Man is a religious being, he asserted in his comments to chapters fifty-five and sixty-two. He possesses creative powers, spontaneously, without willing. He creates. Such a person is holy when he enters the sphere of completeness. Holiness is, therefore, not primarily an attribute of God alone (p. 24), but of the human being as well. For this reason, Buber apparently did not hesitate using von Strauß's the 'holy one' for sage (*sheng-jen*), to describe such a persons's wholeness and godliness.

But Buber obviously chose his vocabulary carefully. This can be seen in his references to God and the divine (*das Göttliche*). It can be, furthermore, seen in the uncertainty of precisely how to deal with *Tao* and the tetragrammaton, a subject extensively discussed by von Strauß in his comments to chapter four-teen.[55] According to von Strauß, the issue of the tetragrammaton was first raised in 1823 when the three characters, *i* 夷, *hsi* 希, and *wei* 微 in the following sentences of chapter fourteen (my translation) were said to represent the tetragrammaton:

> Looking at it, it is not seen; we call it by the name 'ordinary' (*i*).
> Listening to it, it is not heard; we call it by the name 'sparse' (*hsi*).
> Seizing it, it cannot be grasped; we call it by the name 'minute' (*wei*).

Von Strauß, basing himself on the Ho-shang kung commentary, believed that *i* means without colour, *hsi* means without sound, and *wei*, without form. In short, the three characters refer to the same ineffable being the tetragrammaton refers to and which is no other than *Tao*.[56] I, *hsi*, and *wei* were probably pronounced differently, argued von Strauß, closer to the original Hebrew pronunciation. Lao-tzu, no doubt, obtained his knowledge of YAHWE from Jews in China who claimed to have arrived as early as the Han dynasty. (Von Strauß must have read the eighteenth-century Jesuit accounts about the K'aifeng Jews which, citing the 1512 stele inscription, assign the arrival of the Jews in the city to the Han dynasty.) He supported his argument further by stating that the Jews' reluctance to pronounce the Name occurs also in the *TTC* and, therefore, later generations did not know that the three characters referred to God's name.

Buber did not dismiss out of hand the YAHWE-*Tao* identification. The three characters, according to Buber, express something esoteric, the manner of expression is different, the gist being that the attributes spoken of cannot be investigated except when someone experiences their effects and becomes conscious of them (p. 9). Although we cannot know for certain what exactly Buber said, the notes nonetheless indicate that even if he distanced himself from von Strauß's argument he did not reject it.

Perhaps because he now interpreted the *TTC* as a this-worldly rather than as a mystic text, he devoted considerable attention to those portions (altogether six chapters: 29, 30, 57, 61, 78, and 53) which deal with society and the state. The state to him meant community (*Gemeinschaft*). But not community as the sum total of individuals, rather community as a spiritual joining and acting together. Such a community resists domination by anyone person, for it is constituted by the relationship its members have to the person in the center. Buber argued that Lao-tzu considered the political state both a state of human beings and a state of God. 'To Lao-tzu the state consists of the community and legitimate authority', by which he meant the lawful, religious rule of the person who is central to the community (pp. 25–7). Buber, however, did not develop the ideas of the political state and authority, or to what extent the sage (the holy one) was the ruler. He pointed to messianism in chapter forty-nine, stating that the *TTC*'s messianism concerns the sage, but that all messianisms are, in the final analysis, the yearning for a king. His definition of the sage or the holy one in chapter seventy-eight is more in keeping with his own views than the *TTC*'s, when he assigns to him the position of intermediary between God and the world who assumes responsibilities as well as guilt, who steps into the gap that has been created between God and the world (p. 31).

In these chapters, dealing with the state and society, Buber did not resort to von Strauß's commentary and he engaged in free and far-reaching discussions, including remarks on contemporary events. Von Strauß's comments to these chapters had referred to textual matters, and only once, in discussing chapter sixty-one, did he also include some less than complimentary remarks on the Christianity of his day.[57] But Buber's purpose, fifty-odd years later, was not to provide only a learned commentary to the *TTC*. In addition, he seemed interested in these lectures to test the *TTC*'s relevance and applicability to the world of his day. Thus, his discussion of this same chapter (sixty-one) also raised among other topics the problem of Russia where he saw six years after the Revolution a process of dehumanization. A person, said Buber, is not seen in his relationship to others, or the life of the community, but as a cog in a vast, brutal, and senseless machine (p. 29). His remarks to chapter thirty take in World War I which he saw as having begun due to 'the fiction of a mutual threat.' Some people pretended to be pacifists, some made as if to devise plans, yet most people only did what seemed expedient at the moment (p. 28).

TAO-TE-CHING AND *CHUANG-TZU*

Buber returned to several *TTC* chapters in 1942 when he published a Hebrew translation of chapters 17, 29, 30, 31, 57, 58, 66, and 67.[58] It is not clear toward what end he prepared the translations. He may have translated them for use in his courses and then decided to publish them. Or he may have prepared the translations even earlier, perhaps after his arrival in Palestine in 1938 and before Europe was enveloped in the total darkness of World War II. Except for a brief note on the *TTC* and Lao-tzu, no other comments are attached to the translated text. In any event, Buber's translation of fifty years ago – now long forgotten – is, I believe, the first rendition of portions of the *TTC* into Hebrew.

He obviously did not use von Strauß's German text as the source for the Hebrew rendition, and one cannot tell whether he had an English or German original for preparing his translation. A remarkable feature of Buber's Hebrew version is its closeness to the Chinese text.[59] Both the sentence structure and the wording – even, for example, the repetitions that frequently occur in the *TTC* – are singularly felicitous to the original. Yet it is highly unlikely that he was able to translate from the Chinese on his own. Nor is it likely that anyone versed in classical Chinese resided then in Jerusalem. The content of the chapters, however, suggests that they were not chosen at random.

All eight have two themes in common, government and the condemnation of the use of force and instruments of war. Chapters 29, 30, and 31, reject armed force leading to devastation and sorrow. All-under-Heaven (*t'ien-hsia* 天下) can be obtained by abstaining from the use of force, according to chapter 57. In chapter 66, the sage (*sheng-jen*) is above the people, but they do not feel his weight; he is in front, but does not harm the people, and chapter 67 warns not to be first in All-under-Heaven. In a similar vein, chapter 17 states that in antiquity the people merely knew of the ruler's existence, thus implying that they did not feel his rule. Faith between the ruler and the people, moreover, is a prerequisite in governing.

Buber's choice of these and not other chapters may once again reflect his specific concerns at the time. His courses at the Hebrew University in the forties dealt with society and aspects of sociology, such as the sociology of culture or religion, and included materials on social dynamics and the relations between the group and institutions.[60] In Palestine, moreover, a new society and a new state were in the making. The foundation on which both would develop were an important consideration to Buber, and he saw himself as a participant in its construction. In articles which he published after 1938, he addressed the issue of fashioning a new society in various ways: questioning values of Zionism, suggesting the need for a transvaluation of values, proposing to construct the new society from the bottom up and not from the top down.

The concern with society and the state was not new. He had voiced views on this subject earlier, and he had included comments in the 'Ascona Talks'. In Jerusalem, however, he expressed it in a new context and there was an urgency to his proposals.[61] The translated chapters refer not only to the horrors of war, they also suggest the means by which such horrors can be avoided. These *TTC* chapters about society and the state were in many ways then, as others had been earlier, in accord with ideas which preoccupied Buber.

Martin Buber's interest in the *TTC* and his early encounter with the *Chuang-tzu* and the *Liao-chai chih-i* did not apparently lead to a sustained exploration of Taoist ideas in these or other Taoist works. It must be assumed, therefore, that Buber selected and appropriated from the *TTC* those ideas that at various times corresponded to his own, retranslating them into his philosophical discourse.

In this essay the process of retranslation together with the impact on his philosophical works was not discussed, leaving this topic to future investigations. The emphasis in this essay has been on Buber's contact with Taoist philosophical concepts, which ideas were important to him and how he understood them. Thus the *TTC*'s struggle with the namelessness of *Tao*, *Tao*'s reversal, or the notions of spontaneity and being and non-being (*yu* 有 and *wu* 無) did not interest Buber as much as did the ideas of oneness, duality, and non-acting. Although Chuang-tzu's mysticism, his rejection of dichotomies, and insistence on oneness with *Tao* attracted Buber probably initially, the *TTC*'s combination of a practical way of acting (or non-acting) combined with a near-mystic understanding of existence was ultimately more in accord with his own ideas. In the *TTC*, especially in the von Strauß translation (I would rather call it a 'mistranslation'), Buber found affirmation for ideas that he had been formulating. These were ideas of personal oneness or completeness, *Tao*, both as transcendent and immanent, and the personal aspect of the divine.

The *Chuang-tzu*'s rejection of political involvement of any kind may have struck Buber as too passive an attitude toward the world's affairs. The *TTC*'s combination of mystical questioning with practical advice on how individuals manage in society and society manages in the political state, no doubt, appealed more to Buber. Thus the 1924 lectures on the *TTC* took up topics concerned with society, the ruler, and government, and his 1928 comments on Richard Wilhelm's lecture were made in reference to practical issues in post-World War I Germany. Although we cannot be certain exactly when he translated the *TTC* chapters which he published in 1942, their contents similarly indicates that Buber then was drawn to the *TTC*'s condemnation of aggression and rule by force. Buber's interest in the philosophical ideas of Taoism may not have been an isolated phenomenon in pre- and post-World War I Germany. Thus this interest is not significant because it is unique. It is unique, however, because he may have been the first among Jewish philosophers who appropriated ideas from Taoism and integrated these into a specifically Jewish philosophical discourse.

NOTES

1. This essay is based in part on my introduction in Martin Buber, Alex Page, trans., *Chinese Tales, Zhuangzi: Sayings and Parables and Chinese Ghost and Love Stories* (New Jersey and London: Humanities Press International, 1991), pp. ix–xxiii. I wish

to thank the Humanities Press for permission to use portions of the introduction. I also wish to thank Professor Steve Kaplan for his constructive comments. This research was partially supported by the Louis Frieberg Research Fund and the Truman Research Institute.

2. Martin Buber, *Reden und Gleichnisse des Tschuang Tse* (Leipzig: Insel, 1910), and *Chinesische Geister- und Liebesgeschichten* (Frankfurt am Main: Rütten und Loening, 1911). Both volumes were republished a number of times (Zürich [Manesse, 1948 and 1951, respectively]; München [Deutscher Taschenbuch Verlag, 1992]), the *Chuang-tzu* in a revised version.

3. Martin Buber, 'Lao Tzu al hashilton' (Lao-tzu on government), *Hapo'el Hatsa'ir* 35, nos 31–2, May 1942, pp. 6–8.

4. See Maurice Friedman, 'Martin Buber and Asia', *Philosophy East and West* 26, 4, 1976, pp. 411–26, who writes that Buber's '... dialogue with Taoism remained of central importance to him throughout his life' (p. 415). See also Hans Kohn, *Martin Buber, sein Werk und seine Zeit, ein Beitrag zur Geistesgeschichte Mitteleuropas. 1880–1930* (Köln: Joseph Melzer, 1961), pp. 59, 67–8, 82–3, 86, 280. I have not seen a recently completed dissertation by Jonathan Herman, 'The Text of *Chuang Tzu* and the Problem of Interpretation: A Critical Study of Martin Buber's Translation and Commentary' (Ph.D. diss., Harvard University, 1992).

5. Thassilo von Scheffer-Berlin, 'Literarische Wanderung', *Königsberger Allgemeine Zeitung*, January 12, 1913. Jewish National and University Library (JNUL), Arc. Ms. Var. 350/13–46. I wish to thank the JNUL's Buber Archive for making this and other materials available to me. I am especially grateful to Mrs Margot Cohn, archivist, for her patient guidance through the archival collection.

6. Erich Haenisch, 'Die Sinologie an der Berliner Friedrich-Wilhelms-Universität in den Jahren 1898–1945.' *Studium Berolinense* edited by Hans Leussink, et al. (Berlin: Walter de Gruyter, 1960), pp. 554–566. I am grateful to Dr. Hartmut Walravens for setting me straight on the differing functions of the Seminar for Oriental Languages and the Sinological Seminar.

7. *Hundertfünfzig Jahre Rütten und Loening 1844–1969, ein Almanach* (Berlin: Rütten und Loening, 1969), p. 58.

8. According to Buber's foreword in *Chinese Tales*, p. 111, Wang introduced him to the *Liao-chai* stories. P'u Sung-ling (1640–1715), an impoverished and unsuccessful scholar, completed the manuscript of his stories around 1679, but it was not printed and published until nearly one hundred years later. The collection of nearly 500 stories was enormously popular not only in the eighteenth century but later as well. See Chun-shu Chang and Hsueh-lun Chang, 'P'u Sung-ling and His "Liao-chai Chih-i" – Literary Imagination and Intellectual Consciousness in Early Ch'ing China', *Renditions* 13, 1980, pp. 60–81.

9. I am indebted to Dr. Hartmut Walravens for most of the information on Wang Ching-t'ao. I also wish to thank Dr Jonathan Herman for bringing to my attention a book by Wang, *Confucius and China, Confucius' Idea of the State and its Relation to the Constitutional Government* (Shanghai: Commercial Press, 1912). The preface is signed 'Nanking Bureau of Foreign Affairs'. The book is obviously the English translation of a German essay, also mentioned by Dr Walravens, which appeared in *Mitteilungen des Seminars für Orientalische Sprachen. Abt. 1: Ostasiatische Studien* 16, 1913, pp. 1–49. *Min-sheng chu-i jen-k'ou wen-t'i* 民生主義人口問題 (The problem of people's livelihood and population; Shanghai, 1927), was probably also authored by Wang.

10. Herbert A. Giles, *Strange Stories from a Chinese Studio* (London: Thomas de la Rue, 1880), 2 vols. A second revised edition appeared in 1909; and Herbert A. Giles, *Chuang Tzu, Mystic, Moralist and Social Reformer* (London: B. Quaritch, 1889).

11. Alfred Frhr. von Mensio in *Allgemeine Zeitung*, München, November 2, 1911. JNUL, Arc. Ms. Var. 350/48, 13: 'Literarische Wanderung'; Hermann Hesse,

'Chinesische Geistergeschichten', *Neue Zürcher Zeitung*, March 25, 1912. JNUL, Arc. Ms. Var. 350/46, 13. Reviews appeared in numerous newspapers, such as the *Frankfurter Zeitung*, *Schlesische Zeitung*, and *Breslauer Zeitung*.

12. The *Lun-yü* was translated by Wilhelm Schott, *Werke des tschinesischen Weisen Kung Fu-dsu und seiner Schüler* (first part: Halle, 1826; second part: Berlin, 1832). Two early translations of the *Shih-ching* were one by Friedrich Rückert, *Schi-king, chinesisches Liederbuch, gesammelt von Konfuzius* (Altona: J. F. Hammerisch, 1833), the other by Victor von Strauß und Torney, *Schi-king. Das kanonische Liederbuch der Chinesen* (Heidelberg: C. Winter, 1880). The latter was in dreadful rhyme.

13. JNUL, Arc. Ms. Var. 350/45–2. I am grateful to Professor Mendes-Flohr for pointing out that the manuscript is most likely a stenographic record of Buber's talks. Even so, it should reflect his ideas quite accurately.

14. Rita van de Sandt, *Martin Bubers bildnerische Tätigkeit zwischen den beiden Weltkriegen* (Stuttgart: Ernst Klett, 1977), pp. 91–4, lists the courses from the summer semester 1924 to the summer semester 1933.

15. Salome Wilhelm, *Richard Wilhelm, der geistige Mittler zwischen China und Europa* (Düsseldorf: Eugen Diederichs, 1956), p. 346. After 1924, Buber, Hesse, and Wilhelm were apparently in close contact.

16. *Ibid.*, pp. 352, 356. See also Hu Sung-p'ing 胡頌平, *Hu Shih chih hsien-sheng nien-p'u ch'ang-pien ch'u-kao* 胡適之先生年譜長編初稿 (Draft chronological biography of Mr Hu Shih) (Taipei: Lien-ching ch'u-pan she, 1984), vol. 2, p. 658. Hu gave a lecture in October 1926.

17. Salome Wilhelm, *Richard Wilhelm*, pp. 330–9.

18. See JNUL, Arc. Ms. Var. 350/902.

19. Salome Wilhelm, *Richard Wilhelm*, p. 363. Wilhelm's three lectures were constructed around the *yin* concept in Chinese culture. His lecture was printed as 'Sitte in China'. *Chinesisch-Deutscher Almanach für das Jahr Gi Si 1929–30*, pp. 27–35. Buber's comments are on pp. 40–3.

20. This according to a communication from Dr H. Walravens, December 21, 1991.

21. I wish to thank the Leo Beck Institute, New York, for making these letters available to me. Dr H. Walravens has compiled a useful bibliography of Tonn's work which he kindly made available to me. According to it, the Taoist text referred to in Buber's letter is probably the translation of *Ch'ang ch'ing-ching ching* 常清靜經, published in German as 'Das Buch von der Ewigen Reinheit und Ruhe,' *Weiße Fahne* 10, December 1929, pp. 212–15. The *Combined Indices to the Authors and Titles of Books in Two Collections of Taoist Literature*, Harvard-Yenching Institute Sinological Index Series, No. 25, p. 51, lists various annotated editions from different periods, generally entitled *T'ai-shang Lao-chün shuo ch'ang ch'ing-ching ching chu* 太上老君說常清靜經註 (Explanations of the Most High Master Lao's sayings on eternal purity and tranquility). The English translation was published in *China Journal* (September 1939), pp. 112–17. On Chinese Jews Tonn published 'Eine Jüdische Inschrift der Synagoge in K'aifeng fu aus dem Jahre 1512,' *Gemeindeblatt der Jüdischen Gemeinde zu Berlin*, 20 [?], 1930, pp. 360–4. Buber expressed an interest in both the translation and in the work on Chinese Jews in two letters to Tonn, dated March 7, 1927, and January 31, 1931, respectively.

22. JNUL, Arc. Ms. Var. 350/B45 and 350/B50b. The notes which Buber used for his lectures are apparently not in the archive.

23. Unfortunately, not all of Tonn's letters which discuss these points are dated, and those which are, omit the year. I assume that they were written in 1950, and I count one from July 5, another from 22 (?), and a third undated. Courtesy of the Leo Beck Institute, New York.

24. The essay appeared in Martin Buber, *Die Rede, die Lehre und das Lied* (2nd ed., Leipzig: Insel, 1920), pp. 35–94; also in *Werke* (München: Kösel, 1962), vol. I,

pp. 1021–51. The English translation, 'The Teaching of the Tao', is in Maurice S. Friedman, ed., *Pointing the Way, Collected Essays by Martin Buber* (New York: Schocken Books, 1974), pp. 31–60.

25. Friedman, *Pointing the Way*, p. ix. 'Buber's Foreword' to the 1957 collection.
26. Buber, *Chinese Tales*, p. 103.
27. The above was summarized from Buber, 'Afterword', *Chinese Tales*, pp. 81–103.
28. *Ibid.*, pp. 97–100.
29. Benjamin I. Schwartz, *The World of Thought in Ancient China* (Cambridge: Harvard University Press, 1985), p. 193.
30. Kohn, *Martin Buber*, pp. 59, 67–8, 82–3, 86, 280.
31. Martin Buber, *Die Geschichten des Rabbi Nachman* (Frankfurt: Fischer Bücherei, 1955), pp. 18–19.
32. Buber, 'Foreword', *Chinese Tales*, pp. 111–13.
33. Kohn, *Martin Buber*, pp. 77, 87, 100.
34. Van de Sandt, *Martin Bubers bildnerische Tätigkeit*, pp. 20–1.
35. The lecture summarized here is reprinted in Martin Buber, *Der Jude und sein Judentum, gesammelte Aufsätze und Reden*, Introduction by Robert Weltsch (Köln: Joseph Melzer, 1963), pp. 46–65. It was probably delivered in 1915, and was first printed in *Der Neue Merkur* 2, no. 3, June 1915, pp. 353–7.
36. *Ibid.*, p. 53.
37. Kohn, *Martin Buber*, p. 263.
38. JNUL, Arc. Ms. Var. 350/45a-b. Undated notes on *Tao*. From the content I surmise that they were made in conjunction with preparing his discussion at the China-Institut.
39. Martin Buber in *Chinesisch-Deutscher Almanach*, pp. 40–3. Typewritten and corrected ms., entitled 'China und Wir', JNUL, Arc. Ms. Var. 350/2-50a. English translation, 'China and Us', in Martin Buber, *A Believing Humanism, Gleanings*. Maurice Friedman, trans. (New York: Simon and Schuster, 1967), pp. 186–90. See also Maurice Friedman, *Martin Buber's Life and Work, The Middle Years 1923–1945* (New York: E. P. Dutton, 1983), vol. 2, p. 88.
40. The Ascona lectures were privately arranged by a lay group interested in Chinese philosophy. The meetings were held August 10–31, 1924. JNUL, Arc. Ms. Var. 350/627.
41. JNUL, Arc. Ms. Var. 350/2-45. 'Besprechungen mit Martin Buber in Ascona'. The religious questions are recorded in the appendix.
42. Adrian Hsia, *Hermann Hesse und China. Darstellungen, Materialien und Interpretationen* (Frankfurt am Main: Suhrkamp, 1974), pp. 99, 270, and Gerhard Adler, ed., *C. G. Jung Letters* (Princeton University Press, 1973), vol. 95, no. 1 in the Bollingen Series. Letter to Max Rychner, February 28, 1932; pp. 88–9.
43. According to Maurice Friedman, *Martin Buber's Life and Work, The Early Years 1878–1923* (New York: E. P. Dutton, 1981), vol. 1, p. 212, Buber 'imported' the idea of *wu-wei* into the second part of *I and Thou*.
44. Van de Sandt, *Martin Bubers bildnerische Tätigkeit*, pp. 24–5, 75–84.
45. Von Strauß (1809–99) was known as a poet and author. Active in politics for the greater part of his life, he withdrew from public affairs in 1866 and devoted himself to writing and study. He apparently had no formal training in Chinese language or Chinese thought. In addition to his translation of the *TTC* and the *Shih-ching*, he also published in 1885 a study entitled *Ancient Chinese Monotheism*.
46. Victor Friedrich von Strauß und Torney, *Lao-Tse's Tao Te King* (Leipzig: Friedrich Fleischer, 1870), pp. xxvii, xliii.
47. *Ibid.*, pp. xxx–xxxi.
48. *Ibid.*, pp. lv, lxiv–lxv.
49. *Ibid.*, pp. xxxv, xl, xliii. Von Strauß seems to echo here Protestant arguments raging at the time about whether Chinese were mono- or polytheists.
50. *Ibid.*, pp. lxxix, lxxx.

51. In a letter to Franz Rosenzweig, dated August 24, 1922, Buber commented on the Chinese 'Gottesverschwiegenheit' and asserted that to him Taoists were not pagan. See Grete Schaeder, ed., *Martin Buber. Briefwechsel aus sieben Jahrzehnten* (Heidelberg: Lambert Schneider, 1973), vol. 2, pp. 119–20.

52. Ho-shang kung is a problematic figure. He may have lived at the end of the Warring States period or in the Earlier Han dynasty. Yen Ling-feng 嚴靈峰, *Chou, Ch'in, Han, Wei chu tzu chih-chien shu-mu* 周秦漢魏諸子知見書目 (Taipei: Cheng-chung shu-chü, 1975), pp. 3–4, assigns his commentary, *Lao-tzu chang-chü* 老子章句, to 195 BC, during Han Wen-ti's 漢文帝 reign. Ho-shang kung's work would, therefore, predate Wang Pi's 王弼 (226–249) commentary. Arianne Rump and Wing-tsit Chan, trans., *Commentary on the Lao Tzu by Wang Pi* (Honolulu: The University Press of Hawaii, 1979), pp. xxvi–xxvii, argue for a post-Wang Pi dating, and assign the commentary to the Wei-Chin period. Von Strauß did not use Wang Pi's commentary.

53. In the following I cite from the 'Ascona Talks', JNUL, Arc. Ms. Var. 350/45 b. The ms. consists of 42 typewritten pages. Pages 1–35 are the notes to the *TTC* chapters; pp. 36–42 are on related topics not specifically concerned with Chinese thought. When referring to the notes to the *TTC*, I give the page references of the ms.

54. He made a similar point, with somewhat different implications, in the appendix (p. 33). Life, it is stated, is God and men acting together. For belief to be real, the reality of the self must be taken for granted.

55. Von Strauß, *Tao Te King*, pp. 61–79.

56. *Ibid.*, pp. 65–6, 68.

57. *Ibid.*, p. 276.

58. Buber, 'Lao Tzu al hashilton'.

59. Using a more classical (and by now rather old-fashioned) Hebrew, Buber's text, in spite of the extensive use of pronouns which are, of course, not in the Chinese text, nonetheless strikes one as remarkably authentic. Buber's seven chapters compare very favorably with those in a recent Hebrew translation by Dan Daor and Yoav Ariel, *Lao Tzu, Sefer hadereh ve'hasegula* ([Tel Aviv:] Universities Publication, 1981).

60. JNUL, Arc. Ms. Var. 350/17a. There are course titles, but no descriptions of courses.

61. Buber, 'Sie und Wir', and 'Hebräischer Humanismus', for example, in Buber, *Der Jude*, pp. 648–54, 732–44.

17

HEIDEGGER'S HIDDEN SOURCES: EAST ASIAN INFLUENCES ON HIS WORK

Reinhard May

In his introduction to Heidegger's Hidden Sources: East Asian Influences on his Work *(1996), Reinhard May admits that his contribution to Heidegger scholarship involves a certain amount of daring, as it engages, from a transcultural perspective, with certain complex information, hardly broached until now, concerning the hidden sources of Heidegger's work. His primary concern throughout, he declares, is not with an interpretation but rather with a presentation and documentation of the central ideas and key terms of Heidegger's thinking in the light of the basic ideas of Daoism and, where appropriate, Zen Buddhism. He begins his investigation, which is based on the hypothesis that Heidegger's work was influenced by East Asian thought to a hitherto unrecognised extent, by comparing Heidegger's 'From a Conversation on Language' (*Unterwegs zur Sprache, *Pfullingen, 1959, pp. 83–155), with a report by the renowned Japanese Germanist, Tezuka Tomio. This comparison reveals several clues regarding the influence exercised by East Asian thought on Heidegger. He then goes on to reveal other instances of East Asian influence on Heidegger, and to show how Heidegger, in indicating his 'new' path of thinking, may have made a pertinent 'confession' of East Asian influence, 'in his own way'. The following are May's conclusions.*

1.1 The foregoing investigation has shown that Heidegger's work was influenced by East Asian sources to a hitherto unrecognized extent. Moreover, it

Reinhard May, *Heidegger's Hidden Sources: East Asian Influences On his Work* (London: Routledge, 1996), chap. 6, pp. 51–7.

seems highly probable that Heidegger, without stating his sources, in a number of cases of central importance appropriated ideas germane to his work from German translations primarily of Daoist classics but presumably of Zen Buddhist texts as well.

Case 1

As the juxtaposition of relevant textual passages has shown Heidegger adopts almost verbatim, in order to articulate the *topos* 'Nothing' in a non-Western way, locutions from Chapter 22 of the *Zhuangzi* in the translation by Richard Wilhelm (*Dschuang Dsï-Chuang Tzu – Das wahre Buch vom südlichen Blütenland*. Translated with commentary by Richard Wilhelm – Jena: 1912, Düsseldorf/Cologne: 1972) – to the effect that the thingness of the thing cannot itself be a thing.

Case 2

The earlier formulation 'The Being of beings "is" not itself a being' (*Sein und Zeit*, 1927. Tübingen: Max Niemeyer, 1967, 6) apparently anticipates the 'thing'-locution in terms of sentence structure and meaning. Drawing on Victor von Strauss' commentary on Chapter 2 of the *Laozi* (*Lao-Tse, Tao Tê King*. Translated With Commentary by Victor von Strauss – Leipzig: 1870, Zürich 1959) – and the corresponding locution in the *Shinjin-mei* in Ōhazama – Heidegger then writes in further clarification of his 'new' thinking: 'Being and Nothing are not given beside one another. Each uses itself on behalf of the other'. And: 'Nothing and Being the Same'

Case 3

With respect to the *topos* 'Nothing', Heidegger obviously formulates the synonymous *topos* 'Emptiness', drawing this time on Chapter 11 of the *Laozi* in Wilhelm's translation (*Laotse: Tao te king. Das Buch des Alten vom Sinn und Leben*. Translated with a commentary by Richard Wilhelm – Jen: 1911, Düsseldorf/Cologne: 1957, 1972), which has the thingly nature of the container consisting in *emptiness*.

Cases 4 and 5

In his pseudo-dialogue 'From a Conversation on Language', Heidegger adopts almost verbatim, but well hidden, two formulations from a text by Oscar Benl on Noh drama (Oscar Benl, 'Seami Motokiyo und der Geist des Nō-Schauspiels: Geheime kunstkritische Schriften aus dem 15. Jahrhundert'. In *Akademie der Wissenschaften und der Literatur, Abhandlungen der Klasse der Literatur*, Jahrgang 1952, no. 5. Wiesbaden: 1953, pp. 103–249). While these two instances do not affect Heidegger's major ideas of East Asian provenance, they nevertheless provide further evidence of the manner in which he integrates foreign ways of thinking into his own texts without indicating their source.

Case 6

Drawing on the idea of *dao* in the sense of both Way and Saying, as expressed by Richard Wilhelm and Martin Buber (Richard Wilhelm, translation of 1911;

Martin Buber, *Tschuang-Tse*, 'Afterword', 92–3, 'Nachwort', 100), Heidegger clearly formulates his correspondence between Way and Saying.

Further cases beyond these can probably be adduced. Another case of striking correspondence suggests that Heidegger conceived his key idea of 'Appropriation' on the model of the concluding trope of Chapter 25 of the *Laozi*.

Taken together, these cases show that Heidegger very probably thought through and deliberately elaborated his path-breaking ideas from as early as the 1920s on, drawing particularly from the above-mentioned texts of Victor von Strauss, Richard Wilhelm, and mainly from Martin Buber's *Tschuang-Tse*, without ever giving the customary indications of the sources of his thinking. His subsequent appropriation of East Asian ways of thinking, effected through encoded presentations, was presumably furthered in no small measure by his conversations with Chinese and Japanese scholars, though obviously unbeknown to those interlocutors. As became known only after his death, Heidegger's collaboration with Paul Hsiao in the summer of 1946 played an important role in this respect. This is also confirmed in the connection with Hsiao's account by the letter of 9 October 1947 in which Heidegger expresses the desire to continue his conversations with him again soon (Graham Parkes, ed., *Heidegger and Asian Thought*, Honolulu: 1987, p. 102).

1.2 The assumption that these correspondences are merely fortuitous can be rejected on the basis of their nature and quantity; they become especially numerous in the texts from the 1950s, following the period during which Heidegger collaborated with Hsiao on translating the *Laozi*. The nature and quantity of the correspondences suggest a deliberate appropriation of East Asian ways of thinking. It is highly improbable that Heidegger, whose interest in East Asian thought is uncontested, who was able to appreciate it, and even admitted being familiar with most of the relevant texts we have mentioned, should have happened to think and write in such a closely parallel manner in the passages adduced above merely by chance. And the same is of course true for numerous other passages in which Heidegger, as we have seen, thinks in a similarly East Asian way.

The assumption of mere coincidence needs to be rejected also on the basis of Heidegger's 'confession'. In an encoded manner, yet unambiguously, he speaks of a 'deeply hidden kinship' between his own and East Asian thinking. In other words, he speaks of a connection based on his adoption of some essential traits of East Asian thinking which, for reasons easy to understand, he declined to reveal.

In contrast, the passage from the '*Der Spiegel* conversation' ('Only God Can Save Us', *Der Spiegel*'s interview with Martin Heidegger, 1966, published 1976, translated by Maria P. Alter and John D. Caputo, in Richard Wolin, ed., *The Heidegger Controversy: A Critical Reader*, Cambridge, MA and London: 1993, pp. 91–116, 113) must be understood as a tactically necessary 'cover-up' manoeuvre that turned out to be necessary for the preservation of his secret.[1] Heidegger's letter to his Japanese colleague Kojima Takehiko, written on 18 August 1963 and published a year before the *Der Spiegel* conversation ('Briefwechsel mit einem japanischen Kollegen', 6, Hartmut Buchner, ed., *Japan und Heidegger*, Sigmaringen: 1989, p. 224), also speaks in favour of this interpretation. There Heidegger indicates quite decisively, if again in an encoded manner, what has determined his path of thinking: 'above all not a reanimation of the beginning of Western philosophy'[2] – even though one is happy to assume the contrary in the West.

2.1 In so far as Heidegger's work has been influenced by East Asian sources, it is not simply a matter of peripheral topics that are thought about merely incidentally. In the case of the *topos* 'Nothing' it is a matter – bearing in mind the locution 'Nothing and Being the Same' – of *the* major idea, the 'only one' the thinker needs (Martin Heidegger, *What Is Called Thinking?* Translated by J. Glenn Gray, New York: Harper and Row, 1968, 50/20); a matter, then, of an idea that is new to Western thinking, and which Heidegger owes to insight into the teachings of *dao* in the *Laozi* and *Zhuangzi*. For Heidegger, 'Nothing' is not merely a nugatory nothing, the nothingness of nihilism: it is rather the 'Nothing of Being [*Seyn*]', *fullness*. He pursues this thought in his texts continually, which are in this context striking for their repetitions and variations of 'the Same'.[3] To effect a complete and conclusive clarification he eventually (in 1969) adds the 'simple' formula: 'Being: Nothing: Same' ('Seminar in Le Thor', 1969, in *Seminare, Gesamtausgabe*, 15, 1986, p. 101). Corresponding Daoist- and Zen Buddhist-tinged paraphrases are to be found in more or less encoded form, throughout the work that has been published so far.

Whereas in the formula 'Being: Nothing: Same' the 'Same' constitutes a conspicuous key word (*What Is Called Thinking?* 50/20) for a better understanding of Heidegger's work in general, one that holds together in a hidden way all the identifications discussed above, thought of as corresponding *silently* with the spirit of the Daoist teachings, the reader must first laboriously explicate the identification of Way and Saying in order to see that here, too, Heidegger's thinking draws significantly from East Asian sources.

2.2.1 The preceding investigation has not only shown *what* Heidegger has appropriated but also *how* he has paraphrased the adopted ways of thinking and integrated them into his texts in such a way that hardly a trace remains of their East Asian sources. We were able to point at the beginning of the investigation to a valuable document that now assumes considerable weight. For it shows quite explicitly how Heidegger paraphrases a German translation of a passage from *Laozi* 15 in such a way that his text eventually becomes so distant from the wording of the translation that the major *topoi* of the Daoist teachings find expression in his adaptation (and diction) as corresponding key terms in his own thinking.

The document is Heidegger's letter to Hsiao of 9 October 1947, which came to light only after forty years through being printed in the volume *Heidegger and Asian Thought*. In this brief letter Heidegger takes Hsiao's translation of a passage from the *Laozi*, which Hsiao had carefully explained to him character by character during their collaboration the previous year, as the basis for two versions of his own. While the first appears to stem from the earlier collaborative translation work, and renders understandable Hsiao's discomfort with such 'transposition',[4] the second has hardly anything to do with Hsiao's translation, which at best stays in the background 'like the wind-borne echo of a distant call' ('Conversation', 37/131). A comparison of the texts easily reveals to the practised interpreter how Heidegger is proceeding here and what his aim is.

The addition of the phrase 'the *dao* of heaven' may be acceptable in the context of a broadly conceived interpretation,[5] but this is not the case with the question preceding it ['Who is able by making tranquil (*stillend*) to bring something in to Being?']. For here Heidegger would appear to go far beyond the original text in alluding with the word *stillend* (*not* moving, in the sense of the resting of any kind of movement) – posited as synonymous with 'Nothing' in the sense of 'Nothing and Being the Same' – to 'Being'.[6] The result is that Nothing brings, through nothinging [*nichtend*], beings ('something') 'into Being' – something that in Daoism only *dao* could do. This, then, explains the answer Heidegger appended (referring to Hsiao's calligraphy) to the question. His first version could now serve well as a basis for the second. This second version represents a creative and eloquent 'recomposition' influenced by the relationships (discussed above) among *wu* (Nothing), *yu* (Being), and *dao* (Way/Saying), in Heideggerian terminology, such that we have before us the key words that Heidegger drew from Daoist teachings as early as the 1920s and 1930s, and which eventually, after the collaborative translation with Hsiao of the chapters in the *Laozi* dealing with *dao*, extensively condition his subsequent thinking – above all during the 1950s.[7]

One can see in the way Heidegger writes the verb 'move' [*be-wegen*] (playing on *dao*, Way [*Weg*], even though the Chinese word for 'move' in the *Laozi* text does not provide any 'etymological' warrant for this) an indication of how the 'multi-layered meaning of the Chinese text' (Paul Shih-yi Hsiao, *Erinnerung an Martin Heidegger*. Edited by Günther Neske, Pfullingen: 1977, p. 127. Hereinafter cited as *EMH*) can be made 'thinkable and clear in a Western language' (even in Heidegger's idiosyncratic diction and interpretation, which go beyond the original). Our previous investigation (in chapter 4, above) attempted to clarify the way this 'moving' [*be-wegen*] flowed into Heidegger's texts on language (with the 'e'-trema in *wëgen* and other combinations).[8]

2.2.2. In this context Heidegger's often repeated associations of thinking [*Denken*] and poetizing [*Dichten*] gain a special meaning, in so far as the great teachers of classical Daoism are poets as well as thinkers, and Zhuangzi, to whom Heidegger owes so much, is the greatest among them. Heidegger may well have taken Zhuangzi as a significant model to measure himself by, and not only Hölderlin, Rilke, George, or Trakl – to name just a few Western figures who have played a similar role for him. Heidegger the poet, as opposed to Heidegger the thinker, would not then be expected to observe the custom of citing the sources underlying the 'beautiful' work, for knowledge of those, as Thomas Mann so aptly remarks, would 'often confuse and shock, thereby annulling the effects of what is excellent'. That would be fine – if only Heidegger did not lay claim to being understood and taken seriously as a thinker! But thinking and poetizing are so closely intertwined in him that one is hardly to be distinguished from the other.[9] This is because *thinking*, as Heidegger proclaims, has to *poetize* in response to the enigma of Being.[10]

Is it, therefore, so astonishing that one has had to admit – with regard to a thinking that issues in enigmas and likes to create an abundance of encoded locutions (in other words, concealed plays on Daoist teachings which have gone unrecognized) – that, as Walter Biemel has said,[11] we have still not managed to achieve a proper dialogue with Heidegger, because the partner has not been there and we have been genuinely taken aback by this thinking?

2.3 This kind of thinking *and* poetizing under East Asian influence has again taken (post-Nietzsche) as its major task the overcoming of metaphysics, the basic trait of which Heidegger sees as 'onto-theo-logic' (*Identity and Difference*. Translated by Ralph Mannheim, New Haven: Yale University Press, 1959, 59/50). Where this thinking has from early on received its ('silent') directive from[12] is now not difficult to surmise.[13] *From ancient Chinese thought* – for metaphysics, so conceived, was never developed there.[14] Being neither indebted to Aristotelian logic[15] nor receptive to an ontology involving a subject-object dichotomy, nor, above all, being conditioned by any theology, ancient Chinese thought was completely remote from the assertion of 'eternal truths', which belong according to Heidegger 'to the residue of Christian theology that has still not been properly eradicated from philosophical problematics' (*Sein und Zeit*, 1927, p. 229). On this issue, what could be closer to the mark than Heidegger's saying that his thinking (under East Asian influence, to be consistent) could be 'theistic' as little as 'atheistic'.[16]

Thus Heidegger, 'as message-bearer' of his message, recommends underway that the lacunae left in the greatness of the Western beginning (see 'Hölderlin's Earth and Heaven' 36) be gradually filled by the teaching of 'the fullness of Nothing'.[17] This, too, could ultimately communicate Heidegger's 'confession' to us.

3 If one agrees with Walter Biemel's assertion that an interpretation must open the text up and be able to show what lies hidden in a thinker's thought and what it is grounded upon,[18] then the present investigation can also be seen as a small contribution to the interpretation of Heidegger. At any rate, the full extent of its consequences for appropriate future interpretations can at this point hardly be gauged.

In order to gain a new perspective from this 'Heidegger case', we in the West will have to devote ourselves to *non-Western* thinking as thoroughly as to that of our own tradition, not least since Heidegger has, in his own special way, demonstrated the necessity of *transcultural* thinking.

Thanks to Goethe's having rendered great service to the cause of world literature, such a field is now, a good hundred-and-fifty years later, firmly established; but 'world philosophy', by contrast, is still a long way off. Nevertheless, Karl Jaspers sees here 'the unavoidable task of the era'.[19] And to this task Martin Heidegger, too, has paid tribute in a unique way.

NOTES

1. Compare the different interpretation of this passage in Cho, *Bewusstsein und Natursein* 16 [who takes Heidegger's assertion of the irrelevance of Zen Buddhism at face value].
2. 'Briefwechsel mit einem japanischen Kollegen', 6 [*Japan und Heidegger*, 224].
3. On Heidegger's view it is precisely this thought that has been misunderstood in the West.
4. Hsiao writes that he was quite ambivalent about resuming the collaboration with Heidegger the following summer. While, on the one hand, 'a *Laozi* by Heidegger would create a great sensation in the world of philosophy. ... On the other hand, I was slightly perturbed during the collaboration by a feeling that perhaps Heidegger's notes could be going beyond what is afforded by a straight translation' (*EMH* 126).
5. This is how Hsiao seems to have understood Heidegger's supplement in connection with his original calligraphy of the verse for Heidegger (see *Heidegger and Asian Thought*, p. 100).
6. Compare the 'Afterword to "What Is Metaphysics?"'; '"Being" (*Austrag*) as the soundless voice, the voice of stillness [*Stimme der Stille*]' (*Gesamtausgabe* 9:306, footnote f). [The note is appended to the word 'soundless' in the context of the possibility of experiencing Being through not shrinking in the face of 'the soundless voice that summons to the terror of the abyss' (*Wegmarken* 102).]
   The Wilhelm translation makes it clear that the answer to the question 'Who?' is 'the accomplished sages of old'.
7. The role the *Laozi* chapter may have played in Heidegger's 'Discussion of *Gelassenheit*' ['Conversation on a Country Path about Thinking'], which was published in 1959 but supposedly written in 1944/5, is shown, for example, by a short passage (*Discourse on Thinking*, 70, *Gesamtausgabe* 13:51) for which Heidegger drew, presumably before his collaboration with Hsiao, from the version of *Laozi* 15 by Wilhelm (*Laotse*, 134) and/or that by von Strauss (*Lao-Tse*, 74, 230f). The later versions in the letter to Hsiao would then be simply the expression of new (and deeper) endeavours at appropriation.
   The Wilhelm translation of the lines from *Laozi* 15 discussed above reads: 'Wer kann (wie sie) das Trübe durch Stille allmählich klären? / Wer kann (wie sie) die Ruhe durch Dauer allmählich erzeugen? (where the *sie* refers to the masters of old.) In *Gelassenheit* the discussion turns at one point to the extent to which 'rest [*Ruhe*] is the seat and rule of all movement [*Bewegung*]' (*Discourse on Thinking*. Translated by John M. Anderson and Edward Robinson, New York: Harper Torchbooks, 1966, p. 67 / 'Zur Erörterung der Gelassenheit', 1944–5, in *Aus der Erfahrung des Denkens, Gesamtausgabe*, 13, 1983, pp. 37–74; *Gesamtausgabe* 13:51)
8. See section 3 of both 'The Nature of Language' and 'The Way to Language'; the coinage *wëgen* occurs in the latter essay (*On the Way to Language*, 129f, *Unterwegs zur Sprache*, 261f).

9. See 'What Are Poets For?', in *Poetry, Language and Thought* 99–100/*Holzwege* 256; 'The Thinker as Poet', in *Poetry, Language and Thought* 12/*Gesamtausgabe* 13:84. Compare also Karl Löwith, *Denker in dürftiger Zeit* (Göttingen 1953, 1965), 11 [where Löwith writes: 'It is for the most part undecidable whether Heidegger poetizes thinkingly or thinks poetically, so much does he poetically condense a thinking that is associatively disintegrated'].

10. 'The Anaximander Fragment', in *Early Greek Thinking* 58/*Holzwege* 343; compare 'Logos', in *Early Greek Thinking* 78/*Vorträge und Aufsätze* 3:25.

11. See Walter Biemel, 'Dichtung und Sprache bei Heidegger', in *Man and World* 2/4 (1969):487–514, 490; also his *Heidegger* (Hamburg 1973), 129.

12. See 'A Letter to a Young Student', in *Poetry, Language and Thought* 185/*Vorträge und Aufätze* 2:58 [where Heidegger remarks that he finds it 'strange' that people should ask 'from where [his] thinking receives its directive [*Weisung*]').

13. It was not from pre-Socratic thought, nor from Western (theo-)mystical thinking, nor from Nietzsche's poetic thinking, nor even from Hölderlin's poetry that Heidegger received the *essential* impetus for his 'new' poetic thinking. One can hardly help but think that the Western thinkers and poets he mentions simply serve to help him further, step by step, his significant [*wegweisend*] work through so-called dialogue with them, without his attempting or sustaining an *authentic* interpretation of them.

14. See Hajime Nakamurs, *Ways of Thinking of Eastern Peoples: India – China – Tibet – Japan* (Honolulu 1964, 1971), 243–6; Joseph Needham, *Science and Civilization in China*, vol. 2: History of Scientific Thought (Cambridge 1956, 1975), 37.

15. Hsiao instructed Heidegger on this point; see *EMH* 128.
    Hsiao writes: 'Lao-tse's conception of *wu*, Nothing, and his aversion to any kind of rationalism corresponded to Heidegger's ideas' (*EMH* 127). He goes on to say that, in response to his own remark to the effect that 'the Chinese of [Laozi's] time were not acquainted with Aristotelian logic', Heidegger 'spontaneously' remarked: 'Thank God the Chinese weren't acquainted with it' (*EMH* 128).

16. 'Letter on Humanism', in *BW* 230/*Wegmarken* 182.

17. The author is here playing on a locution of Heidegger's in 'Hölderlin's Earth and Heaven', which speaks of 'the preserved greatness of [the] beginning' of the European tradition [*dem gesparten Grossen seines Anfangs*], by writing of 'das Aus*gesparte* des *Grossen*' – the gaps, or lacunae, in the greatness.

18. Walter Biemel, *Heidegger*, 129.

19. Hans Saner, *Jaspers* (Reinbek bei Hamburg 1970), 105 (cf. 103–10).

BIBLIOGRAPHY

(The place of publication is London except where otherwise indicated)

Abe, M., 'In Memory of Paul Tillich', *The Eastern Buddhist* (New Series), 1, 2,1966.

Abe, M., *Buddhism and the Interfaith Dialogue* (Macmillan, 1995).

Abegg, L., *The Mind of East-Asia* (Thames & Hudson, 1952).

Abelson, P., 'Schopenhauer and Buddhism', *Philosophy East and West*, 43, 2, 1993.

Ahmad, A., *In Theory: Classes, Nations, Literatures* (Verso, 1992).

Ajaya, S., *Psychotherapy East and West: A Unifying Paradigm* (Honesdale, PA: The Himalayan International Institute, 1983).

Albert, D. H., 'Thoreau's India: The Impact of Reading in a Crisis', *Proceedings of the American Philosophical Society*, 125, 2, 1981.

Allinson, R. E. (ed.), *Understanding the Chinese Mind: The Philosophical Roots* (Oxford University Press, 1989).

Almond, P. C., 'The Mediaeval West and Buddhism', *The Eastern Buddhist* (New Series), 19, 2, 1986.

Almond, P. C., *The British Discovery of Buddhism* (Cambridge University Press, 1988).

Ames, R. (ed.), *Self as Person in Asian Theory and Practice* (Albany, NY: State University of New York Press, 1994).

Amin, S., *Eurocentrism* (New York: Monthly Review Press, 1989).

Angel, L., *Enlightenment East and West* (Albany, NY: State University of New York Press, 1994).

Appleton, W., *A Cycle of Cathay: the Chinese Vogue in England in the Seventeenth and Eighteenth Centuries* (New York: Columbia University Press, 1951).

Arnold, E., *The Light of Asia* (New York: Crowell, 1884).

Bahm, A., *Comparative Philosophy: Western, Indian and Chinese Philosophies Compared* (Albuquerque, NM: World Books, 1977).

Bailey, P., 'Voltaire and Confucius: French Attitudes towards China in the Early Twentieth Century', *History of European Ideas*, 14, 6, 1992.

Baker, F., (ed.), *Europe and its Other* (Colchester: University of Essex Press, 1985).

Barnes, M., *God East and West* (SPCK, 1991).

Barrows, J. H. (ed.), *The World's Parliament of Religions*, 2 vols (Chicago: The Parliament Publishing Co., 1893).

Batchelor, S., *The Awakening of the West: The Encounter of Buddhism and Western Culture* (HarperCollins, 1994).

Baumer, F. L., *Modern European Thought: Continuity and Change in Ideas, 1600–1950* (New York: Macmillan, 1977).

Bearce, G. D., *British Attitudes towards India, 1784–1858* (Oxford University Press, 1961).

Beck, L. A., *The Story of Oriental Philosophy* (New York: Farrar & Rinehart, 1928).

Benoit, H., *The Supreme Doctrine: Psychological Insights in Zen Thought* (Routledge, 1955).

Bernal, M., *Black Athena: The Afroasiatic Roots of Classical Civilization*, vol. 1, (Vintage, 1987).

Bernstein, R. J., *Beyond Objectivism and Relativism: Science, Hermeneutics and Praxis* (Oxford: Blackwell, 1983).

Berry, T., 'The Religious Life of Modern Man', *Philosophy East and West*, 24, 2, 1974.

Betty, L. S., 'The Buddhist-Humean Parallels: Postmortem', *Philosophy East and West*, 21, 2, 1971.

Bilimoria, P., 'Comparative and Asian Philosophy in Australia and New Zealand', *Philosophy East and West*, 45, 2, 1995.

Billington, R., *East of Existentialism: The Tao of the West*, (Unwin Hyman, 1990).

Bishop, P., *Dreams of Power: Tibetan Buddhism and the Western Imagination* (Athlone, 1993).

Bleicher, J., *The Hermeneutic Imagination* (Routledge, 1982).

Bodde, D., *Tolstoy and China* (Princeton, NJ: Princeton University Press, 1950).

Bodde, D., *Chinese Thought, Science, and Society* (Honolulu: University Press of Hawai'i, 1991).

Bohm, D., *Wholeness and the Implicate Order* (Routledge & Kegan Paul, 1981).

Bookchin, M., *Re-enchanting Humanity* (Cassell, 1995).

Boorstin, D. J., *The Discoverers* (Dent, 1983).

Boss, M., *A Psychiatrist Discovers India* (Wolf, 1965).

Boucher, S., *Turning the Wheel: American Women Creating the New Buddhism* (Boston, MA: Beacon, 1988).

Bouwsma, W. J., *Concordia Mundi* (Cambridge, MA: Harvard University Press, 1957).

Brandon, D., *Zen in the Art of Helping* (Routledge & Kegan Paul, 1976).

Braybrooke, M., *Pilgrimage of Hope: One Hundred Years of Global Interfaith Dialogue* (SCM, 1992).

Breckenridge, C. and P. van der Veer (eds), *Orientalism and the Postcolonial Predicament* (Philadelphia, PA: University of Philadelphia Press, 1993).

Breckenridge, C. and P. van der Veer, (eds), *A Wider Vision: A History of the World Congress of Faiths* (Oxford: Oneworld, 1996).

Brobjer, T. H., 'The Absence of Political Ideals in Nietzsche's Writings: The Case of the Laws of Manu and the Associated Caste-Society', *Nietzsche-Studien*, 17, 1998.

Brockington, J., *Hinduism and Christianity* (Macmillan, 1992).

Brunton, P., *In Search of Secret India* (York Beach: Weiser, 1970).

Bunsen, E. de, *The Angel-Messiah of Buddhists, Essenes, and Christians* (Longmans, 1880).

Burn, E. A., 'What can Western Philosophy Learn from India?', *Philosophy East and West*, 3, 2, 1955.

Burnet, J., *Early Greek Philosophy* (Black, 1908).

Burton, N., P. Hart and J. Laughlin (eds), *The Asian Journal of Thomas Merton* (Sheldon, 1974).

Callicott, J. B. and R. T. Ames (eds), *Nature in Asian Thought: Essays in Environmental Philosophy* (New York: State University of New York Press, 1989).

Campbell, B. E., *Ancient Wisdom Revived: A History of the Theosophical Movement* (Berkeley, CA: University of California Press, 1980).

Campbell, J., *Oriental Mythology* (Souvenir, 1973).

Capra, F., *The Tao of Physics* (Fontana, 1976).

Capra, F., *The Turning Point* (Wildwood, 1982).

Caputo, J., *The Mystical Elements in Heidegger's Thought* (New York: Fordham University Press, 1986).

Caputo, J., *Radical Hermeneutics: Repetition, Deconstruction, and the Hermeneutical Project* (Bloomington, IN: Indiana University Press, 1987).

Carpenter, F. I., *Emerson and Asia* (Cambridge, MA: Harvard University Press, 1930).

Carus, P., *Buddhism and its Christian Critics* (Chicago: Open Court, 1897).

Carus, P. (ed.), *The Gospel of Buddha* (Oxford: One World, 1994).

Casillo, R., *The Genealogy of Demons: Anti-Semitism, Fascism, and the Myth of Ezra Pound* (Evanston, IL: Northwestern University Press, 1988).

Chakov, B. L., *Aldous Huxley and Eastern Wisdom* (Atlantic Highlands, NJ: Humanities Press, 1981).

Chaudhuri, H. and F. Spiegelberg, *The Integral Philosophy of Sri Aurobindo: A Commemorative Symposium* (Allen & Unwin, 1960).

Chaudhuri, N. C., *Scholar Extraordinary: the Life of Professor the Rt. Hon. Friedrich Max Muller, PC* (Chatto & Windus, 1974).

Ching, J., *Confucianism and Christianity: A Comparative Study* (Tokyo: Kodansha, 1977).

Ching, J. and W. Oxtoby (eds), *Discovering China: European Interpretations in the Enlightenment* (Rochester, MA: University of Rochester Press, 1992).

Chishom, L. W., *Fenellosa: The Far East and American Culture* (New Haven, CT: Yale University Press, 1963).

Christy, A., *The Orient in American Transcendentalism* (New York: Columbia University Press, 1932).

Cipolla, C. M., *Guns and Sails in the Early Phase of European Expansion, 1400–1700* (Collins, 1965).

Clarke, J. F., *Ten Great Religions* (Boston, MA: Osgood, 1871).

Clarke, J. J., *Jung and Eastern Thought: A Dialogue with the Orient* (Routledge, 1994).

Clarke, J. J., *Oriental Enlightenment* (Routledge, 1997).

Clarke, J. J., *The Tao of the West* (Routledge, 2000).

Claxton, G. (ed.), *Beyond Therapy: The Impact of Eastern Religions on Psychological Theory and Practice* (Wisdom, 1986).

Claxton, G., *Noises from the Darkroom: The Science and Mystery of the Mind* (Harper Collins, 1994).

Cleary (trans. and ed.), *The Secret of the Golden Flower* (San Francisco, CA: Harper & Row, 1991).

Clifford, J., *The Predicament of Culture: Twentieth-Century Ethnography, Literature, and Art* (Cambridge, MA: Harvard University Press, 1988).

Clifton, R. K. and M. G. Regher, 'Capra on Eastern Mysticism and Modern Physics: A Critique', *Science and Christian Belief*, 1, 1, 1989.

Clooney, F. X., *Theology after Vedanta: An Experiment in Comparative Theology* (Albany, NY: State University of New York Press, 1993).

Cobb, J. B., 'Buddhism and Christianity as Complementary', *Eastern Buddhist* (New Series), 13, 2, 1980.

Cobb, J. B., *Beyond Dialogue: Towards a Mutual Transformation of Christianity and Buddhism* (Philadelphia, PA: Fortress, 1982).

Cobb, J. B. and C. Ives (eds), *The Emptying God: A Buddhist-Jewish-Christian Conversation* (Maryknoll: Orbis, 1971).

Collins, S., *Selfless Persons: Imagery and Thought in Theravada Buddhism* (Cambridge University Press, 1982).

Collis, M., *The Great Within* (Faber & Faber, 1941).

Conze, E., 'Buddhist Philosophy and its European Parallels', *Philosophy East and West*, 13, 1 and 2, 1963.

Conze, E., *Thirty Years of Buddhist Studies* (Oxford: Cassirer, 1967).

Conze, E., *Buddhism: its Essence and Development* (New York: Harper & Row, 1975).

Cook, D. J. and H. Rosemont, 'The Pre-Established Harmony Between Leibniz and Chinese Thought', *Journal of the History of Ideas*, 42, 2, 1981.

Cooper, D., *World Philosophers: An Historical Introduction* (Oxford: Blackwell, 1996).

Cooper, J. C., *Taoism: the Way of the Mystic* (Mandala, 1990).

Coward, H., *Jung and Eastern Thought* (Albany, NY: State University of New York Press, 1985).

Coward, H., *Derrida and Indian Philosophy* (Albany, NY: State University of New York Press, 1990).

Coward, H., 'Taoism and Jung: Synchronicity and the Self', *Philosophy East and West*, 46, 4, 1996.

Cox, H., *Turning East: The Promise and the Peril of the New Orientalism* (New York: Simon & Schuster, 1977).

Critchley S., 'Black Socrates? Questioning the Philosophical Tradition', *Radical Philosophy*, 69, 1995.

Crook, J. and D. Fontana (eds), *Space in Mind: East–West Psychology and Contemporary Buddhism* (Shaftesbury: Element, 1990).

Cushing, J. N., *Christ and Buddha* (Philadelphia, PA: American Buddhist Publications, 1907).

Dallmayr, F., *Beyond Orientalism: Essays on Cross-Cultural Encounter* (Albany, NY: State University of New York Press, 1996).

Danielou, A. and K. F. Hurry, *Shiva and Dionysus, the Religion of Nature and Eros* (New York: Inner Traditions International, 1979).

Danto, A., *Mysticism and Morality: Oriental Thought and Moral Philosophy* (Harmondsworth: Penguin, 1976).

Dasgupta, S., *History of Indian Philosophy*, 5 vols (Cambridge University Press, 1921–55).

Davids, C. A. F. Rhys, *Buddhism: Its History and Literature* (New York: Putnam, 1896).

Davids, C. A. F. Rhys, *Buddhist Psychology: An Inquiry into the Analysis and Theory of Mind in Pali Literature* (Bell, 1914).

Davids, M., *A Scientist Looks at Buddism* (Sussex: Book Guild, 1990).

Davis, C., *Christ and the World Religions,* (New York: Herder & Herder, 1971).

Dawson, R., *The Legacy of China* (Oxford: Clarendon Press, 1964).

Dawson, R., *The Chinese Chameleon: An Analysis of European Conceptions of Chinese Civilization* (Oxford University Press, 1967).

D'Costa, G., *Theology and Religious Pluralism: The Challenge of Other Religions* (Oxford: Blackwell, 1986).

Déchenet, J-M., *Christian Yoga* (Tunbridge Wells: Search Press, 1960).

Deussen, P., *Allgemeine Geschichte der Philosophie*, 7 vols (Leipzig: Brockhaus, 1894–1917).

Deutsch, E., *Advaita Vedanta: A Philosophical Reconstruction* (Honolulu: East-West Center Press, 1968).

Deutsch, E.(ed.), *Culture and Modernity: East–West Philosophic Perspectives* (Honolulu: University Press of Hawai'i, 1991).

Dickinson, G. Lowes, *An Essay on the Civilizations of India, China and Japan* (Dent, 1914).

Dilworth, D. A., *Philosophy in World Perspective: A Comparative Hermeneutic of Major Theories* (New Haven, CT: Yale University Press, 1989).

Dirks, N. (ed.), *Colonialism and Culture* (Ann Arbor, MI: University of Michigan Press, 1992).

Drew, J., *India and the Romantic Imagination* (Oxford University Press, 1987).

Droit, R-P., *L'oubli de l'Inde: une amnésie philosophique* (Paris: Presses Universitaires de France,1989).

Dumoulin, H., *History of Zen Buddhism* (Faber & Faber, 1963).

Dumoulin, H., *Christianity Meets Buddhism* (La Salle, IL: Open Court, 1974).

Dumoulin, H., *Buddhism in the Modern World* (Collier, 1976).

Dumoulin, H., 'Buddhism and Nineteenth-Century German Philosophy', *Journal of the History of Ideas*, 42, 3, 1981.

Dumoulin, H., *Zen Buddhism in History*, 2 vols, (New York: Macmillan, 1990).

Dunne, G. H., *Generation of Giants: The Story of the Jesuits in China* (Burns & Oates, 1962).

Duyvendak, J. J., *China's Discovery of Africa* (Probsthain, 1949).

Eaton, G., *The Richest Vein: Eastern Tradition and Modern Thought* (Faber & Faber, 1949).

Eber, I., 'Martin Buber and Taoism', *Monumenta Serica*, 42, 1994.

Edkins, J., *Religion in China* (Kegan Paul, 1893).

Edmunds, A. J., *Buddhist and Christian Gospels* (Philadelphia, PA: Innes, 1908).

Edwardes, M., *East–West Passage: The Travel of Ideas, Arts and Inventions between Asia and the Western World* (Cassell, 1971).

Eliade, M., *Myths, Dreams and Mysteries* (New York: Harper & Row, 1960).

Emerson, R. W., *Essays* (Dent, 1978).

Eppsteiner, F. (ed.), *The Path of Compassion: Writings on Socially Engaged Buddhism* (Berkeley, CA: Parallax, 1985).

Epstein, M., *Thoughts Without a Thinker: Psychotherapy from a Buddhist Perspective* (Duckworth, 1996).

Evans-Wentz, W. Y. (trans. and ed.), *The Tibetan Book of the Dead* (Oxford University Press, 1960).

Fader, L., 'Arthur Koestler's Critique of D. T. Suzuki's Criticism of Zen', *The Eastern Buddhist* (New Series), 13, 2, 1980.

Faivre, A., *Access to Western Esotericism* (Albany, NY: State University of New York Press, 1994).

Farquar, J., *The Crown of Hinduism* (Oxford University Press, 1930).

Faure, B., *The Rhetoric of Immediacy: A Cultural Critique of Chan/Zen Buddhism*, (Princeton, NJ: Princeton University Press, 1991).

Faure, B., *Chan Insights and Oversights: An Epistemological Critique of the Chan Tradition* (Princeton, NJ: Princeton University Press, 1993).

Fields, K. *How the Swans Came to the Lake: A Narrative History of Buddhism in America* (Boston, MA: Shambhala, 1986).

Figueira, D. M., *Translating the Orient: The Reception of Sakuntala in Nineteenth-Century Europe* (Albany, NY: State University of New York Press, 1991).

Figueira, D. M., *The Exotic: A Decadent Quest* (Albany, NY: State University of New York Press, 1994).

Fingarette, H., *Confucius: The Secular as Sacred* (New York: Harper & Row, 1972).

Flew, A. G. N., *An Introduction to Western Philosophy: Ideas and Arguments from Plato to Sartre* (Thames & Hudson, 1971).

Foster, L. and P. Herzog (eds), *Defending Diversity: Contemporary Philosophical Perspectives on Pluralism and Multiculturalism* (Amherst, MA: University of Massachusetts Press, 1994).

Foucault, M., *Discipline and Punish: the Birth of the Prison* (Tavistock, 1977).

Franke, W., *China and the West* (Oxford: Blackwell, 1967).

Frazier, A. M., 'A European Buddhism', *Philosophy East and West*, 15, 2, 1975.

Fredericks, J., 'Cosmology and Metanoia: A Buddhist Path to Process Thought', *The Eastern Buddhist* (New Series), 22, 1, 1989.

Friedenthal, R., *Goethe: His Life and Times* (Weidenfeld & Nicolson, 1965).

Friedman, L., *Meetings with Remarkable Women: Buddhist Teachers in America* (Boston, MA: Shambhala, 1987).

Friedman, M., 'Martin Buber and Asia', *Philosophy East and West*, 26, 4, 1976.

Fromm, E., *Psychoanalysis and Zen Buddhism* (Mandala, 1986).

Fung Yu-Lan, *A Short History of Chinese Philosophy*, ed. Dirk Bodde (New York: The Free Press, 1996).

Gadamer, H. G., *Truth and Method* (Sheed & Ward, 1975).

Gangadean, A. K., *Meditative Reason: Towards a Universal Grammar* (New York: Lang, 1993).

Garbe, R., *India and Christendom* (La Salle, IL: Open Court, 1959).

Garet, A. E., 'Understanding Oriental Cultures', *Philosophy East and West*, 45, 3, 1995.

Garratt, G. T. (ed.), *The Legacy of India* (Oxford: Clarendon, 1937).

Gellner, E., *Postmodernism, Reason, and Religion* (Routledge, 1992).

Gernet, J., *China and the Christian Impact: A Conflict of Cultures* (Cambridge University Press, 1987).

Gerstering, J., *German Pessimism and Indian Philosophy: A Hermeneutic Reading* (Delhi: Ajanta, 1986).

Goddard, D. (ed.), *A Buddhist Bible* (Boston, MA: Beacon Press, 1994).

Godwin, J., *The Theosophical Enlightenment* (Albany, NY: State University of New York Press, 1994).

Godwin, J., with P. Cash and T. Smith (eds), *Paul Brunton: Essential Readings* (Wellingborough: Crucible, 1990).

Goleman, D., *The Meditative Mind* (Wellingborough: Crucible, 1989).

Goleman, D. and R. A. F. Thurman (eds), *Mind Science: An East–West Dialogue* (Boston, MA: Wisdom, 1991).

Gombrich, R., *Theravāda Buddhism: A Social History from Ancient Benares to Modern Colombo* (Routledge, 1988).

Goodrick-Clarke, N., *The Occult Roots of Nazism. Secret Aryan Cults and their Influence on Nazi Ideology* (Tauris, 1992).

Goody, J., *The East in the West* (Cambridge University Press, 1996).

Graham, A. C., *Disputers of the Tao: Philosophical Argument in Ancient China* (La Salle, IL: Open Court, 1989).

Granet, M., *La pensée chinoise* (Paris: Albin Michel, 1934).

Gray, J., *Enlightenment's Wake: Politics and Culture at the Close of the Modern Age* (Routledge, 1995).

Greenberger, A. J., *The British Image of India: a Study in the Literature of Imperialism* (Oxford University Press, 1969).

Griffiths, B., *The Marriage of East and West* (Collins, 1982).

Griffiths, B., *A New Vision of Reality: Western Science, Eastern Mysticism and Christian Faith* (Collins, 1989).

Griffiths, P., *On Being Mindless: Buddhist Meditation and the Mind-Body Problem* (La Salle, IL: Open Court, 1986).

Gross, R. M., 'Buddhism and Feminism: Towards their Mutual Transformation', *The Eastern Buddhist* (New Series), 19, 1 and 19, 2, 1986.

Gross, R. M., *Buddhism after Patriarchy: A Feminist History, Analysis, and Reconstruction of Buddhism* (Albany, NY: State University of New York Press, 1993).

Gruber, E. and H. Kersten, *The Original Jesus: The Buddhist Sources of Christianity* (Shaftesbury: Element, 1995).

Gudmunsen, C., *Wittgenstein and Buddhism* (Macmillan, 1977).

Guénon, R., *East and West* (Luzac, 1941).

Guénon, R., *Introduction to the Study of Hindu Doctrines* (Luzac, 1945).

Guenther, H., *Buddhism in Western Perspective* (Berkeley, CA: Dharma Publishing, 1989).

Guha, R. and G. Chakravorty (eds), *Selected Subaltern Studies* (New York: Oxford University Press, 1988).

Gulick, S. L., *The East and the West: A Study of their Psychic and Cultural Characteristics* (Rutland: Tuttle, 1963).

Guthrie, W. K. C., *A History of Greek Philosophy*, vol. 2 (Cambridge University Press, 1971).

Guy, B., *The French Image of China Before and After Voltaire* (Geneva: Institut et Musée Voltaire, 1963).

Haas, W. S., *The Destiny of Mind* (Faber & Faber, 1956).

Habermas, J., *The Philosophical Discourse of Modernity* (Oxford University Press, 1987).

Halbfass, W., *India and Europe: An Essay in Understanding* (Albany, NY: State University of New York Press, 1988).

Hall, D. L. and R. T. Ames, *Thinking Through Confucius* (Albany, NY: State University of New York Press, 1987).

Hardy, R. S., *A Manual of Buddhism, in its Modern Development* (Partridge & Oakley, 1853).

Harris, R. B. (ed.), *Neoplatonism and Indian Thought* (Norfolk: International Society for Neoplatonic Studies, 1982).

Hartshorne, C., *Creative Synthesis and Philosophic Method* (La Salle, IL: Open Court, 1970).

Harvey, D., *The Condition of Postmodernity: An Inquiry into the Conditions of Cultural Change* (Oxford: Blackwell, 1990).

Hayward, J. W., *Shifting Worlds, Changing Minds: Where the Sciences and Buddhism Meet* (Boston, MA: Shambhala, 1987).

Hazard, P., *The European Mind, 1680–1715* (Hollis & Carter, 1953).

Hegel, G. W. F., *The Philosophy of History* (New York: Dover, 1953).

Heidegger, M., *On the Way to Language* (New York: Harper & Row, 1971).

Heimann, B., *Indian and Western Philosophy: A Study in Contrasts* (Allen & Unwin, 1937).

Heine, S., *Existential and Ontological Dimensions of Time: Heidegger and Dogen* (Albany, NY: State University of New York Press, 1985).

Heisenberg, W., *Physics and Philosophy: The Revolution in Modern Science* (Allen & Unwin, 1959).

Henderson, H., *Catalyst for Controversy: Paul Carus of Open Court* (Chicago: University of Illinois Press, 1993).

Hermann, J. R., *I and Tao: Martin Buber's Encounter with Chuang Tzu* (Albany, NY: State University of New York Press, 1996).

Hick, J., *God and the Universe of Faiths* (Macmillan, 1973).

Hick, J., *Truth and Dialogue in World Religions* (Philadelphia, PA: Westminster, 1974).

Hick, J., *God has Many Names* (Philadelphia, PA: Westminster, 1982).

Hick, J., *The Metaphor of God Incarnate: Christology in a Pluralistic Age* (SCM, 1993).

Hick, J. and P. Knitter, (eds), *The Myth of Christian Uniqueness* (Maryknoll: Orbit, 1987).

Hillman, J., *Revisioning Psychology* (New York: Harper & Row, 1975).

Hocking, W. E., *The Coming World Civilization* (Allen & Unwin, 1956).

Hodgson, M. G., *Rethinking World History*, Edmund Burke III (ed.), (Cambridge University Press, 1993).

Hoffman, F. J., *Rationality and Mind in Early Buddhism* (Delhi: Motilal Banarsidass, 1987).

Hoffman, Y., *The Idea of Self East and West: A Comparison between Buddhist Philosophy and the Philosophy of David Hume* (Calcutta: Firma, 1980).

Honour, H., *Chinoiserie: the Vision of Cathay* (Murray, 1961).

Hopkins, J., *Meditation on Emptiness* (Wisdom, 1983).

Hourani, A., *Islam in European Thought* (Cambridge University Press, 1991).

Huff, T., *The Rise of Modern Science: Islam, China, and the West* (Cambridge University Press, 1993).

Hulin, M., *Hegel et l'Orient* (Paris: Vrin, 1979).

Hume, D., *Essays Moral, Political, and Literary* (Murray, 1898).

Humphreys, C., *Buddhism* (Harmondsworth: Penguin, 1951).

Huntington, C. W. with Wanchen, G. N., *The Emptiness of Emptiness: An Introduction to Early Mādhyamaka* (Honolulu: University Press of Hawai'i, 1989).

Huntington, S., 'The Clash of Civilizations', *Foreign Affairs*, 72, 3, 1993.

Husserl, E., *The Crisis of European Sciences and Transcendental Phenomenology* (Evanston, IL: Northwestern University Press, 1970).

Huxley, A., *The Perennial Philosophy* (Fontana, 1958).

Inada, K. K., 'Northropian Categories of Experience Revisited', *Journal of Chinese Philosophy*, 19, 1, 1992.

Inada, K. K., and N. P. Jacobson (eds), *Buddhism and American Thinkers* (Albany, NY: State University of New York Press, 1984).

Inden, R., *Imagining India* (Oxford: Blackwell, 1990).

Ingram, P. O., *A Modern Buddhist-Christian Dialogue: Two Universalistic Religions in Transformation* (Queenston: Mellon, 1995).

Ingram, P. O. and F. J. Streng (eds), *Buddhist–Christian Dialogue: Mutual Renewal and Transformation* (Honolulu: University Press of Hawai'i, 1986).

Isaacs, H., *Images of Asia: American Views of China and India* (New York: Random House, 1972).

Isherwood, C. (ed.), *Vedanta for the Western World* (Hollywood, CA: Marcel Rodd, 1945).

Ives, C., *Zen Awakening and Society* (Macmillan, 1992).

Iyer, R. (ed.), *The Glass Curtain Between Asia and Europe: A Symposium on the Historical Encounters and Changing Attitudes of the Peoples of East and West* (Oxford University Press, 1965).

Jackson, C. T., 'The Meeting of East and West: The Case of Paul Carus', *Journal of the History of Ideas*, 29, 1, 1968.

Jackson, C. T., 'Oriental Ideas in American Thought', *Dictionary of the History of Ideas*, vol. 3 (New York: Charles Scribner's Sons, 1973).

Jackson, C. T., *Oriental Religions and American Thought* (Westport, CT: Greenwood, 1981).

Jackson, C. T., *Vedānta for the West* (Bloomington, IN: Indiana University Press, 1994).

Jacobson, N. P., 'The Possibility of Oriental Influence in Hume's Philosophy', *Philosophy East and West*, 19, 1, 1969.

Jacobson, N. P., *Understanding Buddhism* (Carbondale and Edwardsville, IL.: Southern Illinois University Press, 1981).

Jacobson, N. P., *Buddhism and the Contemporary World: Change and Self-Correction*, (Carbondale and Edwardsville, IL: Southern Illinois University Press, 1983).

James, W., *The Varieties of Religious Experience: A Study in Human Nature* (Longmans Green, 1902).

Janaway, C., *The Cambridge Companion to Schopenhauer* (Cambridge University Press, 1999).

Jaspers, K., *The Origin and Goal of History* (New Haven, CT: Yale University Press, 1953).

Jaspers, K., *The Great Philosophers*, 2 vols (Rupert Hart-Davis, 1962).

Jenner, W. J., *The Tyranny of History: The Roots of China's Crisis* (Harmondsworth: Penguin, 1992).

Jennings, H., *The Indian Religions* (Newby, 1858).

Joad, C. E. M., *Counter-Attack from the East* (George Allen & Unwin, 1933).

Johanns, P., *Vers le Christ par le Vedānta*, 2 vols (Louvain: Vallabha, 1932–3).

Johansson, R. E. A., *The Psychology of Nirvana* (Allen & Unwin, 1969).

Johnson, L. E., *A Morally Deep World: An Essay on Moral Significance and Environmental Ethics* (Cambridge University Press, 1991).

Johnson, S., *Oriental Religions and Their Relation to Universal Religion*, vol. 1 (Boston, MA: Osgood, 1873).

Johnston, W., *Christian Zen: A Way of Meditation* (San Francisco, CA: Harper & Row, 1971).

Johnston, W., *The Mirror Mind: Zen–Christian Dialogue* (New York: Fordham University Press, 1981).

Jones, K., *The Social Face of Buddhism: An Approach to Political and Social Activism* (Wisdom, 1989).

Jones, K., *Beyond Optimism: A Buddhist Political Ecology* (Carpenter, 1993).

Jones, R. E., *Ancients and Moderns* (Berkeley, CA: University of California Press, 1965).

Jones, R. H., 'Jung and Eastern Religious Traditions', *Religion*, 9, 2, 1979.

Jones, R. H., 'Against Needham on Taoism', *Journal of Chinese Philosophy*, 8, 2, 1981.

Jones, R. H., *Science and Mysticism: A Comparative Study of Western Natural Science, Theravāda Buddhism, and Advaita Vedānta* (Cranbury, NJ: Associated University Presses, 1986).

Jong, J. W. de, 'A Brief History of Buddhist Studies in Europe and America', *The Eastern Buddhist*, 7, 1 and 7, 2, 1974.

Jung, C. G., *The Archetypes and the Collective Unconscious, Collected Works*, vol. 9i, (Routledge & Kegan Paul, 1959).

Jung, C. G., *Modern Man in Search of a Soul* (Routledge & Kegan Paul, 1961).

Jung, C. G., *The Symbolic Life: Miscellaneous Writings, Collected Works*, vol. 18 (Routledge and Kegan Paul, 1977).

Jung, C. G., *Psychology and the East* (Routledge & Kegan Paul, 1978).

Jung, C. G., *Memories, Dreams, Reflections* (Fontana, 1983).

Jung, C. G., *Synchronicity: An Acausal Connecting Principle* (Routledge & Kegan Paul, 1985).

Kabbani, R., *Europe's Myth of Orient: Devise and Rule* (Macmillan, 1986).

Kalupahana, D. J., *Nāgārjuna: The Philosophy of the Middle Way* (Albany, NY: State University of New York Press, 1986).

Kalupahana, D. J., *The Principles of Buddhist Psychology* (Albany, NY: State University of New York Press, 1987).

Kasulis, T. P., 'The Kyoto School and the West: Review and Evaluation', *The Eastern Buddhist* (New Series), 15, 2, 1982.

Kasulis, T. P. (ed.) *Self as Body in Asian Theory and Practice* (Albany, NY: State University of New York Press, 1993).

Katz, N. (ed.), *Buddhist and Western Philosophy* (New Delhi: Sterling, 1981).

Katz, S. T. (ed.), *Mysticism and Philosophical Analysis* (New York: Oxford University Press, 1978).

Kellogg, S. H., *The Light of Asia and the Light of the World* (Macmillan, 1885).

Keown, D., *Buddhism and Bioethics* (Macmillan, 1995).

Kerouac, J., *The Dharma Bums* (New York: Viking, 1959).

Kiernan, V. G., *The Lords of Human Kind: European Attitudes towards the Outside World in the Imperial Age* (Harmondsworth: Penguin, 1972).

King, R., *Orientalism and Religion* (Routledge, 1999).

King, U., *Towards a New Mysticism: Teilhard de Chardin and Eastern Religions* (Collins, 1980).

King, U., *The Spirit of One Earth: Reflections on Teilhard de Chardin and Global Spirituality* (New York: Paragon, 1989).

King, W. L., *Buddhism and Christianity: Some Bridges of Understanding* (Allen & Unwin, 1963).

King, W. L., 'Is there a Buddhist Ethic for the Modern World?', *The Eastern Buddhist* (New Series), 25, 2, 1992.

King, W. L., 'Engaged Buddhism: Past, Present, Future', *The Eastern Buddhist* (New Series), 27, 2, 1994.

Kitagawa, J. M., *The Quest for Human Unity* (Philadelphia, PA: Fortress, 1990).

Kjellberg, P. and P. J. lvanhoe (eds), *Essays on Skepticism, Relativism, and Ethics in the Zhuangzi* (Albany, NY: State University of New York Press, 1996).

Knitter, P., *No Other Name: A Critical Survey of Christian Attitudes toward the World Religions* (SCM, 1985).

Koestler, A., *The Lotus and the Robot* (Hutchinson, 1960).

Kögler, H. H., *The Power of Dialogue: Critical Hermeneutics after Gadamer and Foucault* (Cambridge, MA: MIT Press, 1986).

Kraemer, H., *World Cultures and World Religions: the Coming Dialogue* (Lutterworth, 1960)

Kraft, K. (ed.), *Inner Peace, World Peace: Essays in Buddhism and Non-Violence* (Albany, NY: State University of New York Press, 1992).

Kung, H. (ed.), *Christianity, and the World Religions: Paths of Dialogue with Islam, Hinduism and Buddhism* (Collins, 1987).

Kung, H. and J. Ching, *Christianity and Chinese Religions* (New York: Doubleday, 1987)

Kung, H. and K.-J. Kuschel (eds), *A Global Ethic: The Declaration of the Parliament of the World's Religions* (SCM, 1993).

Kung, H. and J. Moltmann (eds), *Christianity, Among World Religions* (Edinburgh: T. & T. Clark, 1986).

Lach, D. F., 'The Sinophilism of Christian Wolff', *Journal of the History of Ideas*, 14, 4, 1953.

Lach, D. F., *Preface to Leibniz' Novissima Sinica* (Honolulu: University Press of Hawai'i, 1957).

Lach, D. F., *Asia in the Making of Europe* (Chicago: University of Chicago Press, 1970).

Lach, D. F., *Asia in the Making of Europe*, vol. 2, bk 2 (Chicago: University of Chicago Press, 1977).

Lai, K. L., 'Confucian Moral Thinking', *Philosophy East and West*, 45, 2, 1995.

Lancaster, C., *The Incredible World's Parliament of Religions* (Fontwell: Centaur, 1987).

Larson, G. J. and E. Deutsch (eds), *Interpreting Across Boundaries: New Essays in Comparative Philosophy* (Princeton, NJ: Princeton University Press, 1988).

Leask, N., *British Romantic Writers and the East: Anxieties of Empire* (Cambridge University Press, 1992).

Le Bris, M., *Romantics and Romanticism* (Geneva: Skira, 1981).

Lee, P. K. (ed.), *Confucian-Christian Encounters in Historical and Contemporary Perspective* (New York: Mellen, 1991).

Leibniz, G. W., *Writings on China*, introduction and translation by D. J. Cook and H. Rosemont (eds), (La Salle, IL: Open Court, 1994).

Leites, E., 'Confucianism in Eighteenth-Century England: Natural Morality and Social Reform', *Philosophy East and West*, 18, 2, 1968.

Levenson, J. R. (ed.), *European Expansion and the Counter-Example of Asia* (Englewood Cliffs, NJ: Prentice-Hall, 1967).

Levine, M. M., 'The Use and Abuse of *Black Athena*', *The American Historical Review*, 97, 2, 1992.

Levine, M. P., *Pantheism: A Non-Theistic Concept of Deity* (Routledge, 1994).

Lewis, B., 'The Question of Orientalism', in B. Lewis, *Islam and the West* (Oxford University Press, 1993).

Light, S., *Shuzo Kuki and Jean-Paul Satre* (Carbondale and Edwardsville, IL: South Illinois University Press, 1987).

Lillie, A., *Buddhism in Christendom, or Jesus the Essence* (Kegan Paul, 1887).

Ling, T., *A History of Religion East and West* (Macmillan, 1968).

Ling, T., *The Buddha: Buddhist Civilization in India and Ceylon* (Temple Smith, 1973).

Liu, M.-W. 'The Harmonious Universe of Fa-tsang and Leibniz: a Comparative Study', *Philosophy East and West*, 32, 1, 1982.

Lopez, D. S., 'New Age Orientalism: The Case of Tibet', *Tricycle*, 3, 3, 1994.

Lopez, D. S. (ed.), *Curators of the Buddha: The Study of Buddhism under Colonialism* (Chicago: University of Chicago Press, 1995).

Lopez, D. S. and S. C. Rockefeller (eds), *The Christ and the Bodhisattva* (Albany, NY: State University of New York Press, 1987).

Lovejoy, A. O., *Essays in the History of Ideas* (Baltimore, MD: Johns Hopkins University Press, 1948).

Lowe, L., *Critical Terrains: French and British Orientalisms* (Ithaca, NY: Cornell University Press, 1991).

Loy, D., 'The Clôture of Deconstruction: A Mahayāna Critique of Derrida', *International Philosophical Quarterly*, 27, 1, 1987.

Loy, D., *Non-Duality: A Study in Comparative Philosophy* (New Haven, CT: Yale University Press, 1988).

Mabbett, I. W., 'Nāgārjuna and Deconstruction', *Philosophy East and West*, 45, 2. 1995.

McCarthy, H. E., 'T. S. Eliot and Buddhism', *Philosophy East and West*, 2, 1, 1952.

McDermott, R. A. (ed.), *The Essential Steiner: Basic Writings of Rudolf Steiner* (San Francisco, CA: Harper & Row, 1984).

McEvilley, T., 'Pyrrhonism and Madhyamika', *Philosophy East and West*, 32, 1, 1982.

Macfie, A. L., *Orientalism: A Reader* (Edinburgh: Edinburgh University Press, 2000).

Macfie, A. L., *Orientalism* (Longman, 2002).

Mackenzie, D. A., *Buddhism in Pre-Christian Britain* (Blackie, 1928).

MacKenzie, J. M., *Orientalism: History, Theory and the Arts* (Manchester University Press, 1995).

Mackerras, C., *Western Images of China* (Hong Kong: Oxford University Press, 1989).

McKinney, J. P., 'Can East Meet West?', *Philosophy East and West*, 3, 3, 1953.

Macy, J., *Dharma Development. Religion as Resource in Sarvodaya Self-Help* (West Hartford, CT: Kumarian Press, 1985).

Macy, J., *World as Lover, World As Self* (Berkeley, CA: Parallax, 1991).

Magee, B., *The Philosophy of Schopenhauer* (Oxford: Clarendon, 1987).

Magliola, R., *Derrida on the Mind* (West Lafayette, OH: Purdue University Press, 1986).

Maidenbaum, A. and S. Martin (eds), *Lingering Shadows: Jungians, Freudians and Anti Semitism* (Boston, MA: Shambhala, 1991).

Mallory, J. P., *In Search of Indo-European Language, Archaeology and Myth* (Thames & Hudson, 1989).

Maraldo, J. C., 'Hermeneutics and Historicity in the Study of Buddhism', *The Eastern Buddhist* (New Series), 9, 1, 1986.

Margenau, H., *The Miracle of Existence* (Woodbridge: Ox Bow, 1984).

Marks, J. and R. T. Ames (eds), *Emotions in Asian Thought: A Dialogue in Comparative Philosophy* (Albany, NY: State University of New York Press, 1995).

Marlow, A. N., 'Hinduism and Buddhism in Greek Philosophy', *Philosophy East and West*, 4, 1, 1954.

Marshall, P. J. (ed.), *The British Discovery of Hinduism in the Eighteenth Century* (Cambridge University Press, 1970).

Marshall, P. J. and G. Williams, *The Great Map of Mankind: British Perceptions of the World in the Age of Enlightenment* (Dent, 1982).

Maspero, H., *Taoism and Chinese Religion* (Amhurst: University of Massachusetts Press, 1981).

Masson-Oursel, P., *Comparative Philosophy* (New York: Harcourt Brace, 1926).

Matilal, B. K. and J. L. Shaw, *Analytical Philosophy in Comparative Perspective* (Dordrecht: Reidel, 1985).

Maverick, L. A., *China, A Model for Europe* (San Antonio, TX: Anderson, 1946).

May, Rheinhard, *Heidegger's Hidden Sources: East Asian Influences on his Work*, trans. and with a complementary essay by G. Parkes (Routledge, 1996).

Meadows, T. T., *The Chinese and their Rebellions Viewed in Connection with their Natural Philosophy, Ethics, Legislature and Administration* (Smith, Elder, 1856).

Meckel, D. J. and R. L. Moore (eds), *Self-Liberation: The Jung/Buddhist Dialogue* (New York: Paulist Press, 1992).

Mehta, J. L., *India and the West: The Problem of Understanding* (Chico: Scholars Press, 1985).

Merleau-Ponty, M., *Signs* (Evanston, IL: Northwestern University Press, 1964).

Merton, T., *Mystics and Zen Masters* (New York: Delta, 1961).

Michelson, J. M., 'The Place of Buddhism in Santayana's Moral Philosophy', *Asian Philosophy*, 5, 1, 1995.

Mill, J., *The History of British India* (Madden, 1858).

Mill, J. S., 'On Liberty', *The Collected Works of John Stuart Mill*, vol. 23 (Toronto: University of Toronto Press, 1977).

Minamiki, G., *The Chinese Rites Controversy from its Beginning to Modern Times* (Chicago: Loyola University Press, 1985).

Mistry, F., *Nietzsche and Buddhism: A Prolegomena to a Comparative Study* (Berlin: de Gruyter, 1981).

Mitchell, D., *Spirituality and Emptiness: The Dynamics of Spiritual Life in Buddhism and Christianity* (New York: Paulist Press, 1991).

Moacanin, R., *Jung's Psychology and Tibetan Buddhism: Western and Eastern Paths to the Heart* (Wisdom, 1986).

Monier-Williams, M., *Buddhism, in its Connexion with Brahmanism and Hinduism, and its Contrast with Christianity* (Murray, 1889).

Montaigne, M. E. de, *Essays*, J. M. Cohen (ed.) (Penguin, 1958).

Moore, C. A. (ed.), *Philosophy East and West* (Princeton, NJ: Princeton University Press, 1946).

Moore, C. A., *The Second East–West Philosophers' Conference: A Preliminary Report* (Honolulu: University Press of Hawai'i, 1949).

Moore, C. A. (ed.) *Essays in East–West Philosophy* (Honolulu: University Press of Hawai'i, 1951).

Moore, C. A. (ed.) *The Japanese Mind: Essentials of Japanese Philosophy and Culture* (Honolulu: University Press of Hawai'i, 1967).

Moore, C. A. (ed.), *The Status of the Individual East and West* (Honolulu: University Press of Hawai'i, 1968).

Moore, W., *Schrödinger: Life and Thought* (Cambridge University Press, 1989).

Moore-Gilbert, B. J., *Kipling's 'Orientalism'* (Croom Helm, 1986).

Moss, G. L. *The Crisis of German Ideology: Intellectual Origins of the Third Reich* (New York: Schocken, 1981).

Müller, F. Max, *Sacred Books of the East*, vol. 1 (Oxford University Press, 1879).

Müller, F. Max, *Introduction to the Science of Religion* (Longmans Green, 1893).

Mungello, D., *Leibniz and Confucianism: The Search for Accord* (Honolulu: University Press of Hawai'i, 1977).

Mungello, D., 'Sinological Torque: the Influence of Cultural Preoccupations on Seventeenth-Century Interpretations of Confucianism', *Philosophy East and West*, 28, 2, 1978.

Mungello, D., 'Some Recent Studies on the Confluence of Chinese and Western Intellectual History', *Journal of the History of Ideas*, 40, 4, 1979.

Mungello, D., 'Malebranche and Chinese Philosophy ', *Journal of the History of Ideas*, 41, 4, 1980.

Mungello, D., *Curious Land: Jesuit Accommodation and the Origins of Sinology* (Honolulu: University Press of Hawai'i, 1989).

Murti, T. R., *The Central Philosophy of Buddhism: A Study of the Madhyamika System* (George Allen & Unwin, 1955).

Naito, S., *Yeats and Zen* (Kyoto: Yamaguchi, 1984).

Nakamura, H., *A Comparative History of Ideas* (Routledge & Kegan Paul, 1975).

Nandi A., *The Intimate Enemy: Loss and Recovery of Self under Colonialism* (Delhi: Oxford University Press, 1983).

Naranjo, C. and R. E. Ornstein, *On the Psychology of Meditation* (New York: Viking, 1971).

Nash, R. F., *Wilderness and the American Mind* (New Haven, CT: Yale University Press, 1967).

Nasr, S. H., *Man and Nature: The Spiritual Crisis of Modern Man* (Unwin Hyman, 1990).

Needham, J., *Science and Civilisation in China*, vol. 1 (Cambridge University Press, 1954).

Needham, J., *Science and Civilisation in China*, vol. 2 (Cambridge University Press, 1956).

Needham, J., *The Grand Titration: Science and Society East and West* (George Allen & Unwin, 1969).

Needham, J., *Within Four Seas: Dialogue between East and West* (George Allen & Unwin, 1969).

Needham, J., *The New Religions* (Harmondsworth: Penguin, 1972).

Needham, J., *Three Masks of Tao: A Chinese Corrective for Maleness, Monarchy and Militarism in Theology* (Teilhard Centre for the Future of Man, 1979).

Netland, H. A., *Dissonant Voices: Religious Pluralism and the Question of Truth* (Grand Rapids: Eerdmans, 1991).

Neville, R. C., 'Confucianism as a World Philosophy', *Journal of Chinese Philosophy*, 21, 1, 1994.

Nietzsche, F., *The Anti-Christ* (Harmondsworth: Penguin, 1968).

Nietzsche, F., *Twilight of the Idols* (Harmondsworth: Penguin, 1968).

Nietzsche, F., *The Will to Power* (New York: Vintage, 1968).

Nietzsche, F., *The Gay Science* (New York: Viking, 1974).

Nietzsche, F., *Ecce Homo* (Harmondsworth: Penguin, 1979).

Nivison, D. S., *The Ways of Confucianism: Investigations in Chinese Philosophy*, ed. with an intro. by Bryan W. van Norden (Chicago: Open Court, 1996).

Norris, C., *The Truth About Postmodernism* (Oxford: Blackwell, 1993).

Northrop, F. S. C., *The Meeting of East and West* (New York: Macmillan, 1946).

Nozick, R., *Philosophical Explanations* (Oxford: Clarendon, 1981).

Odajnyk, V. W., *Gathering the Light: A Psychology of Meditation* (Boston, MA: Shambhala, 1993).

Odin, S., *Process Metaphysics and Hua-Yen Buddhism* (Albany, NY: State University of New York Press, 1982).

O'Hanlon, R., 'Recovering the Subject: Subaltern Studies and Histories of Resistance in Colonial Asia', *Modern Asian Studies*, 22, 1, 1988.

Oliver, I. P., *Buddhism in Britain* (Rider, 1979).

Organ, T. W., *The Self in Indian Philosophy* (The Hague: Mouton, 1964).

Organ, T. W., *Western Approaches to Eastern Philosophy* (Athens, OH: Ohio University Press, 1975).

Organ, T. W., *Philosophy and the Self: East and West* (Associated University Presses, 1987).

Organ, T. W., *Third Eye Philosophy: Essays in East–West Thought* (Athens, OH: Ohio University Press, 1987).

Organ, T. W., *Radhakrishnan and the Ways of Oneness of East and West* (Athens, OH: Ohio University Press, 1989).

Ormiston, G. and A. Schrift (eds), *The Hermeneutical Tradition from Ast to Ricoeur* (Albany, NY: State University of New York Press, 1990).

Ornstein, R. E. (ed.), *The Nature of Human Consciousness* (New York: Viking, 1974).

Ornstein, R. E., *The Psychology of Consciousness* (New York: Harcourt Brace, 1977).

Otto, K., *Mysticism East and West: A Comparative Analysis of the Nature of Mysticism* (New York: Meridian, 1957).

Page, R. C. and R. Chang, 'A Comparison of Gestalt Therapy and Zen Buddhist Concepts of Awareness', *Psychologia*, 32, 1, 1989.

Palmer, M., *The Elements of Taoism* (Shaftesbury: Element, 1991).

Palmer, M., *Coming of Age: An Exploration of Christianity and the New Age* (Thorsons, 1993).

Panikkar, R., *The Intrareligious Dialogue* (New York: Paulist Press, 1978).

Panikkar, R., *Myth, Faith, and Hermeneutics* (New York: Paulist Press, 1979).

Panikkar, R., 'The Myth of Pluralism in the Tower of Babel: a Meditation on Non–Violence', *Cross-Currents*, 29, 1979.

Paper, J., *The Spirits are Drunk: Comparative Approaches to Chinese Religion* (Albany, NY: State University of New York Press, 1995).

Parkes, G. (ed.), *Heidegger and Asian Thought* (Honolulu: University Press of Hawai'i, 1987).

Parkes, G. (ed.), *Nietzsche and Asian Thought* (Chicago: University of Chicago Press, 1991).

Parkes, G., 'Nietzsche and East Asian Thought: Influences, Impacts and Resonances', in B. Magnus (ed.), *The Cambridge Companion to Nietzsche* (Cambridge University Press, 1996).

Parrinder, G., *Comparative Religion* (Sheldon, 1962).

Parrinder, G., *The Christian Debate: Light from the East* (Gollancz, 1964).

Peires, W., *Edwin Arnold: Brief Account of his Life and Contribution to Buddhism* (Kandy: Buddhist Publication Society, 1970).

Pelletier, K. K., *Toward a Science of Consciousness* (Berkeley, CA: Celestial Arts, 1985).

Pelletier, K. K. and C. Garfield, *Consciousness East and West* (New York: Harper & Row, 1976)

Peri, J. M. and A. P. Tuck, 'The Hidden Advantage of Tradition: On the Significance of T. S. Eliot's Indic Studies', *Philosophy East and West*, 35, 2, 1985.

Perry, M., *Gods Within: A Critical Guide to the New Age* (SPCK, 1992).

Pickering, J., 'Buddhism and Cognitivism: A Postmodern Appraisal', *Asian Philosophy*, 5, 1, 1995.

Pinot, V., *La Chine et la Formation de l'esprit philosophique en France, 1640–1740* (Paris: Guenther 1932).

Plott, J. C. and P. Mays, Sarva-Darsana-Sangraha: *A Bibliographical Guide to the Global History of Philosophy* (Leiden: Brill, 1969).

Poliakov, L., *The Aryan Myth: A History of Racist and Nationalist Ideas in Europe* (Heinemann, 1971).

Polkinghorne, J., *One World: The Interaction of Science and Theology* (SPCK, 1986).

Popkin, R. H., *The History of Skepticism from Erasmus to Descartes* (New York: Harper & Row, 1986).

Porkert, M., *Chinese Medicine* (New York: Holt, 1982).

Potitella, J., 'Meister Eckhart and Eastern Wisdom', *Philosophy East and West*, 15, 2, 1965.

Potter, K., *Presuppositions of India's Philosophies* (Englewood Cliffs, NJ: Prentice-Hall, 1963).

Powers, J. and D. Curtin, 'Mothering Moral Cultivation in Buddhist and Feminist Ethics', *Philosophy East and West*, 44, 1, 1994.

Prakash, G., 'Orientalism Now', *History and Theory*, 34, 3, 1995.

Pratt, J. B., *Pilgrimage of Buddhism and a Buddhist Pilgrimage* (New York: Macmillan, 1928).

Prebish, C. S., *American Buddhism* (North Scituate, MA: Duxbury, 1979).

Prime, R., *Hinduism and Ecology: Seeds of Truth* (Cassell, 1992).

Pullapilly, C. K. and E. J. Van Kley (eds), *Asia and the West: Encounters and Exchanges from the Age of Exploration* (Notre Dame: Cross Roads, 1986).

Qian, Wen-yuan, *The Great Inertia. Science and Stagnation in Traditional China* (Croom Helm, 1985).

Qian, Zhaoming, *Orientalism and Modernism: The Legacy of China in Pound and Williams* (Durham: Duke University Press, 1995).

Radhakrishnan, S., *Eastern Religions and Western Thought* (Oxford University Press, 1939).

Raghavan, E. and B. Wood, 'Thoreau's Hindu Quotations in A Week', *American Literature*, 51, 1, 1979.

Raju, P. T. and A. Castell (eds), *East–West Studies on the Problem of the Self* (The Hague: Martinus Nijhoff, 1968).

Rao, P. K., *East versus West: A Denial of Contrasts* (George Allen & Unwin, 1939).

Reichwein, A., *China and Europe: Intellectual and Artistic Contacts in the Eighteenth Century* (Kegan Paul, 1925).

Reynolds, J. (trans. and ed.), *Self-Liberation through Seeing with Naked Awareness* (Barrytown: Station Hill, 1989).

Richards, I. A., *Mencius on the Mind: Experiments in Multiple Definition* (Kegan Paul, 1932).

Richardson, A., *East Comes West* (New York: The Pilgrim Press, 1985).

Richardson, M., 'Enough Said', *Anthropology Today*, 6, 4. 1990.

Riencourt, A. de, *The Eye of Shiva: Eastern Mysticism and Science* (New York: Morrow, 1981).

Riepe, D., 'Emerson and Indian Philosophy', *Journal of the History of Ideas*, 28, 1, 1967.

Riepe, D., 'The Indian Influence in American Philosophy: Emerson to Moore', *Philosophy East and West*, 17, 124, 1967.

Riepe, D., *The Philosophy of India and its Impact on American Thought* (Springfield: Thomas, 1970).

Robinson, J., *Truth is Two-Eyed* (SCM, 1979).

Rodinson, M., *Europe and the Mystique of Islam*, (Tauris, 1988).

Rolland, R., *Prophets of the New India* (Cassell, 1930).

Rolston, H., 'Can the East Help the West to Value Nature?', *Philosophy East and West*, 37, 2, 1987.

Ronan, C. A., *The Shorter Science and Civilization in China: An Abridgement of Joseph Needam's Original Text*, 2 vols (Cambridge University Press, 1978).

Ronan, C. E. and B. B. Oh (eds), *East Meets West: The Jesuit in China, 1582–1773* (Chicago: Loyola University Press, 1988).

Ropp, P. S. (ed.), *Heritage of China: Contemporary Perspectives on Chinese Civilisation* (Berkeley, CA: University of California Press, 1990).

Rorty, R., 'A Pragmatist View of Rationality and Cultural Difference', *Philosophy East and West*, 42, 4, 1992.

Rosemont, H. and B. I. Schwartz, (eds), 'Studies in Classical Chinese Thought', *Journal of the American Academy of Religion*, 47, 3, 1979.

Roszak, T., *The Making of the Counter Culture* (Faber & Faber, 1970).

Rougemont, B. de, *The Meaning of Europe* (Sidgwick & Jackson, 1963).

Rouner, L. S. (ed.), *Religious Pluralism* (Notre Dame: University of Notre Dame Press, 1984).

Rowan, J., *Ordinary Ecstasy: Humanistic Psychology in Action* (Routledge & Kegan Paul, 1976).

Rowbotham, A. H., 'The Impact of Confucianism on Seventeenth-Century Europe', *The Far Eastern Quarterly*, 4, 5, 1945.

Roy, O., *Leibniz et la Chine* (Paris: Vrin, 1972).

Ruegg, D. S., 'Ahimsa and Vegetarianism in the History of Buddhism', in S. Balasooriya et al. (eds) *Buddhist Studies in Honour of Walpola Rahula* (Fraser, 1980).

Sadik Jalal al' Azm, 'Orientalism and Orientalism in Reverse', *Khamsin*, 8, 1981.

Saher, P. J., *Eastern Wisdom and Western Thought* (Allen & Unwin, 1969).

Said, E., *Orientalism* (Harmondsworth: Penguin, 1985).

Said, E., 'Representing the Colonized: Anthropology's Interlocutors', *Critical Inquiry*, 15, 2, 1989.

Said, E., *Culture and Imperialism* (Chatto & Windus, 1993).

Said, E., 'Orientalism and After: An Interview with Edward Said', *Radical Philosophy*, 63, 1993.

Said, E., *Orientalism* (with a new Afterword), (Harmondsworth: Penguin, 1995).

Saint-Hilaire, J. B., *The Buddha and his Religion* (Routledge, 1895).

Saunders, K. J., *Buddhist Ideals: A Study in Comparative Religion* (Calcutta: YMCA, 1912)

Sawyer, M., *Marxism and the Question of the Asiatic Mode of Production* (The Hague: Martinus Nijhoff, 1977).

Scharf, R. H., 'The Zen of Japanese Nationalism', *History of Religions*, 33, 1, 1993.

Scharfstein, B.-A., I. Alon, S. Biderman, D. Daor and Y. Hoffmann, *Philosophy East/ Philosophy West: A Critical Comparison of Indian, Chinese, Islamic, and European Philosophy* (Oxford: Blackwell, 1978).

Schipper, K., *The Taoist Body* (Berkeley, CA: University of California Press, 1993).

Schmitz, O. A. H., *Psychoanalyse und Yoga* (Darmstadt: Reich, 1923).

Schopenhauer, A., *The World as Will and Representation*, 3 vols (New York: Dover, 1969).

Schopenhauer, A., *On the Fourfold Root of the Principle of Sufficient Reason* (La Salle, IL: Open Court, 1974).

Schopenhauer, A., *Parerga and Paralipomena*, 2 vols (Oxford: Clarendon, 1974).

Schrag, C., 'Heidegger on Repetition and Historical Understanding', *Philosophy East and West*, 20, 3, 1970.

Schrödinger, E., *What is Life? Mind and Matter* (Cambridge University Press, 1969).

Schuon, F., *The Transcendental Unity of Religions* (Wheaton: Quest, 1984).

Schurmann, F. and Schell, O. (eds), *Imperial China: The Eighteenth and Nineteenth Centuries* (Penguin, 1967).

Schwab, R., *The Oriental Renaissance: Europe's Rediscovery of India and the East, 1680–1880* (New York: Columbia University Press, 1984).

Schweitzer, A., *Indian Thought and its Development* (Boston, MA: Beacon, 1936).

Scott, A., *Buddhism and Christianity: a Parallel and a Contrast* (Edinburgh: Douglas, 1890).

Scott, M., *Kundalini in the Physical World* (Routledge & Kegan Paul, 1983).

Seager, R. H. (ed.), *The Dawn of Religious Pluralism: Voices from the World's Parliament of Religions, 1893* (La Salle, IL: Open Court, 1993).

Seager, R. H., *The World's Parliament of Religions: The East/West Encounter, Chicago, 1893* (Bloomington, IN: Indiana University Press, 1995).

Seidel, A. K., 'Chronicle of Taoist Studies in the West, 1950–1990', *Cahier d'Extrême Asie*, 5, 1989–90.

Shapiro, D. H. and R. N. Walsh (eds), *Meditation: Classic and Contemporary Perspectives* (New York: Aldine, 1984).

Sharpe, E. J., *The Universal Gītā: Western Images of the Bhagavad Gītā* (La Salle, IL: Open Court, 1985).

Sharpe, E. J., *Comparative Religion: A History* (Duckworth, 1986).

Shaw, M., 'William James and Yogacara Philosophy: A Comparative Inquiry', *Philosophy East and West*, 37, 3, 1987.

Shaw, M., *Passionate Enlightenment: Women in Tantric Buddhism* (Princeton, NJ: Princeton University Press, 1994).

Silk, J. A., 'The Victorian Creation of Buddhism', *Journal of Indian Philosophy*, 22, 2, 1994.

Silva, P. de, *An Introduction to Buddhist Psychology* (Macmillan, 1979).

Siu, R. G. H., *The Tao of Science: An Essay on Western Knowledge and Eastern Wisdom* (Chapman & Hall, 1957).

Sivin, N. (ed.), *Science in Ancient China: Researches and Reflections* (Aldershot: Variorum, 1995).

Skiar, D., *The Nazis and the Occult* (New York, Dorset, 1977).

Smart, N., *Beyond Ideology: Religion and the Future of Western Civilization* (Collins, 1981).

Smart, N., *Buddhism and Christianity: Rivals and Allies* (Macmillan, 1992).

Smith, E. F., *Prophets of the New India* (Cassell, 1930).

Smith, J. H., 'Tao Now: An Ecological Testament', in I. G. Barbour (ed.), *Earth Must be Fair: Reflections on Ethics, Religion, and Ecology* (Englewood Cliffs, NJ: Prentice Hall, 1972).

Smith, J. R., 'Nishitani and Nietzsche on the Selfless Self', *Asian Philosophy*, 4, 2, 1994.

Smith, W. C., *Towards a World Theology: Faith and the Comparative Study of Religion* (Macmillan, 1981).

Snelling, J., *Buddhism in Russia* (Shaftesbury: Element, 1992).

Solomon, R. C., and Higgins, K. M. (eds), *From Africa to Zen: An Invitation to World Philosophy* (Lanham: Rowman & Littlefield, 1993).

Sommer, Andreas Urs, 'Ex Oriente Lux? Zur Vermeintlichen "Ostorientierung" in Nietzsches *Antichrist*', *Nietzsche – Studien*, 28, 1999.

Song, Shun-ching, *Voltaire et la Chine* (Aix-en-Provence: Publications Université de Provence, 1989).

Spannhake, B., 'Umwertung Einer Quelle', *Nietzsche – Studien*, 28, 1999.

Sprung, M. (ed.), *The Question of Being: East–West Perspectives* (Philadelphia, PA: Pennsylvania State University Press, 1978).

Stcherbatsky, Th., *Buddhist Logic* ('S-Gravenhage: Mouton, 1958).

Stcherbatsky, Th., *The Conception of the Buddhist Nirvāna* (Varanasi: Bharatiya Vidya Prakashan, 1968).

Steffney, J., 'Mind and Metaphysics in Heidegger and Zen Buddhism', *The Eastern Buddhist* (New Series), 14, 1, 1981.

Stillson-Judah, J., *Hare Krishna and the Counter-Culture* (New York: John Wiley, 1974).

Stokes, E., *The English Utilitarians and India* (Oxford: Clarendon, 1959).

Streng, F., *Emptiness: A Study of Religious Meaning* (Nashville, TN: Abingdon, 1967).

Surette, L., *The Birth of Modernism: Ezra Pound, T. S. Eliot, W. B. Yeats and the Occult* (Montreal: McGill-Queen's University Press, 1993).

Swidler, L., J. B. Cobb, P. F. Knitter and M. K. Hellwig, *Death or Dialogue: From the Age of Monologue to the Age of Dialogue* (SCM, 1990).

Taber, J. A., *Transformation Philosophy: A Study of Sankara, Fichte, and Heidegger* (Honolulu: University Press of Hawai'i, 1983).

Talbot, M., *Mysticism and the New Physics* (New York: Bantam, 1980).

Tarn, W., *The Greeks in Bactria and India* (Cambridge University Press, 1938).

Taylor, C., 'The Politics of Recognition', in A. Gutman, C. Taylor, S. Wolf, S. Rockefeller and M. Walzer (eds), *Multiculturalism and the Politics of Recognition* (Princeton, NJ: Princeton University Press, 1992).

Teilhard de Chardin, P., *The Phenomenon of Man* (Collins, 1968).

Temple, R., *The Genius of China: 3000 Years of Scientific Discovery and Inventions (Prion, 1991)*.

Teng, Ssu-Yu, 'Chinese Influence on the Western Examination System', *Harvard Journal of Asiatic Studies*, 7, 2, 1943.

Thoreau, H. D., *A Writer's Journal* (Heinemann, 1961).

Thundy, Z. P., *Buddha and Christ* (Leiden: Brill, 1993).

Thurman, R. A., *The Central Philosophies of Tibet* (Princeton, NJ: Princeton University Press, 1991).

Tiffin, C. and Lawson, A. (eds), *De-Scribing Empire: Post-colonialism and Textuality* (Routledge, 1994).

Tillich, P., *Christianity and the Encounter of World Religions* (New York: Columbia University Press, 1963).

Titmuss, C., *The Green Buddha* (Totnes: Insight, 1995).

Todorov, T., *On Human Diversity: Nationalism, Fascism, and Exoticism in French Thought* (Cambridge, MA: Harvard University Press, 1993).

Townsend, M., *Asia and Europe* (Constable, 1905).

Toynbee, A., *Civilization on Trial* (Oxford University Press, 1948).

Tracy, D., *Dialogue with the Other: The Inter-Religious Dialogue* (Louvain: Peters, 1990).

Tucci, G., *The Theory and Practice of the Mandala* (Rider, 1969).

Tuck, A. P., *Comparative Philosophy and the Philosophy of Scholarship: On the Western Interpretation of Nāgārjuna* (New York: Oxford University Press, 1990).

Turner, B. S., *Orientalism, Postmodernism, and Globalism* (Routledge, 1994).

Tweed, T. A., *The American Encounter with Buddhism, 1844–1912* (Bloomington, IN: Indiana University Press, 1992).

Tworkov, H., *Zen in America* (New York: Kodansha, 1994).

Varela, F. J.,Thompson, E. and Rosch, E., *The Embodied Mind: Cognitive Science and Human Experience* (Cambridge, MA: MIT Press, 1991).

Verellen, F., 'Taoism', *Journal of Asian Studies*, 54, 2, 1995.

Versluis, A., 'From Transcendentalism to Universal Religion: Samuel Johnson's Orientalism', *American Transcendental Quarterly*, 5, 2, 1991.

Versluis, A., *American Transcendentalism and Asian Religions* (New York: Oxford University Press, 1993).

Viswanathan, G., *Masters of Conquest: Literary Study and British Rule in India* (New York: Columbia University Press, 1989).

Voltaire, F.-M. A., *Essai sur les mœurs* (Paris: Garnier, 1963).

Vyas, R. N., *The Universalistic Thought of India: From the Rigveda to Radhakrishnan* (Bombay: Lalvani, 1970).

Ward, B., *The Interplay of East and West: Elements of Contrast and Cooperation* (George Allen & Unwin, 1957).

Washington, P., *Madame Blavatsky's Baboon: Theosophy and the Emergence of the Western Guru* (Secker & Warburg, 1993).

Watts, A., *Beat Zen, Square Zen, and Zen* (San Francisco, CA: City Light, 1959).

Watts, A., *Psychotherapy East and West* (Harmondsworth: Penguin, 1973).

Webb, J., *The Occult Establishment* (La Salle, IL: Open Court, 1976).

Weber, M., *The Religion of China: Confucianism and Taoism* (New York: The Free Press, 1951).

Weber, M., *The Religion of India: The Sociology of Hinduism and Buddhism* (New York: The Free Press, 1958).

Wehr, G., *Jung: A Biography* (Boston, MA: Shambhala, 1987).

Weiss, P., 'The Gita, East and West', *Philosophy East and West*, 4, 3, 1954.

Welbon, G., *The Buddhist Nirvāna and its Western Interpreters* (Chicago: University of Chicago Press, 1968).

Welburn, A., *The Beginnings of Christianity: Essene Mystery, Gnostic Revelation, and Christian Vision* (Edinburgh: Floris, 1991).

Welwood, J (ed.), *The Meeting of the Ways: Explorations in East/West Psychology* (New York: Schocken, 1979).

West, M. A. (ed.), *The Psychology of Meditation* (Oxford: Clarendon, 1987).

West, M. L., *Early Greek Philosophy and the Orient* (Oxford: Clarendon Press, 1971).

Whorf, B. L., *Language, Thought and Reality: Selected Writings* (Cambridge, MA: MIT Press, 1956).

Wienpahl, P., 'Eastern Buddhism and Wittgenstein's Philosophical Investigations', *The Eastern Buddhist* (New Series), 12, 2, 1979.

Williams, S. W., *The Middle Kingdom*, 2 vols (New York: Scribner's, 1883).

Willson, A. L., *A Mythical Image: The Ideal of India in German Romanticism* (Durham, NC: Duke University Press, 1964).

Wilson, B., ' "From Mirror after Mirror": Yeats and Eastern Thought', *Comparative Literature*, 34, 1, 1982.

Wolin, R. (ed.), *The Heidegger Controversy* (New York: Columbia University Press, 1991).

Wood, R. C., 'British Churches Encounter the Challenge of Pluralism', *The Christian Century*, 19, 1988.

Woodroffe, J. G. (alias Arthur Avalon), *The Serpent Power* (Calcutta: Ganesh, 1919).

Woodroffe, J. G., *The World as Power* (Madras: Ganesh, 1966).

Wright, A. F., *Buddhism in Chinese History* (Stanford, CA: Stanford University Press, 1971).

Wright, B., *Interpreter of Buddhism: Sir Edwin Arnold* (New York: Bookman Associates, 1957).

Yao, X., *Confucianism and Christianity* (Brighton: Academic Press, 1996).

Young, J. D., *Confucianism and Christianity: The First Encounter* (Hong Kong University Press, 1983).

Young, R., *White Mythologies: Writing History and the West* (Routledge, 1990).

Yu Liu, 'From Christian Platonism to Organism: The Two Chinas of Leibniz', *International Philosophical Quarterly*, 41, 4, Issue No. 164, December 2001.

Zaehner, R. C., *At Sundry Times: An Essay in the Comparison of Religions* (Faber & Faber, 1958).

Zaehner, R. C., *Matter and Spirit: Their Convergence in Eastern Religions, Marx, and Teilhard de Chardin* (New York: Harper & Row, 1963).

Zaehner, R. C., *Concordant Discord: The Interdependence of Faiths* (Oxford: Clarendon Press, 1970).

Zaehner, R. C., *Our Savage God* (Collins, 1974).

Zhang Longzi, 'The Myth of the Other: China in the Eyes of the West', *Critical Inquiry*, 15, 1, 1988.

Zhang Longzi, *The Tao and the Logos: Literary Hermeneutics, East and West* (Durham, NC: Duke University Press, 1992).

Zheng, C., *A Comparison between Western and Chinese Political Ideas* (New York: Mellen, 1995).

Zimmer, H., *Philosophies of India* (Princeton, NJ: Princeton University Press, 1951).

Zukav, G., *The Dancing Wu Li Masters: An Overview of the New Physics* (Fontana, 1979).

COPYRIGHT ACKNOWLEDGEMENTS

Grateful acknowledgement is made to the following sources for permission to reproduce material in this book previously published elsewhere. Every effort has been made to trace copyright holders, but if any have been inadvertently overlooked the publisher will be pleased to make the necessary arrangement at the first opportunity.

1. 'Malebranche and Chinese Philosophy' by David E. Mungello, from *Journal of the History of Ideas*, 41:4 (1980)© Journal of the History of Ideas, Inc. Reprinted with permission of The Johns Hopkins University Press.
2. 'The Pre-Established Harmony Between Leibniz and Chinese Thought' by Daniel J. Cook and Henry Rosemont, from *Journal of the History of Ideas*, 42:2 (1981) © Journal of the History of Ideas, Inc. Reprinted with permission of The Johns Hopkins University Press.
3. 'The Sinophilism of Christian Wolff (1679–1754)' by Donald F. Lach, from *Journal of the History of Ideas*, 14:4 (1953) © Journal of the History of Ideas, Inc. Reprinted with permission of The Johns Hopkins University Press.
4. *The French Image of China Before and After Voltaire* by Basil Guy, 1963. Reprinted with permission of the Voltaire Foundation.
5. 'The Possibility of Oriental Influence in Hume's Philosophy' by Nolan Pliny Jacobson, from *Philosophy East and West* 19 (1969), © University of Hawai'i Press. Reproduced by permission.
6. © Oxford University Press 1965. Reprinted from *The Glass Curtain Between Asia and Europe* by Raghavan Iyer (1965) by permission of Oxford University Press.

INDEX